Decorative Arts and Household Furnishings

in America, 1650 – 1920

Distributed by the University Press of Virginia, Charlottesville

Decorative Arts and

Household Furnishings in America

1650–1920

An Annotated Bibliography

EDITED BY

Kenneth L. Ames and Gerald W. R. Ward

Winterthur, Delaware

The Henry Francis du Pont Winterthur Museum

1989

ISBN 0−912724−19−6
Library of Congress Cataloguing-in-Publication Data
appear on page 395.

Contents

Acknowledgments   7

Introduction   9
Kenneth L. Ames

References and Surveys   25

BASIC REFERENCES AND GUIDES TO RESEARCH   27
Neville Thompson
SURVEYS   37
Kenneth L. Ames and Barbara G. Carson

Architecture   59

DOMESTIC ARCHITECTURE   61
David Schuyler

Furniture   77

AMERICAN FURNITURE TO 1820   79
Barbara McLean Ward and Gerald W. R. Ward
AMERICAN FURNITURE, 1820–1920   107
Kenneth L. Ames

Metals   137

AMERICAN SILVER AND GOLD   139
Barbara McLean Ward and Gerald W. R. Ward
PEWTER AND BRITANNIA METAL   159
Barbara McLean Ward
BRASS, COPPER, IRON, AND TIN   169
Deborah A. Federhen

Ceramics and Glass 179

   AMERICAN CERAMICS 181
     Ellen Paul Denker

   CONTINENTAL AND ORIENTAL CERAMICS IN AMERICA 195
     Ellen Paul Denker

   ENGLISH CERAMICS IN AMERICA 201
     George L. Miller and Ann Smart Martin

   AMERICAN GLASS 221
     Kirk Nelson

Textiles 237

   FLOOR COVERINGS 239
     Rodris Roth

   NEEDLEWORK 247
     Susan Burrows Swan

   QUILTS 257
     Susan Roach-Lankford

   TEXTILES 265
     Adrienne D. Hood

Timepieces 281

   CLOCKS AND WATCHES 283
     Thomas S. Michie

Household Activities and Systems 307

   KITCHEN ARTIFACTS AND HOUSEWORK 309
     Donna R. Braden

   PLUMBING, HEATING, AND LIGHTING 319
     Ulysses Grant Dietz

Artisans and Culture 331

   CRAFTSMEN 333
     Edward S. Cooke, Jr.

   THE ARTS AND CRAFTS MOVEMENT IN AMERICA 343
     Cheryl A. Robertson
     with contributions by Thomas Beckman and Robert L. Edwards

Notes on Contributors 359

Index 361

Acknowledgments

I AM GRATEFUL to the many people at Winterthur who provided help or support for this project as it evolved: James Morton Smith, Thomas A. Graves, Jr., Scott T. Swank, Ian M. G. Quimby, Philip D. Zimmerman, Katharine Martinez, Neville Thompson, E. Richard McKinstry, Shirley L. Griesinger, Allison C. Thorp, Linda Carson, Ann Marie Keefer, Jane Mellinger, Patricia Mercer, Karen Sweeney, Dini Silber, Lisa Desmond, Pat Elliott.

The members of Winterthur's Publications Division have been deeply involved in the production of this volume. Thanks are due to Catherine E. Hutchins, Jeanne M. Malloy, Janice E. Ferguson, and, above all, Patricia R. Lisk and Deborah G. Huey for sustained and dedicated work.

For ideas, suggestions, comments, and commentary of various helpful sorts, I am indebted to past and present members of Winterthur's Advanced Studies Office: Robert Blair St. George, Barbara McLean Ward, Kevin M. Sweeney, Nancy L. Garrison, Deborah A. Federhen, Bradley Brooks, and Cheryl Robertson. I also wish to express my gratitude to the many colleagues who wrote sections of this book. They took time away from already busy schedules to share their expertise and insights. I thank them for their valuable contributions to the cause of scholarship.

Much of the value of this bibliography is due to the patient and informed efforts of my coeditor, Gerald W. R. Ward. His knowledge and editorial skills have made this a better book.

This bibliography began, once upon a time, as a class project in the Winterthur Program in Early American Culture. The students who were involved then will probably not recognize the final product, but their enthusiasm helped to get it started. It has long been my belief that its students are Winterthur's greatest treasures. This volume is dedicated, with affection and respect, to Winterthur students—past, present, and future.

KENNETH L. AMES

Introduction

Kenneth L. Ames

*T*HIS BIBLIOGRAPHY provides access and orientation to the study of household furnishings used in the United States from the seventeenth century to the early twentieth century. It is designed for use by the general public, collectors, college and university students at both the undergraduate and the graduate levels, the scholarly community, and librarians and other staff at a variety of cultural institutions. Users will find that this volume simultaneously records the most prominent scholarship on historic household furnishings and offers opportunities for critical reflection on that scholarship.

The descriptor "historic household furnishings" may require clarification. Although some of the titles here can be found listed elsewhere under the headings of antiques and collectibles, decorative arts, or folk art, none of these terms captures the salient, defining feature of domestic usage operative here. This is essentially a bibliography of the material culture of domestic life. The emphasis is on goods used within American homes.

This attention to domestic context distinguishes this bibliography from others published previously and makes it useful to new audiences. It has considerable utility for those interested in the histories of decorative arts, art and architecture, and certain aspects of technology. However, it also offers useful material to those who may wish to examine the history of domesticity, changing male and female roles within the household, housewifery and housework, uses of domestic space, ritual and ceremony, the impact of politics and ideology, and many other issues relating to everyday life in the past.

Readers need to know what this book includes—and what it excludes. It *includes* a thorough overview of household material culture used in the United States by Euramericans and, to a lesser extent, others from the seventeenth century to approximately 1820. This Eurocentrism objectively reflects the current contours of scholarship as well as the numerical and cultural predominance of certain ethnic groups within earlier American society. The story outlined here is largely, but not only, of the westward migration of Euramerican material culture from East Coast origins. This bibliography *excludes* works dealing with the material culture of European settlers prior to 1600. It also does not record publications about the materials of native Americans before or apart from contact with Europeans because they are so well treated in a separate, vast literature. References to Canadian and Mexican materials are deliberately limited. Works dealing wholly with Europe have been listed only when they have clear relevance to the American story.

Within the category of household furnishings, some limits have also necessarily been set. Domestic architecture is discussed, but other forms of architecture are excluded. Technical aspects of building have been omitted, as have detailed treatments of such materials as window glass, hardware, woodwork, and roofing. While paintings, sculpture, prints, and other so-called fine arts were often intended for domestic use, these are dealt with in extensive bibliographies elsewhere and are therefore not included here.

No bibliography could possibly treat all the objects conceivably found in houses, such as toys, games, foodstuffs, packaging, clothing, tools, sporting goods, drugs, cosmetics, musical instruments, photographs, pet supplies, stationery, books, and magazines. Instead, a fairly strict set of guidelines has been drawn up to limit inclusion to equipment considered necessary for furnishing and maintaining households: furniture, clocks, objects associated with the preparation and presentation of food, floor and bed coverings, household textiles of all sorts, the visible or decorated aspects of plumbing, lighting, and heating, objects associated with housekeeping, and objects specifically intended for household decoration. Materials that might be considered supplies are not included. Beyond these broad guidelines, exceptions have been made for artisans and culture. A section on artisans and artisanal culture is included because much of the literature, particularly that dealing with early periods, has stressed makers and the processes of making. A chapter on the arts and crafts movement is provided because that movement has emerged as a major emphasis within scholarship. Because arts and crafts ideology and impact transcend the limits of individual categories of goods, it seemed appropriate to deal with the movement in a separate chapter.

On a more mundane level, readers should know that this bibliography lists and annotates books, articles, catalogues, and reprints of historically significant works. Dissertations, reports, and unpublished studies are not included.

Some words on the organization and intent of this volume may also be helpful. At the start of this project in 1984, I asked a score of authors who were recognized authorities in their areas of scholarship to assume responsibility for individual chapters of the bibliography. All authors were free to select and annotate the titles that they thought were most significant. Each chapter therefore reflects the preferences and intellectual orientation of its author. The resulting diversity of viewpoints is a strength of the book.

All chapters in this bibliography follow the same format. Each is introduced by a short essay contextualizing or analyzing the entries. These essays help readers to understand the internal dynamics of each area of scholarship, identify major concentrations of effort and attention, and in some cases, suggest where future scholarship might be headed. The essays are followed by annotated listings of the most significant works. Because this is a selective bibliography, inclusion of a title means that the author of that chapter thinks that it has some merit. The individual annotations, however, are generally not evaluative, but are intended to convey succinctly and accurately the contents and arguments of each title.

The authors have done an exemplary job of distilling often lengthy and complex works into concise, readable prose. I have consistently found entries that are not only intelligent and cogent but also enjoyable to read. I hope that others will feel the same way. While bibliographies tend to be used by goal-oriented readers, this one well repays browsing. The annotations can be read quickly and easily, making it possible to become familiar with scores of major publications in a matter of minutes. Each chapter is, in a sense, a crash course in an area of historic furnishings scholarship.

The individual chapters in this bibliography are intended to present the major concentrations of historic furnishings scholarship. A chapter on basic references and research guides as well as one focusing on general surveys introduce important scholarship in the field of American decorative arts. A chapter on domestic architecture provides physical context for these furnishings. Most of the writing in the field is organized by material (glass, silver, pewter, ceramics) or function (clocks, furniture, plumbing). Areas with the most extensive bibliographies have been subdivided, while others less written about have been combined. Furniture, for example, is an area with an immense bibliography and is therefore treated in two chapters. The first examines material before 1820; the other, material after that date. Ceramics is another area of extensive publication and is treated in three chapters, each organized according to geographic origin.

The ceramics chapters provide an opportunity to discuss inclusion of non-American goods. In designing this project, we have tried to reflect documented patterns of historic use and ownership in American homes. Where foreign goods were prominent, that prominence is reflected. It is probably accurate to say that the finer ceramics used in American homes have usually been of foreign origin. Asian and English wares have long dominated the market; goods from other nations have also been fashionable or popular at various times. For these reasons, only one of the three ceramics chapters deals with products actually made in this country. All deal with goods used here, however.

The section on household activities, objects, and systems was included because these areas are crucial for household maintenance. Kitchen artifacts, housework, and plumbing, heating, and light- ing systems are often ignored in studies emphasizing luxury goods or issues of style. The rationale for the discussions of artisans and the arts and crafts movement was noted earlier.

This bibliography records the current state of scholarship in the field of historic furnishings. This scholarship has grown and changed significantly over the last two decades. One way to illustrate this growth and change is to examine the state of scholarship as represented in earlier bibliographies. For comparison, two seem particularly relevant. The first is *The Arts in Early American History*, published for the Institute of Early American History and Culture at Williamsburg, Virginia, in 1965.[1] This volume has two components: an essay by Walter Muir Whitehill asserting the validity of studying American arts and an annotated bibliography by Wendell D. Garrett and Jane N. Garrett. Whitehill argued that "the greatest need" was "for every institution possessing pertinent objects to publish promptly as many carefully prepared and liberally illustrated catalogues or picture books, or both, as their time and resources permit" (p. 18). The bibliography compiled by the Garretts substantiated his argument. Of the approximately 115 pages of entries, the majority were given over

[1] Walter Muir Whitehill et al., *The Arts in Early American History* (Chapel Hill: University of North Carolina Press, 1965).

to architecture, painting, and graphic arts. Only about 35 pages were devoted to household furnishings. The greatest number of entries were in the areas of furniture (36) and silver (32). The general area of crafts was represented by 17 titles, textiles by 16, and folk art by 12. Pottery, glass, lighting, and pewter all had 6 or fewer titles (pewter had 2). The total for the entire class of household furnishings was fewer than 150 entries.

The Garrett bibliography made 1826 its terminal date, apparently taking the term *early* seriously. It also excluded "writings on English, Continental, and far Eastern products in porcelain and textiles that were imported and used widely in this country" (p. 42), but offered no rationale for doing so.

Nearly fifteen years later, the second major bibliography appeared. This was the massive, four-volume work titled *Arts in America*.[2] Published by Smithsonian Institution Press with Bernard Karpel as editor, it recorded a dramatic expansion of scholarship within the area of American arts. While historic household furnishings occupied only a portion of one volume, the number of entries was much greater than in the Garrett bibliography. Exact comparisons are difficult because the two works were organized differently. The section within *Arts in America* most nearly equivalent to the relevant section of the Garretts' bibliography was called "Decorative Arts." Edited by Frank H. Sommer, then head of the Winterthur Library, it was more than three times larger than the list compiled by the Garretts. This expansion came in part because Sommer made a deliberate effort to incorporate materials reaching from the earliest settlements to the early twentieth century. His listing of roughly 200 monographs, 100 exhibition catalogues, and nearly 200 articles represents significant gain in all areas.

More than half of the titles in the Garretts' bibliography date from 1949 or before. Sommer, on the other hand, emphasized material written after 1949. Thus it becomes even more evident that a dramatic expansion of scholarly productivity had taken place.

Numbers show activity, but they fail to reveal the pattern of that activity. Sommer felt that most of the writing he recorded tended to be ethnocentric. As he put it, "The vast majority of publications . . . discuss Anglo-American materials of decidedly WASP nature and more especially of a New England brand." Little material dealt with goods produced west of the Alleghenies or south of Baltimore. Sommer argued for a more broad-based study of the art of the United States, incorporating not only the culture of the dominant groups but "other ethnic and racial contributions as well." Sommer succinctly summarized the philosophy guiding his selection of titles: "Snobbery has no place in the objective study of human behavior and of the objects produced by that behavior."

This bibliography is grounded in a similar belief. If anything, it attempts to be even more egalitarian by eliminating invidious or exclusionary dimensions associated with the concepts of art and decorative art. The subjective question "Is it art?" has not been asked here. The ruling questions have been "Does it deal with household furnishings?" and "Is it a publication people should know about?"

Three other previous bibliographies deserve mention. David Sokol's *American Decorative Arts and Old World Influences* (1980) lists and briefly annotates more than 1,000 titles devoted to American

---

[2] Bernard Karpel, ed., *Arts in America: A Bibliography* (Washington, D.C.: Smithsonian Institution Press, 1979).

materials, as well as several hundred on non-American subjects.[3] Sokol's listing, however, does not seem to be selective, and works of varied quality and utility are intermingled.

Simon J. Bronner's *American Folk Art: A Guide to Sources* (1984) has an obviously different focus, but I mention it here because it served in many ways as a model for this bibliography. Finally, my essay, "The Stuff of Everyday Life: American Decorative Arts and Household Furnishings," in Thomas J. Schlereth's edited volume *Material Culture: A Research Guide* (1985), provides an evaluative and analytical overview of scholarship on historic household furnishings. In that essay I maintained that the persisting emphasis on collecting and the cultural conceit of defining household furnishings as decorative arts have simultaneously propelled and constricted scholarship. Readers interested in pursuing those lines of thought should turn to that essay. They may also find the views presented there helpful for contextualizing and analyzing both the organization and the contents of this bibliography.[4]

In comparing the material in this bibliography with that listed by the Garretts and Sommer, significant changes in scholarship appear. Below, I highlight ten of the most noticeable of these, then offer a few explanatory or analytical comments about each.

Information continues to expand. The volume of books, articles, catalogues, and other works seems to grow steadily. Some of these publications reexplore terrain already mapped out, but just as many push off into new territory. The field has its share of glossy, up-scale picture books intended to exploit the visual qualities of the materials they present, but it also has a steady stream of thoughtful, often innovative contributions to our cumulative understanding of household furnishings. Sometimes these are combined, without contradiction, in the same volume. The continuing explosion of knowledge brings with it both the opportunity for new comprehension and a nagging sense that data is expanding so rapidly that no one can keep up with it. On any given day, the New Arrivals shelf at Winterthur holds out the offer of months of informative reading. This explosion of knowledge means that annotated bibliographies, either in their traditional bound format or innovatively reconceived for the computer age, can play increasingly valuable roles in helping people to sort their way through a forest of material that grows deeper and thicker every day.

Surveys are becoming less common. One corollary of the explosion of knowledge is that any competent survey must take into account a much wider range of materials than was necessary or even possible in the past. Surveys are also more difficult to write because the canon of key works, key epochs, or

[3] David M. Sokol, *American Decorative Arts and Old World Influences: A Guide to Information Sources* (Detroit: Gale Research Co., 1980).

[4] Simon J. Bronner, ed., *American Folk Art: A Guide to Sources* (New York: Garland Publishing, 1984). Also serving as a model and precedent for this volume is Charles F. Montgomery, "A List of Books and Articles for the Study of the Arts in Early America," in *A Guide to and Outline of the Winterthur Museum Collections*, ed. R. Peter Mooz and Tessa Craib Cox (Winterthur, Del.: By the museum, 1970). Although intended for staff use only, Montgomery's bibliography contains 136 pages, with material organized under approximately eighty headings. Most entries receive a few sentences of annotation. Kenneth L. Ames, "The Stuff of Everyday Life: American Decorative Arts and Household Furnishings," in *Material Culture: A Research Guide*, ed. Thomas J. Schlereth (Lawrence: University Press of Kansas, 1985), pp. 79–112.

key creators is gradually being dismantled. Eurocentrism, the ethnocentrism mentioned by Sommer, and the emphasis on materials associated with or sanctioned by the ruling classes are all disappearing. Today intellectually and socially responsible surveys must make a fair attempt to reconnoiter and report on all the terrain or explain where and why boundaries are erected. Because dealing with all materials is such an overwhelming task, authors increasingly elect to carve out a manageable part of the whole. In place of sweeping vistas of three or four centuries, we are now more likely to find focused, in-depth examinations of movements, periods, peoples, or styles. The job of synthesis becomes increasingly difficult, and the likelihood of it accordingly more remote.

Studies of nineteenth- and twentieth-century materials dominate current scholarship. The Garretts' bibliography included nothing dealing with the years after 1826, but there was not yet much to include. Sommer, on the other hand, recorded dramatic growth in the later period. This growth continues. This bibliography lists hundreds of titles on nineteenth- and early twentieth-century subjects. For example, furniture writings have so proliferated that a chapter, and a large one at that, deals with furniture between 1820 and 1920. Chapters on plumbing, heating, and lighting; kitchen artifacts and housework; textiles; ceramics; and glass all contain significant complements of titles dealing with the nineteenth century. Two studies in particular, those of quilts and of the arts and crafts movement, are grounded wholly or primarily in nineteenth- and twentieth-century phenomena. The scholarship boom in these two areas is so noteworthy that it deserves separate commentary below. The prominence of these topics, however, underlines the central point that scholarly energies have shifted from the eighteenth and early nineteenth centuries to the late nineteenth and early twentieth centuries.

One of the corollaries of this shift is that the nature of documentation has also shifted. Documentation for earlier materials is often difficult to locate and limited in its range of relevancies. The explosion in both the range and the survival rates of later materials is mirrored in documents as well. There are more types of documents, and they survive in greater numbers. The two most dramatic documentary introductions are trade catalogues and photographs.[5] Both contain vast amounts of contextual information that offer the potential for complex and subtle interpretation.

Quilts have emerged as major focal points for discussing women's issues. Two decades ago, the bibliography on quilts was minimal. Most of it was technical, antiquarian, or sentimental. Today it has become both abundant and highly sophisticated. Quilts have been claimed as women's art, as women's most significant material culture. Although perspectives vary, sometimes dramatically, quilts today serve as key vehicles for the exploration of many issues associated with women and creativity. Quilt literature is expanding at a very rapid rate. Around the country, local and statewide projects are documenting and recording thousands of quilts. The number of quilts known is large today. It will be larger a year from now. The chapter on quilts in this bibliography reports on some of the ongoing

---

[5] On trade catalogues, see E. Richard McKinstry, *Trade Catalogues at Winterthur: A Guide to the Literature of Merchandising, 1750 to 1980* (New York: Garland Publishing, 1984); and Deborah Anne Federhen et al., *Accumulation and Display: Mass Marketing Household Goods in America, 1880–1920* (Winterthur, Del.: Winterthur Museum, 1986). Studies of photography are listed herewith in "Surveys" and "American Furniture, 1820–1920."

activity in this area. Because quilt scholarship is expanding and evolving so rapidly, that chapter can record only a moment in a highly dynamic scenario.

The arts and crafts movement has been reclaimed. The quickening pace of historic rehabilitation so characteristic of our age has brought into prominence objects and ideas associated with a movement that died little more than half a century ago. What makes the arts and crafts movement so unlike the earlier revivals of the nineteenth century is that it was—or appeared to be—an integrated package of aesthetics and philosophy. Grounded in a critique of the social and cultural conditions of the late nineteenth and early twentieth centuries, the arts and crafts movement still carries certain moral and ethical connotations. The chapter here outlines the major contributions to the renewed interest in this movement and its products. As with the heightened interest in quilts, the reclamation of the arts and crafts movement also has political dimensions, although these have rarely been explicitly expressed.[6]

The growing respectability of material culture scholarship has increased the audience for studies of historic furnishings. From the earliest days of scholarship in this field, there have been authors who recognized that household furnishings were significant pieces of American history. Each decade has produced studies conceived within a broad historical vision. Many of those titles appear in this bibliography. The early writers' ambitious dreams of shaping the form and content of American history were rarely realized, however. On one hand, the large number of antiquarian or collector-oriented publications may have made it possible for the majority of academic historians to dismiss this material as trivial or incidental. On the other, historians have their own restricted ideas of what mattered. For many, only words could lead to truth or significance, and the truths or significances they sought pertained to limited aspects of human experience.

There are still many "traditional" historians around. But there are also many others who have developed a holistic perspective that tolerates—and often welcomes—object studies.

The term *material culture* has come to be widely used in historical circles. Material culture means the total range of the material universe shaped by humankind. Schlereth has served as the able chronicler of material culture studies in America. Readers who wish to understand the growth of this scholarship and learn about its major contributions and contributors should consult his works. The key point is that, for a variety of reasons, an increasing number of historians and other students of culture have found tangible materials useful to their studies. Two types of evidence may be sufficient to document this expanded interest. One is the production of a research guide to material culture—including a section on furnishings—initially as a special issue of *American Quarterly* and later, with revisions, as a separate publication. The other is the American Studies Association's 1987 meeting, which was organized around the concept of culture and included sessions on material culture. Many of those dealt with historic furnishings and design.[7]

[6] Fran Kramer, "Arts and Crafts Conference," *Antique Review* 15, no. 4 (April 1989): 26.

[7] Thomas J. Schlereth, *Artifacts and the American Past* (Nashville: American Association for State and Local History, 1980); Thomas J. Schlereth, *Material Culture Studies in America* (Nashville: American Association for State and Local

In sum, the rising visibility of material culture studies has benefited the study of historic household furnishings. One could say that various areas of object-grounded scholarship have banded together under the flag of material culture to achieve impact and status that they might not attain individually. The end result is that material culture is no longer marginal.

Consumers have become as central to current scholarship as producers were to past scholarship. Much earlier writing on historic household furnishings borrowed the creator orientation of art history. Designers of objects, form givers, enjoyed high status. Makers sometimes did too, particularly if it could be shown that they were also designers or artists. Mere artisans or assistants following orders were usually beneath visibility. What happened to the object after it left a shop was also without much consequence. Ownership mattered to the extent that it conferred status on the object and made it worth studying. Thus catalogues usually listed ownership (under the descriptor "provenance") not so much to provide clues to meaning as to lend honorific value. An object was "art" because it had been associated with some member of the early American upper class.

Impetus for change came from at least two different directions. One was the emerging historical interest in the consumer revolution. Much work on this phenomenon focused on the sixteenth, seventeenth, and eighteenth centuries and concentrated on transformations within European society. Scholars of this historical problem recognized that examining the "supply side" illuminated only half of the phenomenon. What actually happened in the minds of people and within their homes was equally critical. The second push for consumer-oriented studies came from the so-called new history of the 1960s and 1970s. The material culture movement that Schlereth chronicled had similar origins. Both were grounded in populist values, in attempts to enfranchise groups and classes of people who had been beneath the gaze of conventional historical scholarship. Many attempted to break down the tyranny of words as evidence. "New historians" recognized that in the past few people wrote and even fewer were written about, but everyone owned or interacted with material culture, however lowly.

Material culture has its own tyrannies, however. Those whose material culture survives are privileged over those whose does not. Yet even if not everyone had the resources to become "consumers" as we understand that term today, the shift toward explorations of acquisition and use have dramatically changed scholarship and opened vast new areas for inquiry and understanding. Many of those new areas are detailed in this bibliography.

More social classes, ethnic groups, and regions are being studied. Sommer's comment about how little scholarship focused on the peoples who lived west of the Alleghenies or south of Baltimore comes to mind here. Even when Sommer wrote, scholarship was being pried loose from its East Coast

---

History, 1982); Thomas J. Schlereth, *Cultural History and Material Culture: Essays on Everyday Life, Landscapes, and Museums* (Ann Arbor: UMI Research Press, 1989). The *American Quarterly* issue was republished as Thomas J. Schlereth, *Material Culture: A Research Guide* (Lawrence: University Press of Kansas, 1985). The 1987 meeting was jointly sponsored with the Canadian Association for American Studies. The theme was "Creating Cultures: Peoples, Objects, Ideas." A listing of all presentations appears in the convention handbook.

moorings. While the WASP materials that Sommer mentioned still have heightened cachet, goods associated with many other groups have been capably dealt with. This bibliography provides ample evidence of that new representation.

Increased scholarship on peoples once considered marginal can be traced in part to the new history and in part to the celebration of ethnicity that accompanied it. The melting-pot ideology of the midcentury reinforced the repression of ethnic and other differences. Recent respect for pluralism has reversed that behavior. American unwillingness to address issues of class has also had a dampening effect on scholarship, but many of the quaint ideological fictions that masked or denied class have been revealed.[8] Writing has become more socially informed.

Scholarship has become increasingly interdisciplinary. The most influential studies and those best known by scholars in other fields tend, not surprisingly, to combine the perspectives of two or more disciplines. Chief among these is anthropology, but a listing of identifiable disciplinary components of contemporary work would also include social, cultural, technological, and art history; archaeology; cultural geography; sociology; psychology; literature and linguistics; and others. While not all fusions are sophisticated or successful, the desire to make them indicates that many believe that traditional demarcations of learning hinder meaningful inquiry. For many scholars today, affiliation with a particular discipline is more a matter of administrative convenience (or necessity) than a statement of intellectual belief. Those operating outside the academy may have even fewer structural restraints on their intellectual affiliation.

Material culture studies' emphasis on innovation has helped to foster interdisciplinary work. It may be fair to say that all major material culture scholars are interdisciplinary. An interdisciplinary orientation is shared by those scholars of historic furnishings who consider themselves part of the material culture movement, or have been adopted by it.

Team projects have become more prominent. The major exhibitions that have defined or redefined areas of the American tangible past have increasingly been the work of teams of museum and academic scholars collaborating. The Museum of Fine Arts, Boston, may have the most distinguished record for collaboration, but the Metropolitan Museum of Art, the Brooklyn Museum, the Wadsworth Atheneum, and others have also completed major projects pooling the talents of many. In some ways, this emphasis on teamwork can be seen as a response to the rapid proliferation of information. Since no one person can write authoritatively about much, the idea of splitting the territory into manageable fragments seems reasonable. Where the goal was to create a holistic vision of a culture, as in Jonathan L. Fairbanks and Robert F. Trent's *New England Begins*, that could only be accomplished by assembling an interdisciplinary group to explore that culture from a variety of perspectives.

---

[8] Nathan Glazer and Daniel Patrick Moynihan, *Beyond the Melting Pot* (Cambridge, Mass.: MIT Press and Harvard University Press, 1963); Werner Sollors, "Theory of American Ethnicity," *American Quarterly* 33, no. 3 (Bibliography 1981): 257–83; Stephan Thernstrom, ed., *Harvard Encyclopedia of American Ethnic Groups* (Cambridge, Mass.: Harvard University Press, 1980). For an irreverent treatment, see Paul Fussell, *Class: A Guide through the American Status System* (New York: Summit Books, 1983).

Teamwork may also be encouraged by the funding requirements of the National Endowment for the Humanities (NEH). Many major examples of teamwork have been recipients of NEH awards. The NEH has been vigorous in requiring significant humanities content in the projects that it funds; the way to obtain NEH funding is to assemble a team of humanities scholars capable of bringing a variety of perspectives and expertises to a given project. This financial carrot has worked well. The NEH can fairly claim to have altered the intellectual content of museum exhibitions in this country.

If the publication of a major bibliography provides an occasion for evaluating the current state of scholarship, it also presents a chance to outline needs and opportunities for future scholarship. The titles listed in this bibliography document a publication explosion, but they also reveal that coverage of the terrain has been spotty. Some areas are still being ignored or dealt with in only cursory ways. Questions and approaches need to be both broadened and diversified. Opportunities for future scholarship are nearly boundless. I have listed below, in only the sketchiest outline, the needs and challenges that I see lying before those who think and write about historic household furnishings.

More Theory. The scholarship of historic household furnishings has a long tradition of expository writing, but has developed little theory. The challenge is to move beyond facts, beyond exposition, to ideas. Those who have used or proposed theory have usually borrowed heavily from other areas of scholarship. Whether historic household furnishings as an area can generate theory is itself a theoretical question. At the very best, those who work with these materials are in a position to contribute more actively than they have to theoretical discussions taking place within the broader material culture community.

Closer attention to objects. This challenge may seem ironic, for the field has sometimes been criticized for a nearly myopic fixation on goods. Yet despite all the looking, or claims for looking, examination-derived insights are not common enough. Words are frequently privileged over objects. Object studies still depend too heavily on the written word and rely too little on the evidence within the object itself. Verbal rhetoric is given more credence than tangible, artifactual reality. Objects need to be looked at more closely precisely because their value and power as historic documents are still not being sufficiently exploited.

More typological histories. There is a real need in the field for thoughtful, methodical, objective historic surveys of all types of goods. Many past studies were either conceived from an art perspective, which compromised objectivity, or based on one collection or a few collections. Some of these early typologies are still valuable, but many more are not. As a result, we still have sketchy impressions of the history of vast numbers of objects. Creating such typological histories may not be glamorous work, but it would be a valuable contribution to the field. Such studies constitute the basic building blocks of material culture history, and we therefore need them.

Reexamination of the familiar. Much territory that is presumed to be known is in reality known only slightly or from limited perspectives. For example, household furnishings of the eighteenth century, for all their heightened economic value, attract relatively little scholarly attention at present. The area is largely devoid of intellectual life. There seems to be a sense that little more can be learned. Yet so many new questions could be brought to the material, so many new ways of conceptualizing and contextualizing it could be conceived. The same fallacious belief that all is known may restrict work on major figures or phenomena of the nineteenth century. In truth, much of the pioneering work on nineteenth-century materials only skimmed the surface, using the most accessible objects or documents. Here again is terrain awaiting new conceptualizations and new insights. That which we assume to be known best may be most in need of reexamination.

Explorations into visual thinking. One way to understand the process of visual thinking is to examine its products. The concept of visual thinking is provocative and suggestive, but it has not been assimilated broadly or pushed to new explanatory levels. Folklorists and historians of technology have been successful in examining visual thinking and other nonverbal aspects of humans' interactions with things, as both makers and users.[9] There are no obvious reasons why those who deal with historic household furnishings should not participate in these examinations — and many good reasons why they should.

Contextual studies. The full range of meanings of the term *context* needs to be appreciated and exploited. When many people say "context," they tend to mean immediate physical surroundings. For every object, however, there exists a wide range of social, cultural, political, ideological, technological, use, reuse, and other contexts. Because context is a factor that shapes meaning, studies of meaning must necessarily address context. Changes or conflicts in meaning may in part be related to changes or conflicts in context. All objects have multiple contexts; all objects have multiple meanings structured by those contexts.

Closer attention to ethnicity and class. Ethnic studies have expanded dramatically in recent years but are hardly inclusive. There is much more to be done. Participating in ethnic studies may be a form of political activism, but it has intellectual rationales as well. Ethnicity is often expressed culturally, which means that it may shape the way people apprehend and evaluate their surroundings. People of different ethnicities *may* hold different views of the world. People of different classes *do* hold different views of the world. Class may be difficult to define, but it shapes — and is manifest in — attitudes, values, and beliefs in significant ways. The concept and reality of class are underused in the writings of Americans who deal with historic household furnishings.

[9] Simon J. Bronner, *Grasping Things: Folk Material Culture and Mass Society in America* (Lexington: University Press of Kentucky, 1986); Michael Owen Jones, *Exploring Folk Art* (Ann Arbor: UMI Research Press, 1987).

Feminist perspectives. Feminist scholars have dramatically reordered literary studies and, to lesser degrees, history and art history.[10] Material culture studies, however, remain largely a male domain. Within the areas of historic household furnishings, feminist arguments have been largely confined to discussions of quilts, needlework, and domesticity. That range seems unnecessarily limited and self-ghettoizing. Many other areas of historic furnishings scholarship would also benefit from feminist critiques. As material culture studies in general become less marginalized, feminists are likely to find additional aspects of the field worth exploring and analyzing.

Marxist perspectives. Some of the most provocative scholarship in the humanities and social sciences is produced by scholars trained in or conversant with Marxist thought. Much of this emanates from Britain and the Continent. In this country, however, the political repression of McCarthyism still stunts intellectual life. In some circles there is very real fear of mentioning Marx or Marxism. Considered objectively, this is sad. Karl Marx was a distinguished philosopher and theorist of the last century. Marxism constitutes a great strand of modern scholarship. Marxist thought has a good deal to contribute to discussions of societies and the things that those societies produce and consume.[11]

Studies of vernacular materials. Only a few years ago the Vernacular Architecture Forum was established. Its membership rapidly grew to several hundred, indicating widespread interest in the subject. There is no organization in this country for the study of vernacular furnishings, but it is clear from publications and collecting activity that there is much interest in this area. The English Regional Furniture History Society might provide a model here. I am not necessarily suggesting the formation of another organization, but only that there is room for the coordinated, systematic study of the vernacular furnishings that were once the contents of vernacular houses. A good deal of work has already been done on the local and regional levels. One next step might be to map regional variations and chart patterns of change or diffusion. Such a study would follow models generated by cultural geography. Another option might be to compile a reader exploring a given class of vernacular materials—furniture, for instance—following the example of *Common Places*, Dell Upton and John Michael Vlach's anthology of vernacular architecture scholarship.[12]

Reconsideration of centers and margins. Can pluralism really work? Are there ways to establish areas of shared knowledge without constructing a canon? Is it necessary to have centers and margins? Are there less invidious ways of thinking about materials from different origins or produced in different contexts? The characteristic Western use of oppositions seems to require that for every up there be

[10] Thalia Gouma-Peterson and Patricia Matthews, "The Feminist Critique of Art History," *Art Bulletin* 69, no. 3 (September 1987): 326–57.

[11] Jean Chesneaux, *Pasts and Futures; or, What Is History For?* (London: Thames and Hudson, 1978); Michael Denning, "'The Special American Conditions': Marxism and American Studies," *American Quarterly* 38, no. 3 (Bibliography 1986): 356–80.

[12] Dell Upton and John Michael Vlach, eds., *Common Places: Readings in American Vernacular Architecture* (Athens: University of Georgia Press, 1986).

a down, for every in, an out. Yet when this familiar way of ordering and ranking is applied to objects—and usually, by association, to people—it has unfortunate effects. New conceptualizations are needed.

Studies of ideologies in goods. Grant McCracken has argued that things are ideologies in tangible form.[13] He maintains that societies often express their most fundamental beliefs in material culture; ideologies expressed in things seem inevitable, the natural order of the world. These ideas need to be tested. If they are valid, material culture is even more useful for documenting societies' basic assumptions than we have recognized. What might grow from these insights is a series of excursions into the ideologies revealed through material culture, or more narrowly, household furnishings. The latter should be particularly useful for explaining the ideologies that shape and structure domestic life.

Systems analysis. A lesson from Ruth Schwartz Cowan's study of household technology is that sometimes objects or events need to be integrated into systems in order to be understood.[14] The obvious explanation for a phenomenon may be the wrong explanation. Factors beyond the object—and invisible in the object—such as trade disputes, price fixing, fuel supplies, or labor shortages, may be critically important in determining the production and use, success or failure, of that object. This approach recognizes that objects cannot be considered in isolation; locating them within systems illuminates the complex and often competing forces that determine their fate. In truth, everything relates to everything else. Materials and forms are in a state of constant competition. The ascendance of one material or form necessarily means the decline of another. The challenge is to determine which factors are operative within a given situation. Such studies may be difficult, but they have the salubrious effect of revealing that complexities often lie behind simplicities.

Cultural energy theory. We know cultural energy when we see it, but we do not know why it happens. Desks and bookcases attract great attention in the eighteenth century but little in the nineteenth. Sideboards are the focus of energies in the nineteenth century but not in the twentieth. Pressed glass was the focus of great energies in the early nineteenth century but generally taken for granted today. Quilts were prominent throughout the nineteenth century, relatively invisible throughout the first half of this century, but once again are charged with meaning. Two sets of questions emerge. First, how or why do certain phenomena rise to crucial cultural visibility? Do different explanations emerge for each instance, or does the data support some general theory? Second, what patterns can be found in charting those goods that have been highly visible at various times? What would we learn if we assembled the "hottest" goods of each decade over the last three or four centuries? Merely doing so could generate a long list of questions and potential research topics.

Diffusion studies. An extraordinary amount of scholarship on historic furnishings traces diffusion of forms, materials, and styles. Relatively little of that work, however, explains that diffusion. Diffusion

[13] Grant McCracken, *Culture and Consumption* (Bloomington: Indiana University Press, 1988), pp. 130–37.
[14] Ruth Schwartz Cowan, *More Work for Mother* (New York: Basic Books, 1983).

is often thought of as a process analogous to the spread of contagious disease; mere contact is enough. Scholars of diffusion recognize that this explanation is inadequate. All diffusion takes place within social contexts. All diffusion is framed within power relationships. When an idea, an object, or a behavior spreads, it is because someone thinks that it is to his or her advantage to adopt the innovation.[15] Within the area of household furnishings, diffusion studies are still in a primitive stage. Rigorous studies of diffusion could contribute to this field and to cultural geography and history.

Under the rubric of diffusion also come studies of cultural transfer. This concept is only loosely understood and usually interpreted mechanistically. A series of studies of cultural transfer within different times and places might bring greater refinement to the concept.

Exlorations of memory. Objects have long been used as prods to memory. Gravestones, public monuments, and portraits are all obvious examples. Household furnishings also are touchstones for memory, albeit usually of a more subtle, less public nature. Some aspects of memory within domestic contexts have been explored but in limited and tentative ways.[16] Further studies might go beyond examinations of individual or personal memory to issues of shared or communal memory. Memory is also a critical dimension of cognition and self-definition. Insofar as objects are related to memory, they too participate in basic aspects of cognition and creation of self.

Constellation studies. We sometimes group historic objects by style, sometimes by origin, and sometimes by material. Within their original contexts of use, however, they may have been grouped according to very different principles. We need to look for constellations of artifacts that in some meaningful ways "go together" within their culture.[17] Many of these patterns of "going together" were obvious to people within that culture, just as they are within ours. Too often these rules remain at the unspoken level and need to be articulated to help us to understand or recreate that culture and its patterns of meaning.

Participation in larger discussions. Household furnishings constitute only a portion of the material universe, but they also constitute significant data for historical and cultural interpretation. Scholars outside the field often seem to recognize the truth of this statement more frequently and fully than those working within the field, as recent books by Asa Briggs and Miles Orvell reveal.[18] Scholars who work with these materials should themselves become contributors to discussions of the consumer revolution or the changing nature of domestic life. Those who work in the field should have much to say about the growth of artifactual literacy, the history of vision, the history of sensory life, and the history of materialism.

[15] Peter J. Hugill and D. Bruce Dickson, *The Transfer and Transformation of Ideas and Material Culture* (College Station: Texas A&M University Press, 1988).

[16] Maurice Halbwachs, *The Collective Memory* (New York: Harper and Row, 1980); Mihaly Csikszentmihalyi and Eugene Rochberg-Halton, *The Meaning of Things* (Cambridge: At the University Press, 1981).

[17] McCracken, *Culture and Consumption*, pp. 118–29.

[18] Asa Briggs, *Victorian Things* (Chicago: University of Chicago Press, 1988); Miles Orvell, *The Real Thing* (Chapel Hill: University of North Carolina Press, 1989).

More interdisciplinary work. The value and impact of interdisciplinary work have already been noted. New ideas and understandings come from traveling up new roads and asking new questions, from making new combinations of perspectives and insights. The value of multidisciplinary work seems self-evident and needs little additional argument here.

Speculative scholarship. At worst, speculative work can be erroneous. At best, it can be brilliantly illuminating. In either case, it can be useful for helping others to reach toward more compelling or refined conclusions. Tentative arguments, partial conclusions, untested hypotheses, unorthodox vistas—these can all be valuable for generating new or more powerful conceptions of the material world and its workings. The point is not to be correct, whatever that might mean, but suggestive; not to end inquiry, but to inspire it; not to close dialogue, but to open it. In the end, there is no historical truth, only ideas or explanations that serve our needs at a given moment in time.

The hundreds of works listed and annotated in this bibliography represent a wide variety of approaches and assumptions. They provide a reliable cross-section of current scholarship in most areas of American household furnishings prior to 1920. Taken together they offer a sumptuous, nearly overwhelming banquet of sensory and intellectual delights. I hope that they will also provide stimulus for continuing and expanding work in this field.

References and Surveys

Basic References and Guides to Research

BIBLIOGRAPHIES AND RELATED WORKS

ENCYCLOPEDIAS, DICTIONARIES, AND RELATED WORKS

PERIODICALS

Surveys

Basic References and Guides to Research

Neville Thompson

REFERENCE BOOKS are the workhorses of any library. Like workhorses, they tend to be functional rather than glamorous, and the results of their use are generally practical rather than ornamental. Also like workhorses, they are indispensable, and they seldom rest. Any librarian will have a mental list of reference sources that are essential to the everyday functioning of the library: some are universal to all libraries, and others are basic to a library serving a defined readership, whether it be research chemists or students of the decorative arts.

This section lists reference materials that have proved to be useful for scholars and students working in the fields of American fine and decorative arts at Winterthur. As with all such selections, it is to some extent subjective and based on experience with this particular readership, but I believe that the works represented are fundamental and should be available in other libraries concerned with similar subject matter. I have omitted reference works of a general nature (such as *Encyclopaedia Britannica* or *Dictionary of American Biography*) and those that deal specifically with other fields. The sources included represent several genres, some of which will be familiar, others probably less so. A few of my choices do not fall within the strict definition of "reference book" at all, but in practice function as such for researchers in these fields.

Bibliographies are basic to research and of course exist in many forms: they may be inclusive (such as Linda Franklin's *Antiques and Collectibles*) or more narrowly defined (such as Simon Bronner's bibliography of American folk art). They may be annotated critically (as is Smithsonian Institution's Archives of American Art set) or factually (such as Etta Arntzen and Robert Rainwater's guide), or they may not be annotated. A few are meant to assist in the formation of a library in the field, such as Louise Lucas's work. A well-compiled bibliography, such as Henry-Russell Hitchcock's exemplary listing of the first century of American architectural publication, with an index by topic and chronological short-title list, can be used to stimulate creative thinking about the subject as well as to verify a name or a date.

Biographical dictionaries that are specific to a field have the virtue of including minor figures that more general compilations cannot cover. They are vital for the few scraps of information they can furnish about the shadowy figures that seem to appear all too often in this field. The dictionary compiled by George Groce and David Wallace for the New-York Historical Society is invaluable for such references. Dictionaries of terminology for defined subject areas, as with the biographical dictionaries already mentioned, are valuable for similar reasons. Many of these are cited here. Yet another type of reference source that has been devoted to one subject area is the periodical index, which can cover less common material: *Art Index* is one of several such tools to cover art periodicals and related journals.

Several sources listed here are more unclassifiable and may be new to some readers. Compilations of newspaper advertisements by craftsmen and artisans emphasize the value of such contemporary sources and may be the only printed records of their work. Harold Lancour's chronological listing of American art auction catalogues provides access to yet another important form of contemporary documentation for the movements of art objects from owner to owner and up and down the financial scale. Household inventories, gathered and published in book form, highlight a third type of record that is important for our understanding of how objects were used and valued by previous owners. Many other fields have similar key reference works that allow researchers to use important resources more easily but which may well be unknown to the general public.

As with many other areas of study, guides have been written to serve as overall introductions to the literature and resources of art history and related disciplines and to the most effective ways of using these resources. A number of these guides were written by art librarians, who may often have found other art librarians to be their most vocally appreciative audience. Such basic guides to research deserve a wide and thoughtful audience among prospective researchers. In addition to providing critical evaluative annotations and lists of printed reference sources, they go into considerable detail about the how-tos of research, from dealing with manuscript materials to coping with the new on-line data bases. Among recent publications of this type (which should be available in most art libraries) are Elizabeth Pollard's *Visual Arts Research: A Handbook* (Westport, Conn., 1986); Elizabeth J. Sacca and Loren B. Singer's *Visual Arts Reference and Research Guide* (Montreal, 1983); Lois Swan Jones's *Art Research Methods and Resources* (Dubuque, Iowa, 1984), and Gerd Muesham's *Guide to Basic Information Services in the Visual Arts* (Santa Barbara and Oxford, 1978). Time spent in consulting one of these sources can result in a more intelligent use of research time in the long run.

Perhaps the most underused resource of all, however, is often neglected by novice and veteran researcher alike: the introduction to the reference work in hand. I cannot emphasize too strongly how valuable skimming such an introduction can be for the potential user. From it, one can learn the exact scope of the work, its inclusions and omissions, the date span and geographical area covered, and often the methodology used in its compilation. Other useful information often appears in the introduction or preface and nowhere else in the body of the text. It can contain explicit instructions for using the work most economically and effectively. In short, careful reading of an introduction is time well spent for the user.

Today's scholars are fortunate to have, as the result of many hours of often tedious labor, the reference works we cannot do without. The next time you use one, remember—if only for a moment—all those authors, editors, and compilers who have devoted so much of their time to allow you to use your time more fruitfully.

Archives of American Art. *Collection of Exhibition Catalogs.* Boston: G. K. Hall, 1979. iv+851 pp.

This collection is an index to a compilation, on microfilm, of thousands of art exhibition catalogues issued in America between the early nineteenth century and the 1960s. The catalogues, located by Archives researchers in public, museum, and historical society collections and in their own holdings, were listed on catalogue cards and filmed in their entirety. This one-volume index reproduces the card listings, which are by exhibiting institution and (in the case of shows of the work of three or fewer artists) by artist and include craftsmen. Each listing is keyed to the microfilm by roll and frame numbers. The microfilm itself may be used at the Archives' field offices in Boston, New York, Washington, and elsewhere or borrowed from the Detroit headquarters. Together, the index and microfilm provide access to a collection of art exhibition catalogues that no one institution alone could possibly house and service. They are research tools of immense value.

Archives of American Art, Smithsonian Institution. *Arts in America: A Bibliography.* Edited by Bernard Karpel. 4 vols. Washington, D.C.: Smithsonian Institution Press, 1979. Indexes.

Intended as a "comprehensive guide to the literature on American art," this series of annotated bibliographies covers the fine arts, the decorative arts, native American art, design, photography, film, theater, dance, and music. It includes separate listings of serials and periodicals, theses and dissertations, and visual resources. Each bibliography was contributed by an authority in his or her field who also prepared introductory essays discussing criteria for inclusion of references cited. Their annotations, while concise, are informative, critical, at times idiosyncratic, but always interesting. While variable in quality and usefulness, *Arts in America* can be browsed for enjoyment as well as used for more conventional bibliographic research.

Arntzen, Etta, and Robert Rainwater. *Guide to the Literature of Art History.* Chicago: American Library Association; London: Art Book Co., 1980. xviii+616 pp.; indexes.

Arntzen and Rainwater's guide stands as the fundamental bibliography of printed material on the fine and decorative arts. Begun as a revision and an update of Mary Chamberlain's basic work, almost half the entries are new. Its audience is the serious researcher, whether graduate student, teaching or museum professional, or librarian. Material on photography and architecture is included, but the fields of aesthetics, archaeology, landscape architecture, and urban planning are omitted, as are monographs on individual artists. Most cited titles are in Western languages, but coverage attempts to be universal for all countries and periods. Excellent annotations summarize the scope and subject matter and provide

information on each work's contents, illustrations, bibliographies, and indexes. The guide is a model of its kind and an essential source of information on the basic works in the fields covered.

Art Index: A Cumulative Author and Subject Index to a Selected List of Fine Arts Periodicals and Museum Bulletins. Vol. 1 –. New York: H. W. Wilson, 1930–.

Art Index is the most comprehensive index to materials appearing in several hundred periodicals in the fine and decorative arts, archaeology, photography, architecture, urban design, and landscape design. The index is issued quarterly in paperback and is cumulated annually and in three-year volumes. Indexed periodicals are selected through review by an editorial board and by subscriber recommendations. Users should check the list of periodicals included in the front of each issue, since titles are both added and dropped. Listings are by subject (including persons) and by author, and citations include volume and issue number, date, pagination, and illustrative material; cross-indexing is extensive. The index includes citations to book reviews and to illustrations without text and a useful listing of ordering information for the periodicals cited. This work is essential for its coverage of major periodicals from many countries and in many languages for art and its related fields. It should be held by every library concerned and consulted by every researcher.

The Arts in Early American History: Needs and Opportunities for Study. Essay by Walter Muir Whitehill; bibliography by Wendell D. Garrett and Jane N. Garrett. Chapel Hill: University of North Carolina Press for the Institute of Early American History and Culture, 1965. xv+170 pp.; index.

The origin of this volume was a conference sponsored by the Institute of Early American History and Culture, Colonial Williamsburg, Archives of American Art, and Winterthur Museum that was devoted to exploring the current state of research and scholarship in the American fine and applied arts to 1826. Whitehill's essay sums up the literature of the field and identifies possible future directions, while the bibliography "attempts to record the most important writings" about the arts in America from the beginning of colonization to 1826. It contains useful evaluative annotations and a helpful section on periodicals. Although much has been written in the field since the publication of this volume, the bibliography remains useful, and the essay is important for our understanding of the growth of the study of American art.

Bronner, Simon J. *American Folk Art: A Guide to Sources.* Garland Reference Library of the Humanities, vol. 464. New York and London: Garland Publishing, 1984. xxxi+313 pp.; 30 plates, indexes.

American Folk Art serves as a guide to the literature of the growing field of folk art studies and is aimed at an audience of students and scholars. The guide is arranged by topic, with each chapter contributed by a different specialist in a particular area. Essays on the literature and present state of scholarship in their chosen subfield are included, followed by annotated bibliographical entries. Diverse media, including films, conference proceedings, and journal articles, are cited. Bronner's introduction surveys the history of folk art studies and comments on possible future directions for the field.

Franklin, Linda Campbell. *Antiques and Collectibles: A Bibliography of Works in English, Sixteenth Century to 1976*. Metuchen, N.J., and London: Scarecrow Press, 1978. xxiii+1,091 pp.; bibliography, indexes.

Franklin attempts to provide the scholar, the collector, and the librarian with a comprehensive listing of works in English on a wide range of man-made objects classifiable as decorative arts, antiques, or collectibles. She cites offprints, theses, dissertations, exhibition catalogues, and monographs and provides locations for many of the pre-1945 works cited. Annotations are used when needed to clarify the subject matter. References are arranged by subject and, within the subject, alphabetically by author. Franklin has indicated with an asterisk works that she considers especially valuable. Although it may lack selectivity, this massive compilation of more than 10,000 references cites material hard to find elsewhere.

Freitag, Wolfgang M. *Art Books: A Basic Bibliography of Monographs on Artists*. New York and London: Garland Publishing, 1985. xxvii+351 pp.; index.

Art Books is a listing of monographic works on 1,870 individual artists from all countries and all historical periods. The fields represented include, in order of amount of coverage, painting and drawing, sculpture, architecture, graphic arts, photography, and decorative and applied arts. Freitag has been selective in his choice of subjects and states that his assumed readership is the graduate student or researcher. He has included such works as treatises, catalogues raisonnés, and autobiographical volumes. Freitag has long been associated with Harvard University Libraries; this bibliography represents his personal selection, both in subject matter and in works cited, based on a distinguished career in the world of art librarianship.

Hitchcock, Henry-Russell. *American Architectural Books: A List of Books, Portfolios, and Pamphlets on Architecture and Related Subjects Published in America before 1895*. New expanded ed. New introduction by Adolf K. Placzek. Da Capo Press Series in Architecture and Decorative Art, edited by Adolf K. Placzek. New York: Da Capo Press, 1976. xvi+150 pp.; index, appendix.

Hitchcock, an eminent American architectural historian, lists all works on the subject of architecture published in the United States from the first publication in 1775 through the end of 1894, excluding journal articles, historical and antiquarian material, and purely technical works. The works are arranged by author and are cited by date of publication. All editions are included and are occasionally accompanied by annotations. The index is arranged by broad subject category and thus reveals the great preponderance of publication on domestic architecture during the period. The chronological short-title list of works cited, compiled by William Jordy, is an important feature of this edition. It would be difficult to imagine undertaking the study of American architectural history without this key work.

Lancour, Harold, comp. *American Art Auction Catalogues, 1785–1942: A Union List*. New York: New York Public Library, 1944. 377 pp.; index.

Lancour lists more than 7,000 catalogues of auction sales of art objects held in the United States from 1785 to 1942, excluding sales of books, maps, stamps, and coins. The listing is chronological by first day of sale, and entries include owners, short title, firm, collation, number of lots, and location of copies of the catalogue. Lancour includes a useful list of auction houses and date spans for their published catalogues. The only such work to deal with American auctions, this book is an essential reference for locating such material for the years covered.

Lucas, E. Louise. *Art Books: A Basic Bibliography on the Fine Arts*. Greenwich, Conn.: New York Graphic Society, 1968. 245 pp.; index.

The word *basic* in the title is a key to this volume's intention and scope. *Art Books* provides an unannotated listing of works in the fine and decorative arts and architecture aimed at the needs of the undergraduate art history student. The author based this work, previously published as the *Harvard List of Books on Art*, on the holdings of Harvard University Libraries, where she served as librarian for many years. Out-of-print books are included, but museum catalogues are omitted. An important feature is the section on basic monographs on individual artists. While the general section on history covers all periods and geographic areas, the sections on architecture, painting, and sculpture are more limited.

McKinstry, E. Richard. *Trade Catalogues at Winterthur: A Guide to the Literature of Merchandising, 1750 to 1980*. New York and London: Garland Publishing, a Winterthur Book, 1984. xv+438 pp.; illustrations, indexes.

McKinstry provides a listing of a rich collection of trade catalogues, primarily American and dating to about 1914, held by Winterthur Library. Entries are arranged in thirty subject categories, with the bulk of material appearing in sections for house furnishings and household goods. Indexes provide access by subject, date, and place of publication. Annotations help to establish the nature of firms and their products as well as the firm's age. This is an exemplary bibliography of a collection of about 2,000 titles, and each catalogue listed is available on microfiche from Clearwater Publishing, New York.

Park, Helen. *A List of Architectural Books Available in America before the Revolution.* New ed., rev. and enl. Foreword by Adolf K. Placzek. Los Angeles: Hennessey and Ingalls, 1973. xv+79 pp.; 11 illustrations.

Park lists and comments on architectural works known to have been sold or owned in this country prior to 1775 and therefore to have been available to American architects and craftsmen. An introduction discusses the state of architectural publication during the period. Included are sources of citations and a list of titles by frequency of citation in eighteenth-century sources. The listing of titles is by author, with variant editions noted. This is an essential reference not only for the study of American building during this period but also for the work of other craftsmen, since such works are known to have been owned and used by cabinetmakers and other artisans.

Reese, Rosemary, comp. *Documentation of Collections.* A Bibliography of Historical Practices, vol. 4, edited by Frederick L. Rath, Jr., and Merrilyn Rogers O'Connell. Nashville: American Association for State and Local History, 1979. xi+218 pp.; appendix, index.

Intended as a guide to information sources on the fine and decorative arts and crafts, this bibliography (one of a series of six on selected topics) was sponsored by the American Association for State and Local History. Its primary audience is nonspecialist museum or historical society staff who must document and identify a variety of objects under their care. Reese's emphasis is on post-1945 publications that are easily locatable. Special features include a "basic reference shelf," which is useful if a reference collection is to be built from scratch, and a chapter on eight major historical organizations and their scope, staff, and activities. After a chapter on general references, the bibliography is divided into sections devoted to artifacts, decorative arts, and fine arts collections, with an emphasis on American objects.

Romaine, Lawrence B. *A Guide to American Trade Catalogs, 1744–1900.* New York: R. R. Bowker Co., 1960. xxiii+422 pp.; bibliography, index.

Commercial catalogues issued by American manufacturers and retailers are listed by category and arranged by company name and date. Categories range from agricultural machinery to windmills and include furniture, glassware, house furnishings, china and pottery, silverware, and lighting. Romaine locates each catalogue listed in at least one library or archive and notes pagination, size, and illustrative material. This is an important and pioneering work that not only focuses attention on this material as important primary sources but also still serves as a useful reference guide.

Roos, Frank J., Jr. *Bibliography of Early American Architecture: Writings on Architecture Constructed before 1860 in the Eastern and Central United States.* Urbana, Chicago, and London: University of Illinois Press, 1968. 389 pp.; index.

Roos has compiled a bibliography of books and periodical articles on the architecture of this country from the East Coast to the "Western edge of the Mississippi Valley," covering buildings constructed before 1860. This work was originally published in 1943 and revised for 1968 publication, although the majority of the material included dates from before 1960. Following a section of general references, the bulk of the entries are arranged by region, then by state, and then by locality. Many references to publications by local historical societies and similar sources are included and are occasionally accompanied by annotations. The bibliography is particularly strong on domestic architecture.

Schimmelman, Janice G. *Architectural Treatises and Building Handbooks Available in American Libraries and Bookstores through 1800.* Reprinted from *Proceedings of the American Antiquarian Society* 95, pt. 2 (October 1985): 317–500. Worcester, Mass.: By the society, 1986. Appendixes.

Schimmelman expands and amplifies (by sixty-five titles) Helen Park's important listing of architectural books available in America before the Revolution, chiefly by adding titles discovered to have been owned by libraries or advertised for sale by bookstores in this country through 1800. By omitting private libraries (unlike Park), Schimmelman focuses attention on the role that public and commercial institutions played in the development of architectural knowledge. The listing is by author. Appendixes cite volumes by date of first appearance in this country, by the number of eighteenth-century references, by bookstore or institution, and, for each institution, by the number of cited titles held.

Schimmelman, Janice G. *A Checklist of European Treatises on Art and Essays on Aesthetics Available in America through 1815.* Reprinted from *Proceedings of the American Antiquarian Society* 93, pt. 1 (April 1983): 95–195. Worcester, Mass.: By the society, 1983. Appendixes.

Lacking the schools, museums, and rich art traditions of England and the Continent, the artist in early America was dependent on imported written and graphic materials as a link with the art world of which he was a distant part. In this compilation, Schimmelman has located references to holdings of forty-five such works and for each has supplied bibliographical information, early locations, and references in contemporary sources. The appendixes list titles by publication date, first recorded American appearance, location, and frequency of citation of the holding source. This book is important for our understanding both of available works on art in this early period and of the transmission of artistic theories and methods from their country of origin to our own.

Sokol, David M. *American Decorative Arts and Old World Influences: A Guide to Information Sources*. Art and Architecture Information Guide Series, vol. 14. Detroit: Gale Research Co., 1980. xii+294 pp.; indexes.

Despite the title, this is not a subject bibliography on New World–Old World design relationships, but rather a basic bibliography of American decorative arts from the seventeenth century to the present, with a small number of entries on arts in other countries. As far as possible, the compiler has attempted to list post-1940 materials published in English, including books, exhibition catalogues, and selected periodical articles, with brief descriptive annotations. This is a useful, basic bibliography of secondary source material.

Yarnall, James L., and William H. Gerdts, comps., with the assistance of Katharine Fox Stewart and Catherine Hoover Voorsanger. *The National Museum of American Art's Index to American Art Exhibition Catalogues, from the Beginning through the 1876 Centennial Year*. Boston: G. K. Hall, 1986. 6 vols.

Yarnall and Gerdts compiled this long-awaited census and index to the contents of 952 catalogues of art exhibited in the United States and Canada through 1876. Each catalogue is indexed by location, owner of individual items, subject, and artist and individual work. One location is given for each catalogue; photocopies are on file at the museum. This work excludes auction catalogues, museum collections, and panoramas and dioramas, and it does not replicate works cited in major existing exhibition records for individual institutions. Begun as a bicentennial project, this massive compilation will be a foundation reference work for all researchers concerned with American art; it also demonstrates the value of the computer for such projects. The indexes will stimulate new thinking about nineteenth-century arts in this country. Users should read the introductory matter carefully, including Gerdts's essay on the art exhibition in its cultural and historical context.

ENCYCLOPEDIAS, DICTIONARIES, AND RELATED WORKS

Comstock, Helen, ed. *The Concise Encyclopedia of American Antiques*. New York: Hawthorn Books, 1965. 848 pp.; 352 plates, 114 line drawings, index.

This work is arranged in the form of topical essays, with glossaries, contributed by a number of specialists on a variety of subjects. Coverage of the field is broad and includes some unusual material, such as art of the Southwest, calligraphy, and stamps. Each section ends with a short, basic bibliography. Although dated and brief, these essays can still be read as useful introductions to their field and as indicators of the state of the art at the time of compilation.

Craig, James H. *The Arts and Crafts in North Carolina, 1699–1840*. Winston-Salem, N.C.: Museum of Early Southern Decorative Arts, Old Salem, 1965. vii+480 pp.; bibliography, index.

Craig documents the arts, crafts, and trades of early North Carolina through newspaper advertisements, apprenticeship indentures, and other records of the period. The volume is organized by craft or trade and, within each trade, by date. Court records of indenture are summarized; other sources are quoted in full. This is a particularly valuable collection of source material in light of the scarcity of newspapers for the period and the compiler's addition of primary materials of other kinds.

Cummings, Abbott Lowell, ed. *Rural Household Inventories: Establishing the Names, Uses, and Furnishings of Rooms in the Colonial New England Home, 1675–1775*. Boston: Society for the Preservation of New England Antiquities, 1964. xl+306 pp.; 14 plates, glossary, index.

Cummings reproduces 109 room-by-room inventories of household goods, the total number recorded for rural towns in Suffolk County, Massachusetts (excluding Boston), during this period. Such primary material is being increasingly employed as a source for understanding the ways in which houses were furnished and lived in at a time that predates photography as a recording device. In his introduction, Cummings explains the ways in which such data can be used and how it can be collected and interpreted. This is a valuable compilation that has helped to draw attention to the inventory as a way of providing insight into the domestic life of the past.

Directory: Historical Agencies in North America. 13th ed. Compiled and edited by Betty Pease Smith. Nashville: American Association for State and Local History, 1986. vi+686 pp.; illustrations, indexes.

This work is the latest edition of a directory of 9,375 historical societies and agencies of all sizes and scope in the United States and Canada. Published since 1944 by the American Association for State and Local History, which solicits relevant information from the agencies listed, the directory includes such related groups as folklore societies, living history groups, and research centers, as well as special listings of National Archives and National Park Service agencies and facilities. Entries include address and telephone number, staff and membership, major publications, programs, and the period covered by collections, and the entries are indexed by the name of the agency and by broad interest category. The directory pulls together a vast amount of information that is vital to anyone in museum work or concerned with American historical materials, and it supplements the listings of *The Official Museum Directory*; together, these two resources are essential.

Dow, George Francis, comp. *The Arts and Crafts in New England, 1704–1775: Gleanings from Boston Newspapers.* Topsfield, Mass.: Wayside Press, 1927. xxxii + 326 pp.; 39 plates, index.

This is the first of several important compilations of advertisements drawn from eighteenth-century American sources (Alfred Prime's, James Craig's, and Rita Gottesman's are others in this genre, inspired by Dow's example). Dow reproduces the texts, with source citations, to hundreds of notices for craftsmen, artisans, trades, and occupations appearing in five Boston newspapers during the first three-quarters of the eighteenth century. As with other compendiums of this sort, Dow has saved future scholars a great deal of searching and provides countless useful leads; in a larger scope, he provides a strong sense of the commercial life of Boston during this period.

Fleming, John, and Hugh Honour. *The Penguin Dictionary of Decorative Arts.* London: Penguin Books, Allen Lane, 1977. 896 pp.; illustrations.

This comprehensive dictionary of styles, techniques, materials, processes, craftsmen, designers, and movements includes notable firms responsible for production of furniture and objects in Europe and North America from the Middle Ages to the present. The compilers selectively list oriental objects that influenced Western arts, but omit jewelry and musical and scientific instruments. Entries range in length from a few lines to an entire page and are generously illustrated. Bibliographical references to standard works have been furnished for many entries, and extensive cross-references are included. This volume, while extremely useful for quick reference, can also be read for pleasure.

[Gottesman, Rita Susswein]. *The Arts and Crafts in New York, 1726–1776: Advertisements and News Items from New York City Newspapers.* Collections of the New-York Historical Society for the Year 1936. The John Watts dePeyster Publication Fund Series, no. 69. New York: By the society, 1938. xviii + 450 pp.; index.
———. *The Arts and Crafts in New York, 1777–1799: Advertisements and News Items from New York City Newspapers.* Collections of the New-York Historical Society for the Year 1948. The John Watts dePeyster Publication Fund Series, no. 81. New York: By the society, 1954. xix + 484 pp.; index.
———, comp. *The Arts and Crafts in New York, 1800–1804: Advertisements and News Items from New York City Newspapers.* Collections of the New-York Historical Society for the Year 1949. The John Watts dePeyster Publication Fund Series, no. 82. New York: By the society, 1965. xx + 537 pp.; index.

These three volumes together provide access to documentary printed references to a great variety of eighteenth-century crafts and trades in New York. The majority of the references are newspaper advertisements and are organized into chapters by craft or trade and then by name of craftsman. Each volume includes a preface by Gottesman that explains the scope and methodology of the volume and lists the newspapers consulted. These collections are invaluable for factual material and for an overall view of the New York scene through contemporary eyes.

Groce, George C., and David H. Wallace. *The New-York Historical Society's Dictionary of Artists in America, 1564–1860.* New Haven: Yale University Press; London: Oxford University Press, 1957. xxvii + 759 pp.; bibliography.

Based on extensive and painstaking searches through primary and secondary sources, this work remains the most authoritative biographical dictionary for both amateur and professional painters, sculptors, graphic artists, and silhouette cutters working in the United States to 1861. The dictionary does not include architects or craftsmen. All entries are documented and include references to key sources where they appear. An extensive introduction explains the scope of and the methods used in searches and compilation of the dictionary. An essential, accurate, and reliable reference work and the first source to turn to for biographical information within its scope, this book is unlikely to be supplanted in the future.

Harris, John, and Jill Lever. *Illustrated Glossary of Architecture, 850–1830.* London: Faber and Faber, 1966. xi + 78 pp. + 224 plates; bibliography.

This work illustrates and defines terminology for architectural styles, details, and elements through photographs of extant buildings and brief written definitions that are cross-indexed to illustrations. The examples shown are exclusively British, and the terminology applies most particularly to British architecture. Many of the entries are concerned with medieval architecture, and the glossary is strongest in this area (and by extension, for the Gothic revival and its literary and pictorial sources). The introduction includes a brief review of previous architectural dictionaries and their strengths and uses. The glossary illustrates the classical orders through excellent plates from literary sources, with individual elements isolated and named. This volume's most useful feature is its ability to illustrate unfamiliar terms. Although the plates are arranged by broad building element (vault, staircase) and then chronologically, it is less handy for locating an element through an illustration and then searching for its written definition.

Lewis, Philippa, and Gillian Darley. *Dictionary of Ornament*. New York: Pantheon Books, 1986. 319 pp.; illustrations, bibliography.

Dictionary of Ornament attempts to define and identify the ornamental styles, themes, and motifs found in the fine and decorative arts and architecture, with principal concentration on European and North American arts from the Renaissance to the present. Heavily illustrated, the dictionary provides as a separate section a visual key to the commonest motifs. In addition, important authors, craftsmen, and designers are included, as are titles of key design books, treatises, schools, and movements. The concise entries are thoroughly cross-indexed.

The Official Museum Directory. Washington, D.C.: American Association of Museums; Wilmette, Ill.: National Register Publishing Co., Macmillan Directory Div. Annual. Indexes.

This directory lists more than 6,000 museums of all kinds in the United States and Canada by state or province and by locality. The publication is issued yearly, with information updated by the institutions listed. Entries include address and telephone number, hours of admission, facilities, activities, selected publications, important collections, and key personnel and are indexed by state, name, and category of collections, with an index for personnel mentioned. Also listed are national, state, and regional organizations and institutions that work closely with museums. Authoritative, detailed, and reliable, this is the first source to turn to for information on American and Canadian museums.

Osborne, Harold, ed. *The Oxford Companion to the Decorative Arts*. Oxford: Oxford University Press, 1975. xiv+865 pp.; illustrations, bibliography.

This one-volume dictionary of wide scope, assembled from contributions by seventy-five experts in various fields, covers "craftsmanship and its exercise on a world-wide basis." Extensive articles cover such broad subjects as furniture or the arts of a particular culture, with shorter entries for individual craftsmen or technical or design terminology. Some articles contain references to the extensive bibliography. The articles are particularly useful for their coverage of ancient and non-Western arts. The longer articles can serve as compact introductions to entire fields of interest.

Pevsner, Nikolaus, John Fleming, and Hugh Honour. *A Dictionary of Architecture*. Rev. and enl. London: Penguin Books, 1975. 556 pp.; illustrations.

Principally the work of the three authors, each a distinguished British architectural historian, with some contributions by specialists, this dictionary of styles, terms, and persons drawn from the history of architecture of all periods and geographic areas includes bibliographical references and cross-references, with line drawings. This is an updated version of a shorter work, originally titled the *Penguin Dictionary of Architecture*, that first appeared in 1966. This edition is a useful reference work, modestly priced, which has stood the test of time.

Prime, Alfred Coxe, comp. *The Arts and Crafts in Philadelphia, Maryland, and South Carolina, 1721–1785: Gleanings from Newspapers*. [Topsfield, Mass.]: Wayside Press for the Walpole Society, 1929. xvi+323 pp.; 42 illustrations, index.

———. *The Arts and Crafts in Philadelphia, Maryland, and South Carolina, 1786–1800: Series Two, Gleanings from Newspapers*. Topsfield, Mass.: Wayside Press for the Walpole Society, 1932. xii+331 pp.; plates, index.

In these two works, selective compilations are drawn from a collection of about 20,000 newspaper advertisements placed by craftsmen and artisans in Philadelphia; Charleston, South Carolina; Baltimore; Annapolis; Richmond; and Trenton, New Jersey. Subjects represented include the fine and decorative arts, crafts, and building trades. Entries are arranged in subject chapters by name of advertiser and reproduce entire text and reference to the source. These volumes, truly a labor of love, have saved countless hours of drudgery for later researchers and emphasize the value of newspaper entries as primary sources for information on the arts and trades of the period.

Steer, Francis W., ed. *Farm and Cottage Inventories of Mid-Essex, 1635–1749*. Essex Record Office Publications, no. 8. Chelmsford: Essex County Council, 1950. [viii]+305 pp.; 14 plates, 21 line drawings, appendixes, map, indexes.

Steer compiles transcriptions of 247 inventories from English rural households and gives extensive commentary on their significance. This work is important for students of early American household furnishings, since many settlers of the period migrated from Essex to this country at about the time this group of inventories was taken. These inventories provide an interesting comparison with those in Abbott Cummings's volume on New England households.

Summerson, John. *The Classical Language of Architecture*. Cambridge, Mass.: MIT Press, 1967. 56 pp.+62 illustrations; glossary, bibliography.

Summerson describes the origin, appearance, and literary sources for the transmission of the five orders basic to classical architecture, developed in antiquity and still in use today. He presents a useful discussion of the varying uses and changes in proportion and detail of these architectural elements in different periods and of the key theoretical treatises in which they have appeared. This small book is written clearly and concisely and remains the best treatment of a topic crucial to the understanding of Western architectural history.

Thieme, Ulrich, and Felix Becker. *Allgemeines Lexikon der bildenden Künstler von der Antike bis zur Gegenwart.* Leipzig: E. A. Seemann, 1908–50. 37 vols.

Compiled in Germany, with contributions by noted scholars, this is a comprehensive list of artists, architects, craftsmen, and workers in the decorative arts of all periods, from the earliest known individuals through the late nineteenth century, and in all countries. Included are biographical articles of varying length, including names and locations of in-

dividual works and useful bibliographical references in all languages. This book has been reprinted: a newly edited Thieme-Becker has begun to appear with volume *Aa–Alexander*, but it will take many years to complete. The original publication, legendary for its comprehensiveness and reliability, remains the first and most important source to consult for biographical information for any pre-twentieth-century artist. In particular, its references to less well known persons often reveal a surprising wealth of information.

PERIODICALS

American Art Journal. Vol. 1–, no. 1–. New York: Kennedy Galleries/Da Capo Press, Spring 1969–.

For years American art was lightly regarded by mainstream art historians and attracted relatively little scholarly publication. The appearance of the *American Art Journal* coincided with a rise in interest in this country's art. From the beginning it has published thoughtful, carefully researched articles on American topics, with particular emphasis on the fine arts. Kennedy Galleries has a long and distinguished record as a specialist in American painting and sculpture. This is an important journal and an essential purchase for any library with holdings in the field.

The American Collector: The Monthly Magazine of Art and Antiques. Vols. 1–17. New York, December 1933–November 1948. Monthly.

The *American Collector* resembles *Antiques* and the *Antiquarian* in subject matter; the periodical's first editor was the prolific Thomas H. Ormsbee, author of many monographs on American decorative arts. This publication is oriented more toward the collector and dealer than the scholar, but, like the other periodicals of the field to appear during this time, it can be valuable for individual articles as well as for the light it sheds on collecting interests.

The Antiquarian: A Monthly Magazine for the Collector of Antiques, Works of Art, and Rarities. Vols. 1–20. New York, 1923–33. Monthly.

Begun as a similar and rival publication to *Antiques*, the *Antiquarian* published many articles on American fine and decorative arts under its first editor, Esther Singleton. Over its ten-year life span, its later problems with establishing a consistent identity and audience led to changes in scope that lessen its value for purposes of this bibliography's audience, but its earlier issues should be consulted.

Antiques. Vol. 1–, no. 1–. New York, January 1922–. Monthly.

Over the years since its first appearance, the *Magazine Antiques* has been the single most valuable periodical for stu-

dents of the American decorative arts, even for its extensive, illustrated advertising sections and wealth of coverage of such topics as silver and furniture. To page through *Antiques* is to gain a sense of changing tides in collecting taste in this country. Although it is now covered in *Art Index*, such coverage is relatively recent, and the lack of one consistent index for earlier volumes can make using the periodical somewhat frustrating, but it is a fundamental source nevertheless. Over the years, *Antiques* has been edited by distinguished authorities in the field: Homer Eaton Keyes, Alice Winchester, and currently Wendell D. Garrett.

Decorative Arts Newsletter. Vol. 1–. [Various places]: Decorative Arts Chapter, Society of Architectural Historians, Summer 1975–.

Issued by the Decorative Arts Society, this newsletter was founded by a chapter of the Society of Architectural Historians in 1975. The contents have varied, but generally include brief news items regarding meetings, workshops, conferences, exhibition and book reviews, news of members, and museum acquisitions. Occasionally longer articles are published. Information in the newsletter is practical, timely, and useful for professionals in the field.

Journal of Early Southern Decorative Arts. Vol. 1–, no. 1–. Winston-Salem, N.C.: Museum of Early Southern Decorative Arts, May 1975–. Biannual. Cumulative indexes.

This scholarly journal is based on field research and assemblage of documentary sources carried out by the Museum of Early Southern Decorative Arts. The research and collection focus of the museum is on the fine and decorative arts and architecture of the southern states to 1820, and these interests are reflected in the journal's contents. The journal includes material on objects made elsewhere but used in the region during this period. Many articles are by museum staff and are based on discoveries made through the institution's research programs. Cumulative author and subject indexes are included. The journal is an important scholarly resource for anyone concerned with the arts of this period and geographic area.

Material History Bulletin / Bulletin d'histoire de la culture matérielle. No. 1–. Ottawa: National Museums of Canada, National Museum of Man, History Division, 1976–. Biannual.

Although this periodical is issued by a Canadian museum and has as its aim the interpretation of the past through examination of "Canadians' relationship to their material world," its scope and value are far greater than these parameters might suggest. Recent issues have covered topics as diverse as the material culture of nineteenth-century childhood and computerized indexing of advertisements in nineteenth-century newspapers as a research tool. Some contributions are in French. Articles are often thought-provoking and always well researched. It is a publication of substance that deserves a wide readership.

Nineteenth Century. Vol. 1, no. 1–vol. 9, nos. 1–2. Philadelphia: Victorian Society in America, January 1975– Spring 1984.

The Victorian Society in America, founded in 1968, was inspired by the example of the British Victorian Society. Since that time it has focused its efforts on the study, appreciation, and preservation of American nineteenth-century arts and architecture and on the social history of the period. The society's journal has gone through several changes in format and publication frequency. It has twice appeared as a year-book devoted to publishing the proceedings of society conferences (on furniture and on hotels and resorts). The journal is uneven in quality, but it is the only American journal devoted wholly to this field.

Winterthur Portfolio. Vols. 1–3. Winterthur, Del.: Henry Francis du Pont Winterthur Museum, 1964, 1965, 1967. Vols. 4–12. Charlottesville: University Press of Virginia, 1968–77. Vols. 13, 14–, no. 1–. Chicago: University of Chicago Press for the Henry Francis du Pont Winterthur Museum, 1979, 1980–.

Founded in 1964 as a publication of Winterthur Museum, the current editorial policy of *Winterthur Portfolio: A Journal of American Material Culture* states that the journal is "committed to fostering knowledge of the American past by publishing articles on the arts in America and the historical context within which they developed." As can be expected, contributions have originated in a wide range of fields, but in the end have converged on man's creation of his own environment through the objects he produces. This triannual periodical, which for its first thirteen volumes was published annually in cloth, has been a source through the years for many notable contributions (and some provocative ones) on a surprising variety of subjects.

Surveys

KENNETH L. AMES AND BARBARA G. CARSON

SURVEYS ARE ATTRACTIVE TO READERS because they provide sweeping, if sometimes brief, vistas of related materials. The prominence of surveys in size, number, and significance of their scholarship indicates that the concept is held in high regard within the field. Important scholarship in the study of American decorative arts appears in surveys included in this section.

Surveys provide entry-level access to the field and are therefore of considerable value to beginning scholars. Because they often juxtapose many different kinds of materials or examine large cultural phenomena, surveys often yield insights and understandings not found in studies defined by material or function. Again, some of the surveys included here constitute major appraisals of American culture; their impact and utility reach far beyond the decorative arts field.

Surveys can be categorized according to their scope, purpose, or both. This essay identifies eight such categories. The first includes those that offer general overviews of the entire field or a major part of it. The second category includes surveys organized around people, while the third and fourth categories use time and place respectively as organizing principles. The fifth category focuses on style. The sixth consists of surveys that examine objects within the broader physical context of the domestic interior, while the seventh looks at objects related by function. An eighth category considers objects linked by symbolic or iconic properties.

The category of general overviews shows that surveys can vary considerably in scope. Probably the most comprehensive volume listed is William Pierson and Martha Davidson's *Arts of the United States*. This extensively illustrated work includes examples of virtually all the visual arts produced in America. The proportion of decorative arts objects is relatively small and necessarily based on the state of learning and interest in 1960. Published in the same year, Daniel Mendelowitz's *History of American Art* also integrates decorative arts into the full artistic picture. Coverage is again necessarily brief, but major movements and trends are concisely and accurately summarized.

Originally published in three volumes between 1967 and 1969, the American Heritage History of Antiques series was the first "modern" survey of the entire range of historic American furnishings. Intended for a popular audience, dramatically and imaginatively illustrated, this lavish production synthesized and disseminated the best scholarship of the period, usually without acknowledgment. Robert Bishop served as picture editor for the series. His sensitivity to the power of exceptional photography is clear in his many subsequent books, including his 1982 coauthored *American Decorative Arts*. Bishop's forte has always been to reveal the visual beauty and appeal of objects. This remarkably handsome book is less a history than an invitation to enjoy the visual delights of outstanding objects depicted in photographs of equally outstanding quality.

General surveys can also be grounded in a single collection, for the decorative arts collections of many major art or history museums have often been conceived and created as surveys. Of the numerous examples available, two are listed here. David Warren's *Bayou Bend* illustrates and discusses the outstanding collection assembled at this Houston country estate. The collection at Bayou Bend was inspired, at least in part, by the treasury of objects preserved and displayed at Winterthur Museum. In his country estate, Henry Francis du Pont drew together thousands of objects dating from the seventeenth century to the middle of the nineteenth. Jay Cantor's artful *Winterthur* is more a history and appreciation of the institution than a history of the objects within it. Yet surveying Winterthur inevitably means surveying a large portion of America's decorative arts.

Under the rubric of general surveys also fall studies that deal less with objects than with the ideas and impulses behind those objects, less with individual monuments than with larger patterns, such as Joan Evans's classic *Pattern* and E. H. Gombrich's *Sense of Order*. Both of these studies deal broadly with the concepts of decoration, pattern, and order. Order, in the sense of temporal sequence and series, is a major concern of George Kubler's magisterial *Shape of Time*, possibly the most challenging yet rewarding book about things written by an American in the last half century. Few studies provide as coherent or usable a conceptual structure for interpreting the ranges of design solutions seen in the series and sequences of related objects.

While *The Shape of Time* speaks with the voice of a single author, the volume edited by Gyorgy Kepes, *The Man-Made Object*, brings together sixteen voices who address a wide range of design issues. Where Kubler is focused, this volume is deliberately an expansive potpourri of observations and arguments about relationships between objects and the people who make and use them.

People make objects, but in all cases some sort of technology is involved. Ian Quimby and Polly Earl's *Technological Innovation and the Decorative Arts* contains essays that explore the impact of or impetus behind the introduction of new technologies for creating furnishings in the past. Most of the examples are drawn from the nineteenth century, when traditional technologies were challenged or superseded by those based on new assumptions and capabilites.

Objects are produced by and for people. The studies in this section draw on objects to help us to understand people, whether a single individual or a distinctive group within the greater society. Warren's and Cantor's works can also be interpreted as focusing on the world as seen by individuals. William Adams's *Eye of Thomas Jefferson* focuses on a single individual but one known for his extraordinary learning and creativity. Nicholas Wainwright examines the lavish house and furnishings of John Cadwalader.

Studies grounded in one person are the exception. The common emphasis is on major ethnic groups. Probably the most studied, at least for their material culture, is the Pennsylvania Germans. The bibliography on their materials reaches back before the turn of the century. Listed here are three inclusive recent works: John Stoudt's *Sunbonnets and Shoofly Pies*, Beatrice B. Garvan and Charles Hummel's *Pennsylvania Germans*, and Scott Swank's *Arts of the Pennsylvania Germans*. The last two were produced in observation of the tricentennial of German settlement in America. Taken together, these volumes provide a rich and informed exploration of a distinctive current of American material culture.

Studies of Afro-American decorative arts or material culture are neither as old nor as numerous as those dealing with the Pennsylvania Germans. The reason lies partly in the chronology of Afro-American historiography and partly in the material culture itself. Pennsylvania German decorative arts are obvious and distinctive; Afro-American material may be neither, at least in the United States. John Vlach has written the first major synthetic study of these materials, and William Ferris brought together several essays that provide more intensive examinations of particular categories of goods. George McDaniel's *Hearth and Home* attempts to reveal the cultural and physical dimensions of daily life as experienced in southern Maryland.

While the Pennsylvania Germans and Afro-Americans dominate studies configured by ethnicity, other groups have also been represented. Most are Germanic, perhaps because Germans constitute the second largest ethnic group in the United States. Charles van Ravenswaay's massive *Arts and Architecture of German Settlements in Missouri* is the most comprehensive look at one of these other groups. John Bivins and Paula Welshimer's *Moravian Decorative Arts in North Carolina* is a more finite exploration of more finite material.

In order to focus on what seems to be the distinctive culture of a given group of people, some of these studies stress traditional artifacts over those that reveal cultural assimilation or accommodation. This is not the case in Carolyn Gilman's *Where Two Worlds Meet*, which examines in subtle detail the ways European and native American cultures were changed through the process of social interaction.

Women's history and the history of childhood are two areas that have witnessed intensified scholarly activity in recent years. Harvey Green's *Light of the Home* sketches the realities of women's lives in Victorian America, drawing heavily on domestic material culture. *A Share of Honour* can also be said to be about place, but its major emphasis is on the history of women in Virginia, told with a wide range of objects. Katharine McClinton provides a descriptive survey of most of the collectible material culture associated with childhood from the seventeenth century to the early twentieth. A fuller historical context is provided in *A Century of Childhood* by Mary Lynn Heininger and others.

The last title in this category deals with people defined by occupation. Not all occupations are equally defined by material culture, but Quimby's *Craftsman in Early America* provides a variety of perspectives on the people responsible for the design and production of early American decorative arts.

Dividing American decorative arts history into a series of units defined by time has proved to be a manageable way of balancing the conflicting needs to be both sweeping and limited. More books have emphasized the earlier periods than the later. Louis Wright and others survey all the visual arts in colonial America; decorative arts occupy only a quarter of his book. Quimby's *Arts of the Anglo-American Community in the Seventeenth Century* is focused more tightly in time but is broader in geographical scope. The most finite in time is *1776: How America Really Looked*. Although only some of America looked like the vision presented here, the group of essays still creates a compelling if partial sense of synchronic material culture.

Issues of nationalism in design are treated in very different ways in two surveys included here. Charles Montgomery and Patricia Kane's *American Art* attempts to find parallels in design to American political separation from Britain. Wendy Cooper gives a celebratory account of American accomplishment in the decorative arts.

Two surveys were written by archaeologists. Ivor Noël Hume's *Guide to Artifacts of Colonial America* suggests that the historical evidence found beneath the ground is not quite the same as that surviving above ground and that it poses special problems of identification and interpretation. James Deetz's *In Small Things Forgotten* is devoted largely to issues of interpretation. It is an effective and influential example of the ways interdisciplinary scholarship, including archaeology, anthropology, and history, can produce original and significant findings. Like Kubler's *Shape of Time*, it also demonstrates that there is no necessary correlation between size and quality. There may even be an inverse correlation: both of these books are slight and unpretentious, but their impact has been extensive.

Surveys of the nineteenth century are less numerous, but the examples listed here provide a concise historiography of that area of scholarship. *The Arts in America* by Wendell Garrett and others can be described as a monument to the new awareness of nineteenth-century material that emerged in the 1960s. It offers a balanced, scholarly treatment of major monuments and trends. *Nineteenth-Century America* marked, in a sense, the Metropolitan Museum of Art's endorsement of nineteenth-century objects. While the museum's emphasis was understandably on costly and exceptional goods, this catalogue effectively defined a new canon of American decorative arts achievement, particularly for the second half of the century. Robert Bishop and Patricia Coblentz's *World of Antiques, Art, and Architecture* offers little that is new historically or interpretively but suggests how the range of materials considered suitable for serious scholarship has continued to expand.

Place has long been a convenient way to organize studies of material culture and decorative arts. Sometimes place and time are combined to provide a sharpened focus on a discrete geographical and temporal culture. Indeed, most studies organized by place are also limited by time, perhaps because the entire chronological sweep, even when limited by geographic boundaries, seems less compelling or comprehensible.

New England has probably been the subject of more place-oriented studies than any other region of the country. For that matter, it still seems to dominate the historiography of the decorative arts, particularly of the earlier periods. The most comprehensive study of any place is Jonathan Fairbanks and Robert Trent's *New England Begins*. This three-volume work on the material universe of seventeenth-century New England is unrivaled in any dimension and will be a major documentary and interpretive reference for many years. It was produced by Boston's Museum of Fine Arts, an institution that has distinguished itself by producing innovative exhibitions and catalogues that put decorative arts into historical and other interpretive frameworks. *Paul Revere's Boston* was their earlier product on a much smaller scale, but it was similarly shaped by the integrative vision that characterizes many of the projects overseen by Fairbanks.

Peter Benes's *Two Towns* is a New England study that adopts an innovative strategy. It compares two early communities with remarkably extensive artifactual survivals. Objects and documents of many kinds work together to generate a thickly textured sense of life in Concord and Wethersfield. Although studies organized by place might seem to hold potential for standardization, in fact they vary considerably. Not only is there no dominant model, but no two studies replicate one another in significant ways. This lack of congruity makes comparisons difficult and accounts, at least in part, for the attractiveness of the *Two Towns* concept.

Each of the remaining place-oriented studies represents a different interpretation of the genre. Dean Failey presents a cultural history of Long Island. *Philadelphia: Three Centuries of American Art*, a bicentennial project by the Philadelphia Museum of Art, spans three centuries of creative history, with no a priori omissions or exclusions. Noël Hume's *Here Lies Virginia* provides an archaeologist's view of colonial life and history. *Frontier America* creates a subtle and comprehensive understanding of the material culture of the American frontier, interpreted here as an attitude or a state of mind as much as a geographical location.

One title in this section is defined by place in a somewhat different sense than the others. Carl Crossman's *China Trade* deals with objects that originated in China but were especially created for an American market. Perhaps this book can also be conceived as dealing with two groups of people: Chinese merchants and artisans and American entrepreneurs and consumers.

Style is a particularly useful tool for making distinctions among objects, particularly when those objects are what Kubler calls "fixed function" objects. Style is a major way that designers, tastemakers of various sorts, and other cultural activists make an imprint on the world or demonstrate authority or control. It is a common feature of most art-historical writing and figures prominently in literature on the decorative arts as well. This section includes four titles, all written by art historians, that deal with major episodes of historic style generated in Europe. John Shearman's *Mannerism* and Hugh Honour's *Neoclassicism* are both products of the same valuable Penguin Books series and offer authoritative and insightful interpretations of their respective styles. Honour also wrote *Chinoiserie*, a classic that is still considered the best treatment of Western dialogues with Chinese design. The oldest title here, Fiske Kimball's *Creation of the Rococo Decorative Style*, is also considered a major exploration of a style that originated in Europe but had a noticeable if limited impact in North America.

Many other style-oriented studies have examined the impact or impress of styles in the United States. Here the dates are significant, for they record the historiographic coming of age of succeeding epochs of American design. Newark Museum's *Classical America* appeared in 1963. The text by Berry Tracy and William Gerdts and the well-chosen selection of objects have helped this volume to wear well. No other major study of classical design impulses in America exists. In 1976 Houston's Museum of Fine Arts published the definitive *Gothic Revival Style in America* by Katherine Howe and David Warren. While studies of the Gothic revival in architecture are numerous, there is no other extensive exploration of its impact on household furnishings.

In 1972 Robert Clark edited *The Arts and Crafts Movement in America*, an area of study that would expand and grow more sophisticated. Two monumental subsequent studies, both based on museum exhibitions, broke the movement into two parts and filled out the picture in lavish and richly documented detail. *In Pursuit of Beauty* by Doreen Burke and others focuses on the achievements of the aesthetic movement in America particularly during the decades of the 1870s and 1880s. Wendy Kaplan's *Art That Is Life* is an equally monumental examination of the arts and crafts movement, with somewhat greater emphasis on materials produced at and after the turn of the century. These two studies, like *New England Begins* and a few others listed here, are noteworthy instances of major contributions to scholarship grounded in museum exhibitions and presented in exhibition catalogues. These major exhibitions, dealing with important cultural movements and written and researched by a team of museum and academic scholars, represent pervasive publication models of the last decade and are key contributions to decorative arts scholarship.

The late nineteenth century has been the focus of at least two other significant interdisciplinary exhibition projects. Brooklyn Museum's *American Renaissance* and Detroit Institute of Art's *Quest for Unity* provide synthetic overviews of many of the visual arts of the late nineteenth century, offering productive and sometimes provocative interpretations of the extraordinary richness and diversity of artistic production of the period. Art nouveau is just one of the stylistic tendencies swirling through design at the turn of the century. Diane Johnson isolates this current of design and offers some of its key examples for examination and discussion.

Is "country" a style, a culture, an attitude? Whatever it is, people seem to know it when they see it. Nina Fletcher Little's *Country Arts in Early American Homes* provides a personal selection of things that seem to have been designed or made outside urban and cosmopolitan centers. Less certain is what constitutes *folk art*, a term that has been unclear since it came into common usage in the 1930s. What might be called the dominant ideology up until the late 1970s is presented in Jean Lipman and Alice Winchester's *Flowering of American Folk Art*, which summarizes and synthesizes more than forty years' work in the field. Kenneth Ames's *Beyond Necessity* is a revisionist essay that attempts to debunk some of the prevalent assumptions and clichés that surround folk art. Quimby and Swank's *Perspectives on American Folk Art* probably contains the greatest diversity of views about and approaches to folk art found in one volume. Milwaukee Art Museum's *American Folk Art* presents the collection of a major folk art devotee while at the same time offering essays that offer dramatically different perspectives on the material. National Gallery of Art's *American Sampler* combines striking images of notable objects with continuing commentary on the definition of folk art.

Goods rarely exist in a void. They are produced in and for a variety of contexts. For much of their existence household goods are located in the physical context of the domestic interior. Many books deal with domestic interiors, but three are particularly informative. Harold Peterson assembles a wide variety of pictorial materials to suggest the appearance of interiors in America from the colonial period through the late nineteenth century. William Seale's *Tasteful Interlude* narrows its chronological focus but deepens its coverage, relying entirely on photographic images to record the look of American interiors from shortly after the middle of the nineteenth century until the early twentieth. Only Edgar Mayhew and Minor Myers attempt to combine the histories of interiors with objects that furnish those interiors by tracing broad configurations of change over more than three centuries.

Of the relatively few studies that have examined the interworkings of constellations of objects within certain settings or ceremonies—or, more specifically, by function—most have focused on objects associated with dining or, more generally, food ways. Louise Belden outlines a history of table decorations, with an emphasis on elegant and wealthy settings. Susan Williams provides a broader view of the material culture and behaviors that were part of dining in Victorian America. The authors in the book edited by Kathryn Grover step back even further to explore specific categories of material culture at length and to analyze issues of propriety and etiquette.

In the eighteenth century, tea drinking was a social ceremony of considerable significance. Rodris Roth's classic work outlines the history of tea and tea drinking in America and describes its political, social, and artifactual impact and significance.

Williams's and Grover's works were both produced under the auspices of the Strong Museum in Rochester, New York. It thus seems appropriate that the only major exploration of the parlor should come from that institution as well. Katherine Grier's *Culture and Comfort* is a massive survey of the idea of comfort, particularly as it was expressed in the parlor between 1850 and 1930, and is an extensive historical treatment of upholstery in America.

The section dealing with symbols is small also. E. McClung Fleming outlines the changing and sometimes conflicting symbolic and allegorical representations of this country from the earliest days until the nineteenth century. Clarence Hornung traces the changing presentations of the bald eagle, a key element of the American symbolic panoply. George Washington, a historic figure of epic proportions, also had a lively symbolic life, which is recounted in Margaret Klapthor and Howard Morrison's study. Symbols have been used actively and effectively in the decorative arts by various groups within society, most prominently by the Masons. *Masonic Symbols in American Decorative Arts* outlines the meaning of these symbols and traces their use in the eighteenth and nineteenth centuries.

Surveys may have many goals and may be organized around a variety of understandings or interests, some of which have been suggested in the categories above; however, this division may obscure a trend that becomes more visible when the titles are arranged chronologically: the growing tendency to see decorative arts as pieces of cultural history. The process of contextualization has grown increasingly sophisticated in the last decade. The most impressive surveys listed here, many of them team efforts associated with major interpretive exhibitions, have combined detailed and learned examination of objects with imaginative inquiry into their relationship to culture and society and constitute works of cultural history of great distinction.

Adams, William Howard, ed. *The Eye of Thomas Jefferson.* Exhibition catalogue. Washington, D.C.: National Gallery of Art, 1976. xli+411 pp.; black and white illustrations, 12 color plates, bibliography, index.

Thomas Jefferson had a lifelong personal commitment to the arts, including the functional and visual design of his household furnishings. When placed in their international context, his achievements demonstrate the considerable significance of his learning and talent. Most of the 605 items in this major bicentennial exhibition and catalogue are architectural renderings and paintings and make up the entire section on nature and landscape gardening. Chairs, tables, silver objects, coins and medals, a guitar, a telescope, a theodolite, a silver pouring vessel replicating a Roman *askos* that Jefferson copied at the Cabinet of Antiquities at Nimes, and a coffee urn and silver goblets made to his design are included in six other sections on the colonial scene, the British connection, the Revolution, Europe of the 1780s, intellectual developments, and Jefferson's own creativity.

Ames, Kenneth L. *Beyond Necessity: Art in the Folk Tradition.* Exhibition catalogue. Winterthur, Del.: Winterthur Museum, 1977; distributed by W. W. Norton.

131 pp.; 111 black and white illustrations, 8 color plates, bibliography.

Ostensibly a catalogue of a 1977 exhibition of 225 folk art objects from Winterthur Museum held at Brandywine River Museum in Chadds Ford, Pennsylvania, this revisionist essay asks, Is folk *art* really *folk* art? Ames takes a cultural approach and seeks a context for the folk and for art, discussing definitions for both terms, and identifies five assumptions that impede understanding of the original context of folk art creations: the myths of individuality, the poor but happy artisan, handicraft, a conflict-free past, and national uniqueness. He examines many examples of folk art (more than 100 are illustrated) and says that their design is characterized by traditional orientation, highly decorated surfaces, and a blend of competence and ineptness in execution. *See also* Quimby and Swank, *Perspectives on American Folk Art.*

Belden, Louise Conway. *The Festive Tradition: Table Decoration and Desserts in America, 1650–1900.* New York and London: W. W. Norton, a Winterthur Book, 1983. xi+340 pp.; 185 black and white illustrations, 15 color plates, recipes, glossary, bibliography, index.

Sweetmeats, jellies, and cakes can be works of art. From the seventeenth to the late nineteenth century, cooks and housewives prepared them and other delicacies in specially designed equipment and served them using elaborate decorative tableware, comfit dishes, step pyramids, and plateaus mostly made of silver, ceramics, or glass set on spotless linen. This book gives recipes, discusses preparation and use of the paraphernalia, and illustrates dessert tables in historical paintings, prints, and drawings as well as in modern recreated settings. The author draws on diaries and letters for her descriptions of the elegant social rituals around these well-set, well-to-do tables.

Benes, Peter. *Two Towns, Concord and Wethersfield: A Comparative Exhibition of Regional Culture, 1635–1850.* Exhibition catalogue. Concord, Mass.: Concord Antiquarian Museum, 1982. xvi+176 pp.; 321 black and white illustrations, 16 color plates, index.

Concord, Massachusetts, and Wethersfield, Connecticut, 90 miles apart, were economically similar but culturally diverse. Benes presents brief catalogue entries that describe the local history of artifacts and two-dimensional materials documented or strongly associated with the landscape, people, domestic architecture, furnishings, agricultural and craft activities, and civil and ecclesiastical affairs and the processes of birth, life, and death in these two richly documented communities. A six-page introduction sketches ways that these materials and a wealth of written historical sources might be used to analyze the genealogical and stylistic relationships among the objects and to interpret their cultural significance within the communities' experiences.

Bishop, Robert, and Patricia Coblentz. *American Decorative Arts: Three Hundred Sixty Years of Creative Design.* New York: Harry N. Abrams, 1982. 405 pp.; 434 black and white and color illustrations, bibliography, index.

Weighing nearly ten pounds, the value of this book is concentrated in illustrations that offer a balanced assortment of furniture, fabrics, and objects made of silver, base metals, ceramics, and glass produced from 1620 to 1980. Occasional makers' labels and trade cards supplement the artifacts, and "Country Styles, 1776–1876" broadens the scope. Illustrations of a few residences and paintings and photographs of interiors offer hints about settings and arrangements, but this work is stronger on the design qualities of artifacts than on their historical contexts.

Bishop, Robert, and Patricia Coblentz. *The World of Antiques, Art, and Architecture in Victorian America.* New York: E. P. Dutton, 1979. 495 pp.; 635 black and white illustrations, 45 color plates, bibliography, index.

The ratio of illustrations to pages indicates a rich visual approach rather than a historical analysis of the world of the American upper class during the years of Queen Victoria's reign (1837–1901). Most categories are customary in inclusive surveys. Architecture and interiors set the scene and are followed by furniture, glass, ceramics, clocks, metals, pictorial art, and sculpture. Nineteenth-century improvements in domestic living are described in sections on heating, lighting, and pleasures and pastimes. The world of age and gender is explored in separate chapters. "Women's World" presents a diverse view through an assortment of sewing, laundry, and kitchen equipment; products of fancy needlework; clothing; and elaborate jewelry. Children are represented mostly by toys, but the selection also includes a 1901 letter from eight-year-old Edsel Ford to Santa Claus. The masculine experience centers on artifacts related to alcohol, tobacco, hunting, and fishing, with references to tailor-made clothes, beekeeping, gardening, and amateur woodwork.

Bivins, John, Jr., and Paula Welshimer. *Moravian Decorative Arts in North Carolina: An Introduction to the Old Salem Collection.* Edited by Frances Griffin. Winston-Salem, N.C.: Old Salem, 1981. 111 pp.; black and white and color illustrations, glossary.

A religious community of Moravians from Pennsylvania and central Europe settled in North Carolina in the second half of the eighteenth century. Bivins and Welshimer argue that although Moravian artisans believed that God directly influenced their work, Germanic traditions, trading contacts in North Carolina, and the communal economic system affected design more than church dogma. These well-documented Moravian paintings, prints, and artifacts—including furniture, pottery, textiles, and metalware—were produced between 1775 and 1840.

Brooklyn Museum. *The American Renaissance, 1876–1917.* Exhibition catalogue. Brooklyn: By the museum, 1979; distributed by Pantheon Books. 232 pp.; 156 black and white and color illustrations, bibliography, index.

The Renaissance label describes a self-confident attitude more than classical principles of design. Although most of the book is devoted to architecture, painting, and sculpture, Dianne H. Pilgrim discusses and illustrates furnishings for houses of the elite. She emphasizes a general state of mind over a coherent style. Other interpretive essays argue that during the industrial revolution and westward expansion at the turn of the century, visual artists were leaders in creating a sense of rational order amid eclectic styles.

Burke, Doreen Bolger, Jonathan Freedman, Alice Cooney Frelinghuysen, David A. Hanks, Marilynn Johnson, James D. Kornwolf, Catherine Lynn, Roger B. Stein, Jennifer Toher, and Catherine Hoover Voorsanger, with the assistance of Carrie Rebora. *In Pursuit of Beauty: Americans and the Aesthetic Movement.* Exhibition catalogue. New York: Rizzoli International Publications in association with the Metropolitan Museum of Art, 1986. 511 pp.; 417 black and white illustrations, 94 color plates, bibliography, index.

Written to accompany an exhibition of 175 objects, this volume stands on its own intellectually and physically. The aesthetic movement, which was popular for approximately a decade bridging the 1870s and 1880s, emphasized art in the production of furniture, metalwork, ceramics, stained glass, textiles, wallpapers, and books. Various authors integrate these expressions of decorative and graphic arts with painting and sculpture, investigate their relationships to architecture and literature, and place the separate topics into their social and cultural milieu. More narrowly they show how the aesthetic movement, like the arts and crafts movement, evolved from British reform ideas, was principally applied in domestic interiors, and offered women new outlets for creative talent. The eighty-seven-page "Dictionary" is a gold mine of facts and bibliographic sources about American and British producers.

Cantor, Jay E. *Winterthur.* Original photography by Lizzie Himmel. New York: Harry N. Abrams, 1985. 240 pp.; black and white illustrations, color plates, index.

Winterthur is a lush evocation of a major museum of early American decorative arts. Cantor's admiring prose traces the history of the mansion, its most famous resident, and the collections that he assembled. Winterthur was begun in 1839 and enlarged several times before Henry Francis du Pont inherited it in 1927. Du Pont had been collecting American antiques since 1923; by 1930 he was acquiring hundreds of objects each year. Cantor recounts the expansion and transformation of the collections as well as changes in du Pont's philosophies of collecting and display. This history is en-

hanced and augmented by many splendid photographs, half in color, that capture the richness and complexity of this museum and its collections.

Clark, Robert Judson, ed. *The Arts and Crafts Movement in America, 1876–1916.* Exhibition catalogue. Princeton: Princeton University Press, 1972. 190 pp.; 295 illustrations, bibliography.

Metropolitan Museum's 1970 exhibition catalogue *Nineteenth-Century America* stimulated this project, which began at Princeton as an idea for a small loan show and grew into an influential traveling exhibition with a catalogue of 293 documented objects. Although brief, many essays were the first to publish new information about makers and objects. Arts and crafts is defined as a reform movement seeking high levels of artistic consideration in craft production. By avoiding specific stylistic criteria, the authors are able to include Gothic, mission, and art nouveau objects. Book arts and art pottery are discussed separately by Susan Otis Thompson and Martin Eidelberg. Three sections organized by regions (the East and West coasts, covered by Clark, and the Midwest, covered by David Hanks) present furniture, metals, stained and leaded glass, leather, wallpaper, and textiles. *See also* "The Arts and Crafts Movement in America."

Classical America, 1815–1845. Text by Berry B. Tracy and William H. Gerdts. Exhibition catalogue. Newark, N.J.: Newark Museum, 1963. 212 pp.; 197 illustrated entries, bibliography.

Classical America illustrates nearly all 295 paintings and objects assembled for an exhibition. The organization is by familiar media: furniture, silver, ceramics, glass, wallpaper, and textiles. An additional section on lamps, stoves, and clocks shows how important these items had become by the early nineteenth century. Brief essays on the European background and the introduction of the classical style into America precede the separate sections. These are introduced by a few paragraphs summarizing visual features, craft practices, and major producers. For a brief analysis of the classical style in the context of the early nineteenth century, see Patrick L. Stewart, "The American Empire Style: Its Historical Background," *American Art Journal* 10, no. 2 (November 1978): 97–105. *See also* "American Furniture to 1820."

Cooper, Wendy A. *In Praise of America: American Decorative Arts, 1650–1830 / Fifty Years of Discovery since the 1929 Girl Scouts Loan Exhibition.* New York: Alfred A. Knopf, 1980. 280 pp.; 308 black and white illustrations, 52 color plates, index.

In Praise of America commemorates the 1929 Girl Scouts Loan Exhibition, a landmark in the history of the study of American decorative arts. For decades, curators, collectors, and scholars accepted and followed the organizing principle that it established—the practice of selecting furnishings according to style periods and arranging them in room settings—and relied on information published in the well-illustrated catalogue. Although the present volume documents an exhibition of objects made in America between 1650 and 1830, it is less a traditional catalogue and more a visual and verbal summary of current approaches to and recent discoveries in the decorative arts. Only one essay, "The Classical Impulse," deals principally with style. Others are more topical: documented objects, upholstered furniture, patronage and commissioned objects, the economy of craft production, regionalism, and design and production of artifacts not usually associated with high-style concepts or centers. *See also* "American Furniture to 1820."

Crossman, Carl L. *The China Trade: Export Paintings, Furniture, Silver, and Other Objects.* Foreword by Ernest S. Dodge. Princeton: Pyne Press, 1972. xii+275 pp.; 216 black and white and color illustrations, appendixes, bibliography, index.

America entered the China trade in 1785. Crossman begins his account with the story of the 1819 voyage of supercargo and captain Benjamin Shreve. Shreve's letters, ship's log, and accounts show how he earned a handsome profit for investors through trading mainly tea, silk, and porcelain. Most of the book discusses less well known categories of goods exchanged throughout the nineteenth century at Canton, such as many types of Western-style paintings by Chinese artists, furniture (bamboo, cane, campaign chests, desks, trunks, and Chinese-style pieces), lacquerware, carvings, fans, silver, pewter, household goods, silks, and wallpaper.

Davidson, Marshall B., ed. *The American Heritage History of Colonial Antiques.* New York: American Heritage Publishing Co., 1967. 384 pp.; 580 black and white and color illustrations, glossary, appendix, index.
——. *The American Heritage History of American Antiques: From the Revolution to the Civil War.* New York: American Heritage Publishing Co., 1968. 416 pp.; 511 black and white and color illustrations, glossary, appendix, index.
——. *The American Heritage History of Antiques: From the Civil War to World War I.* New York: American Heritage Publishing Co., 1969. 415 pp.; 565 black and white and color illustrations, glossary, appendix, index.

The editor and staff of American Heritage dipped into decorative arts scholarship before the late 1960s and offered a three-volume blend of historical facts and pretty things. Organization is chronological by style group. Paintings and prints of landscapes, buildings, and interior views, trade cards, design book illustrations, and so forth accompany photographs of objects such as furniture, glassware, ceramics, metals, and fabrics. Each volume contains a useful glossary. Style charts with line drawings are provided for the 1968 and 1969 volumes. The 1967 volume offers eighty-one illustrations in "Contemporary Notices and Advertisements: 1860s–1870s." Because the editors do not provide footnotes or bibliographies, readers interested in pursuing individual subjects are not shown the way to the scholarship that made these volumes possible.

Deetz, James. *In Small Things Forgotten: The Archaeology of Early American Life.* Drawings by Charles Cann. Garden City, N.Y.: Anchor Press/Doubleday, 1977. 184 pp.; drawings, index.

Although only slightly illustrated, the chapters of this small book relate gravestones, houses, furniture, musical instruments, ceramics, and a wide range of food-related artifacts to the people, largely New Englanders, who used them. Many people were socially and economically privileged, but some, including the members of a postrevolutionary community of free blacks, lived modest lives. Deetz discusses the kind of documentation necessary to put artifacts in a historical context populated by real people, and he demonstrates the value of using an intelligent research design as a foundation for specific studies. His case histories test his influential hypothesis that American colonial culture first tried to replicate, then diverged from, and finally reentered the English cultural community.

Detroit Institute of Arts. *The Quest for Unity: American Art between World Fairs, 1876–1893.* Exhibition catalogue. Detroit: By the institute, 1983. 286 pp.; 21 black and white illustrations, 20 color plates, 182 illustrated entries, bibliography, index.

The Quest for Unity argues that significant changes occurred in American painting, sculpture, and decorative arts in the years between 1876 and 1893. After an introductory essay, 182 objects and accompanying descriptions and historical information are arranged into three sections. "Art at the Centennial" brings together objects exhibited in Philadelphia. Works created later, some of which were exhibited at the World's Columbian Exhibition in Chicago, are divided topically under "Aestheticism" and "The Rationalization of Nature." About a third of the catalogue covers decorative arts. Products by Louis Comfort Tiffany, some of which are accompanied by original drawings, are numerous. Silver manufacturers are represented, as are others who produced glass, ceramics, textiles, and wallpaper. Furniture pieces that are included were sold by several well-known firms or were designed by architects Frank Furness, Richard Morris Hunt, and Henry Hobson Richardson.

Evans, Joan. *Pattern: A Study of Ornament in Western Europe from 1180 to 1900.* 2 vols. 1931. New York: Da Capo Press, 1976. Vol. 1, xxxvi+179 pp.; vol. 2, xvii+249 pp.; 435 illustrations, index.

Although the creation of pattern may employ relief techniques, it is essentially a two-dimensional surface ornament applied to a defined and limited space. Evans traces the development of motifs of ornament and their arrangement into patterns in western Europe from the Gothic period through the nineteenth century. Although the overall organization of the two volumes is chronological, periods give way to motifs and design sources: tracery, naturalism, and heraldry of the Middle Ages; and classicism, Eastern exoticism, the picturesque, and the romantic pastoral of the later periods. Evans finds patterns "a speculum minus of human life, darkly reflecting the web of man's thought and feeling" (1:xxxiii). She also believes that a study of the conditions influencing decorative arts aids an understanding of peasant arts as well as fine arts. This is a thoughtful analysis of the way things look and how people came to ornament them in particular ways. See also Peter Ward-Jackson, "Some Main Streams and Tributaries in European Ornament from 1500 to 1750," *Bulletin*, Victoria and Albert Museum (April, July, October 1967).

Failey, Dean F., with the assistance of Robert J. Hefner and Susan E. Klaffky. *Long Island Is My Nation: The Decorative Arts and Craftsmen, 1640–1830*. Exhibition catalogue. Setauket, N.Y.: Society for the Preservation of Long Island Antiquities, 1976. 304 pp.; 251 illustrations, appendixes.

A survey of historical sources for a cultural history of Long Island turned up a wide range of documents (personal papers, public records, and many craftsmen's account books) and artifacts (furniture, silver, other metalware, textiles, and more). This bicentennial exhibition catalogue ponders over crafts and craftsmen of the seventeenth, eighteenth, and early nineteenth centuries. Noting that the last comprehensive history of Long Island was written in the nineteenth century, it lays the groundwork for future study. Three chronological chapters use artifacts to explore the Anglo and Dutch cultures from 1640 to 1730, the dominance of traditional design over urban fashions in the later colonial period, and mechanization and commercialization of crafts in the postrevolutionary decades before 1830. A fourth chapter and two appendixes discuss craft activities, cite furniture forms and relative quantities recorded in account books of seventeen makers, and list names of craftsmen with biographical sketches for some. *See also* "American Furniture to 1820."

Fairbanks, Jonathan L., and Robert F. Trent. *New England Begins: The Seventeenth Century*. 3 vols. Exhibition catalogue. Boston: Museum of Fine Arts, 1982. Vol. 1, *Introduction: Migration and Settlement*; vol. 2, *Mentality and Environment*; vol. 3, *Style*. xxviii+575 pp.; 84 black and white illustrations, 504 catalogue illustrations, 21 color plates, 13 tables, appendixes, bibliography, index.

Seven years of effort with generous grant support produced a uniquely wonderful project in material culture research. Along with 504 objects from 118 lenders and a program of lectures and films, a seventeenth-century house went up in the museum courtyard, and musicians, dancers, and actors performed to recreate a "total historical experience." The money and energy were spent not only on a temporary exhibition that aimed to change the general public's notion of the settlement era by bringing together maps, portraits,

tombstones, pulpit panels, chairs, tables, tankards, pots, horse furniture, and cowbells but also on three scholarly volumes that follow the organization of the exhibition. Lengthy catalogue entries for each object follow one of ten substantial essays. David Allen discusses mapping, naming, and using the land. Trent writes about arms and armor, the coastal Algonkian culture, turnery and joinery, and, with Albert Roe, the Boston silversmith's trade. Susan Geib interprets the Saugus Ironworks as an example of advanced industrial enterprise. David Hall summarizes and builds on three generations of the intellectual history of Puritanism, Fairbanks analyzes portrait painting, and Robert Blair St. George investigates "everyday life" as a means of understanding cultural values. *See also* "American Furniture to 1820."

Ferris, William, ed. *Afro-American Folk Art and Crafts*. Boston: G. K. Hall, 1983. 436 pp.; 67 illustrations, bibliographies, index.

Scholars often study the sermons, blues, spirituals, and dances of Afro-Americans but usually overlook their arts and crafts. Here twenty essays discuss quilts, sculpture, musical instruments, baskets, pottery, blacksmiths' work, and buildings. Most of the essays are descriptive field reports. When possible, their authors explore the connection between the makers and their work by asking folk artists about their design and purpose. In "African Influence on the Art of the United States," Robert Thompson describes several specific regional examples and identifies visual traits that suggest African influences: monochrome or bichrome colors, smooth luminous surfaces, equilibrated gestures, frozen faces, eye treatment (beads, shells, metal), synoptic vision, and a repertoire of motifs that emphasizes reptiles and human figures. To encourage more fieldwork and analysis of material culture, several scholars have compiled a list of films depicting Afro-American crafts and bibliographies of folklore and black craftsmanship from the colonial era to 1900.

Fleming, E. McClung. "Symbols of the United States: From Indian Queen to Uncle Sam." In *Frontiers of American Culture*, edited by Ray B. Browne et al., pp. 1–24. Lafayette, Ind.: Purdue Research Foundation, 1968. 10 illustrations.

The eagle is not the only symbolic representation of the United States. Fleming discusses the design and significance of six figures who personified the American colonies and the United States between 1755 and 1850. Four female figures— the Indian Princess, the neoclassical Plumed Goddess, American Liberty, and Columbia—date from the eighteenth century. Representing the genteel tradition, they were used for formal, dignified occasions. The use of two robust men, Brother Jonathan and Uncle Sam, indicates the strength of the popular arts between the War of 1812 and the Civil War. Although Fleming does not seek from contemporary writers the meanings they assigned to the different figures, he does explore the origin of their designs, how their appearance changed, and what significance they had for contemporaries.

Garrett, Wendell D., Paul F. Norton, Alan Gowans, and Joseph T. Butler. *The Arts in America: The Nineteenth Century.* New York: Charles Scribner's Sons, 1969. xix+412 pp.; 301 illustrations, bibliography, index.

Garrett's introductory essay summarizes political developments, geographic expansion, industrialization and the American system of manufacturing, disillusionment with industrialization and urbanization and the rise of the rural ideal, popular culture in an egalitarian society, the widening gulf between elite and popular culture toward the end of the century, and romantic idealism. Norton includes a wide range of domestic, public, and industrial architecture in an outline that ranges from Benjamin Latrobe's 1803 design for Dickinson College in Pennsylvania to Frank Lloyd Wright's Robie House of 1908/9. In addition to the works of major painters and sculptors, Gowans offers a few photographs, examples of graphic design, and a frame from a motion picture. Butler's survey of decorative arts focuses on furnishings of the wealthy.

Garvan, Beatrice B., and Charles F. Hummel. *The Pennsylvania Germans: A Celebration of Their Arts, 1683–1850.* Exhibition catalogue. Philadelphia: Philadelphia Museum of Art, 1982. 196 pp.; 133 black and white and color illustrations, checklist, bibliography.

Each of the 133 objects (furniture, books and manuscripts, musical instruments, ironwork, glass, woven fabrics, silver, pewter, and ceramics) has a history of manufacture or ownership by Pennsylvanians with backgrounds or affiliations loosely identified as Germanic. Richly described in lengthy entries, the objects illustrate seven topical essays. Hummel covers European background, patterns of settlement, and acculturation; Garvan treats personal liberty, family life, education, and religion. These objects are a selection of almost twice as many artifacts originally brought together for a major traveling exhibition, and all are fully described and discussed in a microfiche catalogue, *Pennsylvania German Art, 1683–1850.*

Gilman, Carolyn. *Where Two Worlds Meet: The Great Lakes Fur Trade.* St. Paul: Minnesota Historical Society, 1982. vii+136 pp.; 243 black and white and 24 color illustrations, appendixes.

Gilman describes the labors, products, and travels of the native American and European peoples engaged in the fur trade between 1600 and 1850. The trade was rich in objects from both worlds: baskets, pottery, pipestone, flint, shells, war clubs, tools of bone and copper, animal traps, canoes, axes, hatchets, pots, kettles, beads, blankets, firearms, steelyards, and peace medals. In addition to trading goods, both parties exchanged ideas and information about technology, social organization, and human nature. *Communication* is the word that Gilman uses to distill the complexities of the exchange that she analyzes.

Gombrich, E. H. *The Sense of Order: A Study in the Psychology of Decorative Arts.* Ithaca: Cornell University Press, 1979. xi+411 pp.; 354 black and white illustrations, 90 black and white and 11 color plates, index.

In this brilliant, wide-ranging, diversely illustrated, but uneven book, Gombrich investigates the role that the mind plays in choosing what the eye will see. He says that we see but do not notice the infinite variety of decorative motifs and patterns that fill our world; we do not ask questions about why we cover things with ornament or what meanings the dots and scrolls, checkerboard or floral patterns have for us. Repetition or a "sense of order" is expected; sudden breaks catch the eye. Gombrich summarizes the nineteenth-century debate about design, its criticism of ornament, and the rising preference for simplicity. He discusses patternmaking, pattern perception, and the history of particular ornamental shapes. He explores "the force of habit," the persistence of ornamental tradition, and the way motifs and patterns evolve in response to changing styles and fashions. An epilogue of musical analogies concludes the book.

Green, Harvey, with the assistance of Mary-Ellen Perry. *The Light of the Home: An Intimate View of the Lives of Women in Victorian America.* Illustrations from the Margaret Woodbury Strong Museum. New York: Pantheon Books, 1983. xv+205 pp.; 122 illustrations, index.

Before the nineteenth century, generations of women led home-centered lives, but middle-class Victorian women were the first to sanctify their family-oriented activities. Green concentrates on the decades between 1870 and 1910. Following current literature about the cult of true womanhood, he argues that understanding the sanctification of the home and the role of women as priestesses of the domestic altar is integral to an analysis of the way Victorian society pursued self-interest and economic gain. Although only one of seven chapters concentrates on decorating domestic spaces, the others—on courtship and marriage, the cult of motherhood, death and mourning, the tyranny of housework, health, and leisure—use household furnishings to evoke a pattern of daily life.

Grier, Katherine C. *Culture and Comfort: People, Parlors, and Upholstery, 1850–1930.* Exhibition catalogue. Rochester, N.Y.: Strong Museum, 1988; distributed by the University of Massachusetts Press. xi+339 pp.; 288 black and white illustrations, 50 color plates, appendix, index.

A comprehensive analysis of American Victorian parlor upholstery, *Culture and Comfort* argues that to the Victorians both etiquette and upholstery revealed the progress of civilization. Parlors and, within them, upholstery sustained two opposing values: domesticity, expressed as comfort; and gentility, learning, and cosmopolitanism, expressed as culture. Grier describes evolving conceptions of the parlor, "model parlors" in hotels, steamships, and railroad cars, and the principles that shaped middle-class parlors. Individual chapters examine spring-seat upholstery and physical comfort versus standards of deportment, changing aesthetics of upholstery, French and Turkish upholstery (the two most popular styles of the late nineteenth century), parlor suites and lounges, and window and door drapery. The two final chapters comment briefly on homemade and recycled upholstery and the transformation of the Victorian parlor into the twentieth-century living room.

Grover, Kathryn, ed. *Dining in America, 1850–1900.* Amherst: University of Massachusetts Press; Rochester, N.Y.: Margaret Woodbury Strong Museum, 1987. ix+217 pp.; 143 illustrations, index.

Grover has edited a collection of six essays based on papers delivered at the Strong Museum in 1985 in conjunction with the exhibition "Savory Suppers and Fashionable Feasts." Susan Williams, organizer of that exhibition, provides an introduction to the "constellation of ideas" offered in the essays that follow, each of which deals with a different facet of dining. W. J. Rorabaugh discusses social conflicts over alcohol use in the nineteenth century. David Miller explores kitchen reform and the tensions that it revealed and generated, Eleanor Fordyce surveys cookbooks, and John Kasson analyzes Victorian table manners. The book concludes with Clifford Clark's examination of concepts of the dining room and Dorothy Rainwater's overview of Victorian silverware made for dining.

Heininger, Mary Lynn Stevens, Karin Calvert, Barbara Finkelstein, Kathy Vandell, Anne Scott MacLeod, and Harvey Green. *A Century of Childhood, 1820–1920.* Exhibition catalogue. Rochester, N.Y.: Margaret Woodbury Strong Museum, 1984. x+142 pp.; 62 illustrations, index.

In this social and cultural history of childhood published in conjunction with the exhibition, Heininger traces the dramatic changes in America between 1820 and 1920 and how these changes "altered profoundly the ways in which middle-class Americans regarded, instructed, and behaved toward their children" (p. 1). The other authors look at schooling, girlhood, and the impact of scientific knowledge on understanding children and childhood. All the authors deal with objects to some extent, but Calvert's discussion of children's furniture is the most extensive.

Honour, Hugh. *Chinoiserie: The Vision of Cathay.* London: John Murray, 1961. viii+294 pp.; 154 black and white illustrations, 4 color plates, index.

The imagination of the Western world conjured up a vision of the Orient that was often more fanciful than factual. Artistic expressions of this exotic interest, whether in the form of paintings, ceramics, silver, textiles, furniture, buildings, or garden ornaments, are called chinoiserie. After surveying diplomatic and trade relationships between the Chinese em-

pire and Western nations, Honour explores the attitude that created idealized oriental visions from about 1600 to 1900. Although he emphasizes baroque and rococo chinoiserie in France and England, he ranges north to Stockholm and south to Lisbon and extends the chronology to include neoclassical examples and the craze for Japanese design of the 1870s and 1880s. Two more recent books by Oliver Impey (1977) and Madelaine Farm (1981) cover the same topic with glossier pictures but less substantial texts.

Honour, Hugh. *Neo-Classicism.* Middlesex: Penguin Books, 1968. 221 pp.; 109 illustrations, bibliography, index.

In the late eighteenth century, proponents of neoclassicism called it "the true style." They believed that their art would help to create a new and better world governed by the laws of reason and equity. Honour succinctly and with masterful clarity relates architecture, painting, sculpture, and elite decorative arts to Enlightenment philosophy and to the general aspirations of the period. Although nearly all his examples are European, from England to Russia, a few buildings by Benjamin Latrobe and Thomas Jefferson show American readers the relevance of his analysis and selection of examples to expressions of neoclassical art on this side of the Atlantic.

Hornung, Clarence P., ed. *The American Eagle in Art and Design: Three Hundred Twenty-one Examples.* Dover Pictorial Archive Series. New York: Dover Publications, 1978. x+113 pp.; 321 illustrations, bibliography.

The most popular motif in the decorative arts of this country, the bald eagle, is not always shown as officially adopted in 1782—"the Symbol of Supreme Power and Authority, [signifying] the Congress"—"displayed" with its head to its right, with outspread wings and legs, the right talons holding an olive branch and the left holding a bundle of thirteen arrows. Six pages of text describe the official American eagle, discuss its history, and introduce 321 representations of the eagle on domestic crockery, letter boxes, book covers, glass flasks, iron stoves, weather vanes, tavern signs, trademarks, and coins dating from the eighteenth to the twentieth century.

Howe, Katherine S., and David B. Warren. *The Gothic Revival Style in America, 1830–1870.* Exhibition catalogue. Introduction by Jane B. Davies. Houston: Museum of Fine Arts, 1976. viii+101 pp.; 195 black and white and color illustrations, glossary, bibliography, index.

This catalogue of a major loan exhibition at the Museum of Fine Arts provides the first overview of the Gothic revival style. Architectural drawings and furniture dominate the selection of 195 items. Lacy glass compotes, teapots, pickle dishes, wallpaper, birdhouses, iron stoves, and garden furniture also displayed clustered columns, crenellations, crockets, pointed arches, and tracery. The introductory essay concentrates on architecture and traces the style from its lighthearted ornamental beginnings in England to the archaeological correctness and structural "truthfulness" of its maturity. *See also* "American Furniture, 1820–1920."

Johnson, Diane Chalmers. *American Art Nouveau*. New York: Harry N. Abrams, 1979. 311 pp.; 394 black and white illustrations and color plates, bibliography, index.

Chalmers aims to present a broad survey of American art that relates to concepts of art nouveau. She asks questions about the visual characteristics and philosophical basis for diverse examples of late nineteenth-century painting, sculpture, architecture, and applied arts, and she explores the relationships between European and American ideas and products. Although the book includes works of many designers and artists, principal attention is given to the decorative schemes, glass, and silver of the Associated Artists and Louis Comfort Tiffany, to the architecture and ornament of Louis Sullivan, and to the graphic design of Will Bradley.

Kaplan, Wendy. *"The Art That Is Life": The Arts and Crafts Movement in America, 1875–1920*. Exhibition catalogue. Boston: Little, Brown for the Museum of Fine Arts, a New York Graphic Society Book, 1987. xiv+410 pp.; 7 black and white illustrations, color plates, illustrated catalogue, index.

This major catalogue builds on earlier studies of the movement and places its products firmly in their social and intellectual context. Authors of essays and entries appreciate a broad range of design influences including oriental, art nouveau, native American, colonial revival, California, and prairie, as well as medieval and Queen Anne sources. Some expressions are conservative and show nostalgia for a simpler time; others are progressive and link Victorian eclectic design with the international modern style. Separate essays discuss the development of styles and forms, examine methods of reforming craftsmanship and making objects, consider the schools, communities, philanthropic organizations, and publications through which arts and crafts principles were disseminated, and analyze the impact of the movement on domestic life. Although all media categories are well covered, special emphasis is appropriately given to art pottery, needlework, clothing, and book and graphic design. Extensive coverage of architecture and interior design allows readers to envision individual items in contemporary settings. *See also* "The Arts and Crafts Movement in America."

Kepes, Gyorgy, ed. *The Man-Made Object*. New York: George Braziller, 1966. 227 pp.; 246 illustrations.

Illustrated essays by sixteen well-known architects, art critics, designers, artists, aestheticians, and communication specialists such as Marcel Breuer, Sir Herbert Read, Marshall McLuhan, Dore Ashton, Jean Hélion, Joan M. Erikson, and Frederick S. Wright take diverse approaches to the general topic of people and artifacts. Some explore the process—creative, scientific, or technical—whereby designers, crafts-

people, or architects give form to requirements of function. Some emphasize objects in relation to people and social orders; others to people as creative individuals. A few authors analyze things in still-life compositions or study objects and semantics or semiotics. Kepes does not attempt to summarize these idiosyncratic but socially aware statements about the visual and cultural significance of the man-made object.

Kimball, Fiske. *The Creation of the Rococo Decorative Style*. 1943. Reprint. New York: Dover Publications, 1980. xvii+242 pp.+274 illustrations; index.

Without denying the broader cultural context of artistic endeavors, Kimball focuses on visual analysis of form and ornament. After carefully dating and documenting drawings, engravings, and interior decoration, he concludes that the new development in design was wholly French. Its early creators were Jean Berain and Pierre Lepautre, and Juste-Aurele Messonier and Nicholas Pineau gave it a mature asymmetrical character. Although Kimball briefly discusses the way German designers combined baroque interest in spatial and plastic variety with the superficial linear forms of French rococo and the way English neoclassical designers, notably Robert Adam, moved on to new visual expressions, the reader must make his own transatlantic connections.

Klapthor, Margaret Brown, and Howard Alexander Morrison. *G. Washington, a Figure upon the Stage*. Exhibition catalogue. Washington, D.C.: Smithsonian Institution Press, 1982. 231 pp.; 159 black and white and color illustrations.

Scattered references throughout George Washington's correspondence show his calculated use of his house, furnishings, clothing, and other material possessions to create a public image. This catalogue records an exhibition that drew on the wealth of artifacts with documented Washington associations to explore how he consciously acquired and used his possessions "To Perform the Parts Assigned," whether the role was that of Virginia gentleman, militia officer, farmer, commander in chief, president, or retired elder statesman. Looking beyond the man and his achievements, the catalogue records how Washington was venerated at home and abroad. An extraordinary range of artifacts—Horatio Greenough's statue (1841), a "Beetle Bailey" comic strip (1980), ribbons, handkerchiefs, plates, hatchets, greeting cards, stoves, chocolate molds, and a tattoo—produced between his death in 1799 and the 1980s illustrates how he was celebrated, sentimentalized, domesticated, exploited, emulated, and monumentalized: how the man became myth.

Kubler, George. *The Shape of Time: Remarks on the History of Things*. New Haven: Yale University Press, 1962. xii+136 pp.; index.

Less interested in iconographic or symbolic studies than in analyzing the visual appearance of the entire range of man-made things, Kubler explains the mechanisms of formal evolution in a way that offers insight into why at some times some works are accorded more recognition than others. He compares the idea of style to a rainbow, "a phenomenon of perception governed by the coincidence of certain physical conditions" (p. 129). Each work or object is a solution to a problem. It has a place within a sequence of linked solutions in which there are prime objects (successful major products) and replications (variations on a standard theme). Many sequences of linked solutions exist concurrently, with late versions of some overlapping with earlier expressions of others.

Lipman, Jean, and Alice Winchester. *The Flowering of American Folk Art, 1776–1876*. Exhibition catalogue. New York: Viking Press, in cooperation with the Whitney Museum of American Art, 1974. 288 pp.; 410 black and white and color illustrations, appendix, bibliography.

Like the exhibition it accompanied, this book emphasizes the aesthetic aspects of traditional products made between 1776 and 1876. The pictures—portraits, landscapes and seascapes, scenes of daily life, still lifes, penmanship, and religious, literary, and historical subjects—were painted, drawn, or stitched. Sculpture in various media was either decorative (ships' figures) or functional (weather vanes, decoys, toys, shop signs). Other categories include carved and painted architectural ornament, furniture, and accessories (boxes, pie crimpers, molds, trays, ceramic jugs and plates, quilts, and rugs). In a brief introduction, Winchester discusses the authors' visual approach and summarizes the twentieth-century history of interest in these generally accepted categories of folk art. The 410 objects were chosen from nearly 800 photographs, which, with the research notes, are filed at the Archives of American Art.

Little, Nina Fletcher. *Country Arts in Early American Homes*. Foreword by Wendell Garrett. New York: E. P. Dutton, 1975. xv+221 pp.; 190 black and white illustrations, 20 color plates, index.

Here *country* refers less to geography and more to a way of life not influenced by the high styles of urban centers. Most of the houses, views of farms and villages, and artifacts are from New England. The idiosyncratic choice of categories into which the book is organized includes painted fireboards and picture frames, wooden boxes, carvings for houses and barns (figures, tape looms, lemon squeezers, spoon racks, corset busks), schoolgirl and ladies arts, imported and home-made carpets and rugs, flower holders, miniatures (mainly furniture), and ceramic objects made throughout the world but "used by American housewives."

McClinton, Katharine Morrison. *Antiques of American Childhood*. New York: Clarkson N. Potter, 1970; distributed by Crown Publishing. 351 pp.; illustrations, bibliography, index.

Hobbyhorses, velocipedes, metal banks, clothing, books for school and pleasure, and much more fill these pages. Most objects date from the nineteenth century; christening cradles

and portraits survive from the seventeenth; some jumping jacks are as late as circa 1920. All are conveniently arranged into sixteen groups. Children's silver, buttons, furniture, dishes, needlework, indoor and outdoor games, push-pull toys, dolls and dollhouses, and toys of cloth and paper supplement those groups already listed.

McDaniel, George W. *Hearth and Home: Preserving a People's Culture*. American Civilization Series, edited by Allen F. Davis. Philadelphia: Temple University Press, 1982. xxiv+297 pp.; 116 illustrations, appendixes, bibliography, index.

To analyze and interpret nineteenth- and twentieth-century black material culture in five southern Maryland counties, McDaniel examines black tenant farmhouses, artifacts, photographs, and documents as remnants of a disappearing life. He also relies extensively on interviews, both his own and those recorded by the Works Progress Administration in the 1930s. The method allows McDaniel to position objects in domestic spaces and to relate them to patterns of indoor and outdoor activities. He examines the homes of slaves and their descendants as they embody the transmission and transformation of African and American building traditions. For several cases, he records changes made by successive generations or by different families occupying the same premises. Woven throughout are observations on the problems of interpreting Afro-American life-styles in academic scholarship and exhibiting them in museum settings.

Masonic Symbols in American Decorative Arts. Exhibition catalogue. Publications of the Masonic Book Club, vol. 8. Lexington, Mass.: Scottish Rite Masonic Museum of Our National Heritage, 1976. 110 pp.; 147 illustrated entries, glossary, bibliography.

Masonic imagery appears more extensively in American decorative arts than is generally recognized. Freemasonry, which originated in seventeenth-century England, was introduced to America in the 1730s, first to Philadelphia and then to Boston. After the Revolution, American Freemasonry developed independently and acquired its own distinct character. The popularity of Masonic symbols falls into two periods: 1775 to 1830 and 1860 to 1900. Barbara Franco's essay discusses the origins of Masonic symbols and surveys the major forms on which they were used. She emphasizes the earlier period, when imagery was more diverse and often associated with American patriotism. The catalogue includes textiles, hardware, timepieces, jewelry, glassware, ceramics, bed coverings, and furniture. After 1900 Masonic symbols disappeared from American popular culture.

Mayhew, Edgar de N., and Minor Myers, Jr. *A Documentary History of American Interiors from the Colonial Era to 1915*. New York: Charles Scribner's Sons, 1980. xiii+399 pp.; 240 black and white illustrations, 32 color plates, appendixes, bibliography, index.

Although similar to Harold Peterson's *American Interiors* in illustrating interiors, this book's significant additions enhance our understanding of historical domestic settings. These include architectural elevations, house plans, furnishing diagrams, engravings of individual pieces of furniture and other objects, and an extensive assortment of documentary references about details like color, fabric types, and expense of furnishings. Three centuries are divided into twelve time-style periods. A chapter covers the Spanish Southwest; an appendix reviews features of kitchens, bathrooms, and heating systems. *See also* "Domestic Architecture."

Mendelowitz, Daniel M. *A History of American Art.* New York: Holt, Rinehart and Winston, 1960. ix+662 pp.; 570 illustrations, bibliography, index.

With an approach that is both aesthetic and historical, Mendelowitz surveys painting, sculpture, architecture, interior design, household arts, industrial design, and crafts in the United States from prehistory to 1960. His desire to see individual personal expression in relation to social forces weights the selection of objects in favor of better-documented rather than anonymous examples. Although sections of decorative arts are thinner and less numerous than others, major examples from each period are included.

Milwaukee Art Museum. *American Folk Art: The Herbert Waide Hemphill, Jr., Collection.* Exhibition catalogue. Text by Michael D. Hall, Herbert W. Hemphill, Jr., Russell Bowman, and Donald B. Kuspit. Milwaukee: Milwaukee Art Museum, 1981. 112 pp.; black and white and color illustrations, bibliography.

American Folk Art illustrates and provides brief factual information about 105 paintings, sculptures, toys, and utilitarian artifacts from Hemphill's personal collection. Besides collecting and writing about folk art, Hemphill was a founder and the first curator of the Museum of Folk Art in New York. The personal side of a distinguished and influential collection is captured in an edited conversation between the collector and a colleague. Hemphill sees similarities between folk art of the past and modern art. Two related essays in the catalogue explore ways to define and evaluate folk art. The first attributes the attraction of folk art to the ability of the artist to create "a sense of the nature of the world and our place in it" (p. 32). The second relates folk genius to the art of children and to platonic realism. Both build on the revisionist ideas presented by Ames in *Beyond Necessity* and stress the importance of investigating the cultural environment of folk art in order to understand it.

Montgomery, Charles F., and Patricia E. Kane, eds. *American Art, 1750–1800: Towards Independence.* Exhibition catalogue. Boston: New York Graphic Society for the Yale University Art Gallery and the Victoria and Albert Museum, 1976. 320 pp.; black and white and color illustrations, appendixes, index.

Curators at Yale University Art Gallery organized the ambitious bicentennial loan exhibition recorded here. More

than 200 objects from 67 public and private collections traveled to London's Victoria and Albert Museum. Of the five introductory essays, two about English and American culture by J. H. Plumb and Neil Harris are summary and celebratory. Jules David Prown compares the rococo and neoclassical styles, Frank H. Sommer discusses the depiction of Britannia, and Montgomery analyzes the regional preferences and characteristics of decorative arts. One museum director described the objects in the second section, "A Display of American Art," as having "unique vigor and idiosyncrasy." Organization is by medium: paintings, drawings, watercolors, prints, furniture, silver and gold, pewter, brass, ceramics, glass, and textiles. Each object is illustrated, sometimes in two views or with details. In addition, eighty-five figures provide comparative or supplementary visual information. *See also* "American Furniture to 1820."

Museum of Fine Arts, Boston. *Paul Revere's Boston, 1735–1818.* Contributions by Jonathan L. Fairbanks, Wendy A. Cooper, Anne Farnam, Brock W. Jobe, and Martha B. Katz-Hyman. Exhibition catalogue. Boston: By the museum, 1975; distributed by New York Graphic Society. 234 pp.; approximately 180 black and white and color illustrations, bibliography, checklist.

This catalogue begins with an early eighteenth-century gilded copper weather vane and ends with a neoclassical gold reliquary, which holds a lock of George Washington's hair, made by Paul Revere. In between, a selection of imported and domestic objects whose preserve in Boston can be documented tell the story of his life and explore the chronological history of the city where he lived and worked. Paintings, prints, furnishings, and many objects by Revere and other silversmiths offer insight into business affairs, domestic life, war, education, and entertainment in a major American city. Nearly half of the 395 items in the checklist are illustrated and described. *See also* "American Furniture to 1820."

Museum of Fine Arts, Boston, and the Department of American Decorative Arts and Sculpture. *Frontier America: The Far West.* Contributions by Jonathan L. Fairbanks, Roland F. Dickey, Frederick J. Dockstader, John C. Ewers, Anne Farnam, Elisabeth Sussman, William H. Truettner, and Gilian S. Wohlauer. Boston: By the museum, 1975; distributed by New York Graphic Society. 233 pp.; black and white and color illustrations, bibliography.

This catalogue of a bicentennial traveling exhibition interprets the frontier more as attitude than as place: "The theme of the Far West is firmly rooted in our image of self and closely related to the symbols of a growing nation: abundant natural resources, boundless energy, and vast space" (p. 7). Still the authors set limits of place (between the Missouri River and the Pacific), time (before industrialization and urbanization), and cultural identity (Hispanics in the Southwest, Germans in Texas, Mormons in Utah, and assorted pioneers in Colorado, Montana, and Nebraska). More than

350 drawings, paintings, photographs, works of sculpture, and utilitarian objects are featured in short catalogue entries. Brief essays introduce three major sections: native Americans before contact with white men, the period of exploration and conflict, and settlement. The final section, divided into two parts, presents the greatest concentration of artifacts associated with the no-frills life of the frontier and includes a few quilts and coverlets, but it mainly features furniture. Representative examples are the many slat-back side chairs, one of whittled willow, a spare wooden bench with a wooden head rest from a utopian community in Oregon, pie safes, a kitchen table with limestone slab, and antler armchairs.

National Gallery of Art. *An American Sampler: Folk Art from the Shelburne Museum*. Washington, D.C.: By the gallery, 1987. 209 pp.; 126 black and white illustrations, 133 color plates.

From the enormous and diverse collection of the Shelburne Museum, this richly illustrated catalogue concentrates on textiles and sculpture—more specifically, on hooked rugs, coverlets, quilts, weather vanes, decoys, cigar-store Indians, carousel animals, and shop signs. Benjamin L. Mason writes about Electra Havemeyer Webb and her museum. Readers trying to understand the unfinished business of defining American folk art will welcome David Park Curry's clearheaded essay, "Rose-colored Glasses: Looking for 'Good Design' in American Folk Art," which offers a general intellectual context for other works on folk art mentioned in this section.

Nineteenth-Century America: Furniture and Other Decorative Arts. Introduction by Berry B. Tracy; furniture texts by Marilynn Johnson; other decorative arts texts by Marvin D. Schwartz and Suzanne Boorsch. Exhibition catalogue. New York: Metropolitan Museum of Art, 1970; distributed by New York Graphic Society. xxxii+[232] pp.; line drawings, 298 black and white and color illustrated entries, index, bibliography.

This blockbuster exhibition was the first to survey the major styles of nineteenth-century American decorative arts. The magnificent Salem chest-on-chest once attributed to William Lemon leads off the chronological presentation. Furnishings by Frank Lloyd Wright, Gustave Stickley, and Charles and Henry Greene and accessories by Wright and Louis Comfort Tiffany bring up the rear. A paragraph of descriptive and historical information accompanies each entry. The twenty-page introductory essay, illustrated with line drawings, identifies three phases in the neoclassical style, many romantic revival styles (Gothic, French rococo, Renaissance, Louis XVI, néo-Grec), art furniture and oriental exotica, reform furniture with "honest" design and construction, beaux arts neoclassicism, and art nouveau. The exhibition and catalogue stimulated enormous interest and subsequent scholarship in nineteenth-century decorative arts. *See also* "American Furniture, 1820–1920"; "American Furniture to 1820."

Noël Hume, Ivor. *A Guide to Artifacts of Colonial America*. New York: Alfred A. Knopf, 1969. xviii+323 pp.; 100 illustrations, index.

This is not a guide to all artifacts. Noël Hume summarizes the history of artifacts most often found by archaeologists. Identifying ceramic, glass, and metal objects from fragments forces the student to pay attention to salient visual characteristics, especially those significant for dating. Items mainly from the seventeenth and eighteenth centuries are organized into forty-three alphabetical categories from armor, bayonets, beads, and bellarmines, to scissors, seals (lead), silver, spades, and stoneware, to tobacco pipes, toys, and wig curlers. A bibliography accompanies each category. The introductory essay discusses other evidence, especially prints and design books, that is helpful in authenticating and dating archaeological artifacts and in better understanding their use in the past. *See also* "Continental and Oriental Ceramics in America."

Noël Hume, Ivor. *Here Lies Virginia: An Archaeologist's View of Colonial Life and History*. New York: Alfred A. Knopf, 1963. xix+316 pp.; 129 illustrations, bibliography, index.

What is the nature of archaeological evidence? How were "sites" created? How do archaeologists extract information, and what conclusions about the past can they derive from it? Noël Hume, for many years the archaeologist for Colonial Williamsburg Foundation, bases his answers on his experience with Virginia sites. He tells superb research tales, rich with historical detail, which include, chronologically, sixteenth-century Roanoke, seventeenth-century Jamestown, and, for the eighteenth century, parts of Williamsburg, Yorktown, and several outlying plantations (Rosewell, Corotoman, Green Springs, and Tutter's Neck). Excavation of the sites provided information about domestic, governmental (military and penal), commercial (taverns), and manufacturing (ceramic and glassmaking, ironworking, cabinetmaking, and printing) activities. Noël Hume more fully discusses archaeological artifacts in *A Guide to Artifacts of Colonial America*. His recent *Martin's Hundred* concentrates on a group of 1620s James River sites now on Carter's Grove Plantation.

Peterson, Harold L. *American Interiors from Colonial Times to the Late Victorians: A Pictorial Source Book of American Domestic Interiors with an Appendix on Inns and Taverns*. New York: Charles Scribner's Sons, 1971. xviii+[334] pp.; 205 illustrations, appendix, index.

Most collectors and curators of American decorative arts have some curiosity about the original context of objects in their keeping. Originally published as *Americans at Home*, this volume is better identified by its present title. The 205 paintings, sketches, engravings, and photographs with commentaries are arranged chronologically without division into categories. A brief introduction cautions the viewer about biases in visual evidence. An appendix offers images of inns and taverns.

Philadelphia Museum of Art. *Philadelphia: Three Centuries of American Art.* Exhibition catalogue. Philadelphia: By the museum, 1976. xxiv+665 pp.; 546 illustrations, bibliography, indexes.

More than 550 works of every medium are grouped into six chronological periods in the bicentennial loan exhibition that celebrated Philadelphia's artistic achievements. In addition to furniture, silver, and ceramics, the catalogue records many items of female attire and unusual objects like weaving design books, surveying equipment, juvenile engravings, a carved capital and mantelpiece, a fire engine model, and carousel figures. The decorative arts dominate earlier sections but give way to paintings in the twentieth century. No single theme or thesis is advanced in this rich and readable source book on the arts in Philadelphia and its environs.

Pierson, William H., Jr., and Martha Davidson, eds. *Arts of the United States: A Pictorial Survey.* New York: McGraw-Hill Book Co., 1960. x+452 pp.; 4,115 illustrations, appendixes, index.

The Carnegie Corporation of New York sponsored this pictorial survey of American art from prehistory to the 1950s. Its 4,000 photographs and eighteen essays by leading art historians and critics offer the most comprehensive coverage available in a single volume. Examples of architecture, painting, sculpture, decorative arts, graphic arts, Indian arts and artifacts, photography, stage design, costume design, and visual communications (advertisements, greeting cards, billboards) are "representative of the highest quality in the visual arts of the United States, although some items have been included specifically for their ethnological or sociological interests" (p. viii). Slide versions of the 2-by-2-inch images in the book are commercially available.

Quimby, Ian M. G., ed. *Arts of the Anglo-American Community in the Seventeenth Century.* Winterthur Conference Report 1974. Charlottesville: University Press of Virginia for the Henry Francis du Pont Winterthur Museum, 1975. x+299 pp.; 106 illustrations.

This volume begins with E. McClung Fleming's "Place of Research in the Museum's Mission." Original essays by eight European and American scholars demonstrate the value of such research and explore various aspects of the material world of the seventeenth century. Three authors discuss both high-style and vernacular Dutch and English architecture and furnishings. Five authors look at American artifacts—specifically ceramics, silver, textiles, and furniture—of the Connecticut River valley and Middlesex County, Massachusetts. *See also* "American Furniture to 1820."

Quimby, Ian M. G., ed. *The Craftsman in Early America.* New York: W. W. Norton for the Henry Francis

du Pont Winterthur Museum, 1984. 344 pp.; 83 illustrations, 13 tables, index.

Quimby observes in his introduction that the 1979 Winterthur Conference for which these eleven essays were originally prepared felicitously coincided with the thirtieth anniversary of the completion of Carl Bridenbaugh's *Colonial Craftsman.* Like these newer essays, Bridenbaugh focused on makers rather than products, but there the similarity ends. He concentrated on the eighteenth century and used newspapers and secondary sources to write about the life and work of many different urban and rural craftsmen. The present essays depart from his generalizing effort. Different types of scholars (historians, art historians, a folklorist, American studies specialists, and museum curators) have written eight specific case studies: goldsmiths in Boston; woodworkers in southeastern New England; artisans and politics in Philadelphia; the shoe industry in Lynn, Massachusetts; Moravian craftsmen in North Carolina; the relationship between Benjamin Latrobe and his craftsmen; potters; and glassmakers. The complexities that the authors reveal about life, work, individual success, and class identity defy easy generalizations about traditional craftsmen in preindustrial society. The remaining three essays encourage future scholarship by summarizing existing bibliographies, outlining documentary sources, and surveying visual materials.

Quimby, Ian M. G., and Polly Anne Earl, eds. *Technological Innovation and the Decorative Arts.* Winterthur Conference Report 1973. Charlottesville: University Press of Virginia for the Henry Francis du Pont Winterthur Museum, 1974. xiv+373 pp.; 122 illustrations.

Twelve original essays address the question: What is the relationship between decorative arts objects and the technical innovations of the industrial revolution? Ten of them examine specific cases in which new materials or new machines changed the product or where reorganization of labor and management changed working procedures. Topics covered include the exploitation of the principle of electrolysis, Birmingham silver and jewelry (1760–1800), the Harpers Ferry armory, iron castings, pressed glass, Belter furniture, cylinder printing of calico, printed textiles, wallpaper, and new machinery (especially human powered) for furniture production. Two final papers explore museum approaches toward technology and its products.

Quimby, Ian M. G., and Scott T. Swank, eds. *Perspectives on American Folk Art.* New York: W. W. Norton for the Henry Francis du Pont Winterthur Museum, 1980. xvii+376 pp.; 134 illustrations, index.

These twelve essays record a contentious conference held at Winterthur in 1977 following an exhibition of 225 folk art objects from the Winterthur collection at the Brandywine River Museum. They aim to show that a more comprehensive and balanced examination of objects is necessary "to redress a neglect based on previously dominant elitist values"

(p. 6). Swank introduces the subject by describing the limitations of the diffusionist or "top-down" theory of design in dealing with artifacts in a cultural context. Beatrix Rumford surveys the history of collecting folk art in America. Five essays look at regional or ethnic expressions that are popularly regarded as folk art. The last five consider definitional problems and discuss theoretical implications. *See also* Ames, *Beyond Necessity.*

Rice, Kym S., for Fraunces Tavern Museum. *Early American Taverns: For the Entertainment of Friends and Strangers.* Chicago: Regnery Gateway in association with Fraunces Tavern Museum, 1983. xviii+168 pp.; illustrations, bibliography, appendixes, index.

Early taverns combined accommodations for the public with domestic quarters for owners or proprietors and their families. By 1983 more than sixty-five tavern museums in what had been the thirteen original colonies had been restored, furnished with antiques and reproductions, and opened to the public. Drawing on this body of restoration research and much additional evidence, Rice's catalogue records an interpretive exhibition at the Fraunces Tavern Museum and develops ideas introduced there. It summarizes tavern regulations and licensing, shows how taverns changed from the seventeenth through the eighteenth centuries, describes how they differed in rural areas, small settlements, or cities, and portrays the informal social activities and more formal amusements that occurred there. A separate section presents a brief life of Samuel Fraunces, owner of the New York tavern where George Washington gave his 1783 farewell address to his officers and public officials before resigning his military commission.

Roth, Rodris. *Tea Drinking in Eighteenth-Century America: Its Etiquette and Equipage.* United States Museum Bulletin 225. Contributions from the Museum of History and Technology, paper 14, pp. 1–30. Washington, D.C.: Smithsonian Institution, 1961. 22 illustrations.

As tea became cheaper in the eighteenth century, objects associated with it grew larger in size and were available in a wider price range. More people consumed more of it in diverse social situations. The 1767 duty made tea a politically controversial beverage. An early and classic study among the few studies that relate objects to their historical functions, this paper summarizes the history of tea and tea drinking in Western society, describes the ceramic, silver, and other wares found on a well-equipped tea table, presents verbal and visual evidence (mainly American but some British) for polite behavior, and interprets the significance of the tea ceremony in the American colonies.

Seale, William. *The Tasteful Interlude: American Interiors through the Camera's Eye, 1860–1917.* 2d ed., rev. and enl. Nashville: American Association for State and Local History, 1981. 284 pp.; illustrations, index.

Photographs of private home interiors represent the geo-graphic breadth of the United States. Residences of the wealthy and prosperous dominate the economic range, but houses of more ordinary working-class folks and some groups, like Shakers, miners, ranchers, and wolf hunters, are not excluded. A sensible introduction surveys creative and historical revival styles and the arts and crafts movement. Domestic high-style design is related to official and aristocratic European taste and to the mass-manufactured norm of American interior decoration.

1776: How America Really Looked. American Art Journal 7, no. 1 (May 1975). 135 pp.; illustrations, index.

Although the title promises more than the issue delivers, its nine collaborators, all leading scholars, have written sketches of upper-class material life at the time the thirteen colonies declared their independence. Most of the brief essays, each with about twelve illustrations, focus on the years just before the Revolution. Two essays—Wayne Craven's on sculpture and A. Hyatt Mayor's on prints—look back to the seventeenth century. Donald Fennimore's essay on metalwork and Nina Fletcher Little's on floor coverings provide notes. Others by George B. Tatum, E. P. Richardson, Charles F. Montgomery, Ian M. G. Quimby, and Florence M. Montgomery discuss architecture, painting, furniture, silver, and textiles.

"A Share of Honour": Virginia Women, 1600–1945. Essay by Suzanne Lebsock; checklist and catalogue entries by Kym S. Rice. Exhibition catalogue. Richmond: Virginia Women's Cultural History Project, 1984. xix+167 pp.; black and white illustrations, color plates, chronology, checklist.

A committee of twenty-five female scholars, civic leaders, and politicians organized a show "to tell and celebrate the story of women in Virginia." This catalogue and its essays are a permanent record of an exhibition that opened at the Virginia Museum of Fine Arts and traveled to two other locations within the commonwealth. A wide range of artifacts illustrates five chronological chapters based on state-of-the-art research in women's history. Among the seventy-five seventeenth- and eighteenth-century objects are Pocahontas's portrait, native American pottery and baskets, a print of female indentured servitude, a diagram of slave ships, a grubbing hoe, an obstetrical hook, a cradle for an adult invalid, clothing, and an assortment of the usual products of polite elite female accomplishments. More than 200 portraits, photographs, books, and objects dating after 1800 attest to the expansion of women's educational and employment opportunities in later years.

Shearman, John. *Mannerism.* Pelican Books Style and Civilization Series, edited by John Fleming and Hugh Honour. 1967. Reprint. New York: Penguin Books, 1977. 216 pp.; 102 illustrations, bibliography, index.

While a functionalist expression of "less is more" might have been the most efficient sort of design for the settlement of permanent colonies in America, the cultural baggage of early immigrants included one of the least practical and most highly decorative styles known to art history. Shearman explores the artistic expressions and visual sensibilities of mannerism. He tells what its best European examples looked like and what educated contemporaries thought about them. For the relationship between continental elite and American colonial versions, see Robert F. Trent, "The Concept of Mannerism," in Fairbanks and Trent, *New England Begins*, vol. 3.

Stoudt, John Joseph. *Sunbonnets and Shoofly Pies: A Pennsylvania Dutch Cultural History.* New York: A. S. Barnes, 1973. 272 pp.; black and white and color illustrations, index.

Stoudt gives a factual account of Pennsylvania Dutch culture from the eighteenth to the twentieth century. He writes about language, food, folk medicine, humor, and artifact as he describes migration, religious diversity, the failure of pacifism during the French and Indian War and the Revolution, and the agricultural economy. In his discussion of stove plates, glass, dower chests, Fraktur, pottery, textiles, long rifles, tombstones, painted tinware, the Christmas *putz*, and hex signs, Stoudt faces up to problems in interpreting Pennsylvania folk art: How does the art relate to the folk or to the Rhineland? What was "memory art"? What products were innovations in a new land? He argues that over time the most extraordinary characteristic of this ethnic culture has been its persisting dynamic development without any regular contact with its European counterpart.

Swank, Scott T., with Benno M. Forman, Frank H. Sommer, Arlene Palmer Schwind, Frederick S. Weiser, Donald H. Fennimore, and Susan Burrows Swan. *Arts of the Pennsylvania Germans.* Edited by Catherine E. Hutchins. New York: W. W. Norton for the Henry Francis du Pont Winterthur Museum, 1983. x+309 pp.; 297 black and white illustrations, 49 color plates, 26 tables, index.

This richly interpretive study of Pennsylvania German material culture emphasizes the extensive collections assembled by Henry Francis du Pont at Winterthur Museum. Swank's background essays establish a firm foundation for the more specialized examinations of individual genres that follow. His contributions include eight propositions to inform the study of Pennsylvania German material, a history of migration and settlement, analyses of the architectural landscape, patterns of spatial use and furnishings, changing attitudes toward the Pennsylvania Germans, and an account of du Pont as collector. The remaining essays examine furniture, earthenwares, glass, metalwork, textiles, Fraktur, books, periodicals, and manuscripts. Of these, the longest and most innovative is Forman's detailed analysis, "German Influences in Pennsylvania Furniture"; *see* "Craftsmen."

van Ravenswaay, Charles. *The Arts and Architecture of German Settlements in Missouri: A Survey of a Vanishing Culture.* Columbia: University of Missouri Press, 1977. xvi+533 pp.; 605 black and white illustrations, 20 color plates, bibliography, index.

Van Ravenswaay records the survey of architecture and artifacts from an area about 150 miles long and 50 miles wide along the lower Missouri River valley. Settlers of Germanic origin dominated the region from about 1830 to 1870. Equal attention is given to the immigrants, their buildings, and their domestic objects. The latter includes furniture, musical instruments, wood carvings, baskets, firearms, tin and copper, stonecutting and carving, textiles, pottery, drawing, prints, paintings, and miscellaneous crafts by blacksmiths, bookbinders, boxmakers, braziers, broommakers, glassmakers, locksmiths, sabot and woodenware makers, silversmiths, watchmakers, and jewelers.

Vlach, John Michael. *The Afro-American Tradition in Decorative Arts.* Exhibition catalogue. Cleveland: Cleveland Museum of Art, 1978. xii+175 pp.; 99 black and white illustrations, 8 color plates, bibliography.

Ninety-nine examples of the Afro-American craft tradition—basketry, musical instruments, wood carving, quilting, pottery, boatbuilding, blacksmithing, architecture, and graveyard decoration—and approximately that number of photographs and diagrams traveled to major United States museums in 1978 and 1979. A few quilts, other textiles, and face vessels were made in Africa and Jamaica; nearly all other objects and photographs are from the American South. All items range in date from the 1850s to the 1970s. Vlach draws on art history, sociology, and anthropology to explore the mixture of influences on and cultural stamina of the Afro-American tradition.

Wainwright, Nicholas B. *Colonial Grandeur in Philadelphia: The House and Furniture of General John Cadwalader.* Foreword by Henry Francis du Pont. Philadelphia: Historical Society of Pennsylvania, 1964. xii+169 pp.; illustrations, appendix, index.

Considering the three large gilded looking glasses, 152 yards of blue and white fringe for chairs and a sofa, sixty books of gold leaf, and two dragons carved on the pediment of the parlor chimney, it is no wonder that in the 1770s Cadwalader and his heiress wife were said to own Philadelphia's most elegant town house. Using bills and other documents about its construction and furnishings, Wainwright identifies historical terms and prices for fashionable fittings and furnishings. Although the structure was demolished and its furnishings disbursed in the early nineteenth century, comparisons are made with surviving architecture and artifacts. For recent information about extant Cadwalader furniture, see Philip D. Zimmerman, "A Methodological Study in the Identification of Some Important Philadelphia Chippendale Furniture," in *American Furniture and Its Makers: Winterthur*

Portfolio 13, ed. Ian M. G. Quimby (Chicago: University of Chicago Press, 1978), pp. 193–208. For additional architectural and some furnishings comparisons, see John A. H. Sweeney, *Grandeur on the Appoquinimink: The House of William Corbit at Odessa, Delaware* (Newark: University of Delaware Press, 1959); and George B. Tatum, *Philadelphia Georgian: The City House of Samuel Powel and Some of Its Eighteenth-Century Neighbors* (Middletown, Conn.: Wesleyan University Press, 1976).

Warren, David B. *Bayou Bend: American Furniture, Paintings, and Silver from the Bayou Bend Collection.* Foreword by Ima Hogg. Houston: Museum of Fine Arts, 1975; distributed by New York Graphic Society. xvi+192 pp.; 355 black and white and color illustrations, index.

Once a private country estate, Bayou Bend and its collections of Americana were assembled at the Museum of Fine Arts in Houston by Ima Hogg. In this volume the curator presents the collection in two ways: he comments briefly on the main features of room settings that display six major style periods and a series of arrangements devoted to "traditional" (Windsor, country, folk) expressions; and for each style section after the room discussions, he provides concise scholarly commentaries and illustrations of many individual examples of furniture. Separate catalogues of Bayou Bend's entire collection of paintings and silver follow at the end of the book. *See also* "American Furniture to 1820."

Williams, Susan. *Savory Suppers and Fashionable Feasts: Dining in Victorian America.* New York: Pantheon Books in association with the Strong Museum, 1985. xi+335 pp.; illustrations, bibliography, index.

In this major study of the material culture and foods associated with the complex dining ceremonies of Victorian America, Williams begins with brief comments of the emergence of norms for genteel behavior emphasizing ritual, formality, and schedule. Relying heavily on etiquette books, she describes what were promoted as appropriate dining behaviors. She surveys the development of the dining room as a discrete space and the creation of a wide range of furnishings considered necessary or appropriate to it, including furniture, pictures, linens, glass and ceramic tablewares, and silverwares. She also traces changing fashions in food and drink, some of which were related to improvements in canning, refrigeration, and transportation. The last chapter deals with the names, times, and meanings of various meals in the nineteenth century and includes sample menus. The book concludes with a lengthy selection of period recipes.

Wright, Louis B., George B. Tatum, John W. McCoubrey, and Robert C. Smith. *The Arts in America: The Colonial Period.* New York: Charles Scribner's Sons, 1966. xvi+368 pp.; 267 illustrations, diagrams, bibliography, index.

Rich selections of major examples of architecture, painting, and decorative arts are discussed by specialists Tatum, McCoubrey, and Smith. In their separate ways each distinguishes between the derivative and the original in the material legacy of the colonial American past. Wright offers a general historical introduction to the process of transforming the wilderness into a republic and stresses the dominance of British culture, the differences between the North and the South, and the growth of taste.

Architecture

Domestic Architecture

Domestic Architecture

David Schuyler

Eighteenth-century theorists such as Abbé Laugier traced the origins of domestic architecture to the primitive huts erected by the first humans to provide shelter from the elements. Surely the initial dwellings erected by European settlers in colonial North America were little more than temporary rude structures, usually dug into the ground and covered with whatever material was at hand. But as civilization evolved, the house became more than a simple means of protection. As was the case in other forms of architecture, with permanence in construction, residential structures adopted different stylistic expressions and achieved greater elaboration—which often resulted in the specialization of rooms by function as well as the invention of furnishings appropriate to those uses—and embraced new materials and structural technologies. Impermanent shelter became complex artifact, the physical frame that enclosed individual rooms and their contents.

The cultural significance of the home far surpasses an enumeration of these and similar innovations. More important is the set of values and ideals with which individuals and societies have endowed their dwellings. Indeed, many nineteenth-century Americans recognized that domestic architecture and society were inseparable, indistinguishable elements of the cultural matrix that shaped and gave meaning to human existence. Symbolically represented by the image of hearth tended by enlightened motherhood, homes were more than just shelter: they embodied our psychic expectations for self and children. Harriet Beecher Stowe explained the life-shaping qualities of the domestic environment in *Uncle Tom's Cabin* (Boston: John P. Jewett, 1852). At the Shelby plantation, the Christ-like Tom enjoyed a life of domestic harmony. The quarters may have been simple and the food based on inferior ingredients, but with Aunt Chloe's legendary culinary skills and Tom's religious disposition, the tiny cabin was a haven. There, surrounded by wife and children, as well as by a community of owners and fellow slaves, Tom basked in the warmth of the hearth. By contrast, Simon Legree, Tom's last owner, was the product of a broken home. Predictably, having abandoned his mother's Christianity, he lived in a once-grand plantation dwelling, since allowed to deteriorate, a building that attested simultaneously to aspirations of home and to his total disregard for domestic amenities. Kenneth S. Lynn has pointed out that Legree resided in an anarchic environment totally in keeping with his brutal personality.

Most writings about residential architecture published in the United States after 1840 paid homage to this nineteenth-century version of environmental determinism. Such books reinforced a parallel movement: the crusade to make the home a domestic utopia and the optimal setting for the rearing of children. Stowe, coauthor of *The American Woman's Home* (New York: J. B. Ford, 1869), thus called the home "the work of art peculiar to the genius of women" and ranked domesticity above all other human faculties. Like most other writers of her time, Stowe emphasized the importance of a rural or at least a suburban existence, but as more and more Americans began to live in cities, home became haven, with exterior walls and the entrance hall serving as lines of defense that protected members of the family from the dangers and temptations that contemporaries associated with the urban environment. Order prevailed within the home, disorder without.

The pages of nineteenth-century architectural pattern books and treatises on domesticity reveal yet another function ascribed to a properly designed residence. According to Andrew Jackson Downing, the preeminent arbiter of American taste at midcentury, the middle-class home was, at least potentially, a "powerful means of civilization," a battleground on which refinement and culture would vanquish the forces of barbarism. In *The Architecture of Country Houses* (New York: D. Appleton, 1850), he wrote: "So long as men are forced to dwell in log huts and follow a hunter's life, we must not be surprised at lynch law and the use of the bowie knife. But, when smiling lawns and tasteful cottages begin to embellish a country, we know that order and culture are established" (pp. xix–xx). Downing articulated a particular vision of civilization, a middle-class ideology which he believed was appropriate for the American Republic. The political implications of this vision have been remarkably persistent: over time, Americans have considered the single-family home to be central to the maintenance of social order and have justified the reform of domestic architecture as an essential program in the evolution of the nation's republican institutions.

Moreover, as the greatest single investment that most families usually make, these dwellings are part of a broader pattern of consumption: they are statements of self to the world. Downing argued that in its design, the home should be the outward manifestation of the owner's character. A contemporary, Philadelphia architect Samuel Sloan, agreed. In volume 1 of *The Model Architect* (Philadelphia: E. G. Jones, 1852), Sloan noted that when an individual builds a house, "his tact for arrangement, his private feelings, the refinement of his tastes and the peculiarities of his judgment, are all laid bare for public inspection and criticism" (p. 10). The idea of domestic architecture as personal expression persisted throughout the nineteenth century, much as it continues in the present. Looking back on his boyhood in Wilmington, Delaware, Henry Seidel Canby recalled in *The Age of Confidence: Life in the Nineties* (New York: Farrar and Rinehart, 1934): "Homes then did represent some quality of the owner, for the architects, having no style of their own, gave the buyer what he wanted: the nouveau riches got exactly the parapets and ornamental porches and zig-zag sky line they longed for, simple people had simple houses, solid folks solid brick with plate glass windows and heavy metal roofs, and transients, who stayed a year or so and then moved on, precisely the thrown-together houses they deserved. As the Scotch or English farmer was known by the name of his farm, so when I think of many of our citizens I see their homes before I can recall their faces" (pp. 11–12). Russell Lynes, in the opening pages of *The Tastemakers*, which is annotated below, captured the implications of this belief that the home reflected its owner. The prototypical housewife with enough money to redecorate her house becomes totally frustrated when trying to decide which style would be most appropriate. Lynes elevated this seemingly inconsequential event into a powerful allegory: who, after all, would want to convey to the world the wrong image of self?

Shelter, artifact, symbol, familial environment, defense against society, promoter of refinement and civilization, social statement—in its varied yet simultaneous meanings, the home embodies many of the contradictions inherent in American life. As a result, perhaps more than any other artifact the home is the master symbol of American culture. Since Downing's era, the single-family residence as sacred precinct and personal expression has maintained its honored place in the American dream. The federal government provides a generous tax deduction as well as mortgage assistance to promote home ownership, and those who take advantage of such subsidies can turn for advice to professional architects, to dozens of lavishly illustrated magazines that describe the proper arrangement and content of interior spaces, to regular features printed in other mass-circulation journals, or to a weekly supplement of the nation's leading newspapers. Americans take the design of their homes seriously, and for good reason.

Given the values that so many nineteenth-century writers have ascribed to residential architecture and the amount of space domestic design has received in the popular press, it is perhaps surprising that as recently as the 1950s the middle-class home attracted only passing attention from scholars. To be sure, earlier in the century a group of dedicated architects and antiquarians had studied the surviving buildings of the colonial era. Pioneering works by Norman M. Isham, Thomas T. Waterman, J. Frederick Kelly, and others remain the basis for subsequent scholarship. Indeed, Fiske Kimball's *Domestic Architecture of the American Colonies and of the Early Republic* (1922; reprint, 1966) is yet unsurpassed as a study of early residential architecture. Taken together, these books were part of the filiopietistic movement to preserve and restore American antiquities, but with the singular exception of Kimball, their authors were amateur historians. However idealistic the intent, the resulting books portrayed a pattern of life as far removed from the experience of the vast majority of American colonists as it was from the mainstream of contemporary scholarship. During these years, the history of American, particularly domestic, architecture received little academic support or recognition. That would come only after World War II.

George B. Tatum's "Andrew Jackson Downing: Arbiter of American Taste, 1815–1852" (1950) was the first dissertation on an American subject completed under the aegis of the Department of Art and Archaeology at Princeton University. Vincent Scully, who was working at Yale at the same time, reported in his "American Houses: Thomas Jefferson to Frank Lloyd Wright" that while writing *The Shingle Style* he had to overcome two prejudices: "One of them regarded domestic architecture as too insignificant a topic for art-historical investigation; the other reflected a wide-spread aversion to the forms of nineteenth-century 'Victorian' architecture as a whole." If occasionally an incisive book had explored a subject such as the log cabin myth, on the whole, architectural history was something to be studied in foreign places, not at home, and its subject was great edifices, the palaces of emperors and kings, churches, and public buildings, not common houses.

Today, of course, it is unusual to pick up a journal devoted to architecture, material culture, folklore, or interdisciplinary studies that does not contain at least one discussion of American houses. Especially since 1970, energetic scholars have published hundreds of books and articles devoted to styles, types, architects and builders, and similar topics. Many of these studies have borrowed methodologies developed in related academic disciplines and have applied them imaginatively to architecture. Others, building on pioneering works by Fred Kniffen, have studied a range of building types heretofore largely ignored by architectural historians.

Three principal influences help to account for the broadening of architectural history in the last two decades. First is the "new" social history, which traces its roots to the social and political radicalism of the 1960s and which, in its earliest stage, attempted to rewrite history "from the bottom up." Palaces or homes of the rich and famous, to borrow an analogy from Jesse Lemisch, are far less important than the dwellings and the everyday lives of common people. Anyone seriously interested in understanding the past needs to look beyond great individuals and their buildings (or, in literature, the canon of great books) and study the traditional environments, folkways, and normal occurrences that shaped the behavior of the members of society who left no written records.

A second, parallel influence is the evolving discipline of material culture studies. Broadly conceived, material culture attempts to use artifacts—buildings, landscapes, household objects, the entire humanly created environment—to determine patterns of everyday existence. Drawing on such academic disciplines as anthropology, folklore, historical geography, and structural linguistics, students of material culture have examined types of buildings—especially folk or vernacular structures and how they have changed over time—in order to reconstruct the lives, the *mentalité*, of common people in the past.

A third contribution to the recent expansion of architectural history is the broadening of the historic preservation movement. During the last twenty years it has moved beyond the concept of historic "shrine" or personal monument to embrace entire working-class neighborhoods and districts particularly rich in vernacular buildings. In furthering their cause, preservationists have contributed a plethora of useful books to the historiography of American architecture.

These recent innovations have broadened the horizons of architectural history by expanding the corpus of materials worthy of study and by infusing the discipline with new methodologies. Many recent books and articles have encouraged historians to analyze the past more comprehensively, as the affairs not only of great men but also of long-forgotten individuals collectively trying to comprehend and shape their world. In this context, analysis of buildings and their placement on the landscape reveal the persistence of European practices and their adaptation to different environmental and social conditions in the New World, the diffusion of building types, and the evolution of form over time. Moreover, the design and arrangement of interior spaces in houses indicate changing conceptions of public and private realms.

Another area that several recent studies implicitly explore is the discrepancy between the theory and practice of architectural design. The posturing of nineteenth-century writers notwithstanding, their intent usually was prescriptive: they did not describe society as it was, but projected a vision of what they hoped it would become. An astute observation by Alexis de Tocqueville in volume 2 of *Democracy in America* (New York: Vintage Books, 1945) illustrates the divergence between the ideal of the home as a bastion of social order and the reality of a restless people: "In the United States a man builds a house in which to spend his old age, and he sells it before the roof is on; he plants a garden and lets it just as the trees are coming into bearing; he brings a field into tillage and leaves other men to gather the crops; he embraces a profession and gives it up; he settles in one place, which he soon afterward leaves to carry his changeable longings elsewhere" (pp. 144–45). Thus, for all the efforts of architectural and social reformers, the printed texts they left behind are valuable, but in some ways limited, historical documents. Contemporary scholars need to assay the purpose and influence of those writings and use them with some caution.

Three recent books, written by scholars of different ages and academic backgrounds, indicate the emergence of what could become a new synthesis in the history of American architecture: Gwendolyn Wright's *Building the Dream*, Alan Gowans's *Comfortable House*, and Clifford Clark's *American Family Home*. Although each book uses a different methodology and asks different questions of its subject, collectively they represent important new directions in architectural scholarship. Wright, an architectural historian at Columbia University, describes *Building the Dream* as "an interpretative essay that attempts to raise issues about American housing, and that relates the various architectural models this country has adopted." Homes embody symbolic values, of course, and Wright analyzes the almost mythic significance Americans have ascribed to the single-family household—as an environment that shapes character, promotes certain patterns of behavior, and promises to remedy broader social problems. But individual choices in domestic architecture also have implications on public policy, and Wright portrays housing as a social, political, and cultural issue.

Clark's *American Family Home* builds on Wright's work, especially her first book, *Moralism and the Model Home*. Clark examines the relationship between ideals of home and the reality of the middle-class family, which, especially for women, often seemed to be "at odds." As would prove true in subsequent generations, the ideal of middle-class family life caused tension among members of the household.

Gowans's interests range from architecture and painting to popular and commercial arts, but perhaps no subject in his distinguished scholarly career has proved more engaging than *The Comfortable House*. As do Wright and Clark, Gowans believes that the home is "an instrument for promoting stability in society at large and the good life for individuals in families." Whereas Wright and Clark pay close attention to conflict within the household, Gowans juxtaposes the ideal of the single-family home with the failings of modernism.

Until recently, the writing of American architectural history, and especially of domestic architecture, has received far less scholarly attention than its subject merits. Individually and collectively, buildings shape the environment in which most Americans live and work, and none more prominently than homes and houses. A century ago, architectural critic Mariana Griswold Van Rensselaer observed: "It is true that even in our republican land the average does not mean the noblest either among men or buildings. But it means that which is *collectively* most prominent. The general effect of a modern town depends less upon its monumental structures than upon the aggregate of its dwellings, humble in comparison though these individually may be. So there is no architectural branch in which success is more desirable than in the domestic branch" ("Recent Architecture in America, V: City Dwellings," *Century* 31 [November 1885–April 1886]: 548). If few critics heeded Van Rensselaer then, the recent broadening of the field of American architectural history and the maturation of vernacular and material culture studies have enabled talented individuals to write the history of all the buildings that Americans in the past considered homes. As noted by the nineteenth-century writers who championed the home as a domestic utopia, a subject so important deserves such creative syntheses.

Betts, Richard J. "The Woodlands." *Winterthur Portfolio* 14, no. 3 (Autumn 1979): 213–34. 15 illustrations, appendix.

The sophisticated design of the Woodlands, William Hamilton's country estate outside Philadelphia, has long intrigued architectural historians. George B. Tatum noted in *Philadelphia Georgian* that the Woodlands "goes so far beyond anything being attempted by contemporary American builders as to suggest that Hamilton may have brought from London the plans for his new house." Betts's impressive research demonstrates convincingly that the structure was designed in London during winter 1785/86, probably by a lesser-known architect familiar with Robert Adam's and Samuel Sloan's works, in active collaboration with the owner. Careful reading of relevant documents and imaginative interpretation of the building fabric enable Betts to offer a conjectural outline of the changes that Hamilton introduced by adding the famous oval rooms and making other alterations to an older two-story rectangular structure. An appendix of twenty-one letters written by Hamilton documents the owner's supervision of every phase of construction.

Blackburn, Roderick H. *Cherry Hill: The History and Collections of a Van Rensselaer Family*. Albany: Historic Cherry Hill, 1976. viii+176 pp.; illustrations, 192 illustrated entries, appendixes, bibliography.

Blackburn analyzes the evolution of this Georgian structure, built in 1786, as well as the five generations who lived there and the furnishings they accumulated between circa 1730 and the 1860s. He devotes separate chapters to the owners, the farm and buildings, and the primary documents and archival resources. The bulk of the book, however, is six chapters that analyze the furniture, ceramics, textiles, metals, and paintings owned by the Van Rensselaer family. Filiopietism mars this bicentennial publication, but Blackburn nevertheless presents an important collection of documented images and artifacts.

Block, Jean F. *Hyde Park Houses: An Informal History, 1856–1910*. Photographs by Samuel W. Block, Jr. Chicago and London: University of Chicago Press, 1978. xii+156 pp.; 21 illustrations, 76 plates, appendixes, bibliography, index.

Block, a longtime resident of Hyde Park and a librarian at the University of Chicago, has produced a meticulously researched and affectionately written example of neighborhood history. Kenneth T. Jackson notes in the foreword that Block "places the architectural history of the neighborhood within the larger framework of the community's economic and social life" (p. ix). Relying on such evidence as city construction permits, building records, city directories, newspapers, interviews, and the local architectural press, she has examined some 900 buildings designed by more than forty architects in the compact area of Chicago between Forty-seventh and Fifty-ninth streets and from Cottage Grove Avenue to Lake Michigan. Her concern is the area's transformation from "prairie settlement" to prosperous suburb to "heavily populated and thriving urban neighborhood" (p. xi). Especially important are the appendixes, which document the architects who worked in Hyde Park during these years and present a checklist of existing residences built before 1910.

Bloomfield, Anne. "The Real Estate Associates: A Land and Housing Developer of the 1870s in San Francisco." *Journal of the Society of Architectural Historians* 37, no. 1 (March 1978): 13–33. 17 illustrations, appendix.

The Real Estate Associates built more than 1,000 houses in San Francisco principally between 1871 and 1878. The company invested heavily in real estate and then developed blocks of almost identical detached dwellings, most of which were Italianate in design. Bloomfield analyzes its principal leader, William Hollis, and the shaky financial basis of the company, while documenting this attempt to provide decent and attractive housing for the city's working and middle classes.

Bunting, Bainbridge. *Houses of Boston's Back Bay: An Architectural History, 1840–1917*. Cambridge, Mass.: Harvard University Press, Belknap Press, 1967. xvii+494 pp.; 250 illustrations, appendixes, index.

The Back Bay neighborhood of Boston provides a microcosm for studying the development of American architecture. Following the extension of Commonwealth Avenue and the filling in of Charles River, approximately 1,500 private residences and apartment houses were built there between 1857 and 1917. Bunting has reconstructed this building program by examining tax records, building permits, the structures themselves, and other scholarly resources. He focuses on the city house as it evolved stylistically and technologically over time and divides this development into four periods: formative (1844–57), academic hegemony (1857–69), individualistic (1869–85), and revivalistic (1885–1917). He also relates these buildings to social and cultural developments and to the physical fabric of the city. Indeed, Bunting asserts, the development of Beacon Hill "represents one of the country's first concerted efforts to create a homogeneous urban environment on a grand scale" (p. 2). The appendixes, arranged by block, identify each building by street number, date of construction, original owner, and architect if known. This is a meticulously researched and thoughtfully presented book, a classic whose importance extends far beyond the boundaries of neighborhood history.

Byron, Joseph. *New York Interiors at the Turn of the Century.* Text by Clay Lancaster. Photographic essay. New York: Dover Publications in cooperation with the Museum of the City of New York, 1976. xviii+154 pp.; 131 illustrations.

An English immigrant who arrived in New York in 1888, Byron was a professional photographer whose camera recorded the homes of rich and poor alike. This collection of photographs, selected from a much larger group at the Museum of the City of New York, presents eighty-one plates of domestic scenes taken in the years preceding World War I. Other photographs document offices, banks, retail stores, and theaters. Lancaster's introductory essay summarizes Byron's professional career, establishes the urban context in which he worked, and provides a sound guide to interpreting the styles of interiors and furnishings captured in the images.

Carson, Cary, Norman F. Barka, William M. Kelso, Garry Wheeler Stone, and Dell Upton. "Impermanent Architecture in the Southern American Colonies." *Winterthur Portfolio* 16, nos. 2/3 (Summer/Autumn 1981): 135–96. 16 illustrations, appendixes.

This important and imaginative synthesis of research on impermanent domestic architecture in eastern Maryland and Virginia, the combined work of archaeologists and social historians, analyzes the transplanting of an English construction type, the "earthfast" frame building, and its evolution during the seventeenth and eighteenth centuries. Carson and coauthors explain the surprisingly long duration of impermanent domestic architecture and the shift to more durable frame and brick buildings as functions not only of political and social stability but also of greater family stability (due to a decline in mortality rates and an increased birth rate) and the economic shift from reliance on tobacco to the cultivation of grains. Economic stability resulted in permanence of construction. Nevertheless, because of its long duration, many of the construction techniques developed in impermanent architecture became part of the "vernacular mainstream" (p. 163). A richly textured and rewarding analysis distinguishes this essay.

Clark, Clifford E., Jr. "Domestic Architecture as an Index to Social History: The Romantic Revival and the Cult of Domesticity in America, 1840–1870." *Journal of Interdisciplinary History* 7, no. 1 (Summer 1976): 33–56. 4 illustrations.

Clark asserts that the crusade to improve domestic architecture was a major reform movement undertaken in nineteenth-century America. He sketches the aesthetic shift from classic to romantic, the demand for single-family housing, particularly in suburbs, and the emergence of professionalization within the architectural field to meet the needs of specialization within the household. Clark relates these developments to the emergence of a new Protestant theology that emphasized "Christian Nurture." Taken together, these changes "all served to give the advocates of domestic housing reform an unprecedented influence on the American public" (p. 47). As a result, the "family home came to be the major symbol of middle-class values at mid-century" (p. 56).

Clark, Clifford Edward, Jr. *American Family Home, 1800–1960.* Chapel Hill and London: University of North Carolina Press, 1986. xvi+281 pp.; illustrations, bibliography, index.

Drawing on recent social and architectural history, Clark analyzes how homes reflected changing conceptions of family life, from the formality of the Victorian parlor to the more relaxed living spaces of the bungalow or the suburban ranch house. Equally important is his attention to the conflicts between housing reformers, architects, sanitarians, and popular ideas of what constituted a proper home. Throughout this excellent book, Clark places domestic architecture squarely within the social and cultural context in which it was created.

Cohen, Lizabeth A. "Embellishing a Life of Labor: An Interpretation of the Material Culture of American Working-Class Homes, 1885–1915." *Journal of American Culture* 3, no. 4 (Winter 1980): 752–75. 7 illustrations.

Cohen believes that studying furnishings and spatial organization "provides a new way of understanding the historical development of working-class culture." Focusing on consumption preferences, she "interprets how these choices reflected and affected worker social identity" (p. 752). Cohen develops this thesis in three parts: by tracing stylistic development from midcentury styles to the arts and crafts and colonial revival movements; by analyzing the unsuccessful attempts by progressive reformers to "impose" middle-class values on ethnic lower classes; and by demonstrating how urban workers and their families embraced Victorian styles, to the horror of reformers, because such ornamented furnishings suited their rural orientation and satisfied their desire to "adapt to mass-produced goods" (p. 772). This article is an important addition to the bibliography of the "new" urban and social history, to the history of reform, and to the study of architecture as cultural expression.

Cohn, Jan. *The Palace or the Poorhouse: The American House as a Cultural Symbol.* East Lansing: Michigan State University Press, 1979. xii+267 pp.; index.

This ambitious effort of a literary historian examines changing attitudes toward the house from Puritan beginnings to the post–World War II years, paying particular attention to Downing and Wright as well as the contrast between homes for the rich and the poor. Cohn asserts, "the house has been, and continues to be, the dominant symbol for American culture," one that reflects "the complexities and contradictions inherent in American culture" (p. xi). Her sole source of information is the published word, a highly questionable strategy when so much of the material on which she relies is prescriptive in intent. Moreover, in devoting so much energy to what people wrote about houses—which is not necessarily the way they behaved—Cohn presents little information about the buildings themselves. This unwillingness to measure rhetoric against the homes that Americans actually built is symptomatic: Cohn fails to comprehend the complexities of architectural and cultural history.

Cummings, Abbott Lowell. *The Framed Houses of Massachusetts Bay, 1625–1725.* Cambridge, Mass., and London: Harvard University Press, Belknap Press, 1979. xiv+261 pp.; 280 illustrations, appendix, index.

This volume examines the transmission of English building traditions to the New World and their modification through technology and adaptation to climate. Cummings analyzes house plans, the builders and their resources, the construction process, and the chimney, as well as exterior and interior finishes. The final chapter summarizes both the persistence of English culture and the process of adaptation: "English immigrant carpenters were forced from the first moment of their landing to come to grips with a new environment and to find technical solutions for new problems" (p. 209). Appendixes provide information on the dimensions of dwellings, timber grants, inventories, building permits, length of bladed scarfs, and spacing of floor joists. Based on meticulous research in seventeenth-century public records and manuscript sources, as well as on nineteenth- and twentieth-century scholarship and careful examination of the buildings themselves, this product of years of study is a landmark in American architectural history.

Cummings, Abbott Lowell, ed. *Rural Household Inventories: Establishing the Names, Uses, and Furnishings of Rooms in the Colonial New England Home, 1675–1775.* See "Basic References and Guides to Research."

Foley, Mary Mix. *The American House.* Drawings by Madelaine Thatcher; foreword by James Marston Fitch. New York and Cambridge: Harper and Row, 1981. 299 pp.; 320 illustrations, index.

Foley traces the evolution of residential architecture in the United States from the building practices of original settlers through the postmodern movement. While occasionally it places buildings, residents, or architects within social or cultural contexts, this book is admittedly "a guide to style itself" and to "the process of architectural development" (p. 7). Especially noteworthy are Foley's concern for both high-style and vernacular architecture, her comprehensive treatment of regional and ethnic patterns in building, and her attempt to trace the evolution of styles over time. However, the organizational framework—six chapters collectively entitled "The Medieval Echo" followed by eleven devoted to more formal styles—creates problems of chronology. Notable too is the paucity of notes (sixteen in all) for so ambitious an undertaking, which is explained incongruously by Fitch as making the book "refreshingly free of all the usual apparatus of historiography" (p. 6). Some floor plans and views of interiors are included, as are illustrations of exterior architecture.

Friends of the Cabildo. *New Orleans Architecture.* 6 vols. to date. Gretna, La.: Friends of the Cabildo and Pelican Publishing Co., 1971–.

As their individual titles indicate, five of the six volumes in this award-winning series examine the development and evolution of the city's neighborhoods: *The Lower Garden District, The American Sector, The Creole Faubourgs, The Esplanade Ridge,* and *Faubourg Treme and the Bayou Road* (vol. 3 is *The Cemeteries*). Collectively these books comprise perhaps the richest compendium of published material on the architecture of any American city. Initially undertaken to alert citizens to the richness of their city's building heritage and to encourage preservation efforts, this series has become a major contribution to architectural history. It presents a thoroughly textured story based on considerable research (although, alas, only the sixth volume contains notes), enriched by more than fifty color plates and hundreds of black and white illustrations. Volume 6 contains a section entitled "Restoration by Analogy," an imaginative guide to those undertaking the restoration of older residences.

Garrett, Elisabeth Donaghy, comp. *The Antiques Book of Victorian Interiors.* New York: Crown Publishers, 1981. 159 pp.; black and white and color illustrations, bibliography, index.

Garrett has compiled sixteen articles published in *Antiques* between 1974 and 1980. The articles describe buildings that range in location from New England to Texas and from upstate New York to Louisiana. Some, like George W. Vanderbilt's Biltmore and Chateau-sur-Mer in Newport, are vacation homes of the grandest scale; others, like Henry Clay's farmhouse, Ashland, and Theodore Roosevelt's birthplace in New York City (a rare example of a totally reconstructed Victorian building), are more typical upper-class residences of the second half of the nineteenth century. Some, like Mark Twain's Hartford home, represent noteworthy restoration efforts; others, like Frederic Church's Olana, were virtually unaltered in the twentieth century. The texts of these essays vary in length and quality, but each is lavishly illustrated.

Garvin, James L. "Mail-Order House Plans and American Victorian Architecture." *Winterthur Portfolio* 16, no. 4 (Winter 1981): 309–34. 28 illustrations.

In the years following the Civil War, architectural publishing adapted to the need for inexpensive but fashionable housing for the expanding middle and working classes. The result was the mail-order house plan, which, Garvin asserts, was "an important but hidden factor in suburban growth during the decades before 1900." This essay focuses narrowly on the entrepreneurial competition between Palliser, Palliser, and Company and Robert W. Shoppell for control of the mail-order-plan market, but otherwise it helps to explain the transition from the publication of house-pattern books (some of which offered plans for sale) to the mail-order houses that began to dot the American landscape at the turn of the century.

Gillon, Edmund V., Jr., and Clay Lancaster. *Victorian Houses: A Treasury of Lesser-Known Examples.* Photographic essay. New York: Dover Publications, 1973. viii+[117] pp.; 115 plates, index.

With the hope of fostering "enjoyment of nineteenth-century domestic structures through the visual record," this book presents examples of domestic architecture "built by and for people who were never heard of outside their own time and community, and soon forgotten locally" (pp. vii, vi). Drawing largely from the northeastern United States, Gillon and Lancaster include buildings that are modest and grand, both high-style and vernacular examples. Lancaster's introduction provides an "overall vista of the subject" and, together with the lively captions, relates the buildings illustrated to those published in pattern books by Andrew Jackson Downing, Samuel Sloan, George Palliser, and others.

Glassie, Henry. "Artifact and Culture, Architecture and Society." In *American Material Culture and Folklife: A Prologue and Dialogue*, edited by Simon J. Bronner, pp. 47–62. Ann Arbor, Mich.: UMI Research Press, 1985. 3 illustrations.

All building types, Glassie asserts, reflect "orderings of experience"; they represent the "materialization" of ideas about social and political organization (p. 48). Thus, architectural form responds to social change: the vernacular house evolves from an open to a closed one that stands as a barrier against uncertainty and social disorder. In this brief synthesis, Glassie notes that the "key to vernacular technology is engagement, direct involvement in the manipulation of materials (even when the goal is artificiality), and active participation in the process of design, construction, and use" (p. 52). But as the "egalitarian ethic" and active role of the owner cease, vernacular gives way to nonvernacular architecture. Glassie concludes by pleading for the active preservation of vernacular structures.

Glassie, Henry. "Eighteenth-Century Cultural Process in Delaware Valley Folk Building." In *Winterthur Portfolio 7*, edited by Ian M. G. Quimby, pp. 29–57. Charlottesville: University Press of Virginia for the Henry Francis du Pont Winterthur Museum, 1972. 27 illustrations.

In this as in his other writings, Glassie attempts to escape the "methodological limitations of print" by using artifacts to discover the people in the past who left no written records (p. 29). He examines lower Delaware River valley house forms and farm plans during the third quarter of the eighteenth century, a time of "extensive and intensive innovation" (p. 35), when Georgian aesthetics competed with traditional building practices. Glassie argues that the emergence of a "synthetic" house type and the arrangement of farm buildings indicate the beginnings of "the dominant style of America, loose, worried, acquisitive individualism" (p. 57).

Glassie, Henry. *Folk Housing in Middle Virginia: A Structural Analysis of Historic Artifacts.* Knoxville: University of Tennessee Press, 1975. xiv+231 pp.; 86 illustrations, bibliography, index.

This book is part of Glassie's continuing attempt to "battle past wood and stone to begin considering the human beings who left material things as their only legacy" (p. vii). In this analysis of 156 traditional houses in Louisa and Goochland counties, located west of the fall line and east of the Blue Ridge Mountains, he uses the physical fabric of buildings "to reconstruct the logic of people long dead" (p. vii). He establishes the process through which builders determined the basic shape of the house and traces the way they adapted to change during the late eighteenth and nineteenth centuries. Glassie concludes by assessing the significance of the house as a barometer of social change and as an expression of the residents' increasing need to control nature and to impose order on their surroundings. *See also* "Craftsmen."

Gowans, Alan. *Images of American Living: Four Centuries of Architecture and Furniture as Cultural Expression.* 1964. New ed. New York: Harper and Row, 1976. xv+498 pp.; approximately 135 illustrations, indexes.

This pathbreaking book, still fresh in its insights, begins with the premise that architecture and furniture are "by nature arts which represent the collective efforts and ideals of a civilization" (p. xiv). In thirty-six chapters Gowans examines buildings and their furnishings from seventeenth-century beginnings to artistic expression in the post–World War II years. He not only illustrates the evolution of style but also analyzes patterns in American culture—the "progressive conquest over nature," the dynamics of social change, differing conceptions of art and architecture, and "a pattern of evolving democracy, political and economic" (p. xv). *Images* has influenced the writing of numerous books and articles, but none has superseded the original: Gowans's interpretations are thoughtful and challenging, and the book is indispensable.

Gowans, Alan. *The Comfortable House: North American Suburban Architecture, 1890–1930*. Cambridge, Mass., and London: MIT Press, 1986. xv+246 pp.; 209 illustrations, bibliography, index.

During the "confident" years from 1890 to 1929, commercial developments allowed more Americans than ever before to aspire to and own a comfortable suburban house. Mass production and standardization of parts were epitomized by the mail-order home. Instead of dismissing those buildings and lamenting the lack of popular appreciation for a scientific or streamlined house, Gowans takes bungalows and foursquares seriously as cultural expression. Despite the profusion of revival styles, he argues that the "post-Victorian art world, high and low, was a cultural unity." The comfortable house, the result of a commingling of vernacular, popular-commercial, and high-style design, became a recognizable icon of the American landscape. This is an erudite yet affectionate analysis of middle-class ideals of home and comfort.

Handlin, David P. *The American Home: Architecture and Society, 1815–1915*. Boston and Toronto: Little, Brown, 1979. xii+545 pp.; 199 illustrations, index.

Handlin's book represents an ambitious attempt to analyze the relationship between the physical shape of the home and broader social values over a century. In seven lengthy chapters, he explores the "culture of domestic architecture" by analyzing subjects as diverse as the ideology of domesticity, prescriptions for landscaping homes and towns, the impact of attitudes toward ventilation and health on architecture, and advice on the furnishings and upkeep of the household. His impressive range of topics includes the genesis of Arbor Day, cooperative housekeeping, public health, suburbanization, the design of apartment houses for rich and poor, and changing attitudes toward country and city; however, as a result of this diversity, the book lacks coherence. Although flawed, it presents an impressive array of information derived from nineteenth-century books and periodicals.

Hayden, Dolores. *The Grand Domestic Revolution: A History of Feminist Designs for American Homes, Neighborhoods, and Cities*. Cambridge, Mass., and London: MIT Press, 1981. x+367 pp.; illustrations, appendix, index.

Hayden explains the efforts of "the first feminists in the United States to identify the economic exploitation of women's domestic labor by men as the most basic cause of women's inequality" (p. 3). These "material feminists" attempted "to make private domestic work social labor" (p. 310 n. 3). To do so they proposed various schemes for cooperative living or domestic services that would eliminate the split between private and public life as represented by the female-dominated but isolated suburban home and the male-oriented world of business. Their ambitious reformist program attempted to transform the spatial design and material condition of homes, neighborhoods, and cities. Hayden examines macropolitical and economic change as it shapes woman's sphere, as well as the various campaigns of the material feminists to create alternatives to the single-family home so closely identified with the culture of domesticity. This important but polemical book stands as the counterpoint to many of the studies included in this bibliography, especially those that address the Victorian home.

Hayward, Mary Ellen. "Urban Vernacular Architecture in Nineteenth-Century Baltimore." *Winterthur Portfolio* 16, no. 1 (Spring 1981): 33–63. 30 illustrations.

Hayward presents a model for the study of "working-class housing, based on the theory that the design of these houses derived from high-style house types popular in the particular city or region" (p. 33). She examines Federal Hill, a twenty-three-block area overlooking Baltimore's Inner Harbor, which contained every style of working-class housing—from federal to Italianate—built between 1780 and 1890. But for all her efforts to provide a model, Hayward's tautological argument is that working-class houses were smaller-scaled, less-decorated versions of the dwellings of more prosperous people. Because the Federal Hill structures were erected by a handful of wealthy real-estate speculators, the assertion that they are expressions of vernacular culture seems erroneous.

Herman, Bernard L. "Time and Performance: Folk Houses in Delaware." In *American Material Culture and Folklife: A Prologue and Dialogue*, edited by Simon J. Bronner, pp. 155–75. Ann Arbor, Mich.: UMI Research Press, 1985. 12 illustrations.

Herman attempts to establish an "analytical frame" for assessing the changing treatment of vernacular architecture. Using tax assessments, maps, and probate records, as well as analyses of the physical fabric of two eighteenth-century houses in St. Georges Hundred, New Castle County, he examines how those buildings changed over time. Herman is especially concerned with "subsequent performance," and his essay demonstrates the shift toward Georgian forms in the early nineteenth century. This work represents an important effort to merge architecture and the new social history.

Kennedy, Roger G. *Architecture, Men, Women, and Money in America, 1600–1860*. New York: Random House, 1985. xiv+526 pp.; illustrations, bibliography, index.

This book presents a conversationally written, perceptive, and admittedly idiosyncratic survey of American architecture, principally domestic, from its European antecedents to the eve of the Civil War. Although devoted largely to the classical tradition in America, Kennedy ranges broadly and bravely afield from Palladian villas to West Indian plantations, to back-country cabins embellished with classical porticoes, and ending with a nod toward the picturesque of the mid nineteenth century. He delves engagingly into the personalities and relationships of architect and client, but he is equally interested in the interplay among trade economics (including banking and land speculation), politics, and building patterns. He is concerned as well with how personality and the symbolic functions of architecture, particularly as economic and social developments, lead some individuals to become innovative and others conservative in architectural choice. Scholars will undoubtedly complain about the number of mistakes that appear in the text and argue about what Kennedy has chosen not to include, but this is an important, thought-provoking book.

Lancaster, Clay. *The American Bungalow, 1880–1930*. New York: Abbeville Press, 1985. 256 pp.; 191 illustrations, index.

Lancaster traces the bungalow from its origins in India to British and American antecedents (rural homes integrated with nature), its shift in function from occasional house to permanent family home, its migration from the East Coast to the Midwest to California and back again, and its floor plan, furnishings, and landscaping. He is concerned with the bungalow as a livable environment for the middle class, a building type that exemplifies "comfort" rather than "culture." Although he proposes to analyze the style "as an art form and as a document reflecting the life of its era" (p. 11), he pays little attention to the people who lived in these homes (save for his father, who built a bungalow in Lexington, Kentucky) or to recent scholarship on the topic.

Lewis, Peirce F. "Common Houses, Cultural Spoor." *Landscape* 19, no. 2 (January 1975): 1–22. 25 illustrations, bibliography.

Lewis believes that "one's house is more than mere shelter. It is a personal and social testament" (p. 1). This essay attempts to interpret common houses as unconscious statements about the builders and their culture. It examines the four-over-four house, the single-pen cabin, and the I house as each migrates west. Lewis argues that except in the South, increased regional diversity gave way to a national architectural style after the Civil War. He also asserts that regional differences have been replaced by a new architectural variety evident in the chronological and socioeconomic rings of urban growth.

Lynes, Russell. *The Tastemakers: The Shaping of American Popular Taste*. 1954. Reprint. New York: Dover Publications, 1980. xii + 372 pp.; illustrations, bibliography, index.

Americans take taste seriously, Lynes argues, "not only as an ornament of life but as one of its almost inescapable problems. Taste is our personal delight, our private dilemma, and our public facade" (pp. 3–4). He divides his panoramic survey of the development of American taste into three parts. The Age of Public Taste (roughly 1820–80) describes attempts "to discipline everyone to a higher appreciation of the arts and to a nicer sensibility to their surroundings." During the era of Private Taste (roughly 1880–1920), arbiters of culture

charged individuals with maintaining "local standards of refinement and culture." With the dominance of Corporate Taste (post-1920), Madison Avenue and major companies have exploited mass communications to reach unprecedented numbers of people. Lynes pays particular attention to houses and interiors to illustrate the changing conception of taste in America, and for more than thirty years this humorous, insightful book has delighted readers. The new afterword reprints Lynes's celebrated guide to highbrow, middlebrow, and lowbrow.

Maass, John. *The Gingerbread Age: A View of Victorian America*. 1957. New ed. New York: Greenwich House, 1983. 212 pp.; approximately 200 illustrations, bibliography, index.

This affectionate appraisal of the Victorian home is admittedly "not a work of formal scholarship," but is instead "an antidote to long-entrenched clichés" about the Gilded Age and its "monstrosities" (p. 3). In seven chapters Maass presents a short, appreciative introduction to the most popular architectural styles of the second half of the nineteenth century, followed by numerous illustrations and informative captions.

Maass, John. *The Victorian Home in America*. New York: Hawthorne Books, 1972. xiv + 235 pp.; approximately 250 black and white illustrations, 30 color plates, appendixes, bibliography, index.

Beginning with a chapter entitled "How to Think about Houses," Maass examines Gothic, Italianate, octagonal/oriental, French, and eclectic houses (the "nameless period") of Queen Anne, Eastlake, or Richardsonian styles, roughly between 1840 and 1900. The text is punctuated with trenchant observations such as "Nonsense and Sense of Architectural History," "The Mystery of Style," and "Is There an American Architecture?" Maass believes that architecture and interiors are part of "life-style—the way people stand, sit, move, walk, dance, talk, sing, dress, eat, drink, court, and behave" (p. 5), and he presents a collection of richly informative illustrations that capture Victorians in their homes to convey a sense of place and time.

Mayhew, Edgar de N., and Minor Myers, Jr. *A Documentary History of American Interiors from the Colonial Era to 1915*. New York: Charles Scribner's Sons, 1980. xiii + 399 pp.; 240 black and white illustrations, 32 color plates, appendixes, bibliography, index.

"If the true character of Americans is mirrored in their homes," Moreau de Saint-Mery observed at the end of the eighteenth century, then the evolution of domestic interiors and their furnishings provides important information about the changing nature of society and culture (p. ix). In this impressive and well-researched survey, Mayhew and Myers present a comprehensive picture of the architectural design, room functions, and furnishings of American houses over almost 300 years. Paying close attention to the economic status of householders, they interpret a range of visual documents, including prints, drawings, paintings, and photographs that illustrate the kinds of homes in which Americans of different classes resided. The appendixes provide information on household technologies and guide the reader to museums and historical societies with major collections of American furniture. This is the best and most comprehensive study of the subject. *See also* "Surveys."

McDaniel, George W. *Hearth and Home: Preserving a People's Culture. See* "Surveys."

Minhinnick, Jeanne. *At Home in Upper Canada.* Illustration design and drawings by John Richmond. Toronto and Vancouver: Clarke, Irwin, 1970. 228 pp.; illustrations, bibliography, glossary, index.

This study of domestic life and artifacts in the English-speaking area of upper Canada (after 1847 Ontario province) examines the period 1783 to 1867, although the nineteenth century dominates the earlier years. Minhinnick includes her own memories of conversations with grandparents and others who lived in this area after the creation of the Dominion. Her topical approach systematically analyzes the spaces (gardens, parlor, dining room, kitchen), the functions (cooking, homemaking), and the use, decoration, and lighting of interiors, as well as chair- and cabinetmaking. This useful book is the product of a lifetime of experience in restoring and decorating the interiors of some of upper Canada's most important historic buildings. *See also* "Kitchen Artifacts and Housework."

Moe, John F. "Concepts of Shelter: The Folk Poetics of Space, Change, and Continuity." *Journal of Popular Culture* 11, no. 1 (Summer 1977): 219–53. 11 illustrations.

Moe attempts to demonstrate how "concepts of shelter have been articulated in structure and oral narrative" (p. 82). Drawing on interviews with residents as well as other research, he concludes, "inhabitants of traditional folk architecture [in this study the shotgun house, the I house, the upright-and-wing house, and the sod house] are able to attach a conscious value to the type of house in which they live" (p. 87). This value symbolizes the resident's self-identity and membership in a community.

Peterson, Charles E., ed. *Building Early America: Contributions toward the History of a Great Industry.* Radnor, Pa.: Chilton Book Company for the Carpenter's Company of the City and County of Philadelphia, 1976. xvi+407 pp.; 341 illustrations, index.

This collection of essays by notable scholars is a major history of the Anglo-American building industry. Twelve of the twenty papers, all originally presented in 1974 at a symposium celebrating the 250th anniversary of Carpenter's Company, deal with subjects as diverse as building technology, lighting and heating, window glass, and specific con-

struction projects. The other eight provide notable case studies of building preservation, with examples drawn from British, Canadian, and American experiences. This is a seminal work.

Peterson, Harold L. *American Interiors from Colonial Times to the Late Victorians: A Pictorial Source Book of American Domestic Interiors with an Appendix on Inns and Taverns. See* "Surveys."

Pommer, Richard. "The Architecture of Urban Housing in the United States during the Early 1930s." *Journal of the Society of Architectural Historians* 37, no. 4 (December 1978): 235–64. 31 illustrations.

Based on an analysis of major housing projects undertaken in Philadelphia, Cleveland, and New York in the early 1930s, Pommer delineates the interplay of American practice (nineteenth-century philanthropic ideas, the design of apartment houses, and the work of Regional Planning Association of America) with European modernism. Pommer asserts that the ideological basis of modernism clashed with more traditional American planning. Although a few initial projects were successful, as "private initiatives" gave way to increased "bureaucratic control" during the New Deal, the resulting mix left its mark on urban housing design.

Preservation Society of Newport County. *Newport Mansions: The Gilded Age.* Photography by Richard Cheek; text by Thomas Gannon; introduction by David Chase. Little Compton, R.I.: Foremost Publishers, 1982. 89 pp.; 79 color plates.

This spectacularly illustrated book is worthy of its subjects: the eight properties owned by the Preservation Society of Newport County. Seven buildings include the magnificent structures erected around the end of the nineteenth century—the Breakers, Rosecliff, Marble House, and the Elms—as well as the eighteenth-century Hunter House, Upjohn's Gothic revival Kingscote, and the Victorian Chateau-sur-Mer. The eighth property, Green Animals, is a topiary garden. The brief text sketches the history of the buildings and their occupants and explains how they came into the Preservation Society's possession.

Rasmussen, William M. S. "Sabine Hall, a Classical Villa in Virginia." *Journal of the Society of Architectural Historians* 39, no. 4 (December 1980): 286–96. 21 illustrations.

Drawing on Italian and English architectural sourcebooks, Landon Carter apparently designed and began construction of Sabine Hall in 1733. Rasmussen presents a hypothetical reconstruction that demonstrates the evolution of this villa since that time, especially the major changes introduced by Carter's descendants in the 1820s and in 1929. Rasmussen demonstrates that Sabine Hall is illustrative of the "changing attitude toward classical forms that spans two centuries" (p. 296).

Rhoads, William B. "The Colonial Revival and American Nationalism." *Journal of the Society of Architectural Historians* 35, no. 4 (December 1976): 239–54. 16 illustrations.

Around the time of the Centennial, Rhoads argues, the colonial revival became an expression of patriotism and "nationalistic sentiment" (p. 242). Many modern buildings took as their models Mount Vernon or Independence Hall, but most colonial revival structures "were not intended to recall specific patriotic landmarks" (p. 241). Rhoads analyzes the debate over whether the colonial revival was an indigenous American architectural style, but he fails to address the psychological or ideological reasons for its popularity.

St. George, Robert Blair. " 'Set Thine House in Order': The Domestication of the Yeomanry in Seventeenth-Century New England." In Jonathan L. Fairbanks and Robert F. Trent, *New England Begins: The Seventeenth Century*, vol. 2, pp. 159–88. Boston: Museum of Fine Arts, 1982. 13 tables.

St. George is interested in the tension and ambivalence evident in the behavior of the protocapitalistic settlers who attempted to order the landscape of New England. He asserts, "in the patterned structure of their landscape—their farmsteads and houses, personal dress and sense of time—lies evidence as powerful as any sermon of the deeper values that existed in tension at the core of seventeenth-century New England culture" (p. 159). In this richly textured essay, St. George examines the organization of farms and household space, gender roles, stages of life, cycles of labor and seasons, food, and medical practices. He then analyzes how the evolving organization of the material world reflected the emergence of a consumer culture that clashed with traditional practices, resulting in tensions between a hierarchical society and status by ascription and between nature and culture.

Scully, Vincent. "American Houses: Thomas Jefferson to Frank Lloyd Wright." In *The Rise of an American Architecture*, edited by Edgar Kaufmann, Jr., pp. 163–217. New York: Praeger Publishers in association with the Metropolitan Museum of Art, 1970. 53 illustrations, bibliography.

In this essay, Scully examines the evolution of domestic design in the nineteenth century. He argues that Jefferson's Monticello demonstrates two principal ideas that motivated the most talented architects: the desire to "break out of the box" to achieve greater freedom of spatial arrangement (p. 164), and the need to exert human control to express dominion over nature. Scully retraces the development of the shingle and stick styles, as well as the colonial revival, and culminates with Wright, who "created an architecture growing out of the American past but which must be recognized as wholly new as well. It was a cultural achievement of enormous stature" (p. 190).

Seale, William. *Recreating the Historic House Interior.* Nashville: American Association for State and Local History, 1979. x+270 pp.; black and white illustrations, 64 black and white and color plates, bibliography, index.

John Ruskin once asserted that every restoration is a lie, and Seale has read his Ruskin well. Restorers simply cannot exactly recapture an earlier era. But they can recreate, and in this book Seale offers an estimable method for doing so: it is full of common-sense advice on research, writing a historic-house report, and developing strategies for assembling appropriate collections. He also provides useful information about furnishings, "transient objects" (plates, vases, andirons), and such interior details as painting, wall coverings, and flooring. The illustrations, which are accompanied by explanatory captions, combine documentary photographs of interiors with examples of museum settings.

Seale, William. *The Tasteful Interlude: American Interiors through the Camera's Eye, 1860–1917.* See "Surveys."

Sweeney, Kevin M. "Mansion People: Kinship, Class, and Architecture in Western Massachusetts in the Mid Eighteenth Century." *Winterthur Portfolio* 19, no. 4 (Winter 1984): 231–55. 13 illustrations, 5 tables, appendix.

Sweeney asserts that the central-hall and gambrel-roof houses built by the Connecticut valley "River Gods" were attempts "to put social distance between themselves and their neighbors" (p. 231). United by kinship as well as by a sense of self-importance, "these families enhanced their political and economic power in the eighteenth century by maintaining a position of cultural leadership" (p. 232). Sweeney relates architectural style and the differentiation of interior space to status ambitions, to the changing composition of households, and to a desire for greater privacy. He then attributes the River Gods' loss of political power to "a loss of social status, a growing insularity, and the unraveling of the [kinship] web" (p. 250), as a new squirearchy assumed political, economic, and cultural leadership.

Talbot, George. *At Home: Domestic Life in the Post-Centennial Era, 1876–1920.* Exhibition catalogue. Madison: State Historical Society of Wisconsin, 1976. viii+88 pp.; illustrations, appendixes, bibliography.

The brilliant and often haunting photographs that are the core of this publication were selected from some 600 images and objects exhibited at the State Historical Society of Wisconsin during 1976 and 1977. Talbot believes that these photographs "reflect the interaction of taste and social life from the time of the nation's Centennial until the end of World War I" and reveal "how their original owners manipulated their tastes to meet social and emotional demands" (p. iv)—in short, their concerns for status and security in a changing world. He analyzes the photographs as evidence of the way people used artifacts to create environments, and the result is a valuable perspective on work and leisure in the upper Midwest in the late nineteenth and early twentieth centuries.

Tatum, George B. *Philadelphia Georgian: The City House of Samuel Powel and Some of Its Eighteenth-Century Neighbors.* Photographs of Philadelphia architecture by Cortlandt Van Dyke Hubbard. Middletown, Conn.: Wesleyan University Press, 1976. xvii+187 pp.; 66 illustrations, appendixes, bibliography, index.

Despite its modest title, this is the most important single book on eighteenth-century Philadelphia architecture. Tatum provides short, interpretative biographies of the owners, principally the Stedmans and the Powels, and provides a room-by-room analysis of the Third Street structure and its contents. But this book, the product of meticulous research in insurance surveys, diaries and manuscripts, newspapers, pattern books, and extant buildings, also relates the construction of the Powel house to other important Philadelphia residences and provides valuable information on eighteenth-century building and craft practices. Tatum concludes his reconstruction of the building's history by placing its changes within the broader context of the preservation movement; thus, the Powel House is viewed as "not only a monument to the period that first built it, but also in some degree to the period that preserved it" (p. 122).

Upton, Dell. "Pattern Books and Professionalism: Aspects of the Transformation of Domestic Architecture in America, 1800–1860." *Winterthur Portfolio* 19, nos. 2/3 (Summer/Autumn 1984): 107–50. 38 illustrations.

Upton examines "the change from traditional and local forms to popular and national ones in nineteenth-century American architecture." Employing a sociological model of the rise of professionalization, he analyzes "the effort to inject expertise into the process of everyday architectural design" (p. 107). He focuses on the competition between builders and architects to control the course of architectural development. The efforts of Andrew Jackson Downing and others notwithstanding, Upton believes that builders and their clients rejected the professional claims of architects and "created a basis for a popular architecture that lay neither in the realm of elite taste nor in that of traditional architecture" (p. 150). *See also* "Craftsmen."

Upton, Dell. "Vernacular Domestic Architecture in Eighteenth-Century Virginia." *Winterthur Portfolio* 17, nos. 2/3 (Summer/Autumn 1982): 95–119. 28 illustrations, 1 table.

Upton demonstrates how "Virginia's builders started with a traditional architecture forged in the hard years of the seventeenth century and altered and refined it to meet the more complex social and economic structures of the eighteenth" (p. 114). Faced with changing social conditions, local builders adopted elements of the Georgian house plan—most notably the central passage, two-room depth, and symmetry—and grafted those elements to vernacular practices as a way of incorporating additional interior space. Upton examines the evolution of room names and the changing arrangement of domestic spaces as a response to different functions and social structure: as the hall became a public space for entertainment, the dining room, once the chamber, became the family space, while the back room became a private refuge.

Upton, Dell, and John Michael Vlach, eds. *Common Places: Readings in American Vernacular Architecture.* Athens: University of Georgia Press, 1986. xxiv+529 pp.; illustrations, bibliography, index.

This collection of twenty-three essays, all but six published since 1972, is an assertion of the "interdisciplinary nature of the study of vernacular architecture and landscapes" (p. xiii). The work of historians, geographers, folklorists, archaeologists, and preservationists, the essays are grouped into five sections devoted to content, construction, function or use, change, and the process of design, or intention. In their introduction, Upton and Vlach emphasize more recent directions in scholarship, indicate areas worthy of further investigation, and conclude with the point, often overlooked amid measured drawings and charts of quantitative data, that the field of vernacular architecture is "fundamentally a humanistic study" (p. xxiii). This work is an essential beginning point for students and a highly useful compilation for scholars.

Whiffen, Marcus. *The Eighteenth-Century Houses of Williamsburg: A Study of Architecture and Building in the Colonial Capital of Virginia.* Rev. ed. Williamsburg: Colonial Williamsburg Foundation, 1984. xxii+289 pp.; 150 illustrations, appendixes, index.

Originally published in 1960, this book—the result of extensive research in manuscript collections, diaries, account books, public records, newspapers, and scholarly resources—has long been considered a model architectural history. Whiffen divides the book into three parts. In Part 1, five chapters explain the materials used in construction, the training of builders and their tools and books, and the general design and construction details of houses. Part 2, a "cumulative" survey of thirty-six of the more than eighty extant residences, discusses each building's history and restoration. Photographs, floor plans, and interior views illustrate the text, which supplements earlier editions of the book with recent research findings. Part 3, a new addition, explains the history of Carter's Grove, one of the greatest mid Georgian houses in America. Strangely, in this section the historians at Williamsburg who revised the book make no mention of the archaeological evidence uncovered by Ivor Noël Hume and his colleagues at Carter's Grove, which was published in preliminary form more than a decade ago and again with greater elaboration in Noël Hume's *Martin's Hundred* (New York: Alfred A. Knopf, 1982).

Wilson, Richard Guy. "The Early Work of Charles F. McKim: Country House Commissions." *Winterthur Portfolio* 14, no. 3 (Autumn 1979): 235–67. 43 illustrations.

Wilson asserts that during the 1870s McKim "developed the theme of creating an expressive architectural style that would sum up the cultural and historical aspirations of Americans" (p. 235). Using major commissions to analyze the evolution of McKim's style, Wilson demonstrates the emergence of a creative American synthesis out of the English Queen Anne style, an interest in colonial buildings, and the vernacular tradition of wood construction. This essay itself is an imaginative synthesis of architectural and cultural history.

Wright, Gwendolyn. *Building the Dream: A Social History of Housing in America.* New York: Pantheon Books, 1981. xix+329 pp.; 81 illustrations, index.

"For centuries," Wright asserts, "Americans have seen domestic architecture as a way of encouraging certain kinds of family and social life" (p. xv). The home has assumed a kind of mythic significance in American culture: it is an environment that shapes character, promotes certain patterns of behavior, even promises to remedy broader social problems. Wright's book addresses the most important questions the nation has faced in trying to provide adequate shelter for its people and "relates the various architectural and ideological models this country has adopted" (p. xvi). In thirteen chapters, ranging from the Puritans to public housing and suburbanization in the years since World War II, she discusses various "models" of domestic architecture and the values and social aspirations that each one embodies. She deftly juxtaposes plantation manor and slave quarters, workers' housing and the ideal of the independent home, and the rhetoric of domesticity and the changing realities of the twentieth-century woman. In the fourteenth chapter, Wright examines the contemporary housing crisis and offers a prescription that attempts to reconcile the traditional dream of a single-family suburban home with social, economic, and demographic change. This important book is a thoughtful, mul-

tidisciplinary analysis of the aspirations, motivations, and failures of housing reformers.

Wright, Gwendolyn. *Moralism and the Model Home: Domestic Architecture and Cultural Conflict in Chicago, 1873–1913.* Chicago and London: University of Chicago Press, 1980. viii+382 pp.; 52 illustrations, bibliography, index.

Wright presents an excellent examination of the rhetoric of domesticity and the dynamics of architectural and social change in Chicago between the years of the Industrial Exposition of 1873 and the City Club competition for the design of a model suburb forty years later. Her study of cultural conflict analyzes the competing aspirations of architects, builders, construction workers, and housing reformers to control the "course of architectural planning" (p. 15). Based on a careful reading of the professional architects' press, builders' guides, popular journals, and other sources, Wright skillfully reconstructs the changing attitudes of those individuals who created the fabric of the city and suburbs. Perhaps most important, she places the various attempts to improve domestic architecture within their social, economic, and political contexts. Her method and findings are applicable nationally.

Zimmer, Edward F., and Pamela J. Scott. "Alexander Parris, B. Henry Latrobe, and the John Wickham House in Richmond, Virginia." *Journal of the Society of Architectural Historians* 41, no. 3 (October 1982): 202–11. 17 illustrations.

Zimmer and Scott reattribute the design of the Wickham House, heretofore associated with Robert Mills, to Alexander Parris. They examine the evolution of Parris's design, demonstrate the influence of Benjamin Latrobe, and argue that the architect's brief career in Richmond provides the "crucial link" between Parris's "better known early and mature work in New England" (p. 202). This essay also provides important insight into Parris's transition from self-trained master builder to architect, an important step in the professionalization of architecture in the United States.

Furniture

American Furniture to 1820

INTERNATIONAL CONTEXT

TECHNIQUES, TOOLS, WOODS, CONNOISSEURSHIP

AMERICAN FURNITURE TO 1820

American Furniture, 1820–1920

American Furniture to 1820

Barbara McLean Ward and Gerald W. R. Ward

SINCE THE PUBLICATION of Irving W. Lyon's *Colonial Furniture of New England* in 1891, students of furniture have concentrated primarily on questions of identification, attribution to region or maker, nomenclature, construction, and design. It is no easy task to obtain answers to even the simplest questions concerning many pieces of old furniture. Who made it? Where? When? How? What is it made of? Why does it look the way it does? How was it used? The difficulty of answering these basic questions has preoccupied furniture historians, and rightly so, for a firm grounding in objects and documents is the only sound underpinning on which more broadly based studies can be developed. "Great theories must sink a huge anchor in details," Stephen Jay Gould recently noted in a review essay. "Progress in science," Gould cautioned, "often demands that we back away from cosmic questions of greatest scope (anyone with half a brain can formulate 'big' questions in his armchair, so why heap kudos on such a pleasant and pedestrian activity). Great scientists have an instinct for the fruitful and the doable, particularly for smaller questions that lead on and eventually transform the grand issues from speculation to action" (*An Urchin in the Storm: Essays about Books and Ideas* [New York: W. W. Norton, 1987], pp. 26–27).

The titles selected here will help the reader to begin a study of "the fruitful and the doable." We have arranged our selections in three sections. The first group of titles directs readers to a few works that help to place American objects in an international, specifically English, context. Next, we have provided a brief introduction to basic books on technical matters such as techniques, tools, woods, and connoisseurship. These volumes will assist the reader in developing the skills necessary to read old furniture. Last, we have selected a wider range of titles dealing with all aspects of American furniture from 1650 to 1820. These titles represent the common types of furniture publication: the general survey, the collection catalogue, the exhibition catalogue organized around a region or a style, and the biographical sketch. Works representative of each generation of scholarship are included. Thus, the pioneering works of Irving Whitall Lyon, Esther Singleton, and Luke Vincent Lockwood are included, as are the massive pictorial works of the 1920s and 1930s by Wallace Nutting. Works from the 1960s, including Helen Comstock's survey, Charles F. Montgomery's book on federal furniture, and Richard H. Randall, Jr.'s, catalogue of Boston's Museum of Fine Arts collection, represent the beginnings of the modern age. Recent scholarship, with its emphasis on such diverse themes as design sources, shop organization, and the role of furniture as nonverbal communication, is perhaps more heavily represented by the inclusion of titles by John T. Kirk,

Edward S. Cooke, Jr., Benjamin A. Hewitt, Robert Blair St. George, Robert F. Trent, and many others. While the bibliography thus encompasses the basic secondary literature, there are several broad areas of other materials, including design books, price books, auction catalogues, specialized periodicals, and unpublished works, that are also extremely useful.

Design and pattern books were one way in which ornament and form were transferred from England and Europe to America. Relatively little used in this country in the seventeenth century, they began to gain importance here in the mid eighteenth century and were relied on with great frequency and more literalness in the federal period. Specialized and major libraries own copies of most of these in the original or early editions; reprints of many of them have been issued at various times by such houses as Da Capo Press and Dover Publications. The Praeger Library, under the general editorship of Montgomery, issued in 1970 a series of fine-quality reprints with scholarly introductions of Thomas Sheraton's *Cabinet Dictionary* (London, 1803) in two volumes and *Cabinet-Maker and Upholsterer's Drawing-Book* (London, 1791–94), George Smith's *Collection of Designs for Household Furniture and Interior Decoration* (London, 1808), and Joseph Moxon's *Mechanick Exercises* (London, 1703). Simon Jervis's *Printed Furniture Designs before 1650* (London: Furniture History Society, 1974) is a selection with scholarly addenda of published designs; Peter Ward-Jackson's *English Furniture Designs of the Eighteenth Century* (London: Her Majesty's Stationery Office, 1958) provides the same service for the eighteenth century and is a good place to start to gain familiarity with the subject. This work contains selected illustrations from and bibliographical references to many other design books with which one should be familiar, such as those issued by Thomas Chippendale, George Hepplewhite, Robert Manwaring, and the Society of Upholsterers in London.

As Montgomery noted in *American Furniture*, cabinetmakers' and journeymen's price books are manuscript or printed lists of prices for the making of furniture at rates sought by journeymen or agreed on by masters. Although manuscript price books are known from earlier in the century, the first published price books issued in England and America appeared in 1788 and 1794 respectively, although only a 1795 version of the Philadelphia book has survived. Montgomery made extensive use of these, and his bibliography includes a list of published editions from both America and England. In 1982 the Furniture History Society devoted an issue of *Furniture History* to a facsimile of *The Cabinet-Makers' London Book of Prices* (1793).

Since it began publication in January 1922, *Antiques* has provided on a monthly basis an invaluable series of articles about and pictures of early American furniture. Monographs on individual cabinetmakers and regional shop traditions, illustrated surveys of private and public collections, dealers' advertisements, and notices of exhibitions are among the most useful materials to be found in *Antiques*. The care taken by the magazine's editors—Homer Eaton Keyes, Alice Winchester, and Wendell D. Garrett—and their staffs has kept it above the level of other periodicals and tabloids that cover the same ground. For the most part, however, articles in *Antiques* are not included in the following bibliography because of space limitations. About seventy are included in the two anthologies that are listed on seventeeth-century New England furniture and on Philadelphia furniture, edited by Trent and John J. Snyder, Jr., respectively. A good bibliography of furniture articles in *Antiques*, compiled by Garrett and Allison Eckardt, is included in Elizabeth Bidwell Bates and Jonathan L. Fairbanks's *American Furniture to 1620*.

The other periodical literature on American furniture is vast, although largely of indifferent quality. Many in-depth articles on early furniture have been published in *Winterthur Portfolio*; several, but not all, of these have been listed below. Notices of exhibitions, illustrations of new museum acquisitions, book reviews, and brief articles can be found in the *Decorative Arts Newsletter*, published several times a year since 1974 as the journal of the Decorative Arts Society, a chapter of the Society of Architectural Historians. *Furniture History*, the journal of the Furniture History Society, headquartered at Victoria and Albert Museum in London, has been published annually since 1964. Each issue contains several significant articles, usually on English furniture, but an occasional essay on an American subject is included. Of particular interest are special issues: *Furniture in England, France, and the Netherlands from the Twelfth to the Fifteenth Century* by Penelope Eames (vol. 13, 1977) and *The Furnishing and Decoration of Ham House* by Peter Thornton (vol. 16, 1980). The Regional Furniture Society, another English organization, has begun publishing an annual journal devoted to vernacular furniture; the first issue of *Regional Furniture* appeared in 1987.

The thousands of auction catalogues issued since the turn of the century provide a vast archive of illustrations, a record of private collections, and, indirectly, a commentary on the social history of collecting. Catalogues from the major auction houses, including American Art Association/Anderson Galleries, Sotheby Parke Bernet (later Sotheby's), and Christie's, are perhaps the most important resource, although catalogues have been issued by many minor auction houses, often without illustrations. Among the important sales, to mention only a few, are those of the collections of Louis Guerineau Myers (1921), Jacob Paxson Temple (1922), Howard Reifsnyder (1929), Israel Sack (1929, 1932), Philip Flayderman (1930), Benjamin Flayderman (1931), Francis P. Garvan (1931), Roland V. Vaughan (1931), Mrs. J. Amory Haskell (1944/45), Norvin H. Green (1950), Lansdell K. Christie (1972), and Bernice Chrysler Garbisch (1980).

Master's theses written by students in the Winterthur Program in Early American Culture at the University of Delaware form an important corpus of unpublished material. Many have resulted in books, catalogues, or articles that are cited in this bibliography. Others of particular relevance to the study of early furniture include those of Michael K. Brown on Duncan Phyfe (1978); Anne Castrodale (Golovin) on Daniel Trotter of Philadelphia (1962); Raymond B. Clark, Jr., on Jonathan Gostelowe (1956); Margaret Burke Clunie on Salem federal furniture (1976); Cooke on furniture in late eighteenth-century Stratford, Connecticut (1979); Benno M. Forman on seventeenth-century furniture of Essex County, Massachusetts (1968); Morrison H. Heckscher on the organization and practices of the Philadelphia furniture trade in the federal period (1964); John Henry Hill on the furniture trade in Baltimore in the federal period (1967); Charles F. Hummel on the influence of English pattern books on Philadelphia cabinetmakers in the mid eighteenth century (1955); J. Stewart Johnson on New York cabinetmaking prior to the Revolution (1964); Patricia E. Kane on the seventeenth-century case furniture of Hartford County, Connecticut (1968); Snyder on Chippendale furniture of Lancaster County, Pennsylvania (1976); Trent on the seventeenth-century furniture and craftsmen of Middlesex County, Massachusetts (1974); Susan Mackiewicz on the seventeenth-century furniture of Newbury, Massachusetts (1980); Philip Zea on early furniture from the upper Connecticut River valley (1984); and Desirée Caldwell on Germanic influences on Philadelphia mid eighteenth-century seating furniture (1985).

In conclusion, we might just suggest a few of the directions that future research on early American furniture might take, as we attempt to "transform the great issues from speculation to action." Without question, work will continue along the lines already established. John Bivins, Jr.'s, recent study of coastal North Carolina objects, largely from the craftsman's point of view, sets an admirable example that can be followed in related studies of little-understood and little-researched areas, such as Brock W. Jobe's ongoing work on the eighteenth-century furniture of Portsmouth, New Hampshire. Detailed catalogues of collections are still necessary as important building blocks; Charles Venable's work on the Bybee collection at Dallas Museum of Art, scheduled for publication in 1989, and team efforts to catalogue the collections in Milwaukee Art Museum and at the United States Department of State Diplomatic Reception Rooms are examples of the continuing effort to publicize lesser-known collections. More studies of specific styles and eras need to be undertaken, and works that place American objects in cross-cultural and international contexts are especially needed. Such efforts on the baroque style, organized by Cooper-Hewitt Museum in the "Courts and Colonies" exhibition of 1988, and "The American Craftsman and the European Tradition," coordinated by the Minneapolis Institute of Arts and scheduled for 1989/90, demonstrate the potential of this line of inquiry. Research on the evolution of specific forms will continue to be a fruitful avenue; Nancy Goyne Evans's exhaustive study of American Windsor seating furniture, when published, will establish a standard for thoroughness in this genre.

Thus there is much to be done on many fronts. Not all new discoveries and fresh insights will be gained from a study of industrial-era furniture; the older objects make more demands on the researcher but remain a fertile field for investigation. One pressing need is for works of synthesis, especially books that will bring detailed research to two major audiences that tend to overlook scholarly work on early furniture: professional academic historians and the general public. Both groups are apparently intimidated by the exhibition and collection catalogues format, and both obviously have difficulty finding works usually issued in editions of only a few thousand. An increase in the number of scholarly yet literate books on early American furniture—now written by only a handful of authors—will enhance the possibilities of raising the visual literacy of readers with diverse interests and backgrounds.

One area of investigation where advances can be made, for example, is in studies that involve the interaction of people with furniture. Works that explore furniture forms and decoration as evidence of broad-ranging social and demographic trends will enable scholars in other fields to see the potential of material culture evidence in their own areas of inquiry. It is hoped that the titles annotated in the following list will provide some guideposts for those who set out on this exciting task of incorporating the study of early furniture into both the academic and the popular mainstream.

Chinnery, Victor. *Oak Furniture, the British Tradition: A History of Early Furniture in the British Isles and New England*. Woodbridge, Suffolk: Antique Collectors' Club, 1979. 579 pp.; approximately 1,100 black and white illustrations, 16 color plates, appendixes, bibliography, indexes.

The first massive survey of its kind, this work provides an overview of sixteenth- and seventeenth-century British furniture that is essential for the student of American work. The treatment of American production here is cursory, but the information on woods, styles, and construction is helpful, and the number of illustrations is unparalleled. Although this is the most readily available source on English furniture of the period, several small exhibition catalogues issued by Temple Newsam House in Leeds, England, will also be of use to those with a special interest in English provincial and regional furniture, including *An Exhibition of Common Furniture, Illustrating Sub-groups within the Vernacular Tradition* (1982), *Furniture Made in Yorkshire, 1750–1900* (1974), *Oak Furniture from Gloucestershire and Somerset* (1976), and *Oak Furniture from Lancashire and the Lake District* (1973).

Collard, Frances. *Regency Furniture*. Woodbridge, Suffolk: Antique Collectors' Club, 1985. 346 pp.; black and white illustrations, 40 color plates, appendix, bibliography, index.

Collard provides a detailed survey of English furniture from 1790 to 1840 which is "intended to show the development of the different trends which epitomise the Regency in all its eclectic aspects" (p. 11). These include the neoclassical influences of Thomas Sheraton and his pattern books, the Anglo-French taste of Henry Holland, the Greek revival emphasis of Thomas Hope, the French influence in the later Regency, chinoiserie, and historical revivals of Gothic, Old English, and rustic furniture. In the first work of this scale on the subject in nearly four decades, Collard provides an excellent background for understanding American objects of the period.

Edwards, Ralph. *The Shorter Dictionary of English Furniture from the Middle Ages to the Late Georgian Period*. London: Country Life, 1964. 684 pp.; 15 illustrations, illustrated dictionary.

This is "shorter" than the three-volume *Dictionary of English Furniture* by Percy Macquoid and Ralph Edwards in that it omits some material (such as essays on tapestry, carpets, and hangings) and condenses and revises other entries. The information on cabinetmakers, decorative artists, and other craftsmen is grouped at the back in this edition.

The Eye of the Beholder: Fakes, Replicas, and Alterations in American Art. Edited by Gerald W. R. Ward; contributions by Judith Bernstein, Edward S. Cooke, Jr., David Park Curry, Heather Kurzbauer, Francis J. Puig, Kevin Stayton, Diana Strazdes, Barbara McLean Ward, and Beverly Zisla Welber. Exhibition catalogue. New Haven: Yale University Art Gallery, 1977. 95 pp.; approximately 130 illustrations.

This catalogue of a student loan exhibition of 130 objects, including a good deal of furniture, organizes objects into categories labeled misattributions, alterations and adaptations, restorations, fakes, revivals, reproductions, and questionables. It analyzes how objects of any kind reflect the society in which they were produced. Entries are arranged in a series of comparisons. Although a few entries contain errors, both typographical and otherwise (for example, modern potter Lester Breininger is misidentified in cat. 93 as "Lester Breminger"), this remains a valuable example of how connoisseurship can be used to answer questions of both authenticity and cultural content.

Fastnedge, Ralph. *English Furniture Styles from 1500 to 1830*. 1955. Reprint. Baltimore: Penguin Books, 1969. xxii+321 pp.; 101 line drawings, 64 black and white plates, glossaries, index.

Although published more than thirty years ago, this work remains a useful introduction to high-style English furniture. The text is arranged chronologically and is enriched with many quotations from period sources concerning the use of furniture. Most attention is paid to objects and styles from 1740 to 1830, with separate chapters devoted to Robert Adam, George Hepplewhite, Thomas Sheraton, and the Regency period. This is still a good source from which to gain an overview of the English background of American things.

Gilbert, Christopher. *Furniture at Temple Newsam House and Lotherton Hall: A Catalogue of the Leeds Collection*. 2 vols. Leeds: National Art-Collections Fund and the Leeds Art Collections Fund, 1978. 522 pp.; black and white illustrations, color plates, index.

Gilbert provides a complete catalogue, including more than 600 objects, of the holdings at Temple Newsam. Although the strength of the collection is English eighteenth-century furniture, there is a rich assortment of furniture of different forms and from different lands represented, mostly dating from the seventeenth to the early twentieth centuries. Objects from Holland, France, Germany, Italy, Portugal, Cape Colony, Peru, China, Japan, India and Ceylon, Java, and Korea are included. A listing of the Pratt collection of furniture trade catalogues and ephemera is appended. Gilbert's statement of purpose is an excellent and succinct guide to the nature and function of such catalogues.

Gilbert, Christopher. *The Life and Work of Thomas Chippendale*. 2 vols. New York: Macmillan Publishing Co., 1978. Vol. 1, xx+329 pp.; 25 color plates, appendixes, glossary, bibliography, index; vol. 2, 288 pp.; 525 black and white plates.

Gilbert's masterful monograph on Chippendale (1718–79), perhaps the best known English designer of furniture, supersedes all previous studies, including many works of uneven quality. For the student of American furniture, this work provides information of interest not only on design but also on the nature of urban cabinetmaking in the eighteenth century, especially in the chapter "Branches of the Business." While the scale of Chippendale's business was quite different from that of any American firm, in the case of large cabinet-making and upholstery shops in Boston, New York, and Philadelphia, the differences are ones of degree rather than kind.

Gloag, John. *A Short Dictionary of Furniture*. Rev. ed. London: George Allen and Unwin, 1969. 813 pp.; approximately 1,000 illustrations, 2,600 entries.

This dictionary contains more than 2,600 entries that include terms and names used in Britain and the United States. It was first published in 1952; a revised edition appeared in 1965, an abridged paperback version in 1966, and this third revised and enlarged edition in 1969. See also Joseph Aronson, *The Encyclopedia of Furniture* (3d ed.; New York: Crown Publishers, 1965).

Hayward, Helena, ed. *World Furniture: An Illustrated History*. New York and Toronto: McGraw-Hill Book Co., 1965. 320 pp.; 1,177 black and white illustrations, approximately 52 color plates, glossary, bibliography, index.

World Furniture is an anthology of forty-five articles by leading experts on furniture from ancient Egypt to the present. American objects of the seventeenth and eighteenth centuries are discussed by Robert C. Smith; American furniture of the nineteenth century is covered by Joseph T. Butler. English work from 1660 to 1830 is treated in essays by Anthony Coleridge, Helena Hayward, and Clifford Musgrave. Perhaps more important than the work on American and English furniture, however, are the essays on the furniture of France, the Low Countries, Germany, Italy, Spain and Portugal, Poland, Russia, Scandinavia, and the Far and Middle East. This is an essential work for placing American objects in a worldwide context; it is still the most wide-ranging and authoritative survey of its kind.

Hayward, Helena, and Pat Kirkham. *William and John Linnell: Eighteenth Century London Furniture Makers*. 2 vols. New York: Rizzoli International Publications in association with Christie's, 1980. Vol. 1, xiv+206 pp.; 7 black and white illustrations, 19 color plates, glossary, appendixes, genealogies, bibliography, index; vol. 2, 170 pp.; 321 black and white illustrations.

This extraordinarily detailed look at the business of high-style furniture making in the eighteenth century is based on a case study of the prominent firm operated by William Linnell and his son John about 1730–96. The titles of some of the chapters indicate the thoroughness of the work: "Management, Marketing, and Finance," "Workforce and Workshops," "Designing and Its Role," "Style," and "Patrons and Clients." This work gives an essential overview of the balance of taste, economics, workmanship, and design in a large urban shop.

Macquoid, Percy, and Ralph Edwards. *The Dictionary of English Furniture from the Middle Ages to the Late Georgian Period*. Revised and enlarged by Ralph Edwards. 3 vols. London: Barra Books, 1954. [1,110] pp.; black and white illustrations, 40 color plates.

The Dictionary of English Furniture contains an alphabetical listing of illustrated entries that deal primarily with the development of furniture forms. Shorter entries deal with craftsmen, obsolete terms, and many other topics. Although devoted to English furniture, this is an essential starting place for much research. Barra Books has issued a reprint of the 1954 edition in an unabridged format, although the page size has been reduced. *See also* Ralph Edwards, *The Shorter Dictionary of English Furniture*.

Mercer, Eric. *Furniture, 700–1700*. The Social History of the Decorative Arts, edited by Hugh Honour. London: Weidenfeld and Nicolson, 1969. 183 pp.; 187 black and white plates, 16 color plates, bibliography, index.

Although only the last section of this book, which deals with the "emergence of modern furniture" in the seventeenth century, is directly applicable to American furniture, the approach used by Mercer is one that could be (and perhaps should be) adapted by many students of American things. The development of furniture is traced through a modernization paradigm that meshes the study of objects with an examination of changes in housing, education and literacy, technology, the status and role of women, and other areas of social and economic history. Mercer makes excellent use of period paintings and prints.

Pain, Howard. *The Heritage of Country Furniture: A Study in the Survival of Formal and Vernacular Styles from the United States, Britain, and Europe Found in Upper Canada, 1780–1900*. Foreword by Dean A. Fales, Jr.; introduction by William Kilbourn. Toronto and New York: Van Nostrand Reinhold, 1978. 548 pp.; approximately 1,400 black and white and color illustrations, maps, chart, bibliography, index.

Pain's mammoth survey of objects produced in Canada illustrates almost 1,400 examples. After a brief introduction, he examines his subject in relation to ethnic tradition, grouping his material into chapters devoted to various styles, principally Anglo-American, Germanic, Polish, and French Canadian. This is an excellent resource for placing American furniture into context, particularly New England, upstate New York, and German-influenced furniture produced in Pennsylvania, New York, Texas, and elsewhere. The section on French-Canadian furniture should be supplemented by Jean Palardy's classic *Early Furniture of French Canada* (1963).

Thornton, Peter. *Authentic Decor: The Domestic Interior, 1620–1920*. New York: Viking Penguin, 1984. 408 pp.; 532 black and white and color illustrations, index.

This chronological survey focuses strictly on the Western world, and only a handful of American images dating before 1820 are included. Four chapters—those dealing with the periods 1620–70, 1670–1720, 1720–70, and 1770–1820—are of particular relevance here. Thornton's book is illustrated profusely with period paintings and prints. The text and illustrations inevitably are biased toward the middle and upper classes, but this is an extraordinary body of images useful to those interested in room arrangements and decoration.

Thornton, Peter. *Seventeenth-Century Interior Decoration in England, France, and Holland*. New Haven and London: Yale University Press for the Paul Mellon Centre for Studies in British Art, 1978. xii+427 pp.; 320 black and white illustrations, 17 color plates, index.

Thornton's masterful study of high-style interiors, which focuses on the spread of French taste to England and Holland, emphasizes the importance of upholstery and the upholsterer's materials and discusses room use and arrangement. Rich in illustrations of period prints and paintings and engagingly written, this study is primarily concerned with life on a scale not encountered in America and thus helps to place American interiors in a worldwide perspective. The treatment of interiors as a unified whole serves as a reminder that furniture is best studied contextually.

Tomlin, Maurice. *English Furniture: An Illustrated Handbook*. London: Faber and Faber, 1972. 180 pp.+225 black and white plates; 22 black and white illustrations, 8 color plates, glossary, bibliography, index.

Tomlin provides a modern overview of furniture in England

from medieval times to the present, with the greatest attention paid to the 1660–1830 era. A wide variety of forms is discussed, although the emphasis is on high-style examples.

Victoria and Albert Museum. *Georgian Furniture*. New ed. Revised and enlarged by Desmond Fitz-Gerald. London: Her Majesty's Stationery Office, 1969. 30 pp.+144 black and white and color plates.

Georgian Furniture is notable for its large, clear photographs of high-style English furniture that was made between 1715 and 1825 and is now in the collection of Victoria and Albert Museum. The captions are brief and often not particularly helpful to the reader, but the quality of the illustrations makes this a good introduction to urban English work. First published in 1947 and reissued in 1958, this book was considerably enlarged and expanded for this third edition of 1969.

Ward-Jackson, Peter. *English Furniture Designs of the Eighteenth Century*. London: Victoria and Albert Museum, Her Majesty's Stationery Office, 1958. viii+69 pp.+366 plates; index.

This is an essential guide to English furniture designs and pattern books of the period. It contains short biographies, bibliographical references, and illustrations of the work of nearly every known English designer, and it is useful as an introduction to the original works and to the various reprint editions of works by Thomas Chippendale, George Hepplewhite, Thomas Sheraton, Robert Manwaring, and others.

Webster, Donald Blake. *English-Canadian Furniture of the Georgian Period*. Foreword by Charles F. Hummel. Toronto: McGraw-Hill Ryerson, 1979. 232 pp.; illustrations, 309 illustrated entries, bibliography, index.

In his study of the formal furniture of early English Canada before 1830, Webster demonstrates the close relationship between Anglo-Canadian and Anglo-American objects and provides some guidance for distinguishing between the two. This work is of particular importance for students of New England federal-period furniture.

TECHNIQUES, TOOLS, WOODS, CONNOISSEURSHIP

Cescinsky, Herbert. *The Gentle Art of Faking Furniture*. 1931. Reprint. New York: Dover Publications, 1967. ix+168 pp.; 563 illustrations, index.

"Genuine old pieces are a part of the social history of bygone times, be that history ever so unknown or unwritten. To weave romances around a thing of only yesterday—and one the natural life of which has been seriously shortened in the

attempt to give it the spurious appearance of age, and to do this through sheer ignorance—is neither satisfactory nor clever" (p. vii). Written by Cescinsky more than half a century ago, this statement applies with equal force today and almost appears to have been written as a cautionary for some modern historians. The text here is literate and entertaining, and even though the remarks are directed at the collector of English furniture, students of American objects can profit by many of the general observations. See, in particular, the list of questions stated in chapter 5, "Detective Methods and the Problem of Restoration."

Crawley, W. *Is It Genuine? A Guide to the Identification of Eighteenth-Century English Furniture*. New York: Hart Publishing Co., 1972. 188 pp.; 102 illustrations, glossary.

Although devoted to English furniture, this entertaining guide provides a great deal of information on "where to look and what to look for" when examining furniture for authenticity. Crawley claims to "have a record of 53,714 pieces of furniture sold between March 1946 and February 1966, which are either altered or complete fakes" (p. 23), and his stories about the deviousness of the marketplace are rewarding, if sobering, reading. Although he is occasionally dogmatic and some of what he says applies only to English furniture, this is an eye-opening book that can be ignored only at the reader's peril.

Hayward, Charles H. *Antique or Fake? The Making of Old Furniture*. 1970. Reprint. London: Evans Brothers, 1971. 256 pp.; 287 illustrations, glossary, index.

Hayward provides an introductory study of English furniture construction and connoisseurship. Some of the commentary is applicable only to English objects, such as his discussion of period styles and of certain construction techniques, and occasionally his use of English terminology and sparse writing style make the book confusing. Nevertheless, the numerous line drawings and other illustrations help to make construction understandable, and the connoisseurship suggestions are also helpful.

Hoadley, R. Bruce. *Understanding Wood: A Craftsman's Guide to Wood Technology*. Newtown, Conn.: Taunton Press, 1980. xiii+256 pp.; illustrations, 26 tables, appendixes, glossary, bibliography, index.

Understanding Wood is an outstanding guide to the raw material from which furniture is made. While a lot of the text is geared to the woodworking craftsman, there is much essential information here about the properties of wood, wood identification, joining wood, finishing wood, and other topics that will be of use to the student of old furniture. A glossary and an annotated bibliography are included.

Hummel, Charles F. *With Hammer in Hand: The Dominy Craftsmen of East Hampton, New York*. Charlottesville: University Press of Virginia for the Henry Francis du Pont Winterthur Museum, 1968. xiv+424 pp.; 38 illustrations, illustrated catalogue, appendixes, bibliography, index.

Hummel provides a detailed look at the lives and products of three generations of members of the Dominy family of East Hampton, Long Island, who engaged in woodworking, clockmaking, and allied crafts between 1760 and 1840. Included are 176 catalogue entries on woodworking and metalworking tools owned by the Dominys and an additional 79 entries on furniture and clocks made by them. Rich in documentation and precise in its analysis, this remains an unparalleled look at the shop-floor life of a representative group of American woodworkers about whom, due to what Hummel calls "an accident of survival," we know a great deal. Many Dominy family manuscripts, tools, and objects were acquired by Winterthur Museum in the late 1950s, and reconstructed Dominy woodworking and clockmaking shops were installed in the museum. *See also* "Clocks and Watches."

Smith, Nancy A. *Old Furniture: Understanding the Craftsman's Art*. Drawings by Glenna Lang; photographs by Richard Cheek. Indianapolis and New York: Bobbs-Merrill, 1975. 191 pp.; 214 illustrations, glossary, bibliography, index.

This two-part study provides essential guidance for the beginning student. The first section is devoted to furniture-making techniques and includes discussions of furniture woods, joints, hardware, finish, and other aspects of construction. The second section, entitled "What Happens to Furniture with Time," presents information on points of wear, shrinkage, repairs and restorations, and fakes.

Symonds, R. W. *Furniture Making in Seventeenth and Eighteenth Century England: An Outline for Collectors*. London: Connoisseur, 1955. xiv+238 pp.; 363 illustrations, index.

Symonds, a prolific author, examines woods, craftsmen (joiner, chairmaker, cabinetmaker, carver, gilder), color and surface decoration, and fakes. Symonds's photograph collection and papers were acquired by Winterthur Library in 1975, where they form an important source for the study of early furniture.

Welsh, Peter C. *Woodworking Tools, 1600–1900*. United States National Museum Bulletin 241. Contributions from the Museum of History and Technology, paper 51, pp. 178–228. Washington, D.C.: Smithsonian Institution Press, 1966. 66 illustrations, bibliography.

In his richly illustrated and thoroughly documented introduction to woodworking tools, Welsh approaches tools from the viewpoint of specialization, configuration, and change and provides a superb look at them as both functional and decorative objects. For more on tools, see Henry C. Mercer's classic *Ancient Carpenter's Tools* (1929; reprint, Doylestown, Pa.: Bucks County Historical Society, 1960); and W. L. Goodman's *History of Woodworking Tools* (New York: David McKay Company, 1964). *See also* Charles F. Hummel, *With Hammer in Hand*.

American Antiques from the Israel Sack Collection. 8 vols. to date. Washington, D.C.: Highland House Publishers, 1976 –.

This series contains thousands of illustrations of furniture offered for sale by the firm of Israel Sack, initially published in brochures and gathered here in bound volumes. Captions are brief (usually emphasizing the "warm brown patina" of the given object), and the attributions are helpful. Most of the furniture dates from 1730 to 1820, and most is high style, although there are exceptions. Useful indexes help the reader to find documented examples quickly. Later editions of some of the earlier volumes contain notes on changes in ownership of some objects and reflections by members of the Sack family on changes in the marketplace. The series is most useful to the furniture historian as a pictorial reference.

Baltimore Furniture: The Work of Baltimore and Annapolis Cabinetmakers from 1760 to 1810. Exhibition catalogue. Baltimore: Baltimore Museum of Art, 1947. 195 pp.; illustrations, 125 illustrated entries, index.

Now largely of historiographical interest, this catalogue focused attention on Maryland furniture for the first time in a significant way. The objects were selected by Henry Francis du Pont and Joseph Downs, with the help of a steering committee of Mrs. Alexander Stewart, John Schwarz, and Joe Kindig, Jr. Of the 125 objects included, 107 date from the federal period. This work is still a valuable pictorial resource, but it has been superseded by more recent works by William Voss Elder, Lu Bartlett, Gregory J. Weidman, and others. The catalogue includes an elaborate card table (cat. 16) in the Yale collection, which is now recognized as a fake.

Bates, Elizabeth Bidwell, and Jonathan L. Fairbanks. *American Furniture, 1620 to the Present.* New York: Richard Marek Publishers, 1981. xii+561 pp.; approximately 1,300 black and white and 100 color plates, line drawings, glossary, bibliography, index.

In this massive pictorial introduction to American furniture, six chronological chapters cover objects from the seventeenth century to about 1835. Other early examples are discussed in thematic chapters entitled "Away from the Mainstream" and "The Frontier and Vernacular Traditions, 1800–1850." Each chapter begins with a short introduction, followed by illustrations of numerous objects described in lengthy captions. Bates and Fairbanks make good use of line drawings to interpret furniture construction, and the occasional juxtaposition of objects in special "comparison" pages helps to dramatize regional differences in style. Although the text is marred by occasional inaccuracies, the breadth of coverage here is noteworthy. The bibliography, compiled by Wendell Garrett and Allison Eckardt of *Antiques*, is extensive. *See also* "American Furniture, 1820–1920."

Bishop, Robert. *Centuries and Styles of the American Chair, 1640–1970. See* "American Furniture, 1820–1920."

Bivins, John, Jr. *The Furniture of Coastal North Carolina, 1700–1820.* The Frank L. Horton Series. Winston-Salem: Museum of Early Southern Decorative Arts, 1988; distributed by University of North Carolina Press. xiii+562 pp.; approximately 500 illustrations, appendixes, bibliography, index.

The first volume in a projected MESDA series on decorative arts of the South, this book sets an admirable standard for future studies of regional work. The first section, "The Setting," is virtually a book in itself. It provides the context for furniture making with a degree of richness unparalleled in similar works by examining trade networks, the structure of the cabinetmaking trade, materials, and "furniture imports versus the local trade" in rural, eastern North Carolina. The second section, "The Furniture," is arranged by region and presents a comprehensive look at the forms produced by coastal North Carolina makers. Data on individual makers is given in a lengthy appendix. The result is a richly textured look at the Anglo-American tradition in a society characterized by a taste for elegant yet conservative furniture among largely rural farmer-artisans.

Bjerkoe, Ethel Hall, with John Arthur Bjerkoe. *The Cabinetmakers of America.* Foreword by Russell Kettell. Garden City, N.Y.: Doubleday, 1957. xvii+252 pp.; 32 black and white plates, line drawings, glossary, bibliography.

This work represents the first attempt to compile a biographical dictionary of American cabinetmakers on a countrywide basis, and it is still the only book of its kind. Capsule biographies of some 3,000 craftsmen are included, but the coverage is far from complete. A host of regional studies and monographs have corrected some errors by Bjerkoe, augmented the information known about many craftsmen, and identified hundreds, if not thousands, of additional makers who are not represented here. Thus a search for information on a given craftsman should still begin with Bjerkoe, but nearly always additional sources should be consulted as well.

Boston Furniture of the Eighteenth Century. Publications of the Colonial Society of Massachusetts, vol. 48, edited by Walter Muir Whitehill, Jonathan L. Fairbanks, and Brock W. Jobe. Boston: By the society, 1974; distributed by the University Press of Virginia. xvi+316 pp.; 173 illustrations, appendixes, bibliography, index.

Although it lacks the unified outlook of a work by a single author, and the approach taken by the various authors is a traditional one, combining biography and stylistic analysis, this represents the best in furniture scholarship at the time. Of the eight essays, the most relevant to wider concerns are those by Jobe, Margaretta Markle Lovell, and Gilbert T. Vincent. Jobe's detailed study, using the papers of Nathaniel Holmes, Thomas Fitch, Samuel Grant, and other Boston craftsmen, elucidates the importance of specialization, stresses the key role of upholsterers, and documents the introduction of the so-called Queen Anne style to Boston. Lovell traces the development of block-front furniture in Boston and examines the differences in construction between Boston and Newport examples, while Vincent reveals the European origins of the locally popular bombé form. A section on New England timbers by Gordon Saltar, a list of Boston furniture craftsmen compiled by Myrna Kaye, and a selected bibliography enhance the value of the volume.

Bulkeley, Houghton. *Contributions to Connecticut Cabinet Making*. Hartford: Connecticut Historical Society, 1967. 97 pp.; 34 illustrations, index.

This book contains all the articles written by Bulkeley for *Connecticut Historical Society Bulletin* between 1957 and 1966, including studies of Aaron Roberts, Benjamin Burnham, Amos Denison Allen, John I. Wells, George Belden and Erastus Grant, Elias Ingraham, and Norwich cabinetmakers. In "A Discovery on the Connecticut Chest," Bulkeley linked the name of Peter Blin to the group of so-called tulip and sunflower furniture from Wethersfield for the first time.

Burton, E. Milby. *Charleston Furniture, 1700–1825*. Contributions from the Charleston Museum 12. Charleston, S.C.: By the museum, 1955. ix+150 pp.; 149 line drawings and plates, bibliography, index.

This pioneering book is a landmark in the study of southern furniture. Burton, then director of Charleston Museum, examines local products and craftsmen thoroughly, including brief sections on woods, prices of furniture, forms, sources of furniture, and other general topics. As in so many books of this type, much space (here almost half of the book) is given over to biographies of local craftsmen. The numerous illustrations provide an unsurpassed survey of high-style Charleston furniture from many different collections. Eventually, research under way by the Museum of Early Southern Decorative Arts in Winston-Salem, North Carolina, will amplify and perhaps supersede Burton's, but the continuing usefulness of this monograph is underlined by Charleston Museum's decision to issue a reprint in 1968.

Butler, Joseph T. *Sleepy Hollow Restorations: A Cross-Section of the Collection*. Tarrytown, N.Y.: Sleepy Hollow Press, 1983. 310 pp.; 30 color plates, 425 black and white illustrated entries, appendix, index.

Butler compiled this catalogue of the general collections at Phillipsburg Manor, Upper Mills, Van Cortlandt Manor, and Washington Irving's Sunnyside in Tarrytown. Included are entries on about 100 examples of furniture, including many eighteenth-century objects made in New York (some with histories in the Van Cortlandt family) and several superb early nineteenth-century objects of the sort that might have been owned by Irving in his country home.

Classical America, 1815–1845. Text by Berry B. Tracy and William H. Gerdts. Exhibition catalogue. Newark, N.J.: Newark Museum, 1963. 212 pp.; 197 illustrated entries, bibliography.

The decorative arts section of this pioneering catalogue was prepared by Tracy, whose approach focuses on high-style examples and the understanding of American work in a European context. The text is strong in the analysis of English and French pattern and design and stresses French influence throughout the period. The catalogue includes brief entries on eighty-seven examples of furniture, most (but not all) of which are illustrated. *See also* "Surveys."

Clunie, Margaret Burke, Anne Farnam, and Robert F. Trent. *Furniture at the Essex Institute*. Salem, Mass.: By the institute, 1980. 64 pp.; 50 illustrations, bibliography.

Entries on fifty-one objects, primarily of local manufacture, are presented in this work, although some locally owned examples are included. Several objects imported from China, Japan, Italy, Antigua, and India are discussed. See also Anne Farnam, "Furniture at the Essex Institute in Salem, Massachusetts," *Antiques* 111, no. 5 (May 1977): 958–73.

Comstock, Helen. *American Furniture: Seventeenth, Eighteenth, and Nineteenth Century Styles*. New York: Viking Press, a Studio Book, 1962. 336 pp.; 665 black and white illustrations, black and white plates, 8 color plates, bibliography, index.

The first modern survey of American furniture from 1650 to 1870, Comstock's book remains a useful pictorial introduction to the subject for the beginning student. Some objects have changed hands, many attributions have been refined, and stylistic terminology has undergone some modification in the last quarter century, but this remains a helpful source for locating illustrations of objects in collections that have not yet been published. Comstock was on the staff of *Antiques* for many years and was in an excellent position to prepare this substantial survey. Many of the generalizations concerning style, American innovativeness, and other subjects should be examined cautiously in light of more recent work. An unaltered reprint was recently issued by Schiffer Publishing Company, Exton, Pennsylvania.

Comstock, Helen. *The Looking Glass in America, 1700–1825*. New York: Viking Press, a Studio Book, 1968. 128 pp.; 85 illustrations, index.

Comstock presents a general introduction to the looking-glass form, emphasizing styles and documented examples. For more on the subject, see Geoffrey Wills, *English-Looking Glasses: A Study of the Glass, Frames, and Makers (1670–1820)* (New York: A. S. Barnes, 1965); Serge Roche, Germain Courage, and Pierre Devinoy, *Mirrors* (New York: Rizzoli International Publications, 1985); and Herbert F. Schiffer, *The Mirror Book: English, American, and European* (Exton, Pa.: Schiffer Publishing, 1983). A more interpretive look at the symbolic meanings of mirrors is offered in Benjamin Goldberg, *The Mirror and Man* (Charlottesville: University Press of Virginia, 1985).

Connecticut Furniture: Seventeenth and Eighteenth Centuries. Exhibition catalogue. Hartford, Conn.: Wadsworth Atheneum, 1967. xvi+156 pp.; 275 illustrations, bibliography.

This catalogue of 275 objects, arranged by form, provides a look at Connecticut furniture from its founding until the end of the eighteenth century. This was the first exhibition to include a serious discussion of the English background of American furniture, particularly that of the seventeenth century, and several English objects are included. Many other issues, such as the relation of Connecticut objects to Pennsylvania work, the variations in objects produced in different parts of the colony, and Eliphalet Chapin's career, are summarized in an impressive overview that emphasizes looking at Connecticut furniture from an aesthetic point of view. This survey has spawned an impressive body of literature on specialized aspects of Connecticut furniture, as students have focused with increasing intensity on specific counties, towns, and shop traditions during the past twenty years. Many refinements will be found in these studies, but this work remains an invaluable introduction to the subject.

Cooke, Edward S., Jr. *Fiddlebacks and Crooked-backs: Elijah Booth and Other Joiners in Newtown and Woodbury, 1750–1820.* Waterbury, Conn.: Mattatuck Historical Society, 1982. 120 pp.; 35 illustrations, appendixes.

Newtown and Woodbury flank Housatonic River in northwestern Connecticut, separated by only about 18 miles, yet each town had a separate identity, with different attitudes, values, and social structures. In a superb study, Cooke relates objects and craftsmen to these wider issues in a deft weaving of documentary and artifactual evidence. Newtown is seen as a conservative farming community, an egalitarian town in which the furniture maker functioned as a farmer-craftsman producing traditional objects for a closely knit group. In contrast, Woodbury was a growing commercial center, with stronger ties to the outside world and a stratified social system. Furniture makers in Woodbury tended to be independent entrepreneurs who made objects more in keeping with contemporary styles. Cooke provides information on regional construction and ornament idiosyncracies and refines many traditional attributions of objects to Elijah Booth (1745–1823), who is now seen as but one of many Booth family members (and not necessarily the most productive or important one) involved in furniture making. The material here has been expanded and refined in Edward S. Cooke, Jr., "Rural Artisanal Culture: The Preindustrial Joiners of Newtown and Woodbury, Connecticut, 1760–1820" (Ph.D. diss., Boston University, 1984). *See also* "Craftsmen."

Cooke, Edward S., Jr., ed. *Upholstery in America and Europe from the Seventeenth Century to World War I.* Editorial consultants, Susan L. Paxman and Regina Ryan. New York and London: W. W. Norton, a Barra Foundation Book, 1987. 273 pp.; 258 black and white illustrations, 16 color plates, index.

This anthology of twenty articles, many based on presentations at the 1979 conference, represents the first modern book-length study of the important area of historic upholstery. Many of the essays deal with seventeenth- and eighteenth-century topics, and a wide variety of perspectives, both historical and practical, are presented. Chapters on English and French upholstery practices help to place American work in an international context. The many case studies here will help to lay the foundation for a unified study of the subject.

Cooper, Wendy A. *In Praise of America: American Decorative Arts, 1650–1830/Fifty Years of Discovery since the 1929 Girl Scouts Loan Exhibition.* Foreword by J. Carter Brown; photography by Richard Cheek. New York: Alfred A. Knopf, 1980. viii+280 pp.; 308 black and white illustrations, 52 color plates, index.

The Girl Scouts Loan Exhibition was held at American Art Association's galleries in New York in 1929 as a benefit for the Girl Scouts of America. An early example of the "blockbuster" exhibition of American decorative arts, the show included, among many types of objects, more than 300 examples of American furniture dating between 1650 and 1830 drawn from the finest private collections in the country. (The catalogue remains a valuable pictorial resource; now scarce, it was reprinted in 1977.) To commemorate that exhibition, the Girl Scouts commissioned this work, which accompanied a loan exhibition at the National Gallery of Art. It presents a summary and, in some cases, a reassessment of scholarship in decorative arts during the past fifty years. The text is divided into seven chapters, which examine the emergence and importance of documented objects that have come to light; the art of the upholstered object, an area in which much new work has been done; the importance of specially commissioned objects; the economics of fashion and workmanship, as scholars have tried to understand shop organization; old and new approaches to regionalism; the increased study of production outside major style centers; and style in early nineteenth-century America. This synthesis demonstrates that scholars have done much work on many well-known roads of inquiry (such as those of taxonomy, aesthetic evaluation, and increasingly detailed documentation), but rarely have ventured into uncharted territory in their search for understanding. *See also* "Surveys."

Cornelius, Charles Over. *Furniture Masterpieces of Duncan Phyfe.* 1922. Reprint. New York: Dover Publications, 1970. x+86 pp.; 63 illustrations, line drawings.

Cornelius's short monograph, occasioned by an exhibition at Metropolitan Museum of Art, is interesting today chiefly as an early indication of the deep and abiding interest in Phyfe (1768–1854), New York City's leading cabinetmaker in the federal period. The information and attributions should be regarded cautiously; a more recent treatment of the furniture can be found in Nancy McClelland's 1939 monograph, and the documentary record is thoroughly investigated in Michael Brown, "Duncan Phyfe" (M.A. thesis, University of Delaware, 1978).

Dorman, Charles G. *Delaware Cabinetmakers and Allied Artisans, 1655–1855.* Wilmington: Historical Society of Delaware, 1960. 107 pp.; illustrations, appendixes. Also published in *Delaware History* 9, no. 2 (October 1960): 105–217.

Although updated by the more recent work of Deborah Waters, Harold Hancock, and others, this biographical dictionary remains an essential source for the study of Delaware furniture. Dorman draws heavily on surviving account books and newspaper advertisements in his presentation of capsule biographies of several hundred craftsmen. Appendixes include pages from the account book of John Janvier, Sr., 1794–96, and the estate inventories of five craftsmen.

Downs, Joseph. *American Furniture: Queen Anne and Chippendale Periods in the Henry Francis du Pont Winterthur Museum.* Foreword by Henry Francis du Pont. New York: Macmillan Co., 1952. xl+[450] pp.; 401 black and white illustrations, 10 color plates, index.

The first book published by the museum, this catalogue provides illustration of and basic information on 388 examples of eighteenth-century furniture in the Winterthur collection. Downs, Winterthur's first curator, came to the museum after serving as curator of the American Wing at Metropolitan Museum of Art in New York. This catalogue is the major monument of his long and productive career as a curator and an author. His introduction touches briefly on the study of craftsmen, terminology, furniture imports and exports, regional characteristics, and woods, thus setting an agenda of issues that would be examined in more detail by the next generation at Winterthur and elsewhere. Although *American Furniture* remains an incomparable pictorial source, with large, clear, and beautifully reproduced photographs taken by Gilbert Ask, its approach is now dated. It should be used in conjunction with several more recent publications dealing with this aspect of the museum's collection, including Charles F. Hummel's "Queen Anne and Chippendale Furniture in the Henry Francis du Pont Winterthur Museum: Part I," *Antiques* 98, no. 6 (June 1970): 896–914, and his *Winterthur Guide to American Chippendale Furniture.*

The Dunlaps and Their Furniture. Exhibition catalogue. Manchester, N.H.: Currier Gallery of Art, 1970. x+310 pp.; 115 illustrated entries, appendixes.

This exhaustive presentation of information about the Dunlap family of woodworkers in southern New Hampshire in the late eighteenth and early nineteenth centuries is based on a large body of surviving manuscripts, including several account books, tools, and furniture. It examines the distinctive nature of Dunlap furniture, the forms of furniture made by them, their relationships with apprentices and jour-

neymen, their prices, and numerous other topics. A lengthy transcription of John Dunlap's account book spanning the years 1768–87 is included (pp. 171–301). This work has been updated in an unpublished typescript by Charles S. Parsons entitled "More Dunlap" (1976), which is available in some specialized libraries. The body of raw material concerning the Dunlaps is rivaled only by that concerning the Dominy family (see Charles F. Hummel, *With Hammer in Hand*), and it has been treated thoroughly and intelligently here in a traditional manner. There remains a good deal of room for more interpretive studies based on the contents of this catalogue, and more work on the stylistic origins of the distinctive Dunlap style, especially its relationship to Scottish furniture, still needs to be done.

Early Furniture Made in New Jersey, 1690–1870. Exhibition catalogue. Newark: Newark Museum, 1958. 89 pp.; 22 illustrations, bibliography.

About 90 percent of the objects included in this catalogue were made before 1820; unfortunately, relatively few of them are illustrated. Half of the book is devoted to an alphabetical checklist of more than 1,000 New Jersey woodworking craftsmen. This work should be used in conjunction with several more recent catalogues issued by the New Jersey State Museum in Trenton, including *From Lenape Territory to Royal Province: New Jersey, 1600–1750* (1971) and *The Pulse of the People: New Jersey, 1763–1789* (1976).

Elder, William Voss, III, and Lu Bartlett. *John Shaw, Cabinetmaker of Annapolis.* Exhibition catalogue. Baltimore: Baltimore Museum of Art, 1983. 174 pp.; 17 illustrations, 61 illustrated entries, appendixes, bibliography.

John Shaw is an in-depth monograph on the Scottish-born cabinetmaker (1745–1829) whose name "has been synonymous with fine furniture of the federal period in Maryland" (p. 13). Nearly all known examples of Shaw's work, and that of his partnership with Archibald Chisholm, are treated here in sixty-one detailed catalogue entries, and exhaustive documentation of Shaw's life is presented. Contextual material on Annapolis and on the cabinetmaking trade as a whole helps to put Shaw's work and career into perspective. Although one reviewer was critical of Elder and Bartlett because they did not examine Shaw's furniture in a completely systematic, scientific, and objective manner (relying instead on the more empirical type of data-gathering typical of most connoisseurship), this study is in many respects a model investigation of a craftsman and his products along safe, traditional lines.

Fabian, Monroe H. *The Pennsylvania-German Decorated Chest.* Foreword by Frederick S. Weiser. New York: Universe Books, a Main Street Press Book, 1978. 230 pp.; 250 black and white and color plates, bibliography, index.

Fabian thoroughly examines the European background, construction, hardware, surface decoration, use, and makers of this regional form made in great quantities from the 1760s through the nineteenth century. Much nonsense has been published about these objects, but Fabian's judicious handling of evidence, his reliable dating, and the large number of illustrations make a valuable contribution. This book was selected by the Pennsylvania German Society, Breinigsville, as volume 12 in their series of publications.

Failey, Dean F., with the assistance of Robert J. Hefner and Susan E. Klaffky. *Long Island Is My Nation: The Decorative Arts and Craftsmen, 1640–1830.* Exhibition catalogue. Setauket: Society for the Preservation of Long Island Antiquities, 1976. 304 pp.; 251 illustrations, appendixes.

Long Island was an exceptionally interesting rural region due to the intermingling of cultures there, especially during the 1640–1730 period, when the Dutch and English each had communities on the island. As the eighteenth century progressed, English influence became predominant, and objects and designs from both New York and New England affected local production. Although paintings, silver, and other objects are included here, the focus is on furniture. Failey identifies more than 1,000 woodworking craftsmen active 1640–1830, each possessing multiple skills, and a list and biographical sketch of many of them are included in an appendix. *See also* "Surveys."

Fairbanks, Jonathan L., and Robert F. Trent. *New England Begins: The Seventeenth Century.* 3 vols. Exhibition catalogue. Boston: Museum of Fine Arts, 1982. Vol. 1, *Introduction: Migration and Settlement*; vol. 2, *Mentality and Environment*; vol. 3, *Style.* xxviii+575 pp.; 84 black and white illustrations, 504 catalogue illustrations, 21 color plates, 13 tables, appendixes, bibliography, index.

Although a multiauthor work with some unevenness, this catalogue is excellent on the subject of furniture. Two essays by Trent—"The Concept of Mannerism" and "New England Joinery and Turning before 1700"—provide an understanding of the sources and major manifestations of the dominant aesthetic governing seventeenth-century design and an analysis of how design ideas and regional decorative traditions were brought to New England by known joiners and turners. The extensive entries on individual objects are also largely the work of Trent and are notable for the detailed information they contain. Each is a miniessay on form, ornament, provenance, and the works of individual shop traditions, and each represents the most up-to-date scholarship. All the most significant groups of New England furniture are treated, as well as representative English and Continental forms, many with histories of ownership in the region. Unfortunately, because the catalogue covers so many areas and types of artifacts, a listing of joiners and woodworkers is not included. Readers may feel frustrated because many of the entries assume a thorough knowledge of previous scholarship on seventeenth-century furniture. However, this is still the

best, and therefore the first, work that should be consulted when studying furniture of this period. Further information on provenance and the data used in making specific attributions can be found in several works written by Trent that are cited in this bibliography, and in "The Symonds Joinery Shops of Salem and Their Works," *The Ninth Annual Peabody Museum Antiques Show* (Salem, Mass., 1981). *See also* "Surveys."

Fales, Dean A., Jr. *American Painted Furniture, 1660–1880.* Illustrations and design editor, Robert Bishop; general editor, Cyril I. Nelson. New York: E. P. Dutton, 1972. 299 pp.; 511 black and white and color illustrations, bibliography, indexes.

In the first full-length study of painted furniture, focusing on "plain painting, imitative painting, and imaginative or fanciful painting" (p. 5), Fales illustrates and documents the use of paints and stains, a practice that borders on the ubiquitous in early furniture, in a basically chronological fashion. Special attention is given to federal-period fancy furniture, Windsor chairs, and painting on Shaker and Pennsylvania German furniture. Japanning, gilding, and other related techniques are also covered to a degree. More could have been done here with regard to a technical and scientific analysis of painted surfaces, but this remains an excellent overview. *See also* "American Furniture, 1820–1920."

Fales, Dean A., Jr. *Essex County Furniture: Documented Treasures from Local Collections, 1660–1860.* Exhibition catalogue. Salem, Mass.: Essex Institute, 1965. Unpag.; approximately 80 illustrations. Also published in *Essex Institute Historical Collections* 101, no. 3 (July 1965): 165–244.

This catalogue brings together forty-seven objects "made by, attributed to, or strongly associated with local cabinetmakers and chairmakers," twenty-three works "by allied craftsmen such as carvers, decorators, musical instrument makers, clockmakers, upholsterers, frame makers, and looking glass makers," and six "regional types of furniture, some linked with names of craftsmen." Included is a core group of seventeenth-century objects attributed at the time to Thomas Dennis and now associated with Dennis and his master, William Searle. Numerous examples of work by Salem's active cabinetmakers in the federal period are included.

Fales, Dean A., Jr. *The Furniture of Historic Deerfield.* New York: E. P. Dutton, 1976. 294 pp.; 578 black and white and color plates, index.

This book is a pictorial guide to more than 550 examples owned by Historic Deerfield, many of them collected by the institution's founders, Mr. and Mrs. Henry N. Flynt. The objects are arranged by form, with a good deal of information contained in brief captions and in the running text. More than 200 examples of seating furniture are represented. Views of some Deerfield houses and interiors are also included. Although most of the objects are from New England, especially from the Connecticut valley, the collection contains some furniture from England, Europe, and other parts of America. Readers should keep in mind that collections often are not static; for example, since this book was published, a cupboard from the eastern shore of Virginia (cat. 492) has been sold by Historic Deerfield. A price list for cabinetwork agreed on by Hampshire County cabinetmakers in March 1796 is included (p. 286).

Fitzgerald, Oscar P. *Three Centuries of American Furniture*. Englewood Cliffs, N.J.: Prentice-Hall, 1982. xii + 323 pp.; 527 black and white illustrations, 8 color plates, appendix, bibliography, index.

Fitzgerald's sweeping survey of American furniture is perhaps the best of the current generation. The organization of the book, however, reflects some of the problems of current scholarship and underscores the need for still another attempt at a book dealing with American furniture as a whole. Here, for example, the first six chapters are devoted to specific styles, with the antiquated terminology of Jacobean, William and Mary, Queen Anne, and Chippendale retained. Country, southern, and Shaker and Pennsylvania German furniture are given their own separate chapters, rather than being integrated into a more cohesive framework. Unfortunately, given the large amount of work produced on the subject in the 1970s, furniture made before 1730 is given short shrift here. A chapter is devoted to connoisseurship, and Benjamin Lehman's 1786 price list for cabinet- and chairwork is given in an appendix. *See also* "American Furniture, 1820–1920."

Forman, Benno M. *American Seating Furniture, 1630–1730: An Interpretive Catalogue*. New York and London: W. W. Norton, a Winterthur Book, 1988. xxv + 397 pp.; 194 illustrations, catalogue of 92 chairs, appendixes, bibliography, concordance, index.

From 1969 until his death in early 1982, Forman devoted the better part of his teaching and scholarly career at Winterthur Museum to an investigation of American furniture before 1730. His death cut short his major work, a monograph on seventeenth- and early eighteenth-century objects based on a catalogue of the Winterthur collection. This work, published posthumously, is the only volume he was able to bring nearly to completion. It was edited and prepared for publication by Catherine E. Hutchins, with the assistance of two of Forman's students, Robert Blair St. George and Robert F. Trent. It begins with detailed chapters on connoisseurship, woods, and craftsmanship, followed by six catalogue sections devoted to specific types of chairs: turners', joiners', and Cromwellian chairs; cane chairs and couches; carved-top, plain-top, and crooked-back leather chairs; and easy and low chairs. Forman paid particular attention to how various European traditions migrated to America and were developed into specific regional variations. Entries cover

ninety-two chairs in the collection, although many supplementary illustrations are included.

Forman, Benno M. "The Chest of Drawers in America, 1635–1730: The Origins of the Joined Chest of Drawers." *Winterthur Portfolio* 20, no. 1 (Spring 1985): 1–30. 26 illustrations.

An expanded version of an essay first published in 1981, this article explores the origins of the chest of drawers in England in the seventeenth century and its transfer to America through the work of immigrant craftsmen. Forman suggests, for example, that the Boston shops of joiners Ralph Mason and Henry Messenger and of turner Thomas Edsall were the likely makers of the earliest American expressions of the form. He examines the introduction of the high chest of drawers in the 1680s, through the work of immigrant John Brocas, and its subsequent development until about 1715 in the shops of native-born joiners. In conclusion, Forman also discusses the variations of case furniture produced in Pennsylvania during the early years of settlement there. This article is augmented by Robert F. Trent, "The Chest of Drawers in America: A Postscript," pp. 31–48 of the same issue.

Forman, Benno M. "Delaware Valley 'Crookt Foot' and Slat-Back Chairs: The Fussell-Savery Connection." *Winterthur Portfolio* 15, no. 1 (Spring 1980): 41–64. 22 illustrations.

Based on a surviving account book and other documentation, Forman examines the shop organization and production of Philadelphia chairmaker Solomon Fussell between 1738 and 1749, the relationship between Fussell's work and that of his apprentice, William Savery, and the influence of Boston furniture on Philadelphia objects in the Queen Anne style. Forman emphasizes the "complex and highly diversified operation" of Fussell's large shop, which employed specialists or jobbers in the second quarter of the century (p. 42). *See also* "Craftsmen."

Forman, Benno M. "German Influences in Pennsylvania Furniture." In Scott T. Swank et al., *Arts of the Pennsylvania Germans*, edited by Catherine E. Hutchins, pp. 102–70. New York: W. W. Norton for the Henry Francis du Pont Winterthur Museum, 1983. 61 black and white illustrations, color plates, 2 tables.

Forman's study focuses not on the overtly Germanic types of Pennsylvania furniture, but on "the furniture that shows the accommodation of German tastes to life in Pennsylvania" (p. 102). He examines seating furniture, tables, case furniture, and other objects in the origin of their construction and ornament. Forman concludes, "a considerable quantity of furniture that does not 'look' Germanic . . . was made with techniques that could only have been brought to America by craftsmen trained in Germanic Europe" (p. 166), and he discusses ways in which these techniques were assimilated in America. This is a difficult, yet rewarding, essay that considerably expands the parameters of the discussion of American furniture in a worldwide context. *See also* "Craftsmen."

Garvan, Beatrice B. *The Pennsylvania German Collection.* Handbooks in American Art, no. 2. Philadelphia: Philadelphia Museum of Art, 1982. xxviii+372 pp.; color plates, 1,115 illustrated entries, appendix, bibliography, index.

Since its earliest days, the Philadelphia Museum of Art has had a strong interest in the art of the Pennsylvania Germans. Fostered by the interest and support of museum personnel such as Edwin AtLee Barber, and swollen with the addition of several private collections, including that of Titus C. Geesey, their holdings have grown to more than 1,100 objects. This handbook provides a guide to each of these objects, arranged in eight chapters by medium. Each entry includes a photograph, date, written description, dimensions, credit line, and accession number. Some 250 wooden objects are catalogued, including boxes, chests, seating furniture, cupboards, tables, beds, clocks, and a wide variety of tools and utensils.

Goyne, Nancy A. "The Bureau Table in America." In *Winterthur Portfolio 3*, edited by Milo M. Naeve, pp. 24–36. Winterthur, Del.: Henry Francis du Pont Winterthur Museum, 1967. 7 illustrations.

The bureau table, also known as a bureau dressing table, was popular in this country from circa 1760 through the 1790s. It usually consists of a wide drawer running the width of the case and housed above two tiers of smaller, superimposed drawers that flank a central recessed cupboard. Goyne focuses on design sources, price, use, and regional variations.

The Great River: Art and Society of the Connecticut Valley, 1635–1820. Exhibition catalogue. Hartford, Conn.: Wadsworth Atheneum, 1985. xvii+524 pp.; 14 black and white illustrations, 13 color plates, 2 tables, illustrated catalogue.

This large catalogue contains an essay by Philip Zea and ninety entries by Zea and William N. Hosley, Jr., on furniture made in the Massachusetts and Connecticut portions of the valley during the first two centuries of settlement. The interpretation of the objects is based on a regional paradigm that emphasizes the importance of shop traditions. New information on seventeenth-century Connecticut valley carved chests, on mid eighteenth-century Wethersfield furniture, and on the shop practices and drawings of Timothy Loomis III of Windsor is presented.

Green, Henry D. *Furniture of the Georgia Piedmont before 1830.* Exhibition catalogue. Atlanta: High Museum of Art, 1976. 143 pp.; 7 illustrations, 185 illustrated entries.

Based on Green's forty years of experience as a collector, this catalogue represents the first published survey of Georgia-made furniture. It contains 185 objects, arranged by form, many of which were included in a 1976 loan exhibition at High Museum of Art in Atlanta. Most of the objects included date from about 1790 to 1830, and huntboards, sideboards, small tables, chests of drawers, and corner cupboards are well represented. Surprisingly, Green's research uncovered few early chairs. Publication of this volume dramatically increased our understanding of the full scope and variety of American furniture in the 1790–1830 period and represents a key landmark in the evolving literature on southern cabinetmaking.

Greenlaw, Barry A. *New England Furniture at Williamsburg.* The Williamsburg Decorative Arts Series, edited by Graham Hood. Williamsburg: Colonial Williamsburg Foundation, 1974; distributed by the University Press of Virginia. viii+195 pp.; 164 illustrations, index.

In his introduction, Greenlaw discusses the importation of New England furniture into Virginia in the eighteenth century. The catalogue contains 164 objects, including a cross section of high-style and rural furniture dating mostly between 1730 and 1810; only a few earlier objects, mostly chairs, are included. The collection is particularly strong in eighteenth-century beds, small tables, desks, and Windsor chairs.

Griffith, Lee Ellen. *The Pennsylvania Spice Box: Paneled Doors and Secret Drawers.* Edited by Ann Barton Brown and Roland H. Woodward. Exhibition catalogue. West Chester, Pa.: Chester County Historical Society, 1986. 160 pp.; 27 illustrations, 58 illustrated entries, bibliography.

This catalogue of fifty-five examples from Chester County (and a handful from elsewhere) explores the use, construction, materials, inlaid decoration, and makers of this "luxury item used to store and secure valuables and spices" that was very popular in southeastern Pennsylvania in the eighteenth century.

Gusler, Wallace B. *Furniture of Williamsburg and Eastern Virginia, 1710–1790.* Richmond: Virginia Museum, 1979. xxi+194 pp.; 126 black and white and color illustrations, appendix, bibliography, index.

This regional study emphasizes the furniture made in Williamsburg (especially in the shops of Peter Scott and Anthony Hay); objects from Norfolk, Richmond, Fredericksburg, and other parts of eastern Virginia are discussed to a lesser extent. The sophisticated products of the Williamsburg shops, in particular, represent the emergence of "a new and major regional school," one in which the ties to English prototypes remained the strongest among American centers of cabinetmaking in the eighteenth century. Gusler emphasizes the importance of such construction features as full dustboards, paneled backs, and "composite feet" in the Virginia aesthetic and in the identification of shop traditions. A group of five extraordinary ceremonial chairs (two from the capitol in Williamsburg and three Masonic Master's chairs) form an impressive body of objects redolent with cultural meaning. For expanded treatment of Eastern Shore furniture, see James R. Melchor, N. Gordon Lohr, and Marilyn S. Melchor, *Eastern Shore, Virginia, Raised-Panel Furniture, 1730–1830. See also* "Craftsmen."

Heckscher, Morrison H. *American Furniture in the Metropolitan Museum of Art.* Vol. 2, *Late Colonial Period: The Queen Anne and Chippendale Styles.* Edited by Mary-Alice Rogers; photographs by Richard Cheek. New York: Metropolitan Museum of Art and Random House, 1985. 383 pp.; 213 black and white and color illustrations, photographic details, index.

Heckscher's richly detailed and sumptuously illustrated catalogue presents 213 objects arranged by form. The collection is strong in furniture from the Middle Colonies and New England (only a handful of southern objects are included) and is dominated by high-style examples. Entries are lengthy, authoritative on points of connoisseurship, and strengthened by Heckscher's substantive amounts of original research on Newport furniture, New York card tables, easy chairs, and other topics. The retention of the stylistic terms *Queen Anne* and *Chippendale* in the subtitle is unfortunate, since Heckscher recognizes their manifold inadequacies as descriptors of American work. Although this is volume 2, volume 1 in the series of catalogues of the Metropolitan's collection has yet to appear.

Hewitt, Benjamin A., Patricia E. Kane, and Gerald W. R. Ward. *The Work of Many Hands: Card Tables in Federal America, 1790–1820.* Exhibition catalogue. New Haven: Yale University Art Gallery, 1982. 198 pp.; 57 black and white illustrations, 12 color plates, 56 illustrated entries, charts, index.

This catalogue presents a detailed examination of the card table, a fashionable furniture form of the postrevolutionary period, when card playing enjoyed tremendous popularity. Based on Hewitt's computer-assisted statistical analysis of 176 characteristics of each of some 400 surviving tables, the catalogue provides new information about the design and construction of tables from twelve regional centers and establishes norms for the attribution of federal-period objects. While the organization of the data into groups sharing statistically significant characteristics helps to identify regional characteristics, the study also sheds light on the nature of the cabinetmaking trade during these crucial years of transition from craft to industry, including evidence of the various levels of production (ready made, customized, and custom made) and of the use of specialists, such as turners and inlaymakers. The book contains a lengthy essay by Hewitt; detailed entries, prepared by Hewitt and Barbara McLean Ward, on 56 of the tables included in the study; basic information on the 374 tables in the study; numerous line drawings of construction; illustrations, many in color, of the 151

varieties of patterned and pictorial inlay found on the tables in the study; an essay on the role of price and design books by Kane; and some observations on the role of card playing by Gerald Ward. The culmination of a decade of research by Hewitt, this publication marked the first time that a scientific method of connoisseurship was applied to the study of American furniture on this scale and suggests a methodology—rigorous and precise—that can be applied to other large, homogeneous groups of objects.

Hipkiss, Edwin J. *Eighteenth-Century American Arts: The M. and M. Karolik Collection of Paintings, Drawings, Engravings, Furniture, Silver, Needlework, and Incidental Objects Gathered to Illustrate the Achievements of American Artists and Craftsmen of the Period from 1720 to 1820.* Notes on the drawings and prints by Henry P. Rossiter; comments on the collection by Maxim Karolik. Cambridge, Mass.: Harvard University Press for the Museum of Fine Arts, Boston, 1941. xvii+366 pp.; approximately 320 illustrations.

This beautifully printed volume, set in Monotype Bembo and with full-tone collotype illustrations, established a high visual standard for furniture catalogues that was emulated by Joseph Downs in the 1950s and by Morrison Heckscher in the 1980s. The catalogue includes 125 examples of high-style furniture, the vast majority from Massachusetts and Rhode Island, although some superb Philadelphia objects are included. These objects are not included in Richard Randall's 1965 catalogue. Karolik's musings, "As I Reflect upon the Collection," provide a fascinating look at the mind of an idiosyncratic collector. The authenticity of a side chair labeled by Benjamin Randolph (cat. 89) has been questioned; see John T. Kirk, *American Chairs: Queen Anne and Chippendale,* pp. 172–74.

Hornor, William Macpherson, Jr. *Blue Book, Philadelphia Furniture: William Penn to George Washington, with Special Reference to the Philadelphia-Chippendale School.* 1935. Reprint. Washington, D.C.: Highland House Publishers, 1977. xxxii+340 pp.; 502 black and white illustrations, 9 color plates, indexes.

This is an early detailed study of regional furniture, infused with local pride and more than a little snobbish in tone. Hornor made extensive use of primary sources, including price books, tax lists, inventories, bills, invoices, and numerous manuscripts, but to the eternal frustration of later scholars, he failed to footnote his sources, and in some cases they have proved irretrievable. The book is arranged chronologically by style, with the greatest attention paid to the Chippendale period. Much work has been done on Philadelphia furniture in the past fifty years in the form of articles, catalogues, and theses, but no single book has yet superseded Hornor; it remains essential to research on Philadelphia furniture, although careful scholars will be sure to verify the evidence and conclusions contained therein. The 1977 reprint does not include Hornor's original preface.

Hummel, Charles F. *A Winterthur Guide to American Chippendale Furniture: Middle Atlantic and Southern Colonies*. New York: Crown Publishers, a Winterthur Book/Rutledge Books, 1976. 144 pp.; 135 black and white illustrations, 16 color plates, bibliography.

The 151 objects treated here "are a careful sampling of furniture at Winterthur made between 1755 and 1790 in New York, Philadelphia, and the South and, with the exception of the latter, are indicative of the range of forms produced in those areas" (p. 9). Hummel provides new information on some of the objects included in Joseph Downs's earlier catalogue, as well as some objects acquired since the publication of Downs's work in 1952. A short introduction deals with the regional characteristics, design components, and evolution of the rococo style. This is a popular and authoritative guide.

Jobe, Brock, and Myrna Kaye, with the assistance of Philip Zea. *New England Furniture, the Colonial Era: Selections from the Society for the Preservation of New England Antiquities*. Photographs by Richard Cheek. Boston: Houghton Mifflin Co., 1984. xviii+494 pp.; approximately 450 black and white illustrations, 12 color plates, line drawings, bibliography, index.

This work includes introductory essays by Jobe ("Urban Craftsmen and Design") and Zea ("Rural Craftsmen and Design" and "Construction Methods and Materials"). Jobe uses the lives of several representative craftsmen—a turner, an upholsterer, and three cabinetmakers—to illustrate the issues of craft practice and organization and discusses the English sources of American design. Zea's sensitive study of rural furniture makers emphasizes studying these men and their products in light of the context of a seasonal agricultural economy that forced them to make furniture part-time. The essays are followed by 148 detailed entries on selected examples from the vast collection of SPNEA. The entries are arranged by form, and many important documented examples are included, including a group made by joiner Samuel Sewall of York, Maine. A handful of English objects owned in New England is included.

The John Brown House Loan Exhibition of Rhode Island Furniture, including Some Notable Portraits, Chinese Export Porcelain, and Other Items. Text by Joseph K. Ott. Exhibition catalogue. Providence: Rhode Island Historical Society, 1965. xxv+178 pp.; 6 illustrations, 105 illustrated entries.

This catalogue contains entries on ninety-three examples of eighteenth-century Rhode Island furniture and additional entries on local needlework, ceramics, and portraits. The emphasis is on Newport work, but some Providence objects, particularly from the federal period, are included. Also included are transcriptions of a 1756 cabinetmakers' price list of joinery work and its revised form of 1757, the earliest documents of their type in American furniture. The text is strong on the identification of regional characteristics, although Ott's conclusions and attributions should be regarded in the light of more recent research by Morrison Heckscher, Michael Moses, and others. Many important privately owned objects are included.

Kane, Patricia E. *Furniture of the New Haven Colony: The Seventeenth-Century Style*. Exhibition catalogue. New Haven: New Haven Colony Historical Society, 1973. 93 pp.; 34 illustrated entries, appendix.

Kane's loan exhibition catalogue of thirty-four objects produced in central coastal Connecticut identifies four major groups of objects: a New Haven group featuring three-dimensional carving; a Guilford-area group featuring foliated S-scroll carving in conjunction with applied bosses and turnings and geometric moldings; a group of superb cupboards and a board chest (recently attributed by Robert F. Trent to the so-called Russell–Gibbons shops); and a group consisting of turned chairs. The detailed entries are superb studies in connoisseurship, and an appendix includes biographical data on thirty-six New Haven woodworking craftsmen. The judicious handling of documentary and artifactual evidence makes this a useful model when considering how to treat attributions of seventeenth-century furniture.

Kane, Patricia E. "The Joiners of Seventeenth Century Hartford County." *Connecticut Historical Society Bulletin* 35, no. 3 (July 1970): 65–85. 13 illustrations.

In providing biographical information on twenty-eight joiners of Hartford, Wethersfield, Windsor, Farmington, Middletown, Simsbury, and Glastonbury, Kane emphasizes, "perhaps the most significant idea that emerges from this brief survey...is that apprenticeship within a family played a role in providing continuity in craft techniques from generation to generation" (p. 85). She also deals with the lack of specialization in the crafts in a rural community and with customer conservatism as an outgrowth of this inbred conservation of mechanical knowledge coupled with the inability of the community to attract new craftsmen with new ideas.

Kane, Patricia E. *Three Hundred Years of American Seating Furniture: Chairs and Beds from the Mabel Brady Garvan and Other Collections at Yale University*. Boston: New York Graphic Society, 1976. 319 pp.; 18 color plates, 298 illustrated entries, index.

A brief introduction on chairmaking in America precedes detailed information on 298 objects at Yale, including more than 225 that date before 1850. The collection has a broad geographic distribution and a wide variety of forms. The entries are models of connoisseurship.

Kentucky Furniture. Exhibition catalogue. Louisville: J. B. Speed Art Museum, 1974. [84] pp.; 86 illustrations.

This catalogue of a loan exhibition includes many examples of federal-style furniture, all dating somewhat later than related examples from more urban areas, but distinguished by an abundant use of inlaid decoration. See also Mrs. Wade

Hampton Whitley, *A Checklist of Kentucky Cabinetmakers from 1775 to 1859* (Paris, Ky.: By the author, 1969).

Kettell, Russell Hawes. *The Pine Furniture of Early New England.* 1929. Reprint. New York: Dover Publications, [1949]. xxiii+[447] pp.; 230 illustrations, 55 line drawings, bibliography.

Although solely of historiographical interest today, this early survey is frankly celebratory and provides an excellent look at the love of the object that motivated collectors and antiquarians during the first generation of students of American furniture. The book contains illustrations of objects arranged by form, including many from Concord Antiquarian Society (now Concord Museum), where Kettell was the moving force in the 1920s and 1930s. The drawings include "microscopic radial longitudinal sections of pine wood," an early demonstration of interest in the microscopic identification of furniture woods, and about fifty working plans and drawings of furniture designed for the amateur craftsman to follow. This book is still useful for its illustrations, although some of them should be accepted cautiously, and some of the objects have entered museum collections in recent years; for example, a Wethersfield chest (fig. 24) and the Mary Pease Hadley-type chest (fig. 25), then in the Tyler collection, were acquired by the Museum of Fine Arts, Boston, in 1932.

Keyser, Alan G., Larry M. Neff, and Frederick S. Weiser, trans. and eds. *The Accounts of Two Pennsylvania German Furniture Makers—Abraham Overholt, Bucks County, 1790–1833, and Peter Ranck, Lebanon County, 1794–1817.* Sources and Documents of the Pennsylvania Germans, III, edited by Frederick S. Weiser. Breinigsville: Pennsylvania German Society, 1978. xvii+238 pp.; 9 illustrations, glossary.

The transcriptions of these two account books, one privately owned (Overholt) and one in Winterthur Library (Ranck), contain a great deal of information about the daily lives and activities of these rural craftsmen, who practiced farming as well as woodworking. Overholt (1765–1834) was primarily a farmer, although his account book deals with his work as a turner and joiner. He produced spinning wheels and spooling wheels (an example of each has survived, now in Mercer Museum), other equipment used in the processing of fiber, many kinds of household furniture, and a wide variety of farm equipment. His account book contains numerous entries for repairing these sorts of objects as well. Ranck (1770–1851) is best known for the chests he made and decorated, although his account book indicates that he made substantial numbers of beds, tables, and other forms and, like Overholt, engaged in repairwork and many other activities unrelated to woodworking. The lengthy transcriptions are well edited, and a useful glossary is appended. This is a valuable primary source for the study of Pennsylvania German craftsmen and, by extrapolation, other rural woodworkers.

Kindig, Joseph K., III. *The Philadelphia Chair, 1685–1785.* Exhibition catalogue. York, Pa.: Historical Society of York County, 1978. [106] pp.; 80 illustrated entries, bibliography.

A minimum of text accompanies this catalogue of a loan exhibition of seventy chairs arranged chronologically. A section of detail photographs allows for the visual comparison of carving and construction. Dimensions of objects are not given, and little or no documentation is provided.

Kirk, John T. *American Chairs: Queen Anne and Chippendale.* New York: Alfred A. Knopf, 1972. xi+208 pp.; 252 illustrations, appendix, indexes.

Kirk emphasizes the regional approach to American furniture through a study of construction and design details and an analysis of regional aesthetics. Six areas of production are examined: Philadelphia, Massachusetts, New York, Rhode Island, the Connecticut valley, and the South. In the appendix, Kirk links the study of regional furniture to the research on linguistic patterns discerned by Hans Kurath in his work on the distribution of word usage and pronunciation throughout New England. Although Kirk's approach is a visual and an aesthetic one, as in his other work he makes use of the objects as documents of the nature of eighteenth-century society.

Kirk, John T. *American Furniture and the British Tradition to 1830.* New York: Alfred A. Knopf, 1982. xviii+397 pp.; 1,508 black and white and color illustrations, indexes.

Kirk was the first modern scholar seriously to investigate the relationship between American and English furniture, and this important study is the culmination of twenty years of research. Divided into two parts, the book includes a section of nine chapters devoted to "issues relating British to American furniture" and an encyclopedic visual survey, arranged by form, of more than 1,200 objects of British and American manufacture. Kirk debunks many myths concerning the unique quality and originality of American furniture, stressing links in the Anglo-American handling of ornament and construction. With a visual approach in which the objects themselves are used as evidence, he emphasizes a sensitivity of line as the distinctive quality of American furniture and recognizes the innovative aspects of Newport block-and-shell furniture. This is an essential work for those who wish to confront American furniture in a meaningful context, and it is a good example of the derivation of cultural information from a close visual scrutiny of objects.

Kirk, John T. *Early American Furniture: How to Recognize, Evaluate, Buy, and Care for the Most Beautiful Pieces— High-Style, Country, Primitive, and Rustic.* New York: Alfred A. Knopf, 1970. xii+208 pp.; 204 illustrations, 2 line drawings, index.

It is Kirk's gift to be able to *see* furniture and to communicate his understanding of form and ornament to others. This introduction remains the best guide to the essential skill of learning to look. It is not a documentary history of furniture styles, construction, or makers, but rather a primer on how to evaluate the proportion and organization of an object, how to assess the role of small details, and how to recognize the various sources on which an object is based. The classification of objects into the categories included in the subtitle occasionally can be confusing, but the essential point—that objects are made in varying degrees of sophistication and that comparisons should be made between objects of related type—is clear and remains sound. A section on fakes, reproductions, and restorations is helpful, although it is now thought that the chest of drawers illustrated as figure 183 is indeed, at best, the upper case of a high chest to which a new base has been added.

Litchfield County Furniture, 1730–1850. Exhibition catalogue. [Litchfield, Conn.: Litchfield Historical Society, 1969]. 124 pp.; illustrations, 78 illustrated entries, map.

This is a catalogue of seventy-eight objects made in northwestern Connecticut, particularly in Litchfield, county seat and center of local cabinetmaking. Among the more important objects included are several sideboards by Silas E. Cheney, the most productive maker in the federal period; two chests attributed to the elusive Bates How of the Kent-Canaan area; and a selection of chairs by the Hitchcock factory and its local competitors. Capsule biographies of local makers are included. For an update on the entries on furniture associated with the Booth family of Woodbury, see Edward S. Cooke, Jr., *Fiddlebacks and Crooked-backs.*

Lockwood, Luke Vincent. *Colonial Furniture in America.* 3d ed. 2 vols. New York: Charles Scribner's Sons, 1926. Vol. 1, x+398 pp.; vol. 2, 354 pp.; 1,003 illustrations, index.

First published in 1901, this work was reissued in an expanded, two-volume format in 1913. Another printing of the second edition, reduced in scale, appeared in 1921. The third and last edition of 1926 included "Supplementary Chapters" and added 113 illustrations; this was reprinted (two volumes in one) in 1951 and later. Lockwood's stylistic survey was based on a visual analysis of the material, and most of the text is devoted to a written description of the objects illustrated, emphasizing the architectural nature of the moldings and analyzing the success of the design. The objects are arranged by form and chronologically within each section; volume 1 contains case furniture and looking glasses; volume 2 is devoted to seating furniture, tables, and clocks and contains the supplementary chapters. Lockwood (1872–1951) had a long career as collector, author, and museum professional, and his many activities included participation in the Hudson-Fulton exhibition of 1909 and the establishment of influential period rooms in Brooklyn Museum and Museum of the City of New York. This book enjoyed a long life as a principal survey of American furniture and retained its influence for many years.

Luther, Clair Franklin. *The Hadley Chest.* Hartford, Conn.: Case, Lockwood and Brainard Co., 1935. xvi+144 pp.; illustrations, plates.
——— . *Supplemental List of Hadley Chests Discovered since Publication of the Book in 1935, Together with Changes in Ownership as Reported.* Hartford, Conn.: Case, Lockwood and Brainard Co., 1938. 4 pp.

Luther, minister of the Second Congregational Church in Amherst, Massachusetts, devoted years to his pursuit of the Hadley-type chest, a type of object from the Connecticut valley decorated with an allover pattern of tulips and leaves. His 1935 monograph included a catalogue of 109 examples known at that time; a short supplement added three years later brought the total to 114. Subsequent research has pushed that number to 125 or more. These works are still used routinely as pictorial sources, although it is recognized that Luther was overzealous in attempting to link these chests to specific makers and to specific owners on the basis of detective work that was more creative than sound. His pictures and objective data continue to be valuable; his brief text, largely surpassed by later work, nevertheless remains a delight to read, possessing style and flavor not usually encountered in writings on American furniture. Like several other early authors, such as Russell Hawes Kettell, Luther was interested in the microscopic identification of woods. More recent research on the Hadley-type chests has been done by Patricia E. Kane, John T. Kirk, and Philip Zea, and the reader should use Luther only in conjunction with their work.

Lyon, Irving Whitall. *The Colonial Furniture of New England: A Study of the Domestic Furniture in Use in the Seventeenth and Eighteenth Centuries.* Introduction by Dean A. Fales, Jr. 1891, 1925. Reprint. New York: E. P. Dutton, 1977. xxvi+285 pp.; 113 illustrations, appendix, index.

Lyon (1840–96), a Hartford doctor, was an early collector of furniture and decorative arts. Possessed of a logical and analytical mind, his interest in American furniture resulted in this work, the first book on the subject, published in 1891 and reissued with some revisions in 1892 and 1925. The 1977 reprint cited here contains a good introduction by Fales that places Lyon and his book in context. Lyon introduced many techniques still standard in decorative arts research (including the in-depth analysis of estate inventories, the examination of newspaper advertisements, and the study of cabinetmakers' price books), and he traveled abroad to investigate the English origins of seventeenth-century American objects, his greatest love. Some of Lyon's collection eventually was acquired by Francis P. Garvan and given to Yale; Lyon's notebooks, diaries, and papers are in Winterthur Library, along with those of his son, Irving P. Lyon, a noted furniture scholar.

McClelland, Nancy. *Duncan Phyfe and the English Regency, 1795–1830.* Foreword by Edward Knoblock. 1939. Reprint. New York: Dover Publications, 1980. xxix + 364 pp.; 295 plates, bibliography, index.

McClelland is particularly strong in delineating the English background for Phyfe's work and in placing his shop's production in the context of his competitors, both in New York City and elsewhere. Attributions and some of the documentation should be accepted cautiously. Good material on some of Phyfe's customers is provided that is useful in tracing the diffusion and influence of his work. This is still a good place to begin research on Phyfe, although it must be supplemented by more recent work, especially Michael Brown, "Duncan Phyfe" (M.A. thesis, University of Delaware, 1978).

McElroy, Cathryn J. "Furniture in Philadelphia: The First Fifty Years." In *American Furniture and Its Makers: Winterthur Portfolio 13,* edited by Ian M. G. Quimby, pp. 61–80. Chicago and London: University of Chicago Press for the Henry Francis du Pont Winterthur Museum, 1979. 19 illustrations.

Based on McElroy's Winterthur thesis, this remains the only modern monograph on Philadelphia furniture made before 1730. She examines regional characteristics of form and ornament, illustrates a sampling of surviving objects, and traces the popularity and prices of forms through an intensive inventory study.

Maryland Queen Anne and Chippendale Furniture of the Eighteenth Century. Exhibition catalogue. Baltimore: October House for the Baltimore Museum of Art, 1968. 128 pp.; 76 illustrated entries.

This pioneering loan exhibition included entries for seventy-six objects, photographs of known labels of Maryland cabinetmakers, and lists of Maryland cabinetmakers and clockmakers with brief biographical information on each maker. William Voss Elder's introduction and entries are particularly helpful in drawing distinctions between Maryland furniture and its closely related counterparts from the Philadelphia area. More recent work is contained in Luke Beckerdite, "A Problem of Identification: Philadelphia and Baltimore Styles in the Eighteenth Century," *Journal of Early Southern Decorative Arts* 12, no. 1 (May 1986): 21–64.

Melchor, James R., N. Gordon Lohr, and Marilyn S. Melchor. *Eastern Shore, Virginia, Raised-Panel Furniture, 1730–1830.* Norfolk: Chrysler Museum, 1982. 135 pp.; 7 color plates, 2 tables, 107 illustrated entries, bibliography.

This work deals with more than 100 clothespresses, chests, flat-wall cupboards, bookcases, and turkey-breast cupboards produced in Northampton and Accomack counties in a distinctive, conservative local style. A strong emphasis is placed on the relationship of the objects to architecture and the derivation of designs from architectural pattern books. Numerous detail photographs and line drawings accompany the text; however, the book is marred by inelegant design and typography. This work expands on the brief treatment of Eastern Shore furniture in Wallace Gusler, *Furniture of Williamsburg and Eastern Virginia, 1710–1790.*

Miller, Edgar G., Jr. *American Antique Furniture: A Book for Amateurs.* 2 vols. Baltimore: Lord Baltimore Press, 1937. 1,114 pp.; 2,115 illustrations, index.

A Dover reprint of 1966 has given this book a life longer than it perhaps deserves. It is an encyclopedic survey, touching on all styles of furniture from the seventeenth century to about 1840, although emphasis is given to the period 1730–1820. Volume 1 contains general considerations and chapters devoted to seating furniture and case furniture; volume 2 deals with mirrors, tables and stands, and clocks and includes a host of appendixes. This work should be regarded today as primarily of historiographic interest and as a picture resource.

Miller, V. Isabelle. *Furniture by New York Cabinetmakers, 1650 to 1860.* Exhibition catalogue. New York: Museum of the City of New York, 1956. 84 pp.; 144 illustrated entries.

Only about a third of the 144 objects included in this catalogue are illustrated, which seriously hampers its usefulness for the general student. The catalogue is primarily a checklist, but it does record many documented examples in both public and private collections. A few important seventeenth-century objects from Long Island are included. This work represents an update of Joseph Downs and Ruth Ralston, *A Loan Exhibition of New York State Furniture with Contemporary Accessories* (New York: Metropolitan Museum of Art, 1934).

Montgomery, Charles F. *American Furniture: The Federal Period in the Henry Francis du Pont Winterthur Museum.* Foreword by Henry Francis du Pont; photographs by Gilbert Ask. New York: Viking Press, a Winterthur Book, 1966. 497 pp.; black and white and color illustrations, bibliography, index.

This catalogue of federal-period furniture at Winterthur is more than that: it remains the best history of American furniture between 1790 and 1820. It begins with five chapters setting the background of furniture in this period, covering the business of cabinetmaking, price books (here analyzed thoroughly for the first time), the woods used in American furniture (here explored extensively for the first time), upholstery and furnishing fabrics (written by Florence M. Montgomery), and the principles of connoisseurship and attribution. This section is followed by a catalogue, arranged by form, of 491 objects. Also included are details of carving and of cabinetmakers' labels and stamps; biographies of cabinetmakers; and an extensive bibliography.

Montgomery, Charles F., and Patricia E. Kane, eds. *American Art, 1750–1800: Towards Independence*. Exhibition catalogue. Boston: New York Graphic Society for the Yale University Art Gallery and the Victoria and Albert Museum, 1976. 320 pp.; black and white and color illustrations, appendixes, index.

This bicentennial exhibition marked the first time that American decorative arts had been exhibited in England. Spearheaded by Montgomery, it was the last major project of his productive career. The catalogue includes an essay devoted to a stylistic survey of American furniture from 1730 to 1820. The five introductory essays include those by Montgomery on regional preferences and characteristics, 1750–1800, a summary statement on the importance of craft specialization as the factor behind regional characteristics, and Jules D. Prown on style in art, 1750–1800. Much attention is given throughout the book to questions of dependence versus independence in American work, although in the final analysis no clear picture is presented, and American objects generally are regarded in a filiopietistic light. *See also* "Surveys."

Morse, John D., ed. *Country Cabinetwork and Simple City Furniture*. Winterthur Conference Report 1969. Charlottesville: University Press of Virginia for the Henry Francis du Pont Winterthur Museum, 1970. xiv+311 pp.; 57 illustrations, glossary.

This volume contains four traditional essays on furniture and craftsmen (Benno M. Forman on Massachusetts furniture, Charles F. Hummel on the Dominy family, Charles S. Parsons on the Dunlap family, and Nancy Goyne Evans on furniture made and used in Philadelphia) and more theoretical essays by Wendell D. Garrett, R. Peter Mooz, and Bruce R. Buckley on consumers' taste, style, and craftsmen. The goal of the conference was to answer a bevy of questions concerning the evaluation and definition of the "thorny subject" of country furniture, still a worrisome problem for many students of American furniture. These essays, written from a variety of theoretical viewpoints, represent an early attempt to focus attention on the context of furniture and its production.

Moses, Michael. *Master Craftsmen of Newport: The Townsends and Goddards*. Cosponsored by Israel Sack, Inc. Tenafly, N.J.: MMI Americana Press, 1984. xxii+361 pp.; black and white illustrations, 24 color plates, appendixes, bibliography.

Moses's in-depth study in connoisseurship is aimed at "authenticating" the work of John Townsend, John Goddard, and other members of the Goddard–Townsend family of Newport cabinetmakers between 1740 and 1790. He presents a methodology emphasizing a three-pronged test of authenticity based on construction, ornament, and documentation.

When an "unknown" object is compared with a documented example, it is said to be "associated with" the craftsmen if there is a strong similarity in one of the three areas; "authenticated to" if two of the three mesh; and "made by" if there is congruence on all three criteria. The system works well when there is a large body of documented examples to form a control (as with John Townsend) and less well when the body of documented objects is smaller. The text is by Moses; captions are by members of the Sack family of furniture dealers.

Museum of Fine Arts, Boston. *Paul Revere's Boston, 1735–1818*. Contributions by Jonathan L. Fairbanks, Wendy A. Cooper, Anne Farnam, Brock W. Jobe, and Martha B. Katz-Hyman. Exhibition catalogue. Boston: By the museum, 1975; distributed by New York Graphic Society. 234 pp.; approximately 180 black and white and color illustrations, bibliography, checklist.

The material world of Boston—before, during, and after the Revolution—is the focus of this bicentennial exhibition catalogue which includes portraits, silver, ceramics, and other kinds of objects as well as furniture. Only about thirty-five examples of furniture are illustrated and discussed in detailed captions, although many more were included in the show and are represented in the checklist. The objects illustrated chart the general history of style in Boston furniture throughout the period and offer some particularly interesting juxtapositions of English objects known to have been owned in Boston and American objects of related design. For example, the English linen press owned by the Apthorp family and suggested as the inspiration for Boston bombé furniture (cat. 49) is discussed in relation to a desk and bookcase made by Benjamin Frothingham, Sr., or Jr., of Charlestown (cat. 50). Similarly, an English double chair-back settee is played off against a Massachusetts example (cats. 51, 52), and a comparison of an English side chair with an interlaced splat and asymmetrical knee carving (cat. 53) to a Boston armchair (cat. 54), demonstrating the American interpretation of English ornament. The emphasis is on high-style and documented objects, and some major monuments of American furniture are included, such as the John Cogswell chest-on-chest of 1782 (cat. 265) and several objects attributed to John and Thomas Seymour. *See also* "Surveys."

Naeve, Milo M. *The Classical Presence in American Art*. Chicago: Art Institute of Chicago, 1978. iv+36 pp.; 47 black and white and color illustrations, line drawings.

Naeve presents a brief yet helpful study of the pervasive influence of classicism in decorative arts from the seventeenth century to the present, illustrated with examples from the Art Institute of Chicago.

New England Furniture: Essays in Memory of Benno M. Forman. Old-Time New England, vol. 72, no. 259. Boston: Society for the Preservation of New England

Antiquities, 1987. xvii+354 pp.; 218 illustrations, 5 tables.

This anthology contains nine essays that deal with furniture from all six New England states from the seventeenth to the mid nineteenth centuries. The contributions, edited by Brock W. Jobe, include Philip Zea's study of the Hadley chest tradition in western Massachusetts; Gerald W. R. Ward's notes on Connecticut cupboards; a case study of John Cahoone of Newport by Jeanne Vibert; Luke Beckerdite's essay on carving practices in eighteenth-century Boston; Jobe's introduction to the furniture of Portsmouth, New Hampshire; Myrna Kaye's study of the furniture owned in the Sayward-Wheeler house in York, Maine; a survey of Vermont federal furniture by William N. Hosley, Jr.; an examination of transparent furniture finishes in New England, 1700–1825, by Robert D. Mussey, Jr.; and an essay on the upholstery trade in America by Andrew Passeri and Robert F. Trent based largely on two important inventories. A bibliography of Forman's works is also included.

New London County Furniture, 1640–1840. Exhibition catalogue. New London, Conn.: Lyman Allyn Museum, 1974. x+134 pp.; 114 illustrations, appendixes, bibliography.

In this catalogue of 114 objects associated with New London, Norwich, Preston, Stonington, Colchester, and other towns of southeastern Connecticut, emphasis is placed on the work of Samuel Loomis, Benjamin Burnham, and other makers of the "Colchester Chippendale style." The most innovative aspect of the work was the attempt to bring precision to the study of drawer construction and shell carving through a technical and pictorial analysis aimed at organizing related groups and thus providing a basis for attributions. The classification system for drawer construction, for example, emphasized "not the number or the size of the dovetails, but their general arrangement and the handling of the drawer bottoms in relation to the drawer front and sides," and, perhaps more important, the "angle of the dovetail" (p. 94). Although this system allowed the authors to "make some progress in attributions," the results are often confusing and must be regarded as suggestive rather than conclusive. Capsule biographies for local makers are given in an appendix. More recent work on this area is presented by Robert F. Trent and Nancy Lee Nelson in a special 1985 issue of the *Connecticut Historical Society Bulletin* devoted to chairmaking in New London County.

New York Furniture before 1840 in the Collection of the Albany Institute of History and Art. Cogswell Fund Series, no. 2. Albany: Albany Institute of History and Art, 1962. 63 pp.; approximately 50 illustrations, bibliography.

This selective catalogue of a significant group of objects made in New York City and the Albany area includes a group of fourteen objects from Cherry Hill and Albany, including several with documented histories in the Van Rensselaer family, four objects acquired by Stephen Van Rensselaer IV

in 1817 from Charles-Honoré Lannuier, and twenty-seven other objects, many with Hudson valley histories. The magnificent mahogany dining table originally owned by Sir William Johnson (1715–74), superintendent of Indian affairs in North America, is perhaps the single most important object in the collection.

Nineteenth-Century America: Furniture and Other Decorative Arts. Introduction by Berry B. Tracy; furniture texts by Marilynn Johnson; other decorative arts texts by Marvin D. Schwartz and Suzanne Boorsch. Exhibition catalogue. New York: Metropolitan Museum of Art, 1970; distributed by New York Graphic Society. xxxii+[232] pp.; line drawings, 298 black and white and color illustrated entries, index, bibliography.

Although primarily of importance as the first major treatment of American decorative arts made between 1840 and the end of the century, this catalogue contains about fifty entries on furniture made before 1840. The approach is purely aesthetic, and all objects illustrated, including many of the masterpieces of American furniture, are high-style products of major urban shops, such as those of Charles-Honoré Lannuier, Anthony Quervelle, Duncan Phyfe, and John and Thomas Seymour. The introductory essay by Tracy, then curator of the American Wing at the Metropolitan, notes three phases of American neoclassicism: early federal design (1795–1815), late federal design (1815–24), and a Greek revival era (1825–45). *See also* "American Furniture, 1820–1920"; "Surveys."

Nutting, Wallace. *Furniture of the Pilgrim Century, 1620–1720, including Colonial Utensils and Hardware.* Boston: Marshall Jones Co., 1921. ix+587 pp.; approximately 1,000 illustrations, index.

——. *Furniture of the Pilgrim Century (of American Origin), 1620–1720, with Maple and Pine to 1800, Including Colonial Utensils and Wrought-Iron House Hardware into the Nineteenth Century.* Rev. and enl. ed. Framingham, Mass.: Old America Co., 1924. 716 pp.; 1,559 plates, index.

Although Nutting had published *A Windsor Handbook* in 1917, these volumes represent his first major study of early furniture. The two editions are different enough to qualify as separate works. Each is a survey, arranged by form, with numerous illustrations and, somewhat unusual for Nutting, rather lengthy commentary. In the first edition, illustration and text appear on the same page in most cases, facilitating the use of the book. For the 1924 revised edition, Nutting stated, "practically every page has been rewritten and about 600 additional articles have been illustrated," and a few corrections were made and a few objects omitted. Commentary and illustrations were separated by several pages, making this edition more difficult to use. Although the illustrations in these volumes were incorporated into Nutting's *Furniture Treasury*, most of the text was not; thus they occasionally contain nuggets of information of use to the modern researcher. Reprints of both editions have appeared: Bonanza Books reprinted the 1921 edition in 1977, and Dover issued a two-volume reprint of the 1924 edition in 1965. The authenticity of the wrought-iron work illustrated in these volumes has been questioned.

Nutting, Wallace. *Furniture Treasury (Mostly of American Origin): All Periods of American Furniture with Some Foreign Examples in America, also American Hardware and Household Utensils.* (Vol. 3 subtitled, *Being a Record of Designers, Details of Designs and Structure, with Lists of Clock Makers in America, and a Glossary of Furniture Terms, Richly Illustrated.*) 3 vols. Framingham, Mass.: Old America Co., 1928–33. Vols. 1 and 2, approximately 5,000 illustrations, index; vol. 3, 550 pp.; line drawings, index.

Regarded as the bible of furniture collectors for more than fifty years, Nutting's *Furniture Treasury* remains an unsurpassed pictorial dictionary of American furniture; however, the terse captions cannot be relied on, and there have been many changes in ownership and attribution since 1928. (For an analysis of some of these changes, see Helen Comstock, "Wallace Nutting and the *Furniture Treasury* in Retrospect," *Antiques* 80, no. 5 [November 1961]: 460–63.) Volume 1 is devoted to case furniture and tables; volume 2 to chairs, clocks, and other forms. Volume 3 contains line drawings and a good deal of text, written in Nutting's idiosyncratic and entertaining style on such matters as reproductions, fakes, collecting, and numerous other topics. Nutting has been described by William L. Dulaney as "a man of tremendous energy and monumental ego, [who] pronounced upon, photographed, reproduced, bought and sold, and lectured about American antiques with a sweep unmatched before or since" ("Wallace Nutting, Collector and Entrepreneur," in *American Furniture and Its Makers: Winterthur Portfolio 13*, ed. Ian M. G. Quimby [Chicago: University of Chicago Press, 1979], p. 47). Most of Nutting's collection is now at Wadsworth Atheneum in Hartford, Connecticut.

Philadelphia: Three Centuries of American Art. Exhibition catalogue. Philadelphia: Philadelphia Museum of Art, 1976. xxiv+665 pp.; 546 illustrated entries, bibliography, index.

This mammoth catalogue, arranged chronologically, includes some of the best modern writing on Philadelphia furniture. The objects include ten dating from 1676 to 1726, twenty from 1726 to 1776, and twenty from 1776 to 1826. The majority of the entries are by Beatrice B. Garvan, with David Hanks and Page Talbott each contributing a handful of entries on federal-period objects. Lengthy biographies of craftsmen are included for documented objects. Due to the nature of the book (a hefty, triple-column tome with small type, scattered entries, and references placed in parentheses in the text), it is almost impossible to gain an overview of early Philadelphia furniture here. This is particularly distressing since no modern survey of the subject exists.

Plain and Elegant, Rich and Common: Documented New Hampshire Furniture, 1750–1850. Exhibition catalogue. Concord: New Hampshire Historical Society, 1979. 153 pp.; 59 illustrations, 2 maps.

This catalogue presents objects produced in five areas of New Hampshire (the Piscataqua region and the Merrimack, Contoocook and Souhegan, Connecticut, and Saco valleys). Most of the objects date from 1800 to 1850; only a handful can be traced to the last half of the eighteenth century. Biographical sketches of craftsmen whose work appears in the volume are included. This work should be used in conjunction with other catalogues: Richard H. Randall, Jr., *The Decorative Arts of New Hampshire, 1725–1825* (Manchester, N.H.: Currier Gallery, 1964); *The Decorative Arts of New Hampshire: A Sesquicentennial Exhibition* (Concord: New Hampshire Historical Society, 1973); and *The Dunlaps and Their Furniture. See also* "American Furniture, 1820–1920."

Plain and Ornamental: Delaware Furniture, 1740–1890. Introduction by Charles G. Dorman; essay and checklist by Deborah Dependahl Waters. Exhibition catalogue. Wilmington: Historical Society of Delaware, 1984. 60 pp.; 52 illustrations, checklist, index.

Representing the most recent work on Delaware furniture, this catalogue contains a brief introduction by Dorman, author of an earlier biographical dictionary of local makers. His introductory essay and fifty-four catalogue entries summarize what is known about Delaware furniture and stress the conservative nature of local production, particularly vis-à-vis high-style objects from neighboring Philadelphia. As in so many cases (one thinks of the Salem–Boston relationship), patrons in small, micropolitan towns fell within the hegemony of craftsmen in major urban centers and relied on local makers for simple city furniture and repairs. The emphasis here is on documented examples; labeled or attributed objects by John White, James and Daniel McDowell, Ziba Ferris, George Whitelock, members of the Janvier family, and other craftsmen at work before 1820 are included.

Poesch, Jessie J. *Early Furniture of Louisiana.* Exhibition catalogue. New Orleans: Louisiana State Museum, 1972. xviii+85 pp.; approximately 75 illustrations, 61 line drawings.

Poesch's study is the first of Louisiana furniture from the colonial (ca. 1750–1803) and early Republic (1803–ca. 1830) periods. Most of the forty colonial objects illustrated here have a decidedly French appearance, although "they are more austere and less decorated" than their Continental counterparts (p. 1). French influence is also apparent in many of the twenty-one federal-period objects in the catalogue. The most characteristic local forms were the armoire, small tables with thin, tapering, cabriole legs, and slat-back chairs. Poesch takes an important look at a substantial body of early objects that fall outside the mainstream of Anglo-American taste.

Quimby, Ian M. G., ed. *Arts of the Anglo-American Community in the Seventeenth Century.* Winterthur Conference Report 1974. Charlottesville: University Press of Virginia for the Henry Francis du Pont Winterthur Museum, 1975. x+299 pp.; 106 illustrations.

Although each of the nine essays in this volume will be of interest, the contributions by Christopher Gilbert, Robert F. Trent, and Patricia E. Kane are particularly valuable. Gilbert's "Regional Traditions in English Vernacular Furniture" provides an introduction to the sources of design for much American furniture. Trent's "Joiners and Joinery of Middlesex County, Massachusetts, 1630–1730" is an interpretive examination of the documentation provided in his Winterthur thesis. In "The Seventeenth-Century Furniture of the Connecticut Valley: The Hadley Chest Reappraised," Kane builds on the work of Clair Franklin Luther and sets forth a visual analysis of Hadley chests that divides this group of some 125 objects into eight basic groups and several subgroups on the basis of the handling of the Hadley motif of the tulip, leaf, and scroll. Kane's framework has subsequently been refined by Philip Zea in his 1984 Winterthur thesis. *See also* "Surveys."

Randall, Richard H., Jr. *American Furniture in the Museum of Fine Arts, Boston.* Boston: By the museum, 1965. xvii+276 pp.; 218 illustrations, indexes.

The first modern catalogue of a major museum collection, Randall's work has stood the test of time well and recently has been reissued by the Museum of Fine Arts in paperback. It contains entries on 218 objects, but it does not include any of the museum's furniture published in Edwin J. Hipkiss's earlier catalogue of the Karolik collection. Objects are arranged by form, and each catalogue entry contains detailed information on the construction and condition of the object, as well as dimensions, references, a summary of the object's history, and a commentary: in short, Randall borrowed art historical cataloguing methods and established the basic format for modern collection catalogues. Of the objects included, 95 percent are attributed to New England. The Museum of Fine Arts has continued to acquire outstanding examples of American furniture, of course, particularly under the active leadership of Jonathan L. Fairbanks, curator of American decorative arts and sculpture. For highlights of recent acquisitions, see Fairbanks, "A Decade of Collecting American Decorative Arts and Sculpture at the Museum of Fine Arts, Boston," *Antiques* 120, no. 3 (September 1981): 590–636.

Richards, Nancy E. "Furniture of the Lower Connecticut River Valley: The Hartford Area, 1785–1810." In *Winterthur Portfolio 4*, edited by Richard K. Doud, pp. 1–25. Charlottesville: University Press of Virginia for the Henry Francis du Pont Winterthur Museum, 1968. 26 illustrations.

Richards's richly documented study of federal-period furniture in Connecticut's leading commercial center emphasizes the connections between Hartford and New York City and examines several shop traditions in detail.

Rodriquez Roque, Oswaldo. *American Furniture at Chipstone.* Madison: University of Wisconsin Press, 1984. xl+439 pp.; approximately 200 black and white illustrations, 18 color plates, indexes.

This catalogue of 199 objects owned by Mr. and Mrs. Stanley Stone of Milwaukee, Wisconsin, includes case furniture, clocks, seating furniture, tables and stands, and other forms. This extraordinary private collection was formed by the Stones, with the help of John Walton and other dealers, in the years since 1946 and is particularly strong in eighteenth-century Rhode Island furniture, although examples from most regions of early America are included. This catalogue, which begins with a short essay on style in American furniture from 1650 to 1820, provides excellent photographs and detailed information on objects which, as of this writing, are not readily available for study.

Sack, Albert. *Fine Points of Furniture: Early American.* Foreword by Israel Sack; introduction by John Meredith Graham III. New York: Crown Publishers, 1950. xvi+303 pp.; approximately 600 illustrations.

A classic in the field, this book arranges objects by form and usually in groups of three and then evaluates them visually as being "good," "better," or "best." The classification system emphasizes "quality" and is based on subjective, aesthetic value judgments guided by principles of interest to dealers and collectors. Sack is a partner in one of the leading firms specializing in antique furniture and is the son of the firm's founder, Israel Sack. A brief section on "restorations, replacements, and imperfections" suggests guidelines for examining old furniture.

St. George, Robert Blair. "Style and Structure in the Joinery of Dedham and Medfield, Massachusetts, 1635–1685." In *American Furniture and Its Makers: Winterthur Portfolio 13,* edited by Ian M. G. Quimby, pp. 1–46. Chicago: University of Chicago Press for the Henry Francis du Pont Winterthur Museum, 1979. 31 illustrations, appendix.

———. *The Wrought Covenant: Source Material for the Study of Craftsmen and Community in Southeastern New England, 1620–1700.* Exhibition catalogue. Brockton, Mass.: Brockton Art Center/Fuller Memorial, 1979. 132 pp.; illustrations, 83 illustrated entries, checklist, bibliography, appendix.

These two works represent an unusual blend of artifact study and historical ethnography. St. George's intent was to map the role of expressive behavior in everyday life and to integrate social history and material life through investigation of the rules governing society's transformation of natural materials into cultural artifacts. The methodology used in making attributions follows older traditions, but his interpretive structure was largely new to the field in 1979, and these works have continued to have a provocative affect on furniture scholarship. *The Wrought Covenant* includes sections explaining characteristic features of design and construction of objects produced in four distinct subregions in Plymouth Colony. Brief essays are followed by photographs, drawings, and detailed captions for each object. Section 2 lists information on the trade, working or vital dates, location, birthplace, and relationship to other artisans for 428 local woodworkers. Section 3 reprints inventories of tools owned by 15 joiners. Much of this material was further developed by St. George in "Retreat from the Wilderness: Pattern in the Domestic Environment of Southeastern New England, 1620–1700" (Ph.D. diss., University of Pennsylvania, 1982) and in "Fathers, Sons, and Identity: Folk Artisans in Southeastern New England, 1620–1700," in *The Craftsman in Early America*, ed. Ian M. G. Quimby (New York: W. W. Norton, 1984), pp. 89–125. "Style and Structure" is a more complete exploration of artisans in one area, Dedham and Medfield, Massachusetts, and the relationship of the artifacts they produced to the development of those communities. Short biographies of 25 joiners follow the main body of the text. *See also* "Craftsmen."

Scherer, John L. *New York Furniture at the New York State Museum*. Old Town Alexandria, Va.: Highland House Publishers, 1984. 142 pp.; 132 illustrations, bibliography, index.

Scherer has compiled a catalogue of 132 objects, about half of which date before 1830. Most of the objects are labeled or marked by their maker or can be traced to their original owner; thus, this catalogue is an important resource for the identification of unmarked objects and is a significant addition to the relatively scarce literature on early New York furniture. Most of the objects have been acquired by the museum in the last fifteen years, many with the assistance of Wunsch Americana Foundation. Although many of the examples were made in New York City, furniture from other parts of the state is also well represented.

Schiffer, Margaret Berwind. *Furniture and Its Makers of Chester County, Pennsylvania*. Philadelphia: University of Pennsylvania Press, 1966. 280 pp. + 168 illustrations; bibliography.

This book consists almost entirely of an alphabetical list of woodworking craftsmen at work in this rural county outside Philadelphia between 1682 and 1850, followed by a useful gathering of illustrations of local production. A brief section is devoted to characteristics and peculiarities of Chester County objects, particularly the use of berry, herringbone, and line inlay, the local preference for the spice-box form,

and the existence of a distinctive group of Octoraro furniture (named for a creek that forms the western boundary of the county) featuring high, ogee bracket feet with circular cutouts and other characteristics.

Semowich, Charles J., comp. *American Furniture Craftsmen Working prior to 1920: An Annotated Bibliography*. Art Reference Collection, no. 7. Westport, Conn., and London: Greenwood Press, 1984. xi + 381 pp.; appendix, indexes.

Semowich has arranged more than 2,000 entries into four sections: biographies of craftsmen, studies of groups of craftsmen, general works, and furniture trade catalogues. The appendix includes a list of periodicals dealing with the furniture industry and a selected list of manuscript repositories. The indexes (craftsman-biographical, author-title, and subject) are an essential guide to materials that might otherwise be overlooked because of the organization of the book. The quality of the annotations is uneven, the sections on trade catalogues and manuscripts are incomplete, and there are more errors, typographical and otherwise, than there should be in a book of this kind, but it remains the only single-volume bibliography devoted exclusively to American furniture.

Singleton, Esther. *The Furniture of Our Forefathers*. Notes on the illustrations by Russell Sturgis. 1900–1901. Reprint. New York: Benjamin Blom, 1970. xxvi + 655 pp.; approximately 400 illustrations, index.

One of the earliest works on American furniture, this study deals with southern, New England, and New York furniture from the seventeenth until the early nineteenth centuries. Like Irving Whitall Lyon, Singleton (1865–1930) made use of primary documentation, especially in the form of citations from estate inventories, although her statements are not footnoted. She also reprints part of the 1795 Philadelphia cabinetmakers' price book, a type of resource not fully used until Charles F. Montgomery's work in the 1960s. The annotations on the illustrations were provided by Sturgis (1836–1909), an architect and architectural historian.

Snyder, John J., Jr., ed. *Philadelphia Furniture and Its Makers*. Antiques Magazine Library II. New York: Main Street/Universe Books, 1975. 158 pp.; 207 illustrations, index.

This anthology of twenty-six articles originally published in *Antiques* between 1924 and 1975 is arranged in rough chronological order. Introduced with brief notes by Snyder, these articles cover forms, craftsmen, and styles in Philadelphia-area furniture between about 1690 and 1850, with an emphasis on eighteenth-century objects.

Southern Furniture, 1640–1820. Exhibition catalogue. New York: Magazine Antiques, 1952. 64 pp.; approximately 182 illustrations. Also published as a special issue of *Antiques* 61, no. 1 (January 1952): 38–100.

Sponsored by *Antiques*, Colonial Williamsburg, and Virginia Museum, this loan exhibition at the latter institution was the first serious attempt to investigate American southern furniture. The project was spearheaded by Helen Comstock, with the assistance of E. Milby Burton, Joe Kindig, Jr., Charles Navis, Frank L. Horton, Henry D. Green, Mrs. Charlton M. Theus, Alice Winchester, Eleanor Hume Offutt, and others. It organized southern objects into three categories (urban furniture from Charleston, furniture from tidewater Virginia and the related Virginia piedmont, and objects from the valley of Virginia and the related Carolina piedmont) and presented a pictorial survey that still serves as an introduction to the subject. Much new research on southern furniture has been conducted in the last three decades, stimulated in large part by this pioneering effort. Although the information contained here has been superseded in many cases by more recent regional and state monographs, the importance of this catalogue as a landmark in the historiography of American furniture cannot be overestimated.

Stoneman, Vernon C. *John and Thomas Seymour: Cabinetmakers in Boston, 1794–1816.* Boston: Special Publications, 1959. 393 pp.; approximately 300 black and white illustrations, 9 color plates, bibliography.

——. *A Supplement to John and Thomas Seymour: Cabinetmakers in Boston, 1794–1816.* Boston: Special Publications, 1965. [vi]+105 pp.; 75 illustrated entries.

Generally regarded today as the premier example of the phenomenon of overambitious attribution, Stoneman's 1959 monograph attributes about 250 examples of Boston federal-period furniture to John and Thomas Seymour's shop, although only a handful of documented examples were known. In his 1965 supplement, Stoneman attempted (rather lamely) to justify his approach, added some seventy-five objects to his group of works attributed to Seymour, and published a few more documented objects that had come to light since 1959. Simply put, Stoneman confused a regional style with a shop's production; nevertheless, his books are a valuable compilation of illustrations and are a constant reminder that furniture should be attributed to a specific shop only with a great deal of caution. His 1959 book was challenged by Richard H. Randall, Jr.'s, two-part article, "Works of Boston Cabinetmakers, 1795–1825," in *Antiques* (81, no. 2 [February 1962]: 186–89; no. 4 [April 1962]: 412–15), in which he pointed out the overreliance by Stoneman on small details of ornament, especially inlay, as a means of making attributions for furniture produced in an active marketplace in which specialist craftsmen were at work.

Swan, Mabel M. *Samuel McIntire, Carver, and the Sandersons, Early Salem Cabinet Makers.* Salem, Mass.: Essex Institute, 1934. 44 pp.; illustrations, index.

Swan was an indefatigable researcher in period documents, and her studies of Massachusetts furniture resulted in the discovery of numerous important documents and in the reattribution of several examples of furniture. For instance, her work in the Derby family papers at Essex Institute led to the discovery that the famous chest-on-chest with carved allegorical figures in the Yale collection, attributed for many years to McIntire, Joseph True, and others, was actually made by Stephen Badlam of Dorchester Lower Mills and carved by John and Simeon Skillin of Boston. Most of Swan's work resulted in articles published in *Antiques* or local historical society journals, as was the case with this essay which is an expanded version of "Elijah and Jacob Sanderson: Early Salem Cabinetmakers," *Essex Institute Historical Collections* 70, no. 4 (October 1934): 323–64. Here, Swan brought to light McIntire's work as a specialist carver in federal-period Salem and documented the extensive venture-cargo business of Jacob and Elijah Sanderson. Her work reprints a substantial body of original letters and lists of items shipped out of Salem by the Sandersons and other Salem cabinetmakers. She provides an underpinning for the understanding of relationships among craftsmen in the federal period and of the importance of specialists in the creation of regional characteristics.

The Swisegood School of Cabinetmaking. Text by Frank L. Horton and Carolyn J. Weekley; photography by Bradford J. Rauschenberg. Exhibition catalogue. Winston-Salem, N.C.: Museum of Early Southern Decorative Arts, 1973. Unpag.; 20 illustrations.

This monograph focuses on the case furniture of John Swisegood (1796–1874), his master, Mordici Collins, and other craftsmen associated with this shop tradition located in Davidson County in the North Carolina piedmont. Twenty examples are illustrated, most made of native black walnut and all in a restrained version of the federal style, although some may date as late as the 1840s. This work provides a good look at the retention of forms and the transmission of mechanical knowledge through several generations of a shop tradition. *See also* "American Furniture, 1820–1920."

Taylor, Lonn, and Dessa Bokides. *New Mexican Furniture, 1600–1940: The Origins, Survival, and Revival of Furniture Making in the Hispanic Southwest.* Photographs by Mary Peck; additional photography by Jim Bones. Museum of New Mexico Press Series in Southwestern Culture. Santa Fe: Museum of New Mexico Press, 1987. xvi+311 pp.; black and white illustrations, 268 black and white and color plates, glossary, bibliography, index.

The early chapters of this important work examine the relatively small group of furniture produced in the Spanish colonial tradition in New Mexico. The objects, fashioned primarily of Ponderosa pine, are traditional forms such as chests, chairs, tables, benches, and cabinets that feature such design and construction aspects as wedged through-tenons and wedged dovetails and shallow chip carving. Although much of the book deals with furniture making after 1820, this work serves to broaden the parameters of the study of early furniture. *See also* "American Furniture, 1820–1920."

Theus, Mrs. Charlton M. *Savannah Furniture, 1735–1825.* N.p., [1967]. xi+100 pp.; 23 illustrations, index.

In a pioneering study of southern furniture, Theus examines woods used in Savannah and coastal Georgia furniture, investigates the evidence presented by local estate inventories, and provides biographical information on local craftsmen. The types of furniture produced in Savannah are discussed and in some cases illustrated, and the presence of imported furniture is briefly investigated. Although not a sophisticated work and not readily available in most libraries, this study has not yet been superseded by a more recent monograph, although the venture cargo trade is more ably discussed in Katharine Wood Gross, "The Sources of Furniture Sold in Savannah, 1789–1815" (M.A. thesis, University of Delaware, 1967).

Trent, Robert F. "The Emery Attributions." *Essex Institute Historical Collections* 121, no. 3 (July 1985): 210–20. 5 illustrations, 2 tables.

This brief article is representative of the ongoing research on seventeenth-century furniture. Trent discusses a group of furniture (including the famous "vocabulary" chest at Winterthur) previously assigned to the Searle-Dennis workshops and here reattributed to the extended family of Emery joiners, turners, and carpenters in Newbury, Massachusetts. Included are a checklist of twenty-six objects and a discussion of their English and Continental prototypes and parallels.

Trent, Robert F. *Hearts and Crowns: Folk Chairs of the Connecticut Coast, 1710–1840, as Viewed in the Light of Henri Focillon's Introduction to "Art Populaire."* New Haven: New Haven Colony Historical Society, 1977. 101 pp.; approximately 90 illustrations, 7 drawings, appendix.

Trent begins with a short introduction that puts the work of Focillon (1881–1943), a professor of folklore at the Sorbonne and Yale, into historiographical perspective and discusses other theoretical models for the study of folk art. The translation of Focillon's introduction to *Art Populaire* (1931) makes this text widely available and is therefore a significant contribution to the literature. The analysis of coastal Connecticut chairs, although related to the documents, is predominantly visual. The chairs are used primarily to demonstrate concepts of the "abstraction" of forms by rural artisans and stylistic "drift" over time.

Trent, Robert F., ed. *Pilgrim Century Furniture: An Historical Survey.* Antiques Magazine Library 5. New York: Main Street/Universe Books, 1976. 168 pp.; approximately 265 black and white illustrations, 8 black and white and color plates, index.

This anthology of more than thirty articles and notes originally published in *Antiques* between 1923 and 1976 is the most usefully compiled and intelligently edited of the several volumes in the lapsed Antiques Magazine Library series. Trent grouped the articles into five thematic sections, dealing with the early collectors, the "Thomas Dennis Problem," early chairs, the "Connecticut River Valley Problem," and "Late Manifestations and the Emergence of Folk Styles." Included are articles of great historiographic interest by Irving P. Lyon, Clair Franklin Luther, Helen Park, Walter A. Dyer, Esther Stevens Frazer, and others, as well as more recent research by Patricia E. Kane and Benno M. Forman.

Trent, Robert F., with Nancy Lee Nelson. "New London County Joined Chairs, 1720–1790." *Connecticut Historical Society Bulletin* 50, no. 4 (Fall 1985). ix+195 pp.; approximately 65 illustrations, appendix.

A loan exhibition mounted by Connecticut Historical Society in 1985 resulted in this catalogue of sixty-two objects, primarily chairs and needlework. Following a brief introductory essay by Trent, catalogue entries are arranged into six groups, each representing the work of one or more related shop traditions. The entries on individual chairs are extensive and include information on maker, provenance, materials, and dimensions, with a detailed commentary on each object's history, construction, and design features. Needlework entries emphasize the relationship between documented needlework pictures and samplers and coverings on chairs by the same women. These connections help to document the historic ownership of the chairs in question. Based on Nelson's 1984 University of Delaware master's thesis, with significant additional research by Trent, this catalogue demonstrates how detailed genealogical and object research can identify ties between families of makers and families of owners, thus helping us to understand patterns of migration and consumption.

Ward, Gerald W. R. *American Case Furniture in the Mabel Brady Garvan and Other Collections at Yale University.* Photographs by Charles Uht. New Haven: Yale University Art Gallery, 1988. xv+485 pp.; 25 color plates, line drawings, 233 illustrated entries, appendix, index.

In this catalogue of 233 examples at Yale, arranged by form, all but about a dozen objects date before 1830, and the collection includes a broad geographical distribution. Included are some of the finest examples of American furniture known, such as the Boston chest of drawers with doors (cat. 51), and more representative examples as well. Entries are notable for the detailed descriptions of construction and wood use. The introductory essay deals with some of the symbolic and cultural meanings of furniture in a general way.

Ward, Gerald W. R., ed. *Perspectives on American Furniture.* New York and London: W. W. Norton for the Henry Francis du Pont Winterthur Museum, 1988. vi+360 pp.; 179 illustrations, index.

Based on papers originally delivered at the 1985 Winterthur Conference, this anthology includes several essays particularly relevant to the study of early furniture. In essays that assess previous work and suggest avenues for further research, Philip D. Zimmerman examines the usefulness of the concept of regionalism, and Edward S. Cooke, Jr., proposes that we look more carefully at furniture from the maker's point of view. In other chapters dealing with pre-1820 topics, John T. Kirk places early American furniture in an international context, William N. Hosley, Jr., traces the career of joiner Timothy Loomis of Windsor, Connecticut, in the mid eighteenth century, and Nancy Goyne Evans documents the marketing of painted seating furniture from 1750 to 1840. Although the other seven essays focus on topics ranging in date from about 1850 to the present, the methods used by several of the authors will be of interest to all furniture historians.

Warren, David B. *Bayou Bend: American Furniture, Paintings, and Silver from the Bayou Bend Collection.* Foreword by Ima Hogg. Houston: Museum of Fine Arts, 1975; distributed by New York Graphic Society. xvi+192 pp.; 355 black and white and color illustrations, index.

Hogg (1882–1975) was a leading collector of American decorative arts in the 1920s and later. Her collection, installed in some two dozen period rooms in Bayou Bend (a family home in Houston) was given to the Museum of Fine Arts in 1958 and opened to the public in 1966. This catalogue includes entries on some 200 examples of high-style American furniture dating from 1690 to 1815 and an additional chapter devoted to "traditional furniture and arts," as well as illustrations of the Bayou Bend period rooms. A new catalogue of the collection is in preparation. *See also* "Surveys."

Weidman, Gregory R. *Furniture in Maryland, 1740–1940: The Collection of the Maryland Historical Society.* Baltimore: By the society, 1984. 342 pp.; 24 color plates, 260 illustrated entries, checklist, bibliography, index.

This selective catalogue of 260 objects in the collection of Maryland Historical Society includes 180 examples dating before 1840. Each is treated with a standard catalogue entry, although references to condition and previous publication and exhibition history are not given, and notes on structure are often confined to the identification of woods. Most of the objects were made in Maryland, although a substantial number of examples were made elsewhere (particularly in Philadelphia and New York), thus providing at least a partial look at local consumption as well as production patterns. The strength of the collection is the many examples in the federal and empire styles (1790–1840). Arranged chronologically, the book is divided into three main sections, each prefaced by a thorough look at the furniture-making industry during each era. An appendix includes an alphabetical listing of some 4,500 people at work in the furniture industry in Maryland between 1740 and 1860. *See also* "American Furniture, 1820–1920."

Zimmerman, Philip D. "A Methodological Study in the Identification of Some Important Philadelphia Chippendale Furniture." In *American Furniture and Its Makers: Winterthur Portfolio 13*, edited by Ian M. G. Quimby, pp. 193–208. Chicago and London: University of Chicago Press for the Henry Francis du Pont Winterthur Museum, 1979. 9 illustrations.

Intrinsic data (derived from examination of the object) and extrinsic data (provenance, documentation, and evaluation of intrinsic data) are used to reevaluate a group of famous objects regarded in the past as "sample chairs" made by Benjamin Randolph to display his skills. Zimmerman's interpretation of the evidence suggests that they were made instead by Thomas Affleck for John Cadwalader in 1770. He emphasizes "the need to exercise caution in using carving as a means of furniture identification" and the need to study objects "in the full cultural context of which maker identification represents only a part" (p. 208).

Zimmerman, Philip D. "Workmanship as Evidence: A Model for Object Study." *Winterthur Portfolio 16*, no. 4 (Winter 1981): 283–307. 23 illustrations.

Zimmerman advocates a methodology for studying furniture based on examining objects for physical evidence that reveals "consistencies and differences of workmanship techniques instead of formalistic values" (p. 285). Borrowing from David Pye, he stresses the identification of different levels of workmanship, adding "the workmanship of habit" to Pye's workmanship of certainty and of risk. The goal of the research is to identify continuities in shop traditions, often through the study of small details (not unlike Bernard Berenson's reliance on small details for attributing Italian Renaissance paintings to various masters). After a discussion of other methods of analyzing objects and an explication of this approach, the methodology is applied to a group of Philadelphia Chippendale chairs. Zimmerman suggests that the "final object was seldom the product of a single design. Rather, it grew out of a combination of individually designed parts or sections—legs, backs, crest rails, and arms—fitted together" (p. 307).

American Furniture, 1820–1920

Kenneth L. Ames

SCHOLARSHIP ABOUT FURNITURE made after 1820 is a relatively recent development. Only three titles listed here were published before 1960. After that date, titles begin to appear with accelerated frequency. The decade following 1960 is represented by thirteen titles; the 1970s by well more than fifty. The number from the 1980s exceeds that from the 1970s.

A chronological examination of the titles reveals significant changes in emphasis and attitude. The earliest study here is *Shaker Furniture* by Edward Deming Andrews and Faith Andrews, first published in 1937. In the 1930s the trim, spare furnishings of the Shakers fit both modernist and colonial revival preferences for simple and allegedly functional forms. To the Andrewses, Shaker furniture had a spirituality that raised it far above other creations of its time.

The second title is John Hall's *Cabinet Makers' Assistant*, originally published in 1840 and reprinted in 1944 because it was thought to be the first American furniture design book. Carl Drepperd's introduction laments the intersection of this publishing milestone with what he considered "the very eve of our era of poor furniture taste." Drepperd also observed that many of the late classical designs illustrated in Hall's book were still popularly called "colonial" in 1944.

The third title is Siegfried Giedion's monumental *Mechanization Takes Command* (1948). Although dealing only in part with furniture, Giedion introduced to scholarship the vast subject of patented furniture. He also brought to the study of objects of everyday life a level of conceptualization still rare. Yet Giedion's commitment to the modern movement made him intolerant of certain classes of nineteenth-century objects. He was particularly unsympathetic to furniture in historic styles, which he felt lacked creative force and invention.

In the ensuing years many of the opinions and prejudices of the 1940s and 1950s have gradually dissipated. The Shakers now seem not to have been as separate from the world as the Andrewses imagined; today we acknowledge what we call "Shaker Victorian." Drepperd's notion that Victorian design represented the nadir of taste has gradually retreated as the nineteenth century has been reevaluated and scholarship has grown sympathetic. The general contours of furniture history have become so widely known that today few people would mistake late classical forms of the 1840s for colonial. Patented furniture is avidly studied and collected, but so is the "transitory" furniture that Giedion disliked.

Scholarship of the last twenty-five years can be sorted into six different groups: individual firms and makers, styles and design movements, regions, particular furniture forms, the business of making and selling furniture, and historical context and meaning. The most distinguished works in each category are described below.

Studies of individual firms or makers make up by far the largest category. This bibliography could easily have been doubled if all published studies of individual firms had been included. Book-length studies vary considerably in their focus. John T. Kenney's account of Lambert Hitchcock is part of his personal saga of reconstructing the Hitchcock factory and attempting to reproduce Hitchcock chairs for commercial sale. Randell Makinson's *Greene and Greene* draws on extensive documentation to survey the major commissions of this California team at its peak between 1907 and 1911. Marvin Schwartz, Edward Stanek, and Douglas True devote a major portion of *The Furniture of John Henry Belter* to issues of attribution. The most valuable and original chapter in the book is their attempt to formulate an objective system for attributing Belter furniture.

Although the Thonet firm is not American, Christopher Wilk's narrative history is included here because it records the changing processes, products, and fortunes of a company with international reputation and sales. The Wooton desk, on the other hand, was an American product. The two short volumes about Wooton Desk Company approach the subject in different ways. Betty Lawson Walters's *King of Desks* creates a composite history of the firm by drawing on local histories, newspapers, patent office and company records, trade catalogues and periodicals, and city and business directories. Extensive appendixes provide data useful for further interpreting these prestige products of the 1870s and 1880s. *Wooton Patent Desks* is notable for the number of perspectives it brings to these desks. In addition to histories of the company, the personal life and career of William S. Wooton, and the evolution of desks, short essays discuss the development of office spaces and systems in the nineteenth and early twentieth centuries and attempt to understand work processes and conditions in the Wooton factory.

Three other book-length studies deal with less familiar names. Milwaukee Art Museum's *Domestic Scene*, an account of decorator-designer George M. Niedecken, draws on a horde of documentary materials in the Prairie Archives and elsewhere to record the complex and varied career of a multitalented figure. Folklorist Michael Owen Jones's *Hand Made Object and Its Maker* uses the chairs, words, and behaviors of a twentieth-century Kentucky chairmaker, Chester Cornett, to explore relationships between creativity, personal experience, and even neurosis. In dealing with a living chairmaker, Jones had an advantage denied most historians. His descriptions of a creative and complex personality at work serve as useful antidotes to the fragmentary and mechanical individuals who sometimes inhabit historians' worlds. The studies of both Cornett and Niedecken make it clear that designers do not necessarily work in straight lines of development, but simultaneously create in notably different manners and repeatedly return to earlier design ideas.

The third work, *Thomas Day, Cabinetmaker*, provides a sketchy outline of the accomplishments of Day, a free, black cabinetmaker in North Carolina. This exhibition catalogue issued by North Carolina Museum of History contributes to a fuller understanding of the role of Afro-Americans in designing and producing America's material culture and to the study of race relations in the antebellum years.

Most articles on individual firms offer basic documentation of company history and products.

Representative articles include those by Marilynn Johnson Bordes on Christian Herter, David Hanks on Isaac Scott, Hanks and Page Talbott on Daniel Pabst, Dianne Hauserman (Pilgrim) on Alexander Roux, Donald Peirce on Robert Mitchell and Frederick Rammelsberg, and Peter Strickland on Alphonse Lejambre and on Schindler, Roller, and Company, as well as mine on George Henkels.

Some of the articles bring to light significant collections or classes of documents. John Hill's discussion of the Jenkins firm of Baltimore identifies a collection of some 2,500 drawings, still owned by descendants of the company and housed in twenty-nine original uniform containers. Mary Ellen Yehia's account of L. White Chair Company of Boston is based on a cluster of White's business records in Baker Library at Harvard University. Jane Davies's treatment of furniture designed by architect A. J. Davis painstakingly documents Davis's commissions by combining materials of many types, including drawings, record books, bills, letters, and receipts.

Folklorist Warren Roberts uses articles on relatively obscure artisans to document rural life in nineteenth-century Indiana and to address issues of definition and theory. In his study of Ananias Hensel, Roberts examines the life and work of a sometime cabinetmaker who made what is often called "country" furniture. Roberts argues that *country* is a subjective and pejorative expression and should be replaced by the term *traditional*. In his article on Turpin chairs, Roberts uses a lengthy documentary study of a family of seasonal chairmakers to maintain that such craftsmen are under-represented in our scholarship and thinking. Although usually identified as farmers in period documents, the Turpins and many others like them were responsible for many of the chairs purchased in rural areas, particularly the ubiquitous slat-back chairs.

Style is a familiar way of organizing discussions or collections of furniture. Berry Tracy's introduction to *Nineteenth-Century America* is a primer of the major styles of the nineteenth century. Collections like the Crawford at High Museum of Art are often assembled with the goal of acquiring outstanding examples of the various styles. Most publications dealing with nineteenth-century furniture refer to style. While stylistic terms are used freely, however, analyses or histories of those styles are not numerous. Neoclassicism was one of the first to be examined. More than twenty years after publication, Newark Museum's *Classical America, 1815–1845* is still the most extensive survey of that style. The Gothic has been ably outlined in Katherine S. Howe and David B. Warren's 1976 *Gothic Revival Style in America*.

The third style or cultural movement to attract sustained attention is the arts and crafts. Studies of arts and crafts materials are numerous enough to warrant a separate chapter in this bibliography. Here I mention only titles that deal specifically or exclusively with furniture. The early impact of the English design reform movement, sometimes called the aesthetic movement, is well summarized in two complementary publications: *Eastlake-Influenced American Furniture, 1870–1890*, with text by Mary Jean Smith Madigan, is a heavily pictorial catalogue of an exhibition held at Hudson River Museum in 1973; Madigan's "Influence of Charles Locke Eastlake on American Furniture Manufacture, 1870–1890" examines Eastlake's arguments in greater detail and outlines responses to those arguments by American furniture manufacturers.

Hanks's *Isaac E. Scott* provides a case study of a designer who helped to transfer English design reform ideas to the Midwest. Reform design in a commercial shop patronized by the affluent is the topic of Bordes's study of Herter. Active during the same years as Scott in Chicago, the New York Herter Brothers firm was a fashionable decorating house of the period. Herter also figures into Marilynn Johnson's contribution to *In Pursuit of Beauty*, the most recent and most extensive exploration of the aesthetic movement in America.

The complex and apparently confusing period between the classical and the Gothic revivals in the first forty years of the century and the arts and crafts movement of the last thirty has attracted few writers. I have written two short articles on what was known as the "néo-grec" style, a picturesque combination of classical and classicizing elements popular in this country in the 1860s and 1870s. During those same years the colonial revival began to emerge. Rodris Roth was among the first to examine colonial revival furniture. Although the subject is important for understanding issues of both personal taste and cultural politics in the last century, the bibliography on colonial revival furniture remains almost nonexistent. This may be changing, however, for Gregory Weidman's 1984 catalogue of the furniture in Maryland Historical Society discusses many objects in the colonial revival style.

Some styles of furniture are defined by materials or the ways materials are worked. Helaine Fendelman's attractive pictorial survey of tramp art fits in here. Another type of furniture defined by material is wicker. The best account of the history of wicker in America is probably still Katherine Menz's concise essay in *Nineteenth Century Furniture*, edited by Art and Antiques. Illustrations of scores of additional pieces, plus a more extensive historical account and guidelines for restoration, are included in Richard Saunders's works. A third type of furniture defined by nonhistorical references is rustic, characterized by its assertively natural qualities. Craig Gilborn outlines the major forms made or used in the Adirondack Mountain region of New York. Bentwood and bent-metal furniture are also discrete types and are surveyed in the volume edited by Derek Ostergard.

Place has long been an organizing principle of furniture scholarship. Irving Lyon's pioneering study of 1891 focused on New England. Since Lyon's day, many authors have used place to shape, confine, or give heightened meaning to their studies. Place-oriented publications fall into several categories. One extends the study of centers important in colonial America into the nineteenth century. Kathleen Catalano's studies of Philadelphia specifically deal with the transition from eighteenth-century craft to nineteenth-century industry. Studies of Boston also fit here. Each acknowledges documentary or perception problems that have inhibited inquiry into later materials. Page Talbott's articles on Boston empire furniture wrestle with the difficulties of locating documented examples. Edward S. Cooke, Jr.'s, essay on the Boston furniture industry in 1880 explores the theme of decline in quality and quantity. According to Cooke, the Boston fire of 1872 is often thought to have seriously weakened the furniture trade. He finds this notion unsubstantiated and goes on to describe the flourishing furniture business in Boston in 1880.

One recent example of the continuity theme is Weidman's catalogue of Maryland furniture. Here the early accomplishments of Annapolis and Baltimore are juxtaposed with the more flamboyant if less well known products of the mid and later nineteenth century.

Writers seem somewhat surprised to find active and accomplished furniture production in older centers like Maryland, Boston, and, to a lesser degree, Philadelphia. Not so for New York, where the achievements of the nineteenth century far outshine those of the eighteenth century. There is no account of New York furniture manufacturing in the nineteenth century, perhaps because so many of the city's firms have been individually studied.

Studies of nineteenth-century furniture in midwestern cities make no comparisons, invidious or otherwise, with earlier local products; there usually were none. In the case of a city like Grand Rapids, significant settlement began only in the 1840s. The nineteenth century saw not decline, but rapid growth and prosperity. James Bradshaw's account of the expansion of Grand Rapids as a furniture center shows how that city's manufacturers used advanced technology, progressive systems of factory layout and work programming, and innovations in the field of marketing. The swift rise of cities like Grand Rapids also fueled perceptions that Boston and other older eastern areas were in decline.

Research is under way into at least some of the other major furniture centers of the Midwest, including Cincinnati, St. Louis, Milwaukee, Rockford, and Sheboygan. The major producer in the Midwest is the subject of Sharon Darling's monumental account, *Chicago Furniture*. Settled only in 1833, Chicago led the nation in furniture productivity by the end of the nineteenth century. If New York dominated the upper-class market, Chicago seems to have played a critical role for the middle class and middle America. Virtually all aspects of furniture-trade history are recounted in Darling's extraordinarily detailed book. There is no study of any other furniture center so rich in factual material, so well organized, or so comprehensive. Capably written and meticulously documented, *Chicago Furniture* is a landmark of American furniture history.

A second category of studies also uses place as an organizing principle but concentrates on a given form, material, or style. Perhaps the best known example of this genre is William Elder's study of Baltimore's distinctive tradition of painted furniture. Hawaii also had a distinctive tradition, as recorded by Irving Jenkins in a study that emphasizes Hawaii's extensive use of native koa wood.

The kind of value inversion that koa furniture represents is not unusual. In the last few years, regional traditions have taken on heightened significance as focal points for local identity and pride. Edwin Churchill's catalogue of painted furniture made in Maine, *Simple Forms and Vivid Colors*, examines furniture that originally appealed to customers because it provided cheap elegance. This cheap elegance as seen in Georgia plain-style furniture is the focus of *Neat Pieces*. The objects here are appreciated for their design qualities and as manifestations of an aesthetic of plainness.

Something of the same spirit underlies *Made in Ohio*, another state-based furniture study. Charles Muller's introductory comments acknowledge that there is no discernible Ohio style, although certain forms occur in Ohio with greater frequency than elsewhere. While *Made in Ohio* incorporates a far wider range of styles and tastes than *Neat Pieces*, it, too, emphasizes objects of the 1830s and 1840s, many made by traditional artisans in rural areas.

Plain and Elegant, Rich and Common offers an objective commentary on the issue of state-based furniture studies, at least in the case of New Hampshire. The organizers of this work acknowledge that New Hampshire is not a unified cultural entity. Any documentable cultural regionalization joins New Hampshire to several of its neighboring states. Thus, for furniture studies, state lines may be ultimately arbitrary boundaries, marks of political jurisdiction that can make a clear understanding of actual cultural areas and cultural interconnectedness difficult to achieve.

One last group of place-oriented studies blends place and ethnicity. The majority of these deal with German Americans. The second largest immigrant group in this country, Germans have had a major impact on American material culture. German contributions to furniture fall into two distinct groups. The first consists of that extensive body of furniture made by cabinetmakers and manufacturers in major cities. In this furniture, the ethnic dimension is neither obvious nor foremost. When we speak of Belter, Hunzinger, Henkels, or Herter, we tend to think American rather than German, perhaps because the markets to which these firms sold were defined by wealth and taste rather than ethnicity. The second group contains a large mass of furniture in more or less German styles, made by German cabinetmakers for other Germans either because they preferred German-style furniture to Anglo-American goods or because furniture from outside the community was difficult to obtain. Fine studies deal with furniture of this second type in Missouri and Texas. Charles van Ravenswaay's chapter on furniture in his massive *Arts and Architecture of German Settlements in Missouri* provides an extensive survey of furniture forms found in areas settled by Germans. Van Ravenswaay concludes that Missouri German goods are not easily distinguishable from those made in German communities in other parts of the country. The evidence of Texas bears this out, as can be seen in studies by Donald Stover and by Lonn Taylor and David Warren. Both present a broad survey of furniture forms, but the Taylor and Warren study is particularly rich in analyses of the forms and their cultural milieu.

The most recent regional-ethnic study is Taylor and Dessa Bokides's *New Mexican Furniture, 1600–1940*. More than any work produced so far, this book shows how social and cultural history can be told from furniture. Taylor and Bokides rediscovered forgotten cultural richness and dynamism in New Mexico's past, and their study revises several long-standing assumptions about life in the Hispanic Southwest.

Analyzing or describing changes in the shape of given forms over time constitutes a smaller category of writings. Typological studies of specific forms appeal more to historians than to collectors, for they have the potential to raise questions about major social and cultural changes. Giedion's *Mechanization Takes Command* is still the most sweeping and comprehensive study in this class. His objective was to observe the impact of mechanization on a wide range of human behaviors. While today Giedion sometimes seems to have been blinded by doctrinaire modernism, his study offers a greater depth and breadth than any succeeding work. Hanks's *Innovative Furniture in America* is heavily indebted to Giedion in its line of inquiry, but it does not relate developments in furniture to significant shifts in the society around it. A valuable part of the book is Roth's lengthy discussion of patented furniture and the American system of patents.

The most substantial and sustained examination of a single furniture form in the nineteenth century is *The Rocking Chair Book* by Ellen and Bert Denker, who trace the history of that icon of Victorian America from its origins up to the present. Although eminently useful as a guide for collectors who might wish to date or document rocking chairs, the real emphasis of the book is on the cultural context and meaning of the objects. Although less interpretive, Muller and Timothy Rieman's examination of Shaker chairs provides an extensive examination of that form.

Taken together, two articles outline the history of the American hallstand. In "Meaning in Artifacts: Hall Furnishings in Victorian America," I sketch the development of the form to about

1880, then analyze the components and functions of hallstands of the 1870s. Leslie A. Greene continues the story into the early twentieth century, noting changes in the design of hallstands and their gradual elimination from genteel households.

Parlor organs may be musical instruments, but in nineteenth-century America they were also very definitely articles of furniture. A good pictorial overview and capsule history of developments in the musical aspects of the instrument appear in Robert Gellerman's *American Reed Organ*. Food safes found in areas of Virginia and Tennessee are the subject of an article by J. Roderick Moore. There is no overview of the history of desks as such, but *Wooton Patent Desks* illustrates many competing patented forms.

With studies of the tools and processes of furniture manufacture, artisan mobility and status, or the structure of furniture trade, object-centered furniture studies intersect with business, industrial, technological, and labor history. Included here are studies that address issues that reach beyond the furniture itself but that are written from a furniture-centered perspective. Business or labor histories often omit analysis of the product and may be of little value to those seeking material that has some direct utility in interpreting that product. The entries here, although few in number, are written by people sensitive to that need.

The question of the exact nature of the impact of mechanization and technological change on furniture production is one about which a good deal of unsubstantiated opinion was long written as fact. Polly Anne Earl's 1974 "Craftsmen and Machines" made significant strides toward clarification. Earl argued that machines came into general use much later than had been assumed and that mechanization did not mean heavy industry; many machines were powered by foot treadles. In his 1981 article for *Winterthur Portfolio*, Michael Ettema took the argument even further, outlining how machinery did and did not affect furniture, and at what economic levels.

The changing status of journeymen and the decline of the apprenticeship system is a major topic of Kathleen Catalano's treatment of cabinetmaking in Philadelphia. The interrelationships of component parts of the furniture business are outlined in Mary Ellen Yehia's study of the Boston firm of L. White. The kinds of firms dominant in Boston and the major lines produced there are treated in articles by Seidler and Cooke, also mentioned previously. A sense of labor conditions and work schedule appears in excerpts of the journal of Shaker chairmaker Freegift Wills that is reprinted by Muller and Rieman. In Darling's *Chicago Furniture*, locations of firms, partnerships and interrelationships, the role of machinery, sales techniques, typical furniture forms, workers, unions, transportation, and virtually every other aspect of the business are at least touched on; many are dealt with at length.

Interest in the historical context and meaning of objects has expanded in recent years as the study of material culture has encouraged scholars to examine the place of objects in the lives of people of the past. In some cases, context has meant physical location and juxtaposition with other types of furnishings. The comprehensive survey by Edgar Mayhew and Minor Myers recreates the total environment of which furniture was a part. George Talbot's *At Home*, a suggestive study of Wisconsin life recorded in photographs, repeatedly uses interiors with furniture to suggest social and psychological conditions. William Seale's *Tasteful Interlude* is an outstanding collection of images of the interiors of American houses of the nineteenth century which provides a starting point for documenting and interpreting the use and placement of furniture in American homes before World War I.

Another group of studies has examined the ways that objects have heightened the distinctive qualities of certain environments and the experiences associated with them. The Denkers' book-length treatment of the rocking chair notes not only how it changed over time but also how its design was altered for users like women and children or for places like parlors and porches. The articles on the nineteenth-century hallstand describe ways that this form contributed both specific functions and a distinctive artifactural presence to the front hall.

Craig Gilborn's book on rustic furniture of the Adirondacks shows how a variety of distinctive but related designs were made to induce a sense of being in the Adirondacks, both physically and psychologically removed from the customs and complexity of urban life. Taking a somewhat different tack and looking at people who did not have the financial resources to summer in the Adirondacks, Lizabeth Cohen outlines the development of a working-class taste at the turn of the century. This taste was formulated with full awareness of middle-class standards and values, but it selectively rejected certain aspects of that taste to maintain a sense of apartness and identity.

Separateness and identity and a growing sense of specialness lie behind the development of specialized furniture forms for children, as Karin Calvert makes clear in "Cradle to Crib." The development of cribs, high chairs, swings, and perambulators supported idealized and sentimentalized views of childhood while isolating children from adults and suppressing undesirable traits.

Shaker furniture worked in similar ways. As the pioneering work of the Andrewses so compellingly showed, the Shakers fashioned distinctive furniture for themselves precisely to separate themselves from the world and to suppress what they felt were unsuitable actions or thoughts. Shaker furniture remains among the best known of nineteenth-century attempts to influence and constrain behavior by environmental control. But the impulse seemed to be irresistible to the age. Shaker materials stand out from those of the world by their denial of ornament and visual complexity, but the world's ornament and complexity were sometimes as carefully ordered and as much a part of a program or a doctrine as were Shaker goods. Martha McClaugherty's "Household Art" shows the consistency of principles and doctrines of that late nineteenth-century movement and underlines the importance of publications in publicizing and reiterating this design and social ideology.

Groups or arrangements of objects may contain special meanings, but so do many individual objects. Roth's discussion of relic furniture identifies and describes a few products of the nineteenth-century inclination to associate wooden furniture with historic events or personalities. This behavior illuminates the period's considerable regard for furniture and its highly developed historic consciousness. Ellen Marie Snyder's treatment of cast iron, on the other hand, discusses the meanings associated with seating furniture made from a new, progressive material that was widely understood to symbolize progress.

Sometimes meaning is personal or contested. In "Material Culture as Non-Verbal Communication," I discuss the expectations that may have encouraged people to buy parlor organs in the late nineteenth century. Diane Douglas looks at the sewing machine and records contradictory ways that sewing machines were interpreted: as tools to provide freedom and to increase leisure for women or to promote household order and efficiency. These two studies also underline the importance of furniture to the nineteenth-century mind; a musical instrument and a household machine were both cast as, and partially concealed within, furniture forms.

This chapter of the bibliography also includes a small selection of reprinted primary documents, each valuable in a different way. Hall's *Cabinet Makers' Assistant* has already been mentioned. The majority of the designs are in the so-called pillar-and-scroll manner and represent a survey of the major forms of the period. A. J. Downing's *Architecture of Country Houses* not only is a key text in the history of American domestic architecture but also includes a lengthy chapter describing and prescribing furniture available in the middle years of the century. *The Crystal Palace Exhibition* contains little American furniture but is a readily accessible survey of leading styles and forms in western Europe. The catalogue is both evidence of and agent of internationalism in design of the period.

As perhaps the most influential tastemaking book of all time, Eastlake's *Hints on Household Taste* was the first salvo of what McClaugherty calls the household-art movement. As readable and seductive as it was a century ago, *Hints* stills presents a persuasive case for a particular way of furnishing. Clarence Cook's *House Beautiful* is perhaps the best-known American example of a household-art tract. It is also immensely readable and informative, if not always particularly likable. Comments both positive and negative about contemporary furnishings and references to specific firms give *House Beautiful* value as an expression of a particular stance and evidence of the furniture and furnishing trade at the time.

Artistic Houses is included because it records so well the taste and possessions of the wealthy in the 1880s. Never meant as a cross section, it illustrates and describes what were considered at the time particularly outstanding or impressive interiors. Ordinary goods, on the other hand, are the emphasis of *A Victorian Chair for All Seasons*, a reprint of the 1887 catalogue of Brooklyn Chair Company. A juxtaposition of these two publications effectively suggests the range of objects available, as well as the range of life-styles and living conditions, in nineteenth-century America.

Also included here are five titles devoted to British and European furniture. These have been selected less to provide entry into scholarship on that material than to help to place American furniture in an international context.

Agius, Pauline. *British Furniture, 1880–1915*. Woodbridge, Suffolk: Antique Collectors' Club, 1978. 195 pp.; 284 illustrations, bibliography, index.

Agius gives a detailed account of furniture that she finds remarkable for its diversity and original availability to a broad spectrum of society. The period is rich in resources and documents, many of which are drawn on here. Agius devotes chapters to the continuation of earlier Victorian forms, fashionable reproductions, art furniture, woods and finishes, copies and fakes, and the structure of the trade. The most extensive chapter examines progressive furniture and its designers (Morris and Company, William Lethaby, C. F. A. Voysey, C. R. Mackintosh, Baillie Scott, and others). A bibliography lists pattern books and drawings, trade catalogues, period books on taste and style, works on the furniture trade, periodicals, and bibliographies.

Ahlborn, Richard. "Peter Glass, a Maker of American Marquetry." *Antiques* 104, no. 6 (December 1973): 1096–1100. 10 illustrations.

This article records the history of an 1844 emigrant from the Palatinate. Glass settled first in Leominster, Massachusetts, and then moved to Sheboygan County, Wisconsin. In the 1850s and 1860s Glass exhibited at several fairs and won awards. In 1865 he displayed a workstand and center table made for President and Mrs. Lincoln. In 1867 he exhibited at the Paris Universal Exposition and was the only American to win an award in the "mosaic" category. From the late 1860s to about 1890, Glass concentrated on farming and then turned to making workboxes and workstands for members of his family.

Ames, Kenneth. "The Battle of the Sideboards." In *Winterthur Portfolio 9*, edited by Ian M. G. Quimby, pp. 1–27. Charlottesville: University Press of Virginia for the Henry Francis du Pont Winterthur Museum, 1974. 29 illustrations.

International exhibitions of the nineteenth century were intensely competitive events. Ames discusses the sideboard as the prime competitive form for furniture manufacturers. Sideboards exhibited between 1851 and 1876 show France's position of design leadership affirmed, then challenged, and ultimately denied as England moved into primary position. The sideboard initiating the battle was made by Fourdinois of Paris and exhibited in London in 1851. Subsequent English designs emulated French models or sought explicitly English alternatives. European and American objects exhibited in Philadelphia in 1876 show the continuing influence of Fourdinois. The English objects, on the other hand, were in eighteenth-century neoclassical, reformed Gothic, or art furniture styles. American work followed English ideas. After 1876, furniture displays at international exhibitions gradually became less prominent.

Ames, Kenneth. "George Henkels, Nineteenth-Century Philadelphia Cabinetmaker." *Antiques* 104, no. 4 (October 1973): 641–50. 20 illustrations.

This article provides a descriptive account of the life and furniture of Henkels, a well-known Philadelphia furniture maker of the nineteenth century. Trained as a chairmaker, Henkels succeeded Crawford Riddell at a fashionable address on Chestnut Street. Henkels was a prolific writer of articles and pamphlets dealing with furniture, political and economic matters, and even the game of billiards. His furniture figures prominently in Samuel Sloan's *Homestead Architecture* (1861), where it is illustrated in twelve engraved plates. Many of the more elaborate items illustrated are in the Asa Packer house in Jim Thorpe, Pennsylvania, including a spectacular set of richly carved library furniture with a bookcase more than 10 feet high, drawing-room furniture, and two sets of bedroom furniture.

Ames, Kenneth L. "Designed in France: Notes on the Transmission of French Style to America." In *Winterthur Portfolio 12*, edited by Ian M. G. Quimby, pp. 103–14. Charlottesville: University Press of Virginia for the Henry Francis du Pont Winterthur Museum, 1977. 19 illustrations.

Ames reports on the French domination of the decorative arts in the mid nineteenth century. In America one indication of the high status of French products was the frequency with which furniture advertisements referred to French goods or patterns. Cabinetmakers born or trained in France probably kept abreast of French design through family, friends, and visits. Manufacturers without such ties used other means. Philadelphia furniture manufacturer George Henkels apparently relied on two major sources: French publications and direct importation of French furniture. Importation is not documented, although Henkels duplicated a chair made by Ribaillier and Mazaroz of Paris.

Ames, Kenneth L. "Material Culture as Non-Verbal Communication: A Historical Case Study." *Journal of American Culture* 3, no. 4 (Winter 1980): 619–41. 11 illustrations.

Ames argues that nineteenth-century parlor organs were tools for social purposes, parts of social strategies. Parlor organs were most popular between 1870 and 1895. Smaller, cheaper, more compact, and more susceptible to stylistic shifts than pianos, they were extensively purchased by the middle class. Period photographs and advertising images indicate that purchasers also expected these objects to help them to engage in and extend conventionalized social roles, to promote social and cultural continuity over time, to ensure social bonding over space, and to enhance their lives through self-actualization and interaction with others. In particular, parlor organs were agents for inculcating Christian virtues in the home, allowing women to play the dual roles of saint and consumer.

Ames, Kenneth L. "Meaning in Artifacts: Hall Furnishings in Victorian America." *Journal of Interdisciplinary History* 9, no. 1 (Summer 1978): 19–46. 4 illustrations.

This article notes that for much of the second half of the nineteenth century, the entrance hall in middle- and upper-middle-class houses was a narrow passage furnished according to a conventional formula that called for a hallstand, hall chairs, and a card receiver. Hallstands generally incorporated four discrete functions: provisions for umbrellas; hooks or pegs for hats and coats; a looking glass; and a small table, often with a drawer and a marble top. All were synthesized into an architecturally conceived whole. The hallstand "communicated nonverbally about who was or was not home.... It ceremonialized the coming and going, the entry and exit of the members of the household and their guests. And it served as a setting, a theatrical backdrop for the ritual of card leaving, which also took place in the hall" (p. 38). Included are comments on hall chairs, card receivers, and the etiquette of calling cards.

Ames, Kenneth L. "Sitting in (Néo-Grec) Style." *Nineteenth Century* 2, nos. 3–4 (Autumn 1976): 50–58. 15 illustrations.

Néo-grec seating furniture is varied and inventive. It can be divided into two formal categories: one that is based on classical prototypes and a second that is not. Furniture of the second type is commoner. These objects are often loosely patterned after neoclassical furniture of the eighteenth century, but they also may be notably anticlassical in their disregard for conventional hierarchies, balances, and compositions, their use of "agonized joinery," and the openness and expansiveness of their design. Examples following classical precedents experiment with curule and klismos forms. Chairs and sofas from France, New York, and Grand Rapids are illustrated and discussed.

Ames, Kenneth L. "What Is the Néo-Grec?" *Nineteenth Century* 2, no. 2 (Summer 1976): 12–21. 13 illustrations.

Ames describes a distinctive treatment of classical form and ornament popular in America in the 1860s and 1870s. In France it was called néo-grec; in England and America, it was called modern Greek, new Greek, or new Grecian. It constitutes the crest of the metaphoric wave of picturesque eclecticism outlined by C. L. V. Meeks in *The Railroad Station* (1956), sharing design traits with the contemporary high Victorian Gothic style. The néo-grec was disseminated through numerous publications, including Guilmard's *Le Garde-Meuble* and *La Décoration au XIXe Siecle*, and Liénard's *Spécimens*. At the international exhibition of 1862, important examples were shown by Mazaroz-Ribaillier and Marchand. Among the costliest manifestations were polychrome drawing-room cabinets. Fancy goods like wall pockets, small tables and stands, and easels provided the fullest opportunity to express the spirit of the style: gleaming surfaces, strong contrasts of dark wood and gold, light, spiky turnings, and playfully complex construction and contours.

Ames, Kenneth L., ed. *Victorian Furniture: Essays from a Victorian Society Autumn Symposium*. Philadelphia: Victorian Society in America, 1982. 254 pp.; approximately 180 illustrations, 12 tables.

Victorian Furniture contains sixteen essays delivered at a 1978 symposium jointly sponsored by the Decorative Arts Society and the Victorian Society in America. Ames's introduction links scholarly interest in Victorian furniture to five factors: passage of time and growth of nostalgia; impact of the new history and material culture study; influence of the social sciences; fascination with nonverbal communication; and increased prices for Victorian objects on the antiques market. The authors use furniture to examine a wide range of historical problems. Individual essays deal with the meanings of popular styles and motifs; techniques of merchandising; problems of connoisseurship; business and labor structure in Boston and Philadelphia; pianos, folding chairs, spinning wheels, and patented furniture; women's carving; designers and publications; and furniture of both the upper and the working classes.

Andrews, Edward Deming, and Faith Andrews. *Religion in Wood: A Book of Shaker Furniture*. Bloomington: Indiana University Press, 1966. xxi+106 pp.; illustrations, bibliography.

Thomas Merton's introduction to *Religion in Wood* explores similarities between the Shakers and British poet-painter William Blake to capture the "deeply religious and 'monastic' quality" of the Shaker aesthetic (p. viii). The foreword sketches the growing appreciation of Shaker furniture from 1928 to the 1960s. The text discusses Shaker theology and the roles of Mother Ann Lee, Joseph Meacham, and the Millenial Laws. The Andrewses argue that the Shakers sought perfection in all their endeavors, stressing order, usefulness, and simplicity in order to create a society without sin or worldliness. The simplest things, if made without error, were the most useful and the most satisfactory to Shaker conscience. The work of these "humble but consecrated folk" (p. 14) represents the common strain in America's heritage. The illustrations include individual pieces and furniture in Shaker settings, museums, and private homes. Brief notes on western Shaker furniture and craftsmen are included.

Andrews, Edward Deming, and Faith Andrews. *Shaker Furniture: The Craftsmanship of an American Communal Sect*. Photographs by William F. Winter. 1937. Reprint. New York: Dover Publications, 1950. xi+133 pp.; 48 plates, appendixes, bibliography, index.

The Andrewses argue that although much literature deals with the Shakers, few authors examine their finely crafted furniture, the product of "an intensely realized faith, an unusual body of principles, a unique spiritual experience" (p. 3). Regularity, harmony, and order were cardinal principles, and simplicity was valued over decoration. Shaker furniture produces an impression of the "brightness and lightness" of "serene happiness" (p. 25). Subdued elegance and delicacy characterize chairs, small tables, stands, desks, and sewing cabinets. Responsiveness to the needs of groups rather than of individuals gives Shaker furniture distinctive traits. Furniture made by different communities is much the same because of the exchange of artisans, similar shop equipment, concentration of certain industries and distribution of products throughout the order, and the dominance of the New Lebanon colony. The Andrewses discuss craftsmen and working practices. Plates are accompanied by extensive descriptions.

Andrews, John. *The Price Guide to Victorian, Edwardian, and 1920s Furniture (1860–1930)*. Woodbridge, Suffolk: Antique Collectors' Club, 1980. 217 pp.; 609 illustrations, bibliography.

This English publication is intended to help collectors to learn prices. The text deals primarily with furniture available on the antiques market, but it also includes some costly "art" objects to enable readers to understand the relationships between art furniture and commercial production. About thirty pages outline the major stylistic trends of the 1860–1930 period: Victorian rococo, Elizabethan, eighteenth-century reproductions and derivations, Gothic and reformers, art furniture, Anglo-Japanese, the arts and crafts movement, and the 1920s. The remainder of the book presents more than 600 objects arranged by form and includes some non-British goods such as Wooton desks and Thonet chairs. Each illustrated object is accompanied by a description or commentary.

Art and Antiques, ed. *Nineteenth Century Furniture: Innovation, Revival, and Reform.* Introduction by Mary Jean Madigan. New York: Billboard Publications, an Art and Antiques Book, 1982. 160 pp.; black and white and color illustrations, bibliography, index.

This work contains nineteen articles reprinted from *Art and Antiques.* The introduction notes a growing interest in nineteenth-century decorative arts, citing rising prices at auctions and a succession of major exhibitions reaching from the Metropolitan's "Nineteenth Century America" (1970) to Cooper-Hewitt's "Innovative Furniture" (1981). "Scholarship represented by these exhibitions, and by many smaller shows and individual publications during the last decade, has cast new light on the stylistic trends, designers, and makers of nineteenth century furniture" (p. 6). Descriptive articles deal with Philadelphia empire, Hitchcock furniture, John Henry Belter, Daniel Pabst, Egyptian revival, Eastlake-influenced furniture, Kimbel and Cabus, art nouveau, Chicago furniture, Stickley, the Roycrofters, innovative furniture, Hunzinger, wicker, cast-iron, and Adirondack history, as well as several European figures.

Artistic Houses; Being a Series of Interior Views of a Number of the Most Beautiful and Celebrated Homes in the United States. 1883. Reprint. New York: Benjamin Blom, 1971. 400 pp.; 200 illustrations.

This reduced-format, one-volume edition contains luxurious late nineteenth-century folios surveying the homes of the wealthy. The descriptive and laudatory texts identify major attractions in homes of Louis C. Tiffany, Mrs. A. T. Stewart, J. Pierpont Morgan, W. H. DeForest, W. H. Vanderbilt, Henry C. Gibson, George W. Child, H. Victor Newcomb, Henry Villard, and about 100 others. The texts resemble tours, pointing out and praising various features and often identifying designers, makers, or vendors. The volume is rich in documentation of objects, including furniture. It is a useful summary of the taste of the affluent in the 1880s.

Ayres, William. *A Poor Sort of Heaven, a Good Sort of Earth: The Rose Valley Arts and Crafts Experiment.* See "The Arts and Crafts Movement in America."

Baltimore Painted Furniture, 1800–1840. Introduction and commentary by William Voss Elder. Exhibition catalogue. Baltimore: Baltimore Museum of Art, 1972. 132 pp.; 59 illustrated entries, bibliography.

Painted furniture produced in Baltimore from about 1800 to 1840 is a unique contribution to American cabinetmaking. Up to about 1820 the neoclassical furniture of Hugh and John Finlay and others predominated. About 1820 a new style emerged that was characterized by forms based on classical models. Much of this furniture was grained to resemble

rosewood and was stenciled with winged thunderbolts, anthemia, Grecian scrolls, acanthus leaves, and other Greek or Roman devices. This group may represent the largest related body of American furniture based on ancient models. About thirty-five examples are illustrated and discussed, including tables, window seats, couches, and typical Baltimore "wheelback" chairs. Notes on the treatment of painted furniture and a list of cabinetmakers and allied craftsmen are included.

Bates, Elizabeth Bidwell, and Jonathan L. Fairbanks. *American Furniture, 1620 to the Present.* New York: Richard Marek Publishers, 1981. xii+561 pp.; approximately 1,300 black and white and 100 color plates, line drawings, glossary, bibliography, index.

This survey emphasizes the significance of Victorian and post-Victorian work: "Excellent craftsmanship did not die with the industrial boom and the advent of power machinery around the year 1840" (p. xi). Bates and Fairbanks discuss furniture as art and refer to craftsmen as artists. Their major goal is to encourage "a broad public interest in craftsmanship" (p. xii). Nineteenth- and early twentieth-century materials appear in sections entitled "Away from the Mainstream," "Victorian America, 1830–1900," "Frontier and Vernacular Traditions, 1800–1850," and "Craft Revival, Reaction, and Reform, 1870–1930." Brief historical outlines introduce images that are accompanied by essay-length captions discussing forms, styles, makers, functions, owners, or other relevant matters. *See also* "American Furniture to 1820."

Bishop, Robert. *Centuries and Styles of the American Chair, 1640–1970.* Foreword by Charles F. Hummel. New York: E. P. Dutton, 1972. 516 pp.; 923 illustrations, bibliography, index.

Bishop's panoramic survey of seating furniture is about evenly divided between objects made before 1820 and between 1820 and 1920. The illustrations are arranged in roughly chronological order, and each is accompanied by a brief caption. Running text is at a minimum. This work is most valuable for its numerous illustrations drawn from many different collections.

Bordes, Marilynn Johnson. "Christian Herter and the Cult of Japan." In *Aspects of the Arts and Crafts Movement in America,* edited by Robert Judson Clark. *Record of the Art Museum,* Princeton University, 34, no. 2 (1975): 20–27. 5 illustrations.

Under Herter's leadership, the New York Herter Brothers firm became the most famous American decorating house of its day. Bordes notes that some of the company's most important works of the 1870s and 1880s were in the Japanese taste, often also revealing the influence of English designer E. W. Godwin. Herter's masterpiece is the wardrobe in the Metropolitan Museum of Art that was said to have been owned by Lillian Russell. No other object attains the same quality "of Japanese selectivity, sparseness, and restraint" (p. 23). One of Herter's finest Japanese interiors was created 1879–

81 for William H. Vanderbilt's Fifth Avenue home. While later designers like Frank Lloyd Wright and the Greene brothers saw elimination and simplicity as the heart of Japanese art, for Herter it was a decorative vocabulary to be used for exercises in elaboration.

Bradshaw, James Stanford. "Grand Rapids, 1870–1880: Furniture City Emerges." *Michigan History* 55, no. 4 (Winter 1971): 321–42. 3 illustrations.

Bradshaw reports that by 1870 furniture making had become the third largest industry in Grand Rapids. The city's eight firms were already selling goods outside the region. Natural factors were important to the success of the industry, but Grand Rapids also may have been in the forefront of technological change in the woodworking industry. Local firms designed and supplied specialized machinery and wood-curing kilns. The firms were also astutely managed, with progressive and effective systems of plant layout, power, and work programming. The leader in factory operations was John Mowatt, who became almost a legend as a superb planner and systematizer. Indeed, "Grand Rapids furniture manufacturers appear to have been especially innovative and aggressive in the key field of marketing" (p. 337), exhibiting at the Centennial, initiating a semiannual furniture market, and employing trained designers.

Byron, Joseph. *New York Interiors at the Turn of the Century. See* "Domestic Architecture."

Calvert, Karin. "Cradle to Crib: The Revolution in Nineteenth-Century Children's Furniture." In Mary Lynn Stevens Heininger et al., *A Century of Childhood, 1820–1920*, pp. 33–63. Rochester, N.Y.: Margaret Woodbury Strong Museum, 1984. 20 illustrations.

Calvert traces changes in the attitude and practice of raising children. She argues that before the nineteenth century, Anglo-American children had little furniture for their own use. By midcentury, however, furniture specifically for children—cribs, high chairs, swings, perambulators—had become commonplace: "The new furnishings reflected a social climate that was both more permissive and more restrictive than the preceding era had been, for the new forms served an idealized and sentimentalized vision of childhood" (p. 33). The furniture "guarded small children from danger and isolated them from adult activity, simultaneously protecting childhood innocence and suppressing undesirable traits" (p. 42). The most expensive and elaborate furniture form was the perambulator, common after about 1870, which "was designed to show the child off to best advantage, like a jewel on a velvet tray" (p. 58).

Carpenter, Mary Grace, and Charles H. Carpenter, Jr. "The Shaker Furniture of Elder Henry Green." *Antiques* 105, no. 5 (May 1974): 1119–25. 12 black and white illustrations, 2 color plates.

Green joined the Shakers at Alfred, Maine, in 1859 when he

was a boy of fifteen. He "served his community as a cabinetmaker, carpenter, schoolteacher, purchasing agent, salesman, commercial manager, and finally, for more than thirty years, as the spiritual leader of the Shakers at Alfred" (p. 1119). Green worked as a cabinetmaker between about 1870 and 1890, making objects mostly for Shakers. Green's early work is in the familiar reticent manner of the Shakers, but some of his designs from the 1880s take "a Victorian turn" (p. 1121). Particularly notable are the dozen or so writing desks decorated with scrollwork that he made for the sisters. Their Victorian qualities can be attributed to Green's contacts with resort hotels as salesman for Shaker fancy goods. Green's furniture survives today at Sabbathday Lake, where the Alfred community moved in 1931.

Catalano, Kathleen M. "Abraham Kimball (1798–1890), Salem Cabinetmaker." *American Art Journal* 11, no. 2 (April 1979): 62–70. 11 illustrations.

Catalano notes that Salem's furniture trade thrived well into the nineteenth century. The largest number of craftsmen appeared during the empire and early Victorian periods. Kimball's work provides insight into Salem's furniture industry after the "golden age." His career falls into two periods: 1822–43, when he worked in partnership with Winthrop Sargent; and 1843–45, when he worked alone. Only a mahogany veneer worktable has been identified from the first period. A corner cabinet, writing table, bracket, and chair with upholstered back and seat, all in the Gothic taste and made for Fanny Appleton and her new husband, Henry Wadsworth Longfellow, survive from the second; the first three are still in the Longfellow house today. The illustrations are of objects, a label, an advertisement, a bill, and period views of Longfellow house interiors.

Catalano, Kathleen M. "Cabinetmaking in Philadelphia, 1820–1840: Transition from Craft to Industry." In *American Furniture and Its Makers: Winterthur Portfolio 13*, edited by Ian M. G. Quimby, pp. 81–138. Chicago: University of Chicago Press for the Henry Francis du Pont Winterthur Museum, 1979. 5 tables, checklist.

From 1820 to 1840, Philadelphia's "well-organized furniture-making community" of more than "1,290 cabinetmakers, 300 chairmakers, 250 turners, 80 pianoforte makers, 55 framemakers, and 40 chair and ornamental painters" (p. 81) saw furniture making change from an eighteenth-century craft to a modern industry. Catalano discusses how markets expanded dramatically as Philadelphia firms exported wares to more than fifty American cities and twenty foreign ports. The rise of wholesale merchandising took control of retail prices out of manufacturers' hands and encouraged them to cut costs wherever possible. Cheaper labor was hired, wages were lowered, and conflicts erupted. The Society of Journeymen Cabinetmakers opened its own warerooms in 1834; owners retaliated by firing participating cabinetmakers. Apprenticeships were changed by market expansion and wholesaling, becoming little more than cheap labor. "The indentured child of the 1820s and 1830s was not far from becoming the child laborer of later industrial periods" (p. 91).

Churchill, Edwin A. *Simple Forms and Vivid Colors: An Exhibition of Maine Painted Furniture, 1800–1850.* Foreword by Dean A. Fales, Jr. Augusta: Maine State Museum, 1983. xii+117 pp.; 16 black and white and color illustrations, 32 color plates, appendix, bibliography, checklist, index.

Painted furniture appealed to customers because it provided cheap elegance and beauty. It was made of inexpensive materials, usually local white pine, basswood, or maple, was simply and often hastily constructed, and was decorated with graining, painting, stenciling, and striping in some combination. Churchill traces the evolution of decoration, charts regional characteristics, and provides data on decorators. Stephen Weston surveys decorative techniques. Kenneth Jewett describes the history and process of bronze stenciling. Plates illustrate tables, stands, chests, bureaus, boxes, desks, chairs, rockers, and several other forms.

Cogswell, Elizabeth Agee. "The Henry Lippitt House of Providence, Rhode Island." *Winterthur Portfolio* 17, no. 4 (Winter 1982): 203–42. 44 illustrations.

Cogswell describes the Providence mansion of Mary and Henry Lippitt built 1863–65. Not only are the exterior and the interior of the house largely intact, but also the majority of the furnishings survive, along with complete records identifying vendors, prices, and period names. The grandiose hallstand originally costing $625 and furniture for the dining room, reception room, and several bedrooms were sold by the Providence firm of Anthony, Potter, and Denison and are the only known examples of that firm's work. For the drawing room, the Lippitts paid $4,500 to the New York firm of Pottier and Stymus for several pieces of seating furniture, cornices, a center table, an étagère, a bronze cabinet, and a mantel frame, all "Tulip Ebony and Gilt." The survival of so much well-documented material makes the Lippitt house a valuable resource and reference tool.

Cohen, Lizabeth A. "Embellishing a Life of Labor: An Interpretation of the Material Culture of American Working-Class Homes, 1885–1915." *See* "Domestic Architecture."

Cook, Clarence. *The House Beautiful: Essays on Beds and Tables, Stools and Candlesticks.* 1878. Reprint. Croton-on-Hudson, N.Y.: North River Press, 1980. 336 pp.; 111 illustrations.

In this major text on household furnishing, four chapters deal with ways to furnish entrance, living room, dining room, and bedroom. The fifth and last chapter discusses taste in general and the problem of obtaining attractive goods at little cost. Throughout Cook stresses simplicity and utility, recommending a wide variety of oriental, European, and American forms and indicating that people "should put their own taste into their houses and not depend so much on professional help" (p. 336). The text is sprinkled with references to furniture and antiques dealers.

Cooke, Edward S., Jr. "The Boston Furniture Industry in 1880." *Old-Time New England* 70, no. 257 (1980): 82–98. 5 illustrations, appendixes.

Cooke notes that the Boston furniture industry of the late nineteenth century has received little scholarly attention, perhaps because of a belief that the industry declined after the fire of 1872. Relying on census records for 1880, he demonstrates that the industry remained healthy, attracted skilled craftsmen, and accepted technological innovation. Cooke draws from the credit ledgers of the Mercantile Agency to provide information on careers and movements of partners, operations, and products. He divides Boston's furniture industry of 1880 into three categories: firms producing high-quality furniture, usually on order, and acting as interior decorators; firms producing cheap pine goods; and firms concentrating on a specialty (folding chairs, extension tables, lounges, desks).

The Crystal Palace Exhibition. Reprint of *The Art Journal* and *Illustrated Catalogue: The Industry of All Nations.* 1851. New York: Dover Publications, 1970. xxxiv+426 pp.; illustrations.

This work provides engravings of the most interesting and suggestive objects as part of the *Art Journal* campaign to link the fine and industrial arts. It traces background and history of the great exhibition, the role of Prince Albert (to whom the volume is dedicated), the design of prize medals, Joseph Paxton's structure, safety tests for the building, Owen Jones's decoration, and the exhibition's positive impact on international relations. The volume illustrates and comments on hundreds of objects, among them about 150 pieces of furniture. American products include the centripetal spring chairs of American Chair Company, a wicker chair by Topf, an ebony table by Doe, Hazelton, and Company, and pianos by Nunn and Clark, J. Pirsson, and Chickering. Ralph Wornum's prize-winning essay, "The Exhibition as a Lesson in Taste," reports that there is nothing new in ornamental design, the taste of producers is uneducated, the influence of France is paramount, the Renaissance style is the best understood, and quantity of ornament does not imply beauty. Detailed discussions of individual objects are included.

Darling, Sharon. *Chicago Furniture: Art, Craft, and Industry, 1833–1983.* New York and London: W. W. Norton in association with Chicago Historical Society, 1984. xi+416 pp.; black and white illustrations, color plates, appendix, index.

Darling gives a comprehensive descriptive history of furniture making in Chicago. A sparsely settled trading outpost in 1833, "by 1885 Chicago had some 200 furniture factories and led the nation both in the number of employees engaged in that industry and in the amount of its annual production"

(p. 3). The city was a center of innovation, inspired by a variety of aesthetic programs, arts and crafts movements, and designers and architects. Darling deals with virtually all aspects and phases of the trade in Chicago: locations of furniture makers within the city; the introduction of machinery; the growth of specialization; the nature of the work force; the introduction and growth of unions; transportation; the use of trade catalogues and salesmen; mail-order sales; Chicago domination of the parlor furniture business; major and representative manufacturers of all periods; typical furniture forms; patented furniture; wickerwork; commercial furniture; fancy goods; art furniture; the modern Gothic taste; interior decorators; hand-carved furniture and reproductions; the arts and crafts movement; mission furniture; the prairie style; Frank Lloyd Wright; and many other topics. A wide range of illustrative material is included, as is an appendix that lists more than 500 firms.

Davies, Jane B. "Gothic Revival Furniture Designs of Alexander J. Davis." *Antiques* 111, no. 5 (May 1977): 1014–27. 17 black and white illustrations, 8 color plates.

Davies claims that A. J. Davis was the outstanding designer of Gothic revival country houses in America. He also devised some of the finest and most original Gothic revival furniture. Drawings, record books, letters, bills, and receipts document and date his work. Books by J. C. Loudon and the two Pugins seem to have influenced Davis most. The bulk of the article is a chronological survey of Davis furniture, with extensive comments on major commissions at Lyndhurst and Ericstan. Brief biographies of the craftsmen who produced Davis designs—Richard Byrne, Ambrose Wright, and William Burns—are included.

Denker, Ellen, and Bert Denker. *The Rocking Chair Book.* Foreword by Kenneth L. Ames. New York: Mayflower Books, a Main Street Press Book, 1979. 192 pp.; 175 illustrations, bibliography, index.

In this descriptive history of the rocking chair from earliest known examples to the present, the Denkers argue that rocking chairs, in use in this country by the 1740s, combine formal and functional elements derived from cradles and easy chairs. The first chair types to become rockers were children's, nurse, and common slat-back and Windsor armchairs. Early chapters tell how to know if a chair was originally made with rockers or if they were added later, and the Denkers offer extensive documentary evidence for the rocking chair's widespread popularity in the first half of the nineteenth century. Subsequent chapters survey common forms and materials: Boston and Grecian rockers; platform, folding, children's, and rustic rockers; the use of rocking chairs on porches; Shaker, quaint, and colonial revival rockers; and rockers in the twentieth century. Closing comments identify the rocking chair as a symbol of the past, of "the wisdom that comes with old age and the peaceful stability of family life," and of America itself (p. 176).

Dietz, Ulysses G. "Century of Revivals: Nineteenth-Century American Furniture from the Collection of the Newark Museum." *Newark Museum Quarterly* 31, nos. 2–3 (Spring–Summer 1980): 1–63. 55 illustrations.

Dietz highlights the most famous and important examples of Victorian furniture in Newark's collection. He includes objects by David Alling, Michael Allison, Alexander Roux, John Henry Belter, Mitchell and Rammelsberg, George Hunzinger, Collignon Brothers, and Gardner and Company. Prominent among Newark's holdings are more than twenty objects by the local John Jelliff and Company, twelve of which are included here. Each object in the catalogue is illustrated and accompanied by a brief essay commenting on its style, use, and meaning.

The Domestic Scene (1897–1927): George M. Niedecken, Interior Architect. See "The Arts and Crafts Movement in America."

Douglas, Diane M. "The Machine in the Parlor: A Dialectical Analysis of the Sewing Machine." *See* "Kitchen Artifacts and Housework."

Downing, A. J. "Furniture." In *The Architecture of Country Houses including Designs for Cottages, Farm Houses, and Villas,* pp. 406–60. 1850. Reprint. New York: Dover Publications, 1969. 122 illustrations.

Downing states that while the general character of a room depends on architectural forms and lines, its "expression" depends on the manner in which it is furnished. A room filled with furniture in keeping with its uses and the social life of those who use it has variety, intricacy, and significance of meaning. Fashion and good taste are not the same. Furniture in good taste is designed "in accordance with certain recognized styles, and intended to accord with apartments in the same style" (p. 408). Country houses should always be furnished more chastely and simply than town houses. Downing discusses the major styles of furniture that were available: the Grecian, or modern, which "has the merit of being simple, easily made, and very moderate in cost" (p. 412), modern French in the style of Louis Quatorze or Francis I, the Gothic, and Elizabethan and Romanesque.

Dubrow, Richard, and Eileen Dubrow. *Furniture Made in America, 1875–1905.* Exton, Pa.: Schiffer Publishing, 1982. 320 pp.; illustrations.

This work reprints without commentary more than 2,000 illustrations from the trade catalogues of about eighty furniture companies, including A. H. Andrews and Company, Derby and Kilmer Desk Company, Hale and Kilburn, Heywood Brothers, Peter Kehr, E. H. Mahoney, New Haven Folding Chair Company, Phoenix Chair Company, Rockford Union Furniture Company, M. and H. Schrenkeisen, Stickley-Brandt, E. W. Vail, and Wooton Desk Company. Images are arranged by type: parlor and library furniture; bedroom furniture; brass, iron, and folding beds; dining-room furniture; desks and office furniture; children's furniture; invalids' chairs; rocking chairs; folding chairs; hall stands, mirrors, and mantels; rattan and outdoor furniture; and miscellaneous (stands, small cabinets, wall furniture, ottomans, piano stools, and blacking cases).

Earl, Polly Anne. "Craftsmen and Machines: The Nineteenth-Century Furniture Industry." In *Technological Innovation and the Decorative Arts*, edited by Ian M. G. Quimby and Polly Anne Earl, pp. 307–29. Charlottesville: University Press of Virginia for the Henry Francis du Pont Winterthur Museum, 1974. 12 illustrations.

Earl writes that much of our modern vision of craftsmen and craftsmanship is rooted in romantic and nostalgic notions of the preindustrial past. In fact, the distinction between hand and machine labor is not rigid, and the transition from craft to industry was complex. Machines came into use later than is usually assumed; the machines allegedly responsible for the "pillar-and-scroll" style of the 1840s, for example, were not yet in general use at that date. The furniture trade industrialized at different rates, and the introduction of machinery did not necessarily mean heavy industry; many machines ran on human power conveyed through foot treadles.

Eastlake, Charles L. *Hints on Household Taste in Furniture, Upholstery, and Other Details.* New introduction by Joan Gloag. 1878. Reprint. New York: Dover Publications, 1969. xxx+304 pp.; illustrations, 31 black and white and color plates, index.

This work represents the first major tract in the household art movement. Eastlake is full of opinions, which he freely states; he finds deficiencies and absurdities in all aspects of public taste and believes that competition is responsible for the decline in national (British) taste. The "real secret" of old woodwork, he says, lies in its immensely superior workmanship (p. 60). Furniture should be simple but picturesque, rectangular in shape, and made of joined construction. It should not be light and elegant, but "strong and comely" (p. 162). Eastlake provides specific comments and designs for dining tables, sideboards, chairs, bookcases, sofas, beds, and other forms in this key historic text.

Ettema, Michael J. "Forum: History, Nostalgia, and American Furniture." *Winterthur Portfolio* 17, nos. 2/3 (Summer/Autumn 1982): 135–44.

Ettema argues that museum scholarship is unreflective, nostalgic rather than historical. Typical research and writing on American furniture combines aesthetic and historical impulses, the first manifest in subjective judgments of value, the second in the effort to collect facts; together they constitute the antiquarian tradition. Ettema holds that, since its origin, furniture history has demonstrated ideological homogeneity and little conceptual change and that furniture historians have consistently sought the appreciation of artifacts through unsynthesized historical data. The only recent trend is "sci-entific antiquarianism" (p. 137), which uses methodological vigor to maximize the accuracy of object identification. Current writings are assessed in detailed analyses by Ettema.

Ettema, Michael J. "Technological Innovation and Design Economics in Furniture Manufacture." *Winterthur Portfolio* 16, nos. 2/3 (Summer/Autumn 1981): 197–223. 26 illustrations.

In this article, Ettema notes that furniture historians have long assumed that machines and technology were responsible for the elaborate styles of the nineteenth century. They have overestimated the capabilities of machinery and failed to recognize that "furniture production in this country is and always has been a business subject to the same basic economic laws that govern the manufacture of other consumer durable goods" (p. 198). Ettema cites that machinery had little effect on expensive, trend-setting goods; it reduced the cost of operations that were already inexpensive, but did not greatly affect more costly technologies like carving. No practical carving machines were widely used until *after* the period of the most elaborate furniture styles. He discusses how understanding design economics of furniture requires familiarity with the physical and economic capabilities of machines for preparation and joinery (circular saws, planers, sanders, mortisers, tenoners, dovetailers), for forming parts (band saws, scroll saws, lathes), and for decorating (molders, shapers and routers, carvers, embossers).

Fales, Dean A., Jr. *American Painted Furniture, 1660–1880.* Illustrations and design editor, Robert Bishop; general editor, Cyril I. Nelson. New York: E. P. Dutton, 1972. 299 pp.; 511 black and white and color illustrations, bibliography, indexes.

Fales observes that painting preserves and embellishes furniture and is economical. Three basic types occur in America: plain painting, imitative painting, and imaginative or fancy painting. The period from the 1820s to the 1840s was the golden age of American painted furniture. About a third of the book deals with these years and includes sections on painted empire forms, the products of female academies, Hitchcock chairs, and eccentric and colorful forms. The majority of painted furniture is from New England. *See also* "American Furniture to 1820."

Farnam, Anne. "A. H. Davenport and Company, Boston Furniture Makers." *Antiques* 109, no. 5 (May 1976): 1048–55. 11 black and white illustrations, 2 color plates.

A. H. Davenport made furniture for Iolani Palace, the White House, and the mansions of the wealthy. The firm worked with leading architects: Peabody and Stearns; H. H. Richardson and his successors Shepley, Rutan, and Coolidge; Arthur Little; and McKim, Mead, and White. Davenport's high standards of design and production can be attributed in part to Francis H. Bacon, an Ecole des Beaux-Arts–trained architect who served first as designer and later as vice-president. Bacon drew on, and may have helped to assemble, the company's extensive design library, which included historical studies by Irving Lyon, Esther Singleton, and Percy Macquoid, as well as design books by Thomas Chippendale, George Hepplewhite, Thomas Sheraton, and others.

Fendelman, Helaine W. *Tramp Art: An Itinerant's Folk Art*. New York: E. P. Dutton, 1975. 127 pp.; 120 black and white illustrations, 11 color plates, bibliography.

Tramp art is decorative woodcarving in which small geometric notches are chipped or carved out of solid wooden surfaces. Layers of wood decorated this way are then nailed or glued together in elaborately complicated forms, usually small objects like boxes, clock cases, cabinets, mirror and picture frames, comb cases, jardinieres, or whatnots, but also an occasional chest of drawers, sideboard, lounge, and bedstead. Fendelman presents examples of tramp art, which flourished from the late nineteenth century to the 1940s.

Fennimore, Donald L. "American Neoclassical Furniture and Its European Antecedents." *American Art Journal* 13, no. 4 (Autumn 1981): 49–65. 26 illustrations.

Fennimore presents American furniture as an amalgam of European prototypes. He holds that cabinetmakers probably obtained European designs in one of four ways: through training in Europe; from imported furniture books; from American price books published to standardize journeymen's wages and furniture prices; and from actual pieces of imported furniture. Likely instances of each alternative are discussed and illustrated. Whatever their source, few pieces of American furniture were direct copies of European models.

Fitzgerald, Oscar P. *The Green Family of Cabinetmakers: An Alexandria Institution, 1817–1887*. Exhibition catalogue. Alexandria, Va.: Alexandria Association, 1986. 59 pp.; illustrations, 36 illustrated entries, bibliography.

The history and production of a family firm long active in Alexandria, Virginia, are outlined in this catalogue. At their peak in the 1850s, the Greens sold furniture locally and in Washington and shipped their products throughout the country, to the West Indies, and even to Europe. The catalogue portion of this monograph illustrates and discusses thirty-four labeled or otherwise documented objects. Most are middle-level goods and date between 1840 and 1870. Also included are a rare engraved copperplate for a Green advertisement of the 1820s and two volumes of accounts for a rival firm, listing sales for 1807–15, 1857–58, and 1884–88.

Fitzgerald, Oscar P. *Three Centuries of American Furniture*. Englewood Cliffs, N.J.: Prentice-Hall, 1982. xii+323 pp.; 527 black and white illustrations, 8 color plates, appendix, bibliography, index.

In this descriptive survey summarizing and synthesizing research of the last twenty years, relevant chapters are those on American empire, Gothic, rococo, Renaissance, Eastlake, and other revivals and, to a lesser degree, on country, south-ern, and Shaker goods. Fitzgerald approaches furniture "from both a cultural and aesthetic point of view" (p. vii). Most chapters provide comments on background design activity in Europe and examinations of major makers, movements, and forms in this country. Fitzgerald's treatment of Gothic revival furniture outlines demographic and cultural changes in mid nineteenth-century America and discusses the impact of Pugin, Davis, and Downing. Well-chosen illustrations show both costly and commonplace examples. An appendix reprints George Henkel's *Catalogue of Furniture in Every Style*. An annotated bibliography is included. *See also* "American Furniture to 1820."

Gellerman, Robert F. *The American Reed Organ: . . . Its History; How It Works; How to Rebuild It*. Vestal, N.Y.: Vestal Press, 1973. x+173 pp.; 145 illustrations, 10 tables, bibliography, appendixes, index.

The reed organ, not widely built in this country until 1846, reached a peak of popularity about 1890, then was eclipsed by the piano and phonograph. Gellerman provides capsule histories of many firms, including Estey and Company, Mason and Hamlin, and Daniel F. Beatty, and lists critical patents. Music was arranged especially for the reed organ, and several popular songs of the nineteenth century are reprinted here. The text offers guidelines for collectors and technical discussions of stops and voices, restoration, and tuning. An appendix illustrates more than 200 reed organs, most of them in images drawn from period trade catalogues and advertising cards and ranging in date from 1857 to about 1920.

Giedion, Siegfried. *Mechanization Takes Command: A Contribution to Anonymous History*. 1948. Reprint. New York: W. W. Norton, Norton Library, 1969. xiv+743 pp.; 501 illustrations, index.

In his sweeping and encyclopedic inquiry into the effects of mechanization on human beings, Giedion assesses the extent to which mechanization corresponds to or contradicts "the unalterable laws of human nature" (p. v). Furniture is discussed in part 5, "Mechanization Encounters Human Surroundings" (esp. pp. 329–510). Giedion argues that beginning with the empire period, symbols were devalued. Furniture became a dominant object, treated in the spirit of self-sufficient architecture. The upholsterer took on new importance, depriving furniture of any definite shape and obscuring the frame. Giedion defines two categories of objects: transitory and constituent. Transitory objects are short-lived, lacking creative force and invention. Constituent objects are the opposite and form the core of historical growth; patented furniture is the constituent furniture of the nineteenth century. Case studies examine patented furniture for sitting and lying, the mechanization of the barber chair and the reclining chair, and the development of convertible furniture. A lengthy section explores patented furniture for railroad use. After about 1890, inventiveness gradually leaves patented furniture and moves to the kitchen, the bathroom, and laborsaving devices. *See also* "Kitchen Artifacts and Housework"; "Plumbing, Heating, and Lighting."

Gilborn, Craig. *Adirondack Furniture and the Rustic Tradition*. New York: Harry N. Abrams, 1987. 352 pp.; 307 black and white illustrations, 50 color plates, bibliography, index.

Gilborn surveys rustic furniture used in the Adirondacks of New York, much of it within a 10-mile radius of Raquette Lake. He sketches the rustic taste in England and America from the early eighteenth century to the early twentieth and charts the development of Adirondack vacation housing from rough shanties to sprawling and sometimes luxurious cottages. The major emphasis is on two broad categories of furniture: the "twiggy rustic," made locally, and cottage furniture, made elsewhere but considered appropriate for Adirondack settings. The first category includes furniture made of sticks, cedar, roots and burls, peeled poles and branches, applied bark, mosaic twigwork, and animals, both carved and actual. The second includes Indiana hickory, rustic bentwood, Mottville (New York) chairs, and craftsman furniture and the board seats known as Westport and Adirondack chairs. Gilborn concludes with a discussion of regional artisans past and present. The text is beautifully illustrated.

Greene, Leslie A. "The Late Victorian Hallstand: A Social History." *Nineteenth Century* 6, no. 4 (Winter 1980): 51–53. 5 illustrations.

Once a prominent household feature, the hallstand peaked in popularity in the 1870s. After that date it fell from favor with the affluent but remained part of popular culture. Models of 1895–1905 usually added a seat to the mirror, hatrack, and umbrella-stand components common to earlier examples. Authors of decorating books tried to dissuade readers from buying "the ungainly and unpopular" hatrack (p. 51), arguing that it was untidy, unpleasant, and virtually useless. By 1920 changing house plans, the colonial revival, hall closets, and the telephone combined to make the hallstand obsolete. Greene concludes that it was "a fitting symbol of the late Victorian middle class, suggesting affluence within the strictures of economy" (p. 53).

Hall, John. *The Cabinet Makers' Assistant, Embracing the Most Modern Style of Cabinet Furniture*. 1840. Reprint. New York: National Superior, 1944. 40 pp.; 43 plates.

Hall's preface notes, "novelty, simplicity and practicability" characterize cabinetmakers' designs, some of which are original, whereas others are based on work already executed. Throughout, attention has been paid to saving labor, which Hall hopes will make the book attractive to cabinetmakers. The first four plates provide instruction in drawing in perspective, but most of the rest offer designs for entire or parts of bedsteads, pier tables, center tables, sofas, lounges, reclining chairs, hall chairs, worktables, tabourettes, bureaus, toilet tables, wardrobes, bookcases, music stools, and other objects. Each plate is accompanied by a brief explanation.

Hanks, David A. *Innovative Furniture in America from 1800 to the Present*. Introduction by Russell Lynes; essays by Rodris Roth and Page Talbott. Exhibition catalogue. New York: Horizon Press, 1981. 200 pp.; 169 illustrations, bibliography, index.

In his introduction, Lynes argues that there are two kinds of furniture: that on which we impose our wills (friendly furniture) and that which imposes its will on us (disciplinary furniture). Innovative furniture tends to fit into the first category. Hanks acknowledges the volume's debt to Siegfried Giedion's *Mechanization Takes Command* and explains that objects were selected on the basis of their innovative and aesthetic significance. Roth describes how the American patent system works, notes the growing specialization of patented forms throughout the nineteenth century, defines patent terms, and identifies some of the major types of patented furniture. The text groups objects in five categories: techniques of bending and laminating (Samuel Gragg, Belter, Isaac Cole, Gardner and Company, rustic bentwood); materials (cast iron, bent steel, steel mesh, wire, rattan, animal horns, branches); comfort (coil springs, rotary chairs, platform rockers, invalid chairs, Morris chairs); portability (folding chairs); and multiple functions (convertible furniture, library chairs, sofa beds, Wooton desks). Each section is introduced by a brief essay. Illustrations are accompanied by extensive historical and descriptive commentary.

Hanks, David A. *Isaac E. Scott Reform Furniture in Chicago: John Jacob Glessner House*. Chicago: Chicago School of Architecture Foundation, 1974. 31 pp.; 24 illustrations.

Hanks argues that Scott (1845–1920) was one of Chicago's most important nineteenth-century craftsmen and designers. Most of his known work was commissioned by the Glessner family. Although made for this family's previous residence, Scott's furniture was later moved into the house on South Prairie Avenue, which was built for them by H. H. Richardson in 1887. A cabinet-bookcase ordered by the Glessners in 1875 is Scott's earliest piece of documented furniture and his most ambitious. This and other furniture designs suggest that Scott had firsthand familiarity with English furniture of the period. He apparently did his own carving and was active as interior designer, architect, and potter.

Hanks, David A., and Donald C. Peirce. *The Virginia Carroll Crawford Collection: American Decorative Arts, 1825–1917*. Atlanta: High Museum of Art, 1983. 94 pp.; black and white and color plates.

Introductory texts outline the history and justification for this collection of costly and extraordinary objects from the nineteenth and early twentieth centuries. The catalogue includes about fifty pieces of furniture, ranging from a rosewood center table possibly designed by A. J. Davis, cabinets and a table by Alexander Roux, and John Henry Belter seating furniture, to examples by Herter Brothers, Will H. Low,

Frank Furness, Gustave Stickley, and others. Objects are illustrated and accompanied by brief commentary.

Hanks, David A., and Page Talbott. "Daniel Pabst— Philadelphia Cabinetmaker." *Bulletin*, Philadelphia Museum of Art, 73, no. 316 (April 1977): 3–24. 22 illustrations.

Pabst (1826–1910) was among Philadelphia's foremost cabinetmakers in the second half of the nineteenth century. Born and trained in Germany, he settled in Philadelphia in 1849. In 1854 he opened his own shop, patronized by the city's wealthy. The earliest furniture attributable to Pabst was made for historian Henry Charles Lea about 1868 and includes a now-famous sideboard in Philadelphia Museum of Art. In the 1870s Pabst worked in the modern Gothic style of the English reformers, and his major design source was probably Christopher Dresser. Reform ideas found particularly full expression in work apparently designed by Philadelphia architect Frank Furness and executed by Pabst; the most notable was for the house of Theodore Roosevelt, Sr., at 6 West Fifty-seventh Street in New York. Some of this furniture now survives at Sagamore Hill, Oyster Bay, Long Island.

Hauserman, Dianne D. "Alexander Roux and His 'Plain and Artistic Furniture.'" *Antiques* 93, no. 2 (February 1968): 210–17. 17 illustrations.

Born in France, Roux (ca. 1813–86) appears in New York City directories in 1837, listed as an upholsterer. Roux and Company had a long and illustrious history, remaining in business until 1898. As early as 1855 it employed 120 people. Among early examples of Roux's work are four Gothic chairs from 1848, which resemble examples in the White House and Brooklyn Museum. Roux is mentioned in A. J. Downing's *Architecture of Country Houses* and may have made furniture for A. J. Davis. The diversity of styles popular in the 1850s is evident from the furniture that Roux supplied for Rokeby, a house in Tarrytown, New York: Elizabethan slipper chairs, Renaissance cabinets, rococo armchairs, and austere bedroom furniture. Among his most magnificent products is the five-piece bedroom suite in the Henry Shaw House in St. Louis, probably made before 1857. "The quality and diversification of Alexander Roux's craftsmanship rank him with the best of his competitors" (p. 217).

Hill, John H. "Furniture Designs of Henry W. Jenkins and Sons Co." In *Winterthur Portfolio 5*, edited by Richard K. Doud, pp. 155–87. Charlottesville: University Press of Virginia for the Henry Francis du Pont Winterthur Museum, 1969. 30 illustrations, appendix.

Hill reports on the Jenkins firm, founded in Baltimore in 1799. Since 1904 its business has been funerals, not furniture. After 1857, the firm was directed by Henry W. Jenkins, joined by his architect son Thomas W. in 1864. After Henry's death in 1878, the company advertised both a cabinetmaking and an interior decorating house specializing in customwork. A collection of approximately 2,500 Jenkins drawings, some in watercolor and gouache, survive, and most date from the 1870s to about 1900. These are roughly grouped by subject matter (chairs, sofa and divans, tables, cabinets, sideboards, bookcases, and parlor, hall, and chamber furniture) in twenty-nine uniform boxes probably made by the company. Many depict room settings and record period nomenclature, names of patrons, or prices; some indicate that the firm also repaired, reupholstered, and remodeled older pieces. "The greatest single value" of the drawings is that they show "precisely what furniture forms were being made and used during the last quarter of the nineteenth century" (p. 175). Included in the Jenkins materials are many colored and lithographed plates, many published by D. Guilmard of Paris.

Howe, Katherine S., and David B. Warren. *The Gothic Revival Style in America, 1830–1870*. Houston: Museum of Fine Arts, 1976. viii+101 pp.; approximately 200 black and white illustrations, 10 color plates, glossary, bibliography, index.

Jane B. Davies's introduction notes that the Gothic revival style looked to the Middle Ages for inspiration and reintroduced a vocabulary of forms and motifs long out of favor. The Gothic "expressed the very quintessence of Romanticism—bold, dramatic, closely linked to nature, a visual evocation of the brooding melancholy and mystery of the remote Middle Ages" (p. 1). Houses in the Gothic style appeared by the 1830s and were common in the 1840s. Cabinetmakers did not reproduce medieval furniture, but adapted and applied medieval motifs to contemporary forms. Objects produced in this country attained a distinctive American quality. Included in the catalogue are more than 100 pieces of furniture, about half of which are chairs; the rest are couches, settees, tables, desks, wardrobes, bookcases, dressers, hallstands, and other forms. Cabinetmakers and designers represented include Alexander Roux, John and Joseph Meeks, A. J. Davis, Thomas Brooks, James Renwick, George Henkels, John Jelliff, John Needles, Anthony Quervelle, and others less familiar. Objects are illustrated and accompanied by documentation and description. *See also* "Surveys."

Ingerman, Elizabeth A. "Personal Experiences of an Old New York Cabinetmaker." *Antiques* 84, no. 5 (November 1963): 576–80. 10 illustrations.

Ingerman presents a transcription of recollections written by Ernest Hagen in 1908 and now at Winterthur. Hagen was an amateur historian and the first to study Duncan Phyfe. His recollections combine autobiography with comments on other firms and prevailing conditions within the furniture trade. Hagen was born in Hamburg in 1830 and came to the United States in 1844. He wrote that work in the 1840s was all done by hand (except for scroll sawing), that mahogany was the dominant wood, and that among the most prominent cabinetmakers was Henry Weil, who made large bedsteads and case furniture for sale in the South. Small shops employing two to six makers specialized in veneered box sofas, French bedsteads, bureaus, bookcases, card tables, center tables, or chairs. Hagen worked for Charles Baudouine, who made ornate rosewood furniture and oak dining-room furniture "all in French carved style with bunches of fruit and game hanging on the panels" (p. 578), from about 1853 to 1855. Hagen mentions Roux, Rochefort and Skarren, Pottier and Stymus, Marcotte, Herter Brothers, Cottier and Company, and others.

Jenkins, Irving. *Hawaiian Furniture and Hawaii's Cabinetmakers, 1820–1940*. Photographs by Michael D. Horikawa. Honolulu: Editions Limited for the Daughters of Hawaii, 1983. xiii+350 pp.; black and white and color illustrations, map, line drawings, appendixes, bibliography, index.

Jenkins provides a descriptive history of furniture making in the Hawaiian Islands. While most furniture was similar to that made in the United States, Hawaii claims the only American royal furniture and extensive use of koa wood. Koa was found on the five largest islands. Although distinguished by considerable range in figuring and color, koa is difficult to work and therefore rarely exported in the nineteenth century. It was used more out of necessity than because it was admired. Today it has become a prized symbol of the Hawaiian past. Hawaiian furniture making is divided into five phases: missionary work; cabinetmakers of the Kamehameha dynasty; cabinetmakers and furniture companies of the Kalakaua period; Chinese furniture makers; and the twentieth century. Biographies of individual makers and firms are accompanied by color illustrations of examples of their work.

Johnson, Marilynn. "Art Furniture: Wedding the Beautiful to the Useful." In Doreen Bolger Burke et al., *In Pursuit of Beauty: Americans and the Aesthetic Movement*, pp. 142–75. Exhibition catalogue. New York: Rizzoli International Publications in association with the Metropolitan Museum of Art, 1986. 36 black and white illustrations, 8 color plates.

In one of eleven essays on various aspects of the aesthetic movement assembled in a massive volume published to accompany an exhibition at Metropolitan Museum, Johnson argues that late nineteenth-century critics, designers, and collectors all attempted to reunite the beautiful and the useful to repair the split "between art and craft, and between art and manufacture" (p. 143). Her discussion begins with English art furniture and its initial impact in America, then moves to an examination of art furniture exhibited at the Centennial. A brief treatment of Cincinnati carved furniture leads to commentary on trends after the Centennial and an account of some of the premises and products of the colonial revival.

Jones, Michael Owen. *The Hand Made Object and Its Maker. See "Craftsmen."*

Joy, Edward T. *English Furniture, 1800–1851*. London: Sotheby Parke Bernet Publications, Ward Lock, 1977.

318 pp.; black and white illustrations, 8 color plates, index.

Richly illustrated with excellent photographs of individual objects and views of interiors, this study shows how transformations begun in the eighteenth century continued through the first half of the nineteenth century. Joy argues that comfort and elegance became increasingly diffused through a society that was expanding at a prodigious rate. The two most important influences on furniture were the picturesque (which brought romanticism, interdiscipline, historicism, and eclecticism) and the industrial revolution (which encouraged new materials, experimentation, novelty, and comfort). Throughout the period, a tension between the vernacular and the fashionable prevailed. Individual chapters deal with the Regency; Grecian, Egyptian, and Chinese tastes; historic revivals; royal-furniture makers; interiors; patent furniture; the structure of the industry, including a brief discussion of English impact on American furniture; materials and methods; and the exhibition of 1851.

Kassay, John. *The Book of Shaker Furniture*. Amherst: University of Massachusetts Press, 1980. xxii+265 pp.; 254 illustrations, approximately 70 measured drawings, tables, appendix, glossary.

Based on a decade of preparation, this book provides construction plans for all major forms of Shaker furniture. Kassay begins with a brief history of the Shakers and their furniture, which falls into two groups: shop furniture and dwelling furniture. The first served domestic activities and occupations associated with kitchens, laundries, and shops and is usually pine, nail assembled, and painted. The second, for dining, gathering, and retiring rooms, tends to be made of hard woods and represents a higher order of craftsmanship. Shaker furniture also passed through three periods: the primitive, 1790–1820, characterized by forms that were heavy, crude, and plain but strong and functional; the classic, 1820–60, of subtle, elegant, and delicate forms; and Victorian Shaker, after 1860, made with walnut and dark stains, complex turnings and contours, and applied decorative pieces. Kassay comments on working methods, tools, woods, and paints and the difficulty of determining date and origin. The major feature of the book is the extensive collection of photographs and meticulous, measured drawings and the descriptive and evaluative captions that reflect the pragmatic viewpoint of a practicing designer.

Kenney, John Tarrant. *The Hitchcock Chair: The Story of a Connecticut Yankee—L. Hitchcock of Hitchcocks-ville—and an Account of the Restoration of His Nineteenth-Century Manufactory*. New York: Clarkson N. Potter, 1971. x+339 pp.; black and white illustrations, 10 color plates, appendixes, bibliography, index.

A rambling personal account of the discovery and restoration of the Hitchcock factory and reproduction of the chairs made there between 1825 and 1864 flanks a detailed history of

Lambert Hitchcock (1795–1852) and the company he founded. Hitchcock, probably a chairmaker in his youth, came to Barkhamsted, Connecticut, in 1818 at the age of twenty-three and began making chair parts. By 1820 or 1821 he was producing complete chairs and by 1825 had built a new factory, where more than 100 employees made 15,000 chairs per year. Kenney discusses financing, transportation, fabrication and decoration, competition, diversification, partnerships, stores, expansion, changing company structure, Hitchcock's eventual move to Unionville, and his personal life. This work is primarily a pictorial survey of fancy and Windsor chairs, rockers, and settees made by Hitchcock and his contemporaries.

Lapp, Henry. *A Craftsman's Handbook*. Introduction and notes by Beatrice B. Garvan. Philadelphia: Philadelphia Museum of Art in association with Tinicum Press, 1975. Unpag.; 47 color plates.

This work is a reproduction of a small notebook created by deaf and partially mute Amish cabinetmaker Lapp (1862–1904) to display samples of his work to prospective purchasers. Lapp worked in Bird-in-Hand, Lancaster County, Pennsylvania, where he made traditional forms like chests, drop-leaf tables, cupboards, bureaus, wash benches, saltboxes, bedsteads, cradles, and settees. These objects, "as well as games and toys, seed boxes, flower stands, counter boxes, buggies, sleighs, and wagons, give glimpses into the industry, humor, enterprise, and mobility of the people in the heart of the Pennsylvania German farmlands where Lapp was born." Lapp also made frequent trips to Philadelphia, and some forms and finishes reveal influences from beyond Lancaster County. All plates are accompanied by brief notes on form and use.

McClaugherty, Martha Crabill. "Household Art: Creating the Artistic Home, 1868–1893." *Winterthur Portfolio* 18, no. 1 (Spring 1983): 1–26. 19 illustrations, annotated bibliography.

Household art was a distinct movement in the late nineteenth century, propagated through books and articles written by tastemakers who emphasized the moral influence of the home. The first book in the movement was Charles Eastlake's *Hints on Household Taste* (1868); the last was Candace Wheeler's *Household Art* (1893). Drawing on books and articles written between these dates, McClaugherty locates the phenomenon of household art within prevailing perceptions of the home, analyzes major doctrines and aesthetic principles, and reconstructs ideal interiors of the late nineteenth century. Household-art literature shares four traits: organization of material by room or by room components; emphasis on the importance of the domestic environment; reference to the work of leading interior designers; and use of reinforcing illustrations. These manuals told women readers that antique furniture was a sign of exquisite taste and that rooms should be organized around distinct compositions of furnishings. Specific comments are included

on furnishing halls, libraries, dining rooms, drawing rooms, and bedrooms.

Made in Ohio: Furniture, 1788–1888. Exhibition catalogue. Columbus: Columbus Museum of Art, 1984. 128 pp.; 88 black and white and color plates.

This catalogue records the first major exhibition of documented Ohio furniture. Charles Muller's essay points out that Ohio was populated by a mixture of peoples, and, therefore, there is no single Ohio style, but "a rich diversity" (p. 10). Nonetheless, some forms seem typical of Ohio: freestanding corner cupboards; one- or two-drawer stands; punched-tin pie safes; turned-leg drop-leaf tables; two-piece Mennonite wardrobes; and glazed-door flat-wall cupboards. Objects range from a walnut cupboard of 1788, believed to be the earliest surviving example of Ohio furniture, to the massive sideboard made in Cincinnati in 1880 by Henry Fry for President and Mrs. Hayes. Early and rural goods are heavily represented. More than half the objects date between 1820 and 1850; thirty are from the second half of the century. All are illustrated and accompanied by biographical data about the maker and comments on related objects in Ohio and elsewhere.

Madigan, Mary Jean. *Eastlake-Influenced American Furniture, 1870–1890*. Yonkers, N.Y.: Hudson River Museum, 1973. Unpag.; 67 illustrations, bibliography.

Madigan says that the rectilinear furniture with spindles, incising, and conventionalized relief carving called "Eastlake" deserves recognition as a widely manufactured and popular style of the late nineteenth century. More than anyone else, Eastlake was responsible for bringing the principles of the English design reform movement to the United States. In *Hints on Household Taste*, he expounded the principles of simplicity, functionalism, and honesty of construction. Contrary to what is sometimes claimed, however, Eastlake rejected neither machine-made furniture nor veneering and did not advocate any style in particular. In the 1870s and 1880s, American manufacturers made free translations of his designs, assigning his name to nearly anything with rectilinear outlines and incised decoration. Eastlake's most important contribution may have been to raise popular consciousness about furniture's function, construction, and design. This catalogue illustrates and discusses a variety of forms.

Madigan, Mary Jean Smith. "The Influence of Charles Locke Eastlake on American Furniture Manufacture, 1870–90." In *Winterthur Portfolio 10*, edited by Ian M. G. Quimby, pp. 1–22. Charlottesville: University Press of Virginia for the Henry Francis du Pont Winterthur Museum, 1975. 20 illustrations.

Madigan poses three questions: Was there a definable Eastlake style in America between 1870 and 1890? Did furniture of the period conform to Eastlake's dicta on form, construction, and ornamentation? Was it economically feasible to mass produce Eastlake furniture in America? Madigan ultimately answers yes to all three, but her search for answers allows her to record the major teachings of, responses to, and disciples of Eastlake. More popular in this country than in England, Eastlake's ideas were further disseminated by Henry Hudson Holly, Charles Wyllys Elliott, Harriet Spofford, and Clarence Cook. Eastlake-style furniture became common after the Centennial, and the name referred to almost anything in an English reform manner. By the late 1870s, four grades of Eastlake-influenced furniture were available: very expensive, turned out to individual orders by cabinetmakers; moderately expensive, stocked in small quantities and sold retail by its maker-dealers; moderately priced, made in midwestern factories for eastern sales; and inexpensive, for a working-class market. Madigan illustrates and discusses products of Herter Brothers, Daniel Pabst, Kimbel and Cabus, Williamsport Furniture Manufacturing Company, Brooklyn Furniture Company, and others.

Makinson, Randell L. *Greene and Greene: Furniture and Related Designs*. Santa Barbara and Salt Lake City: Peregrine Smith, 1978. 161 pp.; approximately 225 black and white illustrations and 14 color plates, bibliography, index.

This is a companion volume to *Greene and Greene: Architecture as a Fine Art*, also by Makinson, who asserts that if composition and craftsmanship determine quality, then the work of California brothers Charles Sumner Greene and Henry Mather Greene was unsurpassed by other arts and crafts practitioners. Committed to total involvement with the entire spectrum of design, Greene and Greene designed a variety of furnishings to complement their houses, including furniture, lighting fixtures, and hardware. Makinson outlines the chronology of works and evolution of the Greenes' ideas between 1900 and the 1930s. Their early work, 1901 to 1904, was heavily influenced by Gustave Stickley's *Craftsman*. In 1904 they embraced oriental, particularly Chinese, ideas and forms, seen in their furniture for the Adelaide Tichenor house. Greene and Greene enjoyed the height of their popularity between 1907 and 1911. Makinson discusses and illustrates major commissions, describing features of design and construction. After the firm dissolved in 1922, the brothers continued their work individually—Charles in Carmel, and Henry still in Pasadena. *See also* "The Arts and Crafts Movement in America."

Mayhew, Edgar de N., and Minor Myers, Jr. *A Documentary History of American Interiors from the Colonial Era to 1915*. See "Domestic Architecture"; "Surveys."

Moore, J. Roderick. "Wythe County, Virginia, Punched Tin: Its Influence and Imitators." *Antiques* 126, no. 3 (September 1984): 601–13. 23 black and white illustrations, 8 color plates, checklist.

Food safes were both hand made and mass produced in the nineteenth century. Using sheets of punched tin for decoration and ventilation was popular in the Southeast and the Midwest. Moore states that the quality of these tin panels reached a peak in the mid nineteenth century in and around Wythe County. Safes made in that area are larger than those made elsewhere, are of walnut, cherry, or yellow poplar, with yellow poplar secondary wood, and have dovetailed drawers. Many were probably produced by Fleming K. Rich and his family, who ran both a furniture factory and a tinsmithing shop. Surviving papers record the sale of a safe as early as 1830. Between 1840 and 1849, the firm made and sold more than 280 safes in Wythe County as well as elsewhere in Virginia and eastern Tennessee. Moore provides detailed commentary on illustrated examples.

Muller, Charles R., and Timothy D. Rieman. *The Shaker Chair*. Foreword by Jerry Grant; illustrations by Stephen Metzger; photography by Timothy D. Rieman. Canal Winchester, Ohio: Canal Press, 1984. [xx]+232+[17] pp.; black and white and color illustrations, line drawings, appendixes, bibliography, index.

In this book devoted entirely to Shaker chairs, Muller and Rieman attribute them to particular communities on the basis of oral tradition, provenance, design features, historic photographs, and a variety of written documents. The text outlines the elements of Shaker chair style and reprints extensive excerpts for the years 1861–63 from the journal of chairmaker Freegift Wells. Individual chapters describe and illustrate chairs from Watervliet, New York; Enfield and Canterbury, New Hampshire; Harvard, Massachusetts; Enfield, Connecticut; Alfred and Sabbathday Lake, Maine; the Ohio communities; and Pleasant Hill and South Union, Kentucky. The last chapter examines the history of chairmaking at New Lebanon, New York. An appendix discusses non-Shaker manufacturers of Shaker-type chairs.

Neat Pieces: The Plain-Style Furniture of Nineteenth-Century Georgia. Exhibition catalogue. Atlanta, Ga.: Atlanta Historical Society, 1983. vi+204 pp.; black and white illustrations, 8 color plates, checklist.

This catalogue illustrates and describes 126 examples of plain furniture made in Georgia between about 1820 and 1860 to convey impressions of the "simple, strong and rather difficult" (p. 3) everyday life of nineteenth-century Georgians. Religion, humor, and democracy were important in daily life and may have influenced the kinds of furniture that Georgians preferred. The furniture was much like that of the rest of the country, although several typically southern forms were produced, including huntboards (known as sideboards or slabs in period documents), lazy Susan (turn-top or round) tables, cellarettes, sugar chests, and hide-bottom slat-back chairs. An appended checklist of recorded makers includes some 1,300 names.

Nelson, Marion J. "The Material Culture and Folk Arts of the Norwegians in America." In *Perspectives on American Folk Art*, edited by Ian M. G. Quimby and Scott T. Swank, pp. 79–133. New York: W. W. Norton for the Henry Francis du Pont Winterthur Museum, 1980. 43 illustrations.

Between 1836 and 1876, some 200,000 Norwegians came to the United States. Most settled in Illinois, Wisconsin, Iowa, and Minnesota. Nelson discusses their furnishings, which followed the forms and construction of traditional Norwegian items but usually omitted or reduced decoration. Characteristic forms include log and three-legged chairs, benches, bed benches, box tables, chests of drawers, desks, and cupboards. Chests of drawers and desks were among the most finely made pieces, whereas cupboards show the most diversification and the greatest detail and decoration. Major figures whose work survives include Aasmund Aslakson Nestestog, Martin Olson, and Lars Christenson. In the 1930s Norwegian Americans experienced a mass nostalgia resulting in the revival of rosemaling, vigorously encouraged for more than forty years, particularly in Stoughton, Wisconsin. Rosemaling may "ultimately be considered the most important contribution of the immigrants from Norway to folk art in America" (p. 132).

Nineteenth-Century America: Furniture and Other Decorative Arts. Introduction by Berry B. Tracy; furniture texts by Marilynn Johnson; other decorative arts texts by Marvin D. Schwartz and Suzanne Boorsch. Exhibition catalogue. New York: Metropolitan Museum of Art, 1970; distributed by New York Graphic Society. xxxii+[232] pp.; line drawings, 298 black and white and color illustrated entries, index, bibliography.

This survey of high-style decorative arts was published as part of a celebration of Metropolitan Museum's 100th anniversary and includes well over 100 pieces of furniture. Tracy's introduction provides a descriptive outline of design history, citing major stylistic currents, designers, publications, and craftsmen. Tracy divides the period into three phases: 1795–1845, characterized by varieties of neoclassicism; 1845–76, a time of "romantic revivals," westward shift of industry, and changing ethnic makeup of crafts and industries; and 1876–1910, marked by the impact of English reform movements, art furniture, and interest in exotic, colonial, and Old World styles. Every object is accompanied by a succinct essay written by Johnson, who locates it in the sequence that Tracy laid out, analyzes key design and stylistic features, and comments on history, sources, attribution, and use. *See also* "American Furniture to 1820"; "Surveys."

Ostergard, Derek E., ed. *Bent Wood and Metal Furniture, 1850–1946.* Text by Alessandro Alvera, Graham Dry, Robert Keil, Derek E. Ostergard, Christopher Wilk, and Christian Witt-Dörring. New York: American Federation of Arts, 1987. xvi+366 pp.; approximately 120 illustrations, appendix, glossary, bibliography, index.

Ostergard presents the first comprehensive treatment of furniture made from bent materials. "Durable, inexpensive and

often aesthetically distinctive" (p. xi), bent furniture is a leitmotif of the industrial age. Sometimes seen as an adjunct to larger movements, bent furniture has its own discrete international tradition, which is traced in six essays here, four of which deal with material before 1920. Ostergard discusses preindustrial and craft exploration of bending, Alvera deals with Michael Thonet's achievements in bentwood, Dry traces the development of the bentwood furniture industry from 1869 to 1914, and Witt-Dörring describes the impact of Viennese avant-garde design in the early twentieth century. Detailed discussions of 119 objects, all illustrated, are provided.

Otto, Celia Jackson. *American Furniture of the Nineteenth Century.* New York: Viking Press, 1965. 229 pp.; 481 black and white illustrations, 3 color plates, index.

Otto argues that French influence played an important part in the history of American furniture; therefore, French prototypes are illustrated here alongside American examples. The text is organized into six chapters: the classic, empire, restoration, rococo, and Renaissance periods and the 1880s and 1890s. Each chapter is subdivided according to form or by substyle. Although this is primarily a picture book, the text and captions are descriptive and provide the fullest coverage before 1860.

Payne, Christopher. *The Price Guide to Nineteenth Century European Furniture (excluding British).* Woodbridge, Suffolk: Antique Collectors' Club, 1981. 506 pp.; 1,443 black and white illustrations, color plates, bibliography.

This survey of primarily costly Continental furniture is arranged by country of origin. Nearly two-thirds of the volume deal with France. The text provides data on major cabinetmakers, designers, and retailers and presents objects grouped by form, style, decoration, or function (bedroom furniture, Boulle, chinoiserie, desks, Dieppe ivory, the dining room). Other sections provide information about elaborate and expensive furniture made in Germany, Austria and Switzerland, the Iberian peninsula, Italy, the Low Countries, Scandinavia, and even Russia and the Ottoman Empire. Many excellent illustrations are accompanied by comments on style, design, and quality.

Peirce, Donald C. "Mitchell and Rammelsberg: Cincinnati Furniture Manufacturers, 1847–1881." In *American Furniture and Its Makers: Winterthur Portfolio 13,* edited by Ian M. G. Quimby, pp. 209–29. Chicago: University of Chicago Press for the Henry Francis du Pont Winterthur Museum, 1979. 29 illustrations.

Founded by Robert Mitchell and Frederick Rammelsberg in 1847, by 1849 their company employed 150 workers and manufactured furniture worth $145,000. The next thirty-four years of the firm were "marked by continuing expansion and improvement in manufacturing and distribution facilities" (p. 229). In 1870 Mitchell and Rammelsberg employed 600 hands and produced $700,000 worth of furniture, much of it sold throughout the South and Midwest. Peirce describes the growth of the firm, its factories, warerooms, branch stores, products, and prices and illustrates and discusses a large group of surviving Mitchell and Rammelsberg furniture purchased by Abram Gaar for his new home near Richmond, Indiana, in 1877.

Pictorial Dictionary of British Nineteenth Century Furniture Design. Introduction by Edward Joy. An Antique Collectors' Club Research Project. Woodbridge, Suffolk: Baron Publishing, 1977. xlvii+583 pp.; illustrations.

This work presents thousands of images culled from forty-seven design and pattern books to show the complete range of furniture available in Britain from 1800. Sources include books by Thomas Sheraton, George Smith, Thomas King, Henry Whitaker, W. Smee and Son, J. B. Waring, Bruce Talbert, Heal and Son, Morris and Company, and many others. The years from 1820 to 1880 are particularly well represented, with six or seven titles for each decade. Images are grouped into fourteen broad categories (such as bedroom furniture, cabinets, chairs, chests, and couches) and by forms and dates within those categories. Included are a list of key dates in nineteenth-century British furniture history and comments on designers and design books.

Plain and Elegant, Rich and Common: Documented New Hampshire Furniture, 1750–1850. Exhibition catalogue. Concord: New Hampshire Historical Society, 1979. 153 pp.; 59 illustrations, 2 maps.

This exhibition holds that the concept of New Hampshire furniture is artificial. New Hampshire is not a separate cultural or geographical entity; various regions of the state have close historical or commercial links to Maine, Connecticut, Massachusetts, or Vermont. More than 30 percent of the cabinetmakers listed in this catalogue were born and trained out of state. Most New Hampshire furniture, with the notable exception of the famous Dunlap pieces, reflects an aesthetic that pervades well-settled areas of New England. The catalogue includes nineteen documented pieces of furniture produced after 1820; all are illustrated and discussed. Biographical sketches of all cabinetmakers are included. *See also* "American Furniture to 1820."

Reed, Henry M. *Decorated Furniture of the Mahantongo Valley.* Essay by Don Yoder; foreword by Monroe H. Fabian. Exhibition catalogue. Lewisburg, Pa.: Bucknell University, 1987; distributed by the University of Pennsylvania Press. 96 pp.; 61 black and white illustrations, 28 color plates, checklist, bibliography.

Reed examines distinctive furniture from a small region of central Pennsylvania. Two groups have been identified: fifteen chests dating between 1798 and 1828, and fifty-seven case pieces of various types dating from 1827 to 1841. Several noteworthy examples have come to light in recent years. Identifying makers and decorators is still problematic, but

some attributions can be made. The decorative devices found on the furniture also appear on gravestones, Fraktur, and *Scherenschnitten* (scissors cuttings). The study concludes with a transcription of cabinetmaker Johannes Haas's account book and a checklist of known Mahantongo valley pieces.

Roberts, Warren E. "Ananias Hensel and His Furniture: Cabinetmaking in Southern Indiana." *Midwestern Journal of Language and Folklore* 9, no. 2 (Fall 1983): 69–122. 19 illustrations.

Hensel (1832–1913) was a farmer, a minister in the Church of the Brethren, possibly a stonecutter and physician, and definitely a cabinetmaker. Born and trained in Pennsylvania, he moved to Indiana in 1854. Roberts recounts family and personal history, describes Hensel's farm and workshop and the woods used in his furniture, and speculates on his working methods. Surviving Hensel pieces include a secretary desk, a cupboard, a chest, a chest of drawers, two bedsteads, a dry sink, and a drawing for fall-front desks. All are conservative in design and are plainer and simpler than contemporary Victorian forms. While such furniture is sometimes called "country," Roberts argues that "traditional" is a more accurate descriptor that is consistent with folklorists' understanding of genres like folktales.

Roberts, Warren E. "Turpin Chairs and the Turpin Family: Chairmaking in Southern Indiana." *Midwestern Journal of Language and Folklore* 7, no. 2 (Fall 1981): 57–106. 17 illustrations.

Roberts provides a detailed discussion of the strong, durable, comfortable, and lightweight chairs made in rural Indiana by at least three generations of the Turpin family. Although the overall form of their slat-back chairs varied little over time, Jim, Bill, and Joe Turpin's products differed in subtle ways. Roberts describes the processes and tools that Jim Turpin used in making chairs in an area without electricity. The type of slat-back chair made by the Turpins, with bent and flattened rear posts, seems to have been developed in the South around 1800 and remained common there and in midwestern areas well into the twentieth century. Most chairs of this type were made by part-time craftsmen in rural areas who were far commoner than conventional documents reveal.

Roth, Rodris. "American Art: The Colonial Revival and 'Centennial Furniture.'" *Art Quarterly* 27, no. 1 (Spring 1964): 57–81. 24 illustrations.

Roth maintains that the term *Centennial furniture* is a "synonym for nineteenth-century reproductions of colonial pieces," but "no furniture of this kind was ever shown at the 1876 Exposition" (p. 57). The interest in America's colonial past begins before the Centennial and continues independent of it. Roth surveys furniture at the Centennial, locating historic furnishings only in the New England log house and in a display of George Washington relics. Elsewhere, there is abundant evidence of widespread interest in the colonial, and Roth enumerates major books and articles in popular and trade periodicals, as well as other documentation: "Begun in the seventies, nourished and reinforced by the centennial year, the Colonial Revival continued to expand and grow, even though it had been almost completely ignored by the Centennial Exposition of 1876" (p. 76). Centennial furniture should actually be known as "colonial revival."

Roth, Rodris. "Pieces of History: Relic Furniture of the Nineteenth Century." *Antiques* 101, no. 5 (May 1972): 874–78. 8 illustrations.

Relic furniture made between the time of the 1853 New York Crystal Palace Exhibition and the Philadelphia Centennial of 1876 is surveyed in this article. A few examples survive, but others are known only through illustrations and accounts. Examples discussed include a chair made of ironwood from the Castle of San Juan de Ulùa, Vera Cruz, Mexico, commemorating Winfield Scott's capture of that town, by George Henkels; a set of chamber furniture in the style of 1776, made from a maple tree that grew in Independence Square, also by Henkels; a hatrack and two chairs made from hickory cut at Hermitage, Andrew Jackson's Tennessee home, by Daniel Adams; a chair from the Washington Elm, which stood in Cambridge Common and under which Washington took command of the Continental army, by Charles H. Clarke; and a variety of objects, including a piano, bureau, center table, chair, wooden ham, and many wooden nutmegs, made from the wood of Hartford's Charter Oak by John H. Most.

Saunders, Richard. *Collecting and Restoring Wicker Furniture*. New York: Crown Publishers, 1976. [vii]+118 pp.; 156 illustrations, appendix, index.

Saunders states that the "curious renaissance" in the popularity of wicker is due in part to a growing appreciation of the fine craftsmanship involved in its manufacture. The term *wicker* embraces many kinds of woven furniture. Popular in America from the 1860s to 1920s, it has ancient antecedents. Cyrus Wakefield and Levi Heywood were key figures in the development of the American wicker industry. By the 1870s Wakefield's factories and storehouses covered 10 acres. At first wicker was finished natural and used mostly outdoors, but by the 1880s, the golden age of wicker design, it was more often stained or painted and became common indoors. Around the turn of the century, wicker was popular for sun porches and was frequently made in sets. In the twentieth century, angular designs gradually replaced the flowing Victorian contours of earlier years, and the industry was revolutionized by the introduction of fiber reed (imitation wicker made of twisted paper) and the Lloyd loom, which mechanized what had previously been a hand industry. Step-by-step directions for repairing and restoring antique wicker are included.

Saunders, Richard. *Collector's Guide to American Wicker Furniture*. New York: Hearst Books, 1983. 150 pp.; approximately 90 illustrations and 20 plates, line drawings, appendixes, index.

This work is a paraphrase and partial revision of Saunders's earlier title. He defines materials, comments on antecedents, and briefly traces the accomplishments of Cyrus Wakefield, J. and C. Berrian, Samuel Colt, Levi Heywood, and others. He describes the popularity of ornate designs reflecting oriental and exotic design ideas late in the nineteenth century and their subsequent displacement by sedate designs of Austrian and German as well as American reform inspiration. Pictorial chapters document wicker in photographers' studios and other contexts. Final sections discuss investing in wicker and restoration.

Schwartz, Marvin D., Edward J. Stanek, and Douglas K. True. *The Furniture of John Henry Belter and the Rococo Revival: An Inquiry into Nineteenth-Century Furniture Design through a Study of the Gloria and Richard Manney Collection*. Exhibition catalogue. New York: E. P. Dutton, 1981. vii+88 pp.; 30 black and white illustrations, 1 table, 60 illustrated entries, bibliography, index.

This work asserts that Belter (1804–63) was "the outstanding figure in the history of nineteenth-century American furniture" (p. 1). Because of his extraordinary attention to detail and emphatic, flamboyant designs, Belter's work represents the finest American rococo revival furniture. Technical studies by Stanek and True conclude that Belter's laminated furniture was made of veneers about half as thick as those used by others, that the design of seating furniture was organized by sweeping, interconnected "arabesques," and that Belter used cylindrical, conical, and spherical cauls to shape his furniture. Efforts to date Belter pieces are not easy because of evidence that "many designs were used over a long period" (p. 27). Photographs show both details and full views of sixty objects, including chairs, sofas, tables, beds, music stools, a desk, a bookcase, and a chest of drawers.

Seale, William. *The Tasteful Interlude: American Interiors through the Camera's Eye, 1860–1917*. See "Surveys."

Shaker: Furniture and Objects from the Faith and Edward Deming Andrews Collection Commemorating the Bicentenary of the American Shakers. Exhibition catalogue. Washington, D.C.: Smithsonian Institution Press for the Renwick Gallery of the National Collection of the Fine Arts, 1973. 88 pp.; illustrations, bibliography.

In this collection of essays and catalogue celebrating the bicentennial of the Shakers' landing in New York City in 1774, Edward Andrews's reprinted essay outlines the history and theology of the United Society of Believers. Jane Malcolm argues that Shaker design has become a most venerated American craft form. The "strange beauty" of Shaker furniture may be due to "the startling combination of plain, utilitarian forms and craftsmanship of the sort conventionally reserved for ornate aristocratic furniture" (p. 20). A. D. Emerich's interview with Faith Andrews draws forth personal recollections of a career devoted to understanding, recording, and sharing the history and meaning of the Shaker experience. She describes their initial visit to the Shakers in 1923, their first major book, *Shaker Furniture* (1937), and the establishment of Hancock Shaker Village as a museum in 1960. Appended is a bibliography of the Andrewses' writings on the Shakers that includes six books and nearly fifty articles. The catalogue illustrates and discusses about thirty objects.

Snyder, Ellen Marie. "Victory over Nature: Victorian Cast-Iron Seating Furniture." *Winterthur Portfolio* 20, no. 4 (Winter 1985): 221–42. 19 illustrations.

Snyder argues that cast iron was the master material of the nineteenth century. It had previously been reserved largely for utilitarian purposes, but in the nineteenth century it was used for a wide range of artistic and ornamental goods. Mass-produced cast-iron seating was one of the century's innovations. Cast-iron settees were testaments to the growth of civilization and were seen as metaphors for progress. Five major patterns of settees were dominant: rustic, grape, Gothic, fern, and curtain. These showed a conceptual and chronological progression from natural to increasingly artificial forms. Settees were used primarily outdoors on the lawn, in the park, and in the cemetery. In the last setting, their permanent, immutable forms counterbalanced the forces of death and decay.

Stover, Donald L. *Tischlermeister Jahn*. Exhibition catalogue. San Antonio: San Antonio Museum Association, 1978. 62 pp.; 49 illustrations, 33 illustrated entries, appendixes, index.

Johann Michael Jahn (1816–83) was one of the approximately 300 German immigrants who established the Texas settlement of New Braunfels in 1845. Jahn developed a large and flourishing trade, and by the 1860s he was importing knocked-down furniture from New York for resale. In the 1870s he opened a second shop in nearby Seguin. Jahn's furniture in the Biedermeier style is of unusually high quality and is closely related to stylish European examples. In these pieces, the plank, worked into smooth, flat surfaces, is the dominant element. Stover concentrates on furniture made by Jahn, explaining difficulties in attributing pieces to him. Objects are arranged by type: chairs, rocking chairs, worktables, sofas, tripod pedestal tables, washstands, chests of drawers, cupboards, wardrobes, and bedsteads. A checklist of New Braunfels cabinetmakers, 1845–80, is appended.

Stover, Donald Lewis. "Part One: The Furniture of Early Texas." In Cecilia Steinfeldt and Donald Lewis Stover, *Early Texas Furniture and Decorative Arts*, pp. 1–153. Exhibition catalogue. San Antonio: Trinity University Press for the San Antonio Museum Association, 1973. 179 black and white illustrations, 5 color plates.

The objects presented by Stover date from the nineteenth and early twentieth centuries, which "would appear to be a relatively late period for the production of 'early' furniture; however, the unique history of the state of Texas resulted in

the late emergence of the furniture craft and the persistence of that craft long after it had passed in the more industrialized regions of the east and Mississippi Valley" (p. 3). Texas was settled in two waves: from the southern United States and from Europe, especially the Germanic areas. Because of geographical isolation, some regions of Texas remained largely self-sufficient long into the nineteenth century. Furniture was made not only by cabinetmakers but also by carpenters, joiners, wheelwrights, wagoners, and coopers. Shipments of "knocked-down" furniture ended local production. Stover provides extensive and highly detailed descriptions of the forms illustrated, including slat-back chairs, rocking chairs, chests, chests of drawers, desks, settees, sofas, daybeds, tables of many types, food safes, wardrobes, beds, and furniture made from steer horns.

Strickland, Peter L. L. "Furniture by the Lejambre Family of Philadelphia." *Antiques* 113, no. 3 (March 1978): 600–613. 25 black and white illustrations, 5 color plates.

Born near Paris in 1786, Alphonse Lejambre appears in Philadelphia city directories in 1825, listed as an upholsterer. After his death in 1843, Lejambre's business was continued by his widow, Anna, their children, son-in-law Henri, and other members of the family until about 1907. The firm began to manufacture its own furniture in the 1850s. By 1858 the billhead read "French Cabinet Maker and Upholsterer," a designation retained for twenty-five years. A. and H. Lejambre were very successful in the 1860s and 1870s, and most of their documented furniture is from this period. Usually in the French taste, it was patterned after designs in publications like Desiré Guilmard's *Garde-meuble ancien et moderne* and V. L. Quétin's *Magasin de meuble*. The largest known collection of Lejambre furniture was purchased by James Dougherty for his Philadelphia home in 1869, 1870, and 1871. Descriptions and commentary are given for more than twenty documented objects.

Strickland, Peter L. L. "Schindler, Roller, and Company: An Unknown New York Cabinetmaker." *Nineteenth Century* 6, no. 3 (Autumn 1980): 39–43. 14 black and white and color illustrations.

In 1869 manufacturer Andrew Campbell bought a house on Clermont Avenue in Brooklyn. Much of the furniture for that house was provided by Schindler, Roller, and Company. Furniture is still owned by a descendant, along with late nineteenth-century photographs showing it installed in a later house. Bills of sale are at Eleutherian Mills Historical Library. Strickland cites that the firm of Schindler, Roller appears in directories only from 1868 through 1872, although the partners can be traced back to 1861 and 1856. The furniture they sold to Campbell was mostly in the Renaissance revival style "with a liberal use of the incised line of néo-grec frequently highlighted with gilt" (p. 40). Parlor, dining-room, and bedroom pieces are illustrated and discussed.

The Swisegood School of Cabinetmaking. Text by Frank L. Horton and Carolyn J. Weekley; photography by Bradford J. Rauschenberg. Exhibition catalogue. Winston-Salem, N.C.: Museum of Early Southern Decorative Arts, 1973. Unpag.; 20 illustrations.

Between 1800 and 1850 at least fifteen cabinetmakers were active in Rowan and Davidson counties in west central North Carolina. Four of these craftsmen—Mordica Collins, John Swisegood, Jesse Clodfelter, and Jonathan Long—constitute what Horton and Weekley call the Swisegood school of Davidson County, North Carolina. They explain how the 1965 discovery of a desk signed by Swisegood and dated 1821 led to a significant body of related work. On the basis of four signed pieces, about forty others were attributed to these artisans, of whom capsule histories are included. Large, sharp photographs of nineteen case pieces are accompanied by basic data and descriptive and explanatory commentary. *See also* "American Furniture to 1820."

Talbot, George. *At Home: Domestic Life in the Post-Centennial Era, 1876–1920. See* "Domestic Architecture."

Talbott, Page. "Boston Empire Furniture." *Antiques,* pt. 1, 107, no. 5 (May 1975): 878–87; pt. 2, 109, no. 5 (May 1976): 1004–13. 15 black and white illustrations, 3 color plates; 22 black and white illustrations, 4 color plates.

In early nineteenth-century Boston, furniture was often sold by entrepreneurs rather than by makers. Between 1826 and 1832 large quantities were sold at auctions. These auctions forbade obvious labels or stencils, which partially explains the relative rarity of marked Boston furniture of the period. Talbott provides short histories of three representative companies—Emmons and Archibald, Vose and Coates, and Elisha Learnard—and examines labeled examples of their work, for the most part in public collections. Specialists are clustered in certain areas of Boston; looking-glass manufacturers, for example, were located near Court Street and Dock Square. A major concentration of furniture makers and dealers in central Boston occurred in an area defined by State, Union, and Hanover streets and included George and Phillip Graves, William Hancock, Timothy Hunt, Rufus Pierce, Moses Mellen, and George and Jacob Smith. Talbott provides brief outlines of each firm and discusses documented objects.

Taylor, Lonn, and David B. Warren. *Texas Furniture: The Cabinetmakers and Their Work, 1840–1880.* Foreword by Ima Hogg. Austin and London: University of Texas Press, 1975. xi+387 pp.; illustrations, 6 maps, checklist, appendix, glossary, bibliography, index.

In this comprehensive study of Texas furniture made between 1840 and 1880, Taylor and Warren show how geography, settlement patterns, and limited transportation favored local production during that period. They identify six major cabinetmaking areas: Galveston, Austin, Piney Woods, Blackland Prairie, Lower Brazos-Colorado, and Hill Country regions, the last being the origin of the largest body of well-documented furniture. Germans were disproportionately represented in the furniture trade, and their considerable impact is analyzed. The largest portion of the book illustrates and discusses more than 200 objects grouped according to form and accompanied by detailed entries. An annotated checklist provides data on some 874 cabinetmakers working between 1850 and 1870.

Taylor, Lonn, and Dessa Bokides. *New Mexican Furniture, 1600–1940: The Origins, Survival, and Revival of Furniture Making in the Hispanic Southwest.* Photographs by Mary Peck; additional photography by Jim Bones. Museum of New Mexico Press Series in Southwestern Culture. Santa Fe: Museum of New Mexico Press, 1987. xvi+311 pp.; black and white illustrations, 268 black and white and color plates, glossary, bibliography, index.

The medium of furniture is used to explicate more than three centuries of cultural change and interaction in New Mexico and, in the process, overturn long-standing assumptions about the region. Taylor and Bokides demonstrate that the furniture of colonial New Mexico was executed by skilled and specialized artisans according to well-understood design traditions. The region carried on lively trade with New Spain and generated new forms, most notably the *trastero,* a kind of cupboard, and the *harinero,* a flour chest. Later artisans incorporated Anglo-American motifs and developed a Hispanic vernacular. The Spanish colonial revival of the twentieth century had much in common with contemporary antimodernist efforts in other parts of the country, but had little to do with Hispanic furnishing needs or traditions. The text is exceptionally well illustrated. *See also* "American Furniture to 1820."

Thomas Day, Cabinetmaker. Raleigh: North Carolina Museum of History, 1975. 75 pp.; illustrations.

Day (ca. 1801– ca. 1861) worked as a cabinetmaker in Milton, North Carolina, from the 1820s until about 1859 and operated a large furniture-making business. Day was a free black and was subjected to severe legislation restricting mobility, assembly, education, and religion. One major exception was a bill passed by the North Carolina General Assembly allowing Day's Virginia wife to reside legally in the state. In 1850 he employed twelve workers who produced furniture for wholesale and retail sales and did interior carpentry. Interiors for two debating societies at the University of North Carolina, Chapel Hill, are particularly well documented. The catalogue illustrates about sixty objects by or attributed to Day.

Tice, Patricia M. "The Knapp Dovetailing Machine." *Antiques* 123, no. 5 (May 1983): 1070–72. 5 illustrations.

Dovetailers were among the many specialized tools developed in the 1860s and 1870s to accelerate production. Some imitated hand processes, but the Knapp dovetailer produced an alternative machined joint of a scalloped and doweled design. Patented by Charles D. Knapp of Waterloo, Wisconsin, in 1867, the machine was put into production in Northampton, Massachusetts, at Knapp Dovetailing Machine Company, which remained in business into the twentieth century. This dovetailer was exhibited extensively and used by many prominent firms, including Mitchell and Rammelsberg, Nelson, Matter, and Company, and Pottier and Stymus.

Tracy, Berry B. "The Decorative Arts: European Background"; "The Decorative Arts: Furniture." In *Classical America, 1815–1845*, pp. 10–81. Newark, N.J.: Newark Museum, 1963. Illustrations.

Tracy discusses the empire, "Grecian," or "modern" style of the early nineteenth century from its origins in the work of English and French designers to its late American expression in John Hall's *Cabinet Makers' Assistant*. American furniture was largely based on imported design books. English Sheraton and Regency forms were produced by John and Thomas Seymour, Duncan Phyfe, Michael Allison, and others, while French designs were made by immigrant artisans like Charles-Honoré Lannuier, Anthony G. Quervelle, and Michel Bouvier. An American innovation was the use of gilt and bronze painted and stenciled designs in the mode of the expensive metal mounts found on French furniture. Catalogue entries discuss design sources and makers. *See also* "American Furniture to 1820"; "Surveys."

van Ravenswaay, Charles. *The Arts and Architecture of German Settlements in Missouri: A Survey of a Vanishing Culture.* See "Surveys."

A Victorian Chair for All Seasons: A Facsimile of the Brooklyn Chair Company Catalogue of 1887. Watkins Glen, N.Y.: American Life Foundation Library of Victorian Culture, 1978. 137 pp.; 262 illustrations.

This reprint illustrates the line of a typical American chair manufacturer of the late nineteenth century. It contains many design ideas new to the 1880s as well as many older forms. Included are plank, cane, and upholstered seat chairs of many kinds: common kitchen and utility Windsors; Grecians in several patterns; Boston, Grecian, platform, and fancy rockers; fixed- and revolving-seat office chairs; library chairs; dining chairs with and without arms; high chairs; stools; and other forms.

Walters, Betty Lawson. *The King of Desks: Wooton's Patent Secretary.* Washington, D.C.: Smithsonian Institution Press, 1969. 32 pp.; 28 illustrations, appendixes.

The Wooton desk originated on October 6, 1874, when William S. Wooton of Indianapolis patented "Wooton's Patent Cabinet Office Secretary." Two years later Wooton's firm was manufacturing 150 desks per month, exhibiting at the Centennial, and receiving international attention for its products. The desks were made in four grades—ordinary, standard, extra, and superior—and ranged in price from $90 to $750. Smithsonian houses examples once owned by Ulysses S. Grant, Spencer Baird, and Edward Hofma. Wooton also made ladies and rotary desks. Competing products were marketed by several firms, particularly Moore Combination Desk Company. The Wooton desk "is archetypical . . . reflecting America's post–Civil War mania for efficiency, order, and gadgetry" (pp. 21–22). Appendixes list changing names and addresses of the firm, dealers, texts of patents, purchasers, and histories and patents of rival concerns.

Waters, Deborah Dependahl. "Wares and Chairs: A Reappraisal of the Documents." In *American Furniture and Its Makers: Winterthur Portfolio 13*, edited by Ian M. G. Quimby, pp. 161–73. Chicago: University of Chicago Press for the Henry Francis du Pont Winterthur Museum, 1979. 4 illustrations, 1 table.

In 1789 Maskell Ware (1766–1846) settled in Roadstown, New Jersey, where he took up farming and chairmaking. Four generations of his descendants remained active in the chair and furniture trades in Cumberland, Salem, and Cape May counties. Waters recounts capsule career histories of twenty-three members of the Ware family. Despite competition from suppliers of other forms of seating furniture, the Wares continued to sell traditional rush-bottom chairs to southern New Jersey customers for more than 150 years, passing along craft skills through informal apprenticeships within the family.

Weidman, Gregory R. *Furniture in Maryland, 1740–1940: The Collection of the Maryland Historical Society.* Baltimore: By the society, 1984. 342 pp.; 24 color plates, 260 illustrated entries, checklist, bibliography, index.

This catalogue of 259 objects owned by Maryland Historical Society, all either made or used in Maryland, is divided into three sections: 1740–90, 1790–1840, and 1840–1940. The text that introduces the second section discusses "the growth of Baltimore . . . , the evolution of the cabinetmaking trade, the leading cabinetmakers, and the distinctive characteristics of Maryland furniture of the period" (p. 70). The final section continues the discussion of the trade in Baltimore, concentrating on midcentury productions, and turns to colonial revival pieces of the late nineteenth and early twentieth centuries. Every object is illustrated, described, and accompanied by notes on history and structure. *See also* "American Furniture to 1820."

Wilk, Christopher. *Thonet: One Hundred Fifty Years of Furniture.* Woodbury, N.Y., and London: Barron's, 1980. 143 pp.; 181 illustrations, bibliography.

In 1830 Prussian-born cabinetmaker Michael Thonet started to experiment with bending wood into curved shapes. He glued together several layers of veneer, placed them in a warmed wooden frame, and bent them to form curved chair rails. For the next forty years, Thonet continued to search for designs and methods to simplify chairmaking. His bentwood furniture required less labor and material than carved chairs, weighed less, and could be sold cheaper. Chair 14, for example, was constructed of only six pieces of bentwood, ten screws, and two washers. Wilk traces the Thonet firm's designs and techniques through the introduction of mass production in 1857, the first rocking chair in 1860, the end of Thonet's monopoly in 1869, expansion in the 1890s, and diversification into other materials in the twentieth century. Thonet opened an American branch in 1873; its products have been known here ever since.

Wooton Patent Desks: A Place for Everything and Everything in Its Place. Exhibition catalogue. Indianapolis: Indiana State Museum; Oakland, Calif.: Oakland Museum, 1983. 94 pp.; 47 black and white illustrations, 16 color plates.

Wooton desks "are simultaneously the products of a society that placed a high value on order and the tangible components of a strategy to create that order" (p. 9). This publication sandwiches excellent color photographs of these objects between four essays that assess their place in nineteenth-century America. Page Talbott outlines changes in the furnishings and connotations of offices, interpreting Wooton's desks as part of an extensive process of innovation and experimentation that involved desks, typewriters, filing systems, and spatial organization. Betty Lawson Walters recounts the history of the Wooton firm from William S. Wooton's move from Richmond, Indiana, to Indianapolis in 1870, through his several patents and the company's national

and international reputation in the 1870s and 1880s, to his gradual separation from the company and its closing in 1893. Deborah Cooper shows how his desks "addressed the problems of efficient, compact utilization of space as well as convenient access to a comprehensive storage and filing system" (p. 49) and analyzes the four grades of desks. Finally, Susan Dickey pulls together information about Wooton's employees.

Yehia, Mary Ellen. "Chairs for the Masses: A Brief History of the L. White Chair Company, Boston, Massachusetts." *Old-Time New England* 63, no. 2 (Fall 1972): 33–44. Illustrations.

L. White Chair Company (1864–69) made inexpensive "practical" furniture for sale to firms in New England, the Baltimore–Philadelphia area, and the Midwest. Their business books—sales book, ledger, cash book, and trial balance book—are in Baker Library at Harvard. The sales book records daily sales and lists purchasers, quantities, types, and costs per dozen. The ledger records the accounts of each customer. The cash book lists company expenditures, identifying suppliers of tools and materials. The company made cottage chairs—light, delicate, but strong, ranging in price from very low to moderate. Cottage chairs consist mostly of turned parts, have rush or cane seats, and are either varnished or painted and decorated. At its peak, the firm made seventy different designs in four basic categories: Grecian, cottage, nurse, and dining. Production capacity was considerable; in October 1867 alone, White sold 4,776 chairs for $12,543. Yehia includes a detailed discussion of company operations and customers.

Metals

American Silver and Gold

INTERNATIONAL CONTEXT

AMERICAN SILVER AND GOLD

Pewter and Britannia Metal

Brass, Copper, Iron, and Tin

American Silver and Gold

Barbara McLean Ward and Gerald W. R. Ward

THE STUDY OF AMERICAN SILVER has been of interest to antiquarians and art historians for more than 100 years. In his pioneering study *Old Plate*, published by Gorham Manufacturing Company in 1888, John H. Buck was the first to list the names of approximately 160 gold- and silversmiths who were active in the colonies and early Republic before 1800. Although much of his book was cribbed directly from Wilfred Joseph Cripps's *Old English Plate* (1878), Buck's research called into question the general belief that most of the antique silver found in this country had been imported or brought to America by the early settlers from England and Europe and that there was little or no artistic activity in the colonies before the Revolution. *Old Plate* thus interested antiquarians and collectors who were anxious to establish the artistic heritage of America, and by September 1896, when Theodore S. Woolsey published his "Old Silver" in *Harper's New Monthly Magazine*, several enthusiasts were already engaged in the study of early American silver, among the most important of whom were Francis Hill Bigelow, R. T. H. Halsey, and George Munson Curtis.

By researching objects with a long history of ownership in this country, these scholars were able to determine the geographic origin of the objects and to correlate this information with the names of silversmiths gleaned from newspapers and official records. In this way they began the long process of identifying the various maker's marks that appear on old silver. As a result, the thrust of early scholarship in the field was toward the identification of original owners of objects and, subsequently, the identification of makers and marks.

This work first bore fruit in the exhibition of American silver held at the Museum of Fine Arts, Boston, in 1906. This exhibition was soon followed by three loan shows at the Metropolitan Museum of Art in New York, held in 1907, 1909, and 1911. Also in 1911, the Museum of Fine Arts held another major silver exhibition, this one primarily devoted to the silver owned by American churches. Recognizing the trove of well-documented objects owned by the nation's religious institutions, and perhaps inspired by the example of extensive fieldwork conducted by English scholars and antiquarians in their churches in the 1890s and early 1900s (more than thirty monographs on English church silver were published between 1880 and 1913), the National Society of the Colonial Dames of America supported the compilation and publication of E. Alfred Jones's *Old Silver of American Churches*, which appeared in 1913. Various state chapters of the Colonial Dames were instrumental in planning and organizing regional exhibitions of silver as well.

The patriotic sentiment that inspired this early research also motivated early collectors in the field. Many felt that silver objects also represented the highest achievements of American artists of the eighteenth century and made an effort to see to it that these objects found their rightful places in museums. To take one example: In 1910 Judge Alphonso T. Clearwater began to place his collection of American silver on loan to the Metropolitan. He presented his collection to the museum as a gift in 1920, and the gift was celebrated by the publication of C. Louise Avery's *American Silver of the Seventeenth and Eighteenth Centuries*. In 1924 the opening of the American Wing at the Metropolitan marked the beginning of the acceptance of American decorative arts into the permanent collections of major art museums, and silver has held a prominent place in such collections ever since.

In order to satisfy the needs of collectors interested in establishing that pieces were made by American silversmiths, many books were published with illustrations of the makers' marks. The first of these was by Hollis French; his *List of Early American Silversmiths and Their Marks* was published in 1917. French's book was followed by Stephen G. C. Ensko's *American Silversmiths and Their Marks*, published in three editions between 1927 and 1948, and Ernest M. Currier's *Marks of Early American Silversmiths*, issued in 1938. Illustrated with drawings of marks, these books continue to be useful to collectors, but they have been augmented by such works as Louise Conway Belden's *Marks of American Silversmiths in the Ineson-Bissell Collection* and *New York State Silversmiths* (Eggertsville, N.Y.: Darling Foundation, 1964), which include magnified photographs of each mark listed.

During the 1930s and 1940s a host of collective biographies and monographs on individual silversmiths began to appear, marking out additional territories in the manner established in 1913 by George Munson Curtis in his *Early Silver of Connecticut and Its Makers* published by International Silver Company. Many of the books in this category deal with the lives of southern silversmiths, such as *Maryland Silversmiths* by J. Hall Pleasants and Howard Sill, which appeared in 1930. By the mid 1960s most states could boast at least one such geographic survey, Massachusetts being the major exception. Although many rural areas have been covered, large metropolitan centers such as Philadelphia and New York still suffer from incomplete, outdated, or cursory coverage.

Two early collectors of American silver, Francis P. Garvan and Henry Francis du Pont, fostered its study through their support of advanced education in the decorative arts. Garvan was unusual among collectors in that he sought to make his collection comprehensive enough to be used in teaching and of high enough quality to foster an appreciation of the artistic contribution of colonial artisans. He recognized the need to have American decorative arts courses taught at the university level, and when he presented his collection to Yale University in 1930, he did so with a strong commitment to making the history of American art a part of every responsible citizen's education.

Garvan's curator at Yale, John Marshall Phillips, inaugurated a university course in American decorative arts. Phillips's specialty was silver, and he conducted extensive research into the lives of Massachusetts and Connecticut silversmiths and exhaustively searched out important objects to add to the Yale University Art Gallery's collections. Phillips's approach to the study of American silver included an appreciation of the objects as works of art and of the genius of the men who made them. In order to develop a better understanding of the process by which the objects were made, he learned silversmithing himself. Phillips died before he was able to finish so many of the projects he had started, but he still made an enormous contribution to the study of American decorative arts by introducing the subject to a whole generation of Yale undergraduates and by his involvement to some degree in nearly every exhibition and publication on silver for some twenty years.

Many other scholars have added to our knowledge of American silver in significant ways, and many of their works are included in this bibliography. A foremost silver scholar was Kathryn C. Buhler, for many years a member of the staff of the Museum of Fine Arts. During her long career, she catalogued many public and private collections and was responsible for guiding hundreds of privately owned objects into public institutions. Her works are well represented in this bibliography, although many of her shorter articles and catalogues have been omitted.

For many years the study of American silver rested largely in the hands of Phillips and Buhler. Students, feeling that most of the work on silver had been done, did not turn to its study in great numbers, and collectors, finding that much of the best American silver had been funneled into museum collections, looked for other areas in which to collect.

Notable exceptions to this situation were Mr. and Mrs. Henry N. Flynt, Philip Hammerslough, Mr. and Mrs. Frank L. Harrington, and du Pont. The Flynts' silver collection forms the core of the holdings at Historic Deerfield, Hammerslough's collection is now in large part at Wadsworth Atheneum, the Harringtons' is at Hood Museum at Dartmouth College, and du Pont's objects are part of the Winterthur collection. Martha Gandy Fales was one of the relatively few early graduates of the Winterthur Program in Early American Culture to become interested in silver. As her thesis topic, she pursued the study of one important family of silversmiths, the Richardsons of Philadelphia. In her study of this artisan family, later published in revised form as *Joseph Richardson and Family*, she took a comprehensive approach, looking not only at its stylistic attributes but also at the way it was made and at the changes in form and use over time. She also published a catalogue of the Winterthur collection (1958) and collaborated with Henry Flynt on the Heritage Foundation collection (1968).

In recent years, there has been an increasing interest in the study of nineteenth- and twentieth-century silver and gold, particularly among collectors, a phenomenon common to the study of other forms of decorative arts and household objects. An early exhibition to focus on the best of nineteenth-century design in the decorative arts was held at the Metropolitan in 1970. Catalogue entries on silver for the volume reflect the beginning of appreciation for the style and iconography of mass-produced objects. In 1977 another landmark book, *Chicago Metalsmiths*, written by Sharon Darling, was produced to celebrate the Chicago Historical Society's bicentennial exhibition of approximately 500 metal objects made in Chicago between 1804 and 1970. In addition to publishing early pieces made in Chicago, the book brought the silver of the arts and crafts period to the attention of scholars and collectors. Since then there has been much interest in the silver of the late nineteenth and early twentieth centuries, much of which has been highlighted in regional exhibitions, in shows featuring the work of one shop, and in major exhibitions on styles and movements, including the aesthetic movement exhibition at the Metropolitan and the arts and crafts exhibition at the Museum of Fine Arts, both held in 1987.

As silver scholarship moves into the 1990s and beyond, it is liable to follow many well-worn traditional paths, but, it is hoped, it may move in several new directions as well. The study of silver is both blessed and cursed by the phenomenon of its bearing (in many cases) makers' marks, owners' initials, coats of arms, and other identifying inscriptions. Because so much silver can be traced to its maker and original owner, there is an inclination to stress identification and biography as the goals of research. Of all the decorative arts, silver seems to lend itself most easily to studies of an antiquarian nature, a tendency reinforced by silver's traditional and long-standing status as an elite material. Yet this same high level of documentation allows silver scholars to begin their research knowing much of the information about maker and owner that furniture scholars, for example, struggle to acquire and in many cases will never know. The challenge is to use the evidence presented by silver to answer historically significant questions, while continuing to do the basic research that is necessary to fill in the gaps in the literature.

Much more basic work, for example, needs to be done on the identification of makers' marks from the seventeenth century through to 1920 (and beyond). Collective biographies of craftsmen from various regions, such as Massachusetts and Philadelphia, and monographs on various nineteenth-century firms and small arts and crafts shops need to be prepared as well as modern catalogues of collections, like those in progress on Winterthur's silver by Ian M. G. Quimby and on the holdings of the Museum of the City of New York by Deborah Dependahl Waters.

While this research will undoubtedly move ahead, opportunities will be lost if the information gained in such work is not used to greater advantage in studies of wider historical scope. Both the Quimby and the Waters catalogues, for example, are designed to include interpretive essays that will lift their works above the usual examples of the form. More needs to be learned about the craft and technology of silvermaking, about the labor history of silversmiths, and about the history of silver from aesthetic and design points of view. To date, no one has placed American silver in its English and European context to the same degree that John T. Kirk has done for early furniture. There is much to be done on some of the important, yet frequently overlooked, aspects of the silversmith's craft, such as jewelry, the focus of work in progress by Fales.

Some of the most compelling work done on silver to date is found in articles and catalogues that use silver objects to reach a greater understanding of the society in which they were made and produced. Two examples of this in article form are Anthony N. B. Garvan's study of porringers and Edward J. Nygren's work on colonial sugar boxes, each of which analyzes a single form and, while placing the form in context, sheds light on the preoccupations and beliefs of the society that used these objects. The 1987 exhibition catalogue *Marks of Achievement*, prepared by David B. Warren, Katherine S. Howe, and Michael K. Brown of the Museum of Fine Arts, Houston, stands outside the tradition of most silver exhibitions. While maintaining a sensitivity to high-quality design and craftsmanship, the organizers of this show selected the objects to reflect patterns of human interaction, a far different approach than the usual criteria of maker, place of manufacture, or style used for most silver exhibitions. Much more progress could be made along these lines, for example, in studies of church silver in the nineteenth and early twentieth centuries, in works on silver-plated goods in the 1840–1920 period, when silver became accessible to the public at large in significant quantities, and in studies of silver as reflective of inheritance patterns and gender relationships. The ultimate goal is to preserve the strong tradition of silver connoisseurship while simultaneously using the information derived from that study not as an end in itself, but rather as a means toward the goal of a better understanding of people. As we tried to emphasize in *Silver in American Life*, the study of silver can shed light on numerous aspects of the human experience. The many important works annotated below are but the foundation for what promises to be a rich area of research and interpretation in the years ahead.

The following bibliography begins with a generous assortment of titles devoted to English and European silver, for American work is best understood in an international context. Imported wares were also a valuable part of many Americans' silver furnishings throughout the period under consideration here, and the books and articles we have selected will provide an introduction to the identification and interpretation of these objects.

Of the large literature on American silver, we have selected approximately sixty titles with an eye toward representing the major types and genres in the field. We have included some early works that remain important for understanding the development of scholarship, for these pioneering works are often the building blocks for research in the future. A rare booklet—Charles F. Montgomery and Catherine H. Maxwell's *Early American Silver: Collectors, Collections, Exhibitions, Writings*, published by the Walpole Society in 1968—is particularly helpful in generating a sense of perspective. Most of the basic works that we have cited, in turn, contain bibliographies that will lead the reader to more specialized sources that we have omitted because of space limitations.

One large category of works only sparsely represented in this bibliography is the regional or city monograph. Most of these follow a similar pattern and contain capsule biographies of makers and illustrations of their marks. George Barton Cutten, for example, issued works on the silversmiths of Georgia (1958), Northampton, Massachusetts (1939), Poughkeepsie, New York (1945), Utica, New York (1936), New York State, outside New York City (1939), North Carolina (1948), and Virginia (1952). Other important regional studies not annotated below include works by Lilian Baker Carlisle on Vermont (1970), Charles S. Parsons on New Hampshire (1983), Jennifer Faulds Goldsborough on New London, Connecticut (1969), John Devereux Kernan and others on New Haven, Connecticut (1967), Jessie Harrington and Ruthanna Hindes on Delaware (1939 and 1967), Marquis Boultinghouse on Kentucky (1980), Ruth Hunter Roach and Deborah Binder on St. Louis (1967 and 1981), Carl M. Williams on New Jersey (1949), J. Stewart Johnson on Newark, New Jersey (1966), Jerome Redfearn on Indiana (1984), Joan Lynn Schild on Rochester, New York (1944), Elizabeth D. Beckman on Cincinnati (1970), Maurice Brix on Philadelphia (1920), and William Davis Miller on Rhode Island (1928). While few, if any, of these works contain any synthesis, they embody a vast amount of primary material that is often essential to research.

As one might expect, regional and other exhibition catalogues and general books on decorative arts also contain a good deal of information on silver, although we have largely restricted our selection here to works devoted exclusively to silver. Much important work on Philadelphia silver, for example, is included in the Philadelphia Museum of Art's 1976 bicentennial exhibition catalogue. Many of these more general works are cited in "American Furniture to 1820," "American Furniture, 1820–1920," and "Surveys" elsewhere in this volume.

Articles on silver appear in a wide spectrum of periodicals, including *Antiques*, *Winterthur Portfolio*, and many museum bulletins and occasional publications. One collectors' journal, *Silver*, is exclusively devoted to the subject. This bimonthly magazine was first issued in 1967 as *Silver-rama*. The English Society of Silver Collectors, inaugurated in 1958, has issued a regular *Proceedings* which occasionally contains articles on American objects, although the emphasis is primarily on English silver.

Although basic information on the techniques of making silver in both the handcraft and industrial era is included in many of the books cited below, we have not emphasized the technical aspects of the trade in our choice of titles. An excellent introduction to eighteenth-century techniques is given in *The Silversmith at Williamsburg*, a film produced by Colonial Williamsburg in 1971 and now available on videocassette. A wide range of methods is discussed in Oppi Untracht, *Metal Techniques for Craftsmen* (Garden City, N.Y.: Doubleday, 1975).

INTERNATIONAL CONTEXT

Barr, Elaine. *George Wickes (1698–1761), Royal Goldsmith*. New York: Rizzoli International Publications, 1980. xiii+210 pp.; 127 illustrations, bibliography, appendixes, index.

This important work marked a milestone in the documentation of the silversmith's craft. It is based on the surviving ledgers and other accounts of Wickes, a London goldsmith patronized by Frederick, prince of Wales, beginning about 1735. These documents present as detailed a look as we are likely to have of the business practices of an English goldsmith active in the first half of the eighteenth century. They reveal much about shop organization, craft hierarchy, and the routine nature of a silversmith's business, such as renting out plate for special occasions, cleaning silver for clients, and repairwork.

Blair, Claude, ed. *The History of Silver*. New York: Ballantine Books, 1987. 256 pp.; black and white and color illustrations, bibliography, glossary, index.

This anthology is "a survey of the development of silver—and to a lesser extent gold—plate in Europe and European America from the earliest times to the present day" (p. 7). Eight authors provide a sweeping stylistic survey of the finest work in silver and gold made during several millennia. Appendixes on the attributes of silver as a metal, the craft of silversmithing, and the principles of hallmarking conclude the volume. The contributors—nearly all of whom are or have been associated with the Victoria and Albert Museum in London—emphasize English work, although some American objects are included. A similarly broad point of view is taken by Jessie McNab in her fine volume, *Silver* (New York: Cooper-Hewitt Museum, 1981), in the Smithsonian Illustrated Library of Antiques.

Bradbury, Frederick. *History of Old Sheffield Plate*. 1912. Reprint. Sheffield, England: J.W. Northend, 1969. xiii+539 pp.; illustrations, indexes.

"Sheffield plate" is the common name for a type of fused plate in which thin sheets of copper are faced with silver on one or both sides; the two metals are then bonded through heat and pressure. The resulting material can be fashioned into decorative forms which appear to be made of the more expensive sterling alloy. The process was developed in England in the 1730s and was an important industry in Sheffield and elsewhere for more than a century. Many examples of English fused plate were imported and retailed by American silversmiths. This work, written by a descendant of an early Sheffield manufacturer, covers in detail nearly every aspect of the history and technique of the craft.

Brett, Vanessa. *The Sotheby's Directory of Silver, 1600–1940*. London: Philip Wilson Publishers for Sotheby's Publications, 1986; distributed by Harper and Row. 432 pp.; 2,000 illustrated entries, appendixes, bibliography, indexes.

The value of this work lies in the broad scope of its coverage. More than 2,000 examples of silver from Germany, Austria, Switzerland, the Low Countries, Great Britain, Ireland, France, Italy, Russia, and Scandinavia, as well as from North America, provide a useful context for understanding American work. Brief essays on the silver trade, styles, and collecting precede the pictorial directory.

Clayton, Michael. *The Collector's Dictionary of the Silver and Gold of Great Britain and North America*. New York and Cleveland: World Publishing Co., 1971. 351 pp.; 730 black and white illustrations, 48 color plates, bibliography. Published simultaneously at London: Country Life.

This reference includes entries on forms, styles, materials, tools, techniques, and major craftsmen. It remains the first place to look for an authoritative definition of the use and origin of nearly every major object type. Each entry is illustrated, and many include bibliographic citations and documentary references. The emphasis is heavily on English work. Although Clayton's dictionary remains essential, it can be supplemented with a more recent related work, Harold Newman's *Illustrated Dictionary of Silverware* (London: Thames and Hudson, 1987).

Culme, John. *Nineteenth-Century Silver*. London and New York: Hamlyn Publishing Group for Country Life Books, 1977. 232 pp.; black and white and color illustrations, bibliography, index.

Relatively few books deal with nineteenth-century English work. Among the first was *Victorian Silver and Silver-Plate* by Patricia Wardle (1963; reprint, New York: Universe Books, 1970); this larger, more richly illustrated volume by Culme is another. Culme approaches his subject from three principal vantage points: the industry (workshops and operatives), the trade (styles and retailers), and the exhibitions (showmen and craftsmen). His text contains extensive quotations from primary sources and is equally rich in illustrations from period trade catalogues and advertisements. The discussion of forms and styles provides a good background for placing contemporaneous American work in context.

Davis, John D. *English Silver at Williamsburg*. Williamsburg Decorative Arts Series, edited by Graham Hood. Williamsburg: Colonial Williamsburg Foundation, 1976; distributed by the University Press of Virginia. viii+254 pp.; 274 illustrated entries, indexes.

The silver collection at Williamsburg was assembled to include "silver forms similar to those used in the colonial capital in private, public, and commercial capacities" and to contain a few examples for comparison of more stylish and ambitious objects. This thorough catalogue thus includes a wide variety of objects that repay attention by the student of American silver. The catalogue is arranged in sections by form, including lighting equipment and accessories; vessels and accessories for alcoholic beverages, tea, coffee, and chocolate; articles for dining; miscellaneous forms; and fused plate.

Forbes, H. A. Crosby, John Devereux Kernan, and Ruth S. Wilkins. *Chinese Export Silver, 1785 to 1885*. Milton, Mass.: Museum of the American China Trade, 1975. xvi+303 pp.; 304 illustrations, appendixes, bibliography, indexes.

This monograph brought to general attention a large body of objects that had been overlooked or misunderstood by silver scholars until the mid 1960s: silver made in China for the Western market from 1785 to 1885. It includes a well-illustrated catalogue of 299 representative objects, as well as chapters detailing the making, marketing, and marks of this branch of the Chinese export trade. More recent discoveries on the subject are included in John Devereux Kernan, *The Chait Collection of Chinese Export Silver* (New York: Ralph M. Chait Galleries, 1985).

Glanville, Philippa. *Silver in England*. English Decorative Arts. Winchester, Mass.: Allen and Unwin, 1987. xii+366 pp.; 142 black and white illustrations and plates, 4 color plates, bibliography, index.

Comprehensive and engaging, this new book is the most recent general survey of English silver in a long line of distinguished works begun by Sir Charles James Jackson in 1911. Each generation has had its general survey, such as Charles Oman's *English Domestic Silver* (1934), Gerald Taylor's *Silver* (1956), and Judith Banister's *Old English Silver* (1965). Glanville's volume includes the standard material on history, the craft, and design that is found in these earlier works, but gains added distinction through its inclusion of "The Sociology of Silver: Gifts and Obligations" and through its coverage of English silver from its beginnings in medieval times to the present.

Grimwade, Arthur G. *London Goldsmiths, 1697–1837: Their Marks and Lives from the Original Registers at Goldsmiths' Hall and Other Sources*. 1976. 2d ed. London: Faber and Faber, 1982. x+728 pp.; 8 illustrations, appendix.

This reference work, by a dean of English silver scholarship, provides essential information on the marks and names of English eighteenth- and early nineteenth-century silversmiths. Grimwade's introduction provides background on the system of registering marks at Goldsmiths' Hall, the headquarters of the silversmiths' guild, and on the complicated organization of the trades in London during the eighteenth century. A similar reference work on nineteenth-century London silver is John Culme, *The Directory of Gold and Silversmiths and Allied Trades* (Woodbridge, Suffolk: Antique Collectors' Club, 1987).

Gruber, Alain. *Silverware*. New York: Rizzoli International Publications, 1982. 305 pp.; 381 black and white and 28 color illustrations, bibliography, index.

The strength of this work is that, unlike most books on the subject, it concentrates on the history of how silver objects were used and how they were regarded, rather than on how styles changed. Gruber has pulled together an impressive array of prints, drawings, and paintings, most in public collections, showing objects in use. He also cites numerous documentary sources for his statements about changes in manners and table service, although the text is somewhat weakened by the lack of standard scholarly annotations to this material.

Hernmarck, Carl. *The Art of the European Silversmith, 1430–1830.* 2 vols. London and New York: Sotheby Parke Bernet, 1977. [797] pp.; 1,001 plates, bibliography, indexes.

The first volume of this massive work is devoted to a general stylistic survey of silver by country of origin, style period, and development of forms. Hernmarck's treatment of the first two areas is useful, although cursory; the bulk of the narrative is devoted to the history of objects arranged in functional categories—for example, vessels for wine and beer, table silver, furniture and ornaments, and treasury pieces. In each of these sections he treats changes in customs as they influenced stylistic change, and he deals with questions of design origin and transfer. The plates, grouped together in the second volume, provide an unparalleled pictorial resource for the study of the European context of American silver.

Holland, Margaret. *Old Country Silver: An Account of English Provincial Silver, with Sections on Ireland, Scotland, and Wales.* Newton Abbot: David and Charles, 1971. 240 pp.; [39] plates, [49] line drawings, 3 maps, bibliography, index. Published simultaneously at New York: Arco Publishing Co.

Although London has always been the center of the English silversmithing trade, much fine work was produced in the provincial cities of Exeter, York, Newcastle, Norwich, Chester, Birmingham, and Sheffield, as well as in Ireland and Scotland. Some of this provincial silver is closely related to American work and reflects a comparable level of patronage. Much attention is devoted here to minutiae concerning the intricacies of provincial hallmarks, but this book nevertheless provides an introductory view of English silver that is often overlooked in most general surveys.

Hughes, Graham. *Modern Silver throughout the World, 1880–1967.* New York: Crown Publishers, 1967. 256 pp.; 462 black and white and 12 color illustrations, bibliography, index.

After a survey of some of the world's most influential firms, such as Jensen and Bolin of Sweden, this pioneering work moves through nearly a century of modern design thematically. Questions of training, production, the organization of the trade, and marketing are discussed briefly, although the primary strength of the book lies in its numerous illustrations of objects produced throughout the world. In the pre-1920 period, the art nouveau style receives the most detailed attention. Biographies of more than 200 designers and firms are also included.

Jackson, Charles. *English Goldsmiths and Their Marks: A History of the Goldsmiths and Plate Workers of England, Scotland, and Ireland.* 1921. Reprint. New York: Dover Publications, 1964. xvi+747 pp.; index.

Its original, lengthy subtitle explains the continued usefulness of this monumental reference work: "...with over Thirteen Thousand Marks Reproduced in Facsimile from Authentic Examples of Plate, and Tables of Date-Letters and Other Hall-Marks Used in the Assay Offices of the United Kingdom." In several introductory chapters, Jackson explains the assay office system, recounts legislation affecting English silversmiths, discusses the standards for gold- and silverware, and provides a lucid introduction to the English methods of marking silver. First published in 1905, *English Goldsmiths* was issued in a revised second edition in 1921; a 1964 reprint by Dover has made this second edition widely available and sustained its usefulness. A new edition, edited by Ian Pickford, with many corrections and additions, has been published by the Antique Collectors' Club.

Jackson, Charles. *An Illustrated History of Silver Plate.* 2 vols. 1911. Reprint. New York: Dover Publications, 1969. 1,085 pp.; 1,506 illustrations, 76 plates, index.

Although there had been many earlier works on English silver prior to the publication of this volume in 1911, no previous survey attempted "to illustrate the development of form and decoration in the silver and gold work of the British Isles from the earliest known examples to the latest of the Georgian period" (p. x). Nearly eight decades after its appearance and the subsequent publication of many surveys, Jackson's *Illustrated History* remains useful as a pictorial reference and an authoritative introduction to many facets of English work. Jackson divided his book into two volumes: the first contains a chronological overview, followed by a survey of ecclesiastical work; volume 2 includes sixteen chapters devoted to various forms, embracing nearly every type of article fashioned of silver.

Langdon, John E. *Canadian Silversmiths, 1700–1900.* Toronto: Stinehour Press, 1966. xx+249 pp.; 76 plates, illustrated catalogue of marks, appendixes, bibliography, indexes.

This survey is organized geographically, with chapters devoted to Quebec, Nova Scotia and New Brunswick, and Ontario. Each chapter begins with a historical introduction followed by an alphabetical listing of makers and their marks. A special section is devoted to Hendery and Leslie of Montreal, a firm that held a "dominant position" in Canadian silversmithing during the last half of the nineteenth century. Langdon published several other volumes on Canadian silver, usually issued, like this book, in handsomely printed limited editions. Although Langdon covers both English and French traditions, for more detailed coverage of French Canadian traditions, readers may also wish to consult Jean Trudel, *Silver in New France* (Ottawa: National Gallery of Canada, 1974), and Ross Allan C. Fox, *Quebec and Related Silver at the Detroit Institute of Arts* (Detroit: Wayne State University Press, 1978).

Link, Eva. *The Book of Silver.* Translated by Francisca Garvie. New York: Praeger Publishers, 1973. 301 pp.;

black and white and color illustrations, line drawings, glossary, bibliography, index.

Link deals with silver and its significance as a material for coins and precious objects from ancient Greece through the present. The author outlines stylistic changes, but her emphasis is on the social, religious, and political context which either fostered or discouraged the production and ownership of silver objects. Paying particular attention to the relative status of silversmithing as an art in a given culture, she concludes that the increased demand for utilitarian wares toward the end of the sixteenth century ultimately resulted in its decline as a fine art. Special attention is given to German-made objects. Appendixes include stylistic charts with line drawings and an illustrated listing of major hallmarks used in eastern and western Europe.

Oman, Charles. *English Church Plate, 597–1830*. London and New York: Oxford University Press, 1957. xxx+ 326 pp.+199 plates; bibliography, appendixes, indexes.

Oman explores not only the form and ornament of church silver itself but also the changing role of the sacraments and the objects that gave them material manifestation in the Church of England. Beginning with a history of sacramental practice in England, and the origin of the use of vessels made of precious metals, he goes on to discuss the importance of individual forms and to provide conceptual categories for the types of inscriptions they bear: donative, possessive, and scriptural. These general chapters are followed by chapters on the evolution of individual forms, with emphasis on changes in style and liturgical requirements.

Touching Gold and Silver: Five Hundred Years of Hallmarks. Exhibition catalogue. London: Goldsmiths' Hall, 1978. 131 pp.; 200 illustrated entries, bibliography.

Published in conjunction with an exhibition at Goldsmiths' Hall, London, this catalogue is an extremely useful reference tool outlining the histories and major changes in hallmarking in each of the nine English assay offices. It includes excellent detail photographs showing the various marking systems as they appear on objects in the guild's collection. Unfortunately, the brief section on fakes and forgeries and on assaying equipment is only checklists with no illustrations. The exhibition and its catalogue were the work of Susan M. Hare, librarian of the Worshipful Company of Goldsmiths.

AMERICAN SILVER AND GOLD

Avery, C. Louise. *American Silver of the Seventeenth and Eighteenth Centuries: A Study Based on the Clearwater Collection.* Preface by R. T. H. Halsey. New York: Metropolitan Museum of Art, 1920. clix+216 pp.; 141 illustrations, bibliography, index.

Printed in an edition limited to 1,000 copies, this catalogue records basic information on 544 objects in the Alphonso T. Clearwater (1848–1933) collection, one that forms the core of the Metropolitan Museum of Art's holdings in early silver. Following the same general format that she would use a decade later in her *Early American Silver*, Avery included here a general introduction on the history of silver design and the techniques of silversmithing, followed by notes on the evolution of beakers, tankards, mugs, caudle cups, and other principal forms. An unusual addition is a short chapter on classic silver moldings by noted architect Cass Gilbert. The catalogue is arranged chronologically. A modern survey of the Metropolitan's superb holdings is given in Frances Gruber Safford, "American Silver in the American Wing," *Metropolitan Museum of Art Bulletin* (Summer 1983).

Avery, C. Louise. *Early American Silver.* New York and London: Century Co., 1930. xliv+378 pp.; 33 illustrations, 63 plates, bibliography, index.

This survey has stood the test of time well. Published in 1930 and reissued in 1968 by Russell and Russell, it repays reading more than half a century after its publication. The strength of the book is the author's understanding and interpretation of the design of American silver; for example, Avery is particularly strong on the European influences on early New York objects. The book begins with a discussion of the regional styles in silver, with an emphasis on Massachusetts and New York, and concludes with an examination of the evolution of twenty-two principal forms. Although readers may wish to turn to the more recent surveys by Martha Gandy Fales and Graham Hood first, Avery's remains a useful and literate guide to the visual qualities of early American silver.

Belden, Louise Conway. *Marks of American Silversmiths in the Ineson-Bissell Collection.* Charlottesville: University Press of Virginia for the Henry Francis du Pont Winterthur Museum, 1980. 505 pp.; 13 illustrations, illustrated catalogue of marks, glossary, bibliography.

Of the many books on marks, this well-illustrated volume is among the most useful. It contains pictures of some 1,700 marks found on objects in the Ineson-Bissell Collection of Small Silver Objects at Winterthur dating between about 1670 and 1870. Although some rare early marks are not included, this book surpasses earlier related works in its level of documentation. Belden's chapter on the identification of marks is essential reading, and the illustrated glossary of spoon terms helps to clarify some of the confusing nomenclature surrounding the common types of silver objects.

Bigelow, Francis Hill. *Historic Silver of the Colonies and Its Makers*. 1941. Reprint. New York: Tudor Publishing Co., 1948. xxiv+476 pp.; 325 illustrations, bibliography, indexes.

Historic Silver is largely of interest today as the first comprehensive survey of the subject. Although American silver figured in John H. Buck's *Old Plate* (1888), was featured in a handful of exhibition catalogues, and was the focus of E. Alfred Jones's monumental *Old Silver of American Churches* (1913), no author before Bigelow (1859–1933) had attempted a complete survey of American silver. Bigelow organized his book by form, and his wide knowledge of public and private collections enabled him to include more than 300 illustrations, making this survey a valuable reference today.

Bohan, Peter, and Philip Hammerslough. *Early Connecticut Silver, 1700–1840*. Middletown, Conn.: Wesleyan University Press, 1970. xi+288 pp.; 184 plates, bibliography, indexes.

This survey illustrates and describes more than 180 examples of Connecticut silver, many of which are relatively simple objects reflecting the nature of the craft in this state before the industrial era, although fine objects by Cornelius Kierstede, Ebenezer Chittenden, and others are included. The authors see three phases in the development of the craft: an assimilation phase (1700–1740), when silversmiths from Massachusetts, Rhode Island, and New York "adapted their styles to meet the demands of Connecticut patronage"; an indigenous phase (1740–80), when local craftsmen were more innovative; and a final period marked by quantity production (1780–1830), when craftsmen pursued a diverse range of occupations (pp. 19–20). The book concludes with appendixes containing short biographies of some 475 silversmiths and illustrations of their marks as well as a useful annotated bibliography.

Bohan, Peter J. *American Gold, 1700–1860*. Exhibition catalogue. New Haven: Yale University Art Gallery, 1963. 52 pp.; 147 illustrated entries, bibliography.

This small catalogue remains the only scholarly work devoted solely to the scarce objects of gold produced in America before 1860. The entries included here represent a high percentage of the known major examples as well as a sampling of the common forms of clasps, sleeve buttons, and rings. The center of production of ambitious objects such as coral and bells, freedom boxes, spoons, and buckles was apparently New York City.

Bolton, Charles Knowles. *Bolton's American Armory: A Record of the Coats of Arms which Have Been in Use within the Present Bounds of the United States*. 1927. Reprint. Baltimore: Heraldic Book Co., 1964. xxiii+222 pp.; illustrations, glossary, index.

In 1927 Bolton compiled all the known examples of heraldic devices used by American families and meticulously de-

scribed them for this volume. Although not well illustrated, Bolton's book still remains the best single source of information on the coats of arms adopted by key families. It contains full descriptions in standard terminology of all examples and gives the location and other basic information concerning the objects on which the coats of arms are found.

Buhler, Kathryn C. *American Silver, 1655–1825, in the Museum of Fine Arts, Boston*. 2 vols. Boston: By the museum, 1972; distributed by New York Graphic Society. xx+708 pp.; approximately 600 illustrations, appendix, index.

This catalogue contains 566 detailed entries on a collection "unmatched for its wealth of documented New England plate" (1:ix). Volume 1 contains entries on Massachusetts silver; volume 2 is devoted to later work in Massachusetts (including a major group by Paul Revere II), New Hampshire, Connecticut, Rhode Island, New York, and Philadelphia. Brief biographies of craftsmen whose works are represented in the collection are included, and an appendix includes notes on about 125 spoons. Among Buhler's many other works are similarly thorough catalogues of other collections: Mount Vernon (1957); the Harrington collection (1965) now at Hood Museum, Dartmouth College; Yale (1970, with Graham Hood); and Worcester Art Museum (1979).

Buhler, Kathryn C. *Colonial Silversmiths, Masters, and Apprentices*. Boston: Museum of Fine Arts, 1956. 98 pp.; 126 illustrations, 345 illustrated entries.

The conservation of mechanical knowledge through the transmission of skills in the apprenticeship system has long concerned students of early silver. In this catalogue, Buhler attempts "to make a start in associating apprentices with their masters" through a study of documents and through the analysis of surviving objects. Her introduction examines several generations in New England, New York, and Philadelphia, and her points are reinforced through 345 catalogue entries, only a third of which are illustrated. Although some of the relationships postulated by Buhler have been modified by subsequent research, this work remains a basic introduction to one important element of the craft system.

Buhler, Kathryn C., and Graham Hood. *American Silver: Garvan and Other Collections in the Yale University Art Gallery*. 2 vols. New Haven and London: Yale University Press for the Yale University Art Gallery, 1970. Vol. 1, *New England*, xviii+344 pp.; 527 illustrated entries, glossary, bibliography, index. Vol. 2, *Middle Colonies and the South*, xii+300 pp.; 496 illustrated entries, glossary, bibliography, index.

This catalogue contains entries on 1,043 examples of American silver, most made before 1820, drawn from what is generally recognized as the finest collection of early American silver, unrivaled in its number of individual masterpieces and geographic scope. The detailed entries are arranged by region and then chronologically by maker within each section. The superb photographs by E. Irving Blomstrann enhance the value and usefulness of the book. Most of the objects were acquired by collector Francis P. Garvan (1875–1937), many with the assistance of curator John Marshall Phillips (1905–53). Since 1970 the Yale collections have grown, primarily through the addition of post-1850 objects (some of which are represented in Ward and Ward, *Silver in American Life*) and through the acquisition of the Kossack collection in the 1980s, numbering some 4,400 objects, primarily flatware, ranging in date from 1720 to 1890.

Burton, E. Milby. *South Carolina Silversmiths, 1690–1860.* Contributions from the Charleston Museum. Charleston: By the museum, 1942. xvii+311 pp.; illustrations, 16 plates, bibliography, index.

This work was among the first major monographs devoted to silver from a state south of Maryland. It follows the format customary to the genre in that it is primarily a compendium of 320 biographical sketches arranged by community, from Abbeville through York, and based on information drawn from newspapers, land records, marriage lists, and other primary sources. More recent research on South Carolina silver has been conducted by the Museum of Early Southern Decorative Arts.

Carpenter, Charles H., Jr. *Gorham Silver, 1831–1981.* New York: Dodd, Mead, 1982. xii+332 pp.; 295 black and white illustrations, 8 color plates, appendixes, bibliography, index.

Like the Carpenters' earlier work on Tiffany silver, this book broke new ground in the study of another giant in the silversmithing world of the nineteenth century. Here, however, the story of the firm is carried from its nineteenth-century beginnings through to 1981, perhaps reflecting the growing interest in twentieth-century silver in recent years. As in the Carpenters' Tiffany book, *Gorham Silver* contains chapters on specialized forms and product lines, including Gorham bronzes, souvenir spoons, presentation pieces, and Martelé, as well as rich analysis of designers, such as William Christmas Codman, and design sources. Appendixes provide much detailed information on marks, flatware patterns, and other basic source material. *See also* "Craftsmen."

Carpenter, Charles H., Jr., with Mary Grace Carpenter. *Tiffany Silver.* New York: Dodd, Mead, 1978. xix+296 pp.; 331 black and white illustrations, 4 color plates, bibliography, index.

This important monograph represents the first modern study of Tiffany's nineteenth-century years, and its publication marked a new sophistication in the study of silver from the industrial era. The Carpenters trace the history of Tiffany from its beginnings in the late 1830s through its rise to a position of international renown by 1900. Many of their chapters are devoted to specific forms for which Tiffany was

well known, such as presentation pieces, yachting trophies, and elaborate services of holloware and flatware. Other chapters deal with Japanese and other exotic influences on Tiffany's work, with their electroplated goods, and with the making of Tiffany silver. A long section on marks is of use in accurately dating surviving examples.

Clarke, Hermann Frederick. *John Coney, Silversmith, 1655–1722.* 1932. Reprint. New York: Da Capo Press, 1971. xv+89 pp.; plates.

The first in a series of monographs on early Boston silversmiths, this volume set the standard for those that would follow. The short biographical chapter is based on detailed documentary research and includes a facsimile of the inventory of Coney's estate as well as extensive quotations from the funeral sermon preached by his son-in-law Thomas Foxcroft. The following chapter focuses on the dating of Coney's touchmarks and is accompanied by magnified photographs of the marks themselves. The bulk of the book is devoted to a discussion of Coney's works (engravings as well as objects) and a catalogue raisonné of all extant silver known at that time. The catalogue includes dimensions, drawings of marks, engraved initials and coats of arms, original owners, references, and collection or repository. In spite of subsequent discoveries, this is still the most complete listing of Coney's works.

Clarke, Hermann Frederick. *John Hull: A Builder of the Bay Colony.* Portland, Maine: Southworth-Anthoensen Press, 1940. xiv+221 pp.; 15 plates, bibliography, checklist, index.

Hull and his partner Robert Sanderson are renowned as the masters of the first Massachusetts mint and as the earliest of America's productive silversmiths. A civic, religious, and business leader, Hull invested in shipping and other merchant activities while working as an artisan. For the biography, Clarke drew on Hull's personal diaries (transcribed from the originals in American Antiquarian Society and published separately as *The Diaries of John Hull, Mint-Master and Treasurer of the Colony of Massachusetts Bay* [Boston: John Wilson and Son, 1857]) which provided him with detailed information on Hull's attitudes toward the society in which he lived. As a result, he was able to place his subject within a broad historical context. For instance, Clarke's chapter on Hull and Sanderson's coins not only deals extensively with the situation leading up to Massachusetts's decision to establish its own mint but also comments on the appearance of the resulting coins and their chronology. The volume contains a detailed analysis of Hull and Sanderson's silver which is illustrated with photographs of their various marks and of some of their most outstanding objects. Like the other books in the series, this one includes a catalogue raisonné of the artisans' works with dimensions, marks, inscriptions, arms, references, and location. It differs from the other volumes in including a bibliography of historical works used in its preparation.

Clarke, Hermann Frederick, and Henry Wilder Foote. *Jeremiah Dummer: Colonial Craftsman and Merchant, 1645–1718*. Foreword by E. Alfred Jones. Boston: Houghton Mifflin Co., 1935. 205 pp.; 23 plates.

Because of Dummer's stature as a merchant and public servant, Clarke's second monograph on an early Boston silversmith contains more extensive biographical material than his first. The treatment of the silver and the catalogue raisonné follow the same format as those in Clarke's *John Coney*. Of special note is the chapter entitled "Was Jeremiah Dummer a Painter of Portraits?" by Foote. Although Foote clearly reveals that he believed Dummer to be the author of the portraits discovered in 1921, subsequent scholars have rejected them as forgeries. Nonetheless, his arguments are worthy of attention and show the strength of interest in colonial craftsmen during the 1920s and 1930s.

Crescent City Silver: An Exhibition of Nineteenth-Century New Orleans Silver. New Orleans: Historic New Orleans Collection, 1980. vi+130 pp.; 135 illustrated entries, glossary, bibliography, appendixes.

This catalogue follows the traditional pattern of emphasizing biographies and marks of makers from a previously little-studied city. A brief introduction treats the French, German, and American craftsmen who came to New Orleans and dominated the trade there during the nineteenth century. The presence of these immigrant craftsmen, each with distinct ethnic backgrounds, led to the creation of silver objects that reflect these diverse traditions.

Darling, Sharon S. *Chicago Metalsmiths: An Illustrated History*. Exhibition catalogue. Chicago: Chicago Historical Society, 1977. xvi+141 pp.; 155 illustrations, index.

This pioneering work marked the first time that a significant body of silver made in Chicago was brought to general attention. Although the work deals with silver from about 1804 through 1970, the most dramatic objects brought to light here were created during the arts and crafts movement of 1890 to 1918 by the Kalo shop, the Robert Jarvie shop, and other makers whose reputation was revived and established by this book. Darling sets the Chicago school within an international context and provides detailed information on shops and makers. *See also* "Brass, Copper, Iron, and Tin."

Ensko, Stephen G. C. *American Silversmiths and Their Marks III*. New York: Robert Ensko, 1948. 285 pp.; illustrations, maps, bibliography.

This third edition of Ensko's mark book is still useful as a guide to the names and marks of many silversmiths active before 1850. It builds on two earlier editions (1927, 1937) and on such other works as Hollis French, *A List of Early American Silversmiths and Their Marks* (New York: Walpole Society, 1917), and Ernest M. Currier, *Marks of Early American Silversmiths*, ed. Kathryn C. Buhler (Portland, Maine: South-

worth-Anthoensen Press, 1938), and on lists contained in many exhibition catalogues. Later works, such as compilations by C. Jordan Thorn (1949) and Ralph M. and Terry H. Kovel, continue the genre, along with other titles annotated here. The Kovels' *Directory of American Silver, Pewter, and Silverplate* (New York: Crown Publishers, 1961) also serves as an index to earlier literature on each silversmith, thus enhancing its usefulness. Ensko's third edition is enhanced by the inclusion of maps depicting the location of silversmiths' shops in Boston, New York, and Philadelphia and a bibliography of works on silver arranged chronologically.

Fales, Martha Gandy. *American Silver in the Henry Francis du Pont Winterthur Museum*. Photographs by Gilbert Ask. Winterthur, Del.: By the museum, 1958. [57] pp.; 142 illustrations, index.

This short work contains illustrations of and brief descriptive captions about a selection of 171 objects by eighty-six silversmiths in the Winterthur collection largely formed by Henry Francis du Pont (1880–1969). A more detailed catalogue of the entire Winterthur collection is in preparation by Ian M. G. Quimby.

Fales, Martha Gandy. *Early American Silver*. Rev. and enl. ed. New York: E. P. Dutton, 1973. x+336 pp.; 231 illustrations, line drawings, 1 table, glossary, bibliography, index.

The best all-around survey of American silver, this book includes chapters on stylistic change, the development of forms such as drinking vessels and serving pieces, design sources, regional characteristics, the craft of the silversmith and allied artisans, and special features of the metal and marks used by early craftsmen. Fales's thorough understanding of the techniques and tools of the craftsmen and her appreciation of the context within which the objects were produced make this a particularly valuable study. It also includes useful time lines of forms and ornament and a concise glossary of silver terms.

Fales, Martha Gandy. *Joseph Richardson and Family: Philadelphia Silversmiths*. Middletown, Conn.: Wesleyan University Press for the Historical Society of Pennsylvania, 1974. xviii+340 pp.; 180 illustrations, appendixes, bibliography, index.

Francis (1681–1729), Joseph, Sr. (1711–84), Joseph, Jr. (1752–1821), and Nathaniel (1754–1827) Richardson comprised the most prolific silversmithing family in early Philadelphia. Fales places the Richardsons within a broad social, economic, and artistic context. Her chronicle of their lives, their silver, and their business practices is developed through a close analysis of surviving objects and careful examination of surviving documents. The extensive collection of Richardson family papers at Historical Society of Pennsylvania and Winterthur provided her with rare insight into the life of a colonial craftsman. The letter book kept by Joseph Richardson between 1758 and 1774, reprinted here in full, is rich in detail concerning his dealings with English suppliers from whom he imported silver and tools and is an important primary source for anyone studying eighteenth-century American silver.

Fennimore, Donald. "Religion in America: Metal Objects in Service of the Ritual." *American Art Journal* 10, no. 2 (November 1978): 20–42. Illustrations.

Fennimore focuses on American religious diversity and the variety of metal objects that have been produced for ceremonies. He discusses the relative importance of the major religions in America and provides basic information on the ritual and liturgy of each. Thus, rather than concentrating on the common forms, such as the cups or flagons in Protestant churches, he illustrates representative examples of Catholic and Jewish religious silver, including a reliquary, a monstrance, a torah crown, and a menorah. Although the bulk of the article is devoted to a discussion of the eighteenth-century objects, Fennimore briefly extends his treatment into the first half of the nineteenth century.

Fennimore, Donald L. "Thomas Fletcher and Sidney Gardiner: The Stylistic Development of Their Domestic Silver." *Antiques* 102, no. 4 (October 1972): 642–49. 17 illustrations.

Based on the author's 1971 Winterthur thesis, this brief article traces the stylistic evolution of the silver produced between 1808 and 1842 by Fletcher and Gardiner, the nation's largest silver manufacturer at that time. French and English designs influenced the firm's silver in the neoclassical and other revival styles. Although domestic production formed the backbone of the company's production, they were best known for their monumental presentation silver; see Elizabeth Ingerman Wood, "Thomas Fletcher: A Philadelphia Entrepreneur of Presentation Silver," in *Winterthur Portfolio 3*, ed. Milo M. Naeve (Winterthur, Del.: Henry Francis du Pont Winterthur Museum, 1967), pp. 136–71.

Flynt, Henry N., and Martha Gandy Fales. *The Heritage Foundation Collection of Silver, with Biographical Sketches of New England Silversmiths, 1625–1825.* Old Deerfield, Mass.: Heritage Foundation, 1968. xiv+391 pp.; 118 illustrations, bibliography, index.

This book serves a dual purpose: it stands as an introduction to the important collection at Historic Deerfield and as a reference work containing concise biographies and illustrations of the touchmarks of several hundred New England silversmiths active before 1825. The Heritage Foundation collection, assembled by Mr. and Mrs. Flynt, is profiled in a long chapter by Fales in which she discusses its formation and many of its major objects. Brief statements on the "silver climate" in the six New England states are also included, each prepared by a specialist.

French, Hollis. *Jacob Hurd and His Sons, Nathaniel and Benjamin, Silversmiths, 1702–1781.* 1939. Reprint. New York: Da Capo Press, 1972. 147 pp.; 28 illustrations, appendix.

Jacob Hurd was the most prolific of Boston's eighteenth-century silversmiths. He trained Nathaniel and Benjamin Hurd to follow him in his craft, and Nathaniel became known as an extremely able engraver. The book includes a biographical chapter on each man and a catalogue raisonné of the extant silver of all three which contains information on form, decoration, dimensions, engraved initials and coats of arms, original owners, and collection or repository for each object. The biographies are notable for their extensive quotations from documentary sources and the author's painstaking genealogical research. The section on Nathaniel is unusual because, after a brief biography, French concentrates his attention on Nathaniel's career as an engraver in chapters devoted to his seals and dies, his engravings, and his bookplates. Although French deals with an entire family of silversmiths, his aim seems to have been to highlight Nathaniel's career. As a result, there is no significant discussion of the artistry or design sources of Jacob's or Benjamin's works in silver.

Garvan, Anthony N. B. "The New England Porringer: An Index of Custom." In *Annual Report of the Board of Regents of the Smithsonian Institution . . . for the Year Ended June 30, 1958.* Publication 4354, pp. 543–52. Washington, D.C.: Government Printing Office, 1959. 8 illustrations.

This short article represents an attempt to understand silver objects as "an index of values and ideas seldom expressed verbally" (p. 544). Garvan's analysis of a common, popular form—the porringer—suggests to him that its design and stylistic evolution were intimately linked to Puritan "concepts and customs" (p. 545). In particular, he hypothesizes that the intricate piercings on early porringer handles—tablets, hearts, circles, trefoils, and quatrefoils—are symbols with direct references to Puritan ideas about love, marriage, and religion and that the changes in the form in the mid eighteenth century relate to the decline of Puritanism. One need not accept all the author's conclusions to recognize that Garvan's interpretation of the iconography of the voids on porringer handles is an important statement linking objects and ideas.

Gere, Charlotte. *American and European Jewelry, 1830–1914.* New York: Crown Publishers, 1975. 240 pp.; 228 black and white and color illustrations, glossary, bibliography, index.

Although jewelrymaking has always been an important part of the silversmith's craft, and although objects of personal adornment are rich in cultural significance, studies devoted exclusively to American jewelry, especially early jewelry, are scarce. Many broad surveys include some mention of American objects; a more accessible is Marie-Louise d'Otrange Mastai's volume in the Smithsonian Illustrated Library of

Antiques. Gere's book examines nineteenth-century jewelry in relation to the evolution of style and design and includes sections on materials and techniques and biographies of more than 100 jewelers and designers.

Gerstell, Vivian S. *Silversmiths of Lancaster, Pennsylvania, 1730–1850.* Lancaster: Lancaster County Historical Society, 1972. ix+145 pp.; illustrations, appendix, bibliography.

A large inland city located in the rich farming area west of Philadelphia, Lancaster supported more than forty silversmiths during the late eighteenth and early nineteenth centuries. This regional study, a typical example of a common type of silver book, deals with the lives and products of these men in an almost exclusively biographical fashion. Their work, as might be expected, was heavily influenced by Philadelphia designs and preferences. Facsimiles of the estate inventories of six craftsmen are also included.

Gibb, George Sweet. *The Whitesmiths of Taunton: A History of Reed and Barton, 1824–1943.* Harvard Studies in Business History, no. 8, edited by N. S. B. Gras. Cambridge, Mass.: Harvard University Press, 1943. xxxiii+419 pp.; plates, index.

When it appeared in 1943, *The Whitesmiths of Taunton* "was the first in-depth study of a manufacturing enterprise conducted under scholarly auspices at Harvard" (p. xxvi). Gibb's book thus stands outside the fold of the usual object-centered monographs on silver, for although it tells the story of metals and men, its emphasis is on sales, finances, marketing, and the evolution and survival of a business firm. Yet because Reed and Barton's business was "to secure a living by providing America with the appointments of luxurious living" (p. 3), the book has much to say about changing styles and the relationship of technology and taste. Reed and Barton, located in Taunton, Massachusetts, began with the production of Britannia ware, then moved to the manufacture of silver-plated goods, and finally to the production of sterling wares. Their history was representative of a certain level of American silversmithing for a century and a half, giving Gibb's book added importance as a reflection of wider trends. The author's long introduction to the 1969 reprint edition places the book in context and merits attention.

Goldsborough, Jennifer Faulds. *Eighteenth and Nineteenth Century Maryland Silver in the Collection of the Baltimore Museum of Art.* Edited by Ann Boyce Harper. A project supported by the Stieff Company. Baltimore: By the museum, 1975. ix+204 pp.; 207 illustrated entries, appendix, bibliography.

This collection catalogue represents the most inclusive form of the type. It contains a general introduction on Maryland silver (somewhat superseded now, as are other parts of the book, by Goldsborough's subsequent work on the same subject); detailed entries on 207 objects; biographical notes on and illustrations of the marks of Maryland silversmiths; and

a helpful bibliography. Another component further distinguishes this volume. It includes a chapter on the marks of silver fashioned in Baltimore, where a complicated assay office system was in use in the early nineteenth century. Part of the research for this chapter included the testing of 43 objects through X-ray fluorescence spectroscopy to determine if the Baltimore assay office marks were indicative of a standard silver alloy. The results of the scientific examination are included in a separate chapter, the first time that such evidence had been used extensively in a collection catalogue.

Goldsborough, Jennifer Faulds. *Silver in Maryland.* Additional essays by Nancy Baker, Patrick M. Duggan, Catherine B. Hollan, Edward F. LaFond, Jr., and Jane Webb Smith. Exhibition catalogue. Baltimore: Museum and Library of Maryland History, Maryland Historical Society, in cooperation with Historic Annapolis, the Baltimore Museum of Art, and the Peale Museum, 1983. 300 pp.; illustrations, 361 illustrated entries, glossary, bibliography, appendixes.

In 1983 Maryland Historical Society opened an extensive exhibition of silver owned or made in Maryland during the last 300 years. This catalogue, the lasting record of that show, begins with six excellent introductory essays on Annapolis silversmiths, marks on Baltimore silver between 1814 and 1869 (giving extensive new information on marks during the assay office period), Baltimore apprenticeships, clock- and watchmaking, and repeating striking systems in Maryland clocks, as well as a general overview by the author. Dimensions, weights, descriptions of marks, and detailed catalogue entries are given for 361 objects. The appendix lists silversmiths and clock- and watchmakers and allied craftsmen, illustrating many of their marks. However, all known marks could not be illustrated, and the listing therefore does not completely supersede Goldsborough's *Eighteenth and Nineteenth Century Maryland Silver.*

Hogan, Edmund P. *An American Heritage: A Book about the International Silver Company.* Edited by Howard H. Van Lenten. Dallas: Taylor Publishing Co., 1977. 183 pp.; black and white and color illustrations, appendixes, index.

The literature on nineteenth-century manufacturers of silver and silver-plated goods is sketchy and of uneven quality. Although some good company histories exist, this profile of International Silver Company, formed in 1898 by a merger of more than a dozen companies working in the vicinity of Meriden, Connecticut, is typical of a large body of informal publications that nevertheless contain some important information and period illustrations. The book is enriched by the author's long familiarity with International Silver, gained while he worked for the company from 1918 to 1963 and during his retirement, when he served as superintendent of its historical collection. *An American Heritage* can be supplemented by Earl Chapin May, *Century of Silver, 1847–1947:*

Connecticut Yankees and a Noble Metal (New York: Robert M. McBride, 1947).

Hood, Graham. *American Silver: A History of Style, 1650–1900*. American Decorative Arts Series, edited by James Biddle. New York and London: Praeger Publishers, 1971. 256 pp.; 286 illustrations, bibliography, index.

Silver is thoroughly analyzed here from an aesthetic point of view, in a fashion not dissimilar from John Marshall Phillips's survey of 1949. Hood's chapters are arranged by style (as in "Baroque Silver of the William and Mary Period") and progress from the seventeenth century through to the end of the nineteenth. Many of the major masterpieces of American silver are included here, and Hood's exegesis of their visual attributes and qualities provides the reader with an understanding of changing taste and a method of looking at silver objects as works of art.

Jones, E. Alfred. *The Old Silver of American Churches*. 2 vols. Letchworth, England: Arden Press for the National Society of the Colonial Dames of America, 1913. lxxxvii+565 pp.; 145 plates, indexes.

This monumental work includes detailed information on 1,918 items from more than 315 churches in fifteen states and the District of Columbia. Jones, with the help of Francis Hill Bigelow and the cooperation of participating churches, was able to describe each object and record its inscription, coat of arms, and maker's mark. Extensive biographical notes on donors and lengthy quotations from wills and church records make this an extremely valuable book. Jones also included documentary references to silver objects now lost and to pewter vessels and other items owned by the churches. Most of the objects are illustrated in group photographs. Although Jones may be criticized for giving undue attention to English and European silver owned in American churches (these are the only items that appear in photographs by themselves) and for slighting objects made between 1790 and 1840 (few of these are illustrated), the book is the most ambitious one ever written on the subject of American silver. Much of the research first bore fruit in the exhibition and catalogue *American Church Silver of the Seventeenth and Eighteenth Centuries, with a Few Pieces of Domestic Plate* (Boston: Museum of Fine Arts, 1911). Many items included in the exhibition have been on loan to the museum since that date. For years Kathryn C. Buhler kept records of these objects in an annotated copy of *Old Silver* and was compiling corrections for a revised edition when she died. Her copy is still in the library of the Museum of Fine Arts. The relatively poor coverage of southern churches in *Old Silver* was somewhat compensated for by Virginia Museum's exhibition catalogue *Church Silver of Colonial Virginia* (Richmond, 1970), which includes information on the holdings of many churches not covered by Jones.

Kolter, Jane Bentley, ed. *Early American Silver and Its Makers*. Antiques Magazine Library. New York:

Mayflower Books, a Main Street Press Book, 1979. 160 pp.; illustrations, bibliography, index.

This anthology conveniently gathers together thirty-nine articles originally published in *Antiques* between 1922 and 1978 by such authors as John Marshall Phillips, Kathryn C. Buhler, Graham Hood, and Martha Gandy Fales. Many of the articles deal with New York or Massachusetts silver; others focus on specific forms and makers; most contain information not readily available elsewhere. For additional references to pioneering articles on silver published in this journal from 1922 through 1947, see *Antiques* 51, no. 1 (January 1947): 61–64.

McClinton, Katharine Morrison. *Collecting American Nineteenth Century Silver*. New York: Charles Scribner's Sons, 1968. viii+280 pp.; illustrations, glossary, bibliography, index.

This survey treats nineteenth-century silver in a manner usually reserved for the work of seventeenth- and eighteenth-century craftsmen. McClinton first discusses changing styles, which she categorizes as federal and empire (1800–1840), rococo (1840–50), Renaissance revival (1851–70), eclecticism (1870–1900), and art nouveau (1895–1910), including Martelé silver and silver-deposit ware and silver-mounted cut glass. She then includes topical chapters on presentation silver, navy battleship and cruiser silver, church silver, Masonic jewels and medals, and small silver collectibles. Although there has been much research on the nineteenth century during the past two decades, McClinton's book remains a useful introduction for its many illustrations and broad overview.

Miller, V. Isabelle. *Silver by New York Makers: Late Seventeenth Century to 1900*. Exhibition catalogue. New York: Museum of the City of New York, 1937. xvi+71 pp.; 95 illustrations.

Half a century after its publication, this small catalogue is still valuable for its listing of 383 examples of New York City silver and its illustrations of almost 100 of those objects. Miller later compiled a similar work, *New York Silversmiths of the Seventeenth Century* (New York: Museum of the City of New York, 1962), but was not able to complete a projected full-length study of New York silver. To this day, no comprehensive work on New York's important silversmithing history has been published.

Morse, Edward W., ed. *Silver in the Golden State: Images and Essays Celebrating the History and Art of Silver in California*. Oakland: Oakland Museum History Department, 1986. xvi+119 pp.; black and white illustrations, 16 color plates, appendixes.

This book, published in conjunction with an exhibition of the same name, represents two recent trends: it analyzes silver in a wide historical and cultural context, and it reflects a parallel trend to explore the products of regions away from the East Coast and the products of craftsmen working after 1850. The essays contained here include a survey of California objects by Morse; a study of arts and crafts silversmiths Clemens Friedell and Porter Blanchard by Leslie Greene Bowman; two essays on silver mining; and a chapter on the role of silver in the California experience by Gerald W. R. Ward. A note on the scientific examination of some California objects through X-ray fluorescence by John W. Burke is also included.

The New England Silversmith: An Exhibition of New England Silver from the Mid-Seventeenth Century to the Present, Selected from New England Collections. Exhibition catalogue. Providence: Museum of Art, Rhode Island School of Design, 1965. [141] pp.; 84 illustrations, 327 illustrated entries.

The most notable feature of this catalogue is its treatment of New England silver as a continuum from the seventeenth century to the mid 1960s. The exhibition contained 342 objects, although only a fourth are illustrated here. Objects from each New England state except Vermont are represented. The illustrations, grouped chronologically in a separate section, provide a sweeping visual panorama of three centuries of the silversmith's craft.

Nygren, Edward J. "Edward Winslow's Sugar Boxes: Colonial Echoes of Courtly Love." *Yale University Art Gallery Bulletin* 33, no. 2 (Autumn 1971): 38–52. 14 illustrations.

Little work has been done on the iconographic significance of the decorative elements found on American decorative arts objects. Nygren examines the significance of the human and animal representations on three sugar boxes made by Winslow of Boston in 1702. Oval in form, the boxes were meant to resemble the female form, and the symbols of virtuous love that decorate the body and cover were meant to warn intruders away from tasting its sweet contents. Nygren demonstrates how these associations made Winslow's sugar boxes visual embodiments of chivalric ideals.

Paul Revere — Artisan, Businessman, and Patriot: The Man Behind the Myth. Exhibition catalogue. Boston: Paul Revere Memorial Association, 1988. 191 pp.; 50 illustrations, 3 tables, illustrated checklist, bibliography.

Silversmith Revere (1734–1818) has probably received more attention than any other early American craftsman. Esther Forbes's "life and times" biography of 1942 remains the best introduction to Revere's world, but there have been many biographies, exhibitions and catalogues, and other works with Revere as their focus. This modern reassessment takes a rounded look at Revere from several viewpoints. The biographical perspective is taken by Patrick M. Leehey; Revere's silver and shop operations are examined by Janine E. Skerry and Deborah A. Federhen; the often-overlooked aspect of Revere's copper mills at Canton are discussed by Edgard

Moreno; and Revere's life as a Mason is examined by Edith J. Steblecki.

Phillips, John Marshall. *American Silver.* American Crafts Series, edited by Charles Nagel. New York: Chanticleer Press, 1949. 128 pp.; 32 black and white illustrations, 4 color plates, 14 line drawings, bibliography.

Phillips, curator of the Garvan collection and later director of Yale University Art Gallery, was the leading silver specialist of his generation. This brief survey, organized chronologically and couched largely in stylistic terms, is a lasting testament to his wide knowledge of primary sources and collections of objects. Like many other writers of his generation, Phillips had a disdain for objects made after 1850, so as a consequence his survey basically concludes with objects fashioned in the federal period. Written with style and grace, Phillips's book remains a helpful and entertaining introduction to the craft and art of early silver.

Pleasants, J. Hall, and Howard Sill. *Maryland Silversmiths, 1715–1830, with Illustrations of Their Silver and Their Marks and with a Facsimile of the Design Book of William Faris.* Baltimore: Printed by Lord Baltimore Press, 1930. xiv+324 pp.; 67 plates, index.

Begun originally by Sill, this study was completed after his death by Pleasants, his collaborator and friend. The initial chapters offer a narrative survey of silversmithing in Maryland and the prevailing marking systems of different periods. Chapter 3 is a history of the Baltimore assay office and its marks, which until recently was the standard source on the subject. The bulk of the text is devoted to individual biographies of approximately 300 silversmiths and drawings of their marks. Twenty shop drawings, including designs for a coffeepot, teapot, sugar bowl, and creamer, by Faris (1728–1804), now in Maryland Historical Society, are reproduced in the final chapter.

Rainwater, Dorothy T. *Encyclopedia of American Silver Manufacturers.* 3d ed., rev. West Chester, Pa.: Schiffer Publishing, 1986. vi+266 pp.; illustrations, line drawings, bibliography.

First published in 1966, reissued in 1975, and published again in 1986 with minor revisions, this volume is an essential tool for identifying the work of nineteenth- and twentieth-century silver companies. More than 2,200 marks are illustrated, and capsule biographies of some 1,400 firms are included. Rainwater has compiled a related volume, issued by the same publisher, entitled *American Jewelry Manufacturers* (1988).

Rainwater, Dorothy T., ed. *Sterling Silver Holloware.* Princeton, N.J.: Pyne Press, 1973; distributed by Charles Scribner's Sons. [138] pp.; illustrations, bibliography.

Trade catalogues are a rich source of information about the designs, forms, and prices of nineteenth-century goods. This volume contains facsimiles of three different catalogues issued by Gorham Manufacturing Company of Providence, Rhode Island (1888, 1900), and Unger Brothers of Newark, New Jersey (1904). The editor has provided a brief introduction and capsule biographies of each firm. A similar volume, *Victorian Silverplated Holloware* (Des Moines: Wallace-Homestead Book Co., 1972), contains reprints of catalogues from Rogers Brothers Manufacturing Company (1857), Meriden Britannia Company (1867), and Derby Silver Company (1883). The massive Meriden Britannia catalogue of 1886–87 was reprinted as a separate volume by Dover Publications in 1982.

Rainwater, Dorothy T., and H. Ivan Rainwater. *American Silverplate*. Nashville, Tenn.: Thomas Nelson; Hanover, Pa.: Everybodys Press, 1968. 480 pp.; approximately 500 black and white illustrations and line drawings, 6 color plates, glossary, bibliography, index.

Beginning in the late 1840s, electroplating—the process of depositing a thin layer of silver over a base metal in order to obtain the appearance of sterling at a fraction of the cost—was introduced to this country from England. It quickly took hold, and silver-plated goods have been a significant component of the silver market ever since. The appearance of massive quantities of silver-plated goods in the late nineteenth century changed silver's image, as the age-old limitations on its ownership only by the wealthy were shattered. This large volume surveys the various techniques of silver plating, presents a historical overview of its manufacturing and marketing, and discusses the evolution of the many and varied styles and forms of plated wares that were used commercially and in the home. It remains the only single-volume treatment of this important subject.

Rice, Norman S. *Albany Silver, 1652–1825*. Foreword by Laurence McKinney; introduction by Kathryn C. Buhler; design by George Cole; photographs by Helga Photo Studio. Cogswell Fund Series, Publication no. 3. Exhibition catalogue. Albany: Albany Institute of History and Art, 1964. 81 pp.; 156 illustrations, bibliography.

Although New Amsterdam came under English control in 1664, Dutch influence remained strong in the city, in northern New Jersey, and in the Hudson River valley well into the eighteenth century. For example, many of the earliest objects produced in Albany by members of the Ten Eyck family and others reflect the Dutch tradition in form and ornament. By 1800, however, Albany silver was solidly in the Anglo style, although it followed New York City patterns in general. Most of the major objects produced in Albany are gathered here, and, as in most regional studies, biographical notes on the makers are included. The introduction by Buhler briefly discusses the evolution of the craft in Albany.

Roe, Albert S., and Robert F. Trent. "Robert Sanderson and the Founding of the Boston Silversmith's Trade."

In Jonathan L. Fairbanks and Robert F. Trent, *New England Begins: The Seventeenth Century*, vol. 3, pp. 480–89. Boston: Museum of Fine Arts, 1982. Appendixes.

The wealthiest of New England's founders brought with them a vast array of stylish silver. Drawing on Trent's extensive inventory research and Roe's work on Sanderson's career, this essay establishes the link between the objects owned by these early settlers and the first native products of the silversmith's art. Roe provides new information on Sanderson's English career and argues that it was Sanderson, rather than his partner John Hull, who trained their apprentices in the mystery of the craft. Appendixes include a list of most silversmiths active in Boston before 1700, a list of silver forms mentioned in Suffolk and Middlesex county inventories before 1690, probate references to the coining and appraisal of money by silversmiths, and an excerpt from the inventory of the estate of silversmith Joseph Sanderson. *See also* "American Furniture to 1820"; "Surveys."

Rosenbaum, Jeanette. *Myer Myers, Goldsmith, 1723–1795*. The Jacob R. Schiff Library of Jewish Contributions to American Democracy. Philadelphia: Jewish Publication Society of America, 1954. 141 pp.; 12 illustrations, 30 plates, bibliography.

Full-length biographies of early American silversmiths are rare in the literature. This study of an active New York City silversmith is an exception to the rule and followed the lead established by Hollis French and Hermann Frederick Clarke in their earlier work on Boston men. Active for half a century, Myers produced a large body of domestic ware and a few examples of *Rimonim* (scroll ornaments) and other religious objects for his own and other Jewish congregations in Newport and Philadelphia. His work reflects several changes in style and his responsiveness to the demands of patrons with various ethnic and religious backgrounds, thus making Myers's career an interesting case study of the effect of the cultural environment on the work of an artisan. What seems like every shred of evidence concerning Myers's life is gathered here, and a catalogue raisonné of his works, with technical notes by Kathryn C. Buhler, is included.

Roth, Rodris. *Tea Drinking in Eighteenth-Century America: Its Etiquette and Equipage. See* "Surveys."

Southern Silver: An Exhibition of Silver Made in the South prior to 1860. Exhibition catalogue. Houston: Museum of Fine Arts, 1968. [90] pp.; 198 illustrated entries.

This, the first (and to date only) catalogue to treat southern silver as a whole, includes many examples from Maryland, South Carolina, and Virginia, as well as a few objects from Delaware, Kentucky, Georgia, Alabama, North Carolina, Louisiana, and Texas. Curator David B. Warren found that "stylistically, southern silver seems to parallel the products of the North with little evidence of regional characteristics." Approximately 150 objects, primarily hollowware, are illustrated.

Spanish, French, and English Traditions in the Colonial Silver of North America. Winterthur Conference Report 1968. Winterthur, Del.: Henry Francis du Pont Winterthur Museum, 1969. 109 pp.; illustrations, 15 tables.

The importance of this volume lies in its placement of American silver within a North American context in which Spanish and French traditions are considered with the same degree of emphasis as the Anglo-American tradition. The report begins with George A. Kubler's influential "Time's Perfection and Colonial Art," in which he explores the radial geometry of colonialism, the strength of colonial surfaces, and other issues. Essays on silver in New Mexico by Richard E. Ahlborn are followed by John Langdon's and John D. Davis's respective essays on Canadian colonial silver in the French tradition and domestic silver in the American colonies. A computer-assisted study of American church silver by Anthony N. B. Garvan and others is also included, along with a brief statement on the function of church silver by Frank H. Sommer III.

Turner, Noel D. *American Silver Flatware, 1837–1910*. South Brunswick, N.J., and New York: A. S. Barnes, 1972. 473 pp.; illustrations, glossary, bibliography, index.

Turner's massive work discusses the manufacture of flatware in the nineteenth century and its use in the home, in hotels and steamships, for promotion and presentation, and in other contexts. In addition to these aspects of the use of silver as social history, the book is valuable as an aid in identifying and dating surviving objects. One lengthy section, comprising more than 100 pages, contains illustrations of flatware patterns in sterling and electroplate marketed by numerous makers. Almost half the book is devoted to a postscript containing trademarks and trade names of American, English, and Canadian manufacturers and silversmiths and the names and dates of introduction of flatware patterns in both sterling and electroplate.

Vermeule, Cornelius. *Numismatic Art in America: Aesthetics of the United States Coinage*. Cambridge, Mass.: Harvard University Press, Belknap Press, 1971. xix+266 pp.; 249 illustrations, bibliography, index.

The United States minted the first federal coinage in 1792 using Greco-Roman symbolism which is still familiar today. Vermeule traces the origins of the designs used on circulating coins, trade dollars, and medals until the present day. Although his main purpose is to give an aesthetic evaluation of the designs of various coins, he also deals extensively with the economic and political forces that have shaped the bimetallic standard over the last 200 years. For information on the many colonial issues, see the numerous works published by American Numismatic Society, especially Theodore V. Buttrey, Jr., ed., *Coinage of the Americas* (New York: By the society, 1973).

Virginia Museum of Fine Arts. *Masterpieces of American Silver*. Exhibition catalogue. Richmond: By the museum, 1960. 99 pp.; illustrations, 337 illustrated entries.

This catalogue of almost 350 superb objects from public and private collections represents the pinnacle of the masterpiece approach to early silver. It is unlikely that this many monuments of the craft will be assembled together again. Kathryn C. Buhler's authoritative introduction discusses the craft system, the products of more than a dozen cities and regions, types and their uses, and the techniques of the craft. The entries are only descriptive captions, however, and many of the objects are not illustrated, thus diminishing the lasting impact of the exhibition.

von Khrum, Paul. *Silversmiths of New York City, 1684–1850*. New York: By the author, 1978. xx+155 pp.; bibliography.

To create this listing, the author searched all New York City directories published between 1786 and 1840 to obtain more than 2,500 names of silversmiths and craftsmen pursuing related occupations. Surviving objects and other documents provided the names of silversmiths active before 1786, thus creating a useful index to all makers known to have been working in New York through 1850. The author's introduction discusses several technical questions pertaining to date marks, sources of silver, the fineness of silver alloys, and other issues. While not designed for casual reading, this work represents many similar reference volumes that are helpful starting places for beginning research on American silver and silversmiths.

Ward, Barbara McLean. "Boston Goldsmiths, 1690–1730." In *The Craftsman in Early America*, edited by Ian M. G. Quimby, pp. 126–57. New York: W. W. Norton, 1984. 9 illustrations, appendixes.

Using evidence from documentary sources and existing objects, this article examines the socioeconomic conditions of all eighty-two silversmiths active in Boston during this period. This analysis revealed the existence of a hierarchy within the goldsmithing trade, a hierarchy that affected wealth distribution within the craft, the nature of work performed by individual artisans, and the relationships that existed between the wealthier and more socially powerful merchant-producer artisans and the laboring artisans who worked for them as journeymen and jobbers. The paper includes appendixes that list the life and working dates for all the artisans discussed. *See also* "Craftsmen."

Ward, Barbara McLean. "'In a Feasting Posture': Communion Vessels and Community Values in Seventeenth- and Eighteenth-Century New England." *Winterthur Portfolio* 23, no. 1 (Spring 1988): 1–24. 13 illustrations.

Through an analysis of the forms, inscriptions, and origins of 1,044 objects owned by American churches for the service of communion, Ward discusses the interplay between liturgy and material forms and how these reflected the relationship between theology and social order in colonial New England. She demonstrates how patterns in the acquisition of silver communion vessels shed light on lay attitudes toward church polity and social organization and provides a model for the future integration of material culture studies with more traditional historical scholarship.

Ward, Barbara McLean. "Metalwares." In *The Great River: Art and Society of the Connecticut Valley, 1635–1820*, pp. 273–339. Hartford, Conn.: Wadsworth Atheneum, 1985. Illustrations.

This chapter explores silver and other metal objects in the context of the change in consumer preference from imported to locally produced wares. Metalwares are seen as symbols of ethnic and family continuity, particularly for women, who often acquired these objects as part of their portions when they married and left their ancestral homes. These themes, and the correlative concepts of utility and social display, are also explored in the forty-eight accompanying catalogue entries, eighteen of which were prepared by Elizabeth Pratt Fox. *See also* "Pewter and Britannia Metal."

Ward, Barbara McLean, and Gerald W. R. Ward, eds. *Silver in American Life: Selections from the Mabel Brady Garvan and Other Collections at Yale University.* Boston: David R. Godine in association with the Yale University Art Gallery and the American Federation of Arts, 1979. xiii+193 pp.; 217 black and white and 18 color illustrations, bibliography, index.

The goal of this catalogue and its accompanying traveling exhibition was to examine silver's multifaceted nature in as broad a context as possible. This approach led to the articulation of six principal themes: the attributes of silver as a metal, the role of silver in commerce and trade, the evolution of the silversmith's profession, the manner in which silver objects are made and how the techniques involved have changed over time, silver's symbolic and utilitarian roles in society, and the importance of silver objects as a form of artistic expression. These themes are explored in six essays and 196 entries by William A. Lanford, John P. Burnham, Stephen K. Victor, Martha Gandy Fales, Kevin L. Stayton, and the Wards. *See also* "Craftsmen."

Warren, David B. *Bayou Bend: American Furniture, Paintings, and Silver from the Bayou Bend Collection. See* "American Furniture to 1820"; "Surveys."

Warren, David B., Katherine S. Howe, and Michael K. Brown. *Marks of Achievement: Four Centuries of American Presentation Silver.* Introduction by Gerald W. R. Ward. Exhibition catalogue. New York: Harry N. Abrams for the Museum of Fine Arts, Houston, 1987.

207 pp.; 231 black and white and color plates, bibliography, index.

This book, based on objects selected primarily because of their value as documents testifying to specific acts of social interchange, represents a departure from the standard silver catalogues based on style, region, or maker. However, to illustrate their points, the authors (all curators at a major art museum) were able to select examples of high aesthetic quality, including many previously unpublished, to demonstrate their interpretive points. The book examines presentation silver in several categories, including religion and education, industry and progress, pursuits of leisure and avocation, politics and the military, and rites of passage and friendship. Examples illustrating these areas are included in essays and entries on the colonial era by Brown, the century after independence by Warren, and in the years since 1876 by Howe. A short introduction by Ward examines some of the multiple meanings of presentation transactions.

Waters, Deborah Dependahl. "From Pure Coin: The Manufacture of American Silver Flatware, 1800–1860." In *Winterthur Portfolio 12*, edited by Ian M. G. Quimby, pp. 19–33. Charlottesville: University Press of Virginia for the Henry Francis du Pont Winterthur Museum, 1977. 15 illustrations.

Coin silver spoons are perhaps the commonest objects found today in public and private collections. This article discusses the manufacture, silver content, and marketing of such spoons. Several patent drawings for spoonmaking machines are illustrated, and many confusing issues of terminology are clarified. In order to determine if quality marks on spoons (such as "Premium," "Pure coin," and "Coin") reflected the alloy composition of the objects on which they are stamped, Waters tested 114 examples through X-ray fluorescence spectroscopy and learned that there was little correlation between indicated quality and actual composition.

Wroth, Lawrence C. *Abel Buell of Connecticut: Silversmith, Type Founder, and Engraver.* 2d ed., rev. and enl. Middletown, Conn.: Wesleyan University Press, 1958. xiv+102 pp.; 9 illustrations, index.

Wroth's elegantly written profile of the versatile Buell (1742–1822) discusses the career of an individual who combined silversmithing with a variety of other trades. Trained by Ebenezer Chittenden, Buell operated a shop in New Haven at the sign of the Coffee Pot. Silver by him is rare today, perhaps because of his involvement in other activities; Buell was an artist, an engineer, an inventor, a patternmaker, a die cutter, an agricultural-instrument maker, an auctioneer, a quarryman, a shipowner, and a mill owner. Wroth has pieced together the extant information about Buell's life to tell an affecting story of a man with obvious skills who was nevertheless troubled with misfortune throughout his life.

Pewter and Britannia Metal

Barbara McLean Ward

ODERN OBSERVERS, with their vision clouded by current market prices for antique pewter, often forget that in the seventeenth and eighteenth centuries most Americans ate from pewter dishes and drank from pewter vessels. Pewter had the advantages of being relatively cheap, durable, and recyclable, and therefore it was found in the homes of the poor and the wealthy alike.

It was this essential link of pewter to the common man that first allured collectors. Homer Eaton Keyes observed in his foreword to the first, 1925 edition of Howard Herschel Cotterell's *National Types of Old Pewter*: "Pewterware is in itself peculiarly adapted to the requirements of the amateur. From earliest times to within a generation or two it has been an almost universal product of civilized society. Hence it is, even yet, everywhere to be encountered. Its texture and color are delightful; it appears in a fascinating multiplicity of forms. And, lastly, since it is a ware largely of, by, and for the people, it carries with it always a strong savor of nationality."

It was a sense that this legacy from the common man was disappearing that fueled the enthusiasm of the earliest collectors and inspired the first writers on the subject. To paraphrase the words of J. B. Kerfoot, having lost the battle for dominance waged among the great trinity of tablewares—wood, pewter, and china—pewter was rapidly disappearing. In 1887 when a society of English artists decided to hold a discussion on old pewter, H. J. L. J. Massé was appointed to arrange the session "because he was the only member present who owned a piece of pewter" (quoted in Kerfoot, *American Pewter*, p. 4).

From this humble beginning Massé became the outstanding English authority on the subject. His earliest work, *Pewter Plate* (1904), drew heavily on documentary sources and quoted at great length from Charles Welch's monumental *History of the Worshipful Company of Pewterers* (1902). Much attention was given in this and Massé's other early works to the development of forms and their changing functions. In 1905 N. Hudson Moore's *Old Pewter, Brass, Copper, and Sheffield Plate* became the first work to include a lengthy section on American pewter and pewterers and to present gleanings from colonial records. Collectors, however, had been actively pursuing specimens of American makers' works for two decades; Virginia Robie, writing in *House Beautiful* in 1903, already lamented the appearance of fakes on the market.

The first major exhibition to include American pewter was the Hudson-Fulton of 1909, held at the Metropolitan Museum of Art in New York. American objects were displayed with English and

Continental wares in 1916 at the Museum of Fine Arts, Boston, in the first major exhibition (more than 900 objects were included) of antique pewter held in the United States.

The real enthusiasm for American pewter, however, did not begin until Kerfoot's book appeared in 1924. *American Pewter* was the first to provide authoritative information on makers and marks and to establish standards for collecting. Because he believed that rarity was "the very oxygen of the collector's atmosphere," he sought to establish the relative rarity of American pewter objects (most of which were contemptibly common by British standards). There was no American pewter, Kerfoot asserted, that was "not rare enough to be collectible." "The lover of craftsmanship cannot go wrong competitively," he argued, "while following his own bent here. Nor the student of our national past and of our social development. Nor the sentimental patriot hunting eagles."

What made and still makes Kerfoot's book so compelling is its emotionally charged style. A journalist turned antiques dealer, Kerfoot frequently employed military and religious metaphors to invigorate his narrative of the rise and fall of pewter tablewares. Pewter wins its "victory" over wood, only to suffer "defeat and unconditional surrender" to "china" in the nineteenth century. These metaphors must have appealed to the mind-set of the generation of Americans who emerged victorious after World War I. The United States involvement in the affairs of Europe only convinced Americans of the corruption rampant in the rest of the world. Xenophobia and isolationism inspired efforts to educate recent immigrants to the glories of the nation's past. Like most of his contemporaries, Kerfoot saw the products of colonial craftsmen as potent symbols of the "individualism" and "personal pride in personal performance" that formed the essence of the American spirit. One comes away from Kerfoot's book with the distinct impression that he is calling out to collectors to raise these noble but defeated pewter relics from the ashes. We finally see tankards and dishes emerging victorious again, enshrined in the homes of those who would preserve the American past.

Charles F. Montgomery credited Kerfoot with developing an enthusiastic following for American pewter. Although Cotterell and others wrote a series of authoritative articles for *Antiques* on the subject of English and Continental forms, there was only faint criticism of those who would see American pewter in a vacuum. The names and marks of American artisans in pewter were eagerly pursued by men like Louis Guerineau Myers and Charles Calder. And, although the depression slowed the market considerably, in 1934 the American equivalent of the English Pewter Collectors' Society was founded in Boston, bringing a small group of dedicated enthusiasts together.

Always fiercely devoted to promoting knowledge about pewterers and their products, the Pewter Collectors' Club of America immediately began publishing their *Bulletin*, which continues to be the primary organ for the dissemination of current research in the field. The club held the first major exhibition of American pewter at Boston Public Library in 1935, and in 1939 the Metropolitan Museum mounted perhaps the finest exhibition ever devoted to the subject. By then much new information had been accumulated on makers, but no synthesis of the material had been attempted.

Ledlie Irwin Laughlin's *Pewter in America* filled this gap on its publication in 1940. It is a monumental work, unsurpassed in its depth of research and wealth of detail. In many ways it is the best collective biography ever written on a group of American craftsmen. Laughlin covered the full range of individuals engaged in the craft, from the leading masters to the journeymen known only from occasional documentary references. Laughlin, like Kerfoot, recorded these details, however, with little in mind other than the hope of discovering more marks and more forms.

Other than collectors' manuals, little appeared on American pewter for more than a decade after Laughlin's book. In many ways *Pewter in America* was so massive and so completely filled the needs of its readers that it seemed that nothing was left to be said. Museums and private individuals went about the business of collecting objects on the basis of Laughlin's work. Beginning in the 1960s, these efforts bore fruit in several important exhibitions of pewter and numerous collection and exhibition catalogues. Of enormous help to the researcher attempting to locate representative types owned or made in a particular area, most were written merely to chronicle recent museum acquisitions as the early collectors bequeathed or sold their holdings to public institutions. The enormous number of objects in museums is extremely impressive and comprises a significant body of data for the modern researcher.

In the 1960s a renewed interest developed in studying the technology of preindustrial artisans and in linking material remains to the lives of the inarticulate but numerically superior common people. In *History of American Pewter*, Montgomery took a broadly humanistic approach to the subject and attempted to understand the economic and social networks within which artifacts existed. As a result, his book is the finest overall study of the subject. This book and others also demonstrate the tremendous interest in reconstructing historical craft processes that characterized work in the decorative arts in the 1960s and 1970s. Construction and composition of materials have recently become questions of major importance to the historian, the connoisseur, and the collector alike. However, several essential primary works on the craft of the pewterer, specifically Pierre Auguste Salmon's *L'Art du Potier d'Etain* (Paris, 1778) and the section on the pewterer in Diderot's *Encyclopedie* (Paris, 1771), have yet to be fully mined for the information they contain, and as yet no complete study of the American pewterers' business based on documentary and artifactual sources has been undertaken.

The study of the revival of pewtermaking in the twentieth century will no doubt be undertaken in years to come. The recent publication of Carolyn A. Smith and Peggy R. Hixon's *Mystery Era of American Pewter, 1928–1931* (Oklahoma City, Okla.: Universal Press, 1979) and its supplement (1984) and the inclusion of arts and crafts and art deco pewter objects in several recent catalogues already indicate a trend in this direction. Students may find several modern craft manuals to be of interest, especially William H. Varnum's *Pewter Design and Construction* (Milwaukee, Wis.: Bruce Publishing Co., 1926) and Burl Neff Osburn and Gordon Owen Wilber's *Pewter: Spun, Wrought, and Cast* (Scranton, Pa.: International Textbook Co., 1938). (Although these books illustrate colonial and colonial revival objects, the information they contain on techniques is not applicable to early methods.) More recent developments in pewter, now generally hammered from sheet rather than cast in molds, are discussed by Shirley Charron in *Modern Pewter: Design and Techniques* (New York: Van Nostrand Reinhold Co., 1973).

It is difficult today to assess where the study of American pewter is headed. No doubt there will be more books written that clarify our understanding of regional groups of pewterers and that chronicle the shift from preindustrial to industrial technology. Many collections remain to be catalogued. There is some indication, however, that the potential of pewter wares as documents elucidating the lives of past generations is only beginning to be appreciated. The following publications have been selected to aid the researcher attempting to learn about pewter and the history of interest in it. Surely the gleanings and accumulated data represented in the works cited here will be of great value in the future as these new lines of research are pursued.

Allentown Art Museum. *Early American Pewter: John J. Evans, Jr., Collection.* Exhibition catalogue. Introduction by Richard Hirsch. Allentown, Pa.: By the museum, 1966. 27 pp.; 14 illustrations.

Early American Pewter includes 114 items of pewter with related forms in iron, wood, tin, bone, glass, copper, porcelain, and silver, along with a small selection of molds and tools. The objects are arranged by maker, and short biographical notes on each pewterer are included. Only object types are listed; no additional data, such as dimensions, are given.

American Pewter. Exhibition catalogue. Richmond: Virginia Museum, 1976. 84 pp.; 227 illustrated entries, glossary, bibliography.

American Pewter is a catalogue of an exhibition organized by Frederic R. Brandt of pewter objects from public and private collections in Virginia. The entries include information on maker, place and date of manufacture, form, dimensions, location and type of mark (keyed to Ledlie Laughlin's text), and ownership in 1976. A good but brief introduction stressing the influence of technological change on stylistic development and the glossary make this a useful introduction to the subject.

American Pewter: Garvan and Other Collections at Yale. Introduction by Graham Hood. New Haven, Conn.: Yale University Art Gallery, 1965. 55 pp.; 200 illustrated entries, index.

Primarily a checklist of Yale's fine collection of American pewter at the time of publication, this catalogue contains an excellent brief introduction to major craftsmen, craft practices, and stylistic trends. It should be used in conjunction with David Barquist's 1985 supplementary checklist of the holdings at Yale.

American Pewter (c. 1730–c. 1870) in the Collection of Dr. and Mrs. Melvyn D. Wolf. Exhibition catalogue. Flint, Mich.: Flint Institute of Arts, 1973. 40 pp.; 227 illustrated entries.

American Pewter was written to accompany an exhibition of objects from this well-known private collection. The information given on each item is brief, consisting of only form, a terse description of design, maker, touchmark, place of manufacture, and largest dimension. A few touchmarks are illustrated. Primarily this work is useful as a good pictorial resource.

American Pewter in the Museum of Fine Arts, Boston. Photographs by Daniel Farber. Boston: By the museum, 1974; distributed by New York Graphic Society. xiii + 119 pp.; 342 illustrations, checklist, bibliography.

A brief history of materials and methods used in the fabrication of American pewter is provided in the introduction to this work. The catalogue consists of a checklist providing basic data—form, maker, dimensions, location of marks, and place of manufacture—for each of the 411 items in the museum's collection. Although the format of the book sometimes makes it difficult to locate information about a specific object, the catalogue's comprehensiveness and its large, clear illustrations make it an important resource.

Barquist, David L. *American and English Pewter at the Yale University Art Gallery: A Supplementary Checklist.* New Haven, Conn.: By the gallery, 1985. 80 pp.; 272 illustrated entries.

Yale's collection of pewter was first catalogued by Graham Hood in 1965. During Charles F. Montgomery's tenure as curator of the Garvan and Related Collection of American Art (1970–78), he worked steadily to build the pewter collection, making many important additions to the collection. This supplement to Hood's catalogue provides detailed information on acquisitions since 1965, including examples of colonial revival and arts and crafts pewter, as well as on objects omitted from Hood's work. Yale's is primarily a teaching collection, and it is therefore fitting that Barquist has included a section on the study collection. Maker's marks are illustrated.

Brett, Vanessa. *Phaidon Guide to Pewter.* Englewood Cliffs, N.J.: Prentice-Hall, 1982. 256 pp.; black and white illustrations, color plates, line drawings, maps, bibliography, glossary, index.

Brett's survey of pewter made in Europe and North America from about 1600 to the present contains a brief section on pewter marks. This is primarily a collectors' handbook, but it is useful for placing American work in an international context.

British Pewter, 1600–1850. Exhibition catalogue. Manchester, N.H.: Currier Gallery of Art, 1974. 42 pp.; 170 illustrated entries, appendix, bibliography.

Although short, *British Pewter* is a good, concise introduction to the subject, particularly the common forms of flagons, tankards, and measures. The catalogue is arranged by form, and each major section is preceded by a brief essay on the design and use of the object type. The information given on individual items is more extensive than that often provided in catalogues of this length. In addition to form, largest overall dimension, touchmarks, maker, and place of manufacture, entries include information on capacity, provenance, inscriptions, related examples, and explanatory notes.

Bulletin of the Pewter Collectors' Club of America. Vol. 1–, no. 1–. March 21, 1934–.

Published on a regular basis since the founding of the Pewter Collectors' Club in 1934, this journal provides a wealth of technical material concerning pewter objects and the history of pewter collecting in America. See, in particular, Carolyn Denman, "A Bibliography of Pewter," 1, no. 15 (October 1945): 1–21. Indexes have been issued on a regular basis; see William O. Blaney, comp., "Pictorial Index for Volumes 1–6, *Bulletins* nos. 1–69," covering 1934 through 1974. The first five bulletins, originally issued as folders, were reprinted as a supplement to vol. 46, no. 6 (February 1962).

Calder, Charles A. *Rhode Island Pewterers and Their Work.* Providence: E. A. Johnson, 1924. 38 pp.; 41 illustrations, appendix.

In an early work of collective biography, Calder includes extensive quotations from documents relating to Rhode Island pewterers. The book should be used in conjunction with Ledlie Irwin Laughlin's *Pewter in America*, which includes additional information on these artisans.

Carlson, Janice H. "Analysis of British and American Pewter by X-ray Fluorescence Spectroscopy." In *Winterthur Portfolio 12*, edited by Ian M. G. Quimby, pp. 65–85. Charlottesville: University Press of Virginia for the Henry Francis du Pont Winterthur Museum, 1977. 11 illustrations, 19 tables.

X-ray fluorescence spectroscopy is the most sophisticated nondestructive means currently available for the analysis of the elemental composition of decorative arts objects. This article is an excellent introduction to the technique as well as a detailed report on the results of analysis of more than 1,300 pewter objects in the Winterthur collection. Carlson concludes that British pewter exhibits a consistently high quality as measured by tin content, whereas American examples are much more variable in their composition. Further, British pewter declined in quality during the last half of the eighteenth century as the guilds ceased to exercise strict control over their members.

Cocks, Dorothy. *The Pewter Collection of the New Canaan Historical Society.* New Canaan, Conn.: By the society, 1967. 24 pp.; 14 illustrations, bibliography.

The Pewter Collection contains a catalogue of 139 pewter articles from America, Great Britain, and Europe. Geared for the amateur admirer of antiques, the small pamphlet provides interesting descriptions of forms, rather than au-

thoritative attributions. As such, it can be of use to the researcher seeking examples for an exhibition or a catalogue raisonné.

Cotterell, Howard Herschel. *Old Pewter: Its Makers and Marks in England, Scotland, and Ireland.* 1929. Reprint. Rutland, Vt.: Charles E. Tuttle Co., 1963. xxii+432 pp.; 76 illustrations, bibliography, indexes.

Beginning with a detailed discussion of the history of pewter marking and the touchplates used by the London guild for the recording of individual pewterer's marks, Cotterell's book is helpful for an understanding of the early organization and regulation of the pewterers craft in Great Britain. Although some of the information provided on secondary marks and "collector's difficulties" is out of date, much of it remains useful if read in conjunction with more recent works. The listing of makers and marks is still the most comprehensive of its kind and is the standard reference cited in all other works on the subject. It has been updated by Christopher A. Peal's *More Pewter Marks* (n.p.: Pewter Society, 1976) and several addenda. An important feature of *Old Pewter* is the inclusion of oversize, fold-out facsimiles of the five London and two Edinburgh touchplates of pewterers' marks dating as early as 1640.

Cotterell, Howard Herschel, Adolphe Riff, and Robert M. Vetter. *National Types of Old Pewter.* Rev. and exp. ed. New introduction by Charles V. Swain. Princeton: Pyne Press, 1972. vii+152 pp.; illustrations, index.

Few books on Continental pewter are available in English, making this survey a valuable reference. The initial chapters, originally published by Cotterell as a separate volume in 1925, provide an overview of methods of marking and fabrication characteristic of specific countries, a detailed typology of the thumbpieces found on lidded and unlidded vessels, a survey of ecclesiastical and domestic forms, and a brief outline of general methods of manufacture and the composition of various pewter alloys. These chapters are followed by a series of articles by Cotterell, Riff, and Vetter originally published in *Antiques* beginning in 1923. The first article discusses the meaning and distinguishing features of the marks on Continental pewter. Subsequent essays outline the most salient features of French, German, Swiss, Dutch, Austro-Hungarian, and Channel Islands pewter. This work is an invaluable guide to anyone studying pewter owned in this country or the influence of non-English pewter on the work of pewterers in ethnically diverse regions of America.

de Jonge, Eric. "Johann Christoph Heyne: Pewterer, Minister, Teacher." In *Winterthur Portfolio 4*, edited by Richard K. Doud, pp. 169–84. Charlottesville: University Press of Virginia for the Henry Francis du Pont Winterthur Museum, 1968. 18 illustrations.

The work of Heyne (1715–81) includes intriguing Germanic forms that puzzled scholars for many years. This essay outlines the fascinating life of this versatile man who came to

America from Saxony in 1742 with the "First Sea Congregation" of Moravians bound for Philadelphia. Exhaustive research on Heyne's travels during his years as a journeyman revealed that he worked for several years in Sweden. Thus, de Jonge was able to piece together the variety of elements from German and Swedish sources that explain Heyne's exceptional communion flagons. In addition to these studies of design influences, this short biography brings to life the experiences of an unusually well documented eighteenth-century artisan. For more on Heyne, see Donald M. Herr, "Johann Christoph Heyne, Lancaster, Pennsylvania, Pewterer," *Antiques* 117, no. 1 (January 1980): 222–24.

Ebert, Katherine. *Collecting American Pewter*. New York: Charles Scribner's Sons, 1973. v+163 pp.; illustrations, line drawings, bibliography, index.

Collecting American Pewter is a beginners' guide to the subject that touches on many points of interest. Chapters are devoted to the "rise and fall" of pewter; metal, construction, and marks; the first period (1700–1825); the second period (1825–60); lamps; and cleaning, fakes, and reproductions. Ebert includes a list of American pewterers and their marks and an additional list of craftsmen whose work is not known to have survived. The text is not footnoted, although selected references for each chapter are given.

Ely, Elizabeth M. "American Pewter in the Collections of the Society for the Preservation of New England Antiquities"; "A Checklist of American Pewter at the Society for the Preservation of New England Antiquities." *Old-Time New England* 68, nos. 1–2 (Summer–Fall 1977): 38–60. 7 illustrations, 1 table.

Ely presents a brief essay and a checklist of objects, all (with one exception) examples of domestic pewter, many with documented histories. The collection includes 238 objects (102 marked, 136 unmarked), most of which date from the nineteenth century. The checklist does not include the many examples of English pewter in the SPNEA collection.

Fennimore, Donald L. *Silver and Pewter*. The Knopf Collectors' Guides to American Antiques. New York: Alfred A. Knopf, 1984. 478 pp.; 338 color illustrations, line drawings, glossary, price guide, bibliography, index.

Silver and Pewter contains nearly 100 illustrations of pewter (nos. 240–338), each bearing a caption that contains a description, information on marks, dimensions, maker, locality, and date; a brief comment; and some hints for collectors. Geared to the marketplace, this book contains a great deal of authoritative information for students as well as collectors.

Goyne, Nancy A. "Britannia in America: The Introduction of a New Alloy and a New Industry." In *Winterthur Portfolio 2*, edited by Milo M. Naeve, pp. 160–96. Winterthur, Del.: Henry Francis du Pont Winterthur Museum, 1965. 48 illustrations.

The pewter alloy known as Britannia was introduced in England during the 1790s, and the formula for creating this hard, high-luster metal was soon discovered by American pewterers. Because Britannia metal has been associated by collectors with the forms of the early nineteenth century—forms many early collectors disliked—little has been written about the objects produced of the metal. This article, the first serious treatment of the subject, remains definitive. Goyne examines the earliest producers of Britannia in this country, discusses the composition of the metal, and explains the various methods of manufacture used, including casting, spinning, and stamping. The article concludes with a section on the influence of imported wares and the marketing and distribution of American-made objects.

Graham, John Meredith, II. *American Pewter*. Brooklyn, N.Y.: Brooklyn Museum, 1949. 36 pp.; 43 illustrations, appendixes.

Although published forty years ago, much of the text of Graham's short catalogue remains accurate. Many objects have since come to light that make some statements concerning surviving examples out of date, but the essay is informative for what it conveys about the interests of scholars in the 1940s. Each of the sixty-one objects included is illustrated (many in group photographs), and form, largest dimension, maker, date, and place of manufacture are recorded in each entry. Drawn completely from Brooklyn Museum's collection of more than 300 examples, most of the objects included were acquired by the museum from the collection of John W. Poole, a great early collector of American pewter.

Hamilton, Suzanne. "The Pewter of William Will: A Checklist." In *Winterthur Portfolio 7*, edited by Ian M. G. Quimby, pp. 129–60. Charlottesville: University Press of Virginia for the Henry Francis du Pont Winterthur Museum, 1972. 29 illustrations.

Will (1742–98) of Philadelphia "has long been recognized as the outstanding pewterer of eighteenth-century America" (p. 129). Based on Hamilton's 1967 University of Delaware master's thesis, this article presents the major facts of Will's life, a discussion of his known marks, and a survey of surviving objects in museums and private collections. The checklist is arranged by form and includes a brief description, approximate date, dimensions, ownership at the time of publication, and bibliographical references.

Hatcher, John, and T. C. Barker. *A History of British Pewter*. London: Longman, 1974. xii+363 pp.; 7 illustrations, 32 plates, 21 tables, appendixes, bibliography, index.

Commissioned by Worshipful Company of Pewterers to commemorate the 500th anniversary of their Royal Charter of Incorporation in 1474, this economic and social history of pewter was prepared by two historians from the University of Kent at Canterbury. Two-thirds of the book are devoted to pewter before 1700. Like most traditional historians,

Hatcher and Barker do not deal with the artifactual evidence, but rely on standard written sources. The text is strong on manufacturing, marketing, the regulation of the craft, prices, and similar issues. An excellent bibliography is included.

Hedges, Ernest S. *Tin in Social and Economic History.* New York: St. Martin's Press, 1964. xiv+194 pp.; 32 illustrations, index.

Hedges discusses such wide-ranging topics as tin in coinage, "the importance of pewter," and the role of tin in ceremonial observances, decorative arts, music, manufactures, transport, telecommunications, and food preservation. He also served as editor of *Tin and Its Alloys* (London: Edward Arnold Publishers, 1960), an anthology of eleven essays devoted to a similar range of topics.

Hornsby, Peter R. G. *Pewter of the Western World, 1600–1900.* Exton, Pa.: Schiffer Publishing, 1983. 381 pp.; 1,291 illustrations, appendixes, glossary, bibliography, index.

The utility of *Pewter of the Western World* is seriously marred by poor editing and poor documentation. Although Hornsby is a leading pewter dealer in England, much of the information in his introductory chapters is debatable, and without proper footnotes the reader will have difficulty evaluating his conclusions. For the advanced student, however, the illustrations provide a useful pictorial resource. Drawn from private collections, dealers, auction houses, and museums, the objects pictured fully represent pewter made in western Europe (including Russia) and North America. A bibliography includes a good listing of foreign-language publications on pewter.

Jacobs, Carl. *Guide to American Pewter.* Illustrations by Marion B. Wilson. New York: McBride Co., 1957. 216 pp.; 57 illustrations, line drawings, index.

Jacobs's guide is primarily a checklist of American pewterers and their marks that is prefaced by a statement that outlines the general history of pewter's use and comments on the state of the market value of pewter wares to collectors in the 1950s. The text includes short biographical information on each pewterer and the current market prices for a selection of objects bearing their marks. Some names could not be connected with any known maker, but were published in hope of discovering new examples. Line drawings of touches are shown for many of the makers listed. Additional information is provided on the Danforth family of pewterers and on line drawings of characteristic pewter forms. For an updated version that is reduced in size, see Celia Jacobs, *The Pocket Book of American Pewter: The Makers and the Marks* (2d ed.; Boston: Chaners, 1970).

Kauffman, Henry J. *The American Pewterer: His Techniques and His Products.* Camden, N.J.: Thomas Nelson, 1970. 158 pp.; illustrations, line drawings, appendix, bibliography, index.

Kauffman's interpretation of methods of working pewter is suggestive rather than authoritative. His remarks are based more on his experience of reproducing old forms than on documentation, object evidence, or surviving molds. Seriously flawed, his book should be used only in conjunction with other works on the subject, especially Charles F. Montgomery's *History of American Pewter* and John Carl Thomas's *Connecticut Pewterers*, where the discussion of pewtermaking is more reliable. The inclusion here of a reprint of Joseph Downs's *American Pewterers and Their Marks* (New York: Metropolitan Museum of Art, 1942) is of interest to those studying the history of scholarship in the field; however, since this compendium of marks was printed from rubbings, it is much less useful than many more recent works that illustrate photographs.

Kerfoot, J. B. *American Pewter.* 1924. Reprint. New York: Crown Publishers, 1942. xxii+236 pp.; 358 plates, index.

Based primarily on firsthand observations, Kerfoot's personal book is a classic work in the historiography of American decorative arts. Kerfoot (1865–1927) shared the beliefs and biases of his own era and expressed them with such forthright honesty that *American Pewter* gives us unusual insight into the motives and preoccupations of early twentieth-century collectors, dealers, and antiquarians. Although much of his data on pewterers and their craft has been superseded by Ledlie Irwin Laughlin and Charles F. Montgomery, Kerfoot's early chapters have not been significantly revised by more recent works. Particularly suggestive is his analysis of changing preferences in tablewares. At first a luxury, pewter was reserved for making large hollowware forms and large impressive serving platters, with plates and trenchers still being made in wood. But by the middle of the eighteenth century, pewter had become the ordinary tableware—plates and spoons—of the rich and poor alike. It was only when pewter ceased to be the dominant material for tableware that pewterers turned to the production of teapots, coffeepots, and lamps in order to earn a living. In Kerfoot's view, the increased manufacture of larger items in the early nineteenth century is conclusive evidence of the decline in the use of pewter. After these initial chapters, his discussion is devoted to the work of individual pewterers. Classifying makers as "eight-inch-plate men," "coffee-pot men," and "transitional pewterers," Kerfoot's format stresses the role of specialization and marketability rather than geographical region in craft production. Although his "statistical tables" on the productivity of individual pewterers are meant to determine twentieth-century market value for collectors, they also provide the modern researcher with useful information. Kerfoot set the tone for most further scholarship and pewter collecting by establishing rarity of marks and forms as the chief criteria for the relative value of pewter objects to modern collectors.

Laughlin, Ledlie Irwin. *Pewter in America: Its Makers and Their Marks.* 3 vols. Vols. 1, 2. 1940. Reprint. Barre,

Mass.: Barre Publishers, 1969. Vol. 3. Barre, Mass.: Barre Publishers, 1971. Vol. 1, xviii+138 pp.; 58 illustrations; vol. 2, 241 pp.; 78 illustrations, appendixes, bibliography, indexes; vol. 3, xiv+276 pp.; 115 illustrations, appendixes, bibliography, indexes.

Among the most exhaustive and thorough studies of any group of domestic artifacts produced in America, *Pewter in America* is still the definitive work on the subject. The first two volumes, originally published by Laughlin (1890–1977) in 1940, include chapters on European background; the materials, techniques, and business practices of the colonial pewterer; household pewter; ecclesiastical pewter; the care, cleaning, collecting, and connoisseurship of pewter; and biographical sketches of pewterers (along with photographs of objects they made and of their marks) arranged alphabetically by region. The third volume, issued in 1971, follows the same chapter format and was intended to revise and correct the information provided in the first two volumes. Because of this, the researcher should be careful to consult all three volumes on any subject. The 1969 reprint of volumes 1 and 2 also includes brief corrections and additions let into the margins in the appropriate location. In addition to being an essential resource for the identification of pewter objects, Laughlin's biographies of pewterers are a major resource for anyone studying preindustrial artisans. A three-volumes-in-one reprint was issued by American Legacy Press in 1981.

Michaelis, Ronald F. *Antique Pewter of the British Isles*. 1955. Reprint. New York: Dover Publications, 1971. xiv+118 pp.; 75 illustrations, plates, line drawings, bibliography, index.

Antique Pewter is perhaps the best scholarly treatment of the development of designs in pewter from the thirteenth to the early nineteenth centuries. Drawing heavily on the primary documents included in Charles Welch's *History of the Worshipful Company of Pewterers* (London, 1902), Michaelis's discussion of the early history of pewtermaking and period terminology for specific forms is excellent. Each chapter is annotated and is followed by a brief bibliography. Although the final chapter deals with collecting, the emphasis is on the history of pewter wares rather than the concerns of the marketplace.

Montgomery, Charles F. *A History of American Pewter*. Rev. and enl. ed. New York: E. P. Dutton, a Dutton Paperback/a Winterthur Book, 1978. 307 pp.; 238 illustrations, appendixes, bibliography, index.

A History of American Pewter is the best introduction to the subject. The first edition was published in 1973 by Praeger Publishers and was reprinted in 1977 by Weathervane Books. This revised and expanded edition appeared a year later. Although prepared as a catalogue of Winterthur's collection, this book also addresses questions concerning the historical uses of pewter in everyday life, the social conditions of the pewterer, and his methods of fabricating his wares. The

major part of the text is devoted to a consideration of each of the major ecclesiastical and domestic forms commonly made in pewter. The final chapter, "The Collecting of American Pewter before 1950, Incorporating 100 Great Examples of American Pewter," was added to the second edition (issued only in paperback). It provides an engaging and sometimes very personal account of the early pewter collectors, many of whom Montgomery (1910–78) knew. The list of "100 Great Examples" substantially broadens the scope of the book by including numerous objects from collections other than Winterthur's. Photographs of marks and working dates of all pewterers represented make this a useful reference for the identification of specific objects. Also of special interest to collectors is the note on cleaning old pewter; however, the method Montgomery suggests is no longer recommended by museum conservators.

Myers, Louis Guerineau. *Some Notes on American Pewterers*. Garden City, N.Y.: Country Life Press, 1926. xiii+96 pp.; 70 plates.

Myers (1874–1932) was a well-known collector of American decorative arts in the 1920s. His primary interest was in the aesthetic dimension of objects, and he collected pewter, glass, Phyfe-style furniture, and other objects. Some of his pewter collection was acquired by Francis P. Garvan and given to Yale; the remainder was dispersed at auction in 1932. He was closely involved with the Girl Scouts Loan Exhibition of 1929 and wrote much of the catalogue. This book, largely illustrated with pictures of touchmarks, is now principally of historiographical interest as the second major work on American pewter. It includes essays on approximately thirty pewterers and shops that are written in a charming and informal style.

New Haven Colony Historical Society. *An Exhibition of Connecticut Pewter*. Exhibition catalogue. Text by John Devereux Kernan, W. Ogden Ross, F. Farny Eilers, Jr., and W. Ross Fullame. New Haven: By the society, 1969. 72 pp.; 37 illustrations, bibliography, index.

Arranged by maker, this catalogue provides brief biographies as well as basic information on each of the 115 objects exhibited. Data provided include a short description, complete dimensions, touchmark, maker, and place of manufacture. Although not every object is pictured, the full-page illustrations make this a useful pictorial resource, particularly since many of the items are in private collections.

Peal, Christopher A. *Pewter of Great Britain*. Contributions by P. Spencer Davies, C. J. M. Hull, D. A. Mundill, I. D. Robinson, and J. L. Scott. London: John Gifford, 1983. xiii+247 pp.; 203 black and white illustrations, 8 color plates, appendixes, index.

Peal provides an updated and much augmented version of his *British Pewter and Britannia Metal* (1971). Written in a chatty style, *Pewter of Great Britain* includes chapters on the history of pewter collecting in Britain, fakes and forgeries, cleaning and repairing, marking, and the formal evolution of designs in pewter. Peal's discussion of cleaning, repairing, and making rubbings of marks on objects does not always agree with accepted modern conservation techniques. The chronologically arranged chapters on the development of pewter forms from the Roman occupation to the early nineteenth century are filled with details based on Peal's wealth of experience with the actual objects. His chapter on changes in prevailing marking systems is helpful to the beginning student. In addition to the chapters written by Peal, which largely follow the content and organization of his earlier book, several new chapters by other authors have been added as supplements to this volume. The chapter by Robinson, "British Pewter in New England," is of particular interest because it elucidates the role of the makers who specialized in the export trade and includes a chart of the approximately ninety makers who were responsible for 90 percent of the British pewter exported to the colonies in the eighteenth century. Scott's chapter on Britannia wares is largely a condensation of his *Pewter Wares from Sheffield*. Hull, librarian of the Pewterers Company, contributed a chapter on the history of the guild and its collection. Mundill provided "Recognizing European Pewter," and Davies's essay is on Scottish pewter.

Pewter Collectors' Club of America. *Pewter in American Life*. Exhibition catalogue. N.p.: By the club, 1984. 159 pp.; illustrations, appendixes.

Through its authoritative *Bulletin*, the Pewter Collectors' Club of America has been a "clearing house of information on pewter and pewterers" since its founding in 1934. In celebration of the club's fiftieth anniversary, members assembled more than 200 objects from twenty-six public and private collections for an impressive exhibition held at Museum of Our National Heritage in Lexington, Massachusetts. The catalogue is arranged by form, with short introductory statements on use, terminology, and relative rarity at the beginning of each section. The bulk of the text, however, appears in detailed explanatory captions below headings listing form, maker, date, dimensions, and place of manufacture for each object. The volume also includes a short introductory essay on the history of the club and a section on pewterers' tools. The most notable feature of the catalogue is the large and clear illustrations.

Pewter in America, 1650–1900: An Exhibition. Exhibition catalogue. Manchester, N.H.: Currier Gallery of Art, 1968. 75 pp.; 212 illustrated entries.

A checklist of vital data is included in this catalogue. Drawn from private collections as well as the museum's own holdings, the exhibition featured several unusual forms such as a hat mold, a sundial, a pair of scissors, a toy gun, a priest's can, whistles, pewter valves, and other rarely encountered articles. Porringers, teapots, and communion vessels are other forms well represented. It is regrettable that no commentary on

forms or makers is provided to supplement the wide variety of images.

Scott, Jack. *Pewter Wares from Sheffield*. Baltimore, Md.: Antiquary Press, 1980. 261 pp.; 345 black and white illustrations, 6 color plates, line drawings, index.

Based on extensive documentary research, *Pewter Wares from Sheffield* is an authoritative reference on the often neglected subject of Britannia metal wares made in England. Chapters on the history of the industry, the firm of James Dixon and Son, methods of construction, and characteristic features of the wares are very useful. However, because sources and bibliographic information are not provided, the information included is difficult to pursue further. Extensive illustrations from surviving trade catalogues as well as surviving objects make this a valuable pictorial reference. A list of makers and marks provides information not readily available elsewhere.

Stara, D. *Pewter Marks of the World*. Translated by Joy Moss-Kohoutova. London: Hamlyn, 1977. 260 pp.; 1,960 line drawings, indexes.

Stara has compiled images of nearly 2,000 marks, arranged by symbols (man and parts of his body, animals, birds, plants, and so forth), thus providing a place to start when looking for an unknown mark. Also included are brief histories of marking practices in various countries and bibliographical references.

Thomas, John Carl. *Connecticut Pewter and Pewterers*. Hartford: Connecticut Historical Society, 1976. 194 pp.; 194 illustrations, checklist, bibliography, index.

Focusing on the prolific pewterers of the Connecticut valley, their apprentices, and their masters, Thomas investigates design influences (in the form of imported objects and molds inherited from or jointly owned with other pewterers) and the effects of competitive marketing on the craft of the pewterer from the mid eighteenth to the mid nineteenth centuries. Like Ledlie Laughlin, Thomas does this primarily within a format of individual artisan biographies, many of which are illustrated with both objects and the molds and tools used to produce them. Although the bibliography is helpful, the book suffers from a lack of footnotes. Thomas's detailed discussion of the marks of the four Thomas Danforths ends with an interpretation different from that of previous writers. Although his conclusions continue to be the subject of debate, his methodology provides a useful model for the identification of makers' marks. This is among the best recent books on American pewter.

Thomas, John Carl, ed. *American and British Pewter: An Historical Survey*. Antiques Magazine Library VI. New York: Main Street/Universe Books, 1976. 160 pp.; illustrations, index.

Thomas's anthology of articles originally published in *Antiques* is less a historical survey than a compilation of in-depth studies devoted to specific aspects of British and American pewter. With the exception of the good historiographical introduction and the general statements by Thomas, only a few of the articles are intended for the beginning student of American pewter. The others will be most useful to the reader who has mastered the broader surveys such as Charles F. Montgomery's *History of American Pewter* and Christopher A. Peal's *Pewter of Great Britain*. Here the advanced student will find much important information on design influences, new data on the lives of individual pewterers, key specimens from private collections, and studies of specific forms.

Verster, A. J. G. *Old European Pewter*. London: Thames and Hudson, 1958. 106 pp.; plates, bibliography, index.

The text of Verster's survey is tantalizingly brief, tinged with romanticism, and not always entirely satisfactory. Chapters on pewter in the home and tavern and in the church and cloister are the most useful for the student of American pewter. A good bibliography is included. First published in Amsterdam in 1957, this translation was issued a year later.

Ward, Barbara McLean. "Metalwares." In *The Great River: Art and Society of the Connecticut Valley, 1635–1820*, pp. 273–339. Hartford, Conn.: Wadsworth Atheneum, 1985. Illustrations.

"Metalwares" deals with the changing significance of silver, pewter (cats. 190–202), brass, tin, and iron objects made or owned in the region. Ward argues that domestic metalwares, transferred primarily to women through dowry and inheritance, were significant symbols of the cultural and family continuity that linked the settlers to the great trading centers of America and Britain. For this reason, valley residents preferred imported to locally produced objects up until the eve of the Revolution. Their trading networks destroyed, merchants began to recognize the need to encourage local manufacture of wares that had previously been imported. Craft practices in the pewterers' trade were already geared to efficient and profitable quantity productions, and pewterers were among the first to make efficient use of mass-production techniques. *See also* "American Silver and Gold."

[Worshipful Company of Pewterers of London]. *A Short History of the Worshipful Company of Pewterers of London and a Catalogue of Pewterware in Its Possession*. London: By the authority of the Court of Assistants, 1968. 103 pp.; 62 illustrations, bibliography.

Worshipful Company of Pewterers of London. *Supplementary Catalogue of Pewterware*, 1979. London: By the authority of the Court of Assistants, 1978. 132 pp.; illustrations, indexes.

Between 1800 and 1961, Worshipful Company of Pewterers was without a permanent home. Shortly after the new hall was dedicated, the company began to collect outstanding examples of pewter wares dating from the sixteenth century to the present. In addition to a brief history of the company, the 1968 volume contains entries, arranged by form, on 708 objects in its collection, each giving basic catalogue data. The authoritative short essays on the development and use of each form which preface the catalogue sections are especially outstanding. The 1978 supplement presents information on many new acquisitions and includes illustrations of marks.

Brass, Copper, Iron, and Tin

Deborah A. Federhen

BASE-METAL OBJECTS (except those of pewter) have traditionally received considerably less scholarly attention than objects made of silver or gold. The scarcity of makers' marks on items of copper, brass, bronze, iron, and tin-plated sheet iron has made association of these objects with specific regions, dates, and craftsmen much more difficult. In addition, although base-metal objects can be very decorative in both design and ornamentation, many are functional implements intended for active use in the kitchen, fireplace, workshop, or barn. Lacking the intrinsic value, decorative quality, and precise identifications of the precious metals, most base metals unfortunately have been neglected by the collector and the scholar alike.

Much of the early literature on iron and the copper alloys consisted of general surveys, collections of illustrations, or descriptive lists of objects by type or function. Some categories of objects, however, have received fuller attention, especially fireplace accessories and candlesticks: James R. Mitchell, "Marked American Andirons Made before 1840" (Master's thesis, University of Delaware, 1965); and Jean M. Burks, *Birmingham Brass Candlesticks*. Regional studies have also been compiled for Chicago metalsmiths, Pennsylvania blacksmiths, Pennsylvania and Connecticut tinsmiths, and architectural ironwork in Baltimore, Charleston, and Philadelphia. Two recent books have focused on the development of the brass industry in Connecticut during the nineteenth century: Jeremy Brecker, Jerry Lombardi, and Jan Stackhouse, *Brass Valley: The Story of Working People's Lives and Struggles in an American Industrial Region* (Philadelphia: Temple University Press, 1982); and Cecelia Buck et al., *Metal, Minds, and Machines: Waterbury at Work* (Waterbury, Conn.: Mattatuck Historical Society, 1980). There are many rewarding areas for research for regional studies on base metals that are as yet untapped.

Monographs on individual craftsmen are equally scarce. Burks and Charles E. Smart include short biographies of Birmingham brass founders and American instrument makers in their books. Studies of the Hendricks family, Matthew Boulton, Samuel Yellin, and Phillip Simmons published between 1971 and 1981 are an admirable and encouraging beginning to a deeper analysis of the craftsmen who produced base-metal objects. Brian Sipe's 1988 master's thesis for the University of Delaware examines the Bentley family, coppersmiths working in Philadelphia in the nineteenth century, through their account books and existing objects. There remain many more individual craftsmen and metalworking firms who merit detailed and scholarly investigations. There is a great need for a systematic study of account books, bills, and advertisements for craftsmen working in brass, copper, and iron. An expansion of scholarship on the regional, local, and individual levels will enhance the understanding and appreciation of all base-metal objects by helping to overcome the challenges posed by their elusive and somewhat intimidating anonymity.

It is also difficult at present to locate examples of base-metal objects, even in public collections, since few collections of brass, copper, iron, and tin-plated sheet iron have been published. A catalogue of the copper and brass objects in Winterthur's collection is being written by Donald L. Fennimore. Publication of this book will begin to fill a serious void in base-metal scholarship.

During the seventeenth and eighteenth centuries, many of the base-metal objects used in America were manufactured in England and Europe. An awareness of the scholarship on European and British base metals is therefore crucial to the study of base metals in America. Nicholas Goodison's survey of the brassfounders' and brass stampers' trade catalogues at the Victoria and Albert Museum is a useful reference for identifying English sources for the large quantities of furniture hardware, tableware and kitchenware, lighting devices, tools, and architectural embellishments imported from such centers of production as Sheffield and Birmingham. There are large collections of trade catalogues for both English and American companies in several American museums, notably Winterthur and Essex Institute. In addition to published studies of English base metals, many local historical societies in England have checklists of marked metal objects in their collections.

Research on European copper, brass, and iron is less readily accessible. Many texts have not yet been translated into English, like Sigurd Erixon's important study on European brass, *Gammal massing* (Vasteras: ICA-forlaget, 1964). Even when translation of the text is not feasible, these books are valuable for their visual comparisons, since dates and place of origin are usually easily recognizable. Decorative arts scholars have focused primarily on the influence of English goods and English metalworkers on base metals made and used in America. Considerably more attention should be paid to base metals produced in France, Germany, the Netherlands, and Scandinavia, since the influx of immigrants and products from these countries was significant at various periods in American history.

During the last two decades, there have been exciting advances in base-metal scholarship. Systematic examinations of objects and documents have greatly advanced the identification and interpretation of copper, brass, and iron objects and of the craftsmen who produced them. The potential for future research on base metals is particularly rich; the large quantities of objects and documents in the collections of museums, historical societies, and public libraries are a virtually untapped resource for successful and significant research. Much has been accomplished; much more remains to be done.

Alexander, Robert L. "Neoclassical Wrought Iron in Baltimore." *Winterthur Portfolio* 18, nos. 2/3 (Summer/Autumn 1983): 147–86. 58 illustrations, appendix.

Philadelphia and Charleston had flourishing traditions of Georgian architectural ironwork; Baltimore, essentially a nineteenth-century city, developed ironwork in the neoclas-

sical style. This meticulous examination of architectural ironwork in Baltimore includes railings, fences, window guards, gates, and newels on domestic and ecclesiastical buildings. Using examples that survive in their original locations, with old drawings and photographs as documentation, Alexander shows how designer and blacksmith collaborated to produce ironwork incorporating Adamesque, French, and

Greek revival motifs. The changes in technique evident in wrought-iron work of the 1840s and 1850s are interpreted as an adaptation to competition from cast-iron architectural fittings and changing economic conditions. This is an important regional and methodological study.

Bonnin, Alfred. *Tutenag and Paktong: With Notes on Other Alloys in Domestic Use during the Eighteenth Century.* Oxford: Oxford University Press, 1924. xii+98 pp.; 29 plates.

Bonnin uses quotations from seventeenth-, eighteenth-, and nineteenth-century sources such as dictionaries, letters, travel diaries, ship manifests, and books on metallurgy and chemistry to establish *Tutenag* as the commercial name for zinc imported in the East India trade. Paktong is an alloy of copper, nickel, and zinc or tin. The word is derived from the Cantonese pronunciation of *pai-t'ung* (white copper). Bonnin provides contemporary descriptions of paktong dating back to 1597, including the detailed investigations of Swedish chemist Gustave v. Engestrom in 1776. Paktong was always expensive, and the variety of forms cast in it were limited. Bonnin illustrates candlesticks, fire grates, and fenders, and size, weight, date, and location are provided for all objects illustrated. A glossary of forty-two alloys used in the metalworking trades, ranging from the ordinary to the obscure, is included. Until 1970, this was the only book on this subject, and it is still unsurpassed.

Burks, Jean M. *Birmingham Brass Candlesticks.* Charlottesville: University Press of Virginia, 1987. xiii+128 pp.; 120 illustrations, 3 tables, appendixes, bibliography, index.

An outstanding addition to the published material on English brass, this book goes beyond stylistic chronologies to investigate the brass founders who worked in Birmingham and the patented devices they incorporated into their products. It includes short biographies of Birmingham brass founders and American instrument makers.

Campbell, R. *The London Tradesman.* 1747. Reprint. Newton Abbot: David and Charles, 1969. 340 pp.

Campbell includes a description of the products, skills, and responsibilities of all the artisans and professionals working in London in the mid eighteenth century. Craftsmen who worked with base metals include locksmiths, brass founders, ironmongers, jacksmiths, anvilmakers, filemakers, screw- and sawmakers, printer's smiths, stove-grate makers, tin men, cutlers, knife grinders, gunsmiths, watchmakers, mathematical- and optical-instrument makers, needle- and pinmakers, coppersmiths, boltsmiths, anchorsmiths, pewterers, letter founders, and beam- and scalemakers. Although it draws on the London craft scene, this work still helps to identify tasks associated with different trades in America.

Coffin, Margaret. *The History and Folklore of American Country Tinware, 1700–1900.* Camden, N.J., and To-

ronto: Thomas Nelson and Sons, 1968. 226 pp.; approximately 120 black and white and 30 color illustrations, glossary, bibliography, appendixes, index.

Objects made of tin-plated sheet iron, commonly known as tinware, played an important role in American homes of the eighteenth and nineteenth centuries. Coffin notes that tinware was first used in kitchens and dairies where its light weight and low cost were highly desirable. The versatility of tinware, which can be easily cut and shaped, soon made it a popular medium for hundreds of household items, such as containers, lighting devices, and toys. Coffin focuses on the tinsmiths, peddlers, and decorators in Massachusetts, Connecticut, New York, Vermont, and Pennsylvania and farther west. Her book mixes the history of the industry, regional characteristics, and legends of famous smiths and peddlers in a readable guide to these colorful and popular objects. Chapters on the variety of tinware shapes and methods of identifying and preserving old examples are especially valuable for collectors.

Cooke, Lawrence S., ed. *Lighting in America: From Colonial Rushlights to Victorian Chandeliers. See* "Plumbing, Heating, and Lighting."

Darling, Sharon S. *Chicago Metalsmiths: An Illustrated History.* Exhibition catalogue. Chicago: Chicago Historical Society, 1977. xvi+141 pp.; 155 illustrations, index.

This catalogue traces the history of art metalwork in Chicago from 1804 to 1970. While Darling's emphasis is on precious metals, twenty-nine objects are of copper, brass, bronze, and other base metals. *See also* "American Silver and Gold."

Davis, Myra Tolmach. *Sketches in Iron: Samuel Yellin, American Master of Wrought Iron, 1885–1940.* Exhibition catalogue. Washington, D.C.: Dimock Gallery, George Washington University, 1971. Unpag.; 31 illustrations, bibliography.

"Sketches in iron" refers to Yellin's working method of sketching his designs with a "hammer for a pencil and the red hot iron for the drawing paper." Davis's monograph was produced in conjunction with an exhibition of Yellin's work. Born in Poland in 1885, Yellin was trained as a blacksmith in Russia, Belgium, and England before settling in Philadelphia in 1906. He achieved phenomenal success in America. He established Arch Street Metalworker's Studio in 1910, and by the early 1920s more than 200 craftsmen were employed in his forge. In 1925 Yellin was presented the Philadelphia Civic Award and a prize of $10,000 as "the outstanding citizen who had made the finest contribution in the interests of the city." His ironwork enhances important buildings all over the country, including those at Yale, Harvard, and Princeton universities and Bryn Mawr College. Yellin also provided grills, lighting fixtures, gates, rails, balconies, and screens for such structures as Washington Cathedral, Grace Cathedral in San Francisco, and the federal reserve banks in New York and Minneapolis, as well as for the private residences of Vincent Astor, H. H. Flagler, Andrew Jergens, Jr., R. B. Mellon, and Edsel Ford. A checklist of his major works is included. Photographs of Yellin and his apprentices in the studio and examples of his ironwork supplement documentary evidence. Much of the information in Davis's monograph was drawn from family documents.

Deas, Alston. *The Early Ironwork of Charleston*. Illustrated by Richard J. Bryan; introduction by Albert Simons. Columbia, S.C.: Bostick and Thornley, 1941. 111 pp.; 64 illustrations, line drawings, bibliography, index.

This work covers the historic and stylistic background of architectural ironwork in Charleston, particularly the strong English influence of the eighteenth century, and identifies blacksmiths working in Charleston during the eighteenth and nineteenth centuries. Most are known only by their advertisements; no surviving work has been attributed to them. Nineteenth-century craftsmen are associated with specific projects, and most of the book is devoted to scale drawings of surviving architectural ironwork. Captions describe the type of object, building and location, and details of construction. Most of the objects, including wrought-iron gates, grills, railings, balustrades, balconies, brackets, lantern standards, and newels, date from the mid eighteenth century to the 1830s.

DeVoe, Shirley Spaulding. *The Tinsmiths of Connecticut.* Middletown: Wesleyan University Press for the Connecticut Historical Society, 1968. xxiv+200 pp.; 142 illustrations, appendixes, bibliography.

DeVoe, a tinware collector and decorator, traces the history of tinware production in Connecticut from the independent artisans of the mid eighteenth century, like Scottish immigrant Edward Pattison, to the large factories of the nineteenth century, like Goodrich, Ives, and Company. DeVoe discusses manufacturing techniques, apprenticeships, products, and marketing practices of the tinware industry, as well as important figures in manufacturing tinware. Painted decoration became an important component of tin-plated sheet-iron products shortly after 1800. The book contains a list of female painters and japanners and one of craftsmen and companies producing tinware. Appendixes reproduce two typical indenture papers, a peddler's contract, and a company's price list. DeVoe has also published a more comprehensive pictorial survey, *The Art of the Tinsmith: English and American* (Exton, Pa.: Schiffer Publishing, 1981).

Gentle, Rupert. *Brass Candlesticks.* Facsimile of ca. 1800 ed. Milton Lilbourne, Wiltshire: Privately printed, 1973. 28 leaves.

This late eighteenth-century brass founder's trade catalogue (several pages in the original document have watermarks that bear the date 1797) emphasizes candlesticks, which are composed of a variety of square, round, or oval bases with plain, fluted, or baluster columns. In addition, several chamber

sticks, tea bells, and servant bells in nine sizes are pictured. The plates appear to have been selected from a larger assortment, since numbering is irregular and includes leaves numbered as high as fifty-six. The original catalogue was found in Philadelphia and may have been compiled for sales to Pennsylvania merchants.

Gentle, Rupert. *Candlesticks.* Richmond, Va.: Valentine Museum, 1975. [48] pp.; 79 illustrations.

Gentle presents an introduction to an exhibition surveying candlesticks made throughout Europe from the Middle Ages to the end of the eighteenth century. The seventy-nine candlesticks illustrated, all from the G. Dallas Coons Candlestick Collection, present a chronology of the evolution in design and function of European candlesticks over nine centuries. The captions include information on the country of origin, date, size, and composition of each candlestick. Examples are from Germany, Switzerland, Spain, Italy, Scandinavia, France, the Netherlands, and England. Many of these countries are not represented in the larger studies of candlesticks.

Gentle, Rupert, and Rachael Feild. *English Domestic Brass, 1680–1810, and the History of Its Origins.* Foreword by Graham Hood. New York: E. P. Dutton, 1975. xii+204 pp.; 366 plates, appendixes, glossary, bibliography, index.

This comprehensive survey begins with nine chapters that survey the mining, manufacturing, and marketing of brass objects in eighteenth-century England. Technical information on marks, alloys, and decorative processes and materials used in working, decorating, and finishing brass is provided in four appendixes. Approximately half of the book is devoted to illustrations of brass objects arranged in functional categories, including candlelight, hearth and home, kitchen and parlor, accessory and ornament, and brass and the hereafter. As Hood notes in his foreword, "America provided a significant market" for English brass merchants; this book is rich in information on the brass wares used in many eighteenth-century American households.

Goodison, Nicholas. *Ormolu: The Work of Matthew Boulton.* London: Phaidon Press; New York: Phaidon Publishers, 1974; distributed by Praeger Publishers. xii+398 pp.; 174 black and white and 2 color plates, appendixes, index.

Ormolu, from the French *or moulu* (ground gold), was used in the eighteenth century to denote objects made of gilt brass, bronze, or copper. Ormolu ornaments, including candelabra, doorknobs, escutcheons, sconces, inkstands, clock cases, and vases, were produced in large quantities by Matthew Boulton at Soho Manufactory, which operated outside Birmingham, England, from 1768 to 1782. Many documents relating to Boulton's firm are preserved in the library of the Assay Office in Birmingham and form the basis for Goodison's research. The first chapter presents an account of the Boulton and Fothergill button and "toy" manufacturing business and establishes an industrial and financial context for the production of ormolu ornaments. Soho Manufactory produced many other base metalwares, and Goodison discusses the objects, industrial methods of production, markets, and reasons for financial failure. Chapters focus on the ormolu trade at Soho, design sources, manufacturing techniques, and marketing and conclude with a survey of ornaments produced by Boulton and Fothergill. A large section of illustrations includes plates from the company's pattern book and sketches from Boulton's notebook. Appendixes contain the bibliography; a biographical listing of patrons; the indenture of Edward Pardoe, a chaser for Boulton and Fothergill; and sale catalogues for Boulton and Fothergill in 1771 and 1778 with annotations of descriptions, prices, and buyers.

Goodison, Nicholas. "The Victoria and Albert Museum's Collection of Metal-Work Pattern Books." *Furniture History* 11 (1975): 1–30. 60 plates, appendixes.

Goodison surveys forty-one trade catalogues issued by brass founders and stampers between 1770 and 1850 and focuses on the decorative hardware for furniture contained in these catalogues: drawer handles, escutcheon plates, paw-and-ball feet, castors, capitals, finials, hinges, and decorative mounts. Sixty plates from pattern books illustrate a representative range of design, with some emphasis on rococo and neoclassical patterns. Brief entries contain a description of the contents, an approximate date, and any inscriptions or watermarks present. An essay summarizes the range of domestic hardware made by eighteenth- and nineteenth-century brass founders. Goodison ascribes the considerable duplication of patterns among different catalogues to the absence of copyrights for the designs and to the character of the markets served by these catalogues. Catalogues that contain goods designed for American or European markets are noted. He suggests that the anonymity of the catalogues was a deliberate precaution taken by the agents and factors of the founders to prevent their customers from circumventing their services by acquiring goods directly from manufacturers. An appendix presents a list of the domestic fittings offered in a typical catalogue of the 1830s. *See also* "Clocks and Watches."

Gunnion, Vernon S., and Carroll J. Hopf, eds. *The Blacksmith: Artisan within the Early Community.* Foreword by Blanche K. Reigle; introduction by John D. Tyler. Exhibition catalogue. Harrisburg: Pennsylvania Historical and Museum Commission, 1972. 64 pp.; 105 illustrated entries, bibliography.

The Blacksmith includes a catalogue of 105 wrought-iron and steel objects. Tyler's introductory essay explores the difference between a blacksmith, who works in iron, and a whitesmith, who works with steel. He discusses the tools and production methods of these craftsmen and many of the objects they created. Agricultural implements and domestic artifacts are included and display an impressive variety in their func-

tion and design. The practical, decorative, and whimsical potentials of ironwork are well represented by such diverse objects as trivets, crimpers, apple peelers, ladles, escutcheon plates, hinges, andirons, lamps, plows, hoes, Conestoga-wagon fittings, pump handles, weather vanes, and toys. Each object is accompanied by a clear, black and white photograph, a short caption, and measurements.

Haedeke, Hanns-Ulrich. *Metalwork.* Translated by Vivienne Menkes. The Universe Social History of the Decorative Arts, edited by Hugh Honour. New York: Universe Books, 1970. 227 pp.; 249 black and white and 15 color plates, bibliography, index.

Haedeke's history of base-metal work in Europe from the Middle Ages to the early twentieth century describes the evolution of form, function, and decoration of iron objects, the development of metalworking centers with international distributions, the importance of the guilds in the regulation of the metalworking trades and their economic and political influence in many spheres of public life, and the changing role of the craftsman in European society. Examination of metalwork is divided into four large sections by material: copper, bronze and brass, iron, and pewter. Each section begins with a chapter on the mining of the necessary ores, the processing of the raw materials into pure metals or alloys, and the techniques of manufacturing objects with these substances. Haedeke examines domestic, religious, and civic objects made from each metal, proceeding chronologically from the Carolingian period to art nouveau. Contemporary paintings, prints, and book illustrations provide visual evidence of base-metal craft techniques, the operation of metalworking shops, and the domestic uses of base-metal objects.

Hamilton, Henry. *The English Brass and Copper Industries to 1800.* Original introduction by William Ashley; new introduction by J. R. Harris. 1926. Reprint. London: Frank Cass, 1967. xxvi+388 pp.; illustrations, appendixes, bibliography, index.

A new introduction to the second edition by Harris of Liverpool University surveys the literature on copper and brass since 1926 and indicates areas in which this standard work has become dated. Hamilton's comprehensive history of English copper and brass manufacturing from the sixteenth through the eighteenth centuries investigates the mining, manufacturing, and retailing of these metals. One chapter focuses on Birmingham, the most important center of brass founding during the eighteenth century and the source of many of the objects exported to the colonies. Another chapter discusses the establishment of markets for both the raw materials and the finished goods within England and in Europe and America. Fluctuations in trade and changes in the commercial organization of the industry (wages and employment) are also covered. Appendixes contain information on methods of production, reproduce contemporary documents dealing with the value of the ores and the establishment of manufactories, and offer statistics on imports and exports of copper and brass.

Harris, John. *English Decorative Ironwork from Contemporary Source Books, 1610–1836*. London: Alec Tiranti, 1960. vi+18 pp.+168 engraved plates; index.

Harris reproduces plates of architectural ironwork from seventeenth-, eighteenth-, and nineteenth-century design books beginning with Inigo Jones and ending with Henry Shaw. The plates are arranged chronologically, and notes provide historical background and dating information. An introduction traces the dissemination of ironwork patterns from France to England in the early seventeenth century and later from England to the American colonies.

Hayward, Arthur H. *Colonial Lighting*. See "Plumbing, Heating, and Lighting."

John, W. D., and Katherine Coombes. *Paktong: The Non-Tarnishable Chinese "Silver" Alloy Used for "Adam" Firegrates and Early Georgian Candlesticks*. Newport, England: Ceramic Book Co., 1970. xi+25 pp.+50 plates; appendix.

John and Coombes focus on paktong objects made for interiors designed by Robert Adam. Adam's interest in the silvery beauty and noncorrosive properties of paktong is evident in the fire grates, tools, and fenders that he designed for interiors at Nostell Priory, Keddleston, Saltram House, Syon Park House, Osterley Park, and his own London town house at 4 Adelphi Terrace. In addition to illustrating Adam's splendid fireplace equipment, the book includes photographs of paktong candlesticks, andirons, coasters, snuffers, and trays dating from 1725 to 1790, as well as a rare flintlock pistol with paktong fittings. An appendix surveys Adam's training and career as an architect and interior designer and briefly describes his major commissions.

Kauffman, Henry, and Quentin Bowers. *Early American Andirons and Other Fireplace Accessories. See* "Plumbing, Heating, and Lighting."

Kauffman, Henry J. *American Copper and Brass*. 1968. Reprint. New York: Bonanza Books, 1979. 288 pp.; approximately 225 illustrations and line drawings, bibliography, index.

Kauffman's survey is intended to "help the reader to make reasonably positive identification or attribution of objects" and to provide a fuller understanding of American copperware and brassware. He discusses the mining and refining of copper and brass and examines the trades of the coppersmith and brass founder, the extraordinary range of articles made by these craftsmen, and the tools and techniques used to fabricate them. Fifty-two different forms made are illustrated and discussed, with particular emphasis on their construction and use. Illustrations and quotations are taken from many period documents, such as advertisements, dictionaries, di-

rectories, trade cards, ledgers, bills, indentures, and patent specifications, as well as from prints from *The Art of Coppersmithing* (1894). A chapter focuses on the career of coppersmith William Bailey, who worked in Lancaster and York, Pennsylvania, and in Baltimore and maintained branch shops in Chambersburg, Pennsylvania, and Hagerstown, Maryland, during the late eighteenth century. His training, products, and business serve as a case study for exploring the coppersmithing trade in the context of a small inland town and a large coastal city. Kauffman concludes with alphabetical lists of coppersmiths and brass founders active during the eighteenth and nineteenth centuries.

Kauffman, Henry J. *The American Fireplace: Chimneys, Mantelpieces, Fireplaces, and Accessories. See* "Plumbing, Heating, and Lighting."

Kauffman, Henry J. *Early American Ironware: Cast and Wrought*. New York: Weathervane Books, 1966; distributed by Crown Publishers. 166 pp.; 210 illustrations, index.

Early American Ironware considers iron as it was mined, manufactured, and used in America during the seventeenth, eighteenth, and nineteenth centuries. Kauffman's history begins with the processes of manipulating iron at the blast furnace, the forge, and the iron foundry. Subsequent chapters examine the products and practices of ten different ironworking artisans: blacksmith, whitesmith, farrier, edge toolmaker, cutler, locksmith, gunsmith, nailer, wheelwright, and tinsmith who works with tin-plated sheet iron. Ironworkers, in their various permutations, touched all aspects of domestic life. Lighting devices; kitchen utensils; architectural hardware; locks, hinges and latches; fireplace equipment; and weather vanes are among the objects discussed here. Quotations and illustrations are from contemporary advertisements, engravings, trade cards and catalogues, inventories, ledgers, bills, encyclopedias, and dictionaries.

Lasansky, Jeannette. *To Cut, Piece, and Solder: The Work of the Rural Pennsylvania Tinsmith, 1779–1908*. Lewisburg, Pa.: Oral Traditions Project of the Union County Historical Society, 1982. 80 pp.; approximately 280 illustrations, bibliography, index.

Lasansky explores the world of the nineteenth-century tinsmith and traces the impact of mechanized production of tinwares on the craft of tinsmithing through the careers and products of rural Pennsylvania tinsmiths. Many previously unpublished sources are quoted, such as daybooks, ledgers, advertisements, and the full text of a letter from John Jarett, secretary of American Tinned Plate Association, to the *Bulletin of the American and Steel Association* in 1889, describing the process of tinplate production. Lasansky illustrates many different objects, including a significant number of marked examples, and includes a lengthy list of period forms and prices with considerable attention to cookie-cutter patterns.

Lasansky, Jeannette. *To Draw, Upset, and Weld: The Work of the Pennsylvania Rural Blacksmith, 1742–1935.* Lewisburg, Pa.: Oral Traditions Project of the Union County Historical Society, 1980. 80 pp.; illustrations, bibliography, index.

This work begins with a survey of the tools and techniques of metalworking, the plan and organization of the blacksmith's shop, the apprenticeship system, the variety of services performed by general blacksmiths and by specialists such as locksmiths and cutlers, and the changing role of these craftsmen in their society. Lasansky examines account books to determine the types of objects produced by rural Pennsylvania blacksmiths over three centuries and concludes that the character of a smith's work was determined more by individual personality than by geography or date. Many marked examples are illustrated. A separate chapter analyzes the design and decoration of fireplace tools, kitchen implements, lighting devices, and a miscellany of hinges, hasps, and latches. A list of documented blacksmith's marks and biographical information is provided. *See also* "Craftsmen."

Lea, Zilla Rider, ed. *The Ornamented Tray: Two Centuries of Ornamented Trays, 1720–1920, Based on Esther Stevens Brazer's Photographic Collection.* Rutland, Vt.: Charles E. Tuttle Co. for the Historical Society of Early American Decoration, 1971. 255 pp.; 481 black and white illustrations, 6 color plates, bibliography, index.

Pontypool, in South Wales, was an important ironworking center in western Europe during the seventeenth and eighteenth centuries. In 1697 Major John Hanbury was responsible for the invention of rolling mills, which produced uniformly thick sheets of iron. Thomas Allgood, foreman of Hanbury Ironworks from 1670 to 1716, developed a method of protecting the sheet iron from rust by covering the iron plates with a hard, bituminous varnish which resembled oriental lacquer, a process known as japanning. Allgood's son, Edward, further perfected the japanning process and, in the 1720s, developed an alternative method of coating the iron sheets with a thin layer of tin. While tin-plated sheet iron achieved a greater success commercially, colorful japanned wares were widely produced and remained popular into the twentieth century. The tray was a popular form of decorated ironware produced in Pontypool and in England, America, and Russia. Lea examines the history, stylistic development, and techniques of manufacture and decoration of these trays. Each chapter was written by a member of the Historical Society of Early American Decoration and examines a different type of metal or papier-mâché decorated tray: lace-edge trays with pierced borders; trays decorated with gold leaf, ornamented by the freehand bronze technique, or stenciled; and American "country-painted" trays. The last chapter deals exclusively with American-made goods and surveys the American tin industry, the production of decorated tinware in various regions of America, and the identification of regional characteristics in ornamental tray designs.

Light, John D. "The Archaeological Investigation of Blacksmith Shops." *Journal of the Society for Industrial Archaeology* 10, no. 1 (1984): 55–68. 9 illustrations.

Based on archaeological excavations of blacksmithing sites and several working forges in Canada, this article discusses the layout and operation of a blacksmith shop, including its size, location and character of the forge, bellows, anvil, workbench, storage areas, domestic spaces, windows, and waste piles. Analyses of small, broken remains in the soil provide documentation for the types of work done by the smith, the tools he used, and the patterns of movement he customarily followed. Since forges often served as social centers as well as workshops, archaeological studies can yield information on the life-styles and leisure activities of the smith and his clients.

Lindsay, J. Seymour. *Iron and Brass Implements of the English and American House.* Introduction by Ralph Edwards. Rev. and enl. ed. Bass River, Mass.: Carl Jacobs, 1964. vii+88 pp.; 473 illustrations, index.

Still considered an authoritative treatment of domestic brass and iron from the thirteenth century to the early nineteenth century, this work is divided into six sections, each dealing with a different category of domestic object: the hearth, kitchen utensils, lighting devices, tobacco paraphernalia, "American Colonial implements," and miscellaneous objects. Introductory essays for each chapter identify regional characteristics, particularly in ornamentation, evolutionary changes in function and design, and historical factors that influenced the development of iron and brass implements. Many primary sources are quoted in the text. Drawings illustrate hundreds of objects in careful detail and indicate their use and construction.

Lindsay, John Seymour. *An Anatomy of English Wrought Iron.* Chapters in Art, vol. 40. London: Alec Tiranti, 1964. vi+57 pp.; 178 illustrations, index.

Lindsay's survey of English blacksmithing techniques from Nordic influence through the eighteenth century is illustrated with meticulously detailed, measured drawings. The introduction describes twenty-one methods of fashioning iron and depicts a variety of resulting decorative effects. A chronology of balustrades, casement-window fasteners, gates, railings, hinges, locks, and latches supports Lindsay's view that blacksmiths were sculptors in iron.

Mercer, Henry C. *The Bible in Iron: Pictured Stoves and Stoveplates of the Pennsylvania Germans. See* "Plumbing, Heating, and Lighting."

Michaelis, Ronald F. *Old Domestic Base-Metal Candlesticks from the Thirteenth to Nineteenth Century: Produced in Bronze, Brass, Paktong, and Pewter.* Woodbridge, Suffolk: Antique Collectors' Club, 1978. 139 pp.; 202 illustrations, appendix, bibliography.

In the first two chapters, Michaelis deals with candles and candlemakers and metals and methods of manufacture. The remainder of the book is a catalogue of English and European candlesticks from the Middle Ages to the early nineteenth century which are grouped roughly chronologically within evolutionary changes in candlestick styles, such as pricket and "trumpet-based" candlesticks and candlesticks with hollow, incurved conical bases or central drip pans. English examples dominate the sections dealing with the late seventeenth through the early nineteenth centuries. The text is primarily concerned with dating, identifying regional characteristics and unusual features, and establishing a chronology of style. Attributions to country are made broadly. A short chapter deals with special mechanisms incorporated into candlesticks, including ejectors, springs, revolving coil holders, and dousers. The appendix reprints a comparison of the constituents of bronze and brass from 1800 to 1840.

Mitchell, James R., ed. *Antique Metalware: Brass, Bronze, Copper, Tin, Wrought, and Cast Iron*. Antiques Magazine Library. New York: Universe Books, a Main Street Press Book, 1977. 256 pp.; approximately 500 illustrations, index.

Mitchell has selected articles originally published in *Antiques* between 1922 and 1976 that focus on base metals made and used in America up to about 1900. The articles are grouped in seven sections according to function: architectural iron; fireplaces, andirons, and related heating objects; toys; architectural and furniture hardware; instruments, such as tools and nails; architectural appointments; and household objects. A final section includes studies that focus on specific regions or crafts. Many articles are pioneers in the field, but they lack documentation. In some instances, however, they represent all that is currently available on the subject.

Mulholland, James A. *A History of Metals in Colonial America*. University: University of Alabama Press, 1981. xiv+215 pp.; illustrations, 2 maps, 1 table, bibliography, index.

Mulholland surveys precious and base metals as raw materials and as finished products in the English-speaking colonies from their initial settlement through independence. His thesis is that metals were a central element in the material culture of Western civilization and that the successful colonization, sustained growth, and eventual independence of the colonies could not have been achieved without continuous supplies of metals. Mulholland stresses the mining, smelting, and manufacture of raw metals, especially iron, and discusses the development of individual furnaces, mills, and mines, the import and export of raw materials, refined metals, and finished goods, and the tools and techniques for manipulating the metals into usable objects. American metalworking is chronicled from an artisan-based craft, hampered by British regulations and tariffs, to a national industry.

Schiffer, Peter, Nancy Schiffer, and Herbert Schiffer. *The Brass Book: American, English, and European; Fifteenth Century through 1850*. Exton, Pa.: Schiffer Publishing, 1978. 447 pp.; 1,250 illustrated entries, bibliography, index.

The introductory chapter supplies basic information on brass alloys, the European brassmaking business from the fourteenth century to the seventeenth century, and the development of American brass manufacturing. The essay includes a chronological sampling of newspaper advertisements for braziers in Boston, New York, Philadelphia, Baltimore, Annapolis, and Charleston from 1753 to 1820 and a pictorial demonstration of the eighteenth-century process of sand casting. The book's primary strength is its vast compilation of illustrations depicting hundreds of brass objects arranged alphabetically from andirons to warming pans. American, English, Dutch, Flemish, French, and German brass objects are grouped by type into thirty sections, which include the full complement of household furnishings as well as dog collars, bird cages, horse brasses, house fittings, ornaments, armaments, scientific instruments, and tomb plates. The emphasis is on English, American, and Dutch material from 1700 to 1830. There are two particularly strong sections on candlesticks and fireplace equipment. An English brass founder's catalogue, watermarked 1767 and showing mostly furniture hardware, with a few bells, candle sconces, and jamb hooks, is reproduced in its entirety. The same authors and publishers issued a similar volume, *Antique Iron*, in 1979.

Simpson, Marc. *All That Glisters: Brass in Early America*. Exhibition catalogue. New Haven: Yale Center for American Art and Material Culture, 1979. vi+26 pp.; illustrated entries, bibliography.

An illustrated selection of nineteen English- and American-made brass objects used in America during the eighteenth and nineteenth centuries is representative of the eight categories of brass objects defined and discussed by Simpson in his essay: lighting devices, tools of the hearth, armament, locks and handles, scientific instruments, manufacturing and professional tools, musical instruments, and miscellaneous "pieces of Brass." Each item is identified by maker (if known), date, place of manufacture, composition, present location, and size and is accompanied by a short, informative caption. Simpson discusses the production of brass, the characteristics of various alloys used by the brazier, the presence of English brass in the American colonies, and the work of American braziers. Documentation was taken from several seventeenth- and eighteenth-century inventories, newspaper advertisements, and trade cards.

Smart, Charles E. *The Makers of Surveying Instruments in America since 1700*. 2 vols. Troy, N.Y.: Regal Art Press, 1962, 1967. xxvi+282 pp.; black and white and color illustrations, bibliography, index.

Smart examined city directories, newspapers, genealogical records, patents, and published sources for data on companies and products. An introductory section discusses eight types of surveying instruments in detail, touching on the historical origins and subsequent improvements of each, the component parts of the tools, and the mechanics of their use. Entries on each maker are listed alphabetically and are frequently accompanied by an illustration of an object, a trade card, or an advertisement. Also included is a description of all the objects by each maker whom the author was able to locate. In addition to surveying instruments, American makers produced compasses, telescopes, optical equipment, mathematical instruments, bells, and clocks. Many advertised their services as jewelers, clockmakers, brass founders, bell founders, or silversmiths, and some created specialty items, as did William Austin Burt of Detroit, who made the first typewriter in 1829, and Henry Blattner, who developed a "dry plate" for photography. Smart includes a list of patents relating to surveying instruments.

Sonn, Alfred H. *Early American Wrought Iron.* 3 vols. 1928. Reprint. New York: Hacker Art Books, 1978. xvi+263, vi+205, vii+263 pp.; 960 plates, bibliography, index.

Sonn's massive treatise with beautifully detailed sketches of thousands of iron objects initially surveys the history of early American wrought iron to 1850 and stresses the difficulties in studying it because it was seldom signed or dated and was not marketed through published trade catalogues. Several short essays discuss specific categories of ironwork such as hardware, architectural ironwork, and household equipment. The first volume covers door hardware like knockers, latches, and locks. The second includes bolts, hinges, hasps, and doors. The third deals with balconies, braces, railings, newels, gates and grills, weather vanes, wall anchors, gutter supports, foot scrapers, and shutter fasteners and the full range of domestic objects, including andirons, fireplace accessories, kitchen utensils, and lighting equipment. The original location of each object is included in the captions when known, as are the dimensions and a description of any unusual or exceptional features of the object.

Vlach, John Michael. *Charleston Blacksmith: The Work of Philip Simmons.* Athens: University of Georgia Press, 1981. xvi+154 pp.; 82 illustrations, 2 maps, 30 line drawings, appendix, glossary.

Vlach reconstructs the career of black artisan Simmons using field notes and taped interviews to chronicle the early influences that shaped his work as a smith: childhood in a fishing and farming family on Daniel Island near Charleston, apprenticeship with Peter Simmons, and contact with the work of other Charleston blacksmiths. Simmons's ironwork continues the ornamental tradition of architectural iron in Charleston. Thirty of his elaborate gates are illustrated, demonstrating both his technical skill and his competent, sometimes whimsical, sense of design. Vlach examines Simmons's role in preserving craft traditions through his training of apprentices and his views of the future of the craft. An appendix presents step-by-step demonstrations of the construction of two objects, a simple fireplace poker and an ornate wrought-iron gate. *See also* "Craftsmen."

Wallace, Philip B. *Colonial Ironwork in Old Philadelphia: The Craftsmanship of the Early Days of the Republic.* Measured drawings by William Allen Dunn; introduction by Fiske Kimball. New York: Architectural Book Publishing Co., 1930. [vii]+147 pp.; approximately 225 illustrations.

Photographs and measured drawings are used to record examples of architectural ironwork in Philadelphia made before 1850. Captions identify the type of iron shown, the building on which it appears, and the street address. Other than the captions, there is no text.

Whiteman, Maxwell. *Copper for America: The Hendricks Family and a National Industry, 1755–1939.* New Brunswick, N.J.: Rutgers University Press, 1971. viii+353 pp.; illustrations, index.

Whiteman draws on a collection of 20,000 documents at the New-York Historical Society to chronicle the merchandising, shipping, importing, and smelting activities of key members of a family prominent in the history of the American copper industry. Uriah Hendricks (1737–98) and Herman Hendricks (1711–1838) were important pioneers in this industry. The contributions of successive generations of this family are recorded as business responded to advances in mining and increased demands for copper for locomotives, ships, and electricity. Under the ownership of the Hendricks family, Soho Copper Works near Newark, New Jersey, became a successful mill for smelting, refining, and rolling copper. An appendix contains a selection of documents that primarily deal with the establishment of the Soho mill.

Wills, Geoffrey. *Candlesticks. See* "Plumbing, Heating, and Lighting."

Ceramics and Glass

American Ceramics

GENERAL STUDIES AND BIBLIOGRAPHIES

REGIONAL STUDIES

Continental and Oriental Ceramics in America

English Ceramics in America

American Glass

American Ceramics

Ellen Paul Denker

AMERICAN CERAMICS offer all the intellectual excitement inherent in historical study of any medium. For the student of American material culture, the ways in which potters have interacted with the forces of style, taste, tradition, innovation, and technological and economic changes over the years provide endless opportunities for investigation and analysis. A brief account of some terminology and classifications will help to introduce the following selections and annotations.

Ceramic objects are neatly categorized according to type of clay—earthenware, stoneware, and porcelain—but such tidiness belies the diversity and complexity of the interrelationship between the materials, methods of processing, shop organization, and form and decoration. For example, each type of clay body may be further subdivided by color, texture, plasticity, and vitreousness (is it waterproof when fired?). Methods of processing clay to final form and the extent of the division of labor within a pottery distinguish it as being a traditional, industrial, or studio operation. Clay may be hand built, wheel thrown, press molded, or slip cast; a potter can perform all duties related to a pottery's operation (traditional or studio) or may be one worker among few or many others, each with specified duties within the total process (industrial). Furthermore, how an object is to be used and who will use it will affect the final form and surface decoration. Will it be for utility or art or some combination of the two?

Although the general historical movement of ceramics in North America has been in the direction of greater material refinement and fashionable sophistication of form and design, traditional utilitarian coarseware has continued to exist to the present day. Indeed, statistical analysis of the current museum and academic literature would suggest that traditional southern pottery is a more important commodity than mass-market dinnerware or high-technology refractory products. For the national economy, however, nothing could be further from the truth. The current predominance of folkloristic studies of southern pottery represents the maturation of this particular avenue of investigation, while analytical work on American artware and tableware is just beginning to be published.

Historically, traditional pottery, usually of red earthenware (redware) or stoneware, has been contrasted with industrial pottery, generally of refined earthenware, refined stoneware, or porcelain, and both are viewed in opposition to art ceramics, which may be made of any material. Distinctions are drawn in refinement of the clay body, fabrication methods and shop organization, or form and decoration. Although general studies of American ceramics history will touch on most or all these categories, regional considerations tend to focus on only one: traditional, industrial, or art. Traditional and art ceramics of a region have sometimes been combined in exhibitions because both involve the use of hand methods, but these two categories are rarely viewed in conjunction with the industrial ceramics produced in the area.

Preferences of collectors have greatly influenced the kinds of studies that have been published. For example, traditional pottery has been the subject of exhibitions and collectors' guides more frequently than fine porcelain because the former is considered more genuinely American in character, while the latter is viewed as largely, and rather poorly, derivative of foreign sources. In truth, the only indigenous American pottery (and there are those who would argue with this as well) was made by native Americans whose work has had little influence on the products of Euramerican potters. (Native American ceramics are not included in this bibliography because this literature is covered thoroughly elsewhere by anthropologists.) Only recently have collectors turned their attention to fine porcelain tableware and artware; therefore, scholarship on these categories is just beginning to progress beyond the encyclopedic stage, and many monographs are currently in preparation.

Industrial ceramics other than tableware and decorative ware—that is, sanitary products and high-grade electrical-insulation materials—hold almost no charm for collectors and are of little interest to publishers. But the ceramics industry as a whole is moving in this direction, and material culture historians should keep this in mind.

American ceramics received little attention before the late 1960s. Although a few investigations appeared early, the last twenty years have seen a veritable explosion of research published in books and periodicals. Since the pioneering commentaries by Jennie Young (1878) and Edwin AtLee Barber (1893) were released, however, only a few works have considered the overall history of ceramics made in America. The dearth of such studies is understandable. Despite America's short history under Western cultural domination, there is a lot of geography to cover from coast to coast in North America, and the ceramic goods made before 1920 range from medieval utilitarian ware to sophisticated modern works of art. Not only have writers shied away from considering the scope of American ceramics history, but no one has tried to analyze its contents in any way other than from the antiquarian, taxonomical approach. The few efforts at interpretation have been limited by geography or type of goods. For example, Henry Glassie's *Pattern in the Material Folk Culture of the Eastern United States* (1969) lumped ceramics into his theory of the western migration of folk materials. The definition of his subject matter, however, limited the extent of his interpretation to folk pottery, which makes up a relatively small part of American ceramics history.

Despite such shortcomings, the student can get an overall picture of the historical thrust of ceramics made in America. Barber's *Pottery and Porcelain of the United States* and my and Bert Denker's *Pocket Guide to North American Pottery and Porcelain* cover the whole range of American-made wares. Of these two works, ours is more concise and, therefore, less inclusive, while Barber's is out of date and does not include the years after 1909. Marvin Schwartz's *Collector's Guide to Antique American Ceramics* and William Ketchum's *Pottery and Porcelain Collector's Handbook* will fill the bill also, but care should be taken with all these panoramic studies to confirm information on individual potters.

If the comprehensive studies are rare and uneven, individual, local, and regional treatments exist in great quantity. Some sense of this wealth may be gained by considering that Ruth Irwin Weidner's bibliography lists nearly 3,000 citations, most of which have been published. A smaller and still useful bibliography by Susan Strong includes only 629 entries, but offers the advantage of annotations.

In light of these two bibliographies that, taken together, afford easy access to identification and evaluation of many sources, the following section may seem superfluous; but the aim here has been to select sources of information on American ceramics history that are broad in scope or the best available on a particular subject, rather than to list everything in print. Moreover, important work published too recently to be cited by Strong or Weidner has also been included. The citations have been divided into two categories: general considerations of American ceramics history bibliographies and regional studies. General histories also include discussions of specific classifications of ceramics that cut across geographic boundaries—for example, works by Georgeanna H. Greer and Alice C. Frelinghuysen—and compendiums of certain types of goods, including those by Lois Lehner, Paul Evans, and M. Charles Rebert. Studies of individual potteries or of those in a particular city are included under the regional category if the wares were traded widely or if the study presents an especially noteworthy method. All areas of North America for which work is available are represented.

Various approaches have been taken in the regional studies; therefore, an attempt has been made in the annotations to convey a sense of each author's method. Some treatments are strictly encyclopedic, like those by William C. Gates, Jr., and Dana E. Ormerod, who give marks for and brief histories of the many potteries operating in East Liverpool, Ohio, and M. Lelyn Branin, who depends on genealogies and documents as the principal sources about Maine potters and potteries and pays little attention to these potters' products.

Other treatises offer important models for analysis of local and regional ceramics histories. Susan H. Myers uses histories of individual potters and their wares to document the nature of the transition of Philadelphia's early nineteenth-century potteries from preindustrial operations to major manufactories. John A. Burrison and Charles G. Zug bring the folklorist's perspective to examinations of the survival of a traditional craft in Georgia and North Carolina. My own "Ceramics at the Crossroads" uses a local historical collection of utilitarian wares to analyze the trade networks for ceramics in the middle Atlantic region. Finally, Sarah Peabody Turnbaugh gives a cross section of the current analytical methods employed by historical archaeologists.

With analyses such as these in mind, the tedious compilation of local and regional histories comes into clearer focus as the basis for development of a fuller understanding of ceramics as a meaningful medium of material culture. Perhaps more scholars will begin to view such analysis as their primary goal rather than as mere data identification and accumulation.

GENERAL STUDIES AND BIBLIOGRAPHIES

Barber, Edwin AtLee. *The Pottery and Porcelain of the United States: An Historical Review of American Ceramic Art from the Earliest Times to the Present Day; to Which Is Appended a Chapter on the Pottery of Mexico.* 3d ed., rev. and enl. New York: G. P. Putnam's Sons, 1909. xxviii+621 pp.; 333 illustrations, index.

The classic study of American ceramics, this volume is useful for its comprehensiveness as well as for its discussions and illustrations of contemporary production in the United States. The first edition, published in 1893, was reprinted by Century House Americana (Watkins Glen, New York) in 1971; the third edition was reprinted by Feingold and Lewis (New York) in 1976, bound together with a reprint of Barber's *Marks of American Potters* (1904). No one has equalled Barber's contribution, which has stood the test of subsequent research surprisingly well, but two additional early works provide interesting comparison and are important to know for their illustrations and interpretations: John Spargo's *Early American Pottery and China* (New York: Century Co., 1926) and John Ramsay's *American Potters and Pottery* (Boston: Hale, Cushman, and Flint, 1939).

Barber, Edwin AtLee. *Marks of American Potters.* Philadelphia: Patterson and White Co., 1904. 174 pp.; 33 illustrations, approximately 1,000 marks, index.

Barber's classic work is the only comprehensive book on marks of American potters and potteries. It includes marks, dates of operation, and discussion of wares produced. In 1976 this book was reprinted by Feingold and Lewis and bound with Barber's *Pottery and Porcelain of the United States.*

Bruhn, Thomas P. *American Decorative Tiles, 1870–1930.* Exhibition catalogue. Storrs, Conn.: William Benton Museum of Art, University of Connecticut, 1979. 48 pp.; 53 illustrations, bibliography.

This catalogue includes 180 examples that are arranged alphabetically by company name. It also includes a brief but good summary essay on American tile history. Thumbnail sketches of each pottery include location, dates of operation, significant activities, and an individual bibliography. Other considerations of American tiles include E. Stanley Wires, Norris F. Schneider, and Moses Mesre, *Zanesville Decorative Tiles* (Zanesville, Ohio, 1972), and pertinent sections in Julian Barnard, *Victorian Ceramic Tiles* (1972; reprint, New York: Mayflower Books, 1979).

Clark, Garth. *A Century of Ceramics in the United States, 1878–1978: A Study of Its Development.* Exhibition catalogue. New York: E. P. Dutton in association with the Everson Museum of Art, 1979. xxv+371 pp.; 326 black and white illustrations, 40 color plates, bibliographies, index.

The thrust of Clark's essay is that only expressionist ceramics are truly American, all else being derivative. If this bias is overlooked, the volume is useful for the wealth of illustrations and the inclusion of biographies of the many artists represented in the exhibition. It is valuable also for recognizing that the emergence of contemporary studio ceramists was rooted in the art-pottery and porcelain movement following the 1876 Centennial Exhibition. A revised edition by Clark has been published as *American Ceramics, 1876 to the Present* (New York: Abbeville Press, 1987).

Collard, Elizabeth. *Nineteenth-Century Pottery and Porcelain in Canada. See* "English Ceramics in America."

Denker, Ellen, and Bert Denker. *The Main Street Pocket Guide to North American Pottery and Porcelain.* Pittstown, N.J.: Main Street Press, 1985. 256 pp.; approximately 270 black and white illustrations, 50 color plates, bibliography, index. Originally published as Ellen and Bert Denker, *The Warner Collectors' Guide to North American Pottery and Porcelain* (New York: Warner Books, a Main Street Press Book, 1982).

Although billed as a collectors' field guide to quick identification, this volume is useful for its division of North American ceramics into a taxonomy with fifty categories based primarily on the nature of the ceramic body in conjunction with surface decoration. Historical sketches preface each category and, when taken together, present a good general introduction to North American ceramics history.

Derwich, Jenny B., and Mary Latos. *Dictionary Guide to United States Pottery and Porcelain (Nineteenth and Twentieth Century).* Research in United States Pottery and Porcelain. Franklin, Mich.: Jenstan, 1984. 276 pp.; 96 color plates, bibliography.

This work is especially useful for information on many obscure twentieth-century potters and potteries, with facts gained from direct correspondence with the craftsmen or their descendants. Entries are arranged alphabetically by name of potter or pottery; the length and content of the entries vary considerably.

Evans, Paul. *Art Pottery of the United States: An Encyclopedia of Producers and Their Marks.* New York: Charles Scribner's Sons, 1974. 353 pp.; black and white illustrations, 23 color plates, appendixes, index.

The brief but useful introductory essay sets the stage for the rest of this encyclopedic work, which records the histories, products, and marks of the many American potteries that produced artware between 1875 and 1920. Evans's extensive research is well documented by thorough notes that follow each entry. The second edition includes sixty pages of addenda organized by name of pottery; some amend entries in the first edition, while others are newly listed potteries. Also added to the new edition is a twenty-six-page "Directory of Studio Potters Working in the United States through 1960." Short bibliographic essays published between 1970 and 1987 discuss major work on American art potteries and review publications on the history of tilemaking in the United States. For another treatment of similar material, see Ralph and Terry Kovel's *Collector's Guide*.

Frelinghuysen, Alice C. *American Porcelain, 1770–1920.* Exhibition catalogue. New York: Metropolitan Museum of Art, 1989. xv+320 pp.; 52 black and white illustrations, 169 color plates, bibliography, index.

In 1738 Andrew Duché is said to have produced the first porcelain in America, thus predating the making of porcelain in England. Yet the English still want American consumers to believe that there is no tradition for fine porcelain here. From Duché's tentative steps and Bonnin and Morris's first successes in the eighteenth century through the triumphs of early twentieth-century artist potters McLaughlin and Robineau and Lenox's first American-made table service for the White House in 1918, Frelinghuysen disproves this fallacy by tracing more than 150 years of porcelain making in America. That this is the first comprehensive book to be published on the American porcelain industry shows the undeservedly low esteem in which this material has been held previously. A long essay precedes the catalogue of more than 130 examples assembled for an exhibition at the Metropolitan Museum. Frelinghuysen uses period documents (both manuscript and published), family collections, and the objects themselves to explore the technological and economic hurdles that American potters have faced and the design sources that they have used. Each object in the exhibition is given thorough consideration.

Frelinghuysen, Alice Cooney. "Aesthetic Forms in Ceramics and Glass." In Doreen Bolger Burke et al., *In Pursuit of Beauty: Americans and the Aesthetic Movement*, pp. 199–251. Exhibition catalogue. New York: Rizzoli International Publications in association with the Metropolitan Museum of Art, 1986. 52 black and white illustrations, 17 color plates.

European design sources and American cultural milieus are examined to analyze the work of individuals, commercial potteries, and studio potteries producing wares in the aesthetic mode from 1875 to 1885. American potters at the time used a variety of historical styles, including neoclassical, oriental, and Persian, and patterned their designs after examples by contemporary French and English art potters. Frelinghuysen documents Americans' increasing desire to surround themselves with art and culture and the role American potters played in leading and filling these desires on a variety of levels, from classically inspired garden crockery to artistic vases and plaques. Biographies of the potters and decorators are given at the end of the volume.

Gaston, Mary Frank. *American Belleek*. Paducah, Ky.: Collector Books, 1984. 127 pp.; 215 color illustrations, bibliography, index.

About 1870 in Belleek, Ireland, a cream-color porcelain was first slip-cast into extremely thin, extravagant shapes and covered with a pearly glaze. The technology for this ware was transferred to the United States via Trenton, New Jersey, in 1883. Although the glaze was eventually discarded in favor of painted decoration in the English and Austrian manners, the body remained and has been referred to as American belleek. The textual information here for the thirteen New Jersey and American companies that have made belleek is brief and not always accurate, but the illustrations of objects and marks are useful.

Greer, Georgeanna H. *American Stonewares: The Art and Craft of Utilitarian Potters*. Exton, Pa.: Schiffer Publishing, 1981. 286 pp.; approximately 335 black and white illustrations, 16 color plates, line drawings, appendix, glossary, bibliographies, index.

Greer analyzes the European background, history, and technology of American utilitarian stoneware. Southern and midwestern potteries are pictured and discussed in abundance along with the usual northeastern wares. A welcome decision is the inclusion of mundane as well as unusual and beautiful examples. Illustrations include potters at work, tools, and line drawings of form variations as well as photographs of wares.

Guilland, Harold F. *Early American Folk Pottery*. Philadelphia: Chilton Book Co., 1971. vi+322 pp.; black and white and color illustrations, bibliography, index.

The wealth of visual and documentary material contained in the Index of American Design generated by the Works Progress Administration in the 1930s has been tapped for this look at American redware and stoneware. The first quarter of the volume is text, which provides a setting for the many illustrations that seem to have been arranged with no particular method in mind. The essay describes the American colonial world and the earthenware and stoneware traditions of the eighteenth and nineteenth centuries and concludes with some comments on design. Based on old secondary sources, the textual information is stale and not entirely accurate, but the Index pictures and captions taken from documents filed with them are invaluable.

Hillier, Bevis. *Pottery and Porcelain, 1700–1914: England, Europe, and North America*. See "Continental and Oriental Ceramics in America"; "English Ceramics in America."

Ketchum, William C., Jr. *The Pottery and Porcelain Collector's Handbook: A Guide to Early American Ceramics from Maine to California*. New York: Funk and Wagnalls, 1971. xx+204 pp.; approximately 33 illustrations, appendix, index.

When compared with Marvin D. Schwartz's *Collectors' Guide to Antique American Ceramics*, Ketchum's volume is not well illustrated, but it has the advantage of including makers west of East Liverpool, Ohio. Discussion has been divided by type of clay body (redware, stoneware, yellowware, and whiteware) and then by region (East, South, Midwest, and West). The introduction provides a collectors' guide to further research, although its relatively early date precludes the wealth of material published since 1971.

Kovel, Ralph, and Terry Kovel. *The Kovels' Collector's Guide to American Art Pottery.* New York: Crown Publishers, 1974. vi+378 pp.; black and white and color illustrations, bibliographies, index.

No analytical essay relieves the encylopedic nature of this volume as with Paul Evans's *Art Pottery of the United States*, but the Kovels' work is valuable because more potteries have been included, and tilemakers are treated separately (Evans does not cover tilemakers). Footnotes are replaced here with bibliographies for each pottery cited, so information can be confirmed only with difficulty. Collectors and students of American art pottery usually include both Evans's and the Kovels' books in their libraries.

Lehner, Lois. *Complete Book of American Kitchen and Dinner Wares.* Des Moines: Wallace-Homestead Book Co., 1980. 240 pp.; illustrations, bibliography, index.

Lehner's encyclopedia of manufacturers arranged alphabetically includes many twentieth-century potteries not encountered elsewhere. In lieu of an introductory essay, she gives a chronology of whiteware production developments, some definitions, a few points to keep in mind for sorting out identification problems, and a list of various aspects of the industry that might have formed the basis of an introduction if one had been written. For its many illustrations, see also Jo Cunningham, *The Collector's Encyclopedia of American Dinnerware* (Paducah, Ky.: Collector Books, 1982). For a brief overview of the subject from 1735 to 1980 drawn largely from secondary sources, see Susan E. Pickel, *From Kiln to Kitchen: American Ceramic Design in Tableware* (Springfield: Illinois State Museum, 1980).

Leibowitz, Joan. *Yellow Ware: The Transitional Ceramic.* Exton, Pa.: Schiffer Publishing, 1985. 119 pp.; black and white illustrations, approximately 70 black and white and 75 color plates, bibliography, index.

Yellowware is the type of crockery that eventually replaced redware in American kitchens during the third quarter of the nineteenth century. A thick, coarse, serviceable pottery, yellowware has been produced by manufacturers throughout North America since about 1825. After introducing the product, Leibowitz traces its history from the major manufactories in New Jersey and Ohio to smaller companies in New England, the middle Atlantic region, and the Midwest. The many forms of this ware are listed and described in a separate chapter. Leibowitz concludes with a section on English makers that illustrates the difficulty of determining whether England or the United States was the country of origin for any individual unmarked example. This is basically a collectors' guide, but the numerous illustrations from trade catalogues and advertising broadsides add enormously to the book's usefulness. For a similar approach with an attractive presentation, but without the documentary illustrations included in Leibowitz's book, see William C. Ketchum, Jr., *American Country Pottery: Yellowware and Spongeware* (New York: Alfred A. Knopf, 1987).

Maddock, Archibald M., II. *The Polished Earth: A History of the Pottery Plumbing Fixture Industry in the United States.* Trenton, N.J.: Privately printed, 1962. xi+382 pp.; illustrations, appendix, index.

A descendant of the founder of the pottery plumbing-fixture industry in America, Maddock takes the long view, placing his ancestors' contributions within the history of sanitation and hygiene from the birth of civilization to 1960, although he concentrates on the period since 1875. Along the way, he also considers American ceramics history with special reference to the Trenton industry, technological developments in ceramics, and workers' health conditions. This is a rare book, but definitely worth finding for its information on the history of sanitation.

Rebert, M. Charles. *American Majolica, 1850–1900.* Des Moines: Wallace-Homestead Book Co., 1981. 86 pp.; approximately 60 black and white and 30 color illustrations, bibliography, index.

Basically a soft, cheap earthenware, nineteenth-century majolica is most interesting visually for the interplay of brilliant coloring with its rustic, even at times trompe l'oeil, shapes. Rebert provides a collector's approach to identification of wares and recitation of pottery histories, and the introduction purporting to offer historical context is too simplistic to be accurate. But these were popular wares which are well worth studying, and Rebert provides a beginning, at least in the illustrations and identification of American manufacturers of these wares.

Robinson, Dorothy, and Bill Feeny. *The Official Price Guide to American Pottery and Porcelain.* Orlando, Fla.: House of Collectibles, 1980. 550 pp.; illustrations.

The title of this book is extraordinarily misleading. Although it includes a price guide, it contains primarily Robinson's individual histories of Trenton, New Jersey, potteries, her guide to dating Lenox china's marks, and brief biographies of many of Trenton's leading potters and decorators (included only in the first edition). This guide is not interpretive, but provides some important raw data that extends and sometimes corrects Barber's much earlier work. *See* Edwin AtLee Barber, *Marks of American Potters*; Edwin AtLee Barber, *The Pottery and Porcelain of the United States*.

Schwartz, Marvin D. *Collectors' Guide to Antique American Ceramics*. Garden City, N.Y.: Doubleday, 1969. x + 134 pp.; 109 illustrations, index.

Largely illustrated with objects from Brooklyn Museum's important collection of American ceramics, this slim volume offers a general overview of eastern American earthenware, stoneware, and porcelain, with consideration for their foreign antecedents from the earliest days of European settlement through the early 1900s. There is not much detail here; rather, it provides a quick way to learn the basics.

Stradling, Diana, and G. Garrison Stradling, eds. *The Art of the Potter: Redware and Stoneware*. New York: Main Street/Universe Books, 1977. 158 pp.; illustrations, index.

Fifty-six useful articles on American redware and stoneware potteries which were published originally in *Antiques* between 1922 and 1974 have been selected and arranged by the Stradlings, who have also provided an introduction. The articles are divided by material; those on redware are grouped by whether the pottery showed German or English influences, while those on stoneware are organized geographically. A few articles on archaeology and manufacturing techniques are also included. Some of these articles represent the beginning of continuing study on a particular pottery, while others constitute the sum total of what is in print on a given craftsman.

Strong, Susan R. *History of American Ceramics: An Annotated Bibliography*. Metuchen, N.J., and London: Scarecrow Press, 1983. xxii + 184 pp.; indexes.

The 629 entries in this work are divided into twenty-two categories ranging from general history to technical considerations: wares, potters, and potteries are arranged by name. All entries are thoughtfully annotated to provide guidance. Chapters in books not entirely devoted to American ceramics are also included. A useful introduction describes and analyzes the history of publishing on American ceramics.

Sudbury, Byron. "Historic Clay Tobacco Pipemakers in the United States." *British Archaeological Reports International* 60 (1979): 151–341. 69 illustrations, bibliography.

Data summarized from secondary sources, correspondence, and fieldwork is presented for twenty-four states arranged alphabetically. Unfortunately, no overview of the American industry is presented, although clay tobacco pipes have been made here since the seventeenth century.

Webster, Donald Blake. *Decorated Stoneware Pottery of North America*. Rutland, Vt.: Charles E. Tuttle Co., 1971. 232 pp.; 300 illustrations, checklist, glossary, bibliography, index.

A relatively early study of blue-decorated salt-glazed stoneware, Webster's book classifies these goods by motif, a system useful to the student of iconography but useless to one wishing for an economic or historical approach. Webster's book provides a visual collection of the most highly decorated examples from the northeastern states. Although technology is covered, Georgeanna H. Greer's analysis of this aspect, in *American Stonewares*, is much better.

Weidner, Ruth Irwin, comp. *American Ceramics before 1930: A Bibliography*. Westport, Conn.: Greenwood Press, 1982. xx + 279 pp.; indexes.

The 2,922 entries listed by Weidner are divided by type of publication, such as books and pamphlets, chapters, catalogues, trade publications, and periodicals. Although neither annotated nor exhaustive, this bibliography is extremely useful to the student who does not have adequate research facilities at hand.

Wetherbee, Jean. *A Look at White Ironstone*. Des Moines: Wallace-Homestead Book Co., 1980. 159 pp.; 105 illustrations, line drawings, bibliography, index.

White ironstone was a staple tableware in America from the 1840s through the 1890s and was made principally in North America and England. Although most of this volume concentrates on English manufacturers, one chapter is devoted to North American companies that produced wares between 1860 and 1900 and provides a brief overview of the major manufacturers, supplemented with a list of nearly fifty firms. *See also* "English Ceramics in America."

Young, Jennie J. *The Ceramic Art: A Compendium of the History and Manufacture of Pottery and Porcelain*. New York: Harper and Brothers, 1878. 499 pp.; 464 illustrations, index.

Students can easily overlook this volume because it is primarily on foreign ceramics, but it is important in the history of published works on American ceramics because it is the earliest book to include information on the subject, and it is written from a sympathetic American viewpoint (most opinions on American ceramics expressed at the time were derogatory). A lively discussion of manufacturers is especially useful in combination with Edwin AtLee Barber's *Pottery and Porcelain of the United States*.

REGIONAL STUDIES

Adamson, Jack E. *Illustrated Handbook of Ohio Sewer Pipe Folk Art*. Barberton, Ohio: By the author, 1973. [86] pp.; illustrations, glossary.

"Drainage tile" would be a nicer term for the industrial product from which these figures, planters, bookends, lamps, match holders, and assorted whimsies were made, mostly as offhand gifts and souvenirs, beginning in the late nineteenth century. Ohio was the center for this clay genre. This book is composed of photographs and descriptions of Adamson's collection, which also includes advertisements and postcards of tile factories. A list of individuals and companies represented in the collection is appended. Although not interpretive, the book offers a good look at the broad range of forms and styles employed by the laborers who worked this material.

Antonelli, Marylu, and Jack Forbes. *Pottery in Alberta: The Long Tradition*. Edmonton: University of Alberta Press, 1978. 189 pp.; black and white and color illustrations, glossary.

This work emphasizes history and process rather than product. Because the tradition of working clay in Alberta is largely industrial, this volume stands as a welcome foil to the studies of traditional Canadian pottery. *See* David L. Newlands, *Early Ontario Potters*; Donald Webster, *Early Canadian Pottery*.

Barber, Edwin AtLee. *Tulip Ware of the Pennsylvania-German Potters: An Historical Sketch of the Art of Slip-Decoration in the United States*. New introduction by Henry J. Kauffman. 1903. Reprint. New York: Dover Publications, 1970. 233 pp.; 95 illustrations, index.

Potters serving Pennsylvania German communities in eastern Pennsylvania produced some of the most visually and verbally exciting redware in North America between circa 1730 and 1850. Barber analyzes this distinctive ware by placing it within the contexts of Pennsylvania German society, dialect, and literature, of European precedents, and of contemporary production methods and decorations in America.

Barka, Norman F., Edward Ayres, and Christine Sheriden. *The "Poor Potter" of Yorktown: A Study of a Colonial Pottery Factory*. 3 vols. Yorktown Research Series no. 5. Vol. 1, *History*; vol. 2, *Archaeology*; vol. 3, *Ceramics*. Denver: National Park Service, 1984. xvii, xv, xv+615 pp.; 308 illustrations, 26 tables, appendixes.

The Yorktown, Virginia, pottery of William Rogers operated between circa 1720 and circa 1745 and made standard earthenware as well as surprisingly good English-quality brown salt-glazed stoneware. Described to English authorities as that of a "poor potter" by Lt. Gov. William Gooch, Rogers's enterprise was a successful, sizable, highly skilled operation that greatly enhanced his social and economic well-being. This final archaeological report is the culmination of eighteen years' work and is the most complete documentation of a single American colonial pottery site. Divided into three volumes, the report covers the history of the factory and its owner based on written sources, with reference to English mercantilism and colonial manufacture; a detailed description of the site, kilns, factory, and other features with reference to European kilns of the period; and a discussion of the factory's products, including physical features and probable community functions.

Barrett, Richard Carter. *Bennington Pottery and Porcelain: A Guide to Identification*. Photographs by Lloyd Oppenheimer. New York: Crown Publishers, 1958. iv+347 pp.; 462 black and white and 7 color illustrations, index.

Much has been written on the potteries of Bennington, Vermont, because they produced more ware over a longer period of time than other areas in New England, a region that attracted early collectors of Americana. Although some of the work of Bennington's potters was at the forefront of American ceramics design and technology, particularly during the mid nineteenth century, Bennington production usually mirrored the historical development of the American industry in general. For example, collectors still refer to yellowware with a mottled brown glaze (rockingham) as Bennington, although this was only one of many areas from New England to Illinois where it was produced. Barrett's and John Spargo's books have helped to create and sustain this misnomer. Barrett's is the larger of the two works and contains many more illustrations than Spargo's more readable and often reprinted *Potters and Potteries of Bennington* (Boston: Houghton Mifflin Co., 1926).

Bensch, Christopher. *The Blue and the Gray: Oneida County Stoneware*. Exhibition catalogue. Utica, N.Y.: Museum of Art, Munson-Williams-Proctor Institute, 1987. 80 pp.; 180 illustrations, bibliography.

Located on the Erie Canal, Oneida County was a major stoneware center, best known today for work produced in the White family's potteries. This illustrated catalogue is arranged by form, with an introduction that focuses on the roles of stoneware in the nineteenth century and on how changes in public perception of stoneware's usefulness altered the types and decorations produced in Oneida County between 1825 and 1907. During these years, the manufacture of traditional, simple jars, jugs, and churns gave way to a variety of highly ornamented forms related to food and drink, including water coolers, mugs for beer or soft drinks, coffeepots, commercial food packages, and pitchers. Much of the later decoration was influenced by the German heritage of the workers. Although informative in a general way, this should not be construed as the definitive study on the Whites' work.

Bivins, John, Jr. *The Moravian Potters in North Carolina*. Chapel Hill: University of North Carolina Press for Old Salem, 1972. xiii+300 pp.; 276 black and white illustrations, color plates, glossaries, bibliography, index.

The master potters of the Moravian community in North Carolina turned out traditional utilitarian and decorative redware for their brethren during the late 1700s and early 1800s and established a local style adopted by non-Moravians as well, although some attempts were made in the late eighteenth century to produce English-style decorated creamware. Bivins's classic study discusses this folk pottery, which was transported to American soil but was closely tied to its European roots in process and product. He uses archaeology, surviving objects, and records of the brethren to reconstruct this history. *See also* "Craftsmen."

Branin, M. Lelyn. *The Early Makers of Handcrafted Earthenware and Stoneware in Central and Southern New Jersey*. Rutherford, N.J.: Fairleigh Dickinson University Press, 1988. 266 pp.; approximately 90 illustrations, appendixes, bibliography, index.

Centrally located on the East Coast between New York and Philadelphia and blessed with abundant clay resources, New Jersey has a complex ceramics history beginning with the delftware pottery of proprietor Daniel Coxe (ca. 1688) and continuing today with major dinnerware and sanitary, tile, and industrial ceramics factories that are still active. Branin focuses on the traditional and preindustrial potteries in central and southern New Jersey from the seventeenth to the early twentieth centuries and avoids the complexities of the large nineteenth-century industrial developments in the northeastern quadrant of the state and in Trenton after 1850. Using genealogical, census, land, and probate records, along with local and regional commercial directories, extant pottery price lists, and archaeological evidence, Branin details the lives of these potters, which are organized more or less chronologically by the town or region where they lived. Although some wares are illustrated, this is primarily a descriptive documentary study with little interpretation. Due to the enormity of the subject, however, Branin's achievement is formidable and provides excellent material for complex analysis in the future, especially because the sources are well documented in extensive footnotes.

Branin, M. Lelyn. *The Early Potters and Potteries of Maine*. Middletown, Conn.: Wesleyan University Press, 1978. xvi+262 pp.; approximately 65 illustrations, map, appendixes. Simultaneously published at Augusta: Maine State Museum.

Branin's documentary history focuses on traditional and industrial utilitarian pottery divided by locality. Two short introductory chapters set the context and briefly discuss historical trends. A large state with a relatively small rural population, Maine supported barely 100 potteries in fewer than forty-five communities between circa 1740 and circa 1890. While most of these served the local population, Portland's nineteenth-century potteries had a larger vision and, like Susan H. Myers's Philadelphia group, in *Handcraft to Industry*, made the transition from household to industrial forms. Branin includes marks of Maine potters, excerpts of potter's documents, and checklists of early potters and pottery owners.

Bray, Hazel V. *The Potter's Art in California, 1885 to 1955*. Exhibition catalogue. Oakland, Calif.: Oakland Museum Art Department, 1980. viii+86 pp.; 27 duotone illustrations, 10 color plates.

This catalogue is divided into two parts: art potteries and potters working from 1885 to 1930, and studio potters active from 1930 to 1955. Informative biographical entries on fifty-two potteries follow two short essays on these larger divisions. Because artware is only one aspect of California's active pottery industry, this volume should not be regarded as comprehensive.

Burrison, John A. *Brothers in Clay: The Story of Georgia Folk Pottery*. Athens: University of Georgia Press, 1983. xviii+326 pp.; 154 black and white illustrations, 12 color plates, 3 maps, bibliography, indexes.

In this model study of traditional pottery making, Burrison blends documentary research with objects and living craftsmen in an evocative style unlike most ceramics histories. Parts 1 and 2 consider pottery products in the contexts of use and business, the folk potter as artisan and member of a craft dynasty, and the technology of southern ash-glaze stoneware. Part 3 relates a selective history of traditional pottery making in Georgia on a geographic basis from circa 1740 to the present. *See also* "Craftsmen."

Clay in the Hands of the Potter: An Exhibition of Pottery Manufactured in the Rochester and Genesee Valley Region, c. 1793–1900. Exhibition catalogue. Rochester, N.Y.: Rochester Museum and Science Center, 1974. 56 pp.; illustrations, illustrated catalogue, bibliography.

Written records, supplemented by archaeological evidence and surviving examples, form the basis of this catalogue. Extensive historical analysis is absent, but the distinctiveness of the redware and stoneware produced in this region is exciting. These objects include early to mid nineteenth-century redware decorated with marbled and trailed-slip or mottled-lead glazes in the New England style or made up to look like stoneware, as well as later stoneware with fancy blue decoration.

Corbett, Cynthia Arps. *Useful Art: Long Island Pottery*. Setauket, N.Y.: Society for the Preservation of Long Island Antiquities, 1985. 79 pp.; illustrations.

Utilitarian redware and stoneware made on Long Island are the focus of Corbett's study in which many pieces and documents are drawn together. Because this was originally an exhibition catalogue, it is organized as a series of three essays on the major geographic regions of pottery making: Brooklyn, Huntington, and the eastern end of the island. Each essay is followed by illustrations of the wares produced, accompanied by an extensive entry for each object.

Curtis, Phillip H. "The Production of Tucker Porcelain, 1826–1838: A Reevaluation." In *Ceramics in America*, edited by Ian M. G. Quimby, pp. 339–74. Winterthur Conference Report 1972. Charlottesville: University Press of Virginia for the Henry Francis du Pont Winterthur Museum, 1973. 10 illustrations.

William Ellis Tucker's American China Manufactory is considered the first large, commercially successful porcelain enterprise in the United States, although it was ultimately unable to compete in the American marketplace with European manufacturers of wares in the same French empire style. Even today it is difficult to distinguish Tucker's unmarked wares from the large quantities of extant French examples. Curtis used company account books, formula and price books, and line drawings in the collection of Philadelphia Museum of Art for his historical analysis of the company and its production. A review is offered of physical details that might be used to sort out Tucker's unmarked work from similar French wares.

Darling, Sharon S. *Chicago Ceramics and Glass: An Illustrated History from 1871 to 1933*. Photographs by Walter W. Krutz. Exhibition catalogue. Chicago: Chicago Historical Society, 1979. xiii+221 pp.; 221 black and white and color illustrations, index.

A detailed study of ceramics and glass, Darling's book interrelates the makers, their products, and their markets in Chicago, where architectural terra-cotta and hand-painted china were the principal contributions to ceramic arts. Northwestern Terra Cotta Company, Gates Terra Cotta Company, the china painting studios of Pickard, and the development of a distinctive china-decorating style by the ladies of the Atlan Club are covered in depth.

Denker, Ellen Paul. "Ceramics at the Crossroads: American Pottery at New York's Gateway, 1750–1900." *Staten Island Historian* 3, nos. 3–4 (Winter–Spring 1986): 21–36. 31 illustrations.

The impressive collection of locally owned utilitarian pottery now belonging to the Staten Island Historical Society, local inventories, histories of regional potteries, and archaeological remains of Staten Island households are used to analyze regional trade networks for American ceramics. Staten Islanders did not have a viable local pottery industry to draw on for their household needs. Instead, they gathered wares made in potteries along the middle Atlantic coast from Norwalk, Connecticut, to Philadelphia.

Denker, Ellen Paul. *The Kirkpatricks' Pottery at Anna, Illinois*. Exhibition catalogue. Champaign: University of Illinois, 1986. 32 pp.; 25 black and white and 3 color illustrations, checklist.

Brothers Cornwall and Wallace Kirkpatrick made some very imaginative stoneware sculpture along with the sturdy utilitarian stoneware forms that were the stock-in-trade of their late nineteenth-century southern Illinois pottery. Temperance jugs covered with writhing snakes and metaphorical whiskey flasks in the shape of pigs are the best known of their symbolic menagerie. Documentation of the brothers' personal histories, combined with analysis of their wide-ranging sources and meanings of their work, shows that artists in a rural location with rustic imaginations could create artistically sophisticated and intellectually complex sculpture from humble salt-glazed stoneware.

DePasquale, Dan, Gail DePasquale, and Larry Peterson. *Red Wing Stoneware*. Paducah, Ky.: Collector Books, 1983. 160 pp.; approximately 24 black and white and 289 color plates, index.

Between 1877 and 1967, the stoneware potteries of Red Wing, Minnesota, turned out millions of crocks, jugs, water coolers, cuspidors, flowerpots, fruit jars, cooking pots, pie plates, pitchers, and other miscellaneous useful forms. Although more space is devoted to reasons for collecting these wares than to the companies' histories, this small volume illustrates hundreds of pieces of the utilitarian wares produced by the potteries. More work remains to be done, however, on this important pottery town.

Detweiler, Susan Gray. *George Washington's Chinaware*. *See* "English Ceramics in America."

Gates, William C., Jr. *The City of Hills and Kilns: Life and Work in East Liverpool, Ohio*. East Liverpool: East Liverpool Historical Society, 1984. viii+500 pp.; illustrations, 13 tables, index.

Gates traces the growth and development of the economic, social, and political life of East Liverpool, Ohio, where pottery was the foremost industry from circa 1850 until World War II. The rapid rise in this industry from regional to national importance altered East Liverpool from a sleepy river town to an urban center, and the decline in the industry has led to the city's economic depression since the war. Gates's study presents a portrait of an industry as well as a city, because the products of East Liverpool's kilns covered the tables and stuffed the cupboards of middle America. This is not a picture book for light readers, but a serious community study that offers excellent documentation and analysis of the subject despite being somewhat overwritten and cumbersome. For a companion piece on the marks and manufacturers of East Liverpool, see William C. Gates, Jr., and Dana E. Ormerod, "The East Liverpool Pottery District."

Gates, William C., Jr., and Dana E. Ormerod. "The East Liverpool Pottery District: Identification of Manufacturers and Marks." *Historical Archaeology* 16, nos. 1–2 (1982): 1–358. 314 illustrations, appendixes, bibliography, indexes.

Since the Civil War, the bulk of American dinnerware has been made in either East Liverpool, Ohio, or Trenton, New Jersey. Therefore, this volume, designed for use by historical archaeologists, deals with a large proportion of prominent American potteries. It includes a historical introduction to East Liverpool's pottery industry, brief sketches of eighty-five individual firms, and identification of more than 900 marks. For historical and cultural analysis of East Liverpool and its ceramics industry, see William C. Gates, Jr., *The City of Hills and Kilns*.

Hood, Graham. *Bonnin and Morris of Philadelphia: The First American Porcelain Factory, 1770–1772.* An Institute Book on the Arts and Material Culture in Early America. Chapel Hill: University of North Carolina Press for the Institute of Early American History and Culture, 1972. xiii+78 pp.+56 black and white plates; appendixes, index.

Gousse Bonnin and George Morris were the first investors to make porcelain for public consumption in America. Their valiant efforts, however, were undercut by the collapse of the Non-Importation Agreement and the ensuing open competition from European and Asian manufacturers. Hood's fascinating account outlines the brief history of this company and its owners and documents some of their wares through the report of an archaeological investigation of the site. This work adds substantially to what little information existed previously.

Humphreys, Sherry B., and Johnell L. Schmidt. *Texas Pottery: Caddo Indian to Contemporary.* Exhibition catalogue. Washington, Tex.: Star of the Republic Museum, 1976. 45 pp.; black and white and color illustrations, drawings, bibliography.

This work provides a brief and general look at Texas pottery, including native American, traditional Anglo-American utilitarian wares, and contemporary studio art pottery.

Indiana Stoneware. Catalogue by Peggy A. Loar; foreword by Carl J. Weinhardt, Jr.; introduction by Don D. Moore. Exhibition catalogue. Indianapolis: Indianapolis Museum of Art, 1974. 48 pp.; 84 illustrations, appendixes.

This catalogue features stoneware made by nineteenth-century utilitarian potteries as well as twentieth-century artist-potters. The catalogue essay provides background history and perspective.

James, Arthur E. *The Potters and Potteries of Chester County, Pennsylvania.* 1947. 2d ed. Reprint. Exton, Pa.: Schiffer Publishing, 1978. 208 pp.; illustrations, checklist, bibliography.

James presents basically a documentary history, but he includes enough illustrations to define the visual characteristics of nineteenth-century Chester County pottery, such as imaginative figures, inscribed and dated presentation pieces, frilly redware flowerpots, majolica, and stoneware decorated with blue flower vines. Traditional and industrial potteries are also included. Chapters on historical context, technology, and wares precede the main body of the text, which is divided alphabetically by potter's name.

Ketchum, William C., Jr. *Early Potters and Potteries of New York State.* New York: Funk and Wagnalls, 1970. x+278 pp.; 19 illustrations, bibliography, index.

For his discussion of New York State's long and active history of pottery making before 1900, Ketchum divides the territory into geographic regions, beginning with the earliest population centers of Manhattan, Long Island, and the Hudson valley and then moving westward. This is basically a documentary history with little attention paid to actual objects. A short introduction gives an overview of the state's history within the larger context of the Northeast. A preliminary chapter on potters' methods and wares provides technological background for the histories that follow. Also included are a list of New York potters and their marks and a bibliography by county. A greatly revised edition has recently become available as William C. Ketchum, Jr., *Potters and Potteries of New York State, 1650–1900* (Syracuse, N.Y.: Syracuse University Press, 1987).

Lasansky, Jeannette. *Central Pennsylvania Redware Pottery, 1780–1904.* Lewisburg, Pa.: Union County Oral Traditions Projects, 1979. 60 pp.; duotone illustrations, 1 color plate, bibliography, checklist, index.

This book proves to be a model study of what kinds of pictorial, material, written, and oral documentation to accumulate for analysis of a regional pottery industry. Introductory essays on historical development and redware technology provide contexts for the analysis by county. Also included are a list of potters by county and a township list of pertinent collections.

Lasansky, Jeannette. *Made of Mud: Stoneware Potteries in Central Pennsylvania, 1831–1929.* An Oral Traditions Project. University Park: Pennsylvania State University Press, a Keystone Book, 1979. 60 pp.; duotone illustrations, appendix, bibliography, index.

Lasansky documents and illustrates nineteenth-century potters, potteries, and wares of central Pennsylvania. An introduction provides an overall context for the period and places makers in historical perspective for the locale. Her discussion of potteries is by county. Wares, tools, broadsides, and potters at work are illustrated. Also included are a list of potters and marks by location and a time line of potters by location.

Lehner, Lois. *Ohio Pottery and Glass Marks and Manufacturers.* Des Moines: Wallace-Homestead Book Co., 1978. 113 pp.; illustrations, bibliographies, index.

Although arranged by county, manufacturers also can be found by a separate alphabetical listing. Except for the nationally known makers, entries are quite brief. This book is incomplete, but it supplements other studies that focus on a particular city or county in Ohio, such as William C. Gates, Jr., and Dana E. Ormerod, "The East Liverpool Pottery District."

Myers, Susan H. *Handcraft to Industry: Philadelphia Ceramics in the First Half of the Nineteenth Century.* Smithsonian Studies in History and Technology, no. 43. Washington, D.C.: Smithsonian Institution Press, 1980. 117 pp.; 32 illustrations, appendixes.

Potters working in a major East Coast urban center faced a different economic world than their counterparts in the countryside. This important essay analyzes the transition in Philadelphia's potteries from preindustrial to industrial shop organization and products during the first half of the nineteenth century. Key indicators of this transition as noted by Myers may be applied in other studies to determine if potters' experiences were similar in different settings.

Myers, Susan H. "Marketing American Pottery: Maulden Perrine in Baltimore." *Winterthur Portfolio* 19, no. 1 (Spring 1984): 51–66. 11 illustrations, 1 table.

Myers uses the complete 1839/40 daybook of Baltimore utilitarian potter Perrine as a case study of the marketing strategy of an urban East Coast potter during the years that American industry was expanding. Although Perrine's manufacturing methods were basically traditional, his distribution system reflected the changing relationship between producer and consumer in an urban setting.

New Jersey Pottery to 1840. Exhibition catalogue. Trenton: New Jersey State Museum, [1972]. 48 pp.; approximately 85 illustrations, bibliography.

New Jersey has been a major center for ceramic production since the late seventeenth century. This catalogue is still the only recent study that considers early potters and their wares statewide. Its value lies in its illustrations, which should be used in conjunction with information in earlier publications: *The Pottery and Porcelain of New Jersey* (Newark, N.J.: Newark Museum, 1947) and *Early Arts of New Jersey: The Potters' Art c. 1680–c. 1900* (Trenton: New Jersey State Museum, 1956). For the only published consideration of Trenton's important contributions to American ceramics history, see Ellen Denker and Bert Denker, "The Staffordshire of America," in *A Capital Place: The Story of Trenton,* ed. M. A. Quigley and D. Collier (Woodland Hills, Calif.: Windsor Publications,

1984), pp. 56–67. For information on early central and southern New Jersey earthenware and stoneware potters, see M. Lelyn Branin, *The Early Makers of Handcrafted Earthenware and Stoneware.* For histories of Trenton potteries, see Dorothy Robinson and Bill Feeny, *The Official Price Guide to American Pottery and Porcelain.*

Newlands, David L. *Early Ontario Potters: Their Craft and Trade.* Toronto and New York: McGraw-Hill Ryerson, 1979. vii+245 pp.; approximately 240 illustrations, appendixes, bibliography, index.

Newlands's emphasis is on makers of utilitarian wares rather than artistic goods. The illustrations and text of the chapter on the potters' craft would be a valuable introduction to any study of utilitarian wares and their makers. Rarely found images, such as that of the once ubiquitous willow shipping crate, offer exciting surprises. An analysis of the infancy, heyday, and decline of Ontario's pottery industry is followed by the bulk of the text divided into chapters by county.

Osgood, Cornelius. *The Jug and Related Stoneware of Bennington.* Rutland, Vt., and Tokyo: Charles E. Tuttle Co., 1971. 222 pp.; 35 black and white illustrations, 23 black and white and 8 color plates, appendixes, bibliography, index.

Osgood studies Bennington's stoneware made from circa 1820 to circa 1895 specifically, but because the industry there reflected the historical movement of American stoneware, his treatise is applicable to similar objects made across the country. For years Osgood's book was the best source on the technology of stoneware, and it remains useful for its good, clear process descriptions and fine illustrations, although it has recently been superseded by works like Georgeanna H. Greer's *American Stonewares.*

Peck, Herbert. *The Book of Rookwood Pottery.* New York: Crown Publishers, 1968. viii+184 pp.; black and white and color illustrations, bibliography, index.

Rookwood Pottery is the best known of the American art potteries because of its early beginnings, longevity, and the high quality of its work. Begun by Maria Longworth Nichols, a prominent member of Cincinnati society, the pottery maintained for many years a studio atmosphere in which earthenware forms produced by experienced potters and molders were decorated in underglaze slips by academy-trained artists. As a consequence of its important position in the history of American ceramics and the arts and crafts movement, several studies of Rookwood have been published. Peck's is the earliest and most general. For a more specialized study, see Kenneth R. Trapp, *Ode to Nature: Flowers and Landscapes of the Rookwood Pottery, 1880–1940* (New York: Jordan-Volpe Gallery, 1980). A development of Rookwood is discussed in *The Ladies, God Bless 'Em: The Women's Art Movement in Cincinnati in the Nineteenth Century* (Cincinnati: Cincinnati Art Museum, 1976).

Poesch, Jessie. *Newcomb Pottery: An Enterprise for Southern Women, 1895–1940*. Marks and dating by Walter Bob; catalogue by Sally Main Spanola. Exhibition catalogue. Exton, Pa.: Schiffer Publishing, 1984. 160 pp.; 27 black and white illustrations, 78 color plates, drawings, illustrated catalogue, appendixes, bibliography, index.

Newcomb Pottery was founded as part of the art program at Newcomb College, the women's division of Tulane University, because southern women's opportunities for economic survival in the arts were few. Although men did most of the heavy work, women graduates of Newcomb's art program were the decorators. Poesch's excellent history of this organization's principals, artists, and products yields many insights into the roles of women and schools in the arts and crafts movement. Included are biographies of the potters and decorators, Bob's key to dating Newcomb marks, and Spanola's catalogue of the Newcomb Pottery exhibition circulated by Smithsonian Institution Traveling Exhibition Service between 1984 and 1987. An earlier, charming, but less intellectual study is Suzanne Ormond and Mary E. Irvine, *Louisiana's Art Nouveau: The Crafts of the Newcomb Style* (Gretna, La.: Pelican Publishing, 1976).

Regional Aspects of American Folk Pottery. Exhibition catalogue. York, Pa.: Historical Society of York County, 1974. [56] pp.; 121 illustrations.

Regional variations of eastern utilitarian redware and stoneware are described and illustrated in this small catalogue. This is still the best quick introduction to distinctive regional forms and methods of decoration in New England, the middle Atlantic states, Virginia, and North Carolina. The text was written by J. J. Smith.

Schaltenbrand, Phil. *Old Pots: Salt-Glazed Stoneware of the Greensboro–New Geneva Region*. Hanover, Pa.: Everybodys Press, [1977]. ix+89 pp.; 74 illustrations, appendix, bibliography.

Large, nearby clay beds suitable for stoneware provided the basis for development of a major pottery industry in southwestern Pennsylvania. Additional factors in this development were a rapidly increasing population and easy water transportation routes. For nearly a century, beginning about 1840, the stoneware industry thrived in Greensboro and New Geneva, as well as in smaller towns nearby. Schaltenbrand sketches histories for all these potteries, speculates on the reasons for their decline after World War I, and describes the various pottery-making processes that pertain to the period under investigation. This book is primarily useful for identifying pottery from this region.

Smith, Samuel D., and Stephen T. Rogers. *A Survey of Historic Pottery Making in Tennessee*. Division of Archaeology Research Series no. 3. Nashville: Tennessee Department of Conservation, 1979. x+159 pp.; 21 illustrations, drawings, maps, charts, tables, appendixes, bibliography.

Based on two years of archival research and field site surveys, this study divides the information by region (east, middle, and west) and then by county. A discussion of regional distribution and traditions of Tennessee pottery making introduces the entries. Also included are appendixes on potters' marks, pipe production, ceramic grave markers, and technology.

Sweezy, Nancy. *Raised in Clay: The Southern Pottery Tradition*. Washington, D.C.: Smithsonian Institution Press for the Office of Folklife Programs, 1984. 280 pp.; black and white and color illustrations, line drawings, bibliography.

Sweezy's book accompanied an exhibition which was "designed to document the last generation of potters to have direct contact with preindustrial pottery traditions" (p. 10). Chapters giving historical perspective and technological explanations precede entries on thirty-five individual potteries. Entries are divided by type: utilitarian stoneware, unglazed horticultural pottery, and twentieth-century glazed wares. Numerous quotations from the potters provide additional insight into their interaction with process and product.

The Traditional Pottery of Alabama. Essays by E. Henry Willett and Joey Brackner. Exhibition catalogue. Montgomery: Montgomery Museum of Fine Arts, 1983. 69 pp.; 53 black and white and color illustrations, bibliography, checklist.

Willett and Brackner document traditional utilitarian pottery in Alabama from the eighteenth century through the present. They do so untraditionally by focusing the essays on concerns such as the social function of wares and the social status of the potters, the history and technology of glazes, the variety of decorations, usual and unusual forms (grotesque jugs and grave markers), and the survival of the traditional potter in contemporary Alabama.

Turnbaugh, Sarah Peabody, ed. *Domestic Pottery of the Northeastern United States, 1625–1850*. Orlando, Fla.: Academic Press, 1985. xxi+319 pp.; 40 illustrations, 28 tables, bibliography, index.

Fifteen chapters, each by different authors, elucidate current trends in archaeological, anthropological, and historical analysis of ceramics produced in the northeastern United States. Divided into three parts, the articles treat the transplantation of traditional pottery making from Europe, the transformation of production through changing access to local and regional markets, and the emergence of an American ceramics industry by 1850. Although all studies begin with a specific area of pottery, their discussions and conclusions may be applicable to analysis of other situations.

Watkins, Lura Woodside. *Early New England Potters and Their Wares*. 1950. Reprint. Hamden, Conn.: Archon Books, 1968. x+291 pp.+136 plates; appendixes, index.

Watkins records and interprets New England's pottery history through the early twentieth century using documents, account books, broadsides, archaeological materials, and objects. Although rockingham and art pottery are discussed, the primary focus of this early and classic study is on the work of traditional redware and stoneware potters of the region. Information is arranged geographically, but there are also chapters on technology, typical New England redware forms, and a potter's daily work life in the eighteenth century as extracted from the daybooks of John Parker, a Charlestown, Massachusetts, potter.

Webster, Donald. *Early Canadian Pottery*. Greenwich, Conn.: New York Graphic Society, 1971. 256 pp.; black and white illustrations, 16 color plates, glossary, bibliography, index.

Both traditional and industrial Canadian ceramics are covered in this book in a general way, with particular emphasis on objects rather than written documents. Webster includes a chapter on archaeology as a primary research tool. For specific information on potters, see David L. Newlands, *Early Ontario Potters*.

Weiss, Peg, ed. *Adelaide Alsop Robineau: Glory in Porcelain*. Syracuse, N.Y.: Syracuse University Press in association with Everson Museum of Art, 1981. xiv+235 pp.; 361 black and white illustrations, 12 color plates, bibliography, index.

Robineau's contributions to the history of American porcelain, the arts and crafts movement, and the establishment of women's presence in the ceramic arts and the studio-ceramics movement, as well as her role in promoting china decoration as a viable artistic and economic activity for women, make her a key figure in American ceramics and women's history. The papers collected in this volume include Weiss's biography, Martin Eidelberg's analysis of her early design sources, Richard Zakin's and Phyllis Ihrman's technical analyses of her work, and Leslie Gorman's inventory of Robineau porcelains in public collections. In addition, the book contains Frederick Hurten Rhead's reminiscences of the University City, Missouri, venture in which he participated with Robineau and French ceramist Taxile Doat.

Winton, Andrew L., and Kate Barber. *Norwalk Potteries*. New photography by John W. Steer. Canaan, N.H.: Friends of Lockwood House, 1981. vii+40 pp.; illustrations, 50 plates, appendixes. Originally published in *Old-Time New England* 24, nos. 3, 4 (January, April 1934): 75–92, 111–28.

Since originally published, the text has been edited and updated into a single volume with new photographs. The utilitarian redwares and stonewares of Norwalk's potteries received wide distribution along the lower New England and middle Atlantic coasts during the nineteenth century because of family connections to New York shipping. This work contains a chronological history by pottery owner from the late eighteenth through the late nineteenth centuries based on documents, objects, and archaeological research. Although the stoneware is rather standard in appearance, redware plates exhibit a distinctive style in the frequent use of letterforms, names, words, and phrases executed in trailed slip.

Zug, Charles G., III. *Turners and Burners: The Folk Potters of North Carolina*. Fred W. Morrison Series on Southern Studies. Chapel Hill and London: University of North Carolina Press, 1986. xxi+450 pp.; approximately 280 black and white illustrations, 20 color plates, map, charts, bibliography, indexes.

A study of historical North Carolina pottery and the contemporary survivors of the craft, Zug's book is the most thorough, readable, and interesting of the new genre of folklorists' analyses of southern pottery using written and oral sources. Located on the dividing line between the northern salt-glazed and southern alkaline-glazed traditions, North Carolina's history includes both: the first centered in the Piedmont region and the other in the Catawba valley. Zug analyzes both technical and cultural aspects of the craft and its craftsmen, including materials, methods, tools, education, and economics, as well as the place of the wares in the everyday lives of consumers. Moravian earthenware is also discussed, but for a more thorough study, see John Bivins, Jr., *The Moravian Potters in North Carolina*. An early, condensed version of Zug's book is contained in *The Traditional Pottery of North Carolina* (Chapel Hill: Ackland Museum of the University of North Carolina, 1978). For a consideration of this one region of the state, see Daisy Wade Bridges, ed., *Potters of the Catawba Valley* (Charlotte, N.C.: History Department, Mint Museum, 1980).

Continental and Oriental Ceramics in America

ELLEN PAUL DENKER

BOTH FOREIGN AND DOMESTIC CERAMICS have filled the cupboards and decorated the interiors of American homes since the earliest years of European settlement. Although the greatest bulk of foreign wares were made in England, substantial amounts of Chinese, German, French, Spanish, and Dutch ceramic goods have also been used here: Westerwald stoneware and Dutch delft in the seventeenth and eighteenth centuries, fashionable French porcelain in the nineteenth century, and Chinese export porcelain from the very beginning. Since the Civil War, wares have been brought from almost everywhere beyond our shores.

Foreign ceramics in America can be studied from several approaches: scholars have focused on basic identification, artistic and technological contributions, and socioeconomic patterns of fashion, trade, and use. Thus, a variety of publications are available, ranging from encyclopedic studies of the production of individual factories or countries to detailed archaeological reports and descriptions of the goods in a household's cupboards. Any number of these works could have been annotated here; however, this section is limited primarily to general introductory works and studies that consider foreign wares, particularly Continental and oriental objects, in relation to their use in America, to encourage students to learn to identify wares and go on to interpretive studies using ceramics.

Art museum collections, which contain objects chosen primarily for their aesthetic quality, often do not accurately represent the historical record. Thus, information on the accumulations of foreign ceramics preserved from individual households or from local families and the archaeological records of a household or locale provide the best raw data for studying original patterns of consumption and use. At present, archaeological reports are the most numerous, although they offer little actual interpretation of excavation results. Most historic archaeology today is necessitated by modern construction on potentially significant sites, and archaeologists are allowed little time to contemplate their data. In addition, keys to identification of excavated shards, in both origin and form, remain of paramount importance because archaeologists are still grappling with the classification of wares. Visual and laboratory methods for distinguishing imported from domestically made redware and stoneware are very much in their infancy. As a result, some archaeologists concentrate on the function of wares as a more definitive method of characterizing previous lifeways. Even when archaeological analysis is published, it is often written for peers using jargon and with details that confuse the uninitiated reader. The exhibition catalogue *Unearthing New England's Past* is included here as an example of how this data can be interpreted and presented to the public.

House museum collections and the accumulations of local historical societies have the advantage of presenting the student with ceramic objects still largely intact. However, the researcher needs to approach tales of the descent of an artifact with some skepticism. A tea set, for example, may be identified by the donor as having come from a generation that antedates its manufacture by several decades. Such discrepancies underline the importance of connoisseurship, but because ceramics are not studied by most students to the extent that is afforded furniture or silver, material culture historians often have had little experience to apply when analyzing the use of foreign ceramics in America.

Several books of makers' marks, as well as general studies that combine useful illustrations with good historical and descriptive text, are listed to help to place an object within the context of ceramics history. The first step in this process is to identify the ceramic fabric as earthenware, stoneware, or porcelain. When objects fall into either of the first two categories, determining the country of origin is relatively easy, at least in relation to the American market, but doing this for porcelain is more difficult because of the great design interplay between Asia, the Continent, and England. Dwight Lanmon's "It's the Body" (*The Delaware Antiques Show* [Wilmington, 1971]) offers an excellent review of conclusions that can be drawn by careful observation of a porcelain object.

Apart from basic identification, other volumes are listed here for a variety of reasons. Some works are included because they present theoretical solutions to the problems of identification. For example, in their article on early New Amsterdam and New York ceramics, Meta Janowitz, Kate Morgan, and Nan Rothschild propose a shape typology for the study of Dutch-made and Dutch-derived earthenwares in the New World as a way of investigating the persistence of Dutch traditions in New York City. Other studies are included because they speak to the examination of markets. Christina Nelson, for example, offers suggestions for further study of regional preferences for Chinese export porcelain patterns and shapes, while David Sanctuary Howard and Jean Gordon Lee give evidence from New York and Philadelphia that will help to begin this process. Still other works are listed for comparative use, such as those by J. Jefferson Miller II and Lyle M. Stone and by Margaret Brown Klapthor. Finally, some works provide models for relating documents and objects. Jean McClure Mudge's study of American-market Chinese porcelain, Susan Gray Detweiler's analysis of George Washington's ceramics, and Arlene Palmer Schwind's work on the records of New York china merchant Frederick Rhinelander are good examples of this genre.

The interpretation of foreign ceramics used in America is emerging as objects and documents continue to be unearthed, discovered, and analyzed. The future of this area of inquiry is exciting and intriguing for the potential glimpses of the past that it holds.

Cameron, Elisabeth. *Encyclopedia of Pottery and Porcelain: The Nineteenth and Twentieth Centuries.* London and Boston: Faber and Faber, 1986. 366 pp.; black and white illustrations, color plates.

Considering the scope of this work—two centuries of world ceramics—Cameron has assembled an enormous amount of information from disparate sources. Entries are arranged alphabetically, and helpful cross-references are provided when a name that has its own entry also appears in another entry. Bibliographic references are given at the end of each entry. The format is primarily that of an encyclopedia, although a few marks are included. This is a useful, quick reference for this period of ceramics history.

Charleston, Robert J., ed. *World Ceramics: An Illustrated History.* New York: McGraw-Hill, 1968. 352 pp.; 1,019 black and white illustrations, 64 color plates, glossaries, bibliography, index.

Major trends in ceramics art and production are illuminated in this excellent overview of world ceramics history from ancient to modern times and from the Far East to the New World. The strength of the volume is enhanced by the contributions of twenty expert authors and the inclusion of numerous large illustrations. The principal focus is on Asian, Continental, and English ceramics history.

Cushion, J. P., comp., in collaboration with W. B. Honey. *Handbook of Pottery and Porcelain Marks.* 4th ed., rev. and exp. London and Boston: Faber and Faber, 1980. vii+272 pp.; line drawings, index.

Although this is not a comprehensive work, the marks selected are "those most frequently encountered" and include examples from the nineteenth and twentieth centuries, which are usually missing from books on ceramics marks of the world. Most major European and Far Eastern countries are represented here, making this a very useful general book on marks available for quick identification. Further research for individual countries or regions, however, will usually be necessary. Continental porcelain marks from the late nineteenth and twentieth centuries occur frequently in house museum, historical society, and period archaeological materials because of the large European porcelain export business after 1875. These marks, however, are usually the most difficult to identify because few mark books include later firms. Thus, the reader should also be aware of Robert E. Rontgen's *Marks on German, Bohemian, and Austrian Porcelain* (Exton, Pa.: Schiffer Publishing, 1980) and W. Percival Jervis's *Book of Pottery Marks* (Newark, N. J.: By the author, 1897), the latter of which includes contemporary late nineteenth-century marks that may not be found elsewhere.

Deagan, Kathleen. *Artifacts of the Spanish Colonies of Florida and the Caribbean, 1500–1800.* Photographs and drawings by James H. Quine. Vol. 1, *Ceramics, Glassware, and Beads.* Washington, D.C., and London:

Smithsonian Institution Press, 1987. xx+222 pp.; 69 black and white illustrations, 8 color plates, 4 tables, glossary, index.

Descriptions of the sites and samples for this study and an exploration of the economic factors affecting artifact distribution in the Caribbean precede the discussions of ceramics and tiles associated with colonial Spain. These included a variety of Spanish and New World glazed and unglazed colored coarse earthenwares; Spanish majolica in several styles; Italian majolica; New World majolica made in Mexico, Panama, and Guatemala; Chinese porcelain; Rhenish stoneware; Colono ware, made by Indians and used by westerners; and Spanish and Mexican tiles.

de Jonge, C. H. *Delft Ceramics.* Translated by Marie-Christine Hellin. New York and London: Praeger Publishers, 1970. 168 pp.; 156 black and white illustrations, 20 color plates, bibliography, indexes.

Delft and *delftware* are abused terms that can refer to a type of ceramic or to one of the Dutch cities where it was made. Properly called tin-glazed earthenware, it is a coarse-bodied pottery covered with a lead glaze made white by the addition of tin oxide. The Italians call it majolica, the French call it faience, but the English and, historically, the Americans refer to it as delft or delftware because knowledge of the process was transferred to England from the Netherlands, where the city of Delft was a major production center. Most tin-glazed earthenware in eighteenth-century America was English. De Jonge's book is one of only a handful of English-language volumes on Dutch delftware (tin-glazed earthenware made in Delft). Although this account centers on one city, many standard Dutch patterns were made there. This volume covers techniques, antecedents, tiles, and plaques from about 1600 to 1740 and the products of individual potteries from 1670 to 1800 divided by major color (blue, red, polychrome, white) and firing temperature (high, low). See also H.-P. Fourest's *Delftware* (New York: Rizzoli International Publications, 1980), which has the advantage of being organized chronologically but which contains pieces of generally much higher quality than would be found in American households.

Detweiler, Susan Gray. *George Washington's Chinaware.* Prologue and epilogue by Christine Meadows. New York: Harry N. Abrams, a Barra Foundation/Mount Vernon Ladies' Association Book, 1982. 244 pp.; 154 black and white and color illustrations, appendix, bibliography, index.

As the consummate upper-class consumer in colonial and early federal America, Washington bought and used the whole spectrum of foreign ceramics available to Americans: English white, brown, and scratch-blue salt-glazed stoneware; Westerwald stoneware; Chinese export porcelain; English and French porcelain; and English creamware. This volume is both a tribute to him and a detailed study of fashionable taste. Custis and Washington family genealogies are included. *See also* "English Ceramics in America."

Faÿ-Hallé, Antoinette, and Barbara Mundt. *Porcelain of the Nineteenth Century*. New York: Rizzoli International Publications, 1983. 302 pp.; 485 black and white and color illustrations, catalogue of marks, map, bibliography, index. Originally published as *La porcelaine européenne au XIXe siècle* (Fribourg, Switzerland, 1983).

Alexandre Brogniart was appointed director of the Sèvres royal porcelain factory in 1800 and proceeded to collect hundreds of examples of ceramics from around the world for study and comparison of their technical and artistic merits. His curiosity is mirrored in the examples and text assembled here. During the nineteenth century, porcelain production became more widespread in Europe, and technological innovations brought it within reach of the middle classes. More and more Americans shared in this economic and technological prosperity as the century wore on. Indeed, European porcelain had acquired such a cachet of elegance that American manufacturers had difficulty competing in the marketplace. This volume considers Continental and English porcelain during four periods that correspond to the social and artistic history of porcelain: 1800–1830, 1850–80, and 1880 to World War I. The large format, numerous clear illustrations, and engaging text recommend this volume as a good overview of nineteenth-century European porcelain, although many common wares of the later periods are not included.

Feller, John Quentin. "Canton *famille rose* Porcelain, Part I: Rose Medallion." *Antiques* 124, no. 4 (October 1983): 748–58. 7 black and white illustrations, 7 color plates.
——— . "Canton *famille-rose* Porcelain, Part II: Mandarin." *Antiques* 125, no. 2 (February 1984): 444–53. 10 black and white illustrations, 14 color plates.

Many nineteenth-century family collections, at least in the Northeast, include Canton famille rose porcelains, but broad date ranges were assigned to them until this work was published. Feller proposes a chronology using dated and firmly documented examples, many from American families.

Hillier, Bevis. *Pottery and Porcelain, 1700–1914: England, Europe, and North America*. New York: Meredith Press, 1968. 386 pp.; 217 black and white illustrations, 16 color plates, bibliography, index.

Although Hillier is English, she still provides plenty of material on Continental subjects in this chatty but thought-provoking social history of ceramics technology, style, and marketing. The social status of the potter is also considered. A chapter on repairs, reproductions, and fakes includes a brief history of materials and methods used to repair ceramics during the period and describes how fakers adapt to the marketplace. *See also* "English Ceramics in America."

Howard, David Sanctuary, with an essay by Conrad Edick Wright. *New York and the China Trade*. Exhibition catalogue. New York: New-York Historical Society, 1984. xiv+142 pp.; illustrations, 194 black and white and color illustrated entries, bibliography, checklist.

Wright's essay precedes Howard's extensive individual entries on objects gathered for a major exhibition exploring New York's trading relationships with China through the present; the essay, however, examines this interaction to circa 1850 only. The catalogue of the exhibition is divided into four periods: 1620–1780, 1785–90, 1790–1880, and 1880–1984, although the last 100 years are represented in much less detail than pre-1880. Howard was careful to restrict his selection of porcelain objects to archaeological materials and extant pieces with documented New York histories, which provides a good index of this market. Exceptional pieces predominate. A checklist of porcelain with pseudo arms of New York State is included.

Janowitz, Meta F., Kate T. Morgan, and Nan A. Rothschild. "Cultural Pluralism and Pots in New Amsterdam–New York City." In *Domestic Pottery in the Northeastern United States, 1625–1850*, edited by Sarah P. Turnbaugh, pp. 29–48. Orlando, Fla.: Academic Press, 1985. 5 illustrations, 1 table.

This work postulates the persistence of Dutch tradition in New York by analyzing earthenwares excavated from lower Manhattan. A typology of seventeenth- and early eighteenth-century Dutch forms was derived from Dutch genre painting and used for identification of the forms represented by local shards. These forms were compared with a synchronous English-tradition typology from the Chesapeake. Although many areas of overlap were observed, several forms appeared to be unique to each group. The survival of these Dutch forms in post-1664 and post-1674 sites on Manhattan suggests that some aspects of Dutch material culture persisted after English political conquests.

Klapthor, Margaret Brown. *Official White House China, 1789 to the Present*. Washington, D.C.: Smithsonian Institution Press, 1975. 283 pp. ; 97 black and white illustrations and color plates, appendixes, index.

Klapthor reconciles government records pertaining to the presidents' households with surviving china to document the dinnerwares chosen for official use in the White House. Beginning with the 1826 Appropriation Act, the president was directed to furnish the White House with goods of American manufacture "as far as practicable." This did not happen with china until Woodrow Wilson ordered the first Lenox set in 1918. Thus, Klapthor's record serves as an index of fashionable tableware in use in America since 1789, including services made in China, France, England, and the United States. The appendixes include a reprint of Haviland and Company's publication on their 1879 service for Rutherford B. Hayes. For more on china chosen by presidents for personal use while in office, in addition to their official china, see Marian Klamkin, *White House China* (New York: Charles

Scribner's Sons, 1972). For a summary of both Klapthor's and Klamkin's books, see Susan G. Detweiler, *American Presidential China* (Washington, D.C.: Smithsonian Institution Traveling Exhibition Service, 1975). *See also* "English Ceramics in America."

Lee, Jean Gordon, with an essay by Philip Chadwick Foster Smith. *Philadelphians and the China Trade, 1784–1844*. Exhibition catalogue. Philadelphia: Philadelphia Museum of Art, 1984; distributed by University of Pennsylvania Press. 232 pp.; black and white and color illustrations, 267 illustrated entries, glossary, bibliography, index.

In her introduction, Lee details the life and contributions of Nathan Dunn, merchant turned China trader who organized America's first extensive exhibition of Chinese material culture that opened in Philadelphia in 1838. Smith's essay explores trading relationships between the Chinese and the Philadelphians. The bulk of the volume, however, is devoted to the more than 270 items in the exhibition. These are arranged by family of ownership, thus highlighting the contributions to the China trade by Philadelphia's most prominent merchants, shippers, and captains. Porcelains are included, as are furniture, painting, costume, and metals.

Meister, Peter Wilhelm, and Horst Reber. *European Porcelain of the Eighteenth Century*. Translated by Ewald Osers. Ithaca: Cornell University Press, 1983. 320 pp.; 546 black and white and color plates, bibliography, maps, tables, index.

A large format, many clear illustrations, and a variety of approaches make this a useful and informative investigation of eighteenth-century Continental porcelain. Although Chinese export porcelain was used in many eighteenth-century American households, European porcelain was extremely rare here during the period. In addition to giving the definition, historical background, clues to identification, and summaries of factories and artists, Meister and Reber explore style, function, iconography, patronage, and later collecting interests.

Miller, J. Jefferson, II, and Lyle M. Stone. *Eighteenth-Century Ceramics from Fort Michilimackinac: A Study in Historical Archaeology*. Smithsonian Studies in History and Technology, no. 4. Washington, D.C.: Smithsonian Institution Press, 1970. ix+130 pp.; 51 illustrations, bibliography, appendixes, index.

Located on the Mackinac Straits joining Lakes Michigan and Huron, Fort Michilimackinac was established about 1715. It served as a focal point for the fur trade and regulated water travel in the region before it was relocated in 1781. Ceramics archaeologically recovered from the site are classified, illustrated, and discussed by a decorative arts historian and an archaeologist. Delftware; creamware; imported and domestic coarse earthenware; English slipware and refined earthenware; English white salt-glaze, scratch-blue, and red stoneware; Westerwald stoneware; Chinese export porcelain; and English porcelain were found. Appendixes detail shard frequencies and related material from other North American sites. *See also* "English Ceramics in America."

Mudge, Jean McClure. *Chinese Export Porcelain for the American Trade, 1785–1835*. 2d ed. Newark: University of Delaware Press, 1981. xxii+284 pp.; 138 black and white and color illustrations, appendixes, bibliography, index.

First published in 1963, this study focuses primarily on documentation of the American China trade in porcelain and on illustration of the variety of decorations made in China for the American market before 1835. Although this is a thorough study of the early period, Mudge's postulation of decline in this market after 1835 is refuted by evidence presented by John Quentin Feller, Christina H. Nelson, and the Schiffers.

Nelson, Christina H. *Directly from China: Export Goods for the American Market, 1784–1930*. Exhibition catalogue. Salem, Mass.: Peabody Museum of Salem, 1985. 120 pp.; 24 illustrations, illustrated catalogue, bibliography.

Porcelain is considered part of the wide range of goods imported to the United States from China between 1784 and 1930. The existence of regional preferences for forms and decorations is proposed on the basis of documented examples. Some thirty examples of porcelain are included in this catalogue.

Noël Hume, Ivor. *A Guide to Artifacts of Colonial America*. New York: Alfred A. Knopf, 1970. xviii+323 pp.; 100 illustrations, index.

An alphabetical guide to colonial artifacts that might be encountered by archaeologists is preceded by an entertaining and far-reaching essay on the uses of archaeology. Listings range from "armor" to "wig curlers." Although ceramics are listed separately and are divided by origin—English, American, and European—they may also be found under entries for particular forms, such as bellarmines (Rhenish stoneware jugs), bottles, bricks, chamber pots, apothecary's utensils, flowerpots, Chinese porcelain, stoneware, tiles, and tobacco pipes. *See also* "Surveys."

Quimby, Ian M. G., ed. *Ceramics in America*. Winterthur Conference Report 1972. Charlottesville: University Press of Virginia for the Henry Francis du Pont Winterthur Museum, 1973. ix+374 pp.; 124 illustrations, 8 tables.

Although some chapters deal specifically with English and American ceramics topics, there is a wealth of information here on Spanish, German, Chinese, French, and Dutch wares used in America. See especially Charles H. Fairbanks,

"The Cultural Significance of Spanish Ceramics"; John Lunn, "Colonial Louisbourg and Its Developing Ceramics Collection"; and C. Malcolm Watkins, "Ceramics Used in America: Comparisons."

Schiffer, Herbert, Peter Schiffer, and Nancy Schiffer. *Chinese Export Porcelain: Standard Patterns and Forms, 1780–1880.* Exton, Pa.: Schiffer Publishing, 1975. 256 pp.; 682 black and white and color illustrations, bibliography.

Its many illustrations make this book a useful volume for studying form and decoration. Standard patterns are described and then shown as they appear on the variety of forms available during the period. The quantity of material illustrated refutes Jean McClure Mudge's claim, in *Chinese Export Porcelain for the American Trade*, that the trade declined markedly after 1835.

Schwind, Arlene Palmer. "The Ceramic Imports of Frederick Rhinelander, New York Loyalist Merchant." *Winterthur Portfolio* 19, no. 1 (Spring 1984): 21–36. 13 illustrations.

Although most of the goods that Rhinelander imported to New York City were English, a substantial amount of Chinese export porcelain also came to him via the London firm Hodgson and Donaldson. Schwind suggests visual identifications of wares described in Rhinelander's records. *See also* "English Ceramics in America."

Unearthing New England's Past: The Ceramic Evidence. Exhibition catalogue. Lexington, Mass.: Scottish Rite Masonic Museum of Our National Heritage, 1984. 112 pp.; illustrations, bibliography.

This catalogue accompanied an exhibition that interpreted the value of historical archaeology for a popular audience and illustrates materials excavated from a variety of pre-1850 New England sites: forts, potteries, households, ships, a tavern, and an urban hotel. Whole examples from various collections give form to the bits and pieces that made up the original assemblages. The greatest part of the foreign material included is English, although Chinese export porcelain, Rhenish stoneware, and Dutch delft also appear. *See also* "English Ceramics in America."

Wilcoxen, Charlotte. *Dutch Trade and Ceramics in America in the Seventeenth Century.* Albany: Albany Institute of History and Art, 1987. 109 pp.; 33 black and white and 16 color illustrations, bibliography, index.

Wilcoxen reveals the Dutch role in trade between North America and Europe, the extent of which has not been comprehended in the past because much of it was illegal under the English navigation and trade laws (and hence ignored by many previous scholars) and because colonial Dutch documents have begun to be translated only recently. Evidence for Dutch trade in Virginia, Maryland, Plymouth Colony, the Boston and Massachusetts Bay settlements, Rhode Island, Connecticut, and New York (after 1664) is reviewed by colony. The documents are supported by the evidence of archaeologically recovered ceramics in American sites that were made or traded by the Dutch. As an aid to archaeologists, collectors, and curators, Wilcoxen describes three distinctive types of Dutch wares used in America: lead-glazed utility earthenware; tin-glazed ware in the style of the Italian Renaissance, which she calls majolica; and tin-glazed ware decorated in the Chinese manner which she terms faience. She maintains that use of the generic designation *delft* to describe Dutch ceramics has obscured the potential for adequately dating and analyzing site materials. German, Italian, and Chinese ceramics traded by the Dutch in America are also described. Finally, she surveys Dutch-traded ceramics found primarily in New Netherland sites along the Hudson River, but also several along the Connecticut and Delaware rivers.

English Ceramics in America

George L. Miller and Ann Smart Martin

Throughout history, ceramics have been a common part of daily life for most Americans. From inexpensive, sturdy jugs storing water to costly, highly decorated plates serving food, Americans used ceramics to fulfill common tasks ranging from the table to the toilet. Like many categories of material culture, the commoner the object, the less we know from primary sources about how it was used, why it was selected, or the meaning it had.

Yet ceramic objects can be used to answer those very questions of people's motivations in the past. Consumer demand for varying styles and forms are a reflection of the patterning of daily existence. The degree of access a person had to material resources, such as high-priced ceramics, is similarly a measure of his position in society.

The study of ceramics has a greater potential than most types of material culture. First, the use of ceramics was widespread even in the seventeenth century and became nearly universal by the late eighteenth century. Second, a variety of forms and cost levels was available; this variety is used to study changing consumption patterns over time and between socioeconomic classes.

Beyond these extrinsic factors, certain characteristics of the very nature of ceramics make them excellent candidates for study. Styles changed rapidly, providing good dating controls and mediating for frequent replacement. Wares broke easily, causing further demand for new purchases. Once broken, ceramics had minimum potential for recycling, and after they were discarded, they survived well in the ground. Thus, many household ceramics collections survive as archaeological evidence. There are no other types of material culture for which we have both assemblages from the past and the documentary evidence that describes them.

An overwhelming part of the ceramics that Americans used in the past were not American made. With the exception of limited production of coarser wares, the dominance of foreign ceramics, especially British, remained unchallenged until the late nineteenth century.

By the 1770s the introduction of creamware and transfer printing, as well as the brilliant marketing of Josiah Wedgwood, had placed the Staffordshire pottery industry firmly in control of not just the American market but an international market as well. France, Italy, Russia, and other European countries were important outlets for English creamware in the 1770s and 1780s. As various countries began to close their borders to English ceramics through protective trade barriers, the American market became the most important for English potters. From the end of the War of 1812 until the eve of the Civil War, America absorbed between 40 and 50 percent of the pottery exports from England (see J. Potter, "Atlantic Economy, 1815–1860: The U.S.A. and the Industrial Revolution in Britain," in *Studies in the Industrial Revolution Presented to T. S. Ashton*, ed. L. S. Pressnell [London: Athlone Press, 1960], pp. 236–81, esp. 278).

The growing importance of the American market changed the relationship it held with the potters. America in the eighteenth century was often a dumping ground for those styles that had grown cold. After the War of 1812, however, English potters began making patterns for the American trade with views of American scenes and military heroes. Some potters, such as Enoch Wood and William Adams, even adopted the American eagle as part of their trademark.

An American whiteware industry of lasting impact was not established until after the Civil War. Domestic production was aided by higher tariffs and greenback currency issued during the war, both combining to inflate the cost of English ceramics. Yet the American public still considered English wares to be superior, and they continued to dominate the market, despite the strengthened American ceramics industry. Now it was the American potter who copied English pottery marks to pass their products off as British.

By the late nineteenth century, English dominance began to be eroded by American wares as well as by German, Austrian, and Japanese porcelain. English influence, however, remained strong. Even today a large portion of the more expensive tableware purchased is English.

We saw the problem to be addressed by this bibliography as complex. The literature on English ceramics is vast, ranging from collectors' price lists to first-class economic history. Many have no information on the use of these wares in America, but to describe only those works with information specifically about the American market would produce a short list and one of limited use. Therefore, we have included books and articles if they met any one of the following criteria: they are essential for proper identification of the wares; they provide an overview of the development of the English ceramics industry; they reprint important primary documents; they shed light on the evolution of collecting and help to understand the development of collectors' biases, objectives, and terminology; they describe the economic development of the potteries and the marketing of ceramics to North America; they record ceramics collected from or made for the American market; and they analyze assemblages of ceramics from American contexts such as probate, account-book, and archaeological studies.

These criteria are by no means comprehensive. They do, however, contain more than enough information to allow one to begin to identify the wares, study the subject, and expand research.

The quality and reliability of information in the books and articles in this bibliography vary widely. For instance, many collectors' manuals are mere compilations of information. Such a source could be derided, but this group has performed a great service by gathering scattered data that aids in the identification, dating, and establishment of the range of forms for some poorly recorded common wares. These sources are the equivalent of an alphabet, the building blocks of knowledge about ceramics.

Another common group of studies in the bibliography is histories of individual potteries. While these are more comprehensive than collectors' compilations, most do not begin to provide an overview of the pottery trade or the relationship of potteries to consumers. Taking the analogy one step further, these are words in a vocabulary that is necessary to create the prose that will enable us to grasp the role of ceramics in society.

Another major type of reference includes studies of ceramics assemblages from such sources as probate inventories, account books, and archaeological sites. Their importance lies in the ability to relate the ceramics to the people who used them. These studies are the beginnings of a simple grammar that is moving us closer to a social history of ceramics.

Several papers on ceramics in American households are on press. One collection of such works is entitled *Socioeconomic Status and Consumer Choices: Perspectives in Historical Archaeology*, edited by Suzanne Spencer-Wood. A lengthy paper synthesizing ceramics research by historical archaeologists, titled "The Use and Misuse of Nineteenth-Century English and American Ceramics in Archaeological Analysis" by Teresita Majewski and Michael J. O'Brien, is being published in *Advances in Archaeological Method and Theory* (Academic Press). This article will provide a useful survey of the archaeological literature involving English ceramics in an American context.

Another major project that is under way is titled "English Ceramics in America, 1760 to 1860: Marketing, Prices, and Availability." This research has been funded by the National Endowment for the Humanities and is being conducted by Colonial Williamsburg Foundation. It studies importers' records from Boston, New York, Philadelphia, Baltimore, and Virginia as well as records from Staffordshire. We are conducting the research with Nancy S. Dickinson.

The volume and range of information that is becoming available is expanding rapidly. More sophisticated questions are being asked about ceramics and their relationship to those who produced, sold, and used them in America. Because of the dominance of British ceramics in American households, clearly we must study those English wares to understand and interpret American usage. Anyone limited to the study of American ceramics would have less knowledge of ceramics usage in the past than the six blind men had about the elephant that they attempted to describe.

Archer, Michael, and Brian Morgan. *Fair as China Dishes: English Delftware*. Washington, D.C.: International Exhibitions Foundation, 1977. 128 pp.; 88 black and white illustrations, 5 color plates, line drawings, bibliography.

In this brief outline of the development of the English delftware industry and the impact of the introduction of salt-glazed stoneware and creamware, special attention is given to the extensive export trade to the American market, and documentary references to American usage are included. Extensive catalogue entries present both specific information for each vessel and good contextual background.

Arman, David, and Linda Arman. *Historical Staffordshire: An Illustrated Checklist*. Danville, Va.: Arman Enterprises, 1974. 244 pp.; 468 illustrations, bibliography, index.

This text is among the most complete compilations of Amer-ican views and subjects transfer printed on English ceramics. Although many illustrations are included, they are small and of poor quality. Little information is included beyond the pattern name, mark, maker's dates, and type of vessel on which the pattern has been found. For information on these patterns, see Ellouise Baker Larson, *American Historical Views on Staffordshire China*.

Atterbury, Paul, ed. *English Pottery and Porcelain: An Historical Survey*. New York: Universe Books, 1978. 288 pp.; illustrations, index.

A compilation of fifty years of scholarship from *Antiques* magazine, this work traces ceramics production from the seventeenth century to the Victorian era. While many of these short articles have been superseded by more expanded works, this volume provides a good overview. Some of the more important articles are individually discussed in this chapter.

Austin, John C. *Chelsea Porcelain at Williamsburg*. The Williamsburg Decorative Arts Series, edited by Graham Hood. Williamsburg: Colonial Williamsburg Foundation, 1977; distributed by University Press of Virginia. xii+227 pp.; 144 illustrated entries, appendix, index.

In this profusely illustrated and extensively documented catalogue of Chelsea porcelain in Colonial Williamsburg Foundation's collection, Austin briefly summarizes the main periods of Chelsea production, based on marks and stylistic attributes, and provides documentary evidence of the porcelain's usage in colonial America. Appended is a facsimile of a 1755 Chelsea porcelain auction catalogue containing important information on wares and terminology. The introductory sketches provide a quick overview for the untutored reader, while the catalogue itself will satisfy the connoisseur.

Baker, Vernon G. *Historical Archaeology at Black Lucy's Garden, Andover, Massachusetts: Ceramics from the Site of a Nineteenth Century Afro-American*. Papers of the Robert S. Peabody Foundation for Archaeology, vol. 8. Andover, Mass.: Phillips Academy, 1978. xi+122 pp.; 117 illustrations, appendixes.

The recent focus on Afro-American sites in historical archaeology has made important contributions to the understanding of nineteenth-century black life. An early such effort was the 1943 excavation of Black Lucy's Garden. This report is a detailed reexamination of the ceramics from that site to test the extent to which they reflect Afro-American culture. Excellent drawings and photographs of the vessels recovered are amply described with detailed measurements and Munsell color notations.

Beaudry, Mary C. "Ceramics in York County, Virginia, Inventories, 1730–1750: The Tea Service." *The Conference on Historic Site Archaeology Papers 1977* 12 (1978): 201–10.

Beaudry extracts information on teawares from 196 probate inventories and analyzes their placement in households and the association between the ownership of teaware and socioeconomic status. From the evidence gathered, she suggests that colonial Virginia was acquiring new fashions earlier than some of the other colonies.

Beaudry, Mary C., Janet Long, Henry M. Miller, Fraser D. Neiman, and Garry Wheeler Stone. "A Vessel Typology for Early Chesapeake Ceramics: The Potomac Typological System." *Historical Archaeology* 17, no. 1 (1983): 18–43. 1 table, bibliography, appendix.

This article presents an excellent discussion of typology in an attempt to build a folk taxonomy of the commonly found vessel forms from seventeenth-century sites in Virginia and Maryland. Terminology is extracted from probate inven-tories and other sources, and illustrations from excavated vessels are provided.

Blaszczyk, Regina Lee. "Ceramics and the Sot-Weed Factor: The China Market in a Tobacco Economy." *Winterthur Portfolio* 19, no. 1 (Spring 1984): 7–19. 9 illustrations.

Blaszczyk outlines the inventory of ceramics in three Piscataway, Maryland, stores in the second half of the eighteenth century. She briefly describes the trade relationships between the Chesapeake tobacco economy and Glasgow and details the wares and forms available in the stores. Descriptions of the wares from the store inventories are deftly interwoven with documentation from ceramics literature, and the problems of interpreting terminology are discussed.

Bradley, H. G., ed. *Ceramics of Derbyshire, 1750–1795: An Illustrated Guide*. London: By the editor, 1978. xvi+338 pp.; 16 color plates, 470 illustrated entries, maps, bibliography, index.

This catalogue grew out of an exhibition by Morley College Ceramic Circle in 1976. It illustrates many vessels attributed to potteries in Derbyshire and provides short introductions to the various wares and factories by noted English-ceramics historians.

Branner, John Casper. *A Bibliography of Clays and the Ceramic Arts*. Columbus, Ohio: American Ceramic Society, 1906. 451 pp.

Branner's bibliography lists many obscure articles and publications, some of which are primary sources; however, it is difficult to use because there is no subject index. Articles included in the bibliography range from newspaper reports on the potteries to historical studies.

Branyan, Lawrence, Neal French, and John Sandon. *Worcester Blue and White Porcelain, 1751–1790: An Illustrated Encyclopaedia of the Patterns*. London: Barrie and Jenkins; Westfield, N.J.: Eastview Editions, 1981. 367 pp.; illustrations, bibliography, index.

The majority of Worcester wares produced during the first forty years of operation were blue and white. This volume highlights that production in a concise and informative encyclopedia of the patterns, forms, marks, and dates of production. Large photographs and many detailed line drawings enable precise comparison to extant examples. The Worcester factory has been the subject of many scholars, but this study provides an essential companion to factory history by synthesizing a "pattern book" from archaeological, documentary, and curatorial evidence.

Brears, Peter C. D. *The English Country Pottery: Its History and Techniques*. Rutland, Vt.: Charles E. Tuttle Co., 1971. 266 pp.; 31 illustrations, 15 plates, bibliography, index.

In perhaps the best one-volume source for information on potting techniques used by English country potters, Brears clearly describes the processes of decorating with slip, the use of molds, and the firing of kilns. He also compiles a gazetteer of potters from a variety of historical sources, along with a glossary of potting terms and vessel names.

Brown, Marley R., III. "Ceramics from Plymouth, 1621–1800: The Documentary Record." In *Ceramics in America*, edited by Ian M. G. Quimby, pp. 41–74. Winterthur Conference Report 1972. Charlottesville: University Press of Virginia for the Henry Francis du Pont Winterthur Museum, 1973. 3 appendixes.

Brown's study of Plymouth Colony probate inventories is a companion to James Deetz's "Ceramics from Plymouth, 1620–1835." Rather than archaeological evidence used by Deetz to test propositions about ceramics usage in early America, Brown turns to probate inventories as an independent source. He was hindered by unclear probate references either in lumped categories of ceramics or with vague terminology, and he was unable to negate or support many of Deetz's specific propositions. By "reading between the lines," however, the documents proved extremely useful in supporting Deetz's general conclusions about the profound changes in the function of ceramics from the seventeenth through the nineteenth centuries.

Burchill, Frank, and Richard Ross. *A History of the Potters' Union*. Ceramic and Allied Trades Union. Stafford, England: George Street Press, 1977. 292 pp.; 53 illustrations, bibliography, index.

This book provides an excellent overview of the potters' struggles to unionize and their efforts to cope with technological changes and declining wages. One solution attempted in the 1840s was to eliminate the surplus labor by establishing an emigration society that sent surplus potters to Wisconsin to become farmers.

Celoria, Francis. "Reports of the U.S. Consuls on the Staffordshire Potteries, 1883–1892." *Journal of Ceramic History* 7 (1974): 43–67. 6 illustrations.

American trade consuls were established in the Staffordshire potteries in 1869. Their annual reports document the wares being shipped to America along with cost differences between English and American wares and the labor and cost of living for the workers. Celoria has extracted useful information from these reports. In addition, the complete 1892 report by William Burgess entitled "Staffordshire vs. American Pottery" has been reprinted.

Charleston, R. J., ed. *English Porcelain, 1745–1850*. London: Ernest Benn; Toronto: University of Toronto Press, 1965. 183 pp.; approximately 65 black and white illustrations, 12 color plates, bibliography, index.

Thirteen specialists discuss major English factories, concen-

trating mainly on company histories rather than their production of specific wares. While much of this research has been superseded by volumes on each of the subjects, this book provides a good historical framework for further specialized reading and remains a standard source.

Charleston, R. J., and Donald Towner. *English Ceramics, 1580–1830*. London: Sotheby Parke Bernet Publications, 1977. Unpag.; 261 black and white illustrations, 16 color plates.

Commemorating the fiftieth anniversary of the English Ceramic Circle, this catalogue provides a broad pictorial view of the English ceramics industry up to the early nineteenth century. The major types of earthenware and porcelain are represented in excellent, unusually large photographs. These illustrations are the main recommendation for the catalogue, because entries are brief and contextual information is limited. However, cross-references to the literature are helpful.

Collard, Elizabeth. *Nineteenth-Century Pottery and Porcelain in Canada*. 2d ed. Montreal: McGill-Queen's University Press, 1984. 477 pp.; 198 illustrations, bibliography, index.

In a holistic overview of ceramics in a national context, Collard focuses on Canadian ceramics, but she does not make the common mistake of limiting her scope to domestically produced wares. Unfortunately, we do not have an equivalent work on ceramics in America. Yet because the Staffordshire ceramics industry was the dominant one for most of the nineteenth century, information presented in this work is meaningful for understanding the wares being imported to the United States. Collard uses a wealth of newspaper sources, along with other primary documents, to create a view of the seasonality of the trade, the relationship of importers to the potters, and the country trade. She also describes the fledgling Canadian ceramics industry and its problems and limitations.

Cooper, Ronald G. *English Slipware Dishes, 1650–1850*. London: Alec Tiranti, 1968. vi + 144 pp.; 323 black and white illustrations and color plates, bibliography, index.

Cooper traces the development and production of English slipware potters. An overview of the character of slipware from various parts of the world is included, as is regional variation in Britain. Cooper concentrates on the wares of Thomas Toft, illustrating all known attributed examples. His discussion of the symbolism of various motifs and design elements places the slipware into a broad cultural and historical context that is rare in ceramics literature.

Copeland, Robert. *Spode's Willow Pattern and Other Designs after the Chinese*. New York: Rizzoli International Publications in association with Christie's, 1980. x + 182 pp.; approximately 300 black and white illustrations, 4 color plates, appendixes, glossary, bibliography, indexes.

Copeland's major thesis is that the "classic willow" pattern was developed by Josiah Spode. He presents a convincing case along with a detailed description of the technology of transfer printing. In addition, he provides a complete catalogue of early transfer-printed English earthenware in a Chinese style. These wares have long been neglected, although they were the dominant printed patterns from about 1790 until the War of 1812.

Cox, Alwyn, and Angela Cox. *Rockingham Pottery and Porcelain, 1745–1842*. The Faber Monographs on Pottery and Porcelain, edited by R. J. Charleston and Margaret Medley. London and Boston: Faber and Faber, 1983. 262 pp.; 149 black and white illustrations, 10 color plates, line drawings, map, appendixes, bibliography, index.

Rockingham, or Swinton as it was known until 1826, was an important English manufactory of porcelain and earthenware in the first half of the nineteenth century. Using a wide range of sources, the Coxes trace the factory's humble beginnings as "country pot-house" to a well-respected porcelain factory. As many of the earlier wares were unmarked, excavation at the factory enabled the Coxes to make important new attributions. This is a well-organized and information-packed volume.

Coysh, A. W., and R. K. Henrywood. *The Dictionary of Blue and White Printed Pottery, 1780–1880*. Woodbridge, Suffolk: Antique Collectors' Club, 1982. 420 pp.; black and white illustrations, 29 color plates, appendixes, bibliography.

This lengthy volume is a compendium of information about the pottery firms, wares, patterns, and marks of blue-and-white transfer-printed earthenware. Produced in dictionary form with liberal illustration and commentary on the source and subject of many patterns, it is an important reference for the chronology and identification of blue-and-white transfer-printed wares carrying only a pattern name.

Deetz, James J. F. "Ceramics from Plymouth, 1620–1835: The Archaeological Evidence." In *Ceramics in America*, edited by Ian M. G. Quimby, pp. 15–40. Winterthur Conference Report 1972. Charlottesville: University Press of Virginia for the Henry Francis du Pont Winterthur Museum, 1973. 6 illustrations, 1 table.

Deetz's seminal study presents an explanatory model for understanding the cultural significance of ceramics in America. Based on archaeological evidence from sixteen sites at Plimoth Plantation, this study tests three propositions regarding "the place of ceramics in the culture and their relationships to other aspects of that culture." According to Deetz, three successive cultural systems were operative in New England in the period 1620–1835. It is only in the third period that a "Georgian mind-set" impacted the older, medieval-derived folk culture of New England, dissolving regional and rural differences. By the early nineteenth century, this produced the first true horizon in American history and can be seen in individualized food-serving patterns, housing, and gravestone markers.

Detweiler, Susan G. *American Presidential China*. Exhibition catalogue. Washington, D.C.: Smithsonian Institution Traveling Exhibition Service, 1975. 96 pp.; 115 black and white and color illustrated entries, bibliography.

This exhibit was designed to illustrate "one aspect of the evolution of taste and culture in American society as modified by the personalities of the individual presidents and their First Ladies" (p. 94) and traveled throughout the country during the Bicentennial. In contrast to some publications, the personal china of American presidents is stressed as more exemplary of personal taste and current style and as free from the political and economic constraints of "official purchases." The finest special wares were usually French until late in the nineteenth century, although many British services were purchased for common use. This is no mere "picture book," and the brief descriptions provide excellent documentation from official records of purchases, prices, and other sources.

Detweiler, Susan Gray. *George Washington's Chinaware*. Prologue and epilogue by Christine Meadows. New York: Harry N. Abrams, a Barra Foundation/Mount Vernon Ladies' Association Book, 1982. 244 pp.; 154 black and white and color illustrations, appendix, bibliography, index.

Detweiler deftly combines extensive documentation of Washington's purchases, attributed pieces, archaeological evidence, and contemporary accounts and illustrations into a delightful synthesis of the purchase patterns of this wealthy and influential American leader, whose concern for "fashion" and station is clearly documented. Washington bought and used the whole spectrum of foreign ceramics available to Americans: English whiteware, brownware, and scratch-blue salt-glazed stoneware; Westerwald stoneware; Chinese export porcelain; English and French porcelain; and English creamware. Detweiler's study is a clear picture of one household's social and economic evolution in a context of ceramics history. Of great service to the scholar is the extensive reprinting of documentation and attention to terminology, well grounded in the overall context of colonial consumption. *See also* "Continental and Oriental Ceramics in America."

Drakard, David, and Paul Holdway. *Spode Printed Ware*. London and New York: Longman Group, 1983. x + 221 pp.; approximately 876 black and white illustrations, 16 color plates, indexes.

In this rich resource of the printed patterns of Spode Company dating before 1833, many of which continued in production under Spode's successors, Drakard and Holdway discuss the differences between bat and paper printing and illustrate printers' proofs of the pattern from the factory records of the Spode works in Stoke-on-Trent. This is the first catalogue of on-glaze printed patterns and appears to be complete. Extensive use has been made of primary records about the Staffordshire potteries as well as Spode Company.

Earle, Alice Morse. *China Collecting in America.* 1902. Reprint. Rutland, Vt.: Charles E. Tuttle Co., 1973. xv+429 pp.; approximately 65 illustrations, index.

Earle's book is primarily of interest as an early work that set the agenda for collecting and the terminology used to describe the wares. The first such work was Annie Slossen's *China Hunter's Club.* Earle was among the first American scholars to use primary sources such as probate inventories and newspaper advertisements and to focus on presidential china.

Evans, William. *Art and History of the Potting Business Compiled from the Most Practical Sources, for Especial Use of Working Potters.* Hanley, England: Potters' Examiner, 1846. Reprinted in *Journal of Ceramic History,* no. 3 (1970): 21–43.

Evans was a leader in the attempt to organize the Staffordshire potters. Promoting the idea of sending surplus potters to Wisconsin to become farmers, this book was an attempt to make the secrets of the pottery trade available to all as part of the struggle of the potters against their employers. The history is from the working potters' perspective and provides significant information on developments and changing technology in Staffordshire.

Falkner, Frank. *The Wood Family of Burslem.* 1912. Reprint. Yorkshire: EP Publishing, 1972. xx+118 pp.; approximately 180 illustrations, appendixes, genealogical table, index.

Enoch Wood and his sons were major exporters of Staffordshire wares to the American market. Wood took an active interest in the history of the potteries and assembled early examples of Staffordshire wares along with documents related to the trade. Although first published in 1912, Falkner's book is still the major source on the Wood family.

Felton, David L., and Peter D. Schulz. *The Diaz Collection: Material Culture and Social Change in Mid-Nineteenth Century Monterey.* California Archaeological Reports no. 23. Sacramento: California Department of Parks and Recreation, 1983. 120 pp.; 68 illustrations, bibliography.

This book analyzes an extensive collection of ceramics, glass, and faunal remains from a privy pit dating between circa 1843 and 1855. The material was deposited by the family of Manuel Diaz, a Mexican-American merchant in Monterey. Felton and Schulz have addressed the question of the impact of ethnicity and economic class on ceramics consumption patterns. Their conclusions are that economic class has more impact than ethnic background. This book contains the best and most detailed interpretations of an archaeological ceramics collection.

Finer, Ann, and George Savage, eds. *The Selected Letters of Josiah Wedgwood.* London: Cory, Adams and Mackay, 1965. xi+375 pp.; 13 black and white and 2 color plates, bibliography, indexes.

Finer and Savage have thoughtfully selected a group of Wedgwood's correspondence dating from 1762 to his death in 1795. The letters are excellent reading and provide a special insight into the development of Wedgwood and the Staffordshire potteries. For instance, Wedgwood discusses American porcelain clays, the American Revolution, and English potters going to America. The editors have provided a useful biographical index to help scholars to identify to whom Wedgwood was writing.

Fleming, J. Arnold. *Scottish Pottery.* N.d. Reprint. New preface by Peter Walton. East Ardsley, Wakefield, Yorkshire, 1973. 299 pp.; 59 illustrations, index.

Fleming's survey of Scottish ceramics production concentrates on the wares from the mid eighteenth through the nineteenth centuries. Published in 1923, this work is comparable to Llewellynn Jewitt's nineteenth-century study of Staffordshire in its combining of the oral traditions with documentation of small, now-defunct firms. Like Jewitt, some of Fleming's information is inaccurate, but his pioneering work is still the most comprehensive on Scottish potting. He clearly demonstrates that the types of wares produced in England in the nineteenth century were also made in Scotland. Walton's preface is a good roadmap to erroneous, as well as valuable, information and provides historical context to assess Fleming's reporting critically. Of special interest is the discussion of the Delftfield pottery in Scotland and its American connection.

Garner, F. H., and Michael Archer. *English Delftware.* 2d rev. and enl. ed. The Faber Monographs on Pottery and Porcelain, edited by Harry Garner and R. J. Charleston. London: Faber and Faber, 1972. xxi+103 pp.+253 plates; appendixes, bibliography, index.

The standard source for English delftware, this expanded edition traces the evolution of the delftware industry from the sixteenth into the eighteenth centuries, with a useful summary of stylistic attributes of each century's productions. Specific manufactories within the major delftware centers are discussed. Of special note is the discussion of early manufacturing attempts in New Jersey and Pennsylvania.

Gaw, Lina P. "The Availability and Selection of Ceramics to Silcott, Washington, 1900–1930." *Northwest*

Anthropological Research Notes 9, no. 1 (1977): 166–79. 56 illustrations, bibliography.

In an analysis of 192 vessels from four sites, including a country store, in Silcott, Gaw identifies the probable source of the ceramics as the country store, mail-order catalogues, and soap-company giveaways. Because there was only evidence of two sets present, most of the ceramics appear to have been purchased piecemeal.

Godden, Geoffrey. *Staffordshire Porcelain*. London and New York: Granada, 1983. xiv+593 pp.; 737 black and white illustrations, 24 color plates, appendixes, index.

In an overall picture of the vast range of porcelain produced in Staffordshire, "the birthplace of English bone china," Godden and a host of important scholars document more than 200 years of production, including subjects ranging from working conditions of nineteenth-century potters to the products of more than a dozen factories. Heavy emphasis is placed on the huge output of much-neglected nineteenth-century bone chinas. The appendixes include useful checklists of manufacturers, patterns, systems of registration, and problem groups of porcelain.

Godden, Geoffrey A. *Caughley and Worcester Porcelains, 1775–1800*. Woodbridge, Suffolk: Antique Collectors' Club, 1981. xxxvii+336 pp.; 317 black and white plates, 10 color plates, bibliography, index.

Forty-five Chamberlain account books dating from 1788 to 1846 and other documentary sources place the Chamberlain factory among the best-documented porcelain works in England. While indispensable to the study of these wares, the wealth of data included on prices, terminology, decoration, and forms aids in the study of English ceramics in general. Included is "A Day at the Royal Porcelain-Works, Worcester," published in 1843 in *Penny* magazine, which describes and illustrates basic methods of preparation and manufacture.

Godden, Geoffrey A. *Encyclopaedia of British Pottery and Porcelain Marks*. New York: Crown Publishers, 1964. 765 pp.; 4,516 illustrated marks, appendix, glossary, bibliography, indexes.

The standard work in the field, this volume is well illustrated, often with several marks for major firms with dates that each mark was in use. This information is drawn from a variety of primary sources including the Staffordshire rate records, Board of Trade files, Patent Office registers of trademarks, and city directories. It is difficult to imagine working with English ceramics without this valuable source.

Godden, Geoffrey A. *English China*. London: Barrie and Jenkins, 1985. 362 pp.; 1,509 black and white illustrations, 6 color plates, index, bibliography.

This book is an updated synthesis of Godden's earlier works, many of which are out of print. Although the subject is English porcelain, an extensive glossary of all major types of refined English ceramics provides summary capsules, illustrations, and references to major sources. Short but detailed essays on eleven types of English porcelain form the core of the study. Each section is lavishly illustrated and includes updates and corrections to Godden's earlier works.

Godden, Geoffrey A. *Godden's Guide to Mason's China and the Ironstone Wares*. 2d ed. Woodbridge, Suffolk: Antique Collectors' Club, 1980. 316 pp.; 362 black and white plates, 14 color plates, appendix, bibliography, index.

Another of Godden's well-documented studies that includes illustrations of waster shards with whole vessels, the emphasis in this work is again on identification of wares. However, he also discusses the role of Chinese porcelain in the development of the Mason family and its influence on Mason's porcelain and ironstone. In addition to a thorough documentation of Mason's ironstone, Godden provides an extensive catalogue of ironstone produced by other less well known potters. One shortcoming of the book is that it concentrates on decorated ironstone and minimally discusses the plain white ironstone that dominated American households in the second half of the nineteenth century. The section dealing with other ironstone manufacturers, however, does contain information on their trade with America.

Godden, Geoffrey A. *Jewitt's Ceramic Art of Great Britain, 1800–1900; Being a Revised and Expanded Edition of Those Parts of the Ceramic Art of Great Britain by Llewellyn Jewitt, F.S.A., Dealing with the Nineteenth Century*. New York: Arco Publishing Co., 1972. xxviii+282 pp.; black and white illustrations, color plates, bibliography, index.

Jewitt was a nineteenth-century English scholar whose two-volume study of 1878, *The Ceramic Art of Great Britain*, discusses English pottery from the prehistoric period down to the 1870s. Godden has extracted Jewitt's nineteenth-century material and expanded it with additional historical information. One problem created by this is the difficulty in knowing which material is from Jewitt and what has been contributed by Godden.

Godden, Geoffrey A. *Minton Pottery and Porcelain of the First Period, 1793–1850*. London: Herbert Jenkins; New York: Frederick A. Praeger, 1968. xvi+168 pp.+161 black and white and 12 color plates; appendixes, bibliography, index.

While later Minton porcelain is well documented, the early production of earthenware and porcelain is not well known. Godden provides a great service in this volume by publishing many original documents from the Minton archives. Pattern books and bills of sale provide information on Minton's wares, prices, and contemporary terminology.

Godden, Geoffrey A. *Ridgway Porcelains*. Woodbridge, Suffolk: Antique Collectors' Club, 1985. 257 pp.; 218 black and white illustrations, 16 color plates, appendixes, bibliography, index.

Godden has produced a volume chock-full of documentation on patterns, shapes, patents, and prices. Of special interest is a study of the "useful rather than ornamental" Ridgway wares displayed at the 1851 exhibition in Hyde Park. These included items as diverse as architectural elements, fountains, and "fine vitreous earthenware for the United States market."

Grant, Alison. *North Devon Pottery: The Seventeenth Century*. Exeter: University of Exeter, 1983. xvi+156 pp.; 41 black and white illustrations, 30 black and white and color plates, appendixes, bibliography, index.

Unlike most studies of English ceramics, this volume moves beyond chronicling specific history and production. Archaeological and documentary evidence of North Devon wares in seventeenth-century North America and the West Indies leads to a broader synthesis of the trade and personal relationships of early commercial expansion. Grant succeeds on three levels of analysis: a typology of the products of an important early potting center; a study of its rise in a society emergent from a medieval economy and its decline amid expanding industrialization; and use of ceramics evidence to test broader historical questions. These achievements recommend this book to both general historian and specialist.

Haslam, Malcolm. *English Art Pottery, 1865–1915*. Woodbridge, Suffolk: Antique Collectors' Club, 1975. [v]+214 pp.; approximately 95 black and white illustrations, 206 black and white and 16 color plates.

Haslam notes, "By the second half of the nineteenth century, ceramics as a means of artistic expression had all but perished in England, the victim of industrial production and bad taste" (p. 1). This volume is the story of revival and the slow resurgence of ceramics as an art form from 1865 to 1915. Criticism of the products of industrialization, influence of the aesthetic movement, and other factors led to a new appreciation of handmade items. Thus artist-potters and studios where artists decorated industrially produced wares of Wedgwood, Doulton, and others emerged fullfold by the twentieth century. Haslam summarizes this movement and its components. In addition, extensive documentary material from the art magazines of the era is reprinted in full.

Heaivilin, Annise Doring. *Grandma's Tea Leaf Ironstone: A History and Study of English and American Potteries*. Des Moines: Wallace-Homestead Book Co., 1981. 232 pp.; illustrations, bibliography, index.

Tea-leaf ironstone was an extremely popular pattern of table- and teaware during the last quarter of the nineteenth century. Heaivilin compiles information on English- and American-made tea-leaf wares with histories of the companies from secondary sources. Also included are some correspondence

with firms still in business and oral history related to the pattern. While much of the information is extraneous, this book is still a useful source for a common pattern.

Heilpern, Gisela, comp. *Josiah Wedgwood, Eighteenth-Century English Potter: A Bibliography*. Bibliographic Contributions no. 3. Carbondale: Southern Illinois University, 1967. xiv+66 pp.

Because of Wedgwood's role in the development of the English ceramic industry, it is impossible to study the subject without taking him into consideration. In addition to his considerable contribution, his papers have survived, providing some of the best documentation on the industry. Because of these factors, more articles and books have been published on Wedgwood and his products than on any other English potter. This bibliography, which needs updating, provides a helpful guide to the subject. Many articles on Wedgwood wares in American collections are included.

Herman, Bernard L. "Multiple Materials, Multiple Meanings: The Fortunes of Thomas Mendenhall." *Winterthur Portfolio* 19, no. 1 (Spring 1984): 67–86. 25 illustrations, 3 tables.

The leveling of Mendenhall's house in Wilmington, Delaware, led to a study of the structure and the salvage of a large group of ceramics and other artifacts from a related privy. The house was built in the 1780s, and the privy reflects forty years of occupation. Herman's analysis is excellent; he contrasts the historical sources, architecture, and ceramics to gain an insight into the changing fortunes of Mendenhall. From this research, it appears that the ceramics provide a clearer reflection of the reality of the Mendenhall family's economic decline. This is a superb interpretation of a ceramics assemblage.

Herman, Lynne L., John O. Sands, and Daniel Schecter. "Ceramics in St. Mary's County, Maryland, during the 1840s: A Socioeconomic Study." *The Conference on Historic Site Archaeology Papers* 8 (1975): 52–93.

This study examines ceramics consumption patterns in probate inventories of various economic classes in a rural Maryland county in the 1840s. A limitation was that the lower economic classes were generally not probated. However, the authors were able to study consumption of ceramic sets, compare porcelain to earthenware, and evaluate relationships between total ceramics consumption and value of the estate. A most interesting finding was that the value of the ceramics is correlated to wealth only up to a certain level, after which greater amounts of wealth are not reflected by the ownership of more or better ceramics.

Hillier, Bevis. *Master Potters of the Industrial Revolution: The Turners of Lane End*. London: Cory, Adams and Mackay, 1965. vii+96 pp.+73 black and white illustrations and 4 color plates; index.

Hillier is a major English-ceramics historian, and her study of the Turners of Lane End discusses the development of the export trade to France. This relationship has important parallels in the later development of British trade with America. This work is perhaps the best study of a secondary pottery.

Hillier, Bevis. *Pottery and Porcelain, 1700–1914: England, Europe, and North America.* New York: Meredith Press, 1968. 386 pp.; 217 black and white illustrations, 16 color plates, bibliography, index.

Hillier's most readable overview of the relationship between people and pottery is particularly strong on the impact of Chinese porcelain and tea on the development of the English and European pottery industries, the quest for porcelain, the relationship of the potter to society, and the health hazards of the pottery business. She also clearly describes the relationship of fashion to ceramics and the developing market for English wares. *See also* "Continental and Oriental Ceramics in America."

Hodgkin, John Eliot, and Edith Hodgkin. *Examples of Early English Pottery, Named, Dated, and Inscribed.* London: Cassell, 1891. 187 pp.; illustrations.

This early work catalogues dated and inscribed slipware, tinglazed earthenware, and stoneware beginning with the sixteenth century. Like other pioneering works, this volume documents vessels now "lost" to scholars and provides keys to tracing provenances of important pieces. The engravings of inscriptions and vessels are exquisite.

Holgate, David. *New Hall and Its Imitators.* The Faber Monographs on Pottery and Porcelain, edited by Harry Garner and R. J. Charleston. London: Faber and Faber, 1971. xvi+112 pp.+257 black and white and 8 color plates; line drawings, bibliography, index.

Between 1781 and 1835, the new Hall China Manufactory in Staffordshire produced hard-paste porcelain and, later, more economical bone china. Holgate hypothesizes that the partners in this new concern saw a growing middle class that wanted "simple and comparatively cheap gilded and coloured tea-sets" (p. 16) and moved to capture that market. He is able to reconstruct a partial pattern book, and thus an outline, of the factory's production, but he also surveys those wares often mistaken for New Hall products.

Hughes, G. Bernard. *English and Scottish Earthenware, 1660–1860.* London: Lutterworth Press, 1961. 238 pp.; line drawings, 46 black and white and 4 color plates, index.

The most readable introduction and overview of the development of English earthenware, this is a good place for a novice to begin. Information on the Staffordshire potters catering to the American trade is included.

Hughes, G. Bernard. *Victorian Pottery and Porcelain.* 1959. Reprint. London: Spring Books, 1967. 184 pp.; 89 plates, bibliography, index.

Until recently ceramics scholars have often neglected later nineteenth-century wares, dismissing the ornate styles of the Victorian era. This early work is an important exception and remains among the best one-volume introductions to nineteenth-century English ceramics.

Jewitt, Llewellynn. *The Ceramic Art of Great Britain.* 1883. Facsimile. New Orleans: New Orchard Editions, 1985. 642 pp.; 1,816 illustrations, index.

This facsimile of the 1883 edition abridging Jewitt's 1878 two-volume *Ceramic Art of Great Britain* is more of a compilation than a history. It covers the British ceramics industry from prehistoric times to the late 1870s. Jewitt was a firsthand observer of the industry in the third quarter of the nineteenth century. He consistently describes what the contemporary potters were producing and often mentions their involvement in the American trade.

Klamkin, Marian. *American Patriotic and Political China.* New York: Charles Scribner's Sons, 1973. viii+215 pp.; 256 black and white illustrations, 32 color plates, appendix, glossary, bibliography, index.

American historical and political events have long been represented in the ceramics medium. Klamkin compiles these commemorative items and discusses the events that produced them, beginning with the Revolution and leading up to Apollo 11. Her chatty commentary on the political and historical events that are commemorated from transfer-printed plates to small figurines is undocumented, yet she provides a good summary of British production for the American market and briefly lists those firms whose main trade was export to America. The appendix is a useful listing of American commemorative scenes on plates made before 1930.

Klapthor, Margaret Brown. *Official White House China, 1789 to the Present.* Washington, D.C.: Smithsonian Institution Press, 1975. 283 pp.; 97 black and white illustrations and color plates, appendixes, index.

The White House and Smithsonian collections of presidential china have fascinated collectors and historians, as well as first ladies, for almost a century. By using the extensive archival records of publicly funded purchases of official china, Klapthor moves far beyond earlier works to a study of the types, manufacturers, prices, and pieces making up dinner services throughout American history. She provides a useful view of the changes in the "top of the scale" ceramics available and in use. Although this work concentrates on the more elegant state services, the common daily tablewares are also included. *See also* "Continental and Oriental Ceramics in America."

Larsen, Ellouise Baker. *American Historical Views on Staffordshire China*. New York: Doubleday, Doran, 1939. 270 pp.; black and white and color plates, appendixes, bibliography, indexes.

This is an early study that documents print sources for American transfer patterns. In addition to tracing the origins of the patterns, Larson includes good descriptions and photographs of the transfer printing process from the Copeland (Spode) Works in Stoke-on-Trent.

Lewis, John, and Griselda Lewis. *Pratt Ware, 1780–1840*. Woodbridge, Suffolk: Baron Publishing, 1984. 304 pp.; 520 black and white and 57 color illustrations, appendixes, bibliography, index.

Pratt ware is another of the many misnomers in ceramics history. It is used to describe "relief decorated, high temperature fired, underglaze colored cream and pearlware made from about 1780 to 1840." This ware was produced by many British potters, although its name was drawn from F. and R. Pratt of Fenton. The Lewises trace its production through marked pieces and divide the numerous unattributed examples into thematic units. This work is well illustrated and documented and includes an attempt to trace "borrowed" styles and motifs from potter to potter.

Lipski, Louis L. *Dated English Delftware: Tin-Glazed Earthenware, 1600–1800*. Edited and augmented by Michael Archer; contributions by Robert J. Charleston, M. K. Stammers, and Douglas C. Harrod. London: Sotheby Publications, 1984; distributed by Harper and Row. 447 pp.; 16 color plates, 1,790 illustrated entries, indexes.

This remarkable volume differs on two levels from many traditional ceramics sourcebooks. First, it is an extensive compendium of dated pieces that are illustrated chronologically. Second, it groups English delftware by form and function, not by manufacturer or stylistic attributes. These two factors enable a clear view of two centuries of chronological change in delftwares. An introductory essay by Robert Charleston places these changes within a context of social and cultural conditions, particularly in the introduction of forms to fill new needs and developments in "the sister arts and crafts." The many photographs included are clear and well documented, and the index by subject, place, and person makes this a quick and impressive reference source.

Lockett, Terence A. *Davenport Pottery and Porcelain, 1794–1887*. Rutland, Vt.: Charles E. Tuttle Co., 1972. 111 pp.; 104 illustrations, bibliography, index.

Davenport was a major exporter of wares to the American market. Information about the factory was limited, however, until the Foxley papers became available in 1960. Using these documents, Lockett presents good information on the export trade and, to a lesser extent, the American market. Dating and identifying Davenport ware remain the volume's main focus.

Lockett, Terence A., and Pat A. Halfpenny. *Creamware and Pearlware: The Fifth Exhibition from the Northern Ceramic Society*. Exhibition catalogue. Stafford, England: George Street Press, 1986. 106 pp.; 257 black and white plates, 5 color plates, bibliography.

This important catalogue contains nine equally important essays by several noted English ceramics historians. New information is presented on bat printing and the introduction date for pearlware, and excellent overviews of the development of creamware and pearlware are included. Vessels selected for this exhibition illustrate a wide variety of common styles, forms, and types produced in these wares. All vessels from the exhibition are illustrated.

McKendrick, Neil. "Josiah Wedgwood and the Commercialization of the Potteries." In Neil McKendrick, John Brewer, and J. H. Plumb, *The Birth of a Consumer Society: The Commercialization of Eighteenth Century England*, pp. 100–145. Bloomington: Indiana University Press, 1982.

The mastery of production and marketing techniques attained by Wedgwood and Thomas Bentley in the late eighteenth century placed the Staffordshire potteries on the vanguard of the industrial revolution. Whereas most scholars have concentrated on Wedgwood's technical innovations, McKendrick turns to the potter's constant concern for the market, the manipulation of public taste, and the power of social emulation in consumption. To understand both English ceramics and their meaning for users, knowledge of these developments is important. Contemporary correspondence and descriptions are skillfully presented to support McKendrick's compelling case.

Majewski, Teresa, and Michael J. O'Brien. *An Analysis of Historical Ceramics from the Central Salt River Valley of Northeast Missouri*. Publications in Archaeology no. 3. Columbia: American Archaeology Division, Department of Anthropology, University of Missouri, 1984. 121 pp.; 26 black and white illustrations, 5 color plates, bibliography.

In an extensive discussion of ceramics classification and chronology, Majewski and O'Brien argue that a simple classification system is needed that can be used by nonspecialists for the analysis of excavated assemblages. They developed such a system and applied it to ceramics from farm sites in northeastern Missouri. Unfortunately, their system separates some of the major English ceramics types into categories, based on molded or unmolded decoration, that have evolved from common ancestors. The system needs rethinking but has promise. Enough information is available on the vessels from the five sites to make the report of use to anyone studying ceramics consumption patterns.

Mankowitz, Wolf. *Wedgwood.* 1953. Reprint. London: Hamlyn Publishing Group, 1966. xx+284 pp.; 116 black and white plates, 8 color plates, glossary, bibliography, index.

Mankowitz presents a readable overview of Josiah Wedgwood and his products. Of additional value are the reprints of the 1774 and 1817 Wedgwood-shape catalogues. This is a good introduction to Wedgwood, a central figure in the history of English ceramics.

May, John, and Jennifer May. *Commemorative Pottery, 1780–1900: A Guide for Collectors.* London and Toronto: Heinemann, 1972. x+180 pp.; 249 black and white and 8 color plates, index.

As the title indicates, this book is for the collector. The Mays divide the events commemorated into categories and provide a brief historical background, followed by illustrations and suggestions of ceramics forms that may have been used. Because commemorative pieces are generally easily dated, vessels illustrated in this work are useful in tightening chronologies of technology and style. A brief guide to British museum collections is included.

Meteyard, Eliza. *The Life of Josiah Wedgwood from His Correspondence and Family Papers in the Possession of Joseph Mayer, Esq., F.S.A., F. Wedgwood, Esq., C. Darwin, Esq., M.A., F.S.A., Miss Wedgwood, and Other Original Sources, with an Introductory Sketch of the Art of Pottery in England.* 2 vols. London: Hurst and Blackett, 1865–66. Vol. 1, xxxv+504 pp.; vol. 2, xxiv+643 pp.; 267 illustrations, index.

Meteyard's early biography of Wedgwood is rich with primary citations from his letters and papers. She discusses the development of creamware, jasper, and his other contributions, as well as the developing export trade in the eighteenth century. Although reprinted by August M. Kelley, this book is currently out of print. It remains an important source on Wedgwood.

Miller, George L. "Classification and Economic Scaling of Nineteenth-Century Ceramics." *Historical Archaeology* 14 (1980): 1–40. 5 illustrations, 3 tables, appendixes, bibliography.

Arguments are presented for the classification of nineteenth-century ceramics based on their type of decoration rather than ware type. This would be in agreement with the descriptions of the potters, merchants, and consumers in that period. Using potters' price-fixing lists, bills of lading, and account books, Miller establishes sets of price index values for plates, cups, and bowls for the first half of the nineteenth century. These index values are then used to compare the expenditure patterns for ceramics from six archaeological assemblages.

Miller, George L. "George M. Coates, Pottery Merchant of Philadelphia, 1817–1831." *Winterthur Portfolio* 19, no. 1 (Spring 1984): 37–92. 1 illustration, 4 tables.

In this description of the role of a pottery jobber and his relation to the import trade and country merchants, Miller discusses the function of the Staffordshire potters' 1814 price-fixing list in the pottery trade from the end of the War of 1812 to 1850 and the range of ceramics available during that period. The article reprints the 1814 price list. Also included is a study of the cumulative purchases of five country merchants.

Miller, George L. "Marketing Ceramics in North America: An Introduction." *Winterthur Portfolio* 19, no. 1 (Spring 1984): 1–5.

Miller gives an overview of the changes in the marketing of ceramics to North America as the trade evolved from merchant to manufacturer financing in the nineteenth century. This is an introduction to four articles, by Regina Lee Blaszczyk, Bernard L. Herman, Arlene Palmer Schwind, and Miller, on the marketing of ceramics in the eighteenth and nineteenth centuries that were published in a thematic issue of this journal.

Miller, George L. "A Tenant Farmer's Tableware: Nineteenth-Century Ceramics from Tabb's Purchase." *Maryland Historical Magazine* 69, no. 2 (Summer 1974): 197–210. 5 illustrations, 2 tables.

Miller contends that the ceramics from the tenant farmer's household were purchased one or two vessels at a time or possibly at a rate to replace breakage. Even though they were purchased piecemeal, the owner was attempting to build matched sets of dishes. This effort was thwarted because of the continual changes in rim designs for shell-edge plates. Three distinct attempts were made, first with green shell edges, then blue shell edges, and finally with blue willow.

Miller, George L., and Silas D. Hurry. "Ceramic Supply in an Economically Isolated Frontier Community: Portage County of the Ohio Western Reserve, 1800–1825." *Historical Archaeology* 17, no. 2 (1983): 80–92. 3 tables, bibliography.

Prior to the completion of the Erie Canal in 1825, the Ohio Western Reserve was severely limited in products that it could profitably send to market. This, in turn, affected its ability to acquire manufactured goods such as English ceramics. This article employs a variety of sources to establish the nature of the supply system both before and after the canal was completed. Firsthand descriptions and recollections of settlers are used in conjunction with archaeological assemblages to reconstruct the limitations of the supply system and its effect on consumers.

Miller, J. Jefferson, II. *English Yellow-Glazed Earthenware.* Washington, D.C.: Smithsonian Institution Press,

1974. xvii+125 pp.; 74 black and white and 64 color plates, bibliography, appendix, index.

Miller traces the development and production of English yellow-glazed earthenware. This ware is related to creamware and pearlware but has an overall yellow glaze decorated in a myriad of techniques, including enameling, transfer printing, molding, and luster. This volume is important not only because it is the first major study of yellowware but also because it forms a simple, well-documented introduction to early nineteenth-century earthenware. Miller also focuses on those ceramics made specifically for the American market.

Miller, J. Jefferson, II, and Lyle M. Stone. *Eighteenth-Century Ceramics from Fort Michilimackinac: A Study in Historical Archaeology.* Smithsonian Studies in History and Technology, no. 4. Washington, D.C.: Smithsonian Institution Press, 1970. ix+130 pp.; 51 illustrations, bibliography, appendixes, index.

This pioneering study attempts to combine anthropological and art historical approaches to the study of a major collection of ceramics from a complex site. Fort Michilimackinac was occupied by the French from 1715 to 1760 and by the British from 1760 to 1780. Seven years of excavation produced more than 14,000 shards. To analyze this large collection, Miller and Stone set up a simple classification by type and variety, with the major categories being earthenware, stoneware, and porcelain. These groups were further broken down by decoration. Strengths of the study are its presentation of the quantities found and the excellent illustrations of the common types of ceramics. Its major weakness is that the collections are lumped as though they represented one point in time. All dating information comes from external evidence rather than the contexts in which the shards were found. *See also* "Continental and Oriental Ceramics in America."

Mountford, Arnold R. "Documents Relating to English Ceramics of the Eighteenth and Nineteenth Centuries." *Journal of Ceramic History* 8 (1975): 3–41.

Mountford has reprinted twelve primary documents related to the development of the English ceramics industry, making this an important article for scholars studying technology, trade, and prices. Among those documents are Staffordshire potters' price-fixing lists for 1770, 1795, 1796, and 1846. In addition, there are potters' wage lists for 1836, 1850, and 1851.

Mountford, Arnold R. *The Illustrated Guide to Staffordshire Salt-Glazed Stoneware.* The Illustrated Guides to Pottery and Porcelain, edited by Geoffrey A. Godden. London: Barrie and Jenkins; New York: Praeger Publishers, 1971. xxi+88 pp.+244 black and white plates; 7 color plates, appendixes, bibliography, index.

Considered to be the bible on the subject, this guide includes excellent documentary and technological information on the development of white salt-glazed stoneware in Staffordshire. A chronology is constructed by the extensive use of mold blocks, waster shards, and dated vessels. While not a major focus, prices and marketing are also discussed.

Nelson, Christina H. "Transfer-Printed Creamware and Pearlware for the American Market." *Winterthur Portfolio* 15, no. 2 (Summer 1980): 93–115. 32 illustrations.

The introduction of transfer printing in mid eighteenth-century Liverpool ushered in a new era in the ceramics industry. Nelson's study traces the earliest efforts to commemorate historical figures and events, particularly naval ships, on ceramic wares, and seeks to identify the sources for these patterns by examining contemporary prints. She documents that most print sources for English wares with American views were indeed American, even though the ceramic versions varied slightly and were embellished with generalized floral and decorative techniques.

Noël Hume, Ivor. "Creamware to Pearlware: A Williamsburg Perspective." In *Ceramics in America*, edited by Ian M. G. Quimby, pp. 217–54. Winterthur Conference Report 1972. Charlottesville: University Press of Virginia for the Henry Francis du Pont Winterthur Museum, 1972. 17 illustrations.

This important article masterfully blends documentary and archaeological evidence of the development of creamware and pearlware in Staffordshire. It also documents the time lag between the introduction of creamware in England and its importation to Virginia. Ample illustration of these wares is provided from the extensive archaeological collections of Colonial Williamsburg Foundation. This essay provides a sense of what were common, popular wares in Virginia from the 1770s to the 1830s.

Noël Hume, Ivor. *Early English Delftware from London and Virginia.* Colonial Williamsburg Occasional Papers in Archaeology, vol. 2. Williamsburg: Colonial Williamsburg Foundation, 1977. xii+125 pp.; 22 black and white illustrations, 58 black and white plates, 7 color plates, bibliography, index.

In this superb working of documents and ceramics from archaeological contexts, a collection of delft wasters from London were linked with a potter that had investments in Virginia with the governor of the colony. By chance, Noël Hume was involved in the excavation of both sites, and his combination of that information with historical documentation provides an insight into the dating and identification of delftware from the early seventeenth century and its exportation to Virginia.

Noël Hume, Ivor. "Pearlware: Forgotten Milestone of English Ceramic History." In *English Pottery and Porcelain: An Historical Survey*, edited by Paul Atterbury, pp. 42–49. New York: Universe Books, 1978. 10 illustrations.

Noël Hume studies the technological innovation and marketing strategies by Wedgwood that led to the production of pearlware and the decorative techniques that were used to embellish it. Because little fanfare was given its arrival or demise, Wedgwood considered its contribution "more technical than decorative." Extensive research led to Noël Hume's conclusion that what is labeled pearlware today was actually called "pearl white" by Josiah Wedgwood and "china glaze" by other potters.

Noël Hume, Ivor. *Pottery and Porcelain in Colonial Williamsburg's Archaeological Collections.* Colonial Williamsburg Archaeological Series no. 2. Williamsburg: Colonial Williamsburg, 1969. 46 pp.; 43 illustrations, appendix.

This text summarizes the major categories of ceramics recovered from excavations by Colonial Williamsburg Foundation. Eighteenth-century Williamsburg, like most English colonies, was flooded with mercantile goods, and most of the range of ceramics manufactured and used in England were similarly found in homes there. Evidence from both the historical and the archaeological records documents the use of local and imported tablewares, teawares, and utilitarian wares by Williamsburg residents. Noël Hume's extensive research and his incomparable style combine to make this inexpensive popular pamphlet a most authoritative, yet easily read, review of the role of English ceramics in America.

Noël Hume, Ivor. "The Rise and Fall of English White Salt-Glazed Stoneware." *Antiques,* pt. 1, 97, no. 2 (February 1970): 248–55; pt. 2, 97, no. 3 (March 1970): 408–13. 14 illustrations; 9 illustrations.

Development of white salt-glazed stoneware is summarized in this work by using documentary sources, dated vessels, and vessels from tightly dated archaeological contexts. Noël Hume also discusses the transition of patterns from white salt-glazed stoneware to lead-glazed earthenware. Illustrations of common forms are included.

Noël Hume, Ivor. "The What, Who, and When of English Creamware Plate Design." *Antiques* 101, no. 2 (February 1972): 350–55. 9 illustrations.

Noël Hume once again expertly blends documentary sources and vessels excavated from Williamsburg. His subject here is the development and evolution of the common English molded plate patterns from the last half of the eighteenth century.

Oswald, Adrian, in collaboration with R. J. C. Hildyard and R. G. Hughes. *English Brown Stoneware, 1670–1900.* The Faber Monographs on Pottery and Porcelain, edited by R. J. Charleston and Margaret Medley. London: Faber and Faber, 1982. 308 pp.; 195 black and white and 9 color plates, line drawings, appendixes, bibliography, index.

This book is the best source on English brown salt-glazed stoneware. Using excellent documentary evidence, Oswald and coauthors summarize the development of the salt-glazed stoneware industry in England. An extensive listing of dated and marked pieces is included along with drawings of commonly occurring types of decorative motifs.

Otto, John Solomon. "Artifacts and Status Differences— A Comparison of Ceramics from Planter, Overseer, and Slave Sites on an Antebellum Plantation." In *Research Strategies in Historical Archaeology,* edited by Stanley South, pp. 91–118. New York: Academic Press, 1977. 2 illustrations, appendixes.

Otto's study of ceramics excavated from a nineteenth-century Georgia plantation is an attempt to test the often-stated premise that social and economic status may be measured by means of a distributional analysis of ceramics types and forms. His conclusions are that there were discernible differences between the ceramics used by planter, overseer, and slave. For example, mainly shell-edge plates were issued by this planter family to both overseer and slaves, but transfer-print patterns were reserved for their own daily use. In addition, the frequency of serving bowls and flatware shapes similarly indicates differences in diet and food ways that are reflective of social-status differences on early nineteenth-century plantations.

Praetzellis, Mary, Betty Rivers, and Jeanette K. Schulz. *Ceramic Marks from Old Sacramento.* California Archaeological Report no. 22. Sacramento: Department of Parks and Recreation, 1983. 108 pp.; illustrations.

More than 1,000 ceramics marks from excavated vessels in Sacramento are compiled in this work. This type of study is an important step toward defining just which potters were supplying what markets during various periods of time. In addition, this can be used to define when the English dominance began to feel the impact of American production and imports from other countries.

Price, Cynthia R. *Nineteenth Century Ceramics . . . in the Eastern Ozark Border Region.* Southwest Missouri State University Center for Archaeological Research Monograph Series, no. 1. Springfield, Mo.: Center for Archaeological Research, 1979. xi+85 pp.; 6 illustrations, 13 plates, bibliography, appendix.

Price's monograph was written to fill the need for a refined chronology of nineteenth-century ceramics for the dating of undocumented sites in the Midwest. She also presents a brief analysis of several Ozark sites in comparison with other United States and Canadian sites. Basic definitions of ware types and decorations and their respective date ranges are garnered from the ceramics literature and are refined based on archaeological assemblages.

Robacker, Earl F., and Ada F. Robacker. *Spatterware and Sponge: Hardy Perennials of Ceramics.* South Brunswick,

N.J., and New York: A. S. Barnes, 1978. 167 pp.; black and white and color illustrations, bibliography, index.

In their major compilation of information on nineteenth-century spatter- and sponge-decorated wares, the Robackers discuss the potters producing the wares as well as the markets for which they were being made. Some of their reasoning, such as why the majority of sponge- and spatterwares was unmarked, is spurious.

Ross, Lester A. "Transfer Printed Spodeware Imported by the Hudson's Bay Company: Temporal Markers for the Northwestern United States, ca. 1836–1853." *Northwest Anthropological Research Notes* 11, no. 4 (1976): 192–217. Illustrations.

Ross documents the special relationship between Hudson's Bay Company and Staffordshire potters Copeland and Garrett. Excavations at Fort Vancouver by the National Park Service recovered more than 75,000 transfer-printed shards from 135 different patterns. Of those patterns, 60 have been identified as Copeland and Garrett, accounting for 90 percent of the transfer-printed vessels recovered. Ross illustrates 66 different patterns from the fort.

Roth, Rodris. *Tea Drinking in Eighteenth-Century America: Its Etiquette and Equipage. See* "Surveys."

Roussel, Diana Edwards. *The Castleford Pottery, 1790–1821*. Wakefield, West Yorkshire: Wakefield Historical Publications; Belmont, Mass.: Londonderry Press for Wakefield Historical Publications, 1982. xii+[240] pp.; 370 black and white and 4 color plates, line drawings, maps, bibliography, index.

Little is known of the hundreds of secondary English potteries operating in the eighteenth and nineteenth centuries. Thus Roussel's study of the ceramics trade from the perspective of the small D. Dunderdale and Company's Castleford Pottery is an important addition to the literature. Undoubtedly Castleford Pottery would also be relegated to historical anonymity if it were not for the surviving 1796 pattern book and the misapplied generic term *Castleford wares* for high-fired, silver-shape, molded stoneware. Roussel attempts to clarify these errors of classification by defining the pottery's production of this stoneware and highlighting its significant output of creamware and pearlware. An important addition to the text is a reprint of the 1796 pattern book, which consists of some 260 line drawings of vessel forms.

Sandon, Henry. *The Illustrated Guide to Worcester Porcelain, 1751–1793*. 3d ed. London: Barrie and Jenkins, 1980. xvii+96 pp.+149 black and white and 8 color plates; bibliography, index.

As Sandon points out, studies of eighteenth-century Worcester porcelain are well represented in ceramics scholarship, usually basing factory attribution on aesthetic reasons. However, his excavation of the factory site provides new data on

Worcester production that directly contradicts some previous works. For instance, some of the waster shards have characteristics that have been attributed to other factories. The archaeological deposits enable Sandon to provide tighter dating controls on the popularity of various styles. This book does not supersede other scholarship on the subject, but it is important reading to assess the literature critically.

Schwind, Arlene Palmer. "The Ceramic Imports of Frederick Rhinelander, New York Loyalist Merchant." *Winterthur Portfolio* 19, no. 1 (Spring 1984): 21–36. 13 illustrations.

Although most of the goods that Rhinelander imported to New York were English, a substantial amount of Chinese export porcelain also came to him via the London firm Hodgson and Donaldson. Schwind suggests visual identification of wares described in Rhinelander's records and outlines the business and inventory of ceramics of a Loyalist New York importer during the American Revolution and British occupation. The emergence of specialized importers of ceramics and glass, such as Rhinelander, in urban areas in the later eighteenth century marks an important turning point in the history of ceramics in America. Rhinelander's extensive papers are fertile ground for research, and Schwind clearly documents the types of ceramics available, and thus in demand, in American markets. *See also* "Continental and Oriental Ceramics in America."

Shaw, Simeon. *History of the Staffordshire Potteries and the Rise and Progress of the Manufacture of Pottery and Porcelain; with Reference of Genuine Specimens and Notices of Eminent Potters*. 1829. Reprint. Great Neck, N.Y.: Beatrice C. Weinstock, 1968. xxiii+244 pp.; index.

Shaw's history is a primary source on the Staffordshire ceramics industry and is frequently quoted by historians. It is a key document for understanding the development of the wares that captured a world market. Shaw lived in the potteries, had access to many potters, and assembled a great deal of information that is available in no other place.

[Slossen, Annie]. *The China Hunter's Club*. New York: Harper and Brothers, 1878. 274 pp.; 32 illustrations.

This was the first book focusing on china collecting in America, and it is important because it shows a growing historical consciousness that began developing around the time of the Centennial. Slossen describes the beginnings of the "club" as a decision on an activity that her group would undertake for one winter. Out of this grew an extended interest in collecting and studying pottery. These pioneer collectors and this book, along with Alice Morse Earle's *China Collecting in America*, laid the groundwork for future collectors and established terminology. An emphasis was placed on transfer-printed views of America, Chinese porcelain, Wedgwood, and vessels that could be associated with famous people.

Smith, Alan. *The Illustrated Guide to Liverpool Herculaneum Pottery, 1796–1840.* The Illustrated Guides to Pottery and Porcelain, edited by Geoffrey Godden. London: Barrie and Jenkins, 1970. xvi+142 pp.; 191 black and white illustrations, 7 color plates, 8 drawings, 4 maps, appendixes, bibliography, index. Simultaneously published at New York: Praeger Publishers.

Smith's guide is a well-documented history of Herculaneum pottery. In addition, generous documentation related to the American trade in the early nineteenth century is presented. The appendixes contain extracts from primary sources relating to the management of the pottery business and technological information, which shed light on the way the trade functioned.

South, Stanley. "'Evolution and Horizon as Revealed in Ceramic Analysis in Historical Archeology': A Step toward the Development of Archaeological Science." In *The Conference on Historic Site Archaeology Papers 1971* 6, pt. 1, and *The Historical Archaeology Forum* 6, pt. 2, sec. 1, 2, edited by Stanley South (1972): 71–116. 2 tables, bibliography, appendixes.

South proposes a formula for establishing the mean date of archaeological sites by averaging the mean dates of production of excavated ceramic shards. This mean-date formula has become widely used by historical archaeologists and is fairly accurate for eighteenth-century sites. Of special interest are date ranges for common types of ceramics found on American sites. These ranges are based on Ivor Noël Hume's research, which provides a convenient guide for dating.

Stefano, Frank, Jr. "James and Ralph Clews, Nineteenth-Century Potters, Part I: The English Experience." *Antiques* 105, no. 2 (February 1974): 324–28. 6 black and white illustrations, 4 color plates.
———. "James Clews, Nineteenth-Century Potter, Part II: The American Experience." *Antiques* 105, no. 3 (March 1974): 553–55. 3 illustrations.

Ralph and James Clews were major exporters of Staffordshire ware to the American market from after the War of 1812 to 1834. Stefano provides an excellent history of the pottery and its relationship to the American market. After the Clews pottery went bankrupt in 1834, James Clews came to America as part of a venture to produce whiteware near Troy, Indiana. Documentation of this effort is interesting, and it is perhaps the most important part of these articles.

Stone, Garry Wheeler. "Ceramics from Suffolk County, Massachusetts, Inventories, 1680–1775: A Preliminary Study with Divers Comments thereon, and Sundry Suggestions." *The Conference on Historic Site Archaeology Papers 1968* 3 (1970): 73–90.

In a unique study of probate inventories by an archaeologist, ceramics were extracted from 318 inventories and examined by the types of wares owned by different wealth groups. Stone established a relationship between the ownership of porcelain and social status. He also demonstrated a difference in rural versus urban ownership patterns. This article was a "Forum" presentation, and many scholars responded to Stone's paper. These comments and his replies to them are included in the same issue (pp. 91–132).

Stone, Garry Wheeler. "Ceramics from the John Hicks Site, 1723–1743: The Material Culture." In *Ceramics in America*, edited by Ian M. G. Quimby, pp. 103–40. Winterthur Conference Report 1972. Charlottesville: University Press of Virginia for the Henry Francis du Pont Winterthur Museum, 1973. 9 illustrations, 5 tables.

Stone discusses the social significance of ceramics excavated from the mid eighteenth-century Hicks site in St. Mary's County, Maryland. Extensive research by Lois Carr in a companion article preceding Stone's in the same volume provides a compelling background of the social and economic place of Hicks in the cohort of his peers and neighbors. Stone furthers this analysis through the study of ceramics in their probate inventories. He concludes that ceramics were only minimally important to most mid eighteenth-century St. Mary's County residents and that fine ceramics were mostly owned by the elite. The unusually large collection of ceramics excavated from Hicks's home is thus attributed to his background in a British social system that placed a higher value on such status symbols. For additional background on the site, see Lois Green Carr, "Ceramics from the John Hicks Site, 1723–1743: The St. Mary's Town Land Community," in *Ceramics in America*, ed. Ian M. G. Quimby (Charlottesville: University Press of Virginia, 1973), pp. 75–102.

Stonewares and Stone Chinas of Northern England to 1851. Exhibition catalogue. Stoke-on-Trent: City Museum and Art Gallery, 1982. 152 pp.; approximately 20 illustrations, 297 illustrated entries, bibliography.

This publication sketches the wide range of stoneware produced in northern England, first by region, then by type. The exhibition, and hence the catalogue, concentrated on less well known stoneware, such as basaltes and caneware, and attempted to further ceramic history, not merely to give a balanced overview of all production. However, the excellent bibliographic guide points to further reading, and the brief essays are informative and delightful.

Teller, Barbara Gorely. "Ceramics in Providence, 1750–1800: An Inventory Survey." *Antiques* 94, no. 4 (October 1968): 570–77.

Teller's study of the probate inventories of Providence, Rhode Island, is an important early effort to associate ceramics with their owners. She lumped the probate inventories into three groups based on the total value of the estate and examined the ceramics in relation to the occupations of those who owned them. In addition to providing a breakdown of the wares by owner's occupation, Teller provides a generous sampling of the way in which the ceramics were described in the inventories.

Thomas, John. *The Rise of the Staffordshire Potteries*. Preface by G. D. H. Cole. Bath, Somerset: Adams and Dart; New York: Augustus M. Kelley, 1971. xi+228 pp.; 52 illustrations, bibliography, index.

Thomas's study of the Staffordshire industry is undertaken from an economic-historical point of view. This work was distilled from his 1938 dissertation and is focused on production changes, such as the introduction of steam engines into the potteries, clay sources, canals, and labor organization. While the book provides the background information needed to understand the development of the industry, it is rather weak in dealing with marketing, the importance of which has been clearly demonstrated by other scholars; see Neil McKendrick, "Josiah Wedgwood and the Commercialization of the Potteries."

Towner, Donald. *Creamware*. London: Faber and Faber, 1978. 240 pp.; line drawings, 158 black and white plates, 8 color plates, appendixes, bibliography, index.

Towner has written the definitive sourcebook for this ware. The introduction of creamware was one of the pivotal points in ceramics history, and its common occurrence in America in the second half of the eighteenth century is well known. Towner discusses the major sources of creamware manufacture as well as its evolution. Unfortunately, a distorted view of creamware is presented because of his orientation toward decorated wares, whereas most creamware was undecorated. The appendixes are useful compendiums of information on extant pattern books and marks and include line drawings of stylistic elements.

Towner, Donald. *The Leeds Pottery*. New York: Taplinger Publishing Co., 1965. 180 pp.; line drawings, 48 black and white and 4 color plates, appendix, bibliography, index.

In this classic history of a pottery by a dean of English ceramics research, Towner emphasizes the identification of Leeds wares and the range of products produced at the factory. A reprint of the 1814 Leeds catalogue is included as a major source of information for identification and dating. The appendix contains primary sources, such as letters, newspaper advertisements, and indentures.

Turner, William, ed. *William Adams: An Old English Potter, with Some Account of His Family and Their Productions*. London: Chapman and Hall; New York: Keramic Studio Publishing Co., 1904. xxii+252 pp.; 72 plates, appendixes, charts, index.

Despite the title, Turner's subject is actually Adams and three of his descendants with the same name. Adams and his successors exported large quantities of ceramics to the United States, and they made transfer-printed patterns for that market. This book has extensive lists of Adams pieces with American views, as well as primary information on prices, technological developments, and some insight into the export trade.

U.S. Department of Commerce. *The Pottery Industry: Report on the Cost of Production in the Earthenware and China Industries of the United States, England, Germany, and Austria*. Miscellaneous Series no. 21. Washington, D.C.: Government Printing Office, 1915. 709 pp.

This work is a massive government study of cost of production, technology in use, prices, and government regulations of the pottery industries of the United States, England, Germany, and Austria.

Unearthing New England's Past: The Ceramic Evidence. Exhibition catalogue. Lexington, Mass.: Scottish Rite Masonic Museum of Our National Heritage, 1984. 112 pp.; illustrations, bibliography.

Conceived to celebrate the fiftieth anniversary of the China Student's Club of Boston, this catalogue is the result of the cooperation of archaeologists, social historians, and collectors from throughout New England. The first section includes brief essays on the origins, terminology, production, distribution, and archaeological interpretation of ceramics. The remainder of the volume is devoted to brief backgrounds of nine archaeological sites and a catalogue of their significant ceramic artifacts. Extant examples of ceramic vessels provided by members of the club sprinkle the catalogue. The greatest part of the foreign material included is English, although Chinese export porcelain, Rhenish stoneware, and Dutch delft also appear. *See also* "Continental and Oriental Ceramics in America."

Vaisey, D. G., and F. Celoria. "Inventory of George Ecton, 'Potter' of Abingdon, Berks, 1696." *Journal of Ceramic History* 7 (1974): 13–42. Bibliography, index.

Vaisey and Celoria transcribe and annotate a detailed inventory of Ecton, a self-styled seventeenth-century "potter" of the Thames valley. The lack of any reference to potters' tools and materials leads them to suggest that Ecton was a retailer. However, the large number of ceramic and glass vessels in his inventory indicates more specialization than a mercer, grocer, or chandler, the normal retail outlets. This study provides annotations of all the listed vessels with dated references. This is an excellent guide to seventeenth-century terminology, and it provides a glimpse of the forms available and their prices.

Walton, Peter. *Creamware and Other English Pottery at Temple Newsam House, Leeds*. London: Manningham Press, 1976. 293 pp.; 374 black and white illustrations, 17 color plates, bibliography, index.

This work is among the largest and best collections of photographs of creamware and other common wares from the eighteenth and early nineteenth centuries. While this catalogue does not discuss the use of English ceramics in America, it is a very useful source for identification and attribution.

Watkins, Lura Woodside. "Colorful Ceramics of the 1880s in a Family Collection." *Antiques* 93, no. 1 (January 1968): 100–103. 10 illustrations.

A brief discussion of late nineteenth-century ceramics in a family collection, this article points out the explosion of brightly colored wares following the Centennial Exhibition of 1876. These wares contrasted the plain white ironstones that were common in the immediately preceding era.

Watney, Bernard. *English Blue and White Porcelain of the Eighteenth Century*. New York: Thomas Yoseloff, 1964. xii+137 pp.; 4 black and white and color plates, index.

Watney discusses the history and wares of individual English porcelain factories. Although this work has been somewhat superseded by lengthy studies of particular factories, it is still useful in providing a one-volume comparative framework. The small black and white plates, however, are a hindrance to the volume's utility as an identification source.

Weatherill, Lorna. *The Pottery Trade and North Staffordshire, 1660–1760*. London: Manchester University Press, 1971. xviii+174 pp.; 20 illustrations, 12 plates, 7 maps, 16 tables, appendixes, bibliography, index. Simultaneously published at New York: Augustus M. Kelley.

Weatherill analyzes the early development of North Staffordshire as a precedent to the industrial revolution. Solid economic treatment of the raw materials, production, labor, growth, and marketing of the pottery industry is presented, with particular attention given to the development of Staffordshire in relation to the growing pottery industry. Weatherill documents that exports to America and Europe were more extensive in this early era than previously thought.

Weinrich, Peter H. *A Bibliographic Guide to Books on Ceramics—Guide bibliographique des ouvrages sur la céramique*. Ottawa: Canadian Crafts Council, 1976. 272 pp.; index.

This generalized bibliography on ceramics, which is limited to books, contains twenty-three pages of references to English ceramics and seven pages on American wares. These sources cover some titles that are not included in this bibliography. A major weakness of Weinrich's compilation is that it does not include periodicals.

Wetherbee, Jean. *A Look at White Ironstone*. Des Moines: Wallace-Homestead Book Co., 1980. 159 pp.; 105 illustrations, line drawings, bibliography, index.

White ironstone was the most popular type of table- and teaware during the second half of the nineteenth century, although most of the ware was not decorated with molding. In this major compilation of information on white ironstone with molded patterns, Wetherbee provides line drawings of the molded patterns and their makers' marks, making it easy to use for the identification of unmarked vessels. One problem is that it is not always clear which patterns have been named by Wetherbee and which were named by the potters. *See also* "American Ceramics."

Whitehead, James, and Charles Whitehead. *James and Charles Whitehead Manufacturers, Hanley, Staffordshire: Designs of Sundry Articles of Earthen-ware*. Introduction by Reginald Haggar. 1798. Facsimile. Benchley, England: D. B. Drakard, n.d. 25 pp.; 34 illustrations.

Of the few eighteenth-century catalogues to survive, the Whitehead factory's illustrates 170 vessels in creamware. Illustrated shape catalogues like this were produced by Wedgwood, Leeds Pottery, Castleford Pottery, and others. They were sent to importers to facilitate ordering and to provide better communication between importers and potters. This catalogue has text in English, German, Dutch, and French. Although marking on Whitehead pieces is rare, as for most creamware vessels, this is an important source for dating and possibly identifying vessels. Caution should be used, however, as many potters produced similar vessels with the same molded motifs.

Whiter, Leonard. *Spode: A History of the Family, Factory, and Wares from 1733 to 1833*. London: Barrie and Jenkins, 1970. xiii+246 pp.; illustrations, 281 black and white and 9 color plates, drawings, charts, appendixes, bibliography, indexes.

Although Spode did not concentrate on the American market to the extent of some of his competitors, Spode production was of major significance in the Staffordshire industry. It is especially important to ceramics historians because, like Wedgwood, extensive documentation is extant. Whiter's discussion provides a view of the specific Spode production firmly placed within a framework of general industrywide technological practices, innovations, and trends. This balance, as well as Whiter's pleasant style, makes this book a worthy introduction for the novice to the Staffordshire pottery industry itself. The Spode shape book, pattern book, selected prices, and marks, as well as profuse illustration and excellent documentation, should attract the serious scholar as well.

Williams, Howard Y. *Gaudy Welsh China*. Des Moines: Wallace-Homestead Book Co., 1978. 130 pp.; 42 black and white illustrations, 10 color plates, line drawings, map, bibliography.

Gaudy Welsh was inexpensive pottery that enjoyed a limited

range of popularity in the mid nineteenth century and which is rarely marked. Williams's study of these wares is a refreshing change from typical ceramics books because he adds a healthy dose of social and economic history in a readable style. While he is writing for a collecting audience, he points out that these pots had a social context that collectors should be interested in. In addition to his social history sketch, a good discussion of the conditions in the potteries and the technological changes that were taking place is included. This is the only work available on the subject.

Williams, Petra. *Staffordshire Romantic Transfer Patterns: Cup Plates and Early Victorian China*. Jeffersontown, Ky.: Foundation House East, 1978. 763 pp.; illustrations, bibliography, glossary, index.

This photographic catalogue of transfer-printed romantic scenes on Staffordshire pottery, while not all-inclusive, illustrates hundreds of patterns and includes descriptions of scenes, marks, attributions, and dates. Organized by category, such as "Scenic" or "Oriental," and alphabetized by pattern name, this volume is a handy reference guide to the common transfer prints from the second quarter of the nineteenth century. Although the photographs are not well produced, it is among the few books that specialize in these later transfer prints and remains a standard.

Williams, Susan R. "Flow-Blue." *Antiques* 126, no. 4 (October 1984): 923–31. 15 black and white illustrations, 5 color plates.

Beginning in the 1830s and continuing to the early twentieth century, flow-blue, or "halolike," designs were produced on white earthenware, opaque china, and stone china. These were an attempt to copy the slightly fuzzy designs that the public had grown to associate with oriental export tablewares. Generalized Chinese, Japanese, and (later) art nouveau motifs were common. Williams's documentation is excellent, and her discussion of prices from sources such as the Montgomery Ward catalogue provides a cultural context that is often lacking in short, descriptive articles.

Williams-Wood, Cyril. *English Transfer-Printed Pottery and Porcelain: A History of Over-Glaze Printing*. London: Faber and Faber, 1981. 249 pp.; 159 black and white plates, 8 color plates, bibliography, index.

This well-documented history of the development of over-glazed printing on English ceramics includes good technical descriptions of the decorative processes. Unfortunately, some of the information will be supplanted by the research of Paul Holdway, who has demonstrated that most overglaze-printed wares from the eighteenth century were glue-bat printed.

American Glass

KIRK NELSON

NINETEENTH-CENTURY WRITERS addressing the subject of glass frequently extolled its incalculable influence on the character of American life, tirelessly describing the limitless forms it could take and the functions it could serve. In the twentieth century, a formidable mass of literature generated by interest in glassware made and used in America provides ample testimony to the truth of their platitudes. Topics for study within the subject of American glass seem to be truly inexhaustible. More than 400 entries appear under the United States heading of the 1986 "Check List of Recently Published Articles and Books on Glass," a list published annually since 1959 in the *Journal of Glass Studies*. Among them, titles such as "Marbles Made in Navarre in 1890s" or *Historic Shotglasses: The Pre-Prohibition Era* demonstrate the extraordinary specialization of interest often focused on the subject, while Arlene Palmer Schwind's "Glassmakers of Early America," an essay examining the lives of eighteenth- and nineteenth-century glassworkers, addresses for the first time questions that promise to shed new light on many facets of American glassmaking. Reviewing the thousands of books and articles published on American glass (many of which are included in the checklists of the *Journal of Glass Studies*; in the 876-page *History and Art of Glass: Index of Periodical Articles, 1956–1979*, compiled by Louise K. Bush and Paul N. Perrot and published by Corning Museum of Glass in 1982; or in George Sang Duncan's 544-page *Bibliography of Glass: From Earliest Records to 1940*, published in London in 1960), one is struck by the magnitude of information thus far uncovered and, at the same time, by the importance of still unexplored areas and still unposed questions.

With relatively few exceptions, historical interest in American glass has fallen into the collector's domain. For this reason, questions brought to the study of glass have addressed collectors' interests almost exclusively. Literature for collectors is dominated by two different formats. The first is the typological study, where authors scour the landscape for examples of every extant salt dish, pitcher, cup plate, or other form. Like stamp albums, these studies establish perimeters within which collecting activity can be concentrated and against which success can be measured. Factory histories represent the second major format. Unpublished information about glassmakers and manufactories is avidly sought by authors in much the same way that collectors seek rare examples for their collections. Such information occasionally helps to identify the origin and period of specific examples, which represent two other important types of collecting perimeters. More often, however, its ties to attributed glassware are purely associational. The information presented is descriptive rather than analytical and provides a colorful context for glass that conforms to preconceived notions about the past.

Both typological and factory history formats were employed by Edwin AtLee Barber, whose *American Glassware: Old and New* (Philadelphia: David McKay Co., 1900) was the first book on the subject written for collectors. Barber's title is deceptively inclusive, for more than half of this slender volume presents lists of historical flasks and brief histories of the factories producing them. Barber's special interest in flasks that "illustrate events of importance in our nation's progress, or attempt to portray the features of some of the personages who were prominent in the country's history" demonstrates the patriotic incentive felt by many collectors in the late nineteenth century. Barber's interest in cup plates with historical motifs, to which he devotes a short chapter, was similarly motivated, while his desire to chronicle the progress of the industry in America is indicated by short chapters on moldmakers and the "modern" glass of Libbey and Tiffany.

Fourteen years after Barber introduced *American Glassware* to the collecting public, Frederick William Hunter's *Stiegel Glass* set a standard of excellence for factory histories that seldom has been surpassed. Hunter carefully studied the life and glasshouses of Pennsylvania's flamboyant glassmaker, "Baron" Henry William Stiegel, whose romantic riches-to-rags story exerted tremendous collector appeal. Glassware attributed to Stiegel (1763–74) or to the glasshouses of Caspar and Richard Wistar in Wistarburgh, New Jersey (1739–76), topped collectors' lists as the most prestigious pieces to acquire. While Hunter's documentary research was thorough and perceptive, by the early 1920s it had become apparent to some collectors and writers that his attributions were overzealous. Much of the glass ascribed to Stiegel and the Wistars was actually English or Continental or was manufactured by other American glasshouses. George and Helen McKearin helped to straighten out some of Hunter's misconceptions in their monumental *American Glass* by suggesting that, with a few exceptions, glass attributed to Stiegel should be considered "Stiegel type," while glass attributed to the Wistars should be labeled "South Jersey type." Helen McKearin was careful, nevertheless, to emphasize the continuing importance of Hunter's work in her excellent preface to the 1950 Dover reprint of *Stiegel Glass*.

Following the ascendancy of glassware made by Stiegel and the Wistars, the products of Boston and Sandwich Glass Company in Sandwich, Massachusetts, rose to become the third great passion of American collectors in the early 1920s. Sandwich paralleled Stiegel in romantic associations and was given credit for virtually all early pressed glass until the mid 1920s, when the pressed wares of Pittsburgh, Pennsylvania, and Cambridge, Massachusetts, became topics for discussion among collectors. The first book about glassware made in Sandwich was Lenore Wheeler Williams's *Sandwich Glass: A Technical Book for Collectors* (New York: By the author, 1922). A review argued that technical books should substantiate their conclusions and identify their sources. It went on to state: "in this respect, the literature of collecting is notably deficient in scholarly conscientiousness. Borrowing by one writer from others is common enough; but direct references to their works are extremely few. Of such unrecorded borrowings, however, the author of *Sandwich Glass* is to be pretty completely absolved. She criticizes certain unnamed writers by implication and cites one other in support of her position on a mooted point. For the rest she keeps her sources within herself" (*Antiques* 2, no. 3 [September 1922]: 132).

The 1920s were years of active interest in American glass, although much that was written during the decade has been supplanted by more extensive or accurate studies. Collectors' journals such as *Antiques*, which first appeared in 1922, helped to stimulate interest and disseminate information, while a series of encyclopedic studies helped to establish the broader confines of American glass production. The first of these studies was N. Hudson Moore's *Old Glass: European and American* (New York: Frederick A. Stokes Co., 1924). This book was enthusiastically celebrated for providing collectors with illustrations of 322 identified examples of American glass. Although Moore claimed to prefer the designation "early American" to indiscriminate attributions, she closely followed Hunter's classifications and ascribed much midwestern and foreign pressed glass to Sandwich. Despite errors obvious to the modern reader, a reviewer confidently concluded that Moore's was "a work which, for many years to come, will be looked upon as the standard American compendium on glass and glass collecting" (*Antiques* 6, no. 5 [November 1924]: 263).

Only two years later, however, *Antiques* proclaimed the arrival of a still more impressive study. Stephen Van Rensselaer's revised edition of *Early American Bottles and Flasks* (Peterborough, N.H.: Transcript Printing Co., 1926) boasted a 236-page discussion of glass manufactories and an illustrated handbook of more than 1,300 examples. A reviewer triumphantly announced: "Van Rensselaer has covered his field so completely that no one is likely to attempt to dislodge him. On points of controversy some will differ with him; on points of obscurity, subsequent investigations may cast light that will augment that which he supplies. Geniuses in tabulation may devise methods of calculation and reference which they think might lend more speedy guidance than that of this [book]. But no one person is likely very soon to tread anew the long and weary way Mr. Van Rensselaer has traveled, or to attempt to regather, rearrange, and reanimate the wealth of various information which this author has brought together" (*Antiques* 11, no. 3 [March 1927]: 220). This extravagant praise was certainly justified in reference to works that had preceded his, but others were soon to follow that set even higher standards of accuracy and comprehensiveness.

Rhea Mansfield Knittle's *Early American Glass* (New York: Century Co., 1927) stood for more than a decade as the most thorough and well conceived treatment of American glassmaking. Knittle's work was celebrated for suggesting the incredible diversity of glassmaking traditions in America. A reviewer observed: "she has swept together a vast mass of fresh material, given it an orderly arrangement, and set it vividly forth against a broadly painted background of appropriate time and place. She has come as near to writing an industrial epic as we are likely to encounter for many a year" (*Antiques* 13, no. 1 [January 1928]: 56).

In the tradition of Hunter's *Stiegel Glass*, Lura Woodside Watkins published *Cambridge Glass*, an excellent factory history of New England Glass Company. While this company lacked the romance of its rival in Sandwich, its production was more extensive and was of equal if not superior quality. A second important work of the early 1930s was Ruth Webb Lee's *Early American Pressed Glass* (Pittsford, N.Y.: By the author, 1931), which falls more in the tradition of Barber's checklists than Hunter's factory history. It presented little documentary information but was hailed as a great contribution because "pattern glass is interesting, not for its history, its age, or, except in rare instances, its inherent aesthetic appeal, but for its variety of design, its frequently excellent color, and its eminent collectibility" (*Antiques* 21, no. 3 [March 1932]: 148). Comparing Frank Chipman's *Romance of Old Sandwich Glass* (Sandwich, Mass.: Sandwich Publishing Co., 1932) first to Watkins and then to Lee, a reviewer found it "less inclusive, less carefully documented, less convincing in detail than is the one; less analytical, less convenient for reference, and less cautious in statement than the other" (*Antiques* 22, no. 6 [December 1932]: 236).

The appearance of the McKearins' *American Glass* in 1941 marked a great milestone in scholarship on the subject. Their massive tome of 634 pages consolidated research of the preceding four decades, expanded the histories of some of the factories covered in previous studies, introduced new factory histories, and presented collectors with an astounding 3,000 illustrations of identified glassware. It provided collectors with a vastly improved system of tabulation for historical flasks, as well as the first comprehensive treatment of blown three-mold wares. This outstanding achievement was followed nine years later by the publication of their *Two Hundred Years of American Blown Glass*, which provided glass collectors with illustrations of another 380 examples, each discussed more or less extensively on the facing page.

Subsequent contributions to the study of American glass have expanded our understanding of the subject by narrowing the focus of the McKearins' study. In 1972 Kenneth Wilson introduced new information about New England glass and glassmaking factories, drawing especially on period newspapers and city directories. The McKearins devoted only 37 pages to midwestern manufacturers, leaving a gap in coverage that has been partially filled by Lowell Innes's extensive work on Pittsburgh glass production. Estelle Sinclaire Farrar and Jane Shadel Spillman contributed another work focusing on the glass manufactories of an individual city, this time in Corning, New York. Surprisingly, very few in-depth studies have addressed individual manufactories; those by Robert Koch and Arlene Palmer, as well as Corning Museum of Glass's superb study of Amelung in the *Journal of Glass Studies*, represent outstanding exceptions. Equally extensive studies could be undertaken for hundreds of other factories to the great benefit of collectors and scholars.

In the decades following the publication of *American Glass*, tremendous energy has been expended in the compilation of exhaustive typological studies. Pressed glass is especially well suited to such studies, for it provides collectors with innumerable design variations to pursue and amass. Excellent examples of this genre include *American Glass Cup Plates* by Ruth Webb Lee and James H. Rose and *Pressed Glass Salt Dishes of the Lacy Period* by Logan W. Neal and Dorothy B. Neal. Paperweights, ink bottles, salt shakers, and many other forms have received similar treatments. While these works generally do not make substantive contributions to the attribution of the glass they catalogue, they do provide later researchers with a very useful overview of extant glassware. These examples can serve as the "data" for studies directed more specifically toward questions of attribution or for studies using glass and glass history to answer questions about people.

The attribution of glassware has been a persistent concern of writers throughout the twentieth century. Barber relied on factory marks as the basis for his attributions, while Hunter employed family tradition, excavation, geographic concentration, and contemporary description. Although Hunter's conclusions were not entirely sound, his methods have proved more effective for later writers as knowledge about American glassware has grown. Today many individual pieces have been associated with specific glasshouses, yet this group is still incredibly small relative to the amount of glassware that survives. Attempts to bridge the gap between these two groups have not been very successful. Glassworker migration and the use of common working techniques have made stylistic attributions to specific factories virtually impossible and regional attributions questionable. Chemical analysis holds great potential for solving questions of attribution. X-ray fluorescence machines can provide nondestructive analysis of the chemical components of glass and have been used most effectively to identify the products of the Amelung glasshouses. Unfortunately, limitations of the testing process and the use of similar formulas, common sources of raw materials, and a large percentage of old glass, or "cullet," in the glass batch have complicated the interpretation of most test results. As more tests are made and results are analyzed, patterns should emerge that will dramatically improve the accuracy of attributions. This accuracy will be improved further as researchers acquire a better understanding of worker migration and as more information is compiled from professionally directed site excavations, genealogical investigations of families associated with glasshouses, and studies of the many manufactories that have not yet come under careful scrutiny.

While questions relating directly to collecting interests have been pursued vigorously, studies directed toward other interests rarely have been undertaken. Individual studies by Pearce Davis and Warren Scoville are two examples of works using information about glass to deepen our understanding of issues relating to economic and labor history. Questions about the use of glass have remained almost completely unexplored. Information from inventories and the excavation of domestic sites could begin to unravel the meanings that glass held for individuals and demonstrate how these meanings varied from one group to another and from one period to another, as suggested by Olive R. Jones and E. Ann Smith and by Ivor Noël Hume. To what extent did these changing meanings precipitate shifts in production characteristic of the industrial revolution? Other unexplored areas include comparative studies between individuals associated with the glass industry. Who were the financial backers of the glasshouses, and what were their common interests? What can be said about machinists as a group in the glass industry, and what role did they play in the expansion of production from the 1820s onward? The biographies of the glassblowers themselves are still largely unknown. How did the character of their lives differ from that of other artisans, and how did it change from the seventeenth century to the twentieth century? Who were the wholesalers and retailers of glassware, and how did shifts in marketing reflect changing patterns of consumption? Even issues relating to the design of glassware and the shifting popularity of styles rarely have been addressed analytically.

Barlow, Raymond E., and Joan F. Kaiser. *The Glass Industry in Sandwich: Volume 4.* Photographs by Forward's Color Productions, Len Lorette, and Hugo Poisson; edited by Lloyd C. Nickerson. Windham, N.H.: Barlow-Kaiser Publishing Co., 1983. xiv+381 pp.; black and white illustrations, maps, line drawings, approximately 390 color illustrated entries, glossary, bibliography, index.

Many years of collecting experience and research are apparent in this handsomely illustrated work. Barlow and Kaiser are publishing the four volumes of their series in reverse order. Volume 4 treats the latest period of glass production at Boston and Sandwich Glass Company, from roughly 1870 to 1887, and examines the various glassworking enterprises active in Sandwich following the factory's closing in 1888. Many new facts are presented, for the products of this period have only recently aroused serious interest among collectors and researchers. Overshot or frosted glass, vasa murrhina, threaded glass, and iridescent "Travase" glass are each discussed, as are the work of decorators May Gregory and Edward Swan and the cut glass products of Nehemiah Packwoods and J. B. Vodon and Son. Chapters on candlesticks, insulators, and epergnes are included as well. Unfortunately, Barlow and Kaiser do not always footnote their sources or justify their opinions. Many attributions are presumably based on fragments excavated from the site, but the extent of this evidence for each case is not discussed, and the many factors affecting the interpretation of fragments are not evaluated. Despite these shortcomings, the volume makes a significant contribution to the literature.

Bishop, Barbara, and Martha Hassell, eds. *Your Obdt. Servt., Deming Jarves: Correspondence of the Boston and Sandwich Glass Company's Founder, 1825–1829.* Sandwich, Mass.: Sandwich Historical Society, 1984. xii+116 pp.; 22 illustrations.

Sandwich Historical Society has assembled an impressive collection of documents relating to Boston and Sandwich Glass Company, which manufactured glassware in Sandwich from 1826 until 1887. Among the most important of these are approximately forty letters written by or to the company's enigmatic founder. Jarves (1790–1869) was an innovative entrepreneur and businessman who established or helped to establish many of New England's best-known glasshouses, including New England Glass Company, Mount Washington Glass Works, and Cape Cod Glass Works. His letters, reprinted here in their entirety, illuminate the early business operations and products of the company and the many technological problems that occupied his time and thoughts.

Charleston, Robert J. *Masterpieces of Glass: A World History from the Corning Museum of Glass.* New York: Harry N. Abrams, 1980. 239 pp.; 102 color plates, glossary, bibliography, index.

This opulent volume presents a range of glass objects from the time of Tuthmosis to Tiffany in large, glossy color photographs with notes offered as aids to their appreciation. The selection emphasizes the most dazzling, luxurious, and elaborate products of the glassworks of ancient and medieval Europe and the Near East, Venice, Bohemia, the Netherlands, Great Britain, and the United States. An introduction sketches the broad outlines of the history of glass manufacture and decoration. Although the book is a compendium of decorative techniques—threading, engraving, enameling, cutting, and gilding—it finds room for a few plain blown and pressed treasures as well.

Cloak, Evelyn Campbell. *Glass Paperweights of the Bergstrom Art Center.* New York: Crown Publishers, 1969. 196 pp.; 63 color plates, glossary, bibliography, index.

John Nelson Bergstrom Art Center and Museum in Neenah, Wisconsin, owns and displays a major glass paperweight collection. The introductory text is brief, much of it recounting how Evangeline Hoysradt Bergstrom (1872–1958) assembled her collection in the 1930s and 1940s. The principal asset of the book is its color illustrations, which have been divided into four groups: French, British and other European, American, and miscellaneous pieces. This is not an interpretive work; however, owing to the broad scope of the collection, it provides readers with a useful survey of the various paperweight-making traditions. These range from French weights of the "classic" period of the mid nineteenth century to modern sulfides. An extensive bibliography is included. This catalogue is primarily a pictorial archive. *See also* Paul Hollister and Dwight P. Lanmon, *Paperweights.*

Covill, William E., Jr. *Ink Bottles and Inkwells.* Taunton, Mass.: William S. Sullwold, 1971. 431 pp.; 1,780 illustrations, indexes.

The growing popularity of fountain pens in the late nineteenth century and the invention of the ballpoint pen in the 1930s greatly reduced the demand for ink bottles and inkwells. In the eighteenth and nineteenth centuries, however, vessels for holding ink were manufactured in large numbers by virtually every bottle glasshouse in operation. Covill has photographed more than 1,700 examples, 1,500 from his personal collection, to convey the extent and variety of this production. Although the vast majority of his bottles are glass, a few short chapters are included to cover examples in pottery, stone, wood, lead, and horn. Additional chapters treat sanders, quills, and other writing accessories. Covill's text is limited to a short discussion of ink bottle use and to brief chapter introductions. Most examples have not been assigned more than a very general period of manufacture. Nevertheless, this work stands as an exhaustive checklist of ink bottle and inkwell forms, motifs, and marks.

Davis, Pearce. *The Development of the American Glass Industry.* Harvard Economic Studies, vol. 86. 1949. Reprint. New York: Russel and Russel, 1970. xiv+316 pp.; 21 tables, appendixes, bibliography, index.

Davis's work presents a quantitative and qualitative analysis of American glass production through the first quarter of the twentieth century. His emphasis falls primarily on economic and technological developments, which he first examines chronologically and then traces as they affected four major categories of glass production: window, container, pressed and blown, and plate. His analysis, although subject to revision in certain cases, was based on data drawn from a rich variety of primary sources, including government documents, travel accounts, state and local histories, letters, memoirs, brochures, newspapers, trade papers, scientific journals, and other periodicals. Reference to these sources through his extensive footnotes and bibliography provides the reader with an invaluable research tool. In addition to his coverage of economic and technological developments, Davis has carefully examined two issues of fundamental importance to the American glass industry: the tariff question and the labor movement. His treatment of these topics is more complete than that of any other writer.

Doros, Paul E. *The Tiffany Collection of the Chrysler Museum at Norfolk.* Norfolk, Va.: By the museum, 1978. 159 pp.; approximately 160 black and white illustrations and 60 color plates, bibliography.

Walter P. Chrysler, Jr., first made Louis Comfort Tiffany's acquaintance in 1931, and their friendship lasted until Tiffany's death at age eighty-four in 1933. Against the trends of popular taste, Chrysler's appreciation for Tiffany's splendid creations continued unfalteringly through the following decades. He successfully acquired many outstanding works during the low ebb of Tiffany's popularity, and today his collection is unquestionably one of the finest in the world. Doros, as curator of glass at Chrysler Museum, prepared a catalogue of this magnificent collection, which shows Tiffany's glass to excellent advantage. Beautiful color plates capture the shimmering iridescence and rich luminosity of Tiffany's lamps, vases, tiles, and tableware. An informative introduction and extensive descriptions contribute to the catalogue's general usefulness.

Farrar, Estelle Sinclaire, and Jane Shadel Spillman. *The Complete Cut and Engraved Glass of Corning.* New York: Crown Publishers for the Corning Museum of Glass, 1979. [viii]+344 pp.; 753 illustrations, bibliography, index.

This volume presents a detailed exploration of Corning's contribution to cut and engraved glass. It begins with background chapters on Corning, the cut-glass industry, and the various techniques and processes employed. Most of the book examines the scores of firms operating in Corning, some giants in the field and others active for only a few years. Images of hundreds of objects, many taken from catalogues and pattern books, indicate the range of designs and forms executed in this medium. Although the quality of the illustrations occasionally leaves something to be desired, this is

otherwise an admirable presentation of the industry and its role in the history of a city.

Hollister, Paul, Jr. *The Encyclopedia of Glass Paperweights.* New York: Clarkson N. Potter, 1969; distributed by Crown Publishers. vi+312 pp.; 242 black and white and 133 color illustrations, bibliography, glossary, index.

Millefiori is the Italian word for "a thousand flowers." To glass collectors, it describes the effect produced when thin, colored, glass rods are cut into short sections, assembled into flowerlike forms, and covered with a magnifying dome of colorless glass. Hollister traces this process from its appearance in ancient Egypt to its revival in Renaissance Venice and later adaptation for paperweight design. He identified the middle three decades of the nineteenth century as the classical period of millefiori paperweights. The bulk of his study is devoted to the weights, millefiori and others, of this period made at such manufactories as Baccarat, Clichy, Whitefriars, Gillinder and Sons, Boston and Sandwich Glass Company, and New England Glass Company. A special chapter on sulfides and one on modern paperweights complete this solid and richly illustrated study.

Hollister, Paul, and Dwight P. Lanmon. *Paperweights: "Flowers which Clothe the Meadows."* Exhibition catalogue. Corning, N.Y.: Corning Museum of Glass, 1978. 167 pp.; 306 color illustrated entries, glossary, bibliography.

Hollister provides a concise summary of the history and collecting of paperweights at the beginning of this book, but the work's major strength comes from its presentation of 306 extraordinary paperweights, most of which are French and date from the mid or late nineteenth century. Each is illustrated at full size in color and on a smaller scale in black and white. Lanmon points out in his foreword that the objects "were chosen for their quality of design and execution" (p. 8), and surely this is the case. Most of these impressive objects represent some variation of the millefiori technique, but others are decorated with swirls, sulfide portraits or scenes, flowers, fruits, or even snakes and salamanders. This is a splendid pictorial reference.

Hunter, Frederick William. *Stiegel Glass.* Introduction and notes by Helen McKearin. 1914. Reprint. New York: Dover Publications, 1950. xxii+270 pp.; 167 black and white illustrations and plates, 8 color plates, 2 maps, appendix, bibliography, index.

In her introduction to the Dover reprint, McKearin calls this text "a vital member of American glass literature" (p. xii). Her words hold true today, more than thirty years later, for Hunter's work remains the most comprehensive study of this celebrated eighteenth-century Pennsylvania glass manufactory. In the first of two major sections, Hunter provides a detailed biography of Henry William Stiegel and illuminates the account with information drawn from period documents.

Typescripts of many of these documents are presented in the appendix. After a brief overview of the history of glassmaking in America, the second section explores the materials, techniques, and products of the Stiegel glasshouses. McKearin suggests that readers of Hunter's second section substitute "Stiegel type" for "Stiegel," observing that, in his enthusiasm, Hunter was often willing to accept attributions that today seem unlikely or even impossible. While McKearin's footnotes correct many of these errors, attribution of Stiegel glass still poses a serious challenge. James H. Rose has written a suggestive article (*Journal of Glass Studies* 1 [1959]: 95–102) that examines a group of Stiegel-type enameled beakers with English inscriptions, and more recently a positively identified Stiegel wineglass has surfaced (*Glass Club Bulletin* 139 [Winter 1983]: 1–2). Hunter's text, however, remains a valuable source for both scholars and collectors.

Innes, Lowell. *Pittsburgh Glass, 1797–1891: A History and Guide for Collectors*. Boston: Houghton Mifflin Co., 1976. xix+522 pp.; 512 black and white illustrations, 12 color plates, appendixes, bibliography, index.

This comprehensive study spans nearly a century of glass production in Pittsburgh beginning in 1797, when James O'Hara and Isaac Craig founded the first glass factory in that city, and ending in 1891, when nine Pittsburgh companies merged with others in West Virginia and Ohio to form the giant United States Glass Company. Between those dates, Pittsburgh rose to become the largest of American glassmaking centers; more glass was produced there than in any other area in the United States. Innes's monumental book has two major components: a history of the development of the glass industry itself, tracing the careers of such well-known Pittsburgh manufacturers as Bakewell, Robinson, Curling, McKee, Ripley, and Duncan; and a highly personal running commentary on glass products, arranged in roughly chronological order. Chapters examine free-blown glass, cut glass, engraved glass, pattern molding, bottles and flasks, midwestern lacy glass, lamps and chimneys, art glass, and several other topics. While some critics contend that Innes failed to incorporate information that would have significantly enriched this volume, collectors and historians of popular culture will still find it to be of great value.

Jones, Olive R., and E. Ann Smith. *Glass of the British Military, ca. 1755–1820*. Studies in Archaeology, Architecture, and History. Ottawa: National Historic Parks and Sites Branch, Parks Canada, Environmental Canada, 1985. 134 pp.; 137 illustrations, bibliography.

Jones and Smith have skillfully combined contemporary accounts, information from prints, paintings, excavations of British forts in North America, and an examination of surviving glass vessels to suggest the range of glassware used by the British military. Their study extends from the period of the Seven Years' War through the decade following the War of 1812. The nature of the food and drink consumed by officers and men of the military has been carefully researched and

presented in separate chapters on wine, beer, cider, spirits, punch, nonalcoholic beverages, condiments, and desserts. Glass vessels employed during this consumption are divided into categories by use, and the book concludes with an examination of medicinal glassware, toiletries, looking glasses, lighting, inkwells, and sand glasses. This is a refreshing departure from works that list form after form without establishing their cultural contexts.

Journal of Glass Studies 18 (1976). Special bicentennial issue in honor of Helen McKearin. Corning, N.Y.: Corning Museum of Glass, 1976. 279 pp.; 110 illustrations, charts, tables.

The *Journal of Glass Studies* has consistently published articles of exceptional scholarship and played a leading role in presenting new research on all aspects of glass history. The articles in its special bicentennial issue, devoted solely to the study of Amelung glass, represent a definitive treatment of this important eighteenth-century glassworks. The approach is threefold. Dwight P. Lanmon and Arlene Palmer establish the origins and development of the works, beginning with the life of John Frederick Amelung (1741–98) before his emigration from Germany in 1784. Amelung established his glassworks in Frederick County, Maryland, in 1785 and produced a wide variety of goods until its failure in 1795. The best known of these are his elaborately engraved presentation pieces, which probably represent the finest glass produced in eighteenth-century America. Thirty-nine illustrated pieces, each fully described and stylistically analyzed, define and expand our knowledge of that production. The second line of investigation involves excavations of the Amelung site which took place in 1962/63 as a joint operation between Corning Museum of Glass, Smithsonian Institution, and Colonial Williamsburg. Ivor Noël Hume directed the excavations and provides a full report on the information they yielded. The third approach is chemical analysis. Robert H. Brill and Victor F. Hanson report on the chemical compositions of firmly attributed pieces, stylistically related examples, and fragments excavated at the site. This work is a major contribution to the study of early American glass.

Koch, Robert. *Louis C. Tiffany, Rebel in Glass*. New York: Crown Publishers, 1964. 246 pp.; approximately 330 black and white illustrations and 40 color plates, bibliography, index.

A milestone in American decorative arts scholarship, Koch's book put the work of Tiffany (1848–1933) back into the limelight after years of neglect. Koch meticulously recreates Tiffany's career history, beginning with his early experience as a painter studying under George Inness and traveling through Europe and North Africa with fellow painter Samuel Coleman. He details Tiffany's decorating business of the 1880s, his years as a stained-glass maker, and his founding of celebrated Tiffany Glass and Decorating Company in 1892, which produced stained glass, iridescent "Favrile" glass, and other "household art." Koch continues with a study of Tiffany's later years and the artists' foundation at Laurelton Hall in Oyster Bay. He closes with a retrospective of Tiffany's fall from favor, the rebirth of his popularity, and the modern-day influence of his aesthetic. Numerous illustrations and an extensive bibliography of both contemporary and modern sources are included.

Lanmon, Dwight P. "The Baltimore Glass Trade, 1780 to 1820." In *Winterthur Portfolio 5*, edited by Richard K. Doud, pp. 15–48. Charlottesville: University Press of Virginia for the Henry Francis du Pont Winterthur Museum, 1969. 36 illustrations, 5 tables, 1 graph, appendix.

Lanmon has shifted the principal focus of this study away from production to analyze the important subject of glass importation to America in the late eighteenth and early nineteenth centuries. The role of the merchant as purveyor of taste and fashion, the influence of international conflicts on commerce, the effect of tariffs and local products on the glass market, and the specific origins of imported glassware are each considered. Baltimore newspaper advertisements have been carefully quantified to indicate the shifting character and extent of glass importation. The forms, sizes, prices, and sources of glassware listed in these advertisements are then compiled in the appendix and are accompanied by illustrations from two early nineteenth-century catalogues. These catalogues, now at Winterthur, were discovered on Gardiner's Island, New York, and probably represent wares available for importation to the Maryland area.

Lanmon, Dwight P., Robert H. Brill, and George Reilly. "Some Blown 'Three-Mold' Suspicions Confirmed." *Journal of Glass Studies* 15 (1973): 143–73. 40 illustrations, 1 table, appendix.

This major study in glass authentication is based on some remarkable "three-mold" vessels first brought to public attention by George and Helen McKearin in *American Glass*. The objects were attributed at that time to Frederick Mutzer or his son Gottlieb and presumably were made about 1840, although some scholars had doubts about their authenticity. For this study, more than fifty articles belonging to the so-called Mutzer group were examined from virtually every relevant point of view, starting with their history (none could be traced before 1929) and moving to a close look at mold marks, color, variety of forms, and fabrication. The evidence suggested twentieth-century manufacture. Scientific investigation of physical, optical, and chemical properties confirmed this judgment. Wear was insufficient and unusual for glass objects 125 years old, while density, refraction, light transmission, and chemical composition were all at odds with documented period examples. The verdict: "The Mutzer blown three-mold vessels are fakes" (p. 160).

Lee, Ruth Webb. *Antique Fakes and Reproductions*. Enl. and rev. Northborough, Mass.: By the author, 1950. xviii+317 pp.; 166 plates, index.

Most of the early works on American glass by the prolific Lee, a passionate collector and student of American glass, were well conceived and well executed and remain worth consulting, although occasional attributions or points of view may be either untenable or unfashionable today. This particular title is a document of glass and antiques collecting history and perhaps of American commercial impulses as well. By the 1930s the popularity of "antique" American household furnishings had grown large enough to generate a wave of reproductions and forgeries that posed both challenges and threats to collectors. Lee thought that the best defense against fraud came from hands-on experience, and she set out to use her own familiarity with authentic objects to identify various reproductions of blown and pressed glass, lamps and globes, paperweights, historical flasks, and Bohemian glass. The moral is that careful study of originals continues to be the most effective protection against fakes and copies. Other chapters reach beyond glass to deal with mechanical banks, ironwork, and ceramic reproductions. John Marshall Phillips, then curator of the Garvan collection at Yale, contributed a brief essay on silver forgeries. Lee's book provides an intelligent approach to the problem of fakes and reproductions and a record of specific pieces that will be even more deceptive now that they have aged half a century.

Lee, Ruth Webb. *Sandwich Glass: The History of the Boston and Sandwich Glass Company*. 7th ed., rev. and enl. Northborough, Mass.: By the author, 1947. xxvii+590 pp.; 227 plates, index.

Lee's interest in history, her skillfull research, and her lively writing style combine to produce this highly informative and entertaining work. Boston and Sandwich Glass Company was established by Deming Jarves in Sandwich, Massachusetts, in 1825. It became a foremost glass manufactory, and its products have achieved an astonishing level of popularity among collectors. Lee carefully follows its history, using newspaper articles, account books, catalogues, minutes of the director's meetings, and other sources. She develops biographies for the principal figures associated with the company, and, in chapters examining such groups as cup plates, salt dishes, and miniatures, she provides the reader with an extensive catalogue of the company's products. Although many questions remain to be asked of this period in glassmaking history, this work is still considered to be the Sandwich glass collector's bible.

Lee, Ruth Webb, and James H. Rose. *American Glass Cup Plates: The First Classified Check List and Historical Treatise on the Subject*. 3d ed. Northborough, Mass.: Ruth Webb Lee, 1948. xviii+445 pp.; 3 illustrations, 131 plates, indexes.

By the second quarter of the nineteenth century, most English tea drinkers no longer poured their tea from the cup into the saucer to cool. In America, however, this custom remained popular until about 1860, and because the teacup could not be returned to a saucer full of tea, a small pressed-glass plate was often set on the table to receive it. Today glass cup plates represent a tremendous pool of information relating to consumer tastes, business practices, and the mechanization of craft technologies. Their significance as historical documents was recognized by Lee and Rose, who succeeded in compiling much more than a checklist of more than 800 examples. Changes in mold design and construction are identified through a careful study of mold marks on the plates, and historical associations, glass color, chemical makeup, and quality are considered as aids to attribution. Photographs of each plate are accompanied by descriptions of size, rim design, color, origin, age, and relative scarcity. This text sets a standard for observation and analysis that has rarely been matched in glass literature.

McKearin, George S., and Helen McKearin. *American Glass*. Drawings by James L. McCreery. New York: Crown Publishers, 1941. xvi+622 pp.; 262 plates, glossary, bibliography, index.

The McKearins, father and daughter, have written the single most comprehensive volume on glass produced in America from colonial days to the late nineteenth century. They have successfully gathered, classified, and presented an extraordinary mass of material. Their study begins with an examination of the basic properties of glass and the various techniques employed to form and decorate it. The next 200 pages are devoted to a chronological history of major American factories and glass-producing regions. The final 300 pages present an analysis by category of such topics as blown three-mold glass, early pressed and pattern glass, paperweights, art glass, and bottles and flasks. Approximately 2,000 photographs and 1,000 line drawings provide the reader with an extensive library of images. The photographs are assembled into eight groups of plates, with an average of nine separate illustrations per plate. The density of this presentation and the need to refer carefully back and forth between plate groups and text may intimidate some readers, but the richness of the material has provided a foundation on which glass scholars continue to build.

McKearin, Helen. *Bottles, Flasks, and Dr. Dyott*. New York: Crown Publishers, 1970. 160 pp.; 13 illustrations, 10 plates, appendixes, bibliography, index.

Thomas W. Dyott (1777–1861) had appeared in discussions of American glass as a mysterious and flamboyant rags-to-riches figure, yet little of substance about him had ever been verified. McKearin spent close to twenty years accumulating the information that comprises this enjoyable tale. Dyott came to Philadelphia from England in 1804 or 1805 and quickly prospered in the patent medicine business; his early specialty was the cure of venereal diseases. Dyott's medicines soon achieved nationwide distribution, which meant that he needed glass medicine bottles by the thousands. He seems originally to have preferred English bottles, but the War of 1812 forced him to rely on local production. Within a few

years he was deeply involved in glass manufacture in Philadelphia. In 1822 Dyott was responsible for the first recorded mention of historical flasks and by 1824 was peddling flasks ornamented with the figure of Lafayette. Eventually he became "proprietor of the largest, most prolific glass manufacturing complex in the East" (p. 73). McKearin's skillful account follows Dyott to his death and discusses and illustrates the kinds of bottles he probably made. Appendixes provide additional data about Dyott and contemporary glasshouses in Philadelphia and southern New Jersey.

McKearin, Helen, and George S. McKearin. *Two Hundred Years of American Blown Glass*. Garden City, N.Y.: Doubleday, 1950. xvi+382 pp.; 114 black and white and color plates, bibliography, index.

The publication of this book represented a major accomplishment of glass scholarship by two important practitioners in the field, and it has figured prominently in glass bibliographies ever since. About half of the book is devoted to a detailed and methodical account of the history of American blown glass, beginning with a survey of developments in Europe prior to American settlement and ending with a discussion of "the modern renaissance of the art of glass" (p. 132). Between these poles, the McKearins outline the careers and accomplishments of the most important glassblowers and glasshouses and discuss the major forms of glass produced. The second half consists of large, well-printed plates illustrating some 300 pieces of glass that range in date from the eighteenth century to the twentieth century. Each object is described and discussed on a facing page. Subsequent scholarship has revised some of the details of the McKearins' history, and better studies of individual firms are now available; however, those interested in the changing historiography of glass studies or in a still largely accurate overview of blown glass will find the book useful.

McKearin, Helen, and Kenneth M. Wilson. *American Bottles and Flasks and Their Ancestry*. New York: Crown Publishers, 1978. xv+779 pp.; 204 black and white illustrations, 17 color plates, bibliography, index.

The two mainstays of the early American glass industry were windows and containers. Many of these containers, particularly flasks for alcoholic beverages, were decorated, and sometimes they recorded popular events or political sympathies. With recent spectacular prices for rare specimens and many reproductions entering the market, it became necessary to update and expand earlier works on the subject. This has been ably accomplished by McKearin and Wilson. After a review of basic manufacturing techniques and a discussion of the industry's development in the ancient world and Europe, they provide brief histories of seventy-nine American glasshouses that were active bottle producers. Bottles made or used in America from colonial days to about 1870 are examined under such categories as beverage bottles, utilitarian containers, medicine bottles, pattern-molded bottles, and scent and smelling bottles. The longest section is devoted to flasks molded with distinctive historical or geometric motifs, which are tabulated in subject categories and illustrated with line drawings. Wilson has contributed a useful section on modern reproductions and commemorative bottles that copy or resemble the originals. This is unquestionably the most comprehensive single work on the subject.

M'Kee and Brothers. *M'Kee Victorian Glass: Five Complete Glass Catalogs from 1859/60 to 1871.* Introduction and text by Lowell Innes and Jane Shadel Spillman. New York: Corning Museum of Glass in association with Dover Publications, 1981. vi+186 pp.; approximately 115 illustrations.

Trade catalogues can greatly assist scholars and collectors as they seek to identify the makers, dates of production, and pattern names of late nineteenth-century pressed glass. Illustrated with steel-plate engravings that list the price, size, and factory name of each article, these five catalogues survey the production of Pittsburgh's second largest glass manufacturer during the years covered. Pressed glass had become the staple of the glass tableware industry, and successful patterns were quickly copied by competing manufactories. The M'Kee catalogues help to untangle the attribution of these patterns and provide researchers with invaluable data regarding the taste and trade practices of the glass industry in the 1860s.

Measell, James. *Greentown Glass: The Indiana Tumbler and Goblet Company.* Grand Rapids, Mich.: Grand Rapids Public Museum, with the Grand Rapids Museum Association, 1979. x+142 pp.; approximately 325 black and white and color illustrations, bibliography, appendixes, index.

East-central Indiana was once the home of scores of small glass companies. Indiana Tumbler and Goblet Company was located in Greentown, about 10 miles east of Kokomo. From 1894 until its destruction by fire in 1903, the company produced a wide range of pressed tablewares in many colors. Two of its most distinctive and innovative products were chocolate glass and "Holly Amber," an amber-color glass with opalescent highlights. This book is a homage both to Greentown glass and to Ruth Herrick, who first brought the glass to the attention of collectors. Herrick amassed considerable information about the company from excavations of the ruined glass factory and from conventional aboveground sources and wrote the first monograph on the subject in 1959. Her extensive collection is in Grand Rapids Public Museum. Measell updates and amplifies Herrick's earlier book. He includes a history of the company, a description of its glassmaking practices, and detailed examinations of its wares in addition to an account of Herrick's role in glass history.

Neal, L. W., and D. B. Neal. *Pressed Glass Salt Dishes of the Lacy Period, 1825–1850.* Philadelphia: By the authors, 1962. viii+468 pp.; approximately 465 illustrations, index.

Until the late nineteenth century, salt was generally served at the dining table in small, open dishes. With the development of the glass press in the 1820s, these dishes could be inexpensively manufactured in glass. The Neals have published the most comprehensive record to date of this production, listing 465 different salt-dish types. They believed that drawings would provide a more accurate record of pattern details than photographs, which are sometimes subject to the distorting effects of reflected and refracted light. Despite the care exercised in making these drawings, the most reliable sources of data for future research are still provided by photographs coupled with carefully written descriptions. The Neals' careful listing of minute design variations should lead to further refinement of salt-dish attributions and, in turn, to a better understanding of technological and stylistic developments during the period.

Newman, Harold. *An Illustrated Dictionary of Glass.* Introductory survey of the history of glassmaking by Robert J. Charleston. London: Thames and Hudson, 1977. 351 pp.; 608 black and white illustrations, 17 color plates.

In this solid and scholarly dictionary, Newman provides concise definitions for thousands of specific terms relative to glass and glassmaking as well as brief descriptions of manufactories and individuals important to the history of glass. Entries are alphabetical, starting with Alvar Aalto, the celebrated Finnish architect who designed glassware in the 1950s, and ending with *Zwischengoldglas,* the German term for glass featuring encased gold decoration, examples of which can be dated as early as 300 B.C. Entries span the entire history of glassmaking; readers will find discussions of most styles of glass, methods of manufacture and decoration, important glassworking regions, and constituent elements of various objects. The work commences with a brief essay on the history of glass and glassmaking by well-known authority Robert J. Charleston. This is a useful reference to those needing access to both basic and specific information.

Noël Hume, Ivor. *Glass in Colonial Williamsburg's Archaeological Collections.* Colonial Williamsburg Archaeological Series, no. 1. Williamsburg: Colonial Williamsburg, 1969. 48 pp.; 40 illustrations, appendix.

This slender booklet provides a basic introduction to the history of seventeenth- and eighteenth-century glass manufacture in England and America and to the range of glass objects found during the excavation of Colonial Williamsburg sites. Noël Hume uses photographs of glass shards to illustrate stylistic progressions in stemware, bottles, and other table and household wares. At the same time, he analyzes both archaeological and documentary evidence of glass usage to suggest something of the quality of life in Williamsburg during the colonial period. A reference section provides the catalogue number and measurements for each of the objects illustrated. This work is concise, perceptive, and informative.

Palmer, Arlene. "Glass Production in Eighteenth-Century America: The Wistarburgh Enterprise." In *Winterthur Portfolio 11*, edited by Ian M. G. Quimby, pp. 75–101. Charlottesville: University Press of Virginia for the Henry Francis du Pont Winterthur Museum, 1976. 28 illustrations.

In this carefully researched article, Palmer discusses the operation and production of America's first successful glassmaking venture. She begins by placing the firm's founder, German-born Caspar Wistar, in a social and an economic context as an upwardly mobile entrepreneur in colonial Philadelphia. Palmer believes that Wistar entered the glassmaking business in 1739 as an investment venture in partnership with unemployed German glass craftsmen who wished to immigrate to the New World. Palmer describes the technical aspects of Wistarburgh glass production and notes that Wistar was manufacturing glass here and importing finished glassware from overseas for resale. She discusses the forms produced and illustrates documented examples. On the basis of these, Palmer also analyzes several other examples that she attributes to Wistarburgh and many objects with Wistar family associations. She concludes with a discussion of the factors leading to the ultimate closing of the glassworks by Richard Wistar, the founder's son, sometime before the end of 1777.

Pearson, J. Michael. *Encyclopedia of American Cut and Engraved Glass, 1880–1917*. 3 vols. Miami Beach, Fla.: By the author. Vol. 1: *Geometric Conceptions*. 1975. 272 pp.; illustrations, glossary, indexes. Vol. 2: *Realistic Patterns*. 1977. 172 pp.; black and white and color illustrations, indexes. Vol. 3: *Geometric Motifs*. 1978. 259 pp.; 735 black and white and color illustrations, bibliography, indexes.

The period from 1880 to World War I was one of tremendous expansion for the cut-glass industry in America. Hundreds of shops opened across the country to produce cut and engraved glass in thousands of patterns. Although social and economic historians will take exception to Pearson's statement, "it would not serve any useful purpose to include patterns that are poorly conceived, overly common, and without recognizable differences" (p. 9), he has nonetheless succeeded in recording almost 2,000 examples, thereby providing an extensive survey of cut- and engraved-glass production during this period. He has organized the material of his three volumes alphabetically by prominent design features, and considerable effort is required to develop a familiarity with their contents. Each book commences with chatty anecdotes titled "Life among the Antiquers," and none attempts to examine broader historical or aesthetic concerns. Nevertheless, by assembling trade catalogue illustrations, magazine advertisements, patent drawings, and photographs of extant examples, the works do present an extensive and useful body of material.

Peterson, Arthur G. *Four Hundred Trademarks on Glass*. Takoma Park, Md.: Washington College Press, 1968. 51 pp.; illustrations, index.

According to the Trademark Act of 1946, a trademark "includes any word, name, symbol, or device, or any combination thereof adopted and used by a manufacturer or merchant to identify his goods and to distinguish them from those manufactured or sold by others" (p. 5). Peterson's study examines marks registered for use on glassware between 1860 and 1914. An analysis of the history, classification, and value of trademarks on glass is followed by a list of 400 examples pictorially represented and arranged alphabetically by the manufacturer's name. Peterson's information, drawn from the United States Patent Office records, includes the year the trademark was first used, how it was applied, and its owner's name and address. He also provides a list of unregistered trademarks, marks used after 1914, and an explanation of British Registry marks.

Peterson, Arthur G. *Glass Salt Shakers*. Des Moines: Wallace-Homestead Book Co., 1970. 196 pp.; 1,092 black and white illustrations, 1 color plate, appendix, index.

Peterson has condensed a wealth of information on the glass salt shaker into this relatively short work. He illustrates more than 1,000 different types, each accompanied by comments regarding its maker, age, and scarcity. What distinguishes this study from the typical collector's survey is the care taken by Peterson to research and present the history and evolution of the form. Chapters discussing salt and its use are complemented by chapters tracing the technological evolution of the shaker. Because of salt's natural tendency to clump together, great pains were being taken toward the end of the nineteenth century to dispense it from containers with perforated covers. Metal rotating devices were patented to break up the clumps inside the shaker, and finally a process was developed for coating the salt grains with moisture-absorbing agents that prevented clumps from forming. Through patents, trade catalogue illustrations, and surviving salt shakers, Peterson has identified an important aspect of the Victorian fascination with mechanical ingenuity and preoccupation with cleanliness in the home.

Polak, Ada. *Glass: Its Makers and Its Public*. London: Weidenfeld and Nicolson, 1975. 224 pp.; 102 illustrations, 2 maps, bibliography, index.

Polak recounts the history of glass from the Middle Ages to about 1900, starting with a discussion of the properties of glass, its fuels, its furnaces, the organization of glasshouses before the industrial age, and the international mobility of glassworkers. The next few chapters examine glassmaking in forests from the earliest days through the eighteenth century and in cities, most notably Venice. Polak discusses Italian methods of glass decorating, the quest for an artificial rock crystal, and the production of various types of luxury glass. She considers new technology in seventeenth-century England, architectural glass in seventeenth-century France, and the impact of books by Antonio Neri and others. The last few chapters move rapidly over the eighteenth and nineteenth centuries with commentaries on English contributions to glass fashions and the advent of industrialization. The book ends with late nineteenth-century glass and "America's great contribution," Louis Comfort Tiffany (p. 207). Polak's book is not a guide for collectors; it is a social and cultural history organized around glass that explores the full context of glass production, not just the finished product, and places glass in an international setting.

Revi, Albert Christian. *American Art Nouveau Glass.* Camden, N.J., and Toronto: Thomas Nelson and Sons, 1968. 476 pp.; 561 black and white illustrations, 27 color plates, appendixes, bibliography, index.

Profusely and luxuriously illustrated, this work provides an attractive and thorough treatment of American art nouveau glass. The text is organized around eighteen major producers of this colorful and often technically innovative glass, starting with the acknowledged giant in the field, Louis Comfort Tiffany, and moving on through Nash, Quezal, Steuben, Durand, Handel, and others. For each company Revi provides a historical account, often based on his own research and on interviews with surviving artisans, and a commentary on the major types of glass produced. An explanation of manufacturing techniques helps students and collectors to understand processes and identify products. A lengthy chapter discusses lamps of the period, which were important expressions of art nouveau design. Appendixes reprint pages from trade catalogues of four firms. Clear organization and copious illustrations, a remarkable number from Revi's own collection, make this an important collector's reference.

Revi, Albert Christian. *American Pressed Glass and Figure Bottles.* New York and Toronto: Thomas Nelson and Sons, 1964. xi+446 pp.; approximately 725 illustrations, bibliography, indexes.

In this encyclopedia of American pressed glass manufacturers and their products, Revi presents a general history of glass pressing in the nineteenth century. He traces the development from hand- to power-driven presses and discusses technological and stylistic changes in the design, production, and use of molds. Brief essays on seventy-four American glass companies follow, recounting each company's history and location, owners and principal designers, patents, and glass patterns. The majority of these companies operated in Ohio and western Pennsylvania during the second half of the nineteenth century. A concluding chapter discusses the attributions, dates, and designers of approximately 150 blown-molded or pressed-figure bottles, organized into subject groups and chronologically within each group.

Revi, Albert Christian. *Nineteenth-Century Glass: Its Genesis and Development.* New York and Edinburgh:

Thomas Nelson and Sons, 1959. xviii+270 pp.; approximately 140 illustrations, glossary, index.

This volume represents Revi's attempt to cover all the major Western developments in glass in the nineteenth century, which he states "can be considered the Golden Age in glass history—for at no other time, since its discovery more than 5,000 years ago, were more accumulated glass skills and decorative techniques manifested in the comparatively short space of one century" (p. xviii). The text is divided into short chapters on different types of glass (pearl satinglass, amberina, Burmese, Pomona, cameo glass, and many others). Revi's view is international and encompasses American, English, and Continental products. No single chapter constitutes a definitive treatment of its subject, for entire books have been written on some of these glass types, but Revi's compact studies do provide fine capsule overviews. The comprehensive sweep of this work makes it a major guidebook to this topic.

Schaeffer, Herwin. "Tiffany's Fame in Europe." *Art Bulletin* 44, no. 4 (December 1962): 309–28. 23 illustrations.

Schaeffer sketches the roles played by Louis Comfort Tiffany and his colored glass in the development of art nouveau in Europe. Although his designs were not without precedent, Tiffany's technological experiments with luminescent color and mosaic fabrication in stained glass were innovations admired and copied by European artists. Raw materials were imported from America to use in fashioning imitations of the iridescent art glass of Tiffany. Schaeffer attributes the popularity of American stained glass in France, Germany, and Austria during the last decade of the nineteenth century to its abstract quality, bold juxtaposition of brilliant colors, and fragmentation of representational images with heavy, dark lines, characteristics shared with postimpressionist paintings. This article is a notable attempt to correct the blanket assumption that nineteenth-century American decorative arts were always derived from European prototypes and contributed nothing in return.

Scoville, Warren C. *Revolution in Glassmaking: Entrepreneurship and Technological Change in the American Industry, 1880–1920.* Cambridge, Mass.: Harvard University Press, 1948. xvii+398 pp.; 9 illustrations, appendixes, bibliography, index.

American manufactories underwent profound transformations during the late nineteenth century. Some of these changes, such as the expanded scale of production and the introduction of new technology, were symptoms of the widespread transition from craft to industry. Yet the evolution of corporate management and the rapidity with which technology displaced skilled workers varied tremendously from one industry to another. Scoville looks closely at these changes, particularly as they occurred in the glass industry of Toledo, Ohio, between 1880 and 1920. He has attempted to identify the factors responsible for industrial development by examining the effects of technological improvements and entrepreneurship, together with the roles of market development, the availability of raw materials, the discovery of natural-gas sources, protective tariffs, business cycles, and labor-management relationships. Edward D. Libbey's and Michael J. Owens's careers receive special attention, for they demonstrate the accelerating effect that talented individuals could have on the process of industrialization. Scoville's thoughtful analysis represents a major effort to locate the activity of specific glassworks in the broad perspective of American economic and business history.

Shadel, Jane S. "Documented Use of Cup Plates in the Nineteenth Century." *Journal of Glass Studies* 13 (1971): 128–33. 5 illustrations.

The custom of pouring hot tea from a teacup into its saucer to cool led in the 1820s to the introduction of a new article of tableware called the cup plate. Cup plates, generally about 3 inches in diameter and made most commonly of pressed glass, prevented cups from staining the tablecloth as tea drinkers sipped decorously from their saucers. Although cup plates have been collected for many years, Shadel has made the first attempt to examine their actual use. Evidence suggests that in America this custom was practiced only among the emerging middle class, roughly between 1820 and 1860. In England it had gone out of fashion by the late eighteenth century, and Shadel demonstrates that the presence or absence of handles on teacups had nothing to do with the custom's emergence or decline, contrary to popular belief. Her well-tailored article sheds new light on a form of plate that has often puzzled glass enthusiasts and that can contribute to our understanding of American society in the early nineteenth century.

Spillman, Jane Shadel. *American and European Pressed Glass in the Corning Museum of Glass.* The Corning Museum of Glass Catalog Series. Corning, N.Y.: By the museum, 1981. 404 pp.; 1,536 black and white illustrations, 16 color plates, bibliography, index.

No treatment of a pressed-glass collection compares in scale or quality to this volume. With the exception of examples from the Strauss drinking glass collection, all Corning Museum's pressed-glass acquisitions prior to 1981 have been illustrated, described, dated, and attributed. The glass is presented in a uniform format for easy reference, and catalogue entries are complemented with citations to trade catalogues and other primary sources, cross-references to secondary texts, and brief comments regarding historical significance or relative scarcity. Although the catalogue format is not well suited for a conceptual treatment of the subject, Spillman has nevertheless summarized the current understanding of the effects wrought by the introduction of pressing on the industry in general and on the design of glass articles in particular. Entries have been organized into such groups as hand-pressed wares, early machine pressing, lacy glass, cup plates, miniatures, salt dishes, lighting devices, and later

nineteenth-century glass. Within each group, objects are organized by design. Later chapters cover twentieth-century glass, reproductions, and glass made outside the United States.

Toulouse, Julian Harrison. *Bottle Makers and Their Marks.* Camden, N.J., and New York: Thomas Nelson, 1971. 624 pp.; illustrations, index.

Toulouse has designed this book to help collectors to date and attribute their bottles. Following an introductory text of five pages, more than 900 bottle marks are listed alphabetically, dated when possible, and accompanied by relevant historical information. Most company histories are presented in a page or less, but others are more extensive, with changing partnerships, mergers, and subsidiaries neatly diagrammed. The majority of the companies discussed are American or British and operated between 1850 and 1950. Biographical citations are meager. More than 300 later marks and makers recorded from around the world are listed without company histories. While Toulouse provides only the most basic dates on bottles and their makers, identification does represent an essential step in the study of any object.

Watkins, Lura Woodside. *Cambridge Glass, 1818 to 1888: The Story of the New England Glass Company.* Boston: Marshall Jones, 1930. xxi+199 pp.; 80 plates, index.

Before Watkins's book, once-prominent New England Glass Company was virtually unknown to collectors. Yet with a capitalization of $400,000 in 1850, this firm was the largest glass tableware manufactory in New England. During the company's seventy years of production at Cambridge, Massachusetts, its finely cut wares were held in high esteem, and even its standard pressed wares were noted for their quality. All these achievements disappeared in the twentieth century under the shadow of its legendary competitor, Boston and Sandwich Glass Company. Until the publication of this book, collectors routinely assigned glass that did not carry the Sandwich label to either European or midwestern origins. Much of this glass was made in Cambridge. Watkins also estimates that less than a third of the glassware then called Sandwich actually came from that factory. To make her point, she minimizes the role of the Sandwich company, which, although smaller than New England Glass Company, still had a capitalization of $300,000 in 1850. Her general observations are nevertheless correct. This research opened an entirely new area to collectors.

Weiss, Gustav. *The Book of Glass.* Translated by Janet Seligman. New York and Washington, D.C.: Praeger Publishers, 1971. 354 pp.; black and white and color illustrations, maps, appendix, index, glossary, bibliography.

Weiss deals with the entire sweep of world glass history from the Bronze Age to the twentieth century, but his account is "bottom heavy," at least compared with many other studies, and should be appreciated by those frustrated with books that skim these earlier centuries. Unlike many books for British collectors, Weiss devotes relatively little space to English drinking glasses of the eighteenth century; unlike many American publications, he says only a few words about pressed glass. The net effect is to place these two focal points of Anglo and American collector activity within a broader perspective. On the other hand, Weiss's own orientation inclines him to include a large sampling of German and Bohemian glass that may surprise those little familiar with these glass traditions. In any case, this survey is not the familiar Anglo-American view. It is enriched by many maps, tables, and diagrams that show locations of major glassworks, evolutions of forms, and decorations; illustrate marks; or outline periods of activity. This book is useful to those who seek basic background material in glass, particularly before the eighteenth century.

Wilson, Kenneth M. "The Glastenbury Glass Factory Company." *Journal of Glass Studies* 5 (1963): 116–32. 19 illustrations.

In 1962 the planned relocation of Connecticut Route 2, the old Hartford–New London Turnpike, prompted Old Sturbridge Village to conduct an archaeological dig of the threatened Glastenbury glass factory site. Extensive preliminary research turned up important documents relating to the operation of the factory, including town deeds, letters to and from the proprietors, tax lists, and mid nineteenth-century historical accounts. Information garnered from these sources, from the dig, and from a group of vessels associated by family tradition with the works have been combined by Wilson into a succinct history of the factory, which was in operation between 1816 and roughly 1833. Wilson briefly discusses the social background of the founders, the character of the bottles they made, and their relationship to local competitors. Although the foundations of the factory and store could not be precisely located during the dig, the project contributes a great deal to our understanding of this and similar glasshouses founded in the decades following the War of 1812.

Wilson, Kenneth M. *New England Glass and Glassmaking.* New York: Thomas Y. Crowell Co., an Old Sturbridge Village Book, 1972. 401 pp.; 365 illustrations, chronology, bibliography, index.

The first attempt at glassmaking in New England, and probably the second in the United States, took place in Salem, Massachusetts, in 1639 in the glass factory of Obadiah Holmes. From his manufacture of crude window and bottle glass to the output of New England's only remaining factory as of 1972 (Pairpoint Glass Company of Sagamore, Massachusetts), Wilson charts the growth, proliferation, and decline of this important New England industry. Wilson describes imported wares, since much of the demand for glass in New England during the seventeenth and eighteenth centuries was supplied by Great Britain. He discusses the handful of New England glasshouses operating during this early period and follows with informative chapters on the region's nineteenth-century window- and bottle-glass industry. The study concludes with an examination of lead-glass production, which was concentrated in Massachusetts but which also occurred to a lesser degree in Maine, Connecticut, and Rhode Island. This is an extensive and scholarly work.

Textiles

Floor Coverings

Needlework

Quilts

Textiles

Floor Coverings

RODRIS ROTH

LOOR COVERINGS were not common until the late nineteenth century. This fact is easily forgotten, since the literature on the subject tends to focus on expensive goods, suggesting that everyone in the seventeenth and eighteenth centuries seems to have had them, at least among the elite. When looking at the eighteenth century in particular, we must remember not only that rugs and carpets were rare but also that they were seldom found underfoot much before midcentury. Until then their usual place was on tables and cupboards and, in a special form, on beds. Not many floor coverings dating prior to 1800 have survived. Those with known American histories are virtually nonexistent, and those of English origin of the kind imported and used in this country are limited in number. This would seem to inhibit study, but surprisingly it has not. The subject has generated several scholarly publications and conferences.

In 1967 no less than three studies—by Nina Fletcher Little, Ruth Page, and myself—appeared. There also was a spring seminar that year at Pennsbury Manor, near Philadelphia, on American floor coverings, with several speakers including Page, Marian Sadtler Carson, Shirley Spaulding DeVoe, Charles F. Hummel, and Joseph V. McMullan. Until then, however, there had been little information available in print on the subject, let alone interest in it. Cornelia Bateman Faraday, writing in 1929 about American floor coverings in *European and American Carpets and Rugs* (Grand Rapids, Mich.: Dean-Hicks Co., 1929), emphasized hooked and braided rugs, which, at the time, were still associated to some extent with the colonial period. Esther Stevens Fraser recorded a sampling of decorated floors in *Antiques* in 1931, and the identification of George Washington's carpet was offered by Carson, also in *Antiques*, in 1947.

Little's "Decorative Floors" in her masterful *American Decorative Wall Painting, 1700–1850* (Sturbridge, Mass.: Old Sturbridge Village, 1952) was a harbinger of 1967. Besides adding to Fraser's record, Little discussed floorcloths (and, incidentally, other floor coverings), cited directions for making them by Rufus Porter, gave accounts for painting them, examined a book of patterns by John Carwitham, and documented their use with advertisements, accounts, and pictures of the period. Also in the 1950s other kinds of floor coverings began to be examined individually. McMullan, in "The Turkey Carpet in America" (*Antiques* 65, no. 3 [March 1954]: 220–23), explained why only a few types of oriental carpets were appropriate in eighteenth-century America and, with pictures and quotations, described how they were used. The next year, again in *Antiques*, Helen Comstock further documented the floorcloth and pictured a selection of Carwitham's patterns. A decade later, in 1966, floorcloth manufacture was described by DeVoe in the *Antiques Journal*.

Because floor coverings in eighteenth-century America were mostly imported from Britain, British as well as American works must be consulted. The exhibition catalogue by Christopher Gilbert, significant for its scholarship and documented examples, indicates a renewed interest in the subject abroad. Two earlier surveys by Creassey Edward Cecil Tattersall (revised by Stanley Reed) and by W. G. Thompson (revised by G. F. Wingfield Digby) are illustrated with a variety of examples including Brussels, Wiltons, Axminsters, and Moorfields. In addition, individual studies have been done of the latter two rug types by Bertram Jacobs and Wendy Hefford respectively.

The works published in 1967 about floor coverings in eighteenth-century America led to still further publications and conferences. Hummel presented his findings in 1975 at the Textile Museum round table "Imported and Domestic Textiles in Eighteenth-Century America." Sarah B. Sherrill's investigation of oriental carpets was published in 1976. In 1977 Susan H. Anderson completed her monograph, and the reproduction of "The Most Splendid Carpet" was in place in Independence National Historical Park. That year the Philadelphia Antiques Show took the theme "Underfoot" for its exhibition, lecture series, and catalogue. Among the participants were Sherrill, Beverly Gordon, and Helene Von Rosenstiel.

The same people plus Anderson and others presented papers in 1978 at the Pennsbury Manor spring seminar, where, for the second time, the subject was floor coverings. Also speaking on the program, entitled "Floors and Their Coverings: Plain to Fancy," were craftspeople involved in making reproductions. A miniindustry of reproductions had been propagated by these publications from 1967 onward, undertaken in part to determine the appropriate floor treatments for museum installations, restorations, and historic houses. Being copied faithfully as well as freely or with modification from both documented and undocumented pieces were pile-surface Brussels and Wiltons, flat surface ingrain or multiply carpeting, floorcloths or painted canvas, and list or rag rugs.

Eighteenth-century floor coverings continue to attract scholars. Among the most recent entries in the bibliography, for example, is the article by Audrey Michie on floor coverings in South Carolina from 1736 to 1820. By contrast, the nineteenth century, especially after the 1830s, has been virtually ignored, despite the abundance of source material and the survival of examples all around us. The twentieth century also awaits review.

A traditional economic history of the carpet industry has been available since 1941, in Arthur Harrison Cole and Harold F. Williamson's *American Carpet Manufacture*, and *Bigelow*, a traditional business history of the major carpet company, was published by John S. Ewing and Nancy P. Norton in 1955. However, not until Von Rosenstiel's *American Rugs and Carpets*, issued nearly a quarter of a century later, were floor coverings of the nineteenth and twentieth centuries surveyed (aside from Anthony N. Landreau's brief overview in *America Underfoot*). Von Rosenstiel demonstrated, as did Cole and Williamson and Ewing and Norton, that the same kinds of carpets continued to be made in the 1800s as in the 1700s, but in different ways. Previously woven by hand, as the mid nineteenth century approached they were increasingly being woven by machine. The results were an ever-greater quantity, a wider range of quality, and a vast array of patterns. Innovations in looms were a major factor in this change. Material and distribution, labor and management, price and fashion, and domestic and commercial settings also affected, and were affected by, mechanization.

The three other publications on nineteenth-century floor coverings cited are about homemade rugs: *American Hooked and Sewn Rugs*, gathered together by Joel and Kate Kopp, was published in 1975; *Shaker Textiles*, with a section on rugs and floor coverings, documented by Gordon, appeared in 1980; and Jane C. Nylander's concise, informative article on the hearth rug followed in 1983. Often a pastime product, done for one's own pleasure and usually by women, the homemade rug flourished, ironically, side by side with the factory-manufactured carpet. The machine-woven carpets and other floor coverings of the 1800s have received hardly any attention by comparison with the handwoven carpets of the 1700s and homemade rugs of the 1800s; resources for their further exploration are many.

To begin with, dated and identified examples of floor coverings, including hard-surface types such as linoleum, can be examined, photographed, and technically analyzed. Besides constituting a base for comparison and attribution, these floor coverings make up a documented part of the material record of the past. Of course, caution must be exercised in attributions. At one time the Mount Vernon carpet was thought to match one made by William Peter Sprague described in a newspaper of 1791, but later examination, in particular of the structure, showed that it was not by the Philadelphia weaver. Provenance, too, is important. Differentiating between Shaker and non-Shaker work, for instance, is almost impossible without community documentation. Specialized forms such as hearth rugs, doormats, and bedside carpets should not be overlooked, as they too can provide clues to prevailing notions about, for example, comfort, cleanliness, and convenience.

Among the printed resource materials are catalogues and reports of local, state, national, and international fairs. Often the exposition literature is illustrated, occasionally in color, and there may be photographs as well. Other sources for data on both manufacturers and their products, aside from the companies themselves (if still in business), are local histories. Both regional and national institutions such as libraries, government repositories, historical societies, and museums can be consulted. Here one may find primary sources, such as business papers, tax lists, industrial surveys, probate inventories, newspapers, employee accounts, union records, manufacturing censuses, sales reports, and even actual designs used in making the floor coverings. Trade catalogues occasionally include business histories along with the patterns, grades, and prices of the current line of floor coverings. Mail-order catalogues are worth examining also. They date from the late 1800s, as do the trade periodicals, which report on marketing, retailing, and manufacturing.

The patent records for both inventions and designs are available in print and microform, and they point to some of the problems of the period and possible solutions. Housekeeping manuals mention floor coverings, recommending, for instance, how to clean and care for them. Women's magazines offer advice for decoration and purchase as well as maintenance. The use of floor coverings in public settings such as hotels, trains, and boats is another development of the 1800s. Advertisements suggest how floor coverings were perceived, or were meant to be perceived, and their significance in status. And advertisements, along with pictures of the period, may show what floor coverings were actually used as well as how, when, and where. Photographs of interiors are available in increasing numbers as the century advances. They allow us glimpses of the domestic settings of ordinary people as well as the famous, the privileged, and the moneyed few. With other information, they can suggest how common floor coverings were in the homes of people of moderate and even low incomes. Personal accounts and recollections and contemporary comments pertaining to floor coverings can be found in diaries, journals, and letters and in novels and short stories. They extend and humanize our view of the past and may tell us why people had floor coverings and made the choices they did.

Floor coverings are part of the material record of the past. They can be examined from many perspectives, including business, economic, or social history, and as decorative arts, folk art, or textiles. Studying them can reveal attitudes and feelings, for instance, about the home and the family. These, in turn, can lead to insights and a better understanding of some of the larger concerns of society and the nation.

Anderson, Susan H. *The Most Splendid Carpet.* Philadelphia: National Park Service, U.S. Department of the Interior, 1978. x+93 pp.; 52 black and white and color illustrations, bibliography.

Anderson tells the story of reconstructing the carpet of 1791 for the Senate Chamber at Independence National Historical Park. She discusses the maker of the original hand-knotted Axminster, William Peter Sprague (ca. 1750–1808), a British immigrant carpet manufacturer of Philadelphia, but she is mainly concerned with establishing the carpet design and its iconography. Extant British carpets were examined, and symbolic motifs, including the Great Seal of the United States, were studied in arriving at a reconstruction in keeping with the time and place of the original. The final choice of components is convincing. Sprague's carpet for President Washington is also discussed. This article revises the view expressed by Marian Sadtler Carson in "Washington's American Carpet at Mount Vernon" (*Antiques* 51, no. 2 [February 1947]: 118–19) that a carpet belonging to the Mount Vernon Ladies' Association was owned by Washington.

Bartlett, J. Neville. *Carpeting the Millions: The Growth of Britain's Carpet Industry.* Edinburgh: John Donald Publishers, 1978. xiii+296 pp.; 6 illustrations, appendixes, bibliography, index.

This economic history covers British developments up to the 1970s. It is useful for comparison with the United States industry and competition, as imports remained an important part of the floor-covering market here well into the nineteenth century.

Cole, Arthur H., and Harold F. Williamson. *The American Carpet Manufacture: A History and an Analysis.* Harvard Economic Studies, vol. 70. Cambridge, Mass.: Harvard University Press, 1941. [xvii]+281 pp.; 7 illustrations, 17 tables, 10 charts and diagrams, appendixes, bibliography, index.

Cole and Williamson trace the development of the industry in the 1800s, including innovations in looms, evolution of the various companies, and effects of mechanization.

Comstock, Helen. "Eighteenth-Century Floorcloths." *Antiques* 67, no. 1 (January 1955): 48–49. 12 illustrations.

In her article, Comstock documents the use of floorcloths in America with contemporary quotations. The text is illustrated with eleven plates and the title page from the book by John Carwitham, *Floor-Decorations of Various Kinds* (London, 1739).

DeVoe, Shirley Spaulding. "Painted Floor-Cloths." *Antiques Journal* 21, no. 10 (October 1966): 15–17. 4 illustrations.

DeVoe paraphrases the account in the *Illustrated Exhibitor and Art Magazine* (1852) about Smith and Barber's floorcloth manufactory in London and reproduces the accompanying pictures showing the printing room, drying room, and so forth.

Ewing, John S., and Nancy P. Norton. *Broadlooms and Businessmen: A History of the Bigelow-Sanford Carpet Company.* Harvard Studies in Business History, vol. 17. Cambridge, Mass.: Harvard University Press, 1955. xx+439 pp.; black and white and color illustrations, 34 tables, 7 charts, appendixes, index.

In this company history of the giant manufacturer, Ewing and Norton describe the inventions of its namesake, Erastus B. Bigelow, and others. They discuss the various competing and merging firms, the factory, marketplace, and board room, financing and financiers, and workers, managers, and "businessmen." The carpet industry was centered in New England and, to a lesser extent, in New York until its move to the South in this century. It is examined chronologically from the 1820s to the 1950s through brief histories of the many major producers whose number had diminished to a handful by the latter date. Philadelphia carpet manufacturers, who were slow to change from hand to machine and were unrelated to the Bigelow-Sanford evolution, are not considered in this study. Following the invention and introduction of ingrain, Jacquard, and other power looms in the 1840s (the first, by Bigelow, was at Lowell Carpet Company in 1843), factory-made carpets became the norm. Judging from business records and trade literature, the main primary sources used in this work, ingrain was the dominant type made and used in the United States during the nineteenth century rather than pile carpets such as Brussels, Wilton, velvet, and Axminster, almost all of which were imported, principally from Great Britain. Changes in the twentieth century due in large part to the introduction of new material and techniques are also surveyed. A business history of carpet manufacturing, this book reminds us that there is more to floor coverings than covering floors.

Fraser, Esther Stevens. "Some Colonial and Early American Decorative Floors." *Antiques* 19, no. 4 (April 1931): 296–301. 10 illustrations.

A selection of the painted and stenciled floors in New England houses recorded by Fraser are presented. The houses and their decorated floors are not necessarily of the same date.

Gilbert, Christopher, James Lomax, and Anthony Wells-Cole. *Country House Floors, 1660–1850.* Temple Newsam Country House Studies, no. 3. Exhibition catalogue. Leeds, England: Leeds City Art Galleries, 1987. 112 pp.; 91 black and white illustrations, 46 color plates, 78 illustrated entries, bibliography.

Floors—their materials, decoration, and coverings—are the subject of this scholarly, fully illustrated, and useful catalogue that records a special exhibition at Temple Newsam, an English country seat housing a portion of the decorative arts collections of Leeds City Art Galleries. The sections deal with the floors at Temple Newsam, to set the scene; designs for decorated floors, including marble, marquetry, and paint; luxury carpets, such as oriental, Brussels, and Wilton; ingrain carpets; utility floor coverings, specifically Venetian, list, and haircloth; matting; painted floorcloths; protective covers; and maintenance. Each section is introduced with general background information, and the subsections contain specific data followed by the catalogue entries. Seventy-eight items, most of which date between 1800 and 1850, range from carpets to fragments as well as designs and point papers, and all are illustrated except two; twenty-two are reproduced in color. Each entry includes the item's name, date, maker, size, and description (material, weave, pattern, and color), plus references and provenance. Sometimes an additional

paragraph about the object places it in context, compares it with other examples, or quotes a pertinent comment. The original research is based on period records, reports, accounts, pictures, journals, letters, and—most important—dated, documented, and identified floor coverings. The number of examples is significant and reveals what a rich source of material history there is at Temple Newsam. Amazingly, until the publication of this book, we knew more about the subject of floors in the United States than in Great Britain. This publication confirms that fashions underfoot were about the same in both places, the former following the latter. Although dealing with Great Britain and country houses, the catalogue serves as a guide to the treatment of floors on both sides of the Atlantic. It is a major contribution.

Gordon, Beverly. "Rugs and Floor Coverings." In Beverly Gordon, *Shaker Textile Arts*, pp. 95–129. Hanover, N.H., and London: University Press of New England with the cooperation of the Merrimack Valley Textile Museum and Shaker Community, 1980. 25 illustrations.

Gordon presents a study of Shaker-made rugs, including woven rag, braided, hooked, sewn, knitted, and crocheted, some of which were sold to "the world's people." The earliest references to floor coverings mentioned are of the 1830s. Surviving examples duplicate non-Shaker work and date no earlier than the 1840s; most are from later in the nineteenth century or from the twentieth. Without community documentation, a Shaker attribution is almost impossible. Gordon is meticulous in this matter, using only documented pieces in community collections. Salient characteristics of various types and work of different communities are presented; techniques are described and pictured; and material, color, dye, size, and so on are discussed. Appendixes include technical analysis of several Shaker woven rag rugs and a striped one. This text is based on thorough examination of community examples and records.

Hefford, Wendy. "Patents for Strip-Carpeting, 1741–1851." *Furniture History* 23 (1987): 1–7. 8 illustrations.

By 1852 fifty English patents had been issued for strip-carpeting, or carpeting sold by the yard to be sewn together to form a floor covering. Because the most important of these have been treated elsewhere, "only the more interesting little-known patents are examined" here (p. 1). Improvements rather than inventions predominate. Many of the specifications are of a technical nature, but Hefford makes them understandable and assesses their significance—or insignificance. Her emphasis on period technique and terminology leads to more precision in identifying and dating carpets.

Hefford, Wendy. "Thomas Moore of Moorfields." *Burlington* 119, no. 897 (December 1977): 840–48. 11 illustrations.

Hefford provides new information about British weaver

Moore (1700–1788) and about identifying his work. A successful hosiery manufacturer, Moore was making hand-knotted pile or Axminster carpets by the late 1750s. His advertising card of the 1770s shows three looms, one for hosiery and two for carpets (hand-knotted and common). The latter produced strip-carpeting with repeating patterns, which was sewn together to form a large carpet, a type that Moore sold starting in the 1760s (if not earlier), according to Hefford. She has discovered an identifying feature of Moore's carpets that is not found on the work of his competitors, in particular Thomas Witty. Her work is based on original research and close examination of documented Moorfields carpets. This book is a significant contribution.

Hummel, Charles F. "Floor Coverings Used in Eighteenth-Century America." In *Imported and Domestic Textiles in Eighteenth-Century America*, edited by Patricia L. Fiske, pp. 61–92. Irene Emery Roundtable on Museum Textiles Proceedings, 1975. Washington, D.C.: Textile Museum, 1976. 23 illustrations, bibliography.

Hummel discusses the various types of floor coverings used in America during the eighteenth century. His work is based on original research and is enriched with contemporary quotations and pictures.

Jacobs, Bertram. *Axminster Carpets (Hand-Made), 1755–1957.* Leigh-on-Sea, England: F. Lewis, 1970. 80 pp. + 89 plates; illustrations.

Jacobs tells the story of Thomas Witty (1740–99) and his hand-knotted seamless carpets, which are generally known as Axminster. This work also includes the history of successor firms.

Kopp, Joel, and Kate Kopp. *American Hooked and Sewn Rugs: Folk Art Underfoot.* New York: E. P. Dutton, 1975. 128 pp.; 213 black and white and color illustrations, appendix, bibliography.

A wide array of floor rugs dating from the early 1800s to the 1970s is presented by the Kopps. The brief but informed text and captions cover aesthetic as well as technical and historical aspects. Designed by the Kopps, the book is their choice of folk art, a lively and colorful selection. Excluded for the most part are rugs made from commercially manufactured patterns, but they are mentioned and a few are pictured in a two-page section on patterns. There are brief sections on bed rugs (a type of bed cover), and yarn-sewn, shirred, embroidered, and braided floor rugs, but the focus is on hooked rugs. The twentieth-century cottage industry in hooked rugs is also discussed. The emphasis of the book is "visual and not historical" (p. 7). Nevertheless, it is a helpful guide on a popular subject about which little has been published since the 1950s.

Landreau, Anthony N. *America Underfoot: A History of Floor Coverings from Colonial Times to the Present.* Washington, D.C.: Smithsonian Institution Press for the Smithsonian Institution Traveling Exhibition Service, 1976. ix + 76 pp.; 92 black and white and color illustrations, bibliography.

This overview was prepared to accompany an exhibition of the same name. Landreau shows a few examples of recent fiber art. This work was superseded by Helene Von Rosenstiel, but it remains useful for its illustrations and for its technical analysis of the twenty-three floor coverings, also pictured, in the exhibition. It is a good, brief synopsis of existing work on floor coverings.

Lanier, Mildred B. *English and Oriental Carpets at Williamsburg.* Williamsburg: Colonial Williamsburg Foundation, 1975; distributed by University Press of Virginia. xiii + 132 pp.; 56 black and white and color illustrated entries, bibliography, index.

In this catalogue of Williamsburg's collections, fourteen of the forty-nine carpets are English and date from the late 1600s to the early 1800s. Included are turkeywork upholstery, needlework carpets, knotted carpets, and pieces of ingrain. Each entry is pictured, technically analyzed, and described.

Little, Nina Fletcher. *Floor Coverings in New England before 1850.* Sturbridge, Mass.: Old Sturbridge Village, 1967. 82 pp.; 48 illustrations, bibliography.

Little's classic study is based on original research replete with contemporary quotations, examples, and pictures. She covers turkey carpets and turkeywork, ingrain, Brussels, Wilton, and Axminster carpets, painted floorcloths and floors, home-woven carpets, and small homemade rugs (needleworked, braided, yarn sewn, shirred, and hooked). Although limited to New England, the findings concerning ownership are not that different from those applicable to other East Coast regions; that is, although a variety of carpets were available, they were owned by but a handful of people. This text is especially helpful for the early 1800s, a period often overlooked, before handwoven carpets were superseded by machine products. It is also informative about small homemade rugs and the equally prevalent striped, rag, and straw carpets of home, local, national, or foreign origin. Directions are given for making a floorcloth, and suggestions are offered about the selection and use of different types of floor coverings in the setting of the modern period home as well as museum exhibitions and historic houses.

Mayorcas, M. J. *English Needlework Carpets: Sixteenth to Nineteenth Centuries.* Leigh-on-Sea: F. Lewis, 1963. 64 pp. + 94 black and white and color plates; index.

In the first book devoted to the subject, Mayorcas describes but does not analyze the carpets, which are arranged chronologically. The majority of the carpets are dated to the 1700s.

Michie, Audrey. "The Fashion for Carpets in South Carolina, 1736–1820." *Journal of Early Southern Decorative Arts* 8, no. 1 (May 1982): 24–48. 6 illustrations.

This article represents the first study to concentrate on the South and a single colony or state. Information is "drawn primarily from the [Museum of Early Southern Decorative Arts] research files and Charleston County inventories on microfilm" (p. 48). The findings are similar to those for New England and the East Coast as a whole; that is, few people owned carpets in the eighteenth or early nineteenth centuries in South Carolina, but among the carpets mentioned, just about every type was represented. Michie provides standard background information on the different types. Advertisements of the early 1800s for floor coverings in other southern states—Virginia, Kentucky, Tennessee, Maryland—are cited in addition to those from South Carolina, mainly Charleston.

Nylander, Jane. "The Early American Look: Floor Coverings." *Early American Life* 14, no. 2 (April 1983): 13–19. 7 black and white and color illustrations.

Nylander identifies the various kinds of floor coverings, including paint and sand, used in America, mainly in New England. She covers the eighteenth to the twentieth centuries and mentions revivals, but concentrates on the period 1825 to 1850 when machine-woven carpets were beginning to be produced. At the same time, rag carpets and small rugs, newly introduced types, were being made in the home as a result of the increasing availability of factory-produced textiles. Nylander's text is based on written sources and inspection of floor coverings. Illustrated are modern reproductions or adaptations of floorcloths, striped and Brussels carpeting, rag and braided rugs, and straw matting.

Nylander, Jane C. "The Hearth Rug." *Early American Life* 14, no. 6 (December 1983): 50–51, 73–74. 7 color illustrations.

This survey of small rugs in the 1800s extends the section on the subject in Nina Fletcher Little's *Floor Coverings*. Hearth and other small utilitarian rugs that protected the carpet or floor by the fireplace or in other heavily trafficked areas were an acceptable form of aesthetic expression by women and were "worked," or embroidered, in a kind of loop pile. Directions are provided for making one of these rugs, now called a yarn-sewn rug. This is a valuable article based on examination of rugs and contemporary sources.

Page, Ruth. "English Carpets and Their Use in America." *Connecticut Antiquarian* 19, no. 1 (June 1967): 16–25. 5 illustrations, bibliography.

Page outlines the development, manufacture, and importation of English carpets as well as their use up to about 1840. Her work is supported by contemporary accounts, mostly the same as cited by Nina Fletcher Little and Rodris Roth, but some of Connecticut and New Hampshire origin.

Roth, Rodris. *Floor Coverings in Eighteenth-Century America*. United States National Museum Bulletin 250. Contributions from the Museum of History and Technology, paper 59, pp. 1–64. Washington, D.C.: Smithsonian Institution Press, 1967. 28 illustrations.

This and Nina Fletcher Little's monograph were the first to examine floor coverings in eighteenth-century America in depth, and they remain basic for studying the subject. There is some duplication with Little of contemporary accounts and pictures. Roth discusses the major types of floor coverings: oriental, floorcloth, straw, ingrain, Brussels, Wilton, and Axminster. In addition, she mentions sand and needlework, list, and Venetian carpets. For each, the points covered may include characteristics, history, names, manufacture, appearance, size, cost, acquisition, use, and placement. Other topics (considered separately) are sale, miscellaneous use (stairs, entries, passages, bedsides, and hearths), maintenance and upkeep, and selection. Probate inventories, mainly for Suffolk County, Massachusetts, are quoted often and are examined closely for trends and types, as are period comments and advertisements from most of the East Coast. Roth reminds us that floor coverings were owned by few people and consequently were a status symbol, as is evident from their inclusion in portraits and from their mention in period statements.

Sherrill, Sarah B. "Oriental Carpets in Seventeenth- and Eighteenth-Century America." *Antiques* 109, no. 1 (January 1976): 142–67. 22 color plates.

Sherrill provides the guidance essential for the lay person in the enormous and tangled field of oriental or turkey carpets. She demonstrates that they were made in Europe and, like "true" examples from the Middle East, were used in America. Discussion of Axminsters and other kinds of carpets includes the size, the condition and care at the time, and how the carpet was acquired. Misconceptions surrounding oriental carpets, such as what kinds were and were not available in the West, are cleared up. The terms *turkey carpet*, *turkeywork*, and, indeed, *turkey*, are explained, and the construction of both oriental and English carpets is examined in detail. The use of technical data and analysis of carpets is especially effective, pointing up its essential role in the proper identification of carpets whether before us on the floor or depicted in paintings. Sherrill's work is a thorough study incorporating original research.

Tattersall, Creassey Edward Cecil. *A History of British Carpets, from the Introduction of the Craft until the Present Day*. New ed. Revised and enlarged by Stanley Reed. Leigh-on-Sea, England: F. Lewis, 1966. 139 pp.; 176 black and white and color illustrations.

First published in 1934, this updated edition places emphasis on extant handwoven carpets made prior to the early 1800s. Slightly less than half the book is devoted to brief histories of twenty-two extant British manufacturers of woven carpets; samples from their looms are pictured.

Thompson, W. G. "Carpets." Revised by G. F. Wingfield Digby. In Percy Macquoid and Ralph Edwards, *The Dictionary of English Furniture from the Middle Ages to the Late Georgian Period*, vol. 1, pp. 203–18. 2d ed. Revised and enlarged by Ralph Edwards. London: Country Life, 1954. 21 illustrations.

This useful overview of British carpets up to the early nineteenth century is based on contemporary accounts and extant examples. There is some repetition with Creassey Tattersall's *History of British Carpets*.

Von Rosenstiel, Helene. *American Rugs and Carpets from the Seventeenth Century to Modern Times*. New York: William Morrow, 1978. 192 pp.; 232 black and white illustrations, 32 color plates, appendixes, glossary, bibliography, index.

Von Rosenstiel surveys the subject, including linoleum and Amerindian work. This work is especially useful for the post-1850 period, which was virtually ignored by previous writers and seldom illustrated. Original research and period pictures, quotations, and examples are incorporated to cover carpet construction, both hand and machine, to define the various resulting types, and to trace their histories. Von Rosenstiel includes a wide range of information on manufacturing, inventions, imports, appearance, use, sale, and so forth. Gathered together from various primary and secondary sources, such as business histories, trade catalogues, periodicals, collectors' magazines, and advertisements, the information is presented in chapters on floors, matting, rag rugs, floorcloths, and flat-woven, pile, tufted, embroidered, and custom carpets. She deals mainly with residential use; however, commercial use—for instance, in hotels, trains, and boats—is noted. A sweeping look over a wide span of time, this book also points out the many areas awaiting further study.

Needlework

Susan Burrows Swan

WHILE MANY NEEDLEWORK BOOKS AND ARTICLES are published each year, most feature patterns and variations for working the latest popular technique. Historical needlework publications are in the minority and are generally less financially successful. Most historical books discuss only a single type of needlework, and only a few survey the major American techniques practiced.

In preparing this bibliography on American historical needlework, my first criterion was to include only publications that offered new, documentable, and factual information. Those that only emphasized the aesthetic approach or presented a rehash of earlier twentieth-century material were eliminated. In a few cases no publication met these standards fully, but in order to cover a given technique, I used the best one available. In some cases, such as tambourwork and candlewicking, there are no scholarly publications on the subject.

The first substantial history of needlework in the English language is *The Art of Needle-Work* by Mary Margaret Egerton (London: Henry Colburn, 1844). It was followed by a flood of instructional publications issued as inexpensive books and articles, both in the United States and in England. It is amusing to see how nineteenth-century authors renamed the same stitch or technique, apparently to make their publications seem fresh. Sometimes two authors used the same drawings but used different names to describe them. It is no wonder that authors today continue to do the same thing. This lack of consistency has resulted in a mass confusion of terms. The serious student certainly should browse through the nineteenth-century books and articles, since they present the most accurate view of the original emphasis on different needlework forms, names, and techniques. At least two of the late nineteenth-century books have been issued in facsimile form: *The Dictionary of Needlework* by Sophia Francis Anne Caulfield and Blanche C. Saward (New York: Crown Publishers, 1972) and *The Complete Encyclopedia of Needlework* by Th. de Dillmont (1886; reprint, Philadelphia: Running Press, 1972). Both books continue to categorize needlework as "plain" or "fancy" even at this late date.

In selecting books, one of my major goals was to present the widest spectrum of subjects and techniques possible, and these range from lace (Virginia Bath) to the construction of everyday clothing (Ellen J. Gehret). In essence, the titles assembled here represent a basic library for the serious student, collector, or curator. Articles generally more closely adhere to current fashions in collecting, which is why numerous titles on samplers and mourning pictures appear.

Basic reference works for the student include Beverly Gordon's *Domestic American Textiles* and the needlework dictionary compiled by Pamela Clabburn. Therle Hughes's *English Domestic Needlework* demonstrates how American work relates to its most important source, while *Needlework* by Adolph S. Cavallo places American work in an even wider context.

Another criterion in my selection was the availability of the publication. Much fine information appears in historical society bulletins, theses, and antique show and exhibition catalogues, but these publications are difficult to locate. My time frame favors selections from the eighteenth century and the first half of the nineteenth century when the quality of the needlework was at its height.

Sometimes, as in the case of mourning pictures, two authors (for example, Anita Schorsch and Betty Ring) bring different but equally valid approaches to the subject. Sometimes important areas are largely unstudied; only Margery Burnham Howe's *Deerfield Embroidery* deals with revival needlework forms. Interest in this field should increase substantially in the next few years.

Sad as it may be, fancy needlework was women's only major contribution to the decorative arts before 1800. A few publications discuss needlework in this social and historical context; however, many more publications, which I have not included, repeat and perpetuate unsubstantiated facts and romantic notions about needlework and the women who did it. For example, the role of individual creativity and artistic expression, considered to be so essential in today's needlework, cannot be documented as an important consideration in the eighteenth century. Unfortunately, many needlework books continue to apply today's standards, without investigation, to the earlier work. All is not bleak, however. The following works represent solid and responsible scholarship on needlework.

Bath, Virginia Churchill. *Lace*. Chicago: Henry Regnery Co., 1974. 320 pp.; approximately 400 illustrations, 8 color plates, 150 diagrams, appendixes, bibliography, index.

Bath's study of lace includes some forms not made with a needle and only a few forms actually made in the United States. After a brief introduction on the uses of lace, Bath divides her chapters according to overall forms: network, needle lace, bobbin lace, and mixed lace. Excellent close-up photography, old patterns, and contemporary examples accompany descriptions of most forms. The how-to sections enhance the reader's understanding of the complicated historic techniques. While not always using contemporary names, this book's best feature is its clear identification of both machine- and handmade lace techniques.

Bolton, Ethel Stanwood, and Eva Johnston Coe. *American Samplers*. Boston: Massachusetts Society of the Colonial Dames of America, 1921. viii+416 pp.; approximately 115 black and white and 11 color illustrations, index.

American Samplers is a major pioneering effort to record American samplers and schools before 1830. The authors spent five years locating 2,500 samplers to provide data for their study. They discuss the history of samplers by century and indicate gradual changes in style, method, and function. Registers for each century list the samplers alphabetically according to maker. The weakest section is "An Anthology of Sample Verse," which lists 800 different verses arranged by theme and chronology. While this is helpful in locating the authors of some verses, the classification by date does not hold up. Oddly juxtaposed in the last ten pages is a list of hatchments. This book is still a classic in the sampler field.

Cavallo, Adolph S. *Needlework*. The Smithsonian Illustrated Library of Antiques, edited by Brenda Gilchrist. New York: Cooper-Hewitt Museum, 1979. 128 pp.; 107 black and white illustrations, 29 color plates, 1 diagram, glossary, bibliography, index.

Cavallo offers excellent coverage of needlework throughout the world and devotes significant coverage to American work. Cavallo starts by discussing who practiced needlework, why it was made, what kind of training was needed, and what patterns were used. He explodes the popular romantic myth that most needleworkers created their own designs. The second chapter on techniques describes the differences between woven textiles and needlework and the different needle techniques used through the centuries. Other chapters focus on geographical areas of the world. In the final chapter, Cavallo provides his ideas about studying and collecting needlework.

Clabburn, Pamela. *The Needleworker's Dictionary.* New York: William Morrow, 1976. 296 pp.; 350 black and white illustrations, 56 color plates, 300 drawings, bibliography.

A basic tool written by an English author with an American contributing editor (Helene Von Rosenstiel), this dictionary of nearly 2,000 alphabetical entries accomplishes the monumental task of covering needlework terms used worldwide. The definitions often include one or more words that are also unfamiliar; this volume helps the reader by adding an asterisk when one of these words is defined as a separate entry. Valuable for quick references and instructive because of the abundant illustrations (both good photography and descriptive drawings), its only blemish is that many of the names and definitions do not reflect the most recent research.

Cooper, Grace Rogers. *The Copp Family Textiles.* Washington, D.C.: Smithsonian Institution Press, 1971. viii+65 pp.; 68 illustrations, 3 tables, appendix, bibliography.

Cooper's work is noteworthy for cataloguing a rare, surviving cross section of household textiles and clothing owned between 1750 and 1800 by the Copps of Stonington, Connecticut. The Copps, a prosperous but not wealthy family, apparently saved most of the textiles used in their home, including not only expensive and showy items but also much rarer utilitarian goods. Cooper provides a brief account of the family and a history of the collection. This catalogue provides detailed and often technical discussion of common textiles, and the data provides a good basis for future comparative studies. A wide range of forms is covered, such as quilts, candlewicking, Marseilles work, embroidery netting, bed furnishings, table linens, towels, and other textile objects. A well-illustrated and solidly researched section on textile manufacturing in eighteenth-century America and a description of the conservation methods used to preserve the Copp textiles end the catalogue.

Deutsch, Davida Tenenbaum. "Samuel Folwell of Philadelphia: An Artist for the Needleworker." *Antiques* 119, no. 2 (February 1981): 420–23. 6 black and white illustrations, 1 color plate.

Deutsch identifies the artist and the school responsible for the largest recognizable group of federal-period pictorial embroideries presently known. Folwell produced these designs for the students in his wife's school in Philadelphia. From an unfinished example, Deutsch determined that Folwell sketched the basic design, the student did her embroidery, and Folwell added the finishing details and background. Clearly identifying and documenting Folwell's characteristics, this concise monograph is a model for the type of work needed in this field.

Deutsch, Davida Tenenbaum, and Betty Ring. "Homage to Washington in Needlework and Prints." *Antiques* 119, no. 2 (February 1981): 402–19. 25 black and white illustrations, 15 color plates.

"Homage to Washington" surveys needlework pictures commemorating George Washington and the prints from which the needlework derives. The most prevalent category of images depicts one or more mourning figures at a tomb marked with Washington's name and often his portrait. Most are heavily steeped in the classical vocabulary of the early nineteenth century. Deutsch and Ring emphasize the identification of clusters of related work. Extensive, informative captions discuss materials, print sources, and related needlework.

Garoutte, Sally. "Marseilles Quilts and Their Woven Offspring." In *Uncoverings 1982.* Research Papers of the American Quilt Study Group, vol. 3, pp. 115–34. Mill Valley, Calif.: American Quilt Study Group, 1982. 14 illustrations.

Garoutte's monograph focuses on a long-neglected needlework form which later became mechanized. The handmade form is not considered to be a true quilt because Marseilles work is usually composed of two layers; three layers are present only in the design areas where cording or stuffing creates the pattern. Garoutte examines the apparent beginnings of the technique in Provence, France. The English who imported the quilts from the seaport of Marseilles gave them their best-known contemporary name. Several references to loom-made Marseilles work prove that just before and after the 1760s this product was also being sold as Marseilles quilting. Later weavers in England, in their constant search for new names to impress customers, sometimes referred to this loom-made product as Bolton quilting, named for the English city where it was made. Garoutte lists eight other names used before 1925. While not the first study on this subject, this work by the editor of *Uncoverings* adds substantial information and sets a fine standard. Issued once a year by the American Quilt Study Group, *Uncoverings* produces the most consistently scholarly information on quilts.

Garrett, Elisabeth Donaghy. "American Samplers and Needlework Pictures in the DAR Museum." *Antiques* pt. 1, "1739–1806," 105, no. 2 (February 1974): 356–64; pt. 2, "1806–1840," 107, no. 4 (April 1975): 688–701. 12 black and white illustrations, 2 color plates; 14 black and white illustrations, 4 color plates.

Garrett covers the best samplers and needlework pictures owned by DAR Museum. Unable to stress regional characteristics with this limited group, she arranges them chronologically and discusses design sources, characteristic motifs, and what is known of a girl's life. Capable articles like this are essential tools for the serious student, curator, or collector of needlework.

Garrett, Elisabeth Donaghy. *The Arts of Independence: The DAR Museum Collection*. Washington, D.C.: National Society, Daughters of the American Revolution, 1985. 200 pp.; 212 black and white and color illustrations, appendix, bibliography, index.

The format of *The Arts of Independence* differs considerably from the usual survey of a museum's holdings. Instead of a lengthy text with short picture captions, Garrett's book reverses this model. Typical of this style is an embroidered picture (fig. 71) where she describes the woman who did the needlework and what is known of her life and schooling. She also includes a quotation by another young woman who attended this school, a detailed description of the picture and its print source (fig. 72), the characteristics of needlework from this school, and a documented discussion of the style of clothing and headdress depicted. The usual caption details, such as date, place, materials, size, and accession number, are all listed in the back under "Catalogue of Objects." Since the book is so profusely and attractively illustrated, the technique of fuller captions heightens the interest in each object while still subtly covering material normally found in a text. Only a fourth of the images in this book is of needlework, but the volume deserves to be included here because of the high quality of the examples and the scholarly text.

Garrett, Elisabeth Donaghy. "The Theodore H. Kapnek Collection of American Samplers." *Antiques* 114, no. 3 (September 1978): 540–59. 23 black and white illustrations, 17 color plates.

Garrett relies on detailed captions to discuss the examples drawn from one of the largest collections of American samplers formed in recent years. The format allows her to make terse, informative comments and comparisons about each piece. Well researched and well documented, this is an outstanding article covering a diverse collection of samplers.

Gehret, Ellen J. *Rural Pennsylvania Clothing; Being a Study of the Wearing Apparel of the German and English Inhabitants Both Men and Women Who Resided in Southeastern Pennsylvania in the Late Eighteenth and Early Nineteenth Centuries*. Edited by Janet Gray Crosson. York, Pa.: G. Shumway, Liberty Cap Books, 1976. 309 pp.; 303 illustrations, glossary, bibliography, index.

Rural Pennsylvania Clothing is a well-researched and well-documented study examining everyday needlework and textiles. It is informative and valuable because the diagrams of patterns clearly demonstrate every step of making accurate recreations. Gehret provides excellent documentation, photographs, and drawings for both inner and outer male and female clothing; even shoemaking is included.

Gehret, Ellen J. *This Is the Way I Pass My Time: A Book about Pennsylvania German Decorated Hand Towels*. Birdsboro: Pennsylvania German Society, 1985.

xii+253 pp.; 562 black and white and 49 color illustrations, appendixes, bibliography, index.

In the only thorough study of Pennsylvania German hand towels, based on the detailed examination of 1,200 examples, Gehret discusses the various uses of decorated towels as well as where they were hung in the home in both Europe and Pennsylvania. Oddly, the young women from the largest religious element of the Pennsylvania Germans, the Lutheran and Reformed churches, produced the smallest number of towels. The Mennonites, Schwenkfelders, and Amish produced far more than the larger group. Young women made towels at home and probably were instructed by their mothers or other relatives using family designs. In an organized fashion, Gehret covers all aspects of towels: materials used, construction methods, and variations in details like tabs, flaps at the top, stitches, designs, types of drawnwork, leno and netted panels, lettering, borders, finishes, and fringes. The book is profusely illustrated. One appendix is a chart that summarizes 835 examples by date of various stitches, techniques, and materials; another appendix lists names and provides brief genealogical material on 1,424 towels. This is an outstanding, factual book on a popular subject.

Giffen, Jane C. "Susanna Rowson and Her Academy." *Antiques* 98, no. 3 (September 1970): 436–40. 10 illustrations.

Giffen's monograph deals with the unusual career of Rowson, who, after writing a novel and acting on the stage, operated a prominent young ladies' school and academy in the Boston area between 1797 and 1822. Well illustrated with photographs of several needlework techniques, a watercolor picture, and a sewing table painted by a student, it clearly demonstrates the variety of accomplishments considered important to a young woman. Of additional interest are an engraving of Rowson, a view of one of the schools, and the silver medals awarded to proficient pupils.

Ginsburg, Cora. "Textiles in the Connecticut Historical Society." *Antiques* 107, no. 4 (April 1975): 712–25. 15 black and white illustrations, 8 color plates.

Recording some choice pieces in the collection of eighteenth-century needlework and textiles at Connecticut Historical Society, this valuable article primarily covers American crewelwork and silk embroidery. Of special merit is an informative picture of a partially worked coat of arms still attached to its embroidery frame, with some original silk threads in twists and others separated in paper tubes ready to work. Ginsburg's knowledge of costumes allows her to point out the remodeling changes made in the costumes shown.

Gordon, Beverly. *Domestic American Textiles: A Bibliographic Source-book*. Pittsburgh, Pa.: Center for the History of American Needlework, 1978. 217 pp.; index.

Domestic American Textiles consists of 574 briefly annotated bibliographic entries arranged alphabetically by author. In an especially interesting introductory section, "The Fiber of Our Lives," Gordon describes textile trends as reflected in American literature from 1876 to 1976. Included are bar graphs covering publications devoted to general embroidery, crewelwork, coverlets, lace, knitting and crocheting, quilts, samplers, canvaswork, and weaving. Textile exhibitions and their catalogues are listed separately by subject matter. Both historic and currently published magazines devoted solely to textiles or those that consistently include articles about textiles are listed in another section.

Groves, Sylvia. *The History of Needlework Tools and Accessories*. London: Country Life, 1966. 136 pp.; approximately 210 illustrations, index.

This book provides a descriptive historical account of the vast range of tools and accessories associated with needlework. Groves comments on needles and needlecases; thread and thread winders; thimbles, yard measures, darning eggs, and hand coolers; scissors and knives; pins, pincushions, and pin boxes; needlework clamps; sewing caskets, chatelaines, workboxes, and worktables; and the various kinds of apparatuses used in knitting, netting, lacemaking, embroidery, cordmaking, tambourwork, crochet, and other forms of domestic textile handwork. The final chapter deals with *parfilage*, or drizzling, not to be confused with pilfering. *Parfilage* was the practice of unraveling gold or silver threads from worn fabrics in order to recycle the metal. In the eighteenth century it became something of a fad, at least in Europe. Much of Groves's account is oriented to Britain and Europe, but it provides a context for the study of related objects in this country. In general, the objects shown here stress the pre-1850 era when the women who used these tools belonged to the upper level of society and thus had the leisure time to learn and practice fancywork. The lack of a bibliography is an unfortunate omission.

Hanley, Hope. *Needlepoint in America*. New York: Charles Scribner's Sons, 1969. 160 pp.; illustrations, 8 color plates, appendixes, bibliography.

Among needlework techniques, canvaswork—now called needlepoint—has retained its popularity in America longer than any other needlework form. Numerous books cover various aspects of modern work, but no truly outstanding book is devoted to the history of American canvaswork. Hanley's book is perhaps the best. It begins with the European origins of canvaswork, moves on to American work, and continues into the Berlin period. Unfortunately, Hanley uses only popular modern terms and, except for newspaper references, does not document her sources.

Harbeson, Georgiana Brown. *American Needlework: The History of Decorative Stitchery and Embroidery from the Late Sixteenth to the Twentieth Century*. 1938. Reprint. New York: Bonanza Books, n.d. xxxviii+232 pp.; black

and white illustrations, 5 color plates, bibliography, index.

American Needlework covers the history of decorative stitchery and embroidery techniques used by American women. Harbeson begins with good coverage of the work produced by native Americans and follows with a discussion of the fancywork of colonial, federal, and Victorian women. Also included is an early recognition of the revival movements in crewelwork, candlewicking, and netting. The final section is devoted to twentieth-century work and covers revivals and new designs in religious needlework, samplers, silk embroidery, crewelwork, and needlepoint. Harbeson theorizes that women have expressed elements of their cultural environment through their needlework and that as their environment changed, the needlework also changed. The book is amply illustrated with excellent examples and, although written in 1938, still contains valuable information.

Holmes, Edwin F. *A History of Thimbles*. New York: Cornwall Books, 1984. 253 pp.; diagrams, 21 color illustrations, appendixes, bibliography, index.

Holmes's book is the most comprehensive survey of thimbles yet published, and it treats the earliest references and examples as thoroughly as those of the nineteenth and twentieth centuries. A listing of the chapters by materials alone (porcelain, enamel, gold, mother-of-pearl, ivory, tortoiseshell, silver, bone, horn, glass, stone, leather, wood, fabric, brass, iron and steel, nickel, aluminum, and plastic) indicates the depth covered. Included in the text are marks and evaluating and collecting tips that are useful to a curator or collector. The book is voluminously illustrated with examples, diagrams of their manufacture, and pages from trade catalogues. Holmes demonstrates excellent handling of the subject in this expanded version of his earlier book, *Thimbles*.

Holmes, Edwin F. *Thimbles*. Dublin: Gill and Macmillan, 1976. 150 pp.; 118 black and white illustrations, 8 color plates, bibliography, index.

Like many of the commonplace artifacts of everyday life, the thimble is an object of considerable antiquity and yet has not changed significantly over the centuries. In this book entirely devoted to thimbles, Holmes discusses and illustrates examples dating to Roman times. The Roman examples are immediately recognizable as thimbles, as are some of the elaborate sixteenth-century objects that Holmes includes in his study. The dominant mode in thimbles in the last few centuries seems to have been the silver, silver-plated, and white-metal examples so familiar today, yet thimbles have been made of many other materials. Holmes provides succinct discussions of all types, of different forms, and of those having varied uses, such as tailors', children's, and souvenir thimbles. The last two chapters deal with the lively modern business in fakes and offer guidelines for collectors.

Howe, Margery Burnham. *Deerfield Embroidery*. New York: Charles Scribner's Sons, 1976. xiii+240 pp.;

black and white illustrations, 10 color plates, appendix, index.

Howe presents a chatty but factual introduction to Deerfield, Massachusetts, and to four women—sisters Ellen and Margaret Miller and sisters Julia and Margaret Whiting—who developed Deerfield Blue and White Society. The Millers and Margaret Whiting had formal training in art and had previously written and illustrated books. Finding lovely old crewelwork examples in bad condition, they began to draw accurate patterns and to stitch diagrams of them. Aware of John Ruskin's work on village industry, they decided to adopt many of his theories to revive struggling, depressed Deerfield. From 1898 until 1926, embroideries were sold marked with the letter *D* within a spoked wheel. Howe includes references from eighteenth-century diaries and other sources as well as comments by the society's founders on their feelings about their work. Howe makes a contribution because, through photographs, she records old work, a few old patterns, and the patterns and examples created by the society's women. Not all their work was based on old examples; some even strongly reflects an art nouveau trend. For popular appeal, numerous patterns for modern embroiderers to work are included.

Hughes, Therle. *English Domestic Needlework, 1660–1860.* London: Lutterworth Press, 1961. 255 pp.; 48 black and white illustrations, 1 diagram, 3 color plates, index.

If your library could contain only one comprehensive English needlework book of the period from 1660 to 1860, this would be a good choice. The text is divided into chapters on historical background, different types of work (such as metal, wool, or quilted work), and categories of decorated items (such as costume, gloves, and other dress accessories). Thus Hughes distinguishes first between the main styles of embroidery and then regroups these according to their general purpose. Readers should not be put off by the sentimental introduction. The text is carefully researched and enlivened by frequent quotations from primary materials. While the book is mainly oriented to collectors, it provides a good general overview for scholars of the decorative arts as well. Hughes's decision to limit her study to domestic work makes this volume especially pertinent to American domestic needlework of the same period.

Kopp, Joel, and Kate Kopp. *American Hooked and Sewn Rugs: Folk Art Underfoot. See* "Floor Coverings."

Krueger, Glee. *New England Samplers to 1840.* Sturbridge, Mass.: Old Sturbridge Village, 1978. xv+227 pp.; 93 illustrations, appendix, bibliography, index.

This book and Krueger's other 1978 publication, *A Gallery of American Samplers,* show the rising interest in American samplers. *New England Samplers* consists of introductory text that provides brief comments on the historical context for samplers; their definition; the various elements making up samplers, including background fabric, embroidery thread, colors, stitches, and design; the designers and framers of samplers; and descriptive notes organized according to three chronological segments: seventeenth century, eighteenth century, and late eighteenth and early nineteenth centuries. Krueger then presents a collection of ninety-three good photographs of samplers and related images arranged in no apparent order. Unfortunately, the short captions miss an ideal opportunity to draw comparisons between related examples or point out school and regional characteristics. The third part of the book is a valuable listing of "New England schools and/or teachers offering needlework instruction, 1706–1840," organized alphabetically by state, then town, and chronologically within each town, and listing known samplers worked at each school. This volume presents a considerable volume of previously unpublished objects and information.

Krueger, Glee F. *A Gallery of American Samplers: The Theodore H. Kapnek Collection.* New York: E. P. Dutton in association with the Museum of American Folk Art, 1978. 96 pp.; 124 black and white and color illustrations, appendixes, bibliography.

Krueger's introduction provides exceptionally good information on the definition of a sampler, English influence, types of schools offering needlework, teachers, physical characteristics of samplers, designs, and sources. Unfortunately, some references in the text discuss items not pictured and not easily seen. Beautiful black and white and color photographs in the catalogue section are accompanied by enlarged detail photographs which allow close inspection of the stitches and even the ground fabric. Arranging the pictures by date prevents helpful comparison of regions and schools, which is especially sad since the collection contains work from South Carolina north to Maine and west to Ohio. This book is valuable for its examples and the informative introduction.

Lane, Rose Wilder. *Woman's Day Book of American Needlework.* New York: Simon and Schuster, 1963. 208 pp.; black and white and color illustrations, diagrams, index.

Lane's book is basically designed for those who want to recreate historical needlework for themselves or understand the techniques. Viewed as an early book in the most recent revival of historic handcrafts, it has considerable merit. Using diagrams and detailed instructions, the author explains the techniques of embroidery, crewelwork, cross-stitch, needlepoint, patchwork, appliqué, quilting, hooking, crochet, knitting, weaving, candlewicking, and rugmaking. Originally, separate patterns could be purchased with this book. Each chapter concentrates on a single technique and includes a brief background of the technique and an easy needlework project. Fine illustrations and clear directions help the non-needleworker to understand a variety of techniques.

Nylander, Jane C. "Some Print Sources of New England Schoolgirl Art." *Antiques* 110, no. 2 (August 1976): 292–301. 20 black and white illustrations, 4 color plates.

Nylander identifies and discusses more than a dozen print sources for some of the more intricate needlework compositions created by New England schoolgirls in the early years of the nineteenth century. The subjects are primarily literary and historical. Most of the Shakespearean scenes are based on the Boydell prints, published in London between 1789 and 1803. A significant proportion of the rest are drawn from engraved versions of paintings by Angelica Kauffmann. Nylander speculates that schools probably owned portfolios of prints from which students selected their subjects. Lengthy captions accompanying the illustrations provide specific information about individual needlework pictures, their makers, and their schools.

Orlofsky, Patsy, and Myron Orlofsky. *Quilts in America.* New York: McGraw-Hill Book Co., 1974. xiv+368 pp.; 205 black and white illustrations, 109 color plates, bibliography, index.

Beginning with an excellent chapter on the history of quilting, this book contains the best overall factual references on quilts. Succeeding chapters cover tools and equipment; different types of quilts, patterns, and names; signing and initialing; the age of a quilt; and care of quilts. *Quilts in America* dwells more on eighteenth- and early nineteenth-century work than most American quilt books. For example, an excellent section shows quilts using the Hewson fabrics of Philadelphia. The text is interestingly illustrated, not just with whole quilts but with old pictures showing their use, and includes many quotations and testimonies from mid nineteenth-century and twentieth-century women telling how they felt about their quilts. *See also* "Quilts and Quiltmaking."

Pennsylvania Farm Museum of Landis Valley. *The Homespun Textile Tradition of the Pennsylvania Germans. See* "Textiles."

Ring, Betty. *American Needlework Treasures: Samplers and Silk Embroideries from the Collection of Betty Ring.* Exhibition catalogue. New York: E. P. Dutton in association with the Museum of American Folk Art, 1987. 112 pp.; 38 black and white illustrations, 134 color plates, bibliography, index.

This catalogue accompanying an exhibition of Ring's personal collection constitutes the most complete study of regions and schools yet published and is the first major work to organize material according to state of origin. After a brief introduction, the text takes the form of captions placed conveniently near each picture and includes much genealogical information. The book is concise, well organized, and beautifully illustrated. Unusual features are the portraits of needlewomen, the excellent material on original frames and framers, and the inclusion of print sources for some of the designs.

Ring, Betty. *Let Virtue Be a Guide to Thee: Needlework in the Education of Rhode Island Women, 1730–1830.* Exhibition catalogue. Providence: Rhode Island Historical Society, 1983. 276 pp.; 111 black and white illustrations, 60 color plates, appendixes, bibliography, index.

This book belongs to a small group of exhibition catalogues that outline the show they illustrate and make a lasting contribution to their field. Ring devoted years to primary research on this topic. After the introduction, the text comprises four major sections: "Female Education in the Era of Accomplishments: The Renaissance to the Industrial Revolution"; "Newport: The Jewel of a Lively Experiment"; "Providence: Where Freedom of Conscience Flourished"; and "Bristol, Warren, and Warwick: Salubrious Villages on Narragansett Bay." The appendix is divided into three sections covering textiles, patterns, and verses; framing; and a statistical study of the lives of the schoolgirls. As well known as the samplers are the silk-on-silk embroideries from Mary Balch's school. Discussed in this category are both the flowered pictures and a larger group of mourning designs with distinctive marble graining and intricately embroidered lettering on the tombs. Also included in this category are the finely stitched black "print works" which imitate stipple engraving. Ring's work represents some of the best scholarship being published in samplers and mourning pictures.

Ring, Betty. "Mary Balch's Newport Sampler." *Antiques* 124, no. 3 (September 1983): 500–507. 4 black and white illustrations, 10 color plates.

This article is an update on Ring's "Balch School in Providence, Rhode Island" prompted by the recent discovery of Balch's own childhood sampler dated 1773. Also found since the last article was Balch's mother's sampler dated 1746. These two demonstrate how Newport samplers progressed from the English style of the mother's to the fully developed Newport design of the daughter's and her pupils.

Ring, Betty. "Memorial Embroideries by American Schoolgirls." *Antiques* 100, no. 4 (October 1971): 570–75. 9 illustrations.

This is one of the first articles to address only mourning embroideries. Ring sparked more than a decade of collectors', scholars', and museums' attention toward them. She organized this work to show individual, regional, and school characteristics which she later refined in other articles on specific schools.

Ring, Betty. "Mrs. Saunders' and Miss Beach's Academy, Dorchester." *Antiques* 110, no. 2 (August 1976): 302–12. 7 black and white illustrations, 6 color plates.

Ring examines needlework produced between 1803 and the 1830s at a school in Dorchester, Massachusetts, then an elegant suburb of Boston. The school's enrollment peaked about 1810, when thirty-six young ladies attended. "No other girls' school of the Federal period has left so many positively identified examples of delicate and sophisticated pictorial needlework" (p. 304). The captions point out and describe distinctive school characteristics, and the footnotes frequently contain pertinent information and genealogy.

Ring, Betty. "Saint Joseph's Academy in Needlework Pictures." *Antiques* 113, no. 3 (March 1978): 592–99. 5 black and white illustrations, 8 color plates.

Ring discusses the needlework made near Emmitsburg, Maryland, at St. Joseph's Academy, which was founded in 1809 by Elizabeth Ann Seton, the first American-born saint. The most notable characteristic of this work is the representation of the school in needlework compositions, mostly landscapes and mourning pictures. This tradition may have been initiated by Mother Seton herself or by Madame Guerin, who taught French and needlework from 1810 to 1816. The last of these needleworked school portraits dates from the 1830s.

Ring, Betty. "Samplers and Pictorial Needlework at the Chester County Historical Society." *Antiques* 126, no. 6 (December 1984): 1422–33. 15 black and white illustrations, 8 color plates.

Describing the highlights of an exhibition held at Chester County Historical Society, Ring chose examples to demonstrate various styles of samplers found from the area between Philadelphia and Harrisburg. Two photographs of samplers from the English Ackworth Quaker School demonstrate the clear relationship of designs to those of the Quaker schools in Pennsylvania. This is an excellent article on regional samplers except for minor confusion in the Dresden terminology. Figure 3 demonstrates cutwork, not Dresden work, and figure 4 contains both forms. A few pictures also show unusual frames sometimes found in the area; one even encloses a silhouette of the embroideress impressed "Museum," a mark used by the Peales at their museum in Philadelphia, flanked by two watercolors, with the sampler. Abundantly researched and documented, this article does justice to an outstanding collection.

Ring, Betty, ed. *Needlework: An Historical Survey.* New York: Main Street/Universe Books, 1975. 174 pp.; illustrations, index.

This compilation of articles originally published in *Antiques* between 1922 and 1975 reflects the changing fashions in needlework study of the last thirty years. The articles reprinted here are short; their strength lies in their specialized focus. Because of the specific nature of each article, this volume is not actually a comprehensive survey, but is a convenient collection of articles to be consulted when one is dealing with a particular topic or form of needlework.

Rogers, Gay Ann. *An Illustrated History of Needlework Tools.* London: John Murray, 1983. 243 pp.; 193 illustrations, bibliography, index.

Only four major books covering historic sewing tools have been published in this century. In the only one by an American author since 1928, Rogers has produced a well-organized, well-documented, and well-illustrated volume. Unfortunately, the title or subtitle should include "nineteenth century" because almost no mention is made of earlier work. The book is divided into eleven chapters on tools such as needles and needlecases, scissors, and thread containers. Many of the objects pictured were mass produced; thus, women no longer had to be a part of the upper levels of society to do fancy needlework.

Rowe, Ann Pollard. "Crewel Embroidered Bed Hangings in Old and New England." *Bulletin: Museum of Fine Arts, Boston* 71, nos. 365, 366 (1973): 101–66. 39 illustrations, bibliography.

The resurgence of interest in hand embroidery within the last thirty years seemed to start with a renewal of interest in colonial American crewelwork. Because so little crewelwork was done elsewhere, Rowe limited her study to New England bed hangings of the eighteenth century and confined her work to long-term, ambitious projects. For each of the two or three major styles of eighteenth-century crewelwork, Rowe traces design origins, the types of stitches used, and how groups of crewelwork interrelate and form regional schools. The booklet is well illustrated and densely packed with highly detailed information and thus is oriented toward serious and knowledgeable students of embroidery.

Schiffer, Margaret B. *Historical Needlework of Pennsylvania.* New York: Charles Scribner's Sons, 1968. 160 pp.; black and white illustrations, 6 color plates, index.

Schiffer has written probably the first book to survey thoroughly all forms of needlework produced in one large area. This pioneering work begins with comments on the major groups of early settlers in Pennsylvania and on persistent images and symbols in their needlework. The longest chapter is the first, which examines samplers. Schiffer discusses the earliest dated examples; the place of samplers in schooling and education; lace, darning, globe, and map samplers; samplers with architecture; and a variety of others associated with known schools in the early nineteenth century. One minor error is noteworthy: the lace samplers she labeled "Dresden" were called "cutwork" (p. 28) and those she called "drawnwork" were known as "Dresden" (p. 31). The succeeding nine chapters are devoted to specific types of needlework: silk and Florentine embroidery, Moravian and Pennsylvania German needlework, crewelwork, canvaswork, Berlin work, and stumpwork. This is a fine study with good illustrations and good research.

Schorsch, Anita. *Mourning Becomes America: Mourning Art in the New Nation.* Clinton, N.J.: Main Street Press, 1976. Exhibition catalogue. Unpag.; 75 black and white illustrations, 8 color plates, bibliography.

The emphasis in *Mourning Becomes America* is primarily on symbolism of the whole mourning concept and of the individual components that were popular in the first forty years of the nineteenth century. Schorsch credits English artist Angelica Kauffmann with the archetypal design for mourning pictures. Unfortunately, documentation is missing; for example, "eighteen known professional designers of mourning pictures" go unnamed and unfootnoted. While illustrating a fine range of embroideries, many never published before, Schorsch makes no attempt to name or discuss school characteristics of the pieces. The difficult numbering system used for the illustrations makes coordination with the text virtually impossible. The exhibition and catalogue deserve much credit as perhaps the first devoted to needlework mourning themes. Schorsch shows not only the embroideries but also the weaves in related references to literature, ceramics, mourning jewelry, and velvet painting to place the subject in a broader cultural context. She also shows how important mourning symbolism was to the New Republic.

Swan, Susan B. "Worked Pocketbooks." *Antiques* 107, no. 2 (February 1975): 298–303. 6 black and white illustrations, 4 color plates.

Swan's monograph documents the use of American needlework pocketbooks. From dated examples, newspaper advertisements, and diary references, it was determined that needlework pocketbooks were popular between 1740 and 1790. Swan discusses the various needlework techniques used, lists the different things carried in them by men and women, and discusses their relationship to leather pocketbooks. In many respects this is a twofold article, with the other emphasis on the documentation and nomenclature of American canvaswork stitches.

Swan, Susan Burrows. "Appreciating American Samplers." *Early American Life*, pt. 1, 15, no. 1 (February 1984): 41–47, 50; pt. 2, 15, no. 2 (April 1984): 42–45, 72, 93. 6 black and white illustrations, 6 color plates; 5 black and white illustrations, 2 color plates, bibliography.

This two-part series offers practical guidelines for understanding, appreciating, and collecting samplers. The first article covers definitions, plain and fancy types, designs, originality, and regional and chronological developments as well as the place of samplers in the lives of their creators and their current designation as folk art. The second article stresses "specialized" fancy samplers, including examples with colored grounds, darning, lace, solid work, maps, Pennsylvania German motifs, and genealogical designs. The various points to consider when evaluating a sampler are described, such as condition, differences between American samplers and those from other areas, letters used in the alphabets, and fakes.

Swan, Susan Burrows. *Plain and Fancy: American Women and Their Needlework, 1700–1850.* Special photography by George J. Fistrovich. New York: Holt, Rinehart and Winston, a Rutledge Book, 1977. 240 pp.; 123 black and white illustrations, 37 color plates, glossary, bibliography, index.

Written as a history of American needlework, covering both the essential plain sewing worked by ordinary housewives and the fancy needlework practiced by more affluent women, *Plain and Fancy* attempts to interweave the changing styles of needlework with the changing lives of the women who produced it. The book is divided into five chapters concerning plain sewing, the importance of needlework and education, the golden age of needlework (1700–1780), the changes in forms as society encouraged more educational opportunities for women, and the gradual disintegration of the elitism of fancywork with the onslaught of inexpensive, printed patterns and books and magazines in the nineteenth century. Swan tries to rectify the continual misnaming of stitches and techniques and challenges the repeated myths about needlework. The illustrated glossary defines terms and gives period references for their usage. This book joins the small group of needlework titles that covers the entire spectrum of techniques, and it adds new information to the field.

Swan, Susan Burrows. *A Winterthur Guide to American Needlework.* New York: Crown Publishers, a Winterthur Book/Rutledge Books, 1976. 144 pp.; 100 black and white illustrations, 16 color plates, bibliography.

After a short introduction, which discusses the collection at Winterthur and provides general background information about needlework in the past, Swan offers a series of concise, illustrated chapters on several categories of needlework: samplers, canvaswork, crewelwork, silkwork, quilts, tambourwork, knitting, whitework, and several less common forms, including coats of arms and hatchments, bed rugs, and sailors' embroidery. Copiously illustrated with examples from the Winterthur collection, the book provides a good introduction to the subject and to a major museum's collection.

Wadsworth Atheneum. *Bed Ruggs/1722–1833.* Introduction and essay by William L. Warren. Exhibition catalogue. Hartford, Conn.: By the atheneum, 1972. 80 pp.; 49 black and white illustrations, 1 diagram, 4 color plates, glossary, bibliography.

Bed Ruggs is a worthwhile monograph on the bed rug, which is defined as "a heavy needleworked bed covering, with a pile or smooth faced, with or without shaped ends, worked in polychrome or, rarely, monochrome wools on a woven foundation" (p. 10). Warren traces the history of bed rugs found mostly in New England and discusses possible sources for their bold floral and geometric designs. Similar techniques are illustrated by the catalogue's documentation of thirty-eight examples, several hand-stitched floor rugs, a hand-stitched candlework coverlet, and two embroidered blankets. Also given are the origins of terms and how they have changed.

Quilts

Susan Roach-Lankford

TRADITIONAL QUILTMAKING passed on from one generation to the next has continued in the United States for more than three centuries. It serves as the foundation for the quilting productions of contemporary revivalist quilters and fiber artists, who have learned quiltmaking from formal classes, books, and guilds instead of community and family traditions. The dynamic nature of this continuum of quiltmakers—ranging from the traditional folk quiltmaker, to the popular revivalist quilter, to the elite fiber artist—continues to attract numerous studies from both scholarly and popular perspectives. The entries in the following bibliography reflect both of these perspectives and the wide variety of approaches and thematic concerns common in quiltmaking literature.

During the last ten years, the number of publications on a wide variety of aspects of quiltmaking has multiplied, no doubt encouraged by the women's studies movement and the growing popularity of the craft among women without traditional quilting backgrounds. This growth is reflected in the 190 entries under the Quilting subject heading in the 1984–85 edition of *Books in Print*. As in the past 100 years, popular, largely undocumented works continue to outnumber scholarly works. The earlier bibliography on quiltmaking (Susan Roach and Lorre Weidlich, 1974) surveyed books and articles in popular periodicals from *Good Housekeeping* to *Progressive Farmer* to *Popular Mechanics* and revealed an avid, ongoing interest in American quiltmaking throughout the twentieth century. That interest has continued to grow, especially during the 1970s quilting revival. These popular periodical articles, which mainly focus on quiltmaking techniques, patterns, and instructions, have been for the most part excluded from the present bibliography, but because of their accessibility and popularity, they should be recognized as a vital shaping force in contemporary quiltmaking among both traditional and revivalist quiltmakers.

Major popular books, representative of the wide variety of concerns in quilting literature, however, have been included here. Although the numbers of popular books on quiltmaking are overwhelming, many are only of limited use to the quilt scholar. Like popular-periodical articles, the majority are instructional, offering technical advice on techniques, materials, patterns, and innovations such as quilted clothing and original designs especially popular among revivalist quilters and fiber artists. Most of the popular volumes touch only briefly on the history of the development of quilting, but a few such as Averil Colby's *Quilting*, Ruth E. Findley's *Old Patchwork Quilts*, and

Patsy and Myron Orlofsky's *Quilts in America* provide a more detailed and better-documented history of quiltmaking in America.

Also popular are the numerous illustrated volumes on quilt-top patterns usually selected as representative of a historical quilt type or for their visual impact. Generally, these offer little documentation on the history or details of the specific quilts depicted and little concern for the women who made them. During the 1970s, art critics and historians such as Jonathan Holstein took this approach in works that presented quilts for their graphic appeal and their resemblance to American abstract and minimalist painting of the 1960s.

This approach, which virtually ignored the artistic merits of the quiltmakers who produced the art form, in part helped to stimulate feminists' attempts to raise the American public's consciousness of the artistic achievements of quiltmakers, most of whom were women and, therefore, excluded from the male-dominated hierarchy of the art world. Exemplifying this concern, Patricia Mainardi's "Quilts," which considered the artistic, historical, social, and political aspects of quiltmaking, generated additional research in these areas.

This new awareness of the importance of the quiltmaker as artist and the lack of scholarship have provoked several in-depth examinations of quiltmakers and the place of quilting in their lives. These works tend to concentrate on geographic, regional, and ethnic quiltmaking traditions. Amish quilts have probably received the most attention, especially from art historians and quilt revivalists, because of contemporary art tastes for bold graphic designs and striking hot colors. However, most studies of the Amish quilting tradition have given brief overviews of Amish society and offer no specific documentation of individual quiltmakers. On the other hand, in one of the first conscious attempts to focus on both the quiltmaker and her art, Patricia Cooper and Norma Bradley Buferd in *The Quilters* interviewed quiltmakers from the southwestern United States and used the women's oral history accounts to explore the relation of quilting to their lives. The use of oral history and personal memories evoked by quilts continues to be a favorite approach in the literature.

One of the first more scholarly analyses of regional quilting traditions was Mary Washington Clarke's *Kentucky Quilts and Their Makers*. This study investigated the form, techniques, individual pattern preferences, and personality profiles of Kentucky quiltmakers. More scholarly considerations of regional and ethnic quilts also have recently been published in museum catalogues accompanying the increasing numbers of quilt and folk art exhibitions. The most notable ethnic studies deal with the Afro-American quilting traditions first analyzed by John Michael Vlach in his *Afro-American Tradition in Decorative Arts*. Vlach's findings have been developed and expanded in "Aesthetic Principles in Afro-American Quilts" by Maude Southwell Wahlman and John Scully and further detailed and developed in Wahlman's doctoral dissertation. Other regional museum exhibition catalogues considering Afro-American or Anglo-American quilts have proliferated. Representative of these are Roland Freeman's *Something to Keep You Warm*, Ricky Clark's *Quilts and Carosels*, and Dena S. Katzenberg's *Baltimore Album Quilts*. These exhibition publications, in addition to listing and describing the quilts, usually provide basic historical and cultural contexts for the quilts with varying amounts of ethnographic data, thus offering the beginnings of much-needed area-specific research.

The need for specific scholarly research is just beginning to be met in academic circles in doctoral dissertations such as folklorist Joyce Ice's "Quilting and the Pattern of Relationships in Community Life" (University of Texas at Austin, 1984). Important for documenting the role of quilting in women's lives, her study is based on fieldwork with a traditional quilting club in Lytton Springs, Texas. Other folklore dissertations on various regional and ethnic aspects of quiltmaking are presently in progress and tend to focus on present-day traditional folk quilters in their sociocultural context.

Concerned because of the limited number of scholarly studies on quiltmaking, a group of interested artists, quilters, quilt scholars, and devotees formed the American Quilt Study Group and began their own series, *Uncoverings*, to encourage quilt scholarship. Topics range from stories about historical quilts, to revivalist quilters' techniques, to details for documenting quilts. Some publications have also been inspired by the recent quilt documentation projects which locate and register quilts in attempts to record vital information on important historic quilts, regional traditions, and patterns.

With such detailed documentary projects and the recent intense scholarly interest in quiltmaking, the field is certain to amass sufficient data for comparative studies which have been most difficult until this time. The rich variety of quilting literature still developing will have much to interest cultural history, folklore, art, and quilting circles.

Beyer, Jinny. *The Art and Techniques of Creating Medallion Quilts, including a Rich Collection of Historic and Contemporary Examples.* McLean, Va.: EPM Publications, 1982. xii+188 pp.; approximately 70 black and white and 42 color plates, 106 drawings, bibliography, index.

Providing instructions for the recreation of the historic medallion quilt, Beyer, a leader in the contemporary quilt revival, also gives insight into the philosophy of contemporary quilting revivalists.

Bishop, Robert, and Elizabeth Safanda. *A Gallery of Amish Quilts: Design Diversity from a Plain People.* New York: E. P. Dutton, 1976. 96 pp.; 157 illustrations, bibliography.

This work is an attractive pictorial survey of the Amish quilting tradition, which employs striking bold colors and predominantly simple, large-scale geometric patterns. Bishop and Safanda argue that the "dazzling variety" seen in Amish quilts refutes the plain and simple aesthetic attributed to the Amish. The text sketches the geographical and chronological evolution of the Amish quilt and comments on the social aspects of quilting and the relation of the quilt to other material culture of the group. Although unsubstantiated by documentation, this work suggests that the quilt serves as an emotional outlet in restrictive Amish society.

Bishop, Robert, William Secord, and Judith Reiter Weissman. *Quilts, Coverlets, Rugs, and Samplers.* The Knopf Collectors' Guides to American Antiques. New York: Alfred A. Knopf, 1982. 477 pp.; black and white illustrations, 343 color plates, bibliography, glossary, index.

Although also including coverlets, rugs, and samplers, this guide is mainly concerned with quilts. Providing a brief overview of quilt types and quilting stitches, it presents more than 300 quilts dating from the colonial period to the present with information on material, techniques, origin, dates, variations, and maker, if known, along with hints for the collector. It also includes a much-needed price guide, which is especially helpful for those wishing to price older quilts. The information provided on each quilt pictured is much more detailed than in most guides.

Clark, Ricky, ed. *Quilts and Carousels: Folk Art in the Firelands.* Exhibition catalogue. Oberlin, Ohio: Firelands Association for the Visual Arts, 1983. 52 pp.; black and white illustrations, 31 black and white and color plates.

Representative of the numerous recent regional exhibitions of quilts, this catalogue, in addition to presenting photographs of the quilts in the exhibition, also gives a basic history of the Firelands region of Ohio and the role of women in settling the region and relates this history to local quilts.

Clarke, Mary Washington. *Kentucky Quilts and Their Makers.* Lexington: University Press of Kentucky,

1976. viii+120 pp.; 50 black and white illustrations, 8 color plates, index, bibliography.

Clarke focuses on the quiltmaker as well as quilting technology and artifacts. This well-documented work examines the vital quilting tradition in central and western Kentucky counties, drawing on interviews with quilters to understand the social context, techniques, tools, and patterns of quilting. Tradition, changes, and aesthetic preferences are noted in quilts from the past and the present.

Colby, Averil. *Quilting*. New York: Charles Scribner's Sons, 1971. xi+212 pp.; 191 illustrations, appendixes, bibliography, index.

Providing an overview of quilting origins and changing techniques and materials throughout its history, this work is especially important for discussions of both the technical and the historical aspects of the quilting tradition in Britain from the seventeenth through the twentieth centuries and the transfer of this tradition to the United States. Excellent black and white photographs document the complex quilting patterns in historic forms such as whitework and trapunto. Basic instructions are also provided for less common quilting types of gathered patchwork, wadded quilting, flat quilting, cord quilting, and stuffed quilting.

Cooper, Patricia, and Norma Bradley Buferd. *The Quilters: Women and Domestic Art*. Garden City, N.Y.: Doubleday, 1977. 157 pp.; approximately 55 black and white illustrations and 35 color plates, index.

In an early conscious attempt to focus on the life and art of the traditional quiltmaker, Cooper and Buferd use oral history vignettes from quilters in Texas and New Mexico to explore the relation of quilting to the lives of women. Excellent documentary photographs and heavily edited interviews with the quilters are interwoven in an impressionistic manner to provide an affecting picture of the difficult frontier life experienced by these women, who quilted to provide essential warmth and beauty to their often stark surroundings. Through the quilters' own words, quilts are shown to be important not only for carrying special memories of their earlier years and experiences but also for providing a creative pastime during their later years.

Curtis, Phillip H. "American Quilts in the Newark Museum Collection." *Newark Museum Quarterly*, n.s. 25, nos. 3–4 (Summer–Fall 1973): 1–68. Bibliography.

Curtis arranges the approximately 120 quilts in Newark's collection in 1973 into groups: pieced, appliqué, and all white. Several from each type are described at length; many have well-documented New Jersey histories.

Ferris, William. "Pecolia Warner, Quilt Maker." In *Afro-American Folk Art and Crafts*, edited by William Ferris, pp. 98–108. Boston: G. K. Hall, 1983. 1 illustration.

In a rambling narrative taken from taped interviews, Warner, from Yazoo City, Mississippi, speaks of learning to make quilts as a child from her mother, of making string quilts, of her pattern sources, and of other aspects of quilting, along with her religious philosophy and memories of childhood, marriage, and family. The edited interview is important in that it allows a well-known traditional quilter to speak for herself about the significance of quilts in her life.

Findley, Ruth E. *Old Patchwork Quilts and the Women Who Made Them*. Philadelphia: J. B. Lippincott, 1929. 202 pp.; 97 illustrations, 100 diagrams, index.

Long designated by many as the definitive work on patchwork quilts, this book offers basic information on the historical, social, psychological, political, and technical aspects of quiltmaking up to 1880. Findley sees this as the date when a woman finished "the trail of her patchwork," since with new economic and political status, "there would be no need for women to bend patient eyes and fingers over such tasks as patchwork." Little could Findley have known that much of her text would be just as valuable in the twentieth century, when interest in quilting underwent many revivals in the popular literature and never died in areas where quilts were an economic and physical necessity. Much attention is given to the origin, evolution, and typology of quilt names and patterns and their regional variations and migrations. More important are the considerations of the social customs of the quilting bee and making quilts for special occasions, the quilting jargon, and the role of the feminine artist confined to her home.

Freeman, Roland, ed. *Something to Keep You Warm: The Roland Freeman Collection of Black American Quilts from the Mississippi Heartland*. Jackson: Mississippi State Historical Museum, 1981. 46 pp.; 14 black and white illustrations, 25 color plates.

Representing a major collection of blacks' quilts, this catalogue provides excellent photographs of representative quilts and introductory essays entitled "Slave Quilting on Antebellum Plantations," by Gladys Marie Fry, and "The Aesthetics of Afro-American Quilts," by Maude Southwell Wahlman. Also included are brief biographies and documentary photographs of fourteen quilters.

Frye, L. Thomas, ed. *American Quilts: A Handmade Legacy*. Oakland, Calif.: Oakland Museum, 1981. 86 pp.; illustrations.

Published to accompany an exhibition of American quilts and a film on contemporary quiltmakers, this collection of essays and images downplays aesthetic contemplation of quilts in favor of examining their social and psychological roles in women's lives. The longest pieces, Rachel Maine's revisionist, feminist, and pacifist manifesto, calls for museums to collect commonplace goods and for historians to study ordinary people's ability to solve the problems of everyday life and find satisfaction in doing so. As a unit, this publication demonstrates the central role that quilts play in feminist material culture studies.

Gutcheon, Beth. *The Perfect Patchwork Primer*. New York: David McKay Co., 1973. 267 pp.; illustrations, index.

A complete instructional work from the early 1970s quilt revival, this primer provides technical instructions for basic quiltmaking from copying old designs to creating new patterns. Also included are chapters on quilt care, selling, exhibition, and sources of goods and services.

Haders, Phyllis. *Sunshine and Shadow: The Amish and Their Quilts*. Pittstown, N.J.: Mainstreet Press, 1976. 88 pp.; 16 black and white illustrations, 16 color plates.

This expanded edition of Haders's work gives excellent color plates of Amish quilts along with a brief sketch of Amish life, which may have inspired the bold use of color and design in these early quilts.

Hall, Carrie A., and Rose G. Kretsinger. *The Romance of the Patchwork Quilt in America*. Caldwell, Idaho: Caxton Printers, 1936. 299 pp.; 119 illustrations, index.

Although the text is brief and overly romantic, interspersed with verses, the bulk of this book is devoted to illustrations, unfortunately none in color. Nevertheless, it is helpful in identifying older quilt patterns. Each of the black and white plates contains photographs of several quilt blocks with their names and variants.

Holstein, Jonathan. *The Pieced Quilt: An American Design Tradition*. Greenwich, Conn.: New York Graphic Society, 1973. 187 pp.; 42 black and white illustrations, 95 color plates, appendix, bibliography.

Using the thesis that quilts have been undervalued as American abstract design achievements, this pictorial survey presents American pieced quilts chosen on their aesthetic merits as "paintings." The text briefly discusses nineteenth-century developments, the social context of quilting, and some regional variations.

Holstein, Jonathan, and John Finley. *Kentucky Quilts, 1800–1900*. Louisville: Kentucky Quilt Project, 1982. 80 pp.; 14 black and white illustrations, 62 color plates, bibliography.

This work is important for representing the movement in all parts of the country to document older quilts. It is the culmination of the Kentucky Quilt Project, which located and documented more than 1,000 quilts. The finest are presented here. Holstein's text sketches American interest in quilts and comments on the design and construction of all pictured quilts. Finley describes the project and gives vignettes of Kentucky regional history.

Ice, Joyce, and Judith Shulimson. "Beyond the Domestic Women's Traditional Arts and the Creation of Community." *Southwest Folklore* 3, no. 4 (Fall 1979): 37–44.

This in-depth contextual analysis of traditional quiltmaking in Lytton Springs, Texas, explores women's roles, worldview, and aesthetics as they are revealed in quilting club relationships. Based on extensive interviews with and observation of members of the Lytton Springs Quilting Club, this research, which was conducted by folklorists, presents a more thorough view of how quilting functions to establish and preserve relationships in the community and between women.

Irwin, John Price. *A People and Their Quilts*. Exton, Pa.: Schiffer Publishing Co., 1984. 214 pp.; black and white and color illustrations, bibliography, index.

Irwin presents a study of traditional quiltmaking today in the Appalachians that is dominated by beautiful photographs of quiltmakers, their quilts, and their surroundings in the mountain landscape. Also of interest are the oral histories included with the quilts, which explain the meaning and function of quilts in the lives of their makers. Strangely, Irwin, a retired history teacher, devotes one chapter to the quilt as folk art, in which he considers only the idiosyncratic pictorial appliqué quilt to be a work of folk art, thus casting the traditional pieced quilt outside this realm, an idea directly opposed to the views of most folklore scholars.

James, Michael. *The Quiltmaker's Handbook: A Guide to Design and Construction*. Englewood Cliffs, N.J.: Prentice-Hall, a Spectrum Book, 1978. xii+147 pp.; 113 black and white illustrations, 21 color plates, appendixes, bibliography, index.

James discusses quilting materials, design creation, and the technical aspects of quiltmaking from the perspective of a male revivalist quiltmaker. The text is accompanied by detailed illustrations.

Johnson, Bruce, with Susan S. Conner, Josephine Rogers, and Holly Sideford. *A Child's Comfort: Baby and Doll Quilts in American Folk Art*. New York and London: Harcourt Brace Jovanovich in association with the Museum of American Folk Art, 1977. xi+116 pp.; 48 color plates, glossary, bibliography.

The majority of this work is devoted to color plates of baby and doll quilts made chiefly during the latter half of the nineteenth century. Also included are brief essays discussing the quilt's relation to the nineteenth-century child and instructions for making a child's comforter, which are not actually as helpful as those in many other how-to books wholly devoted to quiltmaking.

Jones, Stella M. *Hawaiian Quilts*. Honolulu: Daughters of Hawaii, Honolulu Academy of Arts, and Mission Houses Museum, 1973. 78 pp.; 60 black and white and color plates.

In this updated version of Jones's 1930 monograph, which is supplemented with quilts from a 1973 exhibition, the origins of Hawaiian quilts are traced to New England techniques brought by the American missionaries in the nineteenth century. The Hawaiian design innovations using local flora, sites, and historical events, along with design origins and meanings, are described.

Katzenberg, Dena S. *Baltimore Album Quilts*. Baltimore: Baltimore Museum of Art, 1981. 124 pp.; 99 black and white and color illustrations, bibliography.

The textile origins, design sources, and imagery of some fifty album quilts made in Baltimore from 1846 to 1852 are presented in this well-illustrated account. Katzenberg concludes that most nongeometric designs are traceable to English transfer-decorated ceramics, that a disproportionate number of the quilts are associated with Methodists, and that many were at least in part the work of professional quiltmakers.

Khin, Yvonne M. *The Collector's Dictionary of Quilt Names and Patterns*. Drawings by Yvonne M. Khin; color photographs by Glen Sam Lwin. Washington, D.C.: Acropolis Books, 1980. 489 pp.; approximately 2,400 illustrations, 16 color plates, index.

Including the greatest number of quilt patterns and names in one volume, this index is most useful for researching pattern names and identifying older quilts. The patterns are arranged according to geometrical designs into sometimes confusing groups, making the dictionary somewhat difficult to use at first; however, once understood, it is most helpful.

Laury, Jean Ray. *Quilted Clothing*. Birmingham, England: Oxmoor House, 1982. 154 pp.; black and white illustrations, color plates, index.

This instructional guide for the construction of quilted garments reflects the strong interest of revivalist quilters in producing patchwork and quilting art that has a functional and decorative use outside the home. Pattern and sewing instructions are quite detailed and are simple to follow. Clothing items covered include vests, jackets, kimonos, coats, dresses, skirts, children's clothes, accents and accessories, and decorations.

Leone, Diana. *The Sampler Quilt*. 6th ed. N.p.: Leone Publishing, 1984. 68 pp.; illustrations.

This instructional booklet is representative of the large number of author-published how-to works popular among revivalist quilters and commonly available in quilting supplies stores. Step-by-step instructions for making a sampler quilt are given.

Lewis, Alfred Allan. *The Mountain Artisans Quilting Book*. New York: Macmillan Publishing Co., 1973. 199 pp.; color plates.

Showing how traditional quilters from Appalachia have incorporated modern designs of the late 1960s and early 1970s into traditional quilting and patchwork, this book documents the development of the cottage quilting industry in the region. It contains good photographs of traditional quilters using both traditional and modern methods of patchwork

construction. The text combines pattern and construction description with comments from quilters, which indicate the attitudes of the women.

McMorris, Penny. *Crazy Quilts*. New York: E. P. Dutton, 1984. 127 pp.; 130 color plates, bibliography, index.

A work devoted exclusively to the crazy-quilt type, this predominantly pictorial study discusses the possible influences on the development of the popular Victorian quilt type, techniques of construction, common motifs, and fabrics. Also provided are chapters on the care of the especially fragile crazy quilts of silk and velvet and the design of contemporary crazy quilts.

Mainardi, Patricia. "Quilts: The Great American Art." *Feminist Art Journal* 2 (Winter 1973): 1, 18–23.

In this extensive discussion of the politics of quilts and quilt scholarship, Mainardi argues that the female artistry in quilting has been ignored by the male-dominated artistic hierarchy. Even when critics have compared patchwork quilting to abstract art, the critics have dismissed quiltmakers as artists; similarly, critics have failed to recognize the artistry of appliqué quilts because they cannot be compared with anything produced by male artists. Mainardi also discusses basic types, techniques, and customs and the history of quilting.

Mattera, Joanne, ed. *The Quiltmaker's Art: Contemporary Quilts and Their Makers*. Asheville, N.C.: Lark Books, 1982. 132 pp.; black and white and color illustrations.

A fiber artist herself, Mattera presents the quilted works of thirty fiber artists along with their biographical sketches, which give insight into the professional artist's more self-conscious approach to quiltmaking.

Orlofsky, Patsy, and Myron Orlofsky. *Quilts in America*. New York: McGraw-Hill Book Co., 1974. xiv + 368 pp.; 205 black and white illustrations, 109 color plates, bibliography, index.

Drawing on material from many other works on quilts, this popular survey covers American quilts from their earliest appearance to the twentieth century. The chapters on techniques, tools, types, patterns, signatures, dating, and care are adequate, but the account of the historical development of the quilt in America is oversimplified. Even so, it provides a good overview of the craft and its types. *See also* "Needlework."

Pottinger, David. *Quilts from the Indiana Amish: A Regional Collection*. New York: E. P. Dutton, 1983. 88 pp.; 160 black and white and color plates.

This pictorial volume concentrates on Pottinger's collection of Amish quilts dating from 1875 to 1940 from Elkhart and Lagrange counties in Indiana. In describing how his collection began and developed, Pottinger explains why he terminated his collecting at 1940; after this date, quilters used fewer large-scale patterns and more synthetic fabrics, thus decreasing the appeal of the newer quilts.

Roach, Susan. "The Kinship Quilt: An Ethnographic Semiotic Analysis of a Quilting Bee." In *Women's Folklore, Women's Culture*, edited by Rosan A. Jordan and Susan J. Kalc, pp. 54–64. Publications of the American Folklore Society, new ser., vol. 8. Philadelphia: University of Pennsylvania Press, 1985.

Roach's detailed analysis of conversation occurring among family members at a quilting bee held in rural northern Louisiana reveals the members' quilting aesthetic preferences, their varying degrees of quilting competence and performance, their methods of teaching novices traditional quilting techniques, and their use of quilts for bed covers, baby pallets, "scrapbooks" of past clothing, and heirlooms. The speech at the quilting bee also shows how the quilt functions to communicate worldviews and cultural beliefs, such as the importance of family and the transmission of family values to new generations. The importance of family participation, even of novice quilters, indicates that the aesthetic function does not always dominate in the production of folk art.

Roach, Susan, and Lorre Weidlich. "Quilt Making in America: A Selected Bibliography." *Folklore Feminist Communication* 3 (Spring 1974): 5, 17–28.

This work includes annotations of 36 major books and articles and additional entries of nearly 150 popular-periodical articles from the late 1800s to the 1970s. The articles are arranged alphabetically in sections according to their specific subject matter; categories include American patchwork, exhibitions and collections, historical quilts and patterns, quilts as decoration, quilting in geographic regions, quilting revivals and preservation, techniques of quilting, and quilting newsletters. Noting folklorists' neglect of quiltmaking studies, the introduction summarizes quilt scholarship to 1974 and suggests the research potential that quilts offer for studies in expressive and communicative forms, women's speech and social interaction, symbolism, and interaction of traditional and popular cultures.

Roach-Lankford, Susan. *Patchwork Quilts: Deep South Traditions.* Alexandria, La.: Alexandria Museum, 1980. 9 pp.; 4 illustrations.

Accompanying an exhibition of thirty-two Euramerican and Afro-American quilts from Georgia, Alabama, Mississippi, Louisana, and eastern Texas, this catalogue suggests that a quiltmaker's socioeconomic circumstances and her intended purpose for a quilt (either "everyday" or "fancy") may influence her quiltmaking more than her ethnic background does. This is the first such modification of the ethnic determinism of other studies of Afro-American quilts.

Robacker, Earl F., and Ada F. Robacker. "Quilt Traditions of the Dutch Country." *Pennsylvania Folklife* 21 (Folk Festival Supplement 1972): 31–38. 15 illustrations, bibliography.

Accompanying the twenty-third annual Pennsylvania Dutch Kutztown Folk Festival, this article discusses the different factors taken into account by quiltmakers to produce an aesthetically pleasing, original product and briefly analyzes how different types of quilts grew out of different economic conditions. There is also some consideration of quilt types and customs surrounding them.

Stewart, Susan. "Sociological Aspects of Quilting in Three Brethren Churches in Southeastern Pennsylvania." *Pennsylvania Folklife* 23, no. 3 (Spring 1974): 15–29. 17 illustrations, bibliography.

The meaning of quiltmaking for this conservative Pennsylvania German sect is examined, along with the historic links between quilting and missionary work. For the women of this group, the combination of piety and frugality that quilting represents makes it acceptable as a pastime. Largely a nostalgic activity for the over-sixty women in this sect, quilting fills a void after family rearing and serves both domestic and social functions.

Uncoverings. Research Papers of the American Quilt Study Group, edited by Sally Garoutte. Vol. 1–. Mill Valley, Calif.: By the group, 1980–. Illustrations, index.

This publication is a series written and published by members of the American Quilt Study Group, a nationwide organization interested in the serious study of the history of quilts, textiles, and the women who made them. The essays in the first volume present well-documented articles on Afro-American quilters, midwestern pattern sources, twentieth-century quiltmakers, a Pomo Indian quilt, quilt archives, country quilt design invention, and lettered quilts. Topics covered in the second volume include nineteenth-century cloth, clothing, and quilts; quilts at Chicago fairs; quilts in American literature; contemporary quilters; museum collecting; California's first quilting; an Alabama quilt collection; specific historic quilts; American fabrics in quilts; and the Mariner's Compass pattern. Topics covered in the third volume include Cuna Molas, family quilts, regional quilts, 1809 quilting designs, string quilts, red cross quilts, and many private collections. The fourth volume covers Victorian silk template patchwork, childhood recollections recorded in a quilt, appliqué button blankets in Northwest Coast Indian culture, white perspectives of blacks in quilts, nineteenth-century quilts in North Carolina, chronology of quilt patterns from 1775 to 1825, international patchwork items, and the Kentucky quilt registry.

Vlach, John Michael. "Quilting." In John Michael Vlach, *The Afro-American Tradition in Decorative Arts*, pp. 44–75. Cleveland: Cleveland Museum of Art, 1978. 35 illustrations, 3 color plates.

Although Afro-Americans learned quilting through their plantation experience, Vlach argues that in creating quilts for their own use, black quilters preserved African aesthetic principles by selecting and improvising on American quilt patterns that were similar to African textile designs. He finds African analogs for the appliqué quilts of Harriet Powers in the Fon and other African appliqué textiles. Similar analogs for "string" or "strip" quilts commonly made by black quilters can be found in the strip weaving occurring in western Africa. In addition to the familiar motifs, black quilts frequently employ other African aesthetic preferences such as large-scale design, high-contrast colors, unpredictability, and improvisation. Thus, such quilts are statements of cultural survival rather than cultural surrender.

Wahlman, Maude Southwell, and John Scully. "Aesthetic Principles in Afro-American Quilts." In *Afro-American Folk Art and Crafts*, edited by William Ferris, pp. 78–97. Boston: G. K. Hall, 1983. 2 illustrations, glossary.

This article continues the argument that Afro-American aesthetics are unique and deserving of further appreciation. Scholarship of Afro-American quilts is surveyed, historic references to the quilts are traced, and African textile antecedents are discussed. Five typical design elements are given: the use of strips to construct and organize the surface, large-scale patterns, contrasting colors, off-beat patterning, and multiple rhythms. These ideas formed the basis for Wahlman's further research for her doctoral dissertation at Yale University on Afro-American quilters and her forthcoming book on the subject (Indiana University Press).

Webster, Marie Daugherty. *Quilts: Their Story and How to Make Them*. New York: Doubleday, Page, 1945. xviii + 178 pp.; 69 black and white illustrations, 14 color plates, bibliography, index.

This early work not only provides traditional instructions for making quilts but also surveys the history of quiltmaking and patchwork in antiquity through the Middle Ages to England and America. Chapters on quilt names and the place of quilts in the American home are also included.

Yabsley, Suzanne. *Texas Quilts, Texas Women*. Centennial Series of the Association of Former Students, no. 16. College Station: Texas A and M Press, 1984. 98 pp.; black and white and color plates, bibliography, index.

Representative of the number of regional studies of quiltmaking, this documentary examines the history and development of quilting in Texas. The focus ranges from historic quilts to the recent creations by revivalist quilters. Comparisons are made between the older quilting clubs and the newest revivalist quilt guilds, which Yabsley sees as the dynamic wave of the future.

Textiles

Adrienne D. Hood

N THIS CHAPTER, the words *textile* and *fabric* are used interchangeably to describe woven, dyed, or printed designs. Most of the literature concentrates on fabrics made or used in North America in the seventeenth, eighteenth, and nineteenth centuries. I have tried to include works from the diverse areas of textile research done over the years: literature dealing specifically with textiles in the United States and Canada on a variety of subjects such as coverlets; regional investigations of handweaving and fiber and cloth processing; studies of European textiles that might have been exported to North America; and works on printed fabrics. Literature that provides a more general overview of textiles is included, as are bibliographies and works that clarify terminology.

A broad survey reveals that the majority of the literature attempts to describe not only what textiles might have been made or used here but also their method of manufacture. This is not surprising, given that the survival rate for textiles is much lower than, for example, furniture or silver. Not only do fibers (wool, flax, hemp, cotton, and silk) disintegrate more easily than wood or metal, but in the years prior to the full mechanization of textile manufacture, cloth was costly and often used until worn out. A further difficulty in determining the nature of cloth manufacture is that modern technology has completely replaced that of the earlier period. It is difficult, therefore, to undertake accurate analyses of the types and quantities of textiles that were most commonly used or to assess the scope and organization of local cloth manufacture and its output versus the volume of imported fabrics used. As a result, many researchers have concentrated their energies on creating catalogues of existing collections. This type of analysis, while necessary, unfortunately is biased by the survival rate of textiles (how likely is this type of artifact to be representative if it survives long past its period of use?) and by the nature of collecting (how often do people collect spectacular items while ignoring the more mundane?). However, if one understands these shortcomings, catalogues and descriptive analyses serve the useful and necessary function of illustrating and categorizing objects used in the past, thereby providing a foundation on which to build other research.

There will always be a need for descriptive analyses of fabrics. These can take the form of catalogues, such as Grace Cooper's *Copp Family Textiles*, a description and technical analysis of a collection of one family's textiles now in Smithsonian Institution; or they can be more comprehensive, such as Harold and Dorothy Burnham's *Keep Me Warm One Night*, where the authors not only catalogue eastern Canadian handwoven textiles but also discuss their ethnic origins and evolution in

Canada, the tools and processes with which they were made, their structures, and pertinent weaving information. Descriptive analyses, like Abbott Cummings's *Bed Hangings* and Florence Montgomery's *Textiles in America*, catalogue fabric furnishings and illustrate their use. These two books, however, reflect a bias of collecting because the authors discuss textiles used primarily by the upper classes, the small minority of the population from which many extant artifacts originate.

Another bias resulting from the nature of many collections lies in our interpretation of the extent to which the craft of handweaving occurred on this continent and the ubiquitousness of handwoven products. Part of the problem stems from the high survival rate of woven coverlets, which appeal to weavers as well as researchers, resulting in a disproportionate amount of literature about these artifacts. Because of their visual appeal and high survival rate, coverlets have been collected and documented extensively both in the United States and in Canada in much greater quantities than other bedding and handwoven fabrics. By far the largest percentage of *Keep Me Warm One Night* is devoted to coverlets, and over the years many major museums have produced catalogues on this subject. One of the earlier, although now outdated, of these is *American Hand-Woven Coverlets in the Newark Museum*; more recent and accurate catalogues include Mildred Davison's and Christa Mayer-Thurman's *Coverlets* and John Heisey's *Checklist of American Coverlet Weavers*. Despite the overrepresentation of catalogues of this type, they are useful tools for illustrating the design and technological range of surviving coverlets, thereby giving insights into the skills and tastes of the people who made and used them.

In general, works on coverlets include a description and illustration of an artifact with an analysis of its woven structure, but some of the literature is devoted almost entirely to the latter aspect. Janet Crosson's and Dorothy Burnham's articles on jacquard-woven coverlets fall into this category. Both are valuable contributions to the study of textiles, as the authors demonstrate that, besides helping to document the coverlets, structural analysis can indicate the ethnic origins and European training of the weavers. This kind of research, deriving almost entirely from artifactual investigation, when combined with documentary sources, ultimately could provide new insights into the dissemination of craft skills otherwise not considered.

Coverlets could be identified as the Rolls-Royces of North American handweaving, so it is important to study as wide a range of handwoven products as possible to obtain a balanced view of the subject. *Copp Family Textiles* rounds out our knowledge by describing a collection of one family's utilitarian textiles of the late eighteenth century and the first half of the nineteenth century. Constance Gallagher's *Linen Heirlooms* also does this by illustrating a body of household linens, the majority of which are from New England (this book should be used carefully, however, as it has not been rigorously researched from a historical perspective). Because the authors examine both plain, utilitarian fabrics and those made and reserved for special occasions, the literature about the textile traditions of the Louisiana Acadians and the handweaving of the Pennsylvania Germans and Canadians further enhances our knowledge about the broad range of handwoven textiles produced in North America.

Many of the studies documenting handweaving are regional. Although this is an essential first step in creating a complete picture of early American cloth manufacture, one must be careful not to extrapolate too broadly from regional studies. Frances Little's *Early American Textiles* tackles the issue of regionalism and its effect on textile manufacture. But unlike Little, who attempted a broad synthesis of the subject, many authors examine it from the perspective of a single locale without a sense of whether that area was unique. Coverlet studies have been written for several regions in North America, including Indiana and Ohio, and some researchers have examined the handweaving traditions of specific groups such as the French Canadians, Louisiana Acadians, Pennsylvania Germans, and Shakers. The majority of regional handweaving studies, however, have centered on New England and Pennsylvania, creating the mistaken impression that these areas are representative of preindustrial cloth manufacture throughout North America.

Combined with the literature on handwoven products is a large body of material dealing with the preindustrial manufacture of cloth. Among the earliest of these is Alice Earle's *Home Life in Colonial Days*, published in the late nineteenth century. Earle wrote about colonial cloth production and has been cited frequently by textile researchers; however, her reliance on oral history and surviving remnants of handweaving renders her interpretation romantic and often inaccurate. One should bear in mind that when Earle was writing, the craft of traditional handweaving was on the verge of extinction in much of North America; thus, the information available to her was often incomplete and distorted.

Earle is not the only researcher to paint a romantic picture of early American cloth manufacture. Many of the books annotated in this chapter contain small sections on the background of handweaving, interpreting it as follows: Most early American households had the necessary tools for cloth manufacture. The women, assisted by their children, spun the yarn and wove the cloth needed for the family's use; if the women did not weave the cloth, an itinerant weaver did. This scenario is so well accepted that it is described in many books without supporting documentation, as in Nancy Bogdonoff's *Handwoven Textiles of Early New England*. If, however, one looks at historic account books of weaving or examines the many pieces of equipment used to make the cloth, one realizes that the skills involved in colonial cloth manufacture were much more specialized than the standard picture would indicate.

Informative books that deal with textile manufacture in eighteenth- and nineteenth-century America include two catalogues published by Merrimack Valley Textile Museum (now Museum of American Textile History) that describe linen and wool processing: *All Sorts of Good Sufficient Cloth* and *Homespun to Factory Made*. Although the text is brief and was written to accompany an exhibition in each case, the illustrations provide excellent depictions of the variety of equipment and processes used in preindustrial cloth manufacture. An understanding of these can affect the interpretation of the organization and extent of clothmaking in early America; for example, where were so many devices kept? How did one learn to use these tools? Was it economical or practical for each house to have all the equipment, or did it make more sense for a few specially trained people in a region to do the weaving for a community? Merrimack Valley Textile Museum publications and the Dover reprints of dyers' recipes, weavers' drafts, and nineteenth-century instructions for cloth manufacture issued over the past few decades provide an understanding of the skill involved in and the labor-intensive nature of preindustrial cloth manufacture and thus support the unlikelihood that all households made their own cloth.

The next logical question must be, if North Americans did not manufacture all textiles for their own use, to what extent did they buy and use imported fabrics? This question has recently been addressed by several scholars. In 1975 the Textile Museum in Washington, D.C., devoted a conference to the subject, the proceedings of which were published as *Imported and Domestic Textiles in Eighteenth-Century America*. Other researchers, using household inventories to study seventeenth-, eighteenth-, and early nineteenth-century textiles, have found that the use of imported textiles outweighed the use of those locally made. David-Thiery Ruddel has shown that imported textiles were used not only almost exclusively by urbanites in Quebec City in the late eighteenth and early nineteenth centuries but also in large quantities despite a significant local textile industry in rural Quebec. Ruddel's analysis confirms and adds depth to the earlier work of Robert-Lionel Séguin. Linda Baumgarten demonstrates similar findings, and Susan Schoelwer argues that the majority of textiles used in Philadelphia were functional and imported. Natalie Rothstein describes the silks exported from England to America in the eighteenth century, and in *Textiles in America* Montgomery describes and defines a wide range of imported furnishing fabrics and discusses their use between 1650 and 1870.

Having determined the presence in North America of substantial amounts of imported cloth, much of it manufactured in or exported through Britain, we need to know what the textiles were and how they looked. Consequently, a bibliography of textiles in North America must include works on European and Eastern fabrics. Books such as Judith Bolingbroke's *William and Mary Fabrics* and Peter Thornton's *Baroque and Rococo Silks* are useful in describing European textiles that might have been brought with immigrants or exported for use in America. Montgomery's article on the sample book prepared by Englishman John Holker for the French is an excellent companion to *Textiles in America* as it defines and describes a range of textiles manufactured in Europe, some of which might have been exported to America.

Printed textiles, especially chintz from India and fabrics from England and France, were used by Americans in costumes and furnishings. *Origins of Chintz* by John Irwin and Katharine Brett provides a foundation for understanding the European market for Indian painted fabric and how it was designed, manufactured, and marketed. The English and American printed fabrics are examined in Montgomery's *Printed Textiles*, in Florence Pettit's works, and in *English Printed Textiles*. Margaret Fikioris analyzes late eighteenth-century printed French textile design influences, and Caroline Sloat examines the nineteenth-century American textile printing industry.

General references always give a wider perspective of textile use. Agnes Geijer's *History of Textile Art* is a good example of such a work, although it does not cover North America. Cecil Lubell, gearing his books toward designers, has written excellent guides to textile holdings at museums in North America, Britain, and Europe. In addition to these general works, bibliographies provide more detail on specific areas of textile research, such as those compiled by Beverly Gordon and Clarita Anderson, and several journals provide periodic reviews of textile literature.

The preceding comments make it clear that the study of North American textiles does not fall into large, clear-cut categories. This has always been true of the study of fabrics in general. For years textile historians have been struggling to find effective methods of categorizing, systematizing, and defining fabrics to come to grips with a field that encompasses a wide geographical area and a huge variety of technologies, structures, and uses. Thus I have included several books that, used together, will help researchers to categorize and define textile artifacts. Irene Emery's *Primary Structures of Fabrics* categorizes textiles by structure, Dorothy Burnham's *Warp and Weft* defines textile and weaving terms employed in Europe and North America, and Montgomery's *Textiles in America* gives contemporary definitions and uses for a wide variety of textiles.

The majority of the literature has been written by collectors, antiquarians, craftspeople, and curators. As a result, the artifacts have been examined on two levels: as pieces of weaving that result from certain technologies and as they were used in domestic environments. Clearly, the study of textile history is extremely multidimensional. Weavers and collectors will always be interested primarily in the artifacts themselves. Recently, however, material culture historians have begun to combine what is known about the artifacts with more traditional historical evidence to look at wider sociocultural, economic, and political implications of fabric consumption. While this stage of textile history is in its infancy, what has been done points to new directions of research.

For example, Baumgarten systematically analyzes data from household inventories and finds that instead of the silks and chintzes that are present to such a great extent in textile collections, plain woolens and serges comprised the majority of the fabrics used in seventeenth-century Boston. This represents an important step in altering the often top-heavy interpretation of textile history by demonstrating that in order to create a fully articulated image of North American fabric consumption, it is necessary to move beyond the purely artifactual evidence. Only then will it be possible to determine the similarities and differences in textiles used in rural as opposed to urban areas, the role of social and economic class and ethnicity in determining usage, and how that usage changed. At present there is very little in the literature that attempts to speak to these issues. Ruddel addresses the rural-urban and class concepts, Schoelwer looks at class and temporal influences, and the Burnhams examine ethnic differences. More works like these are needed to enable us to fit textiles into a broader and more complex social and temporal framework.

There is also a need for more information on the variety of textiles used in North America and their origins. What kinds of fabrics did settlers bring with them? How expensive was it to buy textiles imported to America? Did this change over time? What were the similarities and differences of textile usage between North America and Europe or even between the various regions of Europe? How did the industrialization of the textile industry, first in Britain, then in the United States and Canada, affect the supply and demand for fabric consumption in North America? We must remember that prior to the twentieth century, North Americans were dependent on Europe for a great deal of their cloth needs. This fact is clearly presented by Sloat, who argues that because the success of the American textile printing industry depended on the acquisition of British skills and equipment, it is often difficult to distinguish between early Victorian English and American printed textiles.

Finally, we must begin to look at fabrics in their broader social, economic, and political contexts, addressing such issues as their distribution; their impact on a local, national, or international level; the organization of their manufacture; their use as indicators of social status; and, of course, how all this changed over time. In her article on textile furnishings in eighteenth-century Philadelphia, Schoelwer examines the physical and psychological needs that prompted the use of fabric furnishings and asks whether these varied between social or economic class or changed over time. These are not easy questions to answer, but her work provides a preliminary framework and methodology with which to begin, as does Ruddel's article on Quebec textiles. Moreover, Ruddel also touches on the ramifications of British colonial politics on local textile manufacture, another area that should be explored more fully.

Combined with all the above is the necessity to move our research into more modern periods to examine the output of mills and the handmade textiles produced as part of the arts and crafts movement. There is also a need to conduct more comparative looks at Canada and the United States to see the similarities and differences of textile manufacture in two countries with many elements in common and yet some great differences. Eventually, the disparate textile literature should be synthesized to provide a revised general picture of textile manufacture.

Although this bibliography surveys the broad area of textile research and its most important works, it is not intended to be comprehensive. Some of the literature omitted from this chapter had weaknesses in research methodologies and conclusions, thereby undermining its usefulness to students of textile history. This is not to say that the absence of a title condemns it, for undoubtedly I have overlooked some good work. For example, numerous books were published on the subject of textiles in the early decades of this century, but few are included because they often tend to be romantic interpretations of early American cloth manufacture with conclusions revised by more recent works. I have also omitted many short articles that have appeared in *Antiques* over the years; however, this omission is largely compensated for by the inclusion of the volume edited by Anita Schorsch, *The Art of the Weaver*, a compilation of textile articles published in the magazine from 1925 to 1976. Numerous journals and periodicals frequently publish articles on textiles and should be examined for relevant material. Works from some of these have been included, but the articles are too numerous for comprehensive treatment here. Among the important periodicals are *American Folklife*; *Ars Textrina*; *Canadian Collector*; *CIBA Review* (which ceased publication in 1974); *Early American Life*; *Material History Bulletin*; *Shuttle, Spindle, and Dyepot*; *Textile History*; *Weaver's Journal*; *Winterthur Portfolio*; and local historical society and museum journals. The reader should also be aware of the body of literature that deals with the American textile industry that can be found through economic, labor, and social history sources. I have not included the voluminous literature on costume (although much of the cloth made in and imported to North America was for use in clothing), nor have I dealt with works on cashmere and paisley shawls, woven items primarily used as costume but also as furniture accessories. A last body of material not incorporated here is the literature on the textile traditions of native Americans.

Adrosko, Rita J. "Anatomy of a Quilted Counterpane." *Weaver's Journal* 8, no. 4 (Spring 1984): 42–46. Black and white and color illustrations.

This article describes the dismantling of an eighteenth-century counterpane, the components of which were deemed more valuable than the piece as a whole. The step-by-step technical analysis of the various textiles revealed almost a dozen utilitarian fabrics possibly made in the United States in the eighteenth century. It also pointed to the counterpane as being among the oldest in the collection of Smithsonian Institution. Analysis of each fabric includes color, weave structure, thread composition, and sewing stitches.

Adrosko, Rita J. *Natural Dyes and Home Dyeing*. Reprint of *Natural Dyes in the United States*, 1968. New York: Dover Publications, 1971. 160 pp.; 12 illustrations, bibliography, appendixes, index.

Noting the existence of professional dyers using largely imported dyestuffs, part 1 examines the historical background of eighteenth- and nineteenth-century American dyeing. Adrosko also explains that home dyeing may have occurred, but lack of records make this difficult to assess. The most important dyestuffs used during the period were indigo (blue); madder and cochineal (red); fustic and quercitron (yellow); logwood (black); and sumac (neutrals and black). A section on the dyestuffs describes them in detail by the colors they produced, with seventeenth-century illustrations interspersed throughout. Part 2 discusses color and lists dye recipes alphabetically by dyestuff for use by modern artisans. The bibliography includes a list of dye manuals printed in America before 1870. Five appendixes deal with dye chemicals and dyes mentioned in old manuals and include excerpts from some nineteenth-century treatises.

Anderson, Clarita. "Coverlet Bibliography." *Ars Textrina* 2 (1984): 203–15.

Anderson provides exhaustive coverage of the literature on North American handwoven coverlets.

Baumgarten, Linda R. "The Textile Trade in Boston, 1650–1700." In *Arts of the Anglo-American Community in the Seventeenth Century*, edited by Ian M. G. Quimby, pp. 219–73. Winterthur Conference Report 1974. Charlottesville: University Press of Virginia for the Henry Francis du Pont Winterthur Museum, 1975. 1 table, appendixes.

The textile trade of seventeenth-century Boston is examined and evaluated in terms relevant to period restoration. Baumgarten argues that although home production of textiles existed at the time, the colonists could not manufacture enough to meet their own needs and thus relied on large quantities of imported fabrics. The mechanics of trade relations between England and Boston are described, based on merchants' letters. Suffolk County household inventories provide information about the most commonly used fabrics,

which in descending order were wool, linens, cottons, and silks. An appendix defines the fabric names mentioned in the inventories, while another analyzes the fabrics used for household furnishings and finds that plain woolens, serges, and some watered fabrics (many of them green) were used most often.

Beer, Alice Baldwin. *Trade Goods: A Study of Indian Chintz in the Collection of the Cooper-Hewitt Museum of Decorative Arts and Design*. Washington, D.C.: Smithsonian Institution Press, 1970. 133 pp.; 37 black and white illustrations, 4 color plates, bibliography, glossary.

Written to accompany a chintz exhibition presented jointly by the Victoria and Albert and Royal Ontario museums and held at Cooper-Hewitt Museum in 1970, *Trade Goods* examines East Indian chintz from the perspective of the English East India Company. The history of initial European contact with India by sea is discussed, as is the period when the English became dominant in the trade and how it evolved and was organized. Beer describes the materials used in chintz and the techniques of making them and mentions the use of chintz in North America. The catalogue entries with illustrations are very detailed, and the glossary is helpful. Beer draws heavily on Irwin and Brett, *Origins of Chintz*.

Bemiss, Elijah. *The Dyer's Companion*. Introduction and appendixes by Rita J. Adrosko. 3d ed., enl. New York: Dover Publications, 1973. vi+311 pp.; appendixes, index.

This edition is a republication of the second dye manual known to have been printed in the United States (1st ed. 1806). Unlike later works, which were British reprints or French translations, this book was geared specifically to the needs of American dyers. In her introduction, Adrosko sketches Bemiss's history and warns modern dyers of the difficulty of adapting the dyes for home use, since Bemiss's intended audience was professionals who dyed large quantities of material. The text is divided into two parts: the first gives recipes for dyeing wool, silk, cotton, and linen and directions for finishing the cloth; the second contains general recipes, such as how to make ink or furniture polish. There are two appendixes from Adrosko's *Natural Dyes and Home Dyeing* that give names of chemicals used in dyeing and dyes mentioned in American dyers' manuals.

Bird, Michael, and Terry Kobayashi. *A Splendid Harvest: Germanic Folk and Decorative Arts in Canada*. Toronto: Van Nostrand Reinhold, 1981. 240 pp.; 223 black and white illustrations, 41 color plates, glossary, bibliography, index.

Although each textile type is illustrated, *A Splendid Harvest* provides only a superficial examination of textiles made by groups in Ontario and the Prairies within the larger context of their folk art. The weaving, needlework (samplers and show towels), quilting, and rug hooking of the Ontario groups are briefly outlined. Bird and Kobayashi draw heavily on Burnham and Burnham's *Keep Me Warm One Night* for weaving information. An examination of the Prairies groups focuses on late settlements of Mennonites and Hutterites and finds little handweaving but much needlework.

Bogdonoff, Nancy Dick. *Handwoven Textiles of Early New England: The Legacy of a Rural People, 1640–1880*. Harrisburg, Pa.: Stackpole Books, 1975. 192 pp.; black and white illustrations, 20 color plates, bibliography, index.

The local manufacture of textiles in New England in the eighteenth and nineteenth centuries is examined under the following headings: the handweaving era; materials and tools of the weaving trade; table linens; bedding; window curtains; furniture accessories; and rugs and carpeting. Unfortunately, the historical information in this book is superficial, often inaccurate, and abounds with many of the myths associated with North American handweaving. This is compounded by a lack of notes, rendering the sources difficult to check. The bibliography is composed of secondary references.

Bolingbroke, Judith M. *William and Mary Fabrics*. Leigh-on-Sea: F. Lewis, 1969. 99 pp.; 59 illustrations.

This catalogue presents European textiles and textile designs used in England in the late seventeenth and early eighteenth centuries. Changes in designs are noted if they occurred, and the reasons that changes happened are superficially examined. The discussion is not limited to woven fabrics only; it includes silks, chintzes, tapestries, embroideries, and lace. Most of the textiles illustrated are from the Victoria and Albert Museum.

Bronson, J. and R. *Early American Weaving and Dyeing: The Domestic Manufacturer's Assistant and Family Directory in the Arts of Weaving and Dyeing*. Reprint of *The Domestic Manufacturer's Assistant, and Family Directory, in the Arts of Weaving and Dyeing*, 1817. New introduction by Rita J. Adrosko. New York: Dover Publications, 1977. xiii+204 pp.; index.

This reprint of an 1817 weaving manual has a new introduction with instructions that are helpful in interpreting old drafts, dye recipes, and terminology used in the text. Information in the text includes instructions for weaving, dyeing, and sizing wool and cotton, as well as descriptions of some of the cloth being woven in that period.

Burnham, Dorothy K. *The Comfortable Arts: Traditional Spinning and Weaving in Canada*. Exhibition catalogue. Ottawa: National Gallery of Canada, 1981. xvii+238 pp.; 203 illustrations, 95 diagrams, bibliography.

This catalogue of artifacts chosen from museums across the country represents a wide variety of Canadian textile traditions. An introduction discusses the rationale behind the selection of objects, provides general background information, and explains textile terminology and basic technology.

Chapter 1 looks at textile traditions of the native peoples including weft twining, rigid-heddle weaving, and quill and bead weaving, followed by a chapter on braiding by the native people and the French. Chapters 3 through 6 discuss the French, Loyalist, Scottish, Irish, English, and German traditions, adding some new material to, but largely reviewing, the information in Burnham and Burnham's *Keep Me Warm One Night*. A unique contribution to this volume is contained in the last chapter where the author examines and illustrates the twentieth-century weaving of such groups as the Doukhobors, Ukranians, Hutterites, and Icelanders. Each chapter begins with an overview of the traditions and textiles on which it focuses, followed by a photographic catalogue of relevant pieces. The catalogue entries discuss each item, often with a diagram of its weave construction. The section on jacquard coverlets updates and adds the constructions not contained in *Keep Me Warm One Night*.

Burnham, Dorothy K. "Constructions Used by Jacquard Coverlet Weavers in Ontario." In *Studies in Textile History: In Memory of Harold B. Burnham*, edited by Veronika Gervers, pp. 31–42. Toronto: Royal Ontario Museum, 1977. 11 illustrations, diagrams.

Burnham wrote this work as a "postscript" to the chapter on jacquard coverlets in Burnham and Burnham's *Keep Me Warm One Night*, where analyses of weave structures were absent, and notes errors in that chapter. Constructions are described, and each is illustrated with a photograph, a diagram, and a list of all known Ontario weavers using it. Burnham finds twelve variations and feels that they probably relate to the training that weavers received before arriving in Canada, thus giving clues to their origins and Old World influences.

Burnham, Dorothy K. *Unlike the Lilies: Doukhobor Textile Traditions in Canada*. Toronto: Royal Ontario Museum, 1986. ix+102 pp.; 159 black and white illustrations, 23 color plates, glossary, bibliography.

The Doukhobors, a Russian religious sect persecuted for their beliefs, emigrated from the Caucasus region in 1899 and 1900 to Canada, settling first in Saskatchewan and later in British Columbia. Knowledge of their textile traditions still exists among the older generation, many of whom Burnham interviewed. After a brief summary of Doukhobor history, she describes the equipment and processing of flax and wool, including the preparation of the fibers, spinning, and weaving. She then describes some of the clothing, household linens, and bedding made and used by the group. Interesting old photographs and a glossary in English and Russian demonstrate the differences between some of these textiles and those traditionally associated with North American handweaving.

Burnham, Dorothy K. *Warp and Weft: A Textile Terminology*. Adapted and expanded from the *Vocabulary of Technical Terms*, 1964, with permission of the Centre

International d'Etude des Textiles Anciens. Toronto: Royal Ontario Museum, 1980. xiv+216 pp.; illustrations, diagrams, bibliography, appendixes.

Based on vocabularies of Centre International d'Etude des Textiles Anciens at Lyons (CIETA), this book defines textile terms and describes weave structures and weaving equipment not always found in general dictionaries. It is an update of the 1964 English version and encompasses only terms relating to woven fabrics with their equivalents in French, German, Italian, Portuguese, Spanish, and Swedish. The terminology section is arranged alphabetically with many of the terms illustrated by a coherent diagram (drawn by the author), a photograph of a relevant artifact, or both. Definitions are clear and concise, and some are cross-referenced. Where applicable, synonyms are provided. Most of the objects depicted are from the textile collection of Royal Ontario Museum. One appendix provides a table of the weaves that are defined in the text, while another lists specialized French terms.

Burnham, Harold B., and Dorothy K. Burnham. *"Keep Me Warm One Night": Early Handweaving in Eastern Canada.* Toronto: University of Toronto Press, 1972. xv+387 pp.; 491 black and white illustrations, 4 color plates, 4 maps, bibliography, appendix, index.

Providing an extensive survey of handweaving prior to 1900 in Ontario, Quebec, and the Atlantic provinces, this book begins with a historical overview of Canada's settlement by a variety of ethnic groups and the developments in weaving during the period. The authors define the four sources of handweaving traditions (French, Scottish, German, and Loyalist) and survey the types of textiles made by each, providing a look at the tools and equipment and an explanation, with excellent diagrams, of the basic weaves (tabby, twill, and satin) used in cloth construction. The remaining chapters deal with textiles. Each begins with a general discussion of the fabrics, including a historical overview, sometimes a European comparison, and a discussion of the constructions used. The text is followed by a catalogue of the artifacts with clear photographs and a descriptive caption for each. Chapters deal with costume, carpets, blankets, and linens, with the last eight chapters (and the majority of the book) examining coverlets of varying complexity of construction. Beginning with simple two-shaft coverlets, the Burnhams examine others woven in overshot, summer and winter, multiple shaft, twill diaper, and double-cloth constructions, concluding with coverlets woven on looms with jacquard attachments. Because of the great similarities between Canadian and American handwoven products, this is an excellent book for researchers of either country.

Congram, Marjorie. "Haircloth Upholstery." *Nineteenth Century* 6, no. 4 (Winter 1980): 48–50. 10 illustrations.

Haircloth, or fabric made from horsehair, is described in its basic form as plain black cloth and in its pattern variations, with a section on manufacture both in England and in America. Its primary uses as upholstery fabric are described, and other uses of horsehair in clothing, men's hats, bustles, braid trim, and violin bows are listed.

Coons, Martha, and Katherine Koob. *All Sorts of Good Sufficient Cloth: Linen-Making in New England, 1640–1860.* North Andover, Mass.: Merrimack Valley Textile Museum, 1980. 121 pp.; 86 illustrations.

Divided into three sections, this text deals with the manufacture of linen from the first settlement until it was superseded by cotton manufacture in the nineteenth century. History is given first, followed by a discussion of the processing of fiber from plant to fabric, and concluding with the cloth produced. The illustrations and photographs are excellent. When used with *Homespun to Factory Made*, the book provides a good introduction to the processing of yarn and major developments in the textile industry.

Cooper, Grace Rogers. *The Copp Family Textiles.* See "Needlework."

Crosson, Janet Gray. *Let's Get Technical: An Overview of Handwoven Pennsylvania Jacquard Coverlets, 1830–1860.* Lancaster, Pa.: Old Fibers, Weavers, and Coverlets, 1978. 35 pp.; 86 illustrations.

Crosson's pamphlet was written to complement a lecture. Discussion of the basic components of coverlets (yarn, color, design, weave structure), the weave structures of jacquard coverlets, and the jacquard mechanism is followed by an analysis of the various weave structures found in jacquard coverlets made in Pennsylvania. A chronological description of the coverlets is followed by a discussion of the various setups for jacquard-controlled patterning. Crosson believes that knowledge of weave structures and loom setups can help to identify regional coverlets and changes in equipment.

Cummings, Abbott Lowell, comp. *Bed Hangings: A Treatise on Fabrics and Styles in the Curtaining of Beds, 1650–1850.* Boston: Society for the Preservation of New England Antiquities, 1961. ix+60 pp.; 63 illustrations, bibliography.

This treatise is the product of a seminar held in 1960 to examine New England source material on bed hangings. Using information gleaned from period documents such as inventories, letters, and newspapers, the first section discusses the fabrics used, the location of bedsteads in the house, the composition of sets of bed hangings, and the changes in these over time. There is also an alphabetical listing of the fabrics used in bed hangings found in Suffolk County inventories from 1675 to 1810. These are defined where possible with contemporary meanings and some illustrations. Nina Fletcher Little discusses available pictorial evidence, and a final section sheds light on the technical aspects of bed-hanging construction.

Cunningham, Patricia A. "Ohio's Woven Coverlets." *Ars Textrina* 2 (1984): 165–83. 8 illustrations.

Jacquard-woven coverlets are examined in relation to the labor force, potential market, technology, and demographic composition of Ohio. Cunningham argues that various immigrant groups became geographically distinct because they tended to settle in areas of cultural affinity. The greatest numbers of coverlet weavers were among people of German and Pennsylvania German heritage. The materials, equipment, and power available to the weavers are discussed, as are the various types of craft organizations they used in coverlet manufacture. Cunningham finds that weaving occurred on three levels: in the home, in the factory, and in what is called the "residentiary factory." Migrant and immigrant settlers provided both the markets for and the weavers of the coverlets.

Davison, Mildred, and Christa C. Mayer-Thurman. *Coverlets: A Handbook on the Collection of Woven Coverlets in the Art Institute of Chicago.* Chicago: By the institute, 1973. 228 pp.; 164 black and white illustrations, 2 color plates, bibliography.

All the coverlets in the collection of the Art Institute of Chicago (at the time of publication) are featured in this catalogue, with photographs. Part 1 defines coverlets, discusses materials and equipment used in their making, and illustrates them by their construction (overshot, summer and winter, multiple shaft, double cloth, and beiderwand). Part 2 is a state-by-state examination of jacquard coverlets and their makers; within each state they are grouped chronologically.

Earle, Alice Morse. "Flax Culture and Spinning"; "Wool Culture and Spinning, with a Postscript on Cotton"; "Handweaving." In Alice Morse Earle, *Home Life in Colonial Days*, pp. 166–251. 1898. Reprint. Stockbridge, Mass.: Berkshire Traveler Press, 1974. 24 illustrations.

These chapters are an early attempt to describe colonial cloth manufacture. Earle outlines the fiber preparation, processing, and weaving of flax, wool, and cotton used in locally made cloth. While some of her information is accurate, she has a tendency to rely on folklore and oral history with the result that she espouses a romanticized version of colonial cloth manufacture. For example, according to Earle, flax spinning provided "an ever-ready refuge in the monotonous life of the early colonist." Moreover, there are misunderstandings about jacquard weaving, among other things. These are often cited, but they should be used with appropriate critical controls.

Emery, Irene. *The Primary Structures of Fabrics: An Illustrated Classification.* Washington, D.C.: Textile Museum, 1966. xxvi+339 pp.; 382 illustrations, bibliography, index.

In *Primary Structures of Fabrics*, Emery has attempted to create a coherent system of fabric classification to eliminate numerous inconsistencies in this area. She argues that fabric structure provides the best vehicle for doing so because it is common to all fabrics, can almost always be determined, can be observed objectively, and is varied enough to allow it to be categorized. Accordingly, the book is divided into three parts on the basis of ascending structural complexity. The first examines the components of fabrics such as fibers and filaments. The second, and most important, deals with the structures, ranging from nonwoven (felt), to single element (knitting), to two or more elements (plain and compound weaves). The third analyzes structures that are accessory to fabrics, such as embroidery and applied decoration. Each chapter has a short introduction, and the definitions are followed by notes on the uses of the terms. The structures are illustrated clearly, and the bibliography is extensive.

English Printed Textiles, 1720–1836. Exhibition catalogue. Rev. ed. London: Victoria and Albert Museum, Her Majesty's Stationery Office, 1972. 79 pp.; 64 illustrations, bibliography.

This catalogue includes a short text outlining the milestones of the English textile printing industry: woodblock beginning in the last quarter of the seventeenth century; copperplate in the mid eighteenth century; roller printing in the late eighteenth and early nineteenth centuries; and a new dye technology about 1810 to 1835. The author takes a broad look at the design changes over the period and the influence of technology on these changes. A section of photographs with brief descriptions of the textiles is included.

Fikioris, Margaret A. "Neoclassicism in Textile Designs by Jean-Baptiste Huet." In *Winterthur Portfolio 6*, edited by Richard K. Doud and Ian M. G. Quimby, pp. 75–110. Charlottesville: University Press of Virginia for the Henry Francis du Pont Winterthur Museum, 1970. 77 illustrations.

Huet was the chief designer at the Oberkampf factory from 1783 to 1811. Fikioris analyzes his designs, arguing that they reflect the changing tastes of the French public at this period. Early designs portrayed historical anecdotes, political allegories, and genre, romantic, and pastoral scenes. After the mid 1790s, the designs became more academic, reflecting the neoclassical decoration then in vogue. The design motifs on Huet's neoclassical pieces are analyzed to determine their origins. His designs are believed to provide "an encyclopedia of classical figures and motifs enjoyed and understood by the educated classes in both Europe and America at the end of the eighteenth and beginning of the nineteenth centuries" (p. 110).

Fiske, Patricia L., ed. *Imported and Domestic Textiles in Eighteenth-Century America.* Irene Emery Roundtable on Museum Textiles Proceedings, 1975. Washington, D.C.: Textile Museum, 1976. ii+195 pp.; 92 illustrations, bibliographies.

This collection of essays includes five that are of particular interest to students of American decorative arts. Natalie Rothstein describes the eighteenth-century silk trade from Britain and finds that it was piecemeal (probably to meet individual orders), consisting largely of yardage for dress, not furnishing fabrics. Florence Pettit examines the role of European printed textiles in American life and the techniques used for producing them. She believes that the only true American printed fabrics are those with a blue figure on a white ground, used for furnishings. Until a comparative look at similar documented European fabrics has been done, however, it is difficult to claim American origin for these with certainty. Rita Adrosko looks at the organization of the weaving craft in America and finds that most weavers were professionals working in their own workshops; very few were itinerants. She also discusses some mid eighteenth-century textiles at Smithsonian Institution. Mildred Lanier examines textiles in the southern colonies, in particular Virginia, Maryland, and North Carolina, and concludes that the majority of textiles used in these agrarian societies were imported, not manufactured locally. Finally, Dorothy Burnham describes what little is known of Canada's eighteenth-century furnishing fabrics with reference to the various ethnic traditions that influenced the designs of those locally manufactured. Sections in the book also deal with needlework and floor coverings. This is a good compilation of essays by some of the major people working in the field in the mid 1970s.

Forman, Benno M. "The Account Book of John Gould, Weaver, of Topsfield, Massachusetts: 1697–1724." *Essex Institute Historical Collections* 105, no. 1 (January 1969): 36–49.

Gould was a professional weaver who employed two journeymen. Forman provides an analysis of the contents of Gould's account book following a biographical sketch of the weaver. The account book sheds light on the types of cloth he produced and their costs. He did not full or dye cloth, but sent it to a mill; he produced his own wool and flax, but also bought both; and he was not poor. Despite Gould's production, Forman acknowledges that large quantities of textiles were also imported to New England in the seventeenth century. Forman provides an interesting insight into the production, status, and wealth of an early weaver.

Gallagher, Constance Dann. *Linen Heirlooms: The Story and Patterns of a Collection of Nineteenth Century Handwoven Pieces with Directions for Their Reproduction.* Newton Centre, Mass.: Charles T. Branford Co., 1968. xiii+209 pp.; 15 illustrations, 62 diagrams, bibliography, index.

A descendant of a nineteenth-century weaver and a weaver herself, Gallagher focuses on a group of linens (tablecloths, towels, pillowcases, mattress covers, and bags), mostly from New England, woven between 1806 and 1864, which she collected and subsequently gave to Smithsonian Institution. The handlooms and patterns used in making the linens are discussed, and suggestions and weaving drafts helpful in reproducing the old textiles are given. The primary focus is on the fabric structure and the genealogical information relevant to each piece. Historically romantic, this book is aimed at weavers and should be used with caution.

Geijer, Agnes. *A History of Textile Art.* London: Pasold Research Fund in association with Sotheby Parke Bernet, 1979. xi+317 pp.; approximately 200 illustrations, 95 black and white and 4 color plates, bibliography, index.

Geijer's book is mainly concerned with the development of weaving and woven fabrics prior to the industrial revolution. Chapter 1 examines the natural fibers used in cloth production and the methods and tools required to transform these into thread. Chapter 2 discusses a wide variety of weaving implements and their earliest known use. Chapters 3 through 6 look at woven fabrics and the techniques for weaving them. A historical overview of silk weaving as it developed, first in Asia and then in individual countries in Europe, is provided, followed by a discussion of linens and fabrics with pile grounds. Moving away from woven designs, Geijer summarizes the evolution of patterning textiles with dyes. A chapter on miscellaneous textile techniques is followed by one on European textile trade with the Orient and on textiles and textile crafts in the Scandinavian countries. A concluding chapter presents a discussion of how textiles have been and should be preserved and a useful historiographical survey of the major areas of past textile scholarship. Although Geijer does not include North American textiles in her analysis, she provides a broad context for many of the fabric traditions ultimately found in America.

Gilfoy, Peggy S. "The Art of Indiana Coverlets." *Ars Textrina* 2 (1984): 60–93. 20 illustrations, bibliography.

Gilfoy examines the design influences affecting Indiana jacquard coverlet weavers. From the 1840s to the 1870s there were about ninety professional weavers in the state, most of whom were of Scottish, English, or German origins. Many of them were from Kilmarnoch, Scotland, an important ingrain-carpet weaving center in the nineteenth century. Concentrating her analysis on Scottish coverlet weavers, Gilfoy writes that most of them used a double-cloth construction with deep indigo blue wool and white cotton yarns. The design elements distinctly resemble the ingrain carpets made in Scotland. Other possible design sources are illustrated.

Glasgow, Vaughn L. "Textiles of the Louisiana Acadians." *Antiques* 120, no. 2 (August 1981): 338–47. 9 black and white illustrations, 15 color plates.

Surviving Acadian handwoven textiles (the majority of which are bedding) dating from 1860 to 1900 are analyzed in this article. Descriptions of the fabrics indicate that they were made mostly of cotton, rarely of wool, and were woven on two-harness looms, with blue, brown, and white the most frequently used colors. The textiles were sometimes further embellished by *cordons* (strands of heavier cotton), *boutons* (loops of yarn), knitted edges, yarns of two colors plied together, and bands of colors. Although fewer survived, the Acadians also made rugs and clothing material. Glasgow describes the late nineteenth-century interest of the Christian Women's Exchange Shop in Acadian handweaving and the development of market products to be sold in New Orleans over a thirty-year period.

Gordon, Beverly. *Domestic American Textiles: A Bibliographic Sourcebook. See* "Needlework."

Gordon, Beverly. *Shaker Textile Arts*. Hanover, N.H., and London: University Press of New England with the cooperation of the Merrimack Valley Textile Museum and Shaker Community, 1980. xiv + 329 pp.; 139 black and white illustrations, 14 color plates, appendixes, glossary, index.

Gordon provides the only comprehensive analysis of Shaker textiles. The Shakers' philosophy is examined as the context for textile use and manufacture. Gordon argues that many of the group's fabrics are not dramatically different from those of the world around them, although some common characteristics do exist in the simple lines, regular pattern repeats, attention to detail, and careful construction. The fibers used and their processing are described, followed by a detailed analysis of the household textiles made and used by the Shakers, their clothing and personal accessories, and their fancywork. The discussion is not limited to woven fabrics; also included are palm hat- and basketmaking and braided, knitted, hooked, and crocheted items. Appendixes locate Shaker communities on a map, chart the government and organization of two branches of Shakers, provide weaving drafts, analyze some of the textiles, and give recipes for washing, dyeing, and bleaching cloth.

Hargrove, John, comp. *The Weavers Draft Book and Clothiers Assistant*. New introduction by Rita J. Adrosko. AAS Facsimiles, no. 2. 1792. Facsimile. Worcester, Mass.: American Antiquarian Society, 1979. xiii + 28 pp.

The original edition by Hargrove is one of two extant books and may have been among the first printed in the United States. Adrosko sketches the life of Hargrove, outlines eighteenth-century textile manufacture in Maryland, lists other known weavers' books and their locations, compares his work with that of three other weavers, and provides notes on his drafts. Hargrove discusses how to use the drafts, gives general cloth-finishing instructions and local names for patterns, and provides weaving drafts.

Heisey, John W., comp. *A Checklist of American Coverlet Weavers*. Edited and expanded by Gail C. Andrews and Donald R. Walters. Williamsburg: Colonial Williamsburg Foundation, 1978. x + 149 pp.; black and white illustrations, 4 color plates, bibliography, glossary, appendix, index.

Intended to help to identify maker, provenance, and patterns of coverlets, this index contains 942 jacquard weavers and 2,500 coverlets made by them in nineteenth-century America. It provides geographic locations of weavers and discusses their ethnic origin and its influence on the fabric structures used in the coverlets. Also given are the weavers' names alphabetically, known biographical information, the number of coverlets recorded at the time of the survey, and the dates of the first and last known coverlets with scattered illustrations. The book concludes with a pictorial section on weavers' trademarks.

Homespun to Factory Made: Woolen Textiles in America, 1776–1876. Exhibition catalogue. North Andover, Mass.: Merrimack Valley Textile Museum, 1977. 102 pp.; illustrations.

This catalogue is more concerned with processes than products. It shows objects and illustrations that document eighteenth- and nineteenth-century wool manufacture, and for each page of text there is an illustration. The stages of wool processing, technological changes, and nineteenth-century weaving innovations are described and illustrated. When needed, schematic diagrams explain the workings of machinery. This catalogue is a good companion to Coons and Koob's *All Sorts of Good Sufficient Cloth* as an introduction to linen and wool processing in America.

Irwin, John, and Katharine B. Brett. *Origins of Chintz; with a Catalogue of Indo-European Cotton-Paintings in the Victoria and Albert Museum, London, and the Royal Ontario Museum, Toronto*. London: Her Majesty's Stationery Office, 1970. viii + 134 pp.; 60 black and white and 17 color illustrations, 158 black and white plates, appendixes, bibliography, index.

Irwin and Brett examine painted cotton fabrics produced in India in the seventeenth, eighteenth, and nineteenth centuries. The authors argue that the oriental motifs incorporated into the designs were sent to India from England or Holland for the cotton painter to copy or adapt. Because the designs were transformed by the Indian imagination, the textiles were perceived as exotic on their return to Europe. The book focuses on this complicated interchange of art influence.

L'amour de maman: La tradition acadienne du tissage en Louisane. La Rochelle: Musée du Nouveau Monde, 1983. 95 pp.; text in French and English, illustrations.

Written to accompany an exhibition of the same name, *L'amour de maman* is the first comprehensive study of Louisiana Acadian textiles. It traces the origins of the Acadians from France to Canada in the seventeenth century, then, after their expulsion from Canada in 1755, to Louisiana, where they adapted their previous life-style to their new environment. Here *Acadian* became *Cajun*, and their textile traditions continued well into this century due to the group's isolation. The section "Textile Production in Acadian Life" argues that the home production of textiles was associated with social customs integral to Acadian identification. The tradition of a mother making the household textiles for her children's trousseaux, "L'amour de maman," represented almost a lifetime's work. Another section examines how outsiders' perceptions of the Acadians influenced the marketability of their textiles. This is followed by descriptions of the textile manufacturing tools and the regional materials employed, the most identifiable of these being *coton jaune* (brown cotton). Three sections describe the textiles themselves, one discusses the various later attempts to revive outside markets, and a final one provides portraits of several Acadian weavers. The photographs of textiles, tools, and people are captioned only in French in the text but are given in both languages and with more detail at the end. The French text sometimes contains information lacking in the English. For good color illustrations of some of the material discussed here, see Glasgow, "Textiles of the Louisiana Acadians."

La fabrication artisanale des tissus; appareils et techniques. Quebec: Musée du Québec, Ministère des Affaires Culturelles, 1974. 103 pp.; illustrations, bibliography.

This work describes the techniques and tools used in the hand processing of fabrics in nineteenth- and early twentieth-century French Canada. The book is divided into three parts, the first of which outlines the processing of flax and wool, the two main fibers used by the French Canadians. The second part discusses the preparation of the yarn for the loom, including spinning, skeining, dyeing, linen bleaching, bobbin winding, and warping. The third part describes the weaving of the cloth, the fulling of wool cloth, the recycling of old textiles, and wash day. The illustrations accompanying the text are excellent and provide a good comparison for similar processes in other parts of North America.

Little, Frances. *Early American Textiles.* Century Library of American Antiques, edited by Waldo R. Browne. New York and London: Century Co., 1931. xvi+267 pp.; 62 black and white plates, bibliography, index.

Early American Textiles is a pioneering work that examines not only textile manufacturing processes but also the textiles themselves. Little explores the earliest years of settlement in the North and South separately and the development of the textile industry from the seventeenth to the nineteenth centuries. She discusses the beginnings of the machine age in the early nineteenth century, the attempts to manufacture silk in America, the processes used in spinning and weaving, American embroidery, early cotton printing, and the textiles used in colonial houses. The book contains some interesting information but also some inaccuracies; thus, it should be used with care.

Lubell, Cecil, ed. *Textile Collections of the World.* Vol. 1, *United States and Canada.* New York: Van Nostrand

Reinhold Co., 1976. 336 pp.; black and white illustrations, 53 color plates, index.

Directed toward designers, this book examines collections of international textiles in more than seventy North American museums. The emphasis is on the visual, not historical, impact of the artifacts. Listings are alphabetical by city, and each entry includes the museum name, address, telephone number, curator at the time of publication, holdings listed alphabetically by country of origin, approximate size of the holdings, important exhibitions and publications, and occasionally the history of a department and its collecting policies. There are three major essays on North American textile design: "U.S. Textile Traditions" by Robert Riley is a historical overview from earliest times until the present; "Canadian Textiles" by Dorothy Burnham examines Canadian handwoven textiles in eastern Canada and the design traditions influencing the products; and "Fabrics of the North American Indians" by Andrew Whiteford discusses archaeological evidence, basketry, Southwest textile traditions, Pacific Northwest and eastern weaving areas, and applied decoration such as quillwork, beadwork, and ribbonwork. The last half of the book consists of a section of photographs of textiles that is arranged alphabetically by region with no attempt at chronology. The series contains two other volumes dealing with collections in Great Britain and France.

Montgomery, Florence M. "John Holker's Mid-Eighteenth Century *Livre d'Enchantillons.*" In *Studies in Textile History: In Memory of Harold B. Burnham,* edited by Veronika Gervers, pp. 214–31. Toronto: Royal Ontario Museum, 1977. 9 illustrations.

Montgomery analyzes a sample book of 115 swatches from circa 1750 found in the Musée des Arts Décoratifs, Paris. Prepared by Englishman Holker for the French, the sample book lists the types of textiles manufactured in Lancashire, Norwich, and Spitalfields, with English names, dimensions, and value in English money with the French equivalent. It also provides details of fiber processing, weaving, and finishing. Using Holker's notations, Montgomery describes the swatches and, if possible, gives a dictionary definition for each and references from American sources to indicate the importation of certain fabrics to America.

Montgomery, Florence M. *Printed Textiles: English and American Cottons and Linens, 1700–1850.* New York: Viking Press, a Winterthur Book, 1970. 379 pp.; 428 black and white illustrations, 30 color plates, bibliography, index.

Between 1700 and 1800, England manufactured an increasing number of printed textiles, many of which were exported to America. Montgomery examines the designs of many of these fabrics and explores their methods of manufacture and use in bed furniture, window coverings, and slipcovers. She draws largely on the extant examples in the collection at Winterthur, including woodblock-, copperplate-, and cylinder-printed textiles. Montgomery begins with a look at English printed textiles and a survey of technical innovations in the textile printing industry in the eighteenth and nineteenth centuries. After discussing English trade with the colonies, she describes textile furnishings in American homes and the three known eighteenth-century American textile printers, their work, and their history . The book includes a catalogue of artifacts, categorized under technique of manufacture. Montgomery concludes with a look at American plate- and roller-printed textiles and the use of printed fabrics in appliqué and patchwork quilts. The text contains an abundance of contemporary illustrations and photographs of textiles.

Montgomery, Florence M. *Textiles in America, 1650–1870*. New York: W. W. Norton, a Winterthur/Barra Book, 1984. xviii+412 pp.; 217 black and white illustrations, 104 color plates, dictionary, bibliography.

Textiles in America is primarily a dictionary of textile terms and a discussion of the furnishing fabrics of the period. Much of the information in the book has been culled from contemporary swatch books, trade publications, mill pattern books, scrapbooks, household guides, artisans' advertisements, correspondence, and artifacts from a variety of collections. After examining general trends and styles in furnishing practices in England and America, Montgomery describes the use, the changes in style, and sometimes the construction of bed hangings, window curtains, and upholstery. She concludes this section with an evaluation of the problems of using textiles in period rooms. These chapters are well illustrated, and between the text and the dictionary are excellent color plates of fabric swatches arranged by manuscript collection, the majority of which are from the eighteenth century. The dictionary terms are listed alphabetically and include alternate names where applicable, dates when available, quotations from contemporary correspondence and inventories, and an indication of use in America. The bibliography begins with an essay on the types of sources available for this kind of research, followed by an alphabetical listing of primary and secondary references integrated one with the other.

Nylander, Jane C. *Fabrics for Historic Buildings: A Guide to Selecting Reproduction Fabrics*. 3d ed. Washington, D.C: Preservation Press, 1983. 159 pp.; 91 illustrations, appendixes, glossary, bibliography.

This book was written to provide assistance in selecting and ordering fabrics suitable for furnishing historic properties. Nylander discusses the need to preserve original textiles and how to conduct the documentary research necessary to obtain accurate reproductions. Suggestions are given on how to select and order custom reproductions and how to install them. The catalogue section is divided into two parts: a listing of documentary reproduction fabrics arranged by historic period and nondocumentary and plain woven textiles arranged by type. The list of manufacturers and specialty sources and the glossary are especially helpful.

Pennsylvania Farm Museum of Landis Valley. *The Homespun Textile Tradition of the Pennsylvania Germans*. Introduction by Ellen J. Gehret and Alan G. Keyser. Exhibition catalogue. Harrisburg: Pennsylvania Historical and Museum Commission, 1976. Unpag.; 98 black and white and color illustrations, bibliography.

In this brief catalogue of a show of "folk textiles" that were handwoven, homespun, knitted, or vegetable dyed and used on family farms of the Pennsylvania Germans, the text describes the uses and processing of flax (the most widely used fiber), wool, and hemp; the tools needed for fiber preparation; dyeing; weaving; and fulling. The demise of the local fulling mills about 1880 is argued to be the end of the "homespun era." A section on the fabrics manufactured describes and briefly discusses their uses. A final section of photographs illustrates the equipment and textiles with descriptive captions for each. No dates are given unless they appear on the pieces.

Pettit, Florence H. *America's Printed and Painted Fabrics, 1690–1900*. New York: Hastings House Publishers, 1970. 256 pp.; 179 black and white illustrations, 6 color plates, bibliography, index.

As a broad survey of printed fabrics used and made in America, the text is divided into four sections: an overview of the methods of printing fabrics (direct, discharge, mordant, and resist dyeing), a survey of fabric printing prior to the discovery of America, a discussion of printed fabrics produced in America from 1607 to 1775, and a description of the advances in the American textile printing industry in the late eighteenth and early nineteenth centuries. According to Pettit, the major American contributions to textile printing include fabrics made by blue resist dyeing, early folk designs, and advances in textile printing machinery. Despite its title, this book deals more with printed textiles in general rather than those that are specifically American. It is stronger on the technical than the historical material and should be used carefully.

Ponting, K. G. *A Dictionary of Dyes and Dyeing*. London: Mills and Boon, 1980. 207 pp.; illustrations, bibliography.

This dictionary alphabetically lists subjects such as dyestuffs, people associated with major developments in the history of dyeing, colors, chemicals, fibers, and fabrics. Also included are historical entries (such as Babylonian dyers and dyeing), historical dye recipes, various methods of printing fabrics (such as batik and roller printing), and a listing of each volume of *Ciba Review* and its topic from its beginning until it ceased publication in 1974.

Rothstein, Natalie. "The Introduction of the Jacquard Loom to Great Britain." In *Studies in Textile History: In Memory of Harold B. Burnham*, edited by Veronika Gervers, pp. 281–304. Toronto: Royal Ontario Museum, 1977. 17 illustrations.

The jacquard loom was first exhibited in the 1801 Paris exhibition, but it was not used widely in Great Britain until the 1840s. Rothstein examines why. She compares the drawloom and its capabilities to the jacquard loom, compares the designs of fabrics being produced on each, and discusses the weavers and their relationship to their equipment, all of which were major factors. The illustrations include point patterns used in fabric design, textiles, and some equipment.

Ruddel, David-Thiery. "The Domestic Textile Industry in the Region and City of Quebec, 1792–1835." *Material History Bulletin* 17 (Spring 1983): 95–125. 34 illustrations, 7 tables.

Ruddel analyzes more than 400 postmortem estate inventories combined with other evidence (labor contracts, commercial correspondence, newspaper advertisements, and iconographical material) to determine the relationship between homespun and imported cloth, the nature of the occupations in the textile trade, the effect of domestic production on the local market, clothing as a symbol of class and ethnicity, and the impact of politics on the use of homespun. Ruddel argues that the domestic textile industry failed to provide for the clothing needs of the population of either rural or urban Quebec, although more locally made cloth was consumed by the former. This probably was due to the ability of the British to produce cheap cloth combined with their mercantile colonial policy. Despite the heavy emphasis on clothing, Ruddel also discusses other textiles. This examination moves beyond description to analyze the social and economic impact of locally manufactured versus imported textiles.

Safford, Carleton L., and Robert Bishop. "The Overshot Coverlet"; "The Double Weave Coverlet"; "The Summer and Winter Coverlet"; "The Jacquard Coverlet"; "The Candlewick Spread." In Carleton L. Safford and Robert Bishop, *America's Quilts and Coverlets*, pp. 221–89. New York: E. P. Dutton, 1972. 111 black and white and color illustrations.

Safford and Bishop have written brief chapters providing a superficial overview of the various types of woven coverlets produced in the nineteenth century. Some coverlet titles and the names of some professional weavers are listed. This work should be used with care because the history is romanticized and inaccurate, as is some of the information about the artifacts.

Schoelwer, Susan Prendergast. "Form, Function, and Meaning in the Use of Fabric Furnishings: A Philadelphia Case Study, 1700–1775." *Winterthur Portfolio* 14, no. 1 (Spring 1979): 25–40. 8 tables.

Unlike the descriptive textile literature, this article examines textiles in their social and economic context. Schoelwer attempts to determine what physical and psychological needs prompted the use of fabric furnishings and whether these varied between social or economic class or changed over time. She also seeks to learn if occupation or place of residence affected the use of fabric furnishings and how these related to concepts of comfort, style, and status in the eighteenth century. Using estate inventories analyzed at twenty-five-year intervals between 1700 and 1775, Schoelwer looks at the overall patterns of textile use and at chronological, economic, geographic, and occupational patterns. She finds at least partial answers to her questions and challenges some traditional views. She argues that the majority of textiles were imported and that, although they were functional, they were also visible indicators of style and status. As the century progressed and textiles became more easily available, their importance as status indicators declined, and new types of furnishings began to replace the old in the upper levels of society.

Schorsch, Anita, ed. *The Art of the Weaver*. New York: Universe Books, 1978. 256 pp.; illustrations, index.

This book is a compilation of textile articles published in *Antiques* between 1925 and 1976. Each article is reprinted as it appeared originally; therefore, care should be taken in using the information, as more recent research may have revised some of the findings.

Séguin, Robert-Lionel. "L'aménagement intérieur: La lingerie, les rideaux"; "Le costume: Les tissus"; "L'equipement technique: Les instruments servant aux travaux d'artisanat." In *La civilisation traditionnelle de l' "habitant" aux 17e et 18e siècles*, edited by Robert-Lionel Séguin, pp. 386–99, 492–97, 619–25. Montreal and Paris: Fides, 1967. Illustrations.

As part of a larger work examining the culture of the "habitants" in early French Canada, Séguin incorporates several sections about the textiles they used and made. Culling his information largely from postmortem inventories, literary documentation, and earlier secondary sources, he discusses bed and table linens, including *la catalogne* (what we now know as rag floor rugs, but which were originally used as bed coverings) and *boutonné* (woven coverlets with tufted designs of birds, flowers, stars, and so forth). He describes window curtains and clothing fabrics, listing the main textiles used in New France and separating those locally made from the majority that were imported. Séguin discusses how domestically produced textiles were manufactured and describes some of the tools.

Sloat, Caroline. "The Dover Manufacturing Company and the Integration of English and American Calico Printing Techniques, 1825–29." In *Winterthur Portfolio 10*, edited by Ian M. G. Quimby, pp. 51–68. Charlottesville: University Press of Virginia for the Henry Francis du Pont Winterthur Museum, 1975. 8 illustrations.

Sloat looks at the competition between several New England companies to establish cotton printing factories. Until the 1820s there was no capacity for large-scale textile printing on the American continent. Sloat examines three early firms—Taunton, Merrimack, and Dover manufacturing companies—and concentrates on the latter. She argues that their success depended on their ability to acquire British skills and equipment. As a result, it is difficult to distinguish early Victorian English and American printed fabrics.

Textile History. Vol. 1–(December 1968–). Plymouth, England: Latimer Trend.

Textile History publishes "A Review of Periodical Literature on Textile History," which appears annually and is an annotated review of literature published in the preceding year. It was first published December 1968 by David Charles at Newton Abbot and edited by K. G. Ponting.

Thornton, Peter. *Baroque and Rococo Silks.* London: Faber and Faber, 1965. 331 pp.; 120 black and white illustrations, 4 color plates, 4 diagrams, bibliography, index.

Baroque and Rococo Silks traces the development of the patterns of the rich, figured silks produced from approximately 1640 to 1770. Thornton believes that the patterns, designed by professionals, reflect "the various stages of general art history and certain important aspects of the spirit of the sumptuous age in which they were made" (p. 15). He does not dwell on the fabric structure of the textiles, but on their patterns, as dictated by fashion and the limits of the medium. The introduction examines the influence of the French demands of fashion on the varieties of designs produced, noting that the patterns of dress fabric changed more frequently than dress construction. Also included is a discussion of the European centers of silk weaving and their products in descending order of importance and the marketing and use of the fabrics. Chapters 1 through 6 chronologically analyze the design motifs of silks and their changes and evolution, with illustrative diagrams. Chapter 7 is devoted to the designs of furnishing silks, noting the differences between these and the dress silks. Notes precede the plates of dress and furniture fabrics and include the date, attribution, description, location, and relevant information pertaining to each illustrated textile.

Ulasewicz, Connie, Clarita Anderson, and Steven M. Spivack. "Analysis and Documentation of Coverlets." *Ars Textrina* 2 (1984): 113–55. 10 illustrations, bibliography.

A group of double-woven coverlets owned by Ken Colwell that were on loan to the University of Maryland are analyzed by the authors. Through their research, they have developed what they hope will be a systematic method for documenting flat-woven textile artifacts. The analysis of the double-woven coverlets includes their use as bed coverings, their woven structure, the tools and equipment with which they were made, and the tracing of their pattern motifs, where possible, to manuscripts of earlier European weavers.

Walker, Sandra Rambo. *Country Cloth to Coverlets: Textile Traditions in Nineteenth Century Central Pennsylvania.*

Lewisburg, Pa.: Oral Traditions Project of the Union County Historical Society, 1981. 60 pp.; black and white and color illustrations, appendix, bibliography, index.

Beginning with an overview of weaving in central Pennsylvania, including a discussion of the weavers, fibers, tools, account books, fulling and carding mills, and coverlets, *Country Cloth to Coverlets* provides an inventory of the weavers, their history, and their output in eight counties (Centre, Clinton, Columbia, Lycoming, Montour, Northumberland, Snyder, and Union). One section lists all the known weavers in the area, locates them on a map, and charts them on a date graph (the numbers of weavers reached a peak between 1823 and 1825). Throughout the book are illustrations of weavers' inventories, weaving drafts, newspaper advertisements, textiles, and tools. An appendix, with photographs, lists documented interior and border patterns used in jacquard coverlets and the names of weavers known to have used them.

White, Margaret E., comp. *American Hand-Woven Coverlets in the Newark Museum.* Newark, N.J.: By the museum, 1947. 83 pp.; 33 illustrations, bibliography.

Geared to help weavers and collectors to identify old coverlets, this volume catalogues coverlets under three headings: overshot weave, double weave, and jacquard weave. Each coverlet is illustrated, and its history is given when known. Also included is a variety of pattern names. This work is an early attempt to document American handwoven products. With its historical analysis based on folklore and questionable sources, the result is a romantic interpretation of the subject. There are also errors in the technical analysis of the coverlets, but the book is interesting as an early example of coverlet research.

Wilson, Sadye Tune, and Doris Finch Kennedy. *Of Coverlets: The Legacies, the Weavers.* Introduction by Else Regensteiner; photography by Sadye Tune Wilson. Nashville, Tenn.: Tunstede, 1983. 494 pp.; black and white and color illustrations, appendix, bibliography, index.

As part of the Tennessee Textile History Project from 1978 to 1983, Wilson and Kennedy found and documented 1,000 coverlets from the state in order to examine the legacies of the weavers and to preserve the written and photographic records of extant textiles. Analysis is restricted to coverlets, blankets, and counterpanes woven on looms with four shafts. Each coverlet is photographed, the fiber and yarn are analyzed, and the weave structure and size are noted and researched for such things as information on date of manufacture and owner. This is the first of a planned two-volume series, the second of which will include coverlets made on more complex looms, tools, early mills, and more of a historical overview.

Timepieces

Clocks and Watches

GENERAL WORKS AND BIBLIOGRAPHIES

BIOGRAPHIES AND REGIONAL MONOGRAPHS

SOCIAL HISTORY OF TIME AND TIMEKEEPING

TOOLS, WATCHES, AND CLOCK-RELATED CRAFTS

Clocks and Watches

Thomas Michie

WELL BEFORE HENRY WADSWORTH LONGFELLOW composed his evocative tribute "The Old Clock on the Stairs" in 1845, Americans had regarded clocks and timepieces as imposing household sentinels. As the only piece of furniture with an audible "voice," as well as a form that mimics the human body (head, face, hands, feet, waist, and so forth), trustworthy tall clocks naturally presided over families and households and became inextricably linked with their histories in the popular imagination. Writing in 1912, Mary Northend aptly summarized her generation's view of clocks as "quaintly pathetic" objects whose "sociability appeals to all home lovers, as it cheerily ticks the hours away, with a regularity that is almost human" (*Colonial Homes and Their Furnishings*, p. 145).

Before the middle of the nineteenth century, clocks and watches had always been costly personal possessions. In the eighteenth century, they embodied their owners' lofty social status and therefore tended to be preserved and handed down from one generation to the next. Like family portraits, clocks conferred ancestral legitimacy and, if wound, provided both audible and tangible continuity to future generations of owners. Even in today's world of nonmechanical, digital time, watches remain suitable presentation tokens and awards, while modern "grandfather" clocks in colonial guise are promoted as symbols of success and old-fashioned domestic stability.

Clock mechanisms and even some clockmakers have appealed to Americans' persistent fascination with mechanical ingenuity. In the nineteenth century, the instinct for mechanical genius, combined with a keen sense of business acumen, was widely considered to be native to Americans. Nevertheless, to judge from paintings and illustrations of the period, the popular image of the wise and benignly tinkering, independent craftsman was never supplanted by the reality—that clock- and watchmakers had always been industrial entrepreneurs.

The early literature on clocks in this country reflects this dichotomy. On the one hand are the professional journals with national circulation, such as the *Jewelers' Circular*, that were devoted to individual inventions and corporate achievements in the field of manufacturing. On the other hand are the book-length efforts by individual clockmakers to record their life stories. Perhaps prompted by the gradual eclipse of their traditional craft by diversified manufactures, Chauncey Jerome, Henry Terry, and Hiram Camp in Connecticut and Levi Hutchins in New Hampshire all published autobiographies between 1860 and 1890. Their accounts tend to be unabashedly self-congratulatory, yet they present rare firsthand accounts by the craftsmen-turned-entrepreneurs who successfully weathered the fundamental shift in the nineteenth century from the traditional apprenticeship system to diversified modern manufactures. Thanks to recent efforts by American Clock and Watch Museum, the trade catalogues of the major nineteenth-century Connecticut clock manufacturers have been reprinted.

General surveys of the history of clocks and watches begin with Frederick Britten's *Handbook* and his magisterial *Old Clocks and Watches*, both concerned with English clocks and watches but included here as the models for most of the subsequent literature in English. In the next generation of English historians, Granville Baillie sought to update Britten's work and produced the standard bibliography on clocks and clockmaking. More recently, as seventeenth-century clocks have become exceedingly rare and costly, Eric Bruton and Brian Loomes have expanded the range of clocks considered worthy of study and have included American clocks in the appropriate context of provincial English clockmaking traditions.

The American counterparts to Britten and Baillie in the early twentieth century are N. Hudson Moore and Wallace Nutting. Both depended on Britten for their lists of makers, of which Moore's was the first to be published in this country, whereas Nutting's omnium-gatherum of photographs remains a useful reference source today. Other early antiquarians, such as Frances Clary Morse and her sister, Alice Morse Earle, naturally seized on clocks as furniture, tending to borrow their information freely from their contemporaries.

Over the next several decades, Brooks Palmer, William Distin, and Robert Bishop have perpetuated the format of stylistic surveys of clocks with appended lists of makers. Good interpretive histories of clocks and timekeeping are scarce. In this country, the work of Chris Bailey is among the best available. His *Two Hundred Years of American Clocks and Watches* remains the best overall survey, based on primary sources that provide a fresh look at a broad range of objects from three centuries.

Catalogues of museum collections present a different kind of survey whose breadth depends on the range of objects collected. Edwin Battison's and Patricia E. Kane's work on the clocks in the Garvan collection at Yale University followed the format for furniture catalogues recently established by Richard H. Randall, Jr., at Museum of Fine Arts, Boston, and Charles F. Montgomery at Winterthur Museum. In addition, technical notes by Battison of Smithsonian's National Museum of History and Technology accompanied detailed photographs of each clock's movement. Only Edward F. LaFond's forthcoming catalogue of the clocks at Winterthur rivals the range and number of clocks in the Yale catalogue.

Smaller collections of clocks at other museums are often included in more general catalogues of their furniture. Likewise, because silversmiths and engravers frequently supplemented their businesses with clock and watch repair, checklists of silversmiths usually include clock-related craftsmen.

Less conventional collections of what Moore called "curious clocks" can be found in Don and Alice Nicholson's lively compilation of animated "wall pendulettes" or in guides to watch keys and fobs by John Kaduck or Grace Howard Smith and Eugene Randolph Smith. Several valuable studies have been made of specific kinds of clocks, beginning with Ernest Edwardes's pioneering *Grandfather Clock*. This work has only recently been superseded by Tom Robinson's *Longcase Clock*. Apart from biography, investigations of a single type of clock or mechanism account for the greatest number of titles, ranging from carriage clocks to banjo, spring-driven, and bracket clocks, in addition to shorter articles throughout the *Bulletin of the National Association of Watch and Clock Collectors*.

Following general works and museum collection catalogues in this chapter is a larger section that comprises biographies of clockmakers and regional monographs. John Ware Willard's 1911 account of his great-great-grandfather Simon Willard marks the beginning of the anecdotal tradition of clockmakers' biographies, in which historical accuracy is frequently compromised in order to maintain the subject's fabled ingenuity or originality. By midcentury, historians mustered yeoman craftsmen or, in the case of Henry Flynt at Historic Deerfield, entire villages to the front lines of a cold war offensive. Barrows Mussey's 1950 biography of Eli Terry, for example, was intended to inspire "readers in these times when we seem to have lost so much of the spirit, character, and stout-heartedness of our forebears" (*Young Father Time*, p. 5). Far less pious is the contemporary study of Daniel Burnap by Penrose Hoopes, whose careful explication of a craftsman's life by means of his clocks and surviving account books was among the first to depart from the hagiographic tradition established by John Willard. By comparison, Richard W. Husher and Walter W. Welch's study of Simon Willard's clocks is more thorough in a technical sense that is prized by collectors, but ultimately it is less informative for the historian. Brooke Hindle's biography of David Rittenhouse represents the ideal combination of biography and the history of technology, to which Charles F. Hummel's investigation of the Dominys' furniture, clocks, and tools is the apparent heir. A more recent comparative study of Jabez and Jedidiah Baldwin by Philip Zea likewise places the lives and livelihoods of two clockmakers working in different corners of New England into a broader historical and cultural context.

Following from Jerome's and Terry's early efforts to record the progress of the clock industry, Charles Moore's account of Waltham Watch Company represents the traditional historian's documentary approach to a single modern clock manufacturer. In contrast, *Revolution in Time* by David Landes, an economic historian at Harvard, presents a much broader view of the clock industry from its European origins to its virtual extinction by digital, nonmechanical timekeepers, and in the process he poses more provocative questions about the nature of time and technology in modern culture.

As with the study of furniture history in this country, some of the best research on American clocks has emerged in the form of regional monographs, such as Henry Conrad's "Old Delaware Clockmakers." His format of biography followed by entries on specific clocks has in essence been repeated for the intervening century in works on craftsmen and clocks from Vermont to Dixieland and westward to Ohio.

Like the study of other branches of the decorative arts, the literature on clocks has been largely descriptive, with greater emphasis given to an object's aesthetic importance than to its cultural significance. The portion of this bibliography entitled "Social History of Time and Timekeeping" contains a selection of books that considers the issues of time and timekeeping in the broadest cultural sense, often with only passing reference to mechanical clocks.

The enigma of time itself has engendered an extensive literature, most scientific, that is beyond the scope of this bibliography. Studies of nonmechanical timekeeping, such as circadian time, or so-called biological clocks, may extend beyond the needs of the historian of technology, and yet an understanding of circadian time as presented by Martin Moore-Ede and others may be relevant to the social historian. After all, the historian of technology cannot escape the irony of man-made devices, specifically atomic clocks, that are now more accurate than the movement of the earth itself.

Efforts to place clocks and time-consciousness within a broader historical and cultural perspective are rare and relatively recent, yet they represent innovative work in the field. The pioneering book by Carlo Cipolla, *Clocks and Culture*, remains the foundation for this secondary literature, ably followed by *The Study of Time* volumes edited by Julius Fraser. Primary sources are more difficult to come by, since people seldom refer explicitly to their changing attitudes about time. The present list includes two or three items from the late eighteenth and early nineteenth centuries, beginning with two satirical pieces by an anonymous member of the Clockmaker's Guild of London and by Benjamin Franklin. The former was written in response to alleged misperceptions of clockwork metaphors in the novel *Tristram Shandy*; the latter protests the tyranny of other people's clocks, or what Lawrence Wright later aptly called "chronarchy."

Richard Glasser and historians of the Annales school, such as Jacques LeGoff in *Time, Work, and Culture in the Middle Ages* (1980), have written eloquently about the differences between sacred and secular perceptions of time in preindustrial Europe. In this country, Arthur Cole's article on the tempo of mercantile life in eighteenth-century America is the only comparable effort. The impact of clocks and time discipline on the industrial worker is the subject of an influential article by English historian E. P. Thompson.

Clockwork symbols and metaphors in European thought and political theory are the subject of a recent book and a catalogue essay by Otto Mayr, former curator in the Division of Mechanisms at National Museum of American History. Mayr's investigation of the ways in which clocks provide insight into the European societies that used and produced them serves as a model of artifactual analysis and thus is an excellent foil to David Landes's work. Lee Soltow's more limited investigation of clock and watch ownership in Connecticut relies on statistical rather than artifactual evidence. For most of rural America, the only sources of clocks and watches were itinerant peddlers who fanned out across the country in the early nineteenth century. Warmly welcomed at first but eventually regarded as swarthy swindlers, peddlers carried clocks among their wares, and some sold clocks exclusively. The fictitious tales of Samuel Slick by Thomas Chandler Haliburton provide an amusing glimpse of clock consumerism not available in other kinds of sources.

As distinct from traditional investigations of stylistic and technological developments, historians of art and literature have made important contributions to the study of clocks and timekeeping. The most prolific has been Samuel Macey, who has sought to trace themes of time through William Hogarth's paintings and prints as well as in contemporary English literature. Jerome Buckley's study of Victorian concepts of time forms the logical extension of this approach. Preceding them and unsurpassed in its command of iconographic traditions is Erwin Panofsky's study of Father Time and his various incarnations as the agent of revelation and destruction. Images of clocks themselves have been compiled by Alfred Chapuis for an anthology of the fine arts, whereas a home decorator's guide compiled by *Good Housekeeping* is an excellent document of taste and consumerism in the post–World War II era.

The section on tools that follows lists both primary sources, in the form of a facsimile of tool catalogues, and histories of clock- and watchmaking tools and technology. The latter subject was addressed early on by Hoopes and later by Hummel, who were both concerned with the shop methods and tools of individual craftsmen. Many late eighteenth- and early nineteenth-century English hardware catalogues routinely included clock-case accessories, as well as other furniture hardware printed to scale. Examples from two of the best collections of this material, at Victoria and Albert and Winterthur museums, are discussed by Nicholas Goodison and Hummel.

The dearth of material on American watches is directly related to their rarity. Few were actually made here before the mid nineteenth century, and yet thousands were imported from England and the Continent by jewelers, silversmiths, and clockmakers alike. Henry G. Abbott's history of American watch manufacture is an excellent starting point for names and places. Leonard Weiss's history of the trade in England provides a better introduction to the craft in general and watch escapements in particular, and Cecil Clutton provides a well-illustrated general survey of watches over four centuries. A surprising number of books have been published on watch accessories, such as fobs, cases, holders, and winding keys. Watch papers are appealing and informative ephemera that have received little attention apart from Dorothy Spear's extensive work and Robert Emlen's intensive look at a single example.

Any summary of clock-related literature must acknowledge that clocks and watches were products of an extensive collaboration among specialized craftsmen, including metalsmiths, cabinetmakers, decorative painters, and engravers. Although most of these trades are considered in greater detail elsewhere in this volume, several titles deserve particular mention in the context of the clock literature.

The engraved metal dials of clocks were often the work of a local silversmith who would have been familiar with the art of engraving. Few specific instances of this collaboration have been identified, thus making the work of Thomas Johnston of Boston, as documented by Sinclair Hitchings, particularly valuable. The extensive records of William Hunneman, one of Boston's leading brassfounders in the early nineteenth century, are the subject of an article by the indefatigable Mabel Swan, who demonstrates Hunneman's integral role in the clock business of Aaron Willard, Jr.

Decorative painting is an important component of most clocks of the federal period, as painted iron dials replaced the traditional cast-brass and silvered dials. The most comprehensive account of this branch of the arts in early America is Alice Cooney's study of decorative painting in Boston (M.A. thesis, University of Delaware, 1978). That the painted dials of clocks are usually unsigned gives added prominence to the work of the few craftsmen whose names we do know. Carol Andrews's work on John Ritto Penniman, for example, is exhaustive and reveals an artist of considerable talent by any standard. James Keown considers the partnership between the other leading dial painters in Boston, Aaron Willard, Jr., and Samuel Nolen, brothers-in-law whose interrelationship speaks for the tightly knit community of clock-related craftsmen.

Finally, this chapter also comprises a small selection of titles on such virtuoso clockwork as the orrery, as well as on nonmechanical timekeepers such as sundials and hourglasses. Although they stand poles apart technologically, they can be interpreted as coexisting representatives from the realms of science and religion, or public and private life, and symbolic of scientific progress versus the bygone informality of preindustrial time.

GENERAL WORKS AND BIBLIOGRAPHIES

Allix, Charles. *Carriage Clocks: Their History and Development.* Woodbridge, Suffolk: Antique Collectors' Club, 1974. vi+391 pp.; 500 black and white and color illustrations, appendixes, glossary, bibliography, indexes.

Allix presents a generously illustrated and lavishly produced volume on English, French, Swiss, and German carriage clocks. Chapter 12 is a history of American carriage clocks.

Avery, Amos. *New England Clocks at Old Sturbridge Village.* Sturbridge, Mass.: Old Sturbridge Village, 1966. 45 pp.; 40 illustrations.

Avery's introduction is brief and general; however, the photographs of a small selection of clocks and mechanisms from the distinguished J. Cheney Wells Collection remain a useful reference tool.

Bailey, Chris H. *Two Hundred Years of American Clocks and Watches.* Englewood Cliffs, N.J.: Prentice-Hall, 1875. 255 pp.; 285 black and white and color illustrations, index.

This book is the most lucid and best-illustrated survey of American clocks and watches to date. It contains clear photographs of clocks, mostly from American Clock and Watch Museum and private collections. The text is arranged chronologically, with attention to important individual clockmakers. One chapter is devoted to American watches that date from 1800 to 1970. Bailey includes a checklist of clock- and watchmakers in the form of regional time lines.

Baillie, G. H., C. Clutton, and C. A. Ilbert. *Britten's Old Clocks and Watches and Their Makers: A Historical and Descriptive Account of the Different Styles of Clocks and Watches of the Past in England and Abroad Containing a List of Nearly 14,000 Makers.* Frontispiece by L. H. Cresswell; diagrams by F. Janca. 7th rev. ed. London: E. and F. N. Spon, 1956. xx+518 pp.; 183 plates, 40 line drawings, appendixes, checklist, index.

This work is the bible of collectors and clock specialists, perhaps because it illustrates ordinary clocks that one is likely to encounter rather than unique examples found only in museums. It contains the history of timekeeping to about 1830; a chapter on French clocks, 1660–1830; shorter sections on national styles, including American; reprints of documents related to famous makers; and biographies. It

concludes with a list of nearly 14,000 European and American craftsmen, their addresses and working dates, and locations of their works.

Baillie, Granville H. *Clocks and Watches: An Historical Bibliography.* 1951. Reprint. London: Holland Press, 1978. 414 pp.; illustrations, index.

This carefully annotated and illustrated bibliography comprises both printed and manuscript sources in every language on mechanical timepieces up to 1800. Culled from the library of Clockmakers' Company, London Patent Office, National Art Library at Victoria and Albert Museum, British Library, and Bibliothèque Nationale, this monumental work (1,799 items) by a great horological historian remains unsurpassed as a general reference guide to the early literature on clocks. Titles issued between 1951 and 1975 are listed in John Bromley, *The Clockmaker's Library.*

Baillie, Granville H. *Watchmakers and Clockmakers of the World.* 1929. 2d ed. London: N. A. G. Press, 1947. 388 pp.; illustrations.

This early improvement over Frederick James Britten's *Watch and Clock Maker's Handbook* contains a list of approximately 35,000 English, Continental, and American watch- and clockmakers. It includes a listing of initials and monograms used by makers. This volume is most useful in conjunction with Britten's work.

Battison, Edwin A., and Patricia E. Kane. *The American Clock, 1725–1865: The Mabel Brady Garvan and Other Collections at Yale University.* Greenwich, Conn.: New York Graphic Society, 1973. 207 pp.; 48 illustrations, glossary, bibliography, index.

With an introduction by Derek deSolla Price, an essay and technical notes by Battison, and stylistic commentary by Kane, this catalogue of about fifty tall, shelf, and wall clocks at Yale remains among the best available of a single collection. Each entry contains an overall photograph of the clock and details of its movement, a format that became the model for other catalogues of this kind.

Britten, Frederick James. *Britten's Watch and Clock Maker's Handbook, Dictionary, and Guide.* 1878. Rev. ed. London: Printed for Eyre Methuen in association with

E. and F. N. Spon, 1978. viii+355 pp.; appendixes, glossary, bibliography, indexes.

Britten's work remains the standard dictionary for the specialized horologist and amateur collector alike. It has been revised and reprinted in many editions.

Bromley, John, ed. *The Clockmaker's Library: The Catalogue of the Books and Manuscripts in the Library of the Worshipful Company of Clockmakers*. London: Philip Wilson for Sotheby Parke Bernet Publications, 1977. xii+136 pp.; 52 illustrations.

Founded in 1631, the clockmakers' guild in London contains an excellent library (begun in 1814) of books and manuscripts in the field of historical horology. Bromley defers to Granville H. Baillie's annotations in *Clocks and Watches*, although this catalogue includes a broader range of materials, such as portraits and other paintings, prints, drawings, and photographs. The format can be deceptive, as in the case of a single entry (no. 1151) that refers to an entire collection of 1,250 watch papers with its own index.

Bruton, Eric. *Clocks and Watches*. Feltham, England: Hamlyn, 1968. 140 pp.; black and white and color illustrations, index.

In this general, well-illustrated survey of the history of clocks and watches around the world through the ages, Bruton includes one brief chapter on North American clocks and watches, mostly of nineteenth-century Connecticut.

Bruton, Eric. *Clocks and Watches, 1400–1900*. New York and Washington, D.C.: Frederick A. Praeger, 1967. 208 pp.+110 plates; 32 line drawings, appendixes, index.

Bruton's basic introduction to the study of clocks and watches is most useful for its appendixes, which contain lists of public collections and of prominent makers.

Bruton, Eric. *Dictionary of Clocks and Watches*. New York: Archer House, 1963. 201 pp.; 8 illustrations, bibliography.

This is a small but useful handbook of historical and mechanical terms as well as short entries on prominent individuals. Included are many diagrams. It is intended for laymen, but it is a handy reference for specialists as well.

Bruton, Eric. *The Longcase Clock*. 1968. 2d rev. ed. New York: Charles Scribner's Sons, 1977. 233 pp.; 146 illustrations, appendixes, bibliography, index.

For the student, this is perhaps the best of Bruton's many books. As a general introduction to the long-case clock, Bruton rivals Ernest Edwardes's volume, the traditional source. Bruton sets forth the stylistic development of cases, dials, and hands, with separate chapters on thirty-hour clocks and regulators. A chapter on North American clocks and watches is included.

Bulletin of the National Association of Watch and Clock Collectors. 1943–. Published six times yearly.

This is the foremost journal of the history, manufacture, and collecting of American clocks and watches. For the historian, it is most useful as a source for biographies of lesser-known American clockmakers and regional studies of clockmaking, although technical and mechanical studies also abound. The occasional supplemental issues devoted to a single craftsman or region are excellent.

Distin, William H. *The Clock Collection*. Dearborn, Mich.: Henry Ford Museum and Greenfield Village, [1977]. 29 pp.; illustrations, bibliography.

This is a brief handbook to the collection of European and American clocks and watches at Henry Ford Museum, which ranges from the eighteenth to the twentieth centuries.

Distin, William H., and Robert Bishop. *The American Clock: A Comprehensive Pictorial Survey, 1723–1900, with a Listing of 6,153 Clockmakers*. New York: E. P. Dutton, 1976. 359 pp.; 661 black and white and 84 color illustrations, appendix, glossary, bibliography, index.

The American Clock consists of brief historical introductions to each form, followed by illustrations with extended captions. It is useful as a visual reference for a wide range of clock styles and for the list of some 6,153 American clockmakers.

Dreppard, Carl W. *American Clocks and Clockmakers*. 1947. Enl. ed. Boston: Chartles T. Branford Co., 1958. 312+52 pp.; illustrations, bibliography, supplement.

Based on the earlier lists of clockmakers compiled by N. Hudson Moore, Frederick James Britten, and Wallace Nutting, Dreppard also consulted tax lists, church records, account books, and directories for his improved checklist. The enlarged edition contains a supplement with additional names. The entries are liberally illustrated with engravings reprinted from nineteenth-century sales catalogues.

Dworetsky, Lester, and Robert Dickstein. *Horology Americana*. Roslyn Heights, N.Y.: Horology American, 1972. xi+212 pp.; black and white and color illustrations.

This text is illustrated with handsome color photographs of about 200 tall and shelf clocks that range in date from about 1740 to 1880. The chief value of this survey is the unusual number of color photographs and the number of interesting clocks drawn from private collections not published elsewhere.

Eckhardt, George. *United States Clock and Watch Patents, 1790–1890: The Record of a Century of American Horology and Enterprise*. New York: Privately printed, 1960. xii+231 pp.; illustrations, appendix, index.

This is not a book about the significance or impact of clock-related inventions and patents, but it is the best listing of all the American inventors, their patents, their place of work, the date of the patents, and the patent numbers.

Edwardes, Ernest L. *The Grandfather Clock: An Archaeological and Descriptive Essay on the Long-Case Clock with Its Weight-Driven Precursers and Contemporaries.* 4th enl. and rev. ed. Altrincham, England: J. Sherratt, 1980. xvi+215 pp.; 159 illustrations, glossary, index.

Among the first books to deal exclusively with the history and stylistic development of the long-case clock, this volume was more recently updated by Tom Robinson, Eric Bruton, and Brian Loomes. Although restricted to English clocks from 1660 to about 1840, it remains a useful source of solid information about clocks in general and their movements, cases, and dials.

Ela, Chipman P. *The Banjo Timepiece: An In-Depth Study of the Weight-Driven Banjo Clock.* Fryeburg, Maine: Carriage House, 1978. vii+199 pp.; bibliography, index.

Ela's close scrutiny of fifty-three banjo clocks by many makers in several different regions is valuable for gathering under one cover all the various makers of one form of clock. However, the book is marred by its poor black and white photographs and by poorly edited text.

Franklin Institute. *Horological Books and Pamphlets in the Franklin Institute Library.* Compiled by Walter A. R. Petruch and Emerson H. Hilker. 2d ed. Philadelphia: Franklin Institute Library, 1968. 109 pp.

Begun in 1824, the library of Franklin Institute contains more than 1,400 printed books and ephemeral pamphlets on horology, recently built up under the supervision of Penrose Hoopes. Its entire holdings number more than 250,000 items, making it a significant scientific and technical library. Comparable in size and scope to the clockmakers' guild library (see John Bromley, *The Clockmaker's Library*), this collection also ranges from the classics of the seventeenth century to the latest technical books.

Harris, H. G. *Nineteenth Century American Clocks.* Buchanan, N.Y.: Emerson Books, 1981. 256 pp.; 85 illustrations, glossary, bibliography, index.

Harris's popular, general survey is pitched to collectors of nineteenth-century American shelf and wall clocks. He includes chapters on the "preservation" of movements and on the care and repair of wooden clock cases. This work is most useful for its clear photographs of clocks not widely published elsewhere, from the collections of Winterthur Museum, Baltimore Museum of Art, and Illinois State Museum.

Hering, Daniel Webster. *Key to the Watches in the James Arthur Collection: . . . Addendum to "The Lure of the Clock."* New York: New York University Press, 1934. 21 pp.; 14 illustrations.

——. *The Lure of the Clock: An Account of the James Arthur Collection of Clocks and Watches at New York University.* New York: New York University Press, 1932. xiv+114 pp.; index.

The Arthur Collection consists of approximately 220 English, Dutch, German, French, and American clocks and 1,100 watches and watch movements. It is one of the earliest collections formed in the United States and was donated to New York University in 1925. In 1964 the collection was lent to Smithsonian Institution, and in 1983 the bulk of the collection was transferred to National Association of Watch and Clock Collectors Museum in Columbia, Pennsylvania, with the remainder distributed between the Smithsonian and Time Museum in Rockford, Illinois. *Key to Watches* is an index to characteristic features, markings, and makers' names on the European and American watches in the Arthur Collection. In *The Lure of the Clock*, Hering discusses clocks by Eli and Silas Burnham, although the chief emphasis is on European clocks.

Ittman, John. *Clock and Watch Designs: Three Centuries of Horological Design.* Exhibition catalogue. Lawrence: University of Kansas Museum of Art, 1967. 6 pp.

This work is a checklist of an exhibition of engraved and drawn designs for clocks and watches from the sixteenth through the nineteenth centuries lent by Metropolitan Museum of Art.

Jewelers' Circular and Horological Review. New York: Jewelers' Circular Publishing Co., 1869–. Weekly.

This periodical over the years has incorporated the *Jewelers' Circular, Jewelers' Review, Jewelers' Weekly, American Horological Journal,* and other journals. It is an excellent source for information on clockmakers' migrations, especially in the nineteenth century, when news of promotions, changes of shop locations, short biographical articles, and obituaries were published each month.

Langdon, John E. *Clock and Watchmakers and Allied Workers in Canada, 1700 to 1900.* Toronto: Anson-Cartwright Editions, 1976. xix+195 pp.; index.

This volume is the most comprehensive directory of clock-related craftsmen active in Canada. It includes their names, professions, place of work, and references. The information is based on advertisements, censuses, directories and gazetteers, provincial archival documents, family papers, Dun and Bradstreet credit reports, and Canadian newspapers.

Loomes, Brian. *Country Clocks and Their London Origins.* Newton Abbot: David and Charles, 1976. 192 pp.; illustrations, bibliography, index.

More concerned with the stylistic progression of clock design than with technological innovations, this is a well-illustrated survey of English clocks made outside London, many of which relate closely to clocks made in several regions of colonial America.

Loomes, Brian. *The White Dial Clock*. Newton Abbot: David and Charles, 1974. 172 pp.; bibliography, index.
——. *White Dial Clocks: The Complete Guide*. Newton Abbot: David and Charles, 1981. 254 pp.; 90 illustrations, bibliography, index.

In *The White Dial Clock* Loomes redresses the traditional bias against clocks with painted dials, often mistaken for "enamel" and traditionally considered either too late or otherwise inferior to clocks with engraved dials, and thus beyond the ken of most British clock specialists. This stylistic survey of dials and cases made between 1770 and 1870 is particularly useful for students of American clocks, which are briefly examined in chapter 12. The updated sequel contains new chapters on clocks in Scotland and America.

Maust, Don, ed. *Early American Clocks*. 2 vols. Uniontown, Pa.: E. G. Warman Publishing Co., 1971, 1973. 79 pp. each; approximately 200 illustrations each.

Like the Antiques Magazine Library series, these volumes are anthologies of reprinted articles, mostly from *Antiques*, although none is properly identified. They vary in length and range in subject from unusual clocks to labels, finials, and dials of the eighteenth and nineteenth centuries.

Miller, Andrew Hayes, and Maria M. Dalia. *Survey of American Clocks: Calendar Clocks*. Elgin, Ill.: Antiquitat, 1972. 159 pp.; 521 illustrations.

Miller and Dalia discuss forty-seven different makers of calendar clocks, from the mid nineteenth century to the present.

Moore, N. Hudson. *The Old Clock Book*. New York: Frederick A. Stokes Co., 1911. xi+339 pp.; 104 illustrations, index.

An outgrowth of *The Old Furniture Book*, Moore's now-classic volume discusses both English and American clock- and watchmakers. It contains brief biographies of Connecticut, Massachusetts, Rhode Island, and Pennsylvania craftsmen based on documentary evidence from newspapers and other primary sources.

Murphy, John Joseph. "Entrepreneurship in the Establishment of the American Clock Industry." *Journal of Economic History* 26, no. 2 (June 1966): 169–86.

This excellent article is the distillation of Murphy's 1961 dissertation for Yale University. Using clocks as primary evidence, he analyzes the market factors and technical advantages of certain methods of manufacturing over others. The novelty of Eli Terry's and Chauncey Jerome's contributions to the clock industry are central to this study in entrepreneurial history.

Nicholson, Don, and Alice Nicholson. *Novelty and Animated Wall Pendulette Clocks Made by Lux Clock Manufacturing Co., Inc., August C. Keebler Co., Westclox, Columbia Time Products*. Garland, Tex.: Dal-Tex Publishing Co., 1976. x+177 pp.; black and white and color illustrations, appendix, index.

From the animated Jack and Jill and Scotty Dog clocks to the Honey Bunny clock, the Nicholsons identify and discuss about sixty wall clocks from their own remarkable collection, illustrating the impact of television and popular culture on modern clock design.

Nutting, Wallace. *The Clock Book; Being a Description of Foreign and American Clocks*. Framingham, Mass.: Old America Co., 1924. 312 pp.; 250 plates, index.

Nutting's facts are often out of date, but his classic book remains a useful source for photographs of clocks, many of whose location is now unknown, and for the names of early clock collectors. The list of makers provided has been borrowed largely from N. Hudson Moore, and the names of foreign makers from Frederick James Britten. There have been several modern reprints, but the plates in the original edition have yet to be improved on.

Palmer, Brooks. *The Book of American Clocks*. New York: Macmillan Co., 1950. viii+318 pp.; 312 plates, glossary, bibliography.
——. *A Treasury of American Clocks*. New York: Macmillan Co.; London: Collier, Macmillan, 1967. xi+371 pp.; 558 illustrations, appendix.

Palmer's *Book of American Clocks* is closely based on the clock section of Wallace Nutting's *Furniture Treasury*. It includes more than 300 illustrations arranged chronologically and a list of more than 6,000 names of clockmakers. The sequel incorporates additional names and photographs.

Roberts, Deryck. *The Bracket Clock*. Newton Abbot: David and Charles, 1982. 190 pp.; 30 illustrations, line drawings, index.

Roberts presents a chronological survey of bracket clocks in England and makes some reference to clockmaking in France, but he refers less often to America. This is still a useful book, however, since English bracket clocks were imported to America and were frequently imitated by colonial clockmakers.

Robinson, Tom. *The Longcase Clock*. Woodbridge, Suffolk: Antique Collectors' Club, 1981. 467 pp.; 609 black and white illustrations, 22 color plates, glossary, bibliography, indexes.

Among the best surveys of tall clocks, this book contains informative captions that accompany clear photographs of clocks and their movements. Robinson explains changes of style and construction of both the clocks and their cases, thus combining in one volume the merits of Eric Bruton and Brian Loomes.

Shaffer, D. H. *A Survey History of the American Spring Driven Clock, 1840–1860.* Supplement to the *Bulletin of the National Association of Watch and Clock Collectors*, no. 9 (Winter 1973). 102 pp.; 73 illustrations.

Shaffer presents a concise overview of the invention and development of the portable spring-driven clock in America between 1840 and 1860. Beginning with important early contributions by Joseph Ives, he discusses eight or more fusee and spring adaptations developed by other clockmakers who entered this specialized field of production. Shaffer concludes with the solutions developed by Chauncey Jerome. *See also* Kenneth D. Roberts, *The Contribution of Joseph Ives to Connecticut Clock Technology.*

Shaffer, Douglas H. *Clocks.* The Smithsonian Illustrated Library of Antiques, edited by Brenda Gilchrist. New York: Cooper-Hewitt Museum, 1980. 128 pp.; 115 black and white and 30 color plates, glossary, bibliography, appendix, index.

This is a well-illustrated, general historical survey of European and American clocks and watches, although the information is not necessarily drawn from the Cooper-Hewitt or Smithsonian collections.

Smith, Alan, ed. *The Country Life International Dictionary of Clocks.* New York: G. P. Putnam's Sons, 1979. 352 pp.; approximately 850 black and white illustrations, 64 color plates, bibliography, index.

This is an excellent dictionary that is organized in several sections, including history and styles; mechanical parts; tools and methods; makers; and sundials and astrological instruments. It is generously illustrated and contains an excellent index.

Sposato, Kenneth A. *The Dictionary of American Clock and Watch Makers.* White Plains, N.Y.: By the author, 1983. 190 pp.

This checklist of about 7,600 clock- and watchmakers, as well as related craftsmen such as dealers and repairers, includes entries of bibliographic and picture references compiled from thirty-four recently published secondary sources. Sposato's work is marred by a lack of notes for the biographical information, its confusing use of abbreviations, and a lack of cross-references.

Timepieces Quarterly. York, Pa.: American Clock and Watch Foundation, 1948–50.

This periodical is devoted to the history of American and other clocks and watches, the biography of makers and manufacturers, and the bibliography of the science and the art of timekeeping. Only four issues were published, but nevertheless they contain dozens of short articles on clocks and clockmakers, supplementary lists of clockmakers compiled by Carl Dreppard, and occasional book reviews.

Tyler, Eric John. *The Craft of the Clockmaker.* New York: Crown Publishers, 1974. 96 pp.; illustrations, appendix, bibliography, index.

Tyler provides an excellent introduction to the tools, techniques, and shop practices of clock- and watchmakers. His emphasis is on traditional, preindustrial craft practices, although there is a brief chapter on modern industrial developments.

Virginia Museum of Fine Arts. *Catalogue of the Henry P. Strause Collection of Clocks.* Introduction by Edward Morris Davis. Richmond: By the museum, 1937. 70 pp.; 46 illustrations.

This is an old but still useful catalogue of forty-six European and American clocks. It is arranged chronologically and ranges from the mid seventeenth century through the early nineteenth century.

BIOGRAPHIES AND REGIONAL MONOGRAPHS

Albright, Frank P. *Johann Ludwig Eberhardt and His Salem Clocks.* Chapel Hill: University of North Carolina Press for Old Salem, 1978. x+160 pp.; 56 illustrations, appendix, glossary, bibliography, index.

Eberhardt (1758–1839) was a German-trained clockmaker who worked in Salem, North Carolina, between 1799 and 1827. This book includes a biographical sketch, a good description of clockmakers' shops, archival records (inventories, account books, letters), and a catalogue of about thirty-five clocks, with a technical description of their movements.

Ansonia Clock Company. *Illustrated Catalogue of Clocks.* 1880. Reprint. Bristol, Conn.: American Clock and Watch Museum, 1978. 82 pp.; illustrations.

This reprint of an Ansonia catalogue was part of a project by American Clock and Watch Museum to reissue the trade catalogues of all the major nineteenth-century Connecticut clock manufacturers.

Bailey, Chris H. *From Rags to Riches to Rags: The Story of Chauncey Jerome.* Supplement to the *Bulletin of the Na-*

tional Association of Watch and Clock Collectors, no. 15 (1986). 132 pp.; 280 illustrations, 1 map, appendixes.

The combined manufacturing interests of Jerome (1793–1868) were among the largest and most productive in the world in 1850. As a result of too numerous and extended liabilities, however, he was ruined financially and was subsequently maligned by his more vocal erstwhile business partner, P. T. Barnum. Bailey's thoroughly researched and well-illustrated account of Jerome's rise to prominence and his precipitous failure is the best since Jerome's own 1860 autobiography. Appended to the text are documents pertaining to his numerous business ventures, contemporary newspaper reports and obituaries, a family genealogy, his insolvent estate inventory, and an annotated map of Bristol indicating buildings related to Jerome's life. *See also* Chauncey Jerome, *History of the American Clock Business for the Past Sixty Years, and Life of Chauncey Jerome.*

Bailey, Chris H. "One Hundred Sixty Years of Seth Thomas Clocks." *Connecticut Historical Society Bulletin* 38, no. 3 (July 1973): 76–90. 11 illustrations, 2 tables.

Bailey gives a detailed account of the career of Thomas (1785–1859) from his initial partnership with Eli Terry and Silas Hoadley in the first quarter of the nineteenth century to the founding of Seth Thomas Clock Company in 1853 and its successors in the twentieth century. The article contains genealogical data on his children, all of whom were involved in clockmaking and related manufactures. Bailey also provides the working dates and addresses of Elihu Green, whose printed labels can be used to date Thomas's clocks. Unfortunately, this article contains no footnotes, although an annotated version is said to be on file at Connecticut Historical Society.

Bailey, Chris H., and Dana J. Blackwell. *Heman Clark and the "Salem Bridge" Shelf Clocks.* Supplement to the *Bulletin of the National Association of Watch and Clock Collectors,* no. 13 (June 1980). 104 pp.; 137 illustrations, 2 color plates.

Clark (ca. 1783–1838) was Eli Terry's partner working in Plymouth, Connecticut. He developed a thirty-hour shelf clock named for the settlement near Naugatuck. Bailey and Blackwell also consider the work of Spencer and Wooster Company, Spencer, Hotchkiss, and Company, Collins and Bradley and Austin, Ephraim Camp, Osro Collins, Richard Ward, and L. and L. Ward, all clockmakers working in Salem Bridge between 1815 and 1845.

Barber, Laurence Luther. "The Clockmakers of Ashby, Massachusetts." *Antiques* 23, no. 5 (May 1933): 178–80. 5 illustrations.

Barber describes the clockmaking community of Ashby, which included Samuel Edwards, Alexander T. Willard, and John Edwards, who worked between 1790 and 1820.

Barclay, Miriam A. *Daniel Pratt, Jr., Reading (Mass.) Clockmaker.* Supplement to the *Bulletin of the National Association of Watch and Clock Collectors,* no. 2 (Summer 1964). 23 pp.; 16 illustrations.

This is a short biography of Pratt (1797–1871), a shoemaker who became a clockmaker and worked just north of Boston between 1830 and 1870.

Barr, Lockwood Anderson. *Eli Terry Pillar and Scroll Shelf Clocks.* N.p., 1952. 13 pp.; 18 illustrations.

As a study of the sequence of movements and labels, this work is useful for identifying and dating clocks by this prolific clockmaker.

Beckman, Elizabeth D. *An In-Depth Study of the Cincinnati Silversmiths, Jewelers, Watch and Clockmakers through 1850; also Listing the More Prominent Men in These Trades from 1851 until 1900.* Cincinnati: B. B., 1975. xvi+168 pp.; illustrations, bibliography, index.

This alphabetical listing of craftsmen includes short biographies with their working dates, advertisements, touchmarks, and photographs of selected objects. It is marred by a lack of references to original sources.

Boultinghouse, Marquis. *Silversmiths, Jewelers, Clock and Watch Makers of Kentucky, 1785–1900.* Lexington: By the author, 1980. 368 pp.; illustrations, 76 plates, illustrated glossary of marks, appendixes, index.

Short biographical paragraphs are accompanied by illustrations of objects. Included is a glossary of touchmarks.

Burrows, G. Edmond. *Canadian Clocks and Clockmakers.* Oshawa, Ontario: By the author through Kalabi Enterprises, 1973. 506 pp.; 322 illustrations.

In addition to the checklist of clock- and watchmakers of Ontario, Quebec, Nova Scotia, and New Brunswick, Burrows includes a chapter on clocks made by Seth Thomas for dealers in Ontario.

Burt, Edwin B., Sr., and Fraser R. Forgie. *Clockmakers of the Concord, Massachusetts, Community.* Supplement to the *Bulletin of the National Association of Watch and Clock Collectors,* no. 5 (Summer 1967). 37 pp.; 48 black and white illustrations, 2 color plates, bibliography.

This volume presents excellent histories of Joseph Mulliken (1765–1802), Daniel Munroe, Jr. (1775–1859), Nathaniel Munroe (1777–1861), William Munroe (1778–1861), Lemuel Curtis (1790–1857?), Samuel Whiting (b. 1778), James Nye Dunning (1793–1841), and Joseph Dyer (1795–1850). For complementary photographs, see *Clockmakers of Concord, Massachusetts, as Gathered at the Concord Antiquarian Museum.*

Burt, Owen, and Jo Burt. "Walter H. Durfee: His Clocks, His Chimes, His Story." *Bulletin of the National Associ-*

ation of Watch and Clock Collectors 23, no. 6 (December 1981): 556–83. 27 illustrations.

Durfee (1857–1939) worked in Providence, Rhode Island, and is considered by many to be the father of the modern tall clock, which he designed in many revival styles and marketed in large numbers. He is well known for importing large quantities of European clock movements and placing them in antique American cases and for his patented chimes. Durfee was also a furniture dealer who influenced several early collectors in Providence and is thus emerging as an important figure in the colonial revival movement. Although said to be based in part on Durfee's own papers, a conspicuous lack of notes makes this study more suggestive than conclusive.

Burt, Owen H., and Jo Burt. *The Welch, Spring, and Company.* Supplement to the *Bulletin of the National Association of Watch and Clock Collectors*, no. 12 (February 1978). 108 pp.; 125 illustrations, 1 table.

This work documents the partnership of Elisha N. Welch, financier, Solomon C. Spring, manager and engineer, and Benjamin B. Lewis, inventor, between 1868 and 1884. The firm made high-grade regulators, shelf clocks, and calendar wall clocks in Bristol, Connecticut.

Camp, Hiram. *A Sketch of the Clock Making Business, 1792–1892.* New Haven, Conn., n.d. 8 pp.

Camp (1811–93) is less well known today than his uncle Chauncey Jerome, for whom he worked between 1829 and 1844 and to whom he sold his shop in 1851. In 1853 Camp founded New Haven Clock Company, supplied clock movements to his uncle, and later acquired the bankrupt Jerome firm. Camp wrote this account shortly after his retirement at age eighty-one and shortly before his death two years later.

Carlisle, Lilian Baker. "New Biographical Findings on Curtis and Dunning, Girandole Clockmakers." *American Art Journal* 10, no. 1 (May 1978): 90–109. 22 illustrations.

Carlisle gives an excellent summary of the earlier literature on the girandole clock, which was first invented by Lemuel Curtis in Concord, Massachusetts, and later made in partnership with Joseph Dunning in Burlington, Vermont. Carlisle traces the history of the girandole form, which was probably inspired by Willard's banjo timepiece and has no European counterpart. She also describes the various styles and subjects of their reverse-painted glass decoration and adds new biographical information that supersedes the research of Walter Durfee ("The Clocks of Lemuel Curtis," *Antiques* 4, no. 6 [December 1923]: 281–85).

Carlisle, Lilian Baker. *Vermont Clock and Watchmakers, Silversmiths, and Jewelers.* Burlington: By the author, 1970. xi + 313 pp.; illustrations, index.

This directory of approximately 1,000 craftsmen working between 1778 and 1878 illustrates objects, touchmarks, and facsimiles of advertisements.

Champlin, Richard L. "James Wady: 'The Life so Short, the Craft so Long to Learn'—Chaucer." *Newport History* 48, pt. 4 (Fall 1975): 348–57. 5 illustrations.

Champlin gives a brief biographical sketch of Wady (d. 1759), an important Newport clockmaker and brazier who was William Claggett's son-in-law and apprentice. Only six clocks by Wady are known today, three of which Champlin illustrates and discusses.

Champlin, Richard L. "Quaker Clockmakers of Newport." *Newport History* 50, pt. 4 (Fall 1977): 77–89. 4 illustrations.

Champlin considers the work of seven clockmakers who worked in Newport, with particular emphasis on David Williams, Stephen Gould, Job Wilbur, and Walter Cornell. The lives of Robert Proud, John Easton, Jr., and Christopher Townsend are set forth in a more cursory manner. Several of these craftsmen evidently cleaned and repaired rather than made clocks.

Champlin, Richard L. "Thomas Claggett: Silversmith, Swordsman, Clockmaker." *Newport History* 49, pt. 3 (Summer 1976): 57–68. 7 illustrations.

Claggett (ca. 1730–97) was a versatile and prominent Newport clockmaker, goldsmith, and sometime fencing instructor who was James Wady's brother-in-law and by whom fewer than a dozen clocks have survived. This brief biographical sketch is largely informed by the surviving business records of Newport merchant John Bannister.

Champlin, Richard L. *William Claggett and His Clockmaking Family.* Supplement to the *Bulletin of the National Association of Watch and Clock Collectors*, no. 11 (Summer 1976). 48 pp.; 30 black and white illustrations, 1 color plate.

Claggett was born in Wales, immigrated to Boston circa 1708, and was working in Newport by 1716. In this book, Champlin presents a historical account of three generations of Rhode Island clockmakers, expanded from his earlier article "High Time: William Claggett and His Clockmaking Family," *Newport History* (Summer 1974): 157–85.

Chandlee, Edward E. *Six Quaker Clockmakers.* Philadelphia: Historical Society of Pennsylvania, 1943. xvii + 260 pp.; 163 illustrations, bibliography, appendix, index.

This is still the best account of the lives and work of Abel Cottey, Benjamin Chandlee, Jr., Goldsmith Chandlee, Ellis Chandlee, and Isaac Chandlee, five generations of a single family that originally emigrated from Ireland and subsequently worked in Pennsylvania, Maryland, and Virginia between 1709 and about 1811. Some sixty-five clocks and surveying instruments are illustrated and are accompanied by details of their dials.

Chase, Ada R. "Two Eighteenth-Century Craftsmen of Norwich." *Connecticut Historical Society Bulletin* 25, no. 3 (July 1960): 84–88. 2 illustrations.

Two short biographies are presented in this article: one of Nathaniel Shipman (1764–1853), clockmaker and goldsmith who was apprenticed to Thomas Harland and who made clock dials; and one of Felix Huntington (1749–1822), a Norwich cabinetmaker who made clock cases. The information is based on two account books and a daybook now belonging to the Society of the Founders of Norwich at Leffingwell Inn.

Chase, Ada R. "Two Eighteenth-Century Clockmakers." *Antiques* 38, no. 3 (September 1940): 116–18. 7 illustrations.

This short account of Reuben Ingraham (1744–1811), goldsmith and clockmaker of Plainfield, Connecticut, includes a discussion of six clocks signed by him. His probate inventory is also reproduced. Chase introduces for the first time Edward Spalding (1732–85), who was born in Plainfield but settled and worked in Providence, Rhode Island.

Clockmakers of Concord, Massachusetts, as Gathered at the Concord Antiquarian Museum. Concord: Concord Antiquarian Society, 1966. 36 pp.; approximately 35 illustrations.

Clockmakers contains an illustrated checklist, without text, of an exhibition celebrating the 150th anniversary of the girandole clock. Twenty-four photographs of Concord tall and wall clocks, many from private collections, are arranged chronologically. For complementary biographies, see Edwin B. Burt, Sr., and Fraser R. Forgie, *Clockmakers of the Concord, Massachusetts, Community.*

Conrad, Henry Clay. *Old Delaware Clockmakers.* Wilmington: Historical Society of Delaware, 1898. 34 pp.; 7 illustrations.

Conrad's paper, read before the Delaware Historical Society by its librarian in 1897, includes short, illustrated biographies of about twenty clockmakers who worked in Delaware. The information was updated and reprinted in James W. Gibbs, "Early Delaware Clockmakers," but without Conrad's vintage photographs of the craftsmen and their shops.

Cutten, George Barton. *The Silversmiths, Watchmakers, and Jewelers of the State of New York Outside of New York City.* Hamilton, N.Y.: Privately printed, 1939. 47 pp.; index.

——. *The Silversmiths of Georgia, together with Watchmakers and Jewelers, 1733 to 1850.* Savannah: Pigeonhole Press, 1958. viii + 154 pp.; illustrations, index.

——. *The Silversmiths of Virginia, together with Watchmakers and Jewelers, from 1694 to 1850.* Richmond: Dietz Press, 1952. xxiv + 259 pp.; illustrations, index.

Each of these books contains a brief historical overview of

metalsmithing in a specific geographical area followed by a list of makers, arranged alphabetically under the towns in which they worked.

The Decorative Arts of New Hampshire, 1725–1825. Exhibition catalogue. Manchester: Currier Gallery of Art, 1964. 73 pp.; 106 illustrations.

Included in this survey of 106 objects are 16 shelf, wall, and tall clocks from the late eighteenth through the early nineteenth centuries. The clockmakers represented include William Fitz of Portsmouth; Silas Parsons of Swanzey; Timothy Chandler, Abiel Chandler, and Levi Hutchins of Concord; Benjamin Morrill and Joseph Chadwick of Boscawen; Jeremiah Fellows of Kensington; Richard Blasdel of Chester; Edward Moulton and James Cole of Rochester; Philip Brown of Hopkinton; and Benjamin Clark Gilman of Exeter.

DeVoe, Shirley S. "Hopkins and Alfred, Clockmakers of Harwinton." *Connecticut Historical Society Bulletin* 35, no. 4 (October 1970): 122–26. 5 illustrations.

DeVoe gives a brief account of the shelf clocks with wooden works made by Edward Hopkins (b. 1797) and Augustus Alfred (1808?–64), who worked together in Harwinton, Connecticut, between 1829 and 1841. DeVoe, a japanner and the author of *Tinsmiths of Connecticut,* addresses the stenciled decoration on clock cases. She attributes many of the dials and reverse-painted panels on Hopkins and Alfred's clocks to Benjamin Ely of East Campville and to Samuel Brown of Harwinton.

Drost, William E. *Clocks and Watches of New Jersey.* Elizabeth, N.J.: Engineering Publishers, 1966. xi + 291 pp.; approximately 225 illustrations, bibliography, glossary, index.

Drost's book is divided into three sections: clockmakers, followed by a list of craftsmen working 1710–1966; watchmaking in New Jersey, also followed by a list of craftsmen; and a short section on New Jersey watch papers.

Eckhardt, George H. *Pennsylvania Clocks and Clockmakers: An Epic of Early American Science, Industry, and Craftsmanship.* New York: Devin-Adair Co., 1955. xviii + 229 pp.; approximately 60 illustrations, appendixes, indexes.

This book on Pennsylvania clocks and their makers from about 1682 through 1850 is mostly historical, although Eckhardt includes some technical background and two outdated chapters on the care, repair, and appraisal of old clocks. Also included are lists of Philadelphia clockmakers and of craftsmen working outside Philadelphia.

Emlen, Robert P. "A Masterful William Claggett Clock: A Short Story in a Long Case." *Antiques* 118, no. 3 (September 1980): 502–7. 11 black and white illustrations, 1 color plate.

Emlen gives an excellent description and analysis of one of Claggett's most elaborate and best documented tall clocks. Its japanned case is signed and dated 1736 by Robert Davis of Boston, as well as by two generations of Providence japanners and gilders in the nineteenth century. The movement bears other inscriptions by the notable clockmakers who repaired it in the course of a century, including Christopher Townsend of Newport and George Whiting, Simon Willard, and Elnathan Taber of Boston. Emlen sets forth the history of this horological palimpsest and illustrates each of its inscriptions and attached documents.

Fredyma, James P. *A Directory of Maine Silversmiths and Watch and Clock Makers*. Hanover, N.H.: Paul J. Fredyma and Marie-Louise Fredyma, 1972. v+26 pp.; bibliography.

Fredyma, John J. *A Directory of Connecticut Silversmiths and Watch and Clock Makers*. Hanover, N.H.: Paul J. Fredyma and Marie-Louise Fredyma, 1973. iv+60 pp.; bibliography.

Fredyma, Paul J. *A Directory of Vermont Silversmiths and Watch and Clock Makers*. Hanover, N.H.: Privately printed, 1974. iv+58 pp.; bibliography.

Fredyma, Paul J., and Marie-Louise Fredyma. *A Directory of Boston Silversmiths and Watch and Clock Makers*. Hanover, N.H.: By the authors, 1975. iv+46 pp.; bibliography.

The directories in this series by the Fredymas include names, locations, working dates, and bibliographical references.

Gibbs, James W. *Buckeye Horology: A Review of Ohio Clock and Watch Makers*. Columbia, Pa.: Art Crafters Printing Co., 1971. x+128 pp.; approximately 60 illustrations, bibliography, appendix, index.

Gibbs, a past president of National Association of Watch and Clock Collectors, has compiled a list of clock- and watchmakers in Ohio. The list is arranged by county, with information gleaned from local libraries, historical societies, and secondary sources. The list includes jewelers, repairmen, dealers, and patent holders. Selected newspaper advertisements are reproduced in the appendix.

Gibbs, James W. *Dixie Clockmakers*. Gretna, La.: Pelican Publishing Co., 1979. 191 pp.; 59 illustrations, bibliography, index.

Gibbs provides biographical sketches of clockmakers and illustrations of selected clocks made in Delaware, Maryland, the District of Columbia, Virginia, North Carolina, and "the balance of Dixieland": Alabama, Florida, Georgia, Kentucky, Louisiana, Mississippi, Tennessee, and West Virginia.

Gibbs, James W. "Early Delaware Clockmakers." *Bulletin of the National Association of Watch and Clock Collectors* 12, no. 8 (February 1967): 712–15.

Short biographies of twelve Delaware clockmakers are given

with liberal quotations from Henry Clay Conrad's *Old Delaware Clockmakers* of seventy years before. Gibbs incorporates some new information from the notes of George Eckhardt, but he omits Conrad's original illustrations.

Gibbs, James W. "Horologic Rhode Island Visited." *Bulletin of the National Association of Watch and Clock Collectors* 14, no. 149 (December 1970): 801–11. 5 illustrations.

This checklist of sixty-four clockmakers with brief biographies is arranged by the towns in which they worked. The information is compiled from an article originally published in the *New York Sun* which forms part of a scrapbook in Gibbs's possession.

Gibbs, James W. "Horology in Vermont." *Bulletin of the National Association of Watch and Clock Collectors* 18, no. 5 (October 1976): 420–35. 12 illustrations, bibliography.

Short biographies of about forty clockmaking firms and individuals are accompanied by useful references to related articles elsewhere in the *Bulletin*. Gibbs concludes with a checklist of "unsubstantiated" makers compiled by earlier researchers, a list of Vermont patent grantees, and Vermont watch papers.

Gibbs, James W., and Robert W. Meader. "Shaker Clockmakers." Supplement to the *Bulletin of the National Association of Watch and Clock Collectors*, no. 7 (Summer 1972). 31 pp.; 44 illustrations, bibliography.

This is a brief biographical inventory of about ten Shaker clockmakers, with attention given to the clocks they produced and the details of their dials and movements.

Heffner, Syvilla L., ed. *Ohio Clock Exhibit: Guide to the Collection*. [Lebanon, Ohio]: Warren County Historical Society Museum, 1984. ii+33 pp.; 65 illustrations.

Written to accompany an exhibition of tall and shelf clocks made in Ohio between 1810 and 1892, this catalogue illustrates thirty-five clocks by nineteen individual clockmakers and firms. Many of the makers represented had learned their trade in Connecticut before moving to Ohio to claim land granted for service in the revolutionary war. Some came with clocks from Connecticut to sell as agents; others brought the skills to establish the first clock manufactories in Ohio.

Hindle, Brooke. *David Rittenhouse*. Princeton: Princeton University Press, 1964. xiii+394 pp.; 12 illustrations, bibliography, index.

Hindle's biography of Rittenhouse remains the standard work on a leading American figure of the Enlightenment. Rittenhouse's life is traced from his beginnings as a mechanic and clockmaker to his achievements as astronomer; his work in experimental optics, magnetism, and psychology; his career as a public servant in the Pennsylvania Assembly and as surveyor and munitions expert; and his role in the establishment of the National Mint. As a self-made savant whose interests and reputation were global, Rittenhouse embodies the Enlightenment in America. Hindle's biography helps to place his exceptionally sophisticated clocks in the widest possible context.

Holly, Forrest M. *For Generations to Come: The Life Story of Elias Ingraham*. Old Rappan, N.J.: Fleming H. Revell Co., 1975. 224 pp.; 16 illustrations, index.

Holly has written a fine biography of Ingraham, the founder of a successful and long-lived (1831–1967) American clock company.

Hoopes, Penrose R. *Connecticut Clockmakers of the Eighteenth Century*. 1930. 2d ed. New York: Dover Publications, 1974. 182 pp.; 66 illustrations, appendix, bibliography, index.

Brief but thorough essays deal with early brass, wooden, and public clocks. The second part contains biographies of some seventy-nine Connecticut clockmakers, with illustrations of selected clocks. The appendix to the second edition, "Some Minor Connecticut Clockmakers" (reprinted from *Antiques* 28, no. 3 [September 1935]: 104–5), adds seven new names.

Hoopes, Penrose R. *Shop Records of Daniel Burnap, Clockmaker*. Hartford: Connecticut Historical Society, 1958. viii+188 pp.; 56 plates, appendixes, index.

Based on shop records, account books, and Burnap's surviving tools, Hoopes's exemplary account of Burnap's life and work is an excellent study of an individual clockmaker. Burnap worked in the prosperous river town of East Windsor, Connecticut, as a clockmaker, an instrument maker, a silversmith, and a brass founder. Hoopes includes a complete transcription of his memorandum book and illustrations of clocks, dials, movements, and tools. Thanks to the wealth of surviving documents, Hoopes presents an unusually complete and eloquent picture of Burnap's life and livelihood by combining the techniques of the historian and the art historian.

Hummel, Charles F. *With Hammer in Hand: The Dominy Craftsmen of East Hampton, New York*. Charlottesville: University Press of Virginia for the Henry Francis du Pont Winterthur Museum, 1968. xiv+424 pp.; 38 illustrations, illustrated catalogue, appendixes, bibliography, index.

The second half of this book is devoted to a catalogue of approximately forty clocks and fifty pieces of documented furniture now at Winterthur. Like Penrose Hoopes's exemplary account of Daniel Burnap, Hummel's approach combines furniture, technology, and economic histories. *See also* "American Furniture to 1820."

Husher, Richard W., and Walter W. Welch. *A Study of Simon Willard's Clocks*. Nahant, Mass.: By the authors,

1980. vi+292 pp.; black and white and color illustrations, bibliography, appendixes.

The first book devoted to Simon Willard and his clocks since John Ware Willard's pioneering memoir of 1911, this work is based on extensive and close scrutiny of many clocks. Husher and Welch devote separate chapters to each type of clock that Willard is known to have made, including thirty-hour wall clocks, shelf and tower clocks, orreries, tall clocks and the patented timepiece, roasting jacks, regulators, gallery clocks, and lighthouse alarm clocks. (For information on his regulator clocks, see Albert L. Partridge, "Simon Willard's Regulator Clocks," *Old-Time New England* 46 [October–December 1955]: 29–35.) Excellent photographs of clocks accompany the text, with details of their movements. In the appendix are reprinted some of the few surviving bills and Willard's correspondence with early business partner Paul Revere. No hint is provided of contemporary clockmakers and clockmaking in Boston, nor of the many Willard apprentices. Despite little interpretive meat and careless editing, this book remains the best work to date on Willard.

[Hutchins, Levi]. *The Autobiography of Levi Hutchins; with a Preface, Notes, and Addenda, by His Youngest Son*. Cambridge: Printed by Riverside Press, 1865. iv+188 pp.

After fourteen pages of genealogical notes on William Hutchins's descendants follows a narrative of the life and career of Levi Hutchins (1761–1855), Simon Willard's successful apprentice, who, together with his brother Abel, worked in Concord, New Hampshire, from around 1786 until 1807. Hutchins records his subsequent interludes as a textile manufacturer (ca. 1812) and several clock-related incidents.

Ingraham, Edward, John C. Losch, William F. Pritchett, Fraser R. Forgie, and William L. Wadleigh, Jr. *Eli Terry, Dreamer, Artisan, and Clockmaker*. Supplement to the *Bulletin of the National Association of Watch and Clock Collectors*, no. 3 (Summer 1965). 42 pp.; 32 illustrations, bibliography.

This anthology of articles is the outgrowth of a seminar devoted to Terry at the national convention of the National Association of Watch and Clock Collectors.

James, Arthur E. *Chester County Clocks and Their Makers*. 2d ed., enl. and rev. Exton, Pa.: Schiffer Publishing, 1976. xiii+222 pp.; 54 illustrations, bibliography.

Originally published under the auspices of Chester County Historical Society, this volume by James presents the biographies of Chester County clockmakers with illustrations of selected clocks they made.

Jerome, Chauncey. *History of the American Clock Business for the Past Sixty Years, and Life of Chauncey Jerome*. New Haven: F. C. Dayton, Jr., 1860. 144 pp.

As the title suggests, the life of Jerome (1793–1868) was

inextricably linked with the history of clockmaking in Connecticut during the first part of the nineteenth century. This was the first autobiography by an American craftsman and entrepreneur. Jerome's tone is self-aggrandizing, although more recent research, by Chris H. Bailey, "From Rags to Riches to Rags," corroborates most of Jerome's story.

Kernodle, George H. "Concerning the Simon Willard Legend." *Antiques* 61, no. 6 (June 1952): 523–25. 5 illustrations.

This article represents an early attempt to reassess Willard's mythic stature that grew unchecked in the early part of the century and to replace him in the context of contemporary craft practices, where machine-made parts, for example, were no less honorable than handmade ones.

Miller, Andrew Hayes, and Dalia M. Miller. *Illinois Horology: A Brief View into the Land of Lincoln*. Chicago: Published for the 33rd National Convention of the NAWCC, 1977. 64 pp.; 114 illustrations, bibliography, index.

This work contains short biographical sketches of clockmakers and manufacturers from the nineteenth through the twentieth centuries.

Mussey, Barrows. *Young Father Time: A Yankee Portrait*. New York, San Francisco, and Montreal: Newcomen Society in North America, 1950. 44 pp.; approximately 25 illustrations.

Mussey, Barrows, and Ruth Mary Canedy. *Terry Clock Chronology*. Bristol, Conn.: Charles Terry Treadway, 1948. 30 pp.

Young Father Time, Mussey's short biography of Eli Terry (1772–1852), is based on notes compiled by Charles Terry Treadway, Terry's great-great-grandson. It illustrates clocks and some of Terry's furniture still in Treadway's possession. Mussey and Canedy's *Terry Clock Chronology* contains a year-by-year chronology of Terry's clocks.

Parsons, Charles S. *New Hampshire Clocks and Clockmakers*. Exeter: Adams Brown Co., 1976. 356 pp.; 550 illustrations.

The product of twenty-five years of research by the leading authority on New Hampshire furniture and silver, this book contains excellent descriptions of case design and construction, clockmakers' tools, and clock movements. Parsons includes up-to-date biographical information on 285 New Hampshire clockmakers.

Péladeau, Marius B. "Silas Hoadley, Connecticut Clockmaker." *Antiques* 102, no. 1 (July 1972): 90–95. 11 illustrations.

After partnerships with Eli Terry and Seth Thomas, Hoadley (1786–1870) continued to manufacture tall clocks with thirty-hour and eight-day wooden movements and shelf clocks with an "upside-down" mechanism. Péladeau traces the sequence of Hoadley's work and discusses several tall and shelf clocks made by him in Plymouth, Connecticut.

Proper, David R. "Edmund Currier, Clockmaker." *Essex Institute Historical Collections* 101, no. 4 (October 1965): 281–88.

This is a brief but thorough biography of Currier (1793–1853), a Salem clockmaker.

Roberts, Kenneth D. *The Contribution of Joseph Ives to Connecticut Clock Technology, 1810–1862*. Bristol, Conn.: American Clock and Watch Museum, 1970. xiv+338 pp.; 69 illustrations, bibliography.

This documentary study of Ives from 1810 to 1862 is primarily concerned with the technical analysis of his clock mechanisms and patented improvements.

Roberts, Kenneth D. *Eli Terry and the Connecticut Shelf Clock*. Bristol, Conn.: Ken Roberts Publishing Co., 1973. xvi+320 pp.; illustrations, appendix, index.

This thorough and well-documented history of Terry and his clocks is illustrated with examples from Roberts's collection, other private collections, and American Watch and Clock Museum, Bristol, where Roberts was curator. An appendix includes a useful checklist of Connecticut firms that manufactured shelf clocks through 1833.

Roberts, Kenneth D. *Some Observations concerning Connecticut Clockmaking, 1790–1850*. Supplement to the *Bulletin of the National Association of Watch and Clock Collectors*, no. 6 (Summer 1970). 43 pp.; 29 illustrations.

Roberts discusses marketing, sales, exports, methods of manufacturing, and specific technological developments in Connecticut clockmaking during the first half of the nineteenth century.

Shaub, Elizabeth W. "The Gorgas Family of Cocalico Valley: Grandfather Clockmakers." *Journal of the Lancaster County Historical Society* 66, no. 4 (Autumn 1962): 167–75. 2 illustrations.

Genealogical information is given on the six clockmakers among four generations of the Gorgas family, who worked in Ephrata, Germantown, Greensburg, and elsewhere in Pennsylvania from the seventeenth through the nineteenth centuries. The text includes descriptive notes on approximately ten clocks located by Cocalico Valley Historical Society, although none are illustrated.

Shelley, Frederick. *Aaron Dodd Crane: An American Original*. Supplement to the *Bulletin of the National Association of Watch and Clock Collectors*, no. 16 (1987). 120 pp.; 197 illustrations, bibliography, index.

Crane (1804–60) is best known today for his sophisticated astronomical timepiece first patented in 1841 and unique for its torsion pendulum. Brought up in Newark, New Jersey, Crane was a self-taught mechanical genius, a notion supported by the highly unorthodox movements and escapements that he developed well outside the mainstream of American clockmaking in Connecticut. Shelley reconstructs Crane's career in Newark and in Boston and discusses his tower, shelf, and astronomical-year clocks in great detail. He explains clearly the most innovative aspects of Crane's inventions, which are well illustrated.

Stretch, Carolyn Wood. "Early Colonial Clockmakers in Philadelphia." *Pennsylvania Magazine of History and Biography* 56, no. 2 (1932): 225–35. 5 illustrations.

Stretch briefly outlines the lives of Peter and Thomas Sketch, Owen Biddle, and John Wood, Jr.

Terry, Henry. *American Clock Making: Its Early History and Present Extent of the Business*. 1870. Reprint. Bristol, Conn.: American Clock and Watch Museum, 1974. 94 pp.; illustrations.

Henry Terry (1801–77), son of Eli Terry, worked in his father's firm until 1829, when he continued in the clock business under his own name. His short history of the clock industry in America is generally accurate and is profitably compared with other clockmakers' autobiographies, such as those by Chauncey Jerome, Levi Hutchins, and Hiram Camp. Terry concentrates on the lives of the most prominent Connecticut craftsmen and describes the various models of shelf, marine, parlor, calendar, and tower clocks they made. Appended to the reprinted edition is the 1885 illustrated catalogue of Terry Clock Company of Pittsfield, Massachusetts, the last of the family concerns, founded in 1867 by Eli's son Silas Burnham Terry (1772–1852) and moved from Waterbury in 1880. Included is a brief history of the firm and biographical notes by Chris Bailey.

Whitney, Philip. *The Clocks of Shenandoah*. Stephens City, Va.: Commercial Press, 1983. 93 pp.; illustrations, bibliography, index.

Whitney's brief historical introduction is followed by lists of clock- and cabinetmakers. The text is accompanied by measured drawings.

Willard, John Ware. *Simon Willard and His Clocks*. 1911. Reprint. New York: Dover Publications, 1968. 128 pp.; black and white illustrations, 38 black and white and color plates, line drawings.

Written by Simon Willard's great-grandson, this is an anecdotal and genealogical history of the family, not an analysis of Willard the craftsman and entrepreneur. It includes useful biographies of several of the collaborating craftsmen in the Willards' circle in Roxbury, as well as an outdated checklist of twenty-five of Simon Willard's clocks. *See also* Richard W. Husher and Walter W. Welch, *A Study of Simon Willard's Clocks*.

Williams, Carl M. *Silversmiths of New Jersey, 1700–1825; with Some Notice of Clockmakers Who Were Also Silversmiths*. Philadelphia: George S. MacManus Co., 1949. xii+164 pp.; 46 illustrations, bibliography, index.

Williams provides biographies of sixty-four craftsmen, arranged by their place of residence.

Wood, Stacy B. C., Jr. "The Hoff Family: Master Clockmakers of Lancaster Borough." *Journal of the Lancaster County Historical Society* 81, no. 4 (1981): 169–225. 23 illustrations, appendixes.

After recording the scant facts of George Hoff's life, Wood turns to a discussion of Hoff's clocks, paying particular attention to the Germanic features that set his clocks apart from those by other mid eighteenth-century craftsmen working in the English tradition. Wood also describes the lives of Hoff's three clockmaking sons, John (1776–1818), John Jacob (b. 1784), and John George (1788–1822), who worked as clock- and watchmakers into the 1820s. In five appendixes, Wood provides a family genealogy, probate inventories, and a most valuable annotated transcription of John Hoff's clock order book from 1800 to 1812.

Wood, Stacy B. C., Jr. "Rudy Stoner, 1728–1769: Early Lancaster, Pennsylvania, Clockmaker." *Bulletin of the National Association of Watch and Clock Collectors* 19, no. 1 (February 1977): 21–32. 7 illustrations, appendix.

Wood provides a biography of Stoner, an early clockmaker who settled in Lancaster County, circa 1755, and a transcription of his extensive estate inventory. This article is reprinted from *Journal of the Lancaster County Historical Society* 80, no. 2 (Easter 1976): 112–27.

Wood, Stacy B. C., Jr. *Two Hundred Twenty-five Years of Timepieces: A Lancaster County Legacy*. Columbia, Pa.: NAWCC Museum, 1979. 83 pp.; illustrations, bibliography.

In this catalogue and checklist from the first annual exhibition of National Association of Watch and Clock Collectors Museum, Wood discusses twenty-seven clocks ranging in date from the 1750s to the 1870s. Following the text is a checklist of watches, chronometers, and horological instruments and tools used in Lancaster County.

Wood, Stacy B. C., Jr., Stephen E. Kramer III, and John J. Snyder, Jr. *Clockmakers of Lancaster County and Their Clocks, 1750–1850*. New York: Van Nostrand Reinhold Co., 1977. 224 pp.; illustrations, indexes.

Based on a survey of ninety-seven clocks representing forty-seven of the ninety-four craftsmen known to have been working in Lancaster County between 1750 and 1850, this well-illustrated survey begins with a biographical directory of clockmakers compiled by Wood from tax and church records, deeds, wills, newspapers, and genealogies. Snyder contributed the chapter on the clock cases, of which none is signed or labeled, and considers them in the broader context of Lancaster County furniture. The final two chapters provide clear, full-page illustrations with descriptive captions of each dial and movement. These are introduced by brief essays defining the English and German clockmaking traditions that were often interestingly modified or combined by Lancaster County clockmakers, as discussed in greater detail in Stacy B. C. Wood, Jr., "The Hoff Family."

Woodbury, Robert S. "The Legend of Eli Whitney and

Interchangeable Parts." *Technology and Culture* 1, no. 3 (Summer 1960): 235–53.

Although not exclusively concerned with clocks, Woodbury discusses the Connecticut clock industry as the first link in the chain that would become known as the American System of Manufactures.

Zea, Philip. "Clockmaking and Society at the River and the Bay: Jedidiah and Jabez Baldwin, 1790–1820." *See* "Craftsmen."

SOCIAL HISTORY OF TIME AND TIMEKEEPING

Ayensu, Edward S., and Philip Whitfield, eds. *The Rhythms of Life.* New York: Crown Publishers, 1982. 109 pp.; black and white and color illustrations, appendix, index.

Ayensu has written a provocative study of the large, long-term cyclical rhythms governed by patterns of daylight and darkness that affect all living things: seasons, sexual behavior, population, emotions, health, and disease, known collectively as circadian timing systems.

Buckley, Jerome Hamilton. *The Triumph of Time: A Study of the Victorian Concepts of Time, History, Progress, and Decadence.* Cambridge, Mass.: Harvard University Press, Belknap Press, 1966. xi+187 pp.; index.

With the rise of Darwinism and the study of natural history in general, concepts of time began to change radically in the nineteenth century. Buckley relies mostly on literary sources for his conclusions, rather than on artifactual evidence.

Chapuis, Alfred. *De horologiis in arte: L'horloge et la montre a travers les ages, d'apres les documents du temps.* Editions du journal suisse d'horlogerie et de bijouterie. Lausanne: Scriptar, 1954. 154 pp.; 210 black and white illustrations, 2 color plates.

This is a valuable compendium of images of clocks and watches as depicted in sculpture, paintings, prints, and drawings dating from the twelfth through the nineteenth centuries. The arrangement is chronological, with a separate chapter on the Far East. Captions are written in French, English, and German. Although no American images appear, both "fine" and "popular" European sources have been included.

Cipolla, Carl M. *Clocks and Culture, 1300–1700.* New York: W. W. Norton, 1978. 192 pp.; illustrations, index.

In this eloquent social history of clocks and timekeeping, Cipolla begins with the rise of urban populations in late medieval Europe and traces "the utilitarian spirit, born of the

medieval urban civilization, fostered by the Baconian philosophy, that expressed itself in an ever-growing craze for new machines" (p. 34). He discusses public clocks of the fourteenth century and the proliferation of domestic clocks in the seventeenth century and traces the rise of specialized clockmaking centers in Germany, France, Switzerland, and England, with particular attention paid to changes within the industry caused by broad cultural changes and brought about by improved timekeeping. The second half of the book examines the "self-ringing bells," a rare instance of Chinese fascination with Western goods in the sixteenth century, and the different responses of China and Japan to the mechanical clock and to early Western technology in general.

The Clockmakers Outcry against the Author of the Life and Opinions of Tristram Shandy. London: J. Burd, 1760. 44 pp.

This farcical page-by-page response to the alleged lewdness of Sterne's clock-inspired punning in *Tristram Shandy* provides a rare view of eighteenth-century humor and specifically of the language relating to clocks and popular attitudes toward them.

Clocks in Home Decoration. Edited in collaboration with *Good Housekeeping.* La Salle, Ill.: Westclox, 1965. 98 pp.; black and white and color illustrations.

This home decorator's handbook shows the many opportunities for "added beauty and usefulness through careful selection and placement of appropriate clocks in every room" and "the fascinating potential in clocks as dramatically effective home design elements" (p. 96). The text includes the adaptive reuse of old clocks for wall vitrines and curio cabinets and room settings ranging from early American to the impeccably modern.

Cole, Arthur H. "The Tempo of Mercantile Life in Colonial America." *Business History Review* 33, no. 3 (Autumn 1959): 277–99. 3 tables.

Cole presents a statistical study of the working habits of seven merchants active in Boston, New York, Providence, and Yorktown around 1750, as revealed by their surviving letters and other business papers. By calculating the average volume of correspondence, numbers of daily business transactions, credit sales, and time elapsed between letters overseas, Cole clarifies business methods of the day and concludes, "business in colonial times had not yet become an end in itself nor a dominant means for self-expression" (p. 227).

de Solla Price, Derek J. *On the Origin of Clockwork, Perpetual Motion Devices, and the Compass*. United States National Museum Bulletin 218. Contributions from the Museum of History and Technology, paper 6, pp. 81–112. Washington, D.C.: Smithsonian Institution, 1959. 22 illustrations, appendix.

In this important early article, de Solla Price advances the controversial thesis that clocks were an early by-product of astronomical timekeepers, which were more important to early cultures than the need to keep accurate civic or domestic time.

Franklin, Benjamin. "How to Make a Striking Sundial." In *The Papers of Benjamin Franklin*, vol. 7, *October 1, 1756, through March 31, 1758*, edited by Leonard W. Labaree et al., pp. 75–76. New Haven: Yale University Press, 1963.

Franklin's satirical treatise includes instructions for a sundial with an explosive striking mechanism, "by which not only a man's own family, but all his neighbors for ten miles round, may know what o'clock it is" (p. 75).

Fraser, J. T. *Of Time, Passion, and Knowledge*. New York: George Braziller, 1975. xiii+529 pp.; index.

This book provides an abstract discussion of the philosophical dimension of time and the varying perceptions of time through history.

Fraser, J. T., ed. *The Voices of Time: A Cooperative Survey of Man's Views of Time as Expressed by the Sciences and by the Humanities*. New York: George Braziller, 1966. xxv+710 pp.; illustrations, bibliography, index.

Fraser presents the best introduction to the role of time in language, music, biology, analytic psychology, quantum theory, and other disciplines.

Glasser, Richard. *Time in French Life and Thought*. Translated by C. G. Pearson. 1936. Manchester: University of Manchester Press; Totowa, N.J.: Rowman and Littlefield, 1972. 306 pp.; indexes.

This historical survey from medieval times to the nineteenth century is based primarily on linguistic evidence.

Grant, John, and Colin Wilson, eds. *The Book of Time*. North Pomfret, Vt.: David and Charles, 1980. 320 pp.; illustrations, index.

This interdisciplinary anthology of seven essays focuses on the relationships of philosophy, history, anthropology, horology, and the physical sciences to both mechanical and nonmechanical timekeeping. Grant and Wilson present an excellent survey of this subject, although they are more attentive to scientific than historical issues.

Haliburton, Thomas Chandler. *The Clockmaker; or, The Sayings and Doings of Samuel Slick, of Slickville*. 1st American ed. Philadelphia: Carey, Lea, and Blanchard, 1837. vi+220 pp.

——. *Sam Slick*. Edited by Ray Palmer Baker. New York: George H. Doran Co., 1923. 430 pp.; bibliography.

Published many times since, *The Clockmaker* is the picaresque adventures of Slick, a fictitious clock peddler "from Slickville, Onion County, State of Connecticut, United States of America," who comments on the manners and social customs of his American and Canadian customers and, indirectly, on the ubiquitous clock peddlers, who later came to be universally mistrusted. The story of this character continues in *Sam Slick*.

Howse, Derek. *Greenwich Time and the Discovery of the Longitude*. New York: Oxford University Press, 1980. xviii+254 pp.

This is the best account of the search for a prime meridian and a universal time standard and their subsequent impact on horology.

Landes, David S. *Revolution in Time: Clocks and the Making of the Modern World*. Cambridge, Mass.: Harvard University Press, Belknap Press, 1983. 482 pp.; 32 black and white illustrations, 8 color plates.

Landes's study considers the impact of clocks and watches on the multiple activities of modern life, work, leisure, travel, technology and culture, politics, and personalities. Landes is a professor of history and economics at Harvard and a watch collector. As a sequel to his *Unbound Prometheus: Technological Change and Industrial Development in Western Europe from 1750 to the Present* (1969), this book examines the single invention that he considers a major catalyst of Europe's progress from medieval times to the scientific revolution in the seventeenth through the eighteenth centuries. In three sections he traces the invention of the mechanical clock in Europe and China. The race for precision timekeeping in England, France, and Switzerland emerges largely through anecdotes of individual craftsmen. Landes also examines the rise and fall of America's watch industry and the ultimate triumph of Japan, Hong Kong, and the digital electronic quartz movement over traditional mechanical timepieces.

Landesberg, Peter T., ed. *The Enigma of Time*. Bristol: Adam Hilger, 1982. xii+248 pp.; glossary, bibliography, index.

This anthology of essays from about 1920 to 1980 examines the struggle in various academic disciplines, but primarily among physicists, to comprehend the nature of time. Particularly useful are the essays by Ernst Gombrich, "Moment and Movement in Art," and W. J. Ong, "Evolution, Myth, and Poetic Vision," which discuss the traditional problem of depicting the passage of time in the arts.

Macey, Samuel L. "The Changing Iconography of Father Time." In *The Study of Time III: Proceedings of the Third Conference of the International Society for the Study of Time*, edited by J. T. Fraser et al., pp. 540–77. New York and Berlin: Springer-Verlag, 1978. 9 illustrations.

Macey presents an iconographic study of a persistent image, Father Time, who has existed in various guises beginning with the ancient Greek Chronos. Still unsurpassed, however, is Erwin Panofsky's 1939 "Father Time."

Macey, Samuel L. "Clocks and Chronology in the Novels from Defoe to Austen." *Eighteenth-Century Life*, n.s. 7, no. 2 (January 1982): 96–104.

In a special issue devoted to "science and technology and their cultural contexts," Macey analyzes the relationship of clocks to time-consciousness in eighteenth-century literature. In particular, he examines changing responses to the clocklike qualities of characters in the novels of Defoe, Richardson, Fielding, Sterne, and Austen. He traces the occurrence of time-related words that increased in proportion to the number of clockmakers working in London as ownership of clocks and watches became common. Macey also considers the positive connotations of watches early on and the gradual reactions after about 1760 against clocklike order and regularity.

Macey, Samuel L. *Clocks and the Cosmos: Time in Western Life and Thought*. Hamden, Conn.: Archon Books, 1980. 260 pp.; illustrations, index.

Macey traces the use of the clock as an analogy for order, mostly through literary sources. This book is useful in conjunction with the essay by Otto Mayr in Klaus Maurice and Otto Mayr, eds., *The Clockwork Universe*.

Macey, Samuel L. "Hogarth and the Iconography of Time." In *Studies in Eighteenth-Century Culture*, vol. 5, edited by Ronald C. Rosbottom, pp. 41–53. Madison: University of Wisconsin Press for the American Society for Eighteenth-Century Studies, 1975. 4 illustrations.

In this iconographical analysis of Hogarth's numerous engraved images of time, clocks, and hourglasses, Macey compares the images with other contemporary artists' depictions of the same subjects.

Maurice, Klaus, and Otto Mayr, eds. *The Clockwork Universe: German Clocks and Automata, 1550–1650*. Exhibition catalogue. New York: Neale Watson Academic Publications for the Smithsonian Institution, 1980.

ix + 321 pp.; 85 illustrations, illustrated catalogue, glossary, index.

Within this lavish volume, written to accompany an exhibition of the same title, are several excellent essays on the social history of clocks, notably, Mayr's "Mechanical Symbol for an Authoritarian World," Francis Haber's "Clock as Intellectual Artifact," and Silvio Bedini's "Mechanical Clock and the Scientific Revolution." Mayr examines the basis of man's fascination with clocks and why, from the moment of its invention in the fourteenth century, the mechanical clock became such an important basis for comparison in figures of speech. By means of scientific, philosophical, and art historical evidence, Mayr documents the spread of the clockwork metaphor from Dante to the seventeenth century in three central human concerns: celestial spheres, the human body, and political states. Haber examines the gulf between the eager reception of clocks as intellectual artifacts in the pre-industrial era and the nineteenth-century perception of machines as the enemy of spiritual values. Bedini traces the rise of a specialized clockmaking profession in the seventeenth century from the related arts of the blacksmith, locksmith, and gunfounder. He postulates that endeavors brought scientists into closer contact with craftsmen and that the astronomical sciences required mechanisms of greater and greater precision. Improved pendulum and escapement designs were both cause and effect of the scientific revolution, from which ultimately grew the modern industry of precision scientific instruments.

Mayr, Otto. *Authority, Liberty, and Automatic Machinery in Early Modern Europe*. Johns Hopkins Studies in the History of Technology Series no. 8. Baltimore and London: Johns Hopkins University Press, 1986. xviii + 265 pp.; 38 illustrations, index.

Pursuing themes first published in his essay for *The Clockwork Universe* (ed. Klaus Maurice and Mayr), Mayr examines clockwork metaphors in politics in this discussion of the relationships among machinery, technological thought, and European culture. He traces the divergence between a Continental commitment to values of authority and its symbol, the clock, and the British preference for more liberal values of balance, equilibrium, and self-regulation, which found their own mechanical correlatives. Together with David Landes (*Revolution in Time*) and Brooke Hindle (*Emulation and Invention*), Mayr is the most eloquent proponent of the idea that "technology is a cause as well as a consequence of the values and norms of the society in which it flourishes — technology is both a social force and a social product" (p. xviii).

Moore-Ede, Martin C., Frank M. Sulzman, and Charles A. Fuller. *The Clocks That Time Us: Physiology of the Circadian Timing System*. Cambridge, Mass., and London: Harvard University Press, 1982. xii + 448 pp.; 154 illustrations, glossary, bibliography, index.

This is the best introduction to the elusive science of biological rhythms and "internal" clocks. For more on this subject, see Edward S. Ayensu and Philip Whitfield, eds., *The Rhythms of Life*.

Nowotny, H. "Time Structuring the Time Measurement: On the Inter-relation between Timekeepers and Social Time." In *The Study of Time II*, edited by J. T. Fraser and N. Lawrence, pp. 325–42. New York and Berlin: Springer-Verlag, 1975.

In Nowotny's theoretical essay, he considers the changing value of time in society.

Panofsky, Erwin. "Father Time." In Erwin Panofsky, *Studies in Iconology: Humanistic Themes in the Art of the Renaissance*, pp. 69–93. New York: Oxford University Press, 1939. Illustrations.

This is the most thorough and scholarly study of the changing iconography of Father Time from classical antiquity through the nineteenth century. It is still unsurpassed by Samuel Macey's more recent "Changing Iconography of Father Time."

Priestly, J. B. *Man and Time*. Garden City, N.Y.: Doubleday, 1964. 319 pp.; black and white and color illustrations, index.

Priestly presents a general history of time in physics, fiction, and drama, from ancient to modern times.

Soltow, Lee. "Watches and Clocks in Connecticut, 1800: A Symbol of Socioeconomic Status." *Connecticut Historical Society Bulletin* 45, no. 4 (October 1980): 115–22. 2 illustrations, 3 tables.

Soltow provides a statistical study of watch owners and their status in four Connecticut towns. Based on tax lists for 1795–99, this study bears the bias of its evidence, but it suggests one technique of determining the value of watches to their owners.

Thompson, E. P. "Time, Work-Discipline, and Industrial Capitalism." *Past and Present* 38 (December 1967): 56–97.

The study of work and leisure has been variously approached in religious ideology, issues of labor and management, and even drinking habits. In this now-classic article, Thompson, a Marxist historian, examines the imposition of work-discipline and its relation to the consciousness of time.

Wright, Lawrence. *Clockwork Man: The Story of Time, Its Origins, Its Uses, Its Tyranny*. New York: Horizon Press, 1969. 260 pp.; illustrations, appendixes, bibliography, index.

Wright discusses changing popular attitudes toward time and its increasing role in people's lives, from medieval times to the present. Beginning with the limited horizons of medieval farmers, in both time and space, he traces the steady advance of the domestic timetable later and later into the day, aided by artificial light, to the pervasive importance of time in the modern industrial era. Wright examines popular concepts of time, history, and the future; secular and religious divisions of time; how timekeeping devices affect our manners and behavior; and, ultimately, whether modern people are now enslaved by "chronarchy."

TOOLS, WATCHES, AND CLOCK-RELATED CRAFTS

Abbott, Henry G. [pseud. of George Henry Abbott Hazlitt]. *The Watch Factories of America Past and Present*. Chicago: George K. Hazlitt, 1883. 145 pp.; 50 illustrations.

Abbott's early history of watchmaking in the United States, from 1809 to 1888, includes sketches of celebrated individual craftsmen and entrepreneurs.

Andrews, Carol Damon. "John Ritto Penniman (1782–1841), an Ingenious New England Artist." *Antiques* 120, no. 1 (July 1981): 147–70. 15 black and white illustrations, 16 color plates, checklist.

This is a thorough account of Penniman, a dial painter associated with the Willard circle of clockmakers in Boston and Roxbury. Andrews illustrates several signed clock dials and includes a checklist of other known or documented dials by Penniman.

Ashton, Thomas Southcliffe. *An Eighteenth Century Industrialist: Peter Stubs of Warrington, 1756–1806*. Publications of the University of Manchester, no. 226. Manchester, 1939. x+156 pp.; index.

Ashton presents a thorough study of a British manufacturer of watch files and includes an account of the craftsman and his materials, market, and shop practices.

Burton, Stanley H. *The Watch Collection of Stanley H. Burton*. London: B. T. Batsford, 1981. 439 pp.; illustrations, index.

Burton illustrates more than 100 watches ranging in date from the seventeenth century to the twentieth century, citing mostly European examples but including several American watches. Each entry is accompanied by brief descriptive notes. Indexes to the names of the watchmakers and to specific watch features are included.

A Catalogue of Tools for Watch and Clock Makers by John Wyke of Liverpool. Introduction and technical commentary by Alan Smith. Facsimile. Charlottesville: University Press of Virginia for the Henry Francis du Pont Winterthur Museum, 1978. vii+153 pp.; 19 illustrations, illustrated catalogue, appendixes.

Wyke's Liverpool catalogue is the earliest known English printed source of clock-related tools. Smith has written an introductory essay, "The Lancashire Watch and Watch Tool Trade," as well as excellent technical commentary that accompanies each plate.

Clutton, Cecil, and George Daniels. *Watches: A Complete History of the Technical and Decorative Development of the Watch.* 1965. 3d rev. and enl. ed. London: Philip Wilson Publishers for Sotheby Parke Bernet Publications, 1979; distributed by Biblio Distribution Center. 159 pp.; 16 color plates, 387 illustrated entries, appendix.

Containing biographies of watchmakers, this large and well-illustrated book covers the history of watches and watchmaking from approximately 1500 through 1900. A glossary of technical terms and a short annotated bibliography are included.

Cousins, Frank W. *Sundials: The Art and Science of Gnomonics.* New York: Pica Press, 1970. 247 pp.; 107 illustrations, appendixes, bibliography, indexes.

Cousins's general, although largely technical, history of the sundial from ancient to modern times is arranged according to type—for example, spherical, analemmatic, pillar. The text is well illustrated with museum and civic examples. An excellent bibliography divides the pre-1800 from the post-1800 literature.

Crom, Theodore R. *Horological Shop Tools, 1700 to 1900.* Melrose, Fla.: By the author, 1980. xiv+678 pp.; approximately 1,325 black and white and color illustrations, bibliography, index.

The text includes excerpts from early treatises on watch- and clockmaking, beginning with Joseph Moxon (1678) and continuing with English, French, and American sources into the twentieth century. Crom explains the uses of various tools and includes a list of museums with horological tool collections.

Crom, Theodore R. *Horological Wheel Cutting Engines, 1700 to 1900.* Gainesville, Fla.: By the author, 1970. ix+150 pp.; 142 illustrations, bibliography, index.

Crom's comprehensive study of French, Spanish, German, Swiss, English, and American wheel-cutting engines used specifically by clock- and watchmakers is useful for its detailed photographs of various types of engines and its clear explanations of their history and application.

Cummins, J. M. "Small New England Clocks, Minimal Cases Hide Elegant Works." *Fine Woodworking*, no. 41 (July–August 1983): 74–77. Black and white and color illustrations.

This article presents a woodworker's view of the economical case construction and workmanship behind the shelf and wall clocks of the Willards, Curtis and Dunning, Joshua Wilder, and Eli Terry.

Daniels, George. *English and American Watches.* London and New York: Abelard-Schuman, 1967. 128 pp.; illustrations, appendix, index.

In his good popular history of watches from the seventeenth century to the present, Daniels illustrates about fifty watches, each photographed to show the case as well as the exposed movement.

Dolan, Winthrop W. *A Choice of Sundials.* Brattleboro, Vt.: Stephen Greene Press, 1975. xii+148 pp.; 73 illustrations, bibliography, index.

Dolan's historical survey and technical explanation of sundials includes a chapter with a brief discussion of specific sundials from seventeenth-century Massachusetts to the modern era.

Earle, Alice Morse. *Sun Dials and Roses of Yesterday.* New York: Macmillan Co., 1902. xxiii+461 pp.; illustrations.

This is a popular, general history of European and American sundials by an American collector and antiquarian.

Elgin Reminiscences: Making Watches by Machinery. 1869. *Excerpts from 1873 Elgin Almanac and Other Sources.* Bristol, Conn.: Ken Roberts Publishing Co., 1972. 32 pp.; illustrations, bibliography.

Selected by the former curator of American Clock and Watch Museum, these excerpts have been culled from Elgin Watch Company's illustrated almanac. It is an excellent record of the clock movements and the factory buildings and machine shops in which they were made.

Emlen, Robert P. "Christopher Townsend, Jr.'s, Watch Paper." *Antiques* 121, no. 2 (February 1982): 483. 1 illustration.

In this short notice of an acquisition by Rhode Island Historical Society, Emlen documents and interprets the only known impression of a watch paper by little-known Newport watchmaker Townsend (1738–1809). Within its numerical chart for adjusting a watch by local solar time is an unusual engraved illustration of the clockmaker with his sundial beside a tall clock.

Gatty, Mrs. Alfred. *The Book of Sun-Dials.* Edited by H. K. F. Eden and Eleanor Lloyd. 1872. 4th rev. ed.

London: George Bell and Sons, 1900. xvii+529 pp.; 9 illustrations, index.

An extensive survey of antique British sundials, this book is largely based on Gatty's own collection, begun around 1835. The examples range from the Middle Ages through the nineteenth century, and most are illustrated by line drawings. The second half of the book contains transcriptions of nearly 1,700 epigrams and their translations, which, like gravestone epitaphs and clock dials, provide a glimpse of contemporary attitudes toward mortality and the passage of time.

Gillingham, Harrold E. "The First Orreries in America." *Journal of the Franklin Institute* 229, no. 1 (January 1940): 81–89. 8 illustrations.

Gillingham discusses and illustrates the three most famous orreries produced in America: the Rittenhouse orrery at University of Pennsylvania; Harvard's by Joseph Pope of Boston; and Aaron Willard, Jr.'s, for West Chester Academy, now at Chester County Historical Society.

Goodison, Nicholas. "The Victoria and Albert Museum's Collection of Metal-Work Pattern Books." *Furniture History* 11 (1975): 1–30. 60 plates, appendixes.

This survey of Victoria and Albert Museum's extensive collection of eighteenth- and nineteenth-century trade catalogues illustrates many clock ornaments and related brass hardware, with dimensions and prices. These are the sort of sale catalogues used by American hardware merchants and preserved in the greatest numbers at Winterthur Museum and Essex Institute. Goodison's survey is useful if considered in conjunction with Charles F. Hummel, "English Tools in America." *See also* "Brass, Copper, Iron, and Tin."

Hitchings, Sinclair. "Thomas Johnston." In *Boston Prints and Printmakers, 1670–1775*, pp. 83–132. Publications of the Colonial Society of Massachusetts, vol. 46. Boston: By the society, 1973; distributed by the University Press of Virginia. 28 illustrations.

Hitchings's paper contains a brief discussion and illustrations of clock faces engraved by Johnston, a versatile craftsman.

Hummel, Charles F. "English Tools in America: The Evidence of the Dominys." In *Winterthur Portfolio 2*, edited by Milo M. Naeve, pp. 27–46. Winterthur, Del.: Henry Francis du Pont Winterthur Museum, 1965. 5 illustrations.

An illustrated checklist of about twenty firms that produced tools used by the Dominy family of Easthampton, Long Island, and preserved by Winterthur includes descriptions of their marks and profiles of their manufacturers, based on Sheffield directories. The checklist is preceded by a historical introduction documenting toolmakers in America, particularly those in New York and numerous planemakers in Pennsylvania, by means of newspaper advertisements and records

kept by merchants. *See also* Charles F. Hummel, *With Hammer in Hand*.

Hummel, Charles F. "Samuel Rowland Fisher's Catalogue of English Hardware." In *Winterthur Portfolio One*, pp. 188–97. Winterthur, Del.: Henry Francis du Pont Winterthur Museum, 1964. 16 illustrations.

Hummel presents several examples of clock-related hardware made in England and imported to America. This work is useful when considered in conjunction with Nicholas Goodison, "The Victoria and Albert Museum's Collection of Metal-work Pattern Books."

Kaduck, John M. *Collecting Watch Fobs: A Price Guide*. Des Moines: Wallace-Homestead Book Co., 1973. 100 pp.; illustrations, appendix, index.

This guide is useful for its illustrations of 530 watch fobs, all of which are illustrated and arranged according to the subjects they depict.

Keown, J. R. " 'Willard and Nolen': Ornamental Painters." *Bulletin of the National Association of Watch and Clock Collectors* 25, no. 2 (April 1983): 140–63. 24 illustrations.

Keown traces the history of the partnership formed in 1806 between Aaron Willard, Jr., and Spencer Nolen, the best-known sign and clock-dial painters in federal Boston. The text includes brief biographical sketches and a stylistic analysis of signed work on clocks by the Willards, Elnathan Taber, and David Wood. Keown attributes other unsigned clock dials that relate to the documented examples. Unfortunately, he relies on John Ware Willards' outdated research, perpetuating the myth that Nolen may be the "English" dial painter said to have worked for the Willards.

[Keyes, Homer Eaton]. "The Editor's Attic: Harvard Has an Orrery." *Antiques* 31, no. 3 (March 1937): 112–15. 7 illustrations.

In his brief discussion of Harvard's orrery, made by Joseph Pope of Boston and dated 1786, Keyes pays particular attention to the mahogany case and the bronze figures of Benjamin Franklin, James Bowdoin, and Isaac Newton repeated in the corners of "this sturdy shrine," here attributed to John and Simeon Skillin.

Moore, Charles W. *Timing a Century: History of the Waltham Watch Company*. Harvard Studies in Business History 11. Cambridge, Mass.: Harvard University Press, 1945. xxxiv+362 pp.; 18 illustrations, appendixes, bibliography, index.

Moore's comprehensive scholarly study of a large American watchmaking concern traces the origins, rise, and decline of the watch company from 1850 through the Second World War.

Niebling, Warren H. *History of the American Watch Case*. Philadelphia: Whitmore Publishing Co., 1971. xi+192 pp.

In this history of a single manufacturer, Keystone Watch Case Company of Philadelphia, Niebling has compiled lists of watch-case makers, illustrations of trademarks used by American case manufacturers, and illustrations of watch-case designs for various patent applications.

Niehaus, James J. *A Guide to Watch Holders*. St. Mary's, Ohio: Hunter Publishing Co., 1978. 37 pp.; 57 illustrations.

Niehaus examines the decorative pedestals and cases for storing and displaying watches. The examples illustrated are drawn from his collection of eighteenth- and nineteenth-century European watch holders.

Rees, Abraham. *Rees's Clocks, Watches, and Chronometers (1819–1820): A Selection from the Cyclopaedia; or, Universal Dictionary of Arts, Sciences, and Literature*. 1819. Reprint. Newton Abbot: David and Charles Reprints, 1970. vii+287 pp.; illustrations, index.

This book contains a selection of articles and engraved illustrations of watch, chronometer, and other movements taken from Rees's *Cyclopaedia*, the first encyclopedia to put primary emphasis on technological subjects.

Rohr, René R. J. *Sundials: History, Theory, and Practice*. Toronto: University of Toronto Press, 1970. x+142 pp.; 57 illustrations, 104 line drawings, appendixes, bibliography, index.

Rohr's history of sundials is organized according to type of construction. It is well illustrated with historical examples, although his interest is more technical than historical.

Shugart, Cooksey. *The Complete Guide to American Pocket Watches, 1981*. Cleveland, Tenn.: Overstreet Publications, 1981. 252 pp.; approximately 500 illustrations.

This guide for the identification and evaluation of watches made between 1809 and 1950 contains mainly lists of serial numbers, the names of common watch models, and data on their manufacturers.

Smith, Grace Howard, and Eugene Randolph Smith. *Watch Keys as Jewelry: Collecting Experiences of a Husband and Wife*. Syracuse: Syracuse University, 1967. [xii]+135 pp.; black and white and color illustrations, index.

A private collection of watch keys from all countries is presented in this illustrated survey with extended captions.

Spear, Dorothea E. *American Watch Papers; with a Descriptive List of the Collection in the American Antiquarian Society*. Worcester, Mass.: By the society, 1952. 76 pp.; 3 plates. Also published in *Proceedings of the American Antiquarian Society* 61, pt. 2 (October 1951): 297–370.

Spear provides a brief historical introduction to the use and occurrence of watch papers in America, a form of advertising that also protected watches within their cases. They help to document watchmakers and are often interesting for their engraved illustrations. The introduction is followed by a complete list of about 200 examples, mostly from the nineteenth century, in American Antiquarian Society's collection. Spear provides biographical information about the watchmakers and engravers as well as bibliographical references and a separate geographical listing.

Sternfield, Joseph. *Hour Glasses*. Supplement to the *Bulletin of the National Association of Watch and Clock Collectors* (February 1953). 22 pp.; 2 illustrations, bibliography.

Sternfield outlines the history of hourglass production and decoration and their varied functions in church and state as well as in navigation.

Swan, Mabel M. "The Man Who Made Brass Works for Willard Clocks." *Antiques* 17, no. 1 (June 1930): 524–26. 7 illustrations.

Based on the little-known ledgers of William C. Hunneman (1769–1856), Boston brass founder, Swan documents his extensive collaboration with the Willards and other craftsmen in Roxbury.

Swan, Mabel M. "The Man Who Made Simon Willard's Clock Cases: John Doggett of Roxbury." *Antiques* 15, no. 3 (March 1929): 196–200. 7 illustrations.

Although it is doubtful that Doggett, a carver and gilder, actually made the tall-clock cases that Swan illustrates, there is no doubt that he supplied parts for the cases of Willard's patented timepieces, as documented by Doggett's surviving ledger, now at Winterthur.

Weiss, Leonard. *Watchmaking in England, 1760–1820*. London: Robert Hale, 1982. 304 pp.; illustrations, bibliography, index.

Weiss provides a clear introduction to watchmaking tools and their uses, the nature of different watch escapements, and the organization of the watchmaking shops and trade in general.

Woodbury, Robert S. *History of the Gear-Cutting Machine: A Historical Study in Geometry and Machines*. Technology Monographs, Historical Series no. 1. Cambridge, Mass.: Technology Press of MIT, 1958. v+135 pp.; 56 illustrations, bibliography, index.

This work is more technical than Theodore R. Crom's *Horological Wheel Cutting Engines* and is broader in scope. Woodbury considers the production of gear-cutting machines through the 1920s and includes a careful examination of patents and trade journals. Chapter 2 concerns the first gear-cutting machines used by clockmakers and instrument makers.

Household Activities and Systems

Kitchen Artifacts and Housework

Plumbing, Heating, and Lighting

PLUMBING

HEATING

LIGHTING

Kitchen Artifacts and Housework

Donna R. Braden

For decades the study of kitchens and housework had been largely ignored by collectors and historians, at least in part because related objects were generally plain and usually unmarked and had often been passed over for more decorative, refined, and datable household furnishings. Recently kitchens, housework, and their related artifacts have been brought under closer historical scrutiny. Current scholarship in this field has come from many directions and as the result of varied circumstances.

Objects related to food and domestic activities have recently become highly collectible because of their affordability, their highly personal and familiar nature, and the recent nostalgic appeal of "primitives" and "country kitchens." Many publications, including several collectors' newsletters (such as *Kitchen Collectibles News* edited by Linda Campbell Franklin), point to this recent interest. As more objects are uncovered and acquired by collectors, more information about these types of artifacts should be revealed.

Museum staff are continually seeking better documentation for objects in their collections. Efforts to revise outdated exhibits, furnish historic kitchens, or understand more about a certain class of objects have encouraged several publications. A few studies from the museum perspective include those by Frank White, John Tyler, and Harvey Green and the exhibition catalogues in this listing.

Other contributions have been provided by historians. The recent interest in women's studies has resulted in many insightful works relating housework to the role of women in American society. Some historians of technology have also geared their efforts toward studying the effect of technology and mechanization in the home. Another field that has recently supplemented our knowledge is the study of food ways and gastronomy. Several excellent works on the historical roles of various foods in American culture also have discussed the related artifacts.

The following annotations include works pertaining to the history of American kitchens, kitchen furnishings and equipment, housework, and household technology. Other related subjects are highlighted by recent works in this listing—namely, sewing machines, pressing irons, and baskets. Sources on woodenware are included, but those related to most other specialized materials, such as metals and ceramics, are left for other sections. Likewise, specific sources on heating and lighting are covered in another section, although some of the sources on household technology contain overlapping information.

The subjects of changing women's roles and the history of gastronomy relate closely to housework and kitchen artifacts, but only those sources that deal specifically with the subjects at hand were included. Because of the cutoff date of 1920 in this book, sources relating to these subjects that primarily emphasize the twentieth century are also excluded.

The titles chosen are drawn from collector's guides, food histories, women's history studies, and other sources that document or describe aspects of the kitchen or housework. Collector's guides mainly serve to document and identify certain classes of objects. Some are more helpful, and some are more basic, than others. Because there are so few useful sources relating to specific categories of artifacts, most of the general survey works in this field are included, such as those by Geraldine Cosentino and Regina Stewart, Linda Franklin, Mary Gould, Louise Lantz, and Mary Norwak. I recommend that researchers form conclusions about specific subjects or artifacts by combining a number of these sources.

Technological developments within given categories of objects are covered in many of the sources, and these are also described in the annotations. See especially works included by David Hounshell and Siegfried Giedion, both of whom use technology as their primary emphasis.

Sources relating the social context of kitchen and housekeeping artifacts are more difficult to evaluate. The studies listed here, such as those by Jane Carson, Marjorie Kreidberg, Frances Phipps, and Audrey Noël Hume, connect the artifacts to food and food-related activities in certain regions during specific times. Other authors view the objects in the context of changing values and attitudes within the American home, including Ruth Cowan, Caroline Davidson, Susan Strasser, Harvey Green, and William and Deborah Andrews.

Numerous exhibition catalogues also involve kitchen artifacts, usually because of their material. *The American Hearth* and *Objects for Preparing Food* are included because of their excellent documentation, special emphasis on food-related artifacts, and unique perspectives.

The American Hearth: Colonial and Post-Colonial Cooking Tools. Exhibition catalogue. Binghamton, N.Y.: Cojac Printing for the Broome County Historical Society, 1976. Unpag.; 160 illustrations.

This catalogue surveys the many types of American cooking tools used for preparing food around the hearth. In the preface, collector and antiquarian DeVere Card, who provided many of the objects for the exhibition, describes major developments in fireplace and early stove cooking, baking, and fire starting. The 225 pieces of fireplace cooking equipment in the original exhibition were judged on their design and historical importance. Of these objects, 160 are illustrated, including andirons, broilers, cranes, griddles, spits, toasters, and numerous other forms. Lengthy captions describe each object's function, provenance, measurements, and unusual features or special design elements. While there is little attempt to place the artifacts into a broader cultural context, the catalogue provides an initial approach to organizing, documenting, and comparing the scores of generally anonymous pieces of fireplace cooking equipment that have survived.

Andrews, William D., and Deborah C. Andrews. "Technology and the Housewife in Nineteenth-Century America." *Women's Studies* 2, no. 3 (1974): 309–28. 6 illustrations.

The Andrewses examine the social significance of technology as it was introduced into the American home in the nineteenth century. They argue that the complex relationship between technology and the housewife was a reflection of greater changes in American society, especially the changing perceptions of women's roles. Evidence of the relationship between housework and mechanization from various types of popular writings is studied, with an emphasis on the contrasting symbols of home and factory, the cult of domesticity, the campaign to professionalize housekeeping, and the use of technology to help to elevate women's role in the home. The exhibits and activities at the women's buildings of the

1876 Centennial Exhibition are analyzed to illustrate these points further. Aimed at students and academics in the fields of women's studies, American studies, and sociology, this article combines popular literature, material culture, and social history.

Bailey, Beth. "Learning to Accept the Sewing Machine, 1854–74." *Henry Ford Museum and Greenfield Village Herald* 12, no. 2 (1983): 66–75. 15 illustrations.

Bailey describes attempts by manufacturers to make sewing machines not only acceptable to but also welcomed by American women (and their husbands) in the third quarter of the nineteenth century. At first viewed as an unfeminine activity and a threat to accepted home values and morals, sewing machines became increasingly respectable additions to the middle-class home through the late nineteenth century. Manufacturers emphasized their elegance and ease of operation, promising health and mental relaxation to the women who bought and used them. Not until they also became less expensive did families consider purchasing them, but such companies as Singer realized the value of effective marketing strategies that became so important as the competition between manufacturers intensified. Bailey uses extensive historical sources to describe public and manufacturers' attitudes toward sewing machines in the nineteenth century. Illustrations, including the machines and related advertisements, are from Henry Ford Museum and Greenfield Village. Easy to read, this article is aimed at a popular audience as well as more serious scholars.

Berney, Esther S. *A Collector's Guide to Pressing Irons and Trivets*. New York: Crown Publishers, 1977. 182 pp.; 358 illustrations, chronology, bibliography, index.

A more recent study of irons than A. H. Glissman's *Evolution of the Sad-Iron*, Berney's work is primarily a collectors' guide but with more effort to incorporate social history. She relates developments in ironing devices to changes in housework and American society, especially the transition from drudgery toward greater comfort, convenience, efficiency, and safety. Early irons, specialized irons and ironing devices, self-heating irons, tailor and laundry irons, and trivets are discussed. Additional sections include collectors' information on cleaning and displaying irons and a chronology of important iron inventions and developments in the world. Most irons included are indigenous to America, although a few foreign examples help to clarify how American ironing instruments evolved. Profuse illustrations with detailed captions include photographs of irons and a variety of graphic sources ranging from advertisements to patent records. Berney's guide is best used for documenting specific irons and their manufacture.

Carson, Jane. *Colonial Virginia Cookery: Procedures, Equipment, and Ingredients in Colonial Cooking*. Drawings by Linda Funk. 1968. Reprint. Williamsburg: Colonial Williamsburg Foundation, 1985. xxi + 145 pp.; illustrations, index.

Carson describes the foods, methods, and objects used in colonial Virginia cooking. Prepared in 1968, this study was undertaken to attain more accurate preservation and restoration and to enhance interpretation at Colonial Williamsburg. Primary sources are used extensively, especially cookbooks, travel accounts, and inventories. Specific chapters pertain to provisions and menus, a description of the Virginia kitchen, the fireplace and its equipment, baking and cooking methods, and food preservation. Historical recipes have been edited for modern use. Carson closely relates artifacts to specific foods and cooking methods. Illustrations are hand drawn from items in the Colonial Williamsburg collections. Although intended to aid Williamsburg in its overall presentation, the book covers a subject of broad interest and is aimed at a wide general audience that includes collectors, cooks, historians, and museum people.

Clark, Hyla M. *The Tin Can Book: The Can as Collectible Art, Advertising Art, and High Art*. New York: New American Library, 1977. 128 pp.; 261 black and white and color illustrated entries, bibliography.

Clark surveys the history of the tin can from the early nineteenth century to the present, both in its role in food storage and as the bearer of fine graphic design. A section on the history of the tin-plated canister, which includes information on various manufacturing and printing processes, is supplemented by contemporary photographs and renderings of the interiors of tin-can manufactories. A larger section illustrates many varieties of often brilliantly colored and fascinatingly designed tin containers sought by collectors today. Arranged by type, such as vegetable tins, coffee and tea containers, roly-poly tobacco tins, and peanut butter pails, each grouping of clear, detailed plates is preceded by a brief explanatory essay and captioned with measurements and additional information of particular interest to tin collectors. Information on modern canning processes is included.

Cooper, Grace Rogers. *The Sewing Machine: Its Invention and Development*. Washington, D.C.: Smithsonian Institution Press for the National Museum of History and Technology, 1976. ix + 238 pp.; 219 illustrations, appendixes, bibliography, indexes.

The sewing machine was considered the mechanical wonder of the nineteenth century and had wide appeal from the start. Although only a few companies were in business in the 1850s, by 1877 the number was well over 100. Cooper provides a compact history of sewing machine developments, beginning by tracing attempts to mechanize sewing and describing several of the earliest American patents, starting with John J. Greenough's on February 21, 1842. Chapters detail attempts to refine and perfect earlier machines, again drawing heavily on evidence provided by patents; comment on the sewing machine trust, formed in 1856; and discuss cheaper machines, many powered by hand and of unusual design. Copious appendixes include comments on commercial uses of sewing machines, lists of American sewing machine companies of the nineteenth century, illustrated catalogues of machines, outlines of styles, histories of companies, names of machines made in this century, chronological lists of patents, and biographies of key figures. This work is an expanded version of a study first published in 1968.

Cosentino, Geraldine, and Regina Stewart. *Kitchenware: A Guide for the Beginning Collector.* New York: Golden Press, 1977. 128 pp.; black and white and color illustrations, bibliography, index.

Kitchenware describes a variety of kitchen artifacts from the colonial period to the early twentieth century, concentrating on items that are marked or are the most collectible. The book is divided into several sections, each reporting about the use and history of a specific category of objects. Photographed pieces, representative of those most readily found in the market today, are identified in accompanying captions. Additional chapters give a brief history of the American kitchen, care for kitchenware, and ideas for displaying, purchasing, and collecting implements. As the title indicates, this book is aimed at collectors, but it could also prove valuable as a general survey and in identifying specific objects. Other sources must be consulted for more thorough history, documentation, and cultural context of these objects.

Cowan, Ruth Schwartz. *More Work for Mother: The Ironies of Household Technology from the Open Hearth to the Microwave.* New York: Basic Books, 1983. xiv + 257 pp.; 45 illustrations, bibliography, index.

This recent social history of housework drawn from Cowan's articles on the subject represents the most up-to-date scholarship in the field on the effects of industrialization on the American household. Following an analysis of preindustrial housework and domestic equipment, Cowan describes the massive change in housework and household technology from the second half of the nineteenth century to the mid twentieth. Throughout she argues that the effects of industrialization on housework increasingly separated men from women and that they did not decrease women's work, but shifted it to other forms of labor. Photographic essays between chapters further document the arguments. Cowan's use of primary and secondary sources is exhaustive; her annotated bibliography in itself is a valuable reference.

Davidson, Caroline. *A Woman's Work Is Never Done: A History of Housework in the British Isles, 1650–1950.* London: Chatto and Windus, 1982. vi + 250 pp.; 113 illustrations, appendix, bibliography, index.

Davidson studies the impact of the industrial revolution on housework in England between 1650 and 1950 and attempts to illustrate how housework offers insights into a society's values and cultural characteristics as well as its economic and industrial development. Contents of this clearly written and well-organized book are arranged thematically rather than chronologically. Sections describe technological developments in the use of water, gas, and electricity in the home,

cooking, heating, lighting, cleaning, laundering, the use of servants, time spent on housework, and women's attitudes toward housework. Primary sources are referred to extensively, and illustrations are profuse. Davidson's major interest (and thus, emphasis) is on English lower and middle classes of the seventeenth and eighteenth centuries, but this book's social history approach and overall framework may be relevant to the study of similar aspects of American domestic life.

Douglas, Diane M. "The Machine in the Parlor: A Dialectical Analysis of the Sewing Machine." *Journal of American Culture* 5, no. 1 (Spring 1982): 20–29. 10 illustrations.

Douglas examines the complex interplay between the sewing machine and nineteenth-century American attitudes and values. She argues that when the sewing machine entered the home, it brought into that private, female-dominated, and spiritual space part of the outer masculine world of power and industry. Primarily a tool used by women, the sewing machine became a focal point in debates over women's appropriate role and was preempted for arguments on both sides of the issue of women's liberation. Douglas uses contemporary texts and images to show how the machine was manipulated in debates over social issues, then turns to an analysis of the physical form of the sewing machine, indicating how patterns of reconciliation of social alternatives were paralleled in reconciliations of design alternatives.

Ewers, William, and H. W. Baylor. *Sincere's History of the Sewing Machine.* Phoenix, Ariz.: Sincere Press, 1970. 256 pp.; 239 illustrations, bibliography.

Ewers and Baylor describe the history of the sewing machine industry. Written by two people who worked in the industry at one time, this book presents a somewhat different viewpoint than that of museum curator Grace Rogers Cooper's *Sewing Machine.* Much of the information repeats that in Cooper's book, but Ewers and Baylor describe twentieth-century developments more extensively, with a strong emphasis on inventors and company history. Many of the photographs are of poor quality.

Franklin, Linda Campbell. *America in the Kitchen, from Hearth to Cookstove: An American Domestic History of Gadgets and Utensils Made or Used in America from 1700 to 1930, a Guide for Collectors.* Photographs by Paul Persoff. Florence, Ala.: House of Collectibles, 1976. xv + 271 pp.; 1,155 illustrations, appendixes, bibliography, index.

The subtitle of this volume is not quite accurate; it is not a history, but a dictionary that helps readers to identify various kitchen artifacts. The text is an alphabetical presentation of some 650 kitchen gadgets and utensils, each identified in boldface and defined and usually illustrated. For some entries Franklin also includes relevant quotations from period publications, a cursory account of varied forms of the object, or a more or less related recipe. Some categories—apple parers, chopping knives, egg beaters, graters, waffle irons, and a few others—are represented by a range of illustrations that demonstrate how varied different solutions to the same problem can be. Appendixes include comments on approximate values of each object in 1976, a table of patent numbers, and a guide to public collections where kitchen utensils can be seen. This book is richest in material from 1870 to 1930.

Giedion, Siegfried. "Mechanization Encounters the Household." In Siegfried Giedion, *Mechanization Takes Command: A Contribution to Anonymous History*, pp. 511–627. 1948. Reprint. New York: W. W. Norton, Norton Library, 1969. 106 illustrations.

Giedion was among the first historians to research the social and technological history of housework. This work explores the effects of mechanization and its relationship to the American home. Giedion justifies gaps in the text by explaining that it was difficult to track down sources for this study of "anonymous history." He argues that the mechanizing of housework between the mid nineteenth and mid twentieth centuries was not unlike that of industry, occurring first through the mechanization of various tools and then through the reorganization of the work process. His survey of this process includes the mechanization of the hearth, heating, and refrigeration; aids to the mechanical comfort of the home, especially those for cleaning; and the reorganization of the kitchen and of housework in general. His views must be regarded in the context of his time, when *automation* and *streamlining* were buzzwords both in industry and in the home. Despite gaps and occasional subjectivity, this is still a significant source on the technological and social history of housework. *See also* "American Furniture, 1820–1920"; "Plumbing, Heating, and Lighting."

Glissman, A. H. *The Evolution of the Sad-Iron*. Carlsbad, Calif.: By the author, 1970. 282 pp.; 387 illustrations.

Glissman surveys the evolution of irons made and used during the last 100 years. Supposedly the first of its kind, this book was written to identify specific irons for collectors. The author drew information from many primary sources and from other collectors. Each chapter describes specific types or origins of irons or ironing equipment. A brief introduction to each section is followed by several identified illustrations. Several trade catalogue excerpts, mostly from European sources, and many patents are included at the end. This is mainly a collector's guide, with no attempt to provide a cultural context for the tools.

Gould, Mary Earle. *The Early American House: Household Life in America, 1620–1850*. Rev. ed. Rutland, Vt.: Charles E. Tuttle Co., 1965. 152 pp.; illustrations, index.

Gould surveys the various domestic activities undertaken and artifacts used by early Americans. Because this book is the result of her hobby of collecting woodenware, tinware, and fireplace equipment, the illustrations and text mainly center around New England. Specific related chapters discuss antique kitchenware and how it was used, food and drink, and everyday life throughout the year. The text contains almost no documentation, and, although there is some attempt at dating, most objects and activities are grouped under such phrases as "early American" or "from the olden days." Gould provides some useful information about America's preindustrial economy, when the home and local community were centers of production. Recommended for general readers, this book should not be passed over by scholars, but must be supplemented with better-documented sources.

Gould, Mary Earle. *Early American Wooden Ware and Other Kitchen Utensils*. Rev. ed. Rutland, Vt.: Charles E. Tuttle Co., 1962. xii+243 pp.; approximately 130 illustrations, index.

This is a highly personal account of various types of woodenware and baskets made and used during America's "wooden age." When written, it was the best reference book on this subject and has served as a model and source for later works. The heavy New England emphasis reflects the nature of Gould's collection. Intended as a popular book for the layman and student, this book contains sections on authenticating woodenware, construction methods, tools, types of wood, and various categories of woodenware, including those related to food service, preparation, storage, and eating. It also includes a tangential chapter on the New England kitchen. Within these sections, Gould tries to distinguish origins, regional differences, use, and manufacture of numerous wooden items. Illustrations consist mainly of fuzzy groupings of objects from Gould's collection. This book is useful for helping beginners to identify and understand the range of wooden domestic objects in America's past; however, it is also simplistic, with mostly personal, nostalgic descriptions rather than serious attempts to document the objects with historical sources.

Green, Harvey. "Cleanliness and Godliness: The Tyranny of Housework." In Harvey Green, with the assistance of Mary-Ellen Perry, *The Light of the Home: An Intimate View of the Lives of Women in Victorian America*, pp. 59–92. New York: Pantheon Books, 1983. 21 illustrations, index.

Green combines social history with artifact analysis to reach a better understanding of the domestic life of middle-class women in the late nineteenth and early twentieth centuries. He argues that the domestic artifacts and common wares of the late nineteenth century are evidence of middle-class customs, ideals, and attitudes toward the home. In this chapter, he relates the nature of housework—cooking, cleaning, laundering, sewing, baking, and preserving—to middle-class values and the role of women in the society of the time. The domestic science movement, the relation of sewing to changing fashions, and the role of domestic servants are also mentioned. By comparing printed contemporary sources, diaries, and artifacts themselves, Green depicts the tension created in women's lives between advice and realities, a tension that was also reflected in American culture in general between 1870 and 1910. The text and illustrations are taken from a related exhibit at the Strong Museum and point to the affinity between museum artifacts, contemporary sources, and recent methods of social history. Illustrations, including advertisements and three-dimensional objects, are accompanied by lengthy captions and are usually related to a portion of the text. Written for a popular audience, this work might be considered somewhat generalized by some scholars. Its major contribution is its material culture approach.

Harrison, Molly. *The Kitchen in History.* New York: Charles Scribner's Sons, 1972. 142 pp.; 49 illustrations, 73 plates, bibliography, index.

The primary perspective of this work is British, and its time frame is quite broad, starting with prehistoric times and proceeding from Roman Britain through the Middle Ages to the twentieth century. Several primary sources have been used, but these, as well as most of the illustrations, are English. American kitchens are mentioned in the nineteenth and twentieth centuries, but the text is very sketchy. Various aspects of kitchens, housework, and domestic activities are surveyed, but most of the information is either too general or too specific (for example, Mrs. Beeton is quoted so often that one would think she was the only writer on domestic subjects in the nineteenth century). Although about English kitchens and written as a popular history, this book presents useful information for the student of American kitchens. However, a far more useful and insightful examination of this subject from a British perspective is Caroline Davidson's *Woman's Work Is Never Done.*

Hounshell, David A. "The Sewing Machine and the American System of Manufactures." In David A. Hounshell, *From the American System to Mass Production, 1800–1932: The Development of Manufacturing Technology in the United States,* pp. 66–123. Studies in Industry and Society, no. 4, edited by Glenn Porter. Baltimore: Johns Hopkins University Press with the Eleutherian Mills-Hagley Foundation, 1984. 26 illustrations.

In this scholarly historical study of the ways in which the sewing machine industry related to the evolution of mass production technology in nineteenth-century America, Hounshell argues that through woodworking, reapers, bicycles, automobiles, and sewing machines, this kind of technology was spread and improved by a close-knit network of key mechanics who originally worked in the armories. In this chapter, three different sewing machine companies are discussed, all of which began production during the 1850s. During this decade, each manufacturer could choose between available methods of hand and machine production. While the Wheeler and Wilson and Willcox and Gibbs companies began using modern mass-production techniques with ex-

perienced arms mechanics almost from the outset, Singer Manufacturing Company continued producing machines with extensive amounts of hand fitting and custom design for at least the next decade. Hounshell maintains that I. M. Singer's reputation as the sewing machine "giant" of the nineteenth century is not attributable to his use of advanced production technology, but to his superior marketing strategy. The book is superbly illustrated with period photographs and engravings.

Jones, Joseph C., Jr. *American Ice Boxes: A Book on the History, Collecting, and Restoration of Ice Boxes.* Humble, Tex.: Jobeco Books, 1981. ix+100 pp.; approximately 85 illustrations, bibliography.

Jones surveys the history of the icebox, including its major technological developments, manufacturers, and the related growth of the ice industry. He does not relate the refrigerator to any larger context, such as its tremendous significance in changing food and eating habits across the country. The bibliography reveals that most of his sources are recent trade publications and magazine articles, not sources of the period. Many of the numerous illustrations are from advertisements and trade catalogues of the mid nineteenth to early twentieth centuries, and some are of poor quality. Mainly geared toward collectors, *American Ice Boxes* includes sections on refrigerators as investments, where to find them, and how to refinish them. This book is a first step toward documenting a domestic artifact that has recently become highly collectible.

Ketchum, William C., Jr. *American Basketry and Woodenware: A Collector's Guide.* New York: Macmillan Publishing Co.; London: Collier Macmillan, 1974. ix+228 pp.; 83 illustrations, appendix, bibliography, index.

Ketchum surveys several of the major types of wooden objects and baskets made and used by various groups of immigrants in the United States. The first section describes the materials and uses of various baskets. The section on woodenware is divided into types of usage, such as tableware, cooking, washing, and ironing utensils, and dairy equipment. Descriptions of individual objects within each category emphasize their use, but Ketchum also tries to address their importance in daily life as well as their techniques of manufacture, guidelines for dating, places of origin, and availability to the modern collector. Illustrations consist of groupings of historical objects. The appended list of manufacturers provides some additional assistance in documenting these types of objects. Many references to primary sources are included. Several objects described in the book, such as maple-sugaring equipment, are rarely discussed in other secondary studies. However, the sketchiness and inconsistency of the descriptions keep this work from being more than a starting point on the subject.

Kreidberg, Marjorie. *Food on the Frontier: Minnesota Cooking from 1850 to 1900, with Selected Recipes.* St. Paul:

Minnesota Historical Society Press, 1975. viii + 313 pp.; illustrations, indexes.

Despite the regional and culinary references in the title, *Food on the Frontier* is an invaluable source for studying the cultural context of late nineteenth-century food-related artifacts and the kitchen. Intended as a regional study of Minnesota, this book also reflects the increasing similarity of food distribution, availability, and domestic activities across the country as America changed from a rural, agrarian country to an urban, industrial nation. Making major use of primary sources, especially from the rich collections at Minnesota Historical Society, Kreidberg describes various aspects of food and food-related activities in the home from the mid nineteenth to the early twentieth centuries. A lengthy chapter on kitchens and "kitchenry" provides insightful descriptions of furnishings and equipment, especially stoves and refrigerators. Numerous woodcuts and engravings are intended to clarify the text, but they are not identified and serve mainly as border decoration. The text is straightforward and well footnoted and is appropriate for both a popular and a scholarly audience.

Lantz, Louise K. *Old American Kitchenware, 1725–1925.* Camden, N.J., and New York: Thomas Nelson; Hanover, Pa.: Everybodys Press, 1970. 289 pp.; illustrations, bibliography, index.

Lantz surveys American kitchenware from the eighteenth to the early twentieth century; however, the great bulk of the material ranges between about 1870 and 1925. In the first three chapters Lantz gives general and sketchy descriptions of what eighteenth-century, Victorian, and early twentieth-century kitchens looked like. Her examination of individual objects is more useful; however, her treatment of the subject is so vast, the objects or images of objects so available, and the topic so unexplored that at best this volume amounts to notes toward a history. The range of goods examined includes apple parers and cherry stoners, bedwarmers and footwarmers, bottle and can openers, brooms and rug beaters, butter churns, molds, and cutters, coffee roasters and grinders, eggbeaters and cream whippers, graniteware, hornware, ice accessories, ironing boards, and so on alphabetically through nearly two dozen more categories. Many of the illustrations are from period advertisements and trade catalogues, and the text does little more than repeat or describe what is visible in these images. This work should be used only as a descriptive introduction to the material.

Lasansky, Jeannette. *Willow, Oak, and Rye: Basket Traditions in Pennsylvania.* University Park: Pennsylvania State University Press for Union County Oral Traditions Projects, a Keystone Book, 1978. 60 pp.; illustrations, bibliography, index.

In this study of the types of farm and household utility baskets made and used in nineteenth- and early twentieth-century Pennsylvania, Lasansky gives an overview of the basketmaking traditions brought to the state, provides new insight into the life and craft of the basketmaker, and takes a detailed look at construction methods that points to regional variations in design and technique. She examines the material, form, and function of baskets made from peeled and unpeeled willow, round and splint oak, and coiled rye straw. The text is heavily illustrated with crisp black and white photographs of baskets and of contemporary and old-time basketmakers at their work. Lasansky's book is a useful model for further research on baskets and their makers in given geographic regions.

Lifshey, Earl. *The Housewares Story: A History of the American Housewares Industry.* Chicago: National Housewares Manufacturers, 1973. 384 pp.; black and white and color illustrations, index.

Lifshey traces the complex development and organization of the housewares industry. Not so much a history of objects as of the people and companies who made major contributions to the industry, the book contains sections on prehistoric cooking utensils, markets, changing patterns of distribution, the evolution of the kitchen, bathroom wares, electricity, housecleaning, "gadgets," and plastics. The text is richly illustrated, although the captions are often general. Because this book was intended to "celebrate" the modern housewares industry, it is often subjective, and its contents are geared to its members. Some topics are extremely general (for example, a section in the chapter on the evolution of the kitchen titled "From 1800 to 1900" is only one paragraph), while other subjects, because they have major significance in the modern industry, are overemphasized (the section on bathroom scales is one and one-half pages long). The last 100 years are heavily stressed, while earlier history is vague. Nevertheless, the exhaustive descriptions of major inventions, companies, and technological developments of such products as enamelware and aluminum are extremely valuable. The overall text, subjective as it is, confirms the tremendous changes that took place in the technology, materials, production, distribution, and marketing of household goods.

Lynes, Russell. "The Kitchen." In *The Domesticated Americans*, pp. 115–37. New York: Harper and Row, 1963. 14 illustrations, index.

Lynes surveys some of the major developments in and popular attitudes toward the kitchen from the nineteenth century to the mid twentieth century, with a heavy emphasis on the late nineteenth. Some aspects of the kitchen are covered in great detail, such as developments in cookstoves, refrigeration, food availability, and window screens, but others are completely lacking, are vague, or are covered briefly, such as kitchen arrangements and furnishings. Lynes uses a social history approach, but writes in a popular style for a general audience, making for enjoyable reading.

Minhinnick, Jeanne. "Kitchens"; "Cooking and Heating"; "Keeping Clean." In Jeanne Minhinnick, *At Home in Upper Canada*, pp. 51–70, 89–100, 101–14.

Toronto and Vancouver: Clarke, Irwin, 1970. Illustrations.

Minhinnick presents an account of domestic life and furnishings in upper Canada from pioneer settlement to the confederation (1867). Combining historical sources and personal reminiscences, she describes changing tastes, activities, and artifacts related to cooking, heating, and various aspects of housework. Specific topics include the location and arrangement of the kitchen, kitchen equipment and furnishings, food preservation, developments in fireplace and stove cooking, housecleaning, laundering, personal cleanliness, and the evolution of plumbing devices and the bathroom. Artifacts are often placed within a broader cultural context, especially relating to early industrialization and changing modes of distribution. Several photographs and drawings illuminate the text, primarily from historic sites in upper Canada. This is one of the few books pertaining to domestic artifacts and activities in the Canadian home. It is, unfortunately, difficult to distinguish between conclusions drawn from historical sources and those derived from Minhinnick's often nostalgic personal viewpoint. *See also* "Domestic Architecture."

Noël Hume, Audrey. *Food.* Colonial Williamsburg Archaeological Series no. 9. Williamsburg: Colonial Williamsburg Foundation, 1978. 68 pp.; 44 illustrations.

Noël Hume uses archaeological evidence to expand the knowledge of food ways in Colonial Williamsburg. This ninth monograph of the popular Colonial Williamsburg Archaeological Series compares the physical remains of food and containers with historical documentation to draw some conclusions about their origins and use. Meal components, food-preservation methods, various kinds of foods, and kitchen equipment are discussed. This work points out the strong relationship between food, methods of preparing it, and food-related artifacts. Both the photographs of excavated materials and the comparative historical illustrations help to elucidate the text and provide visual documentation of many objects that have rarely survived today. *Food* is geared toward the popular audience, but is also useful to scholars, archaeologists, and museum staff.

Norwak, Mary. *Kitchen Antiques.* New York: Praeger Publishers, 1975. 135 pp.; black and white and color plates, index.

Kitchen Antiques describes various types of kitchen equipment from a collector's point of view. Norwak believes that through kitchen antiques (defined in the book as those objects made before World War I), one can trace economic developments, the changing face of fashion, and relationships between rural and urban cultures within and between countries; however, these complex concepts actually are only touched on within the book. Specific chapters discuss fireplace and cooking equipment, kitchen furniture (including much tangential information on Windsor chairs, apparently of special interest to Norwak), the dairy, laundry, housecleaning, storage and preservation, molds, cutters and serving

equipment, labor-saving devices, convenience foods, and cleaning materials (two subjects rarely discussed in collector's guides). A separate section describes primary sources for documenting kitchen artifacts. The emphasis of the text is primarily British, although many American innovations are discussed, especially in the chapter on labor-saving devices. Most of the illustrated objects and advertisements are from British and American museums, chosen to help collectors to identify some of the more unusual objects.

Objects for Preparing Food. Exhibition catalogue. Washington, D.C.: Renwick Gallery of the National Collection of Fine Arts, Smithsonian Institution; New York: Museum of Contemporary Crafts of the American Crafts Council, 1972. Unpag.; 244 illustrations.

Renwick Gallery and Museum of Contemporary Crafts collaborated on the preparation of this catalogue and associated exhibition exploring cross-cultural relationships and differences through a comparison of food preparation objects and related environments. Objects are grouped according to specialized operations, such as heating, chilling, cutting, mixing, measuring, and forming, so that visual comparisons can be made between the varied utensils. Selections include manufactured and handcrafted contemporary and historical objects from America, Europe, and the Orient as well as from primitive cultures. Short essays that explain the function and various aspects of each food-preparing operation are accompanied by groups of identified illustrations. A sketchy section describes food-preparing environments of various cultures and periods and presents a somewhat confusing analysis of structural changes by an environmental designer. The essays tend toward the philosophical, but it is always valuable to take a step back from our scrutiny of American historical artifacts to assess their significance within a broader context, against both other cultures and contemporary society. The catalogue is a thought-provoking publication that is intended for the general public, designers, members of the housewares industry, historians, and museum people.

Phipps, Frances. *Colonial Kitchens, Their Furnishings, and Their Gardens.* New York: Hawthorn Books, 1972. xxii+346 pp.; black and white illustrations, color plates, glossaries, bibliography, index.

This highly readable description of colonial kitchens and their accompanying gardens as they developed in seventeenth- and eighteenth-century America contains an occasionally confusing mixture of historical materials on early settlements, accounts of kitchen furnishings, a survey of major colonial foods and garden features, and kitchen activities other than those related to food, such as dyeing and candlemaking. Phipps uses numerous primary sources, especially journals, diaries, and estate inventories. A glossary of common utensils, beverages, and foods and illustrations of surviving kitchen implements are included. Illustrations are not identified. The book provides comprehensive information for people trying to restore and recreate kitchens in historic homes.

Russell, Loris S. *Handy Things to Have around the House.* Toronto, Montreal, and New York: McGraw-Hill Ryerson, 1979. 176 pp.; 167 illustrations, bibliography, indexes.

Handy Things surveys nineteenth-century domestic appliances in the United States and Canada. Some of Russell's text belabors the obvious, as in his discussion of fire and fuel—"Logs were chopped or sawn to lengths somewhat less than the width of the fireplace" (p. 13)—but other discussions deal with less familiar practices and artifacts. In six chapters the book covers the fireplace, the cooking stove, objects for preparing food, lighting, artifacts related to textiles and clothing, and implements for household cleaning. Russell's surveys of objects for food preparation and cleaning are particularly useful. Not a history in the usual sense, the text moves rapidly and does little more than identify items and explain their functions. This book perhaps best serves as a guide to explain the uses of these gadgets and when they came into use.

Stephenson, Sue H. *Basketry of the Appalachian Mountains.* New York, Cincinnati, and Toronto: Van Nostrand Reinhold Co., 1977. 112 pp.; 129 illustrations, 41 plates, bibliography, index.

Stephenson describes and preserves the rapidly disappearing specialized craft technology and the history of Appalachian basketry, which was originally brought to the area by British immigrants. The book combines historical information, ethnological insights from Stephenson's personal experience, and practical instructions. Specific sections of the book include basket terminology; uses and origins of common baskets, particularly those for storing and transporting things; preparation of materials; instructions for making baskets; guidelines for cleaning and conserving old baskets; advice to collectors on finding, purchasing, and pricing baskets; and sources for supplies in making them. Illustrations involve photographs of historical and contemporary Appalachian baskets with accompanying text and clear diagrams for their construction. Like Lasansky's *Willow, Oak, and Rye*, this book documents a distinct regional basket style.

Strasser, Susan. *Never Done: A History of American Housework.* New York: Pantheon Books, 1982. xvi+365 pp.; illustrations, index.

Never Done traces the history of American housework from colonial times to the present. Through a description of household chores and technology, Strasser demonstrates how post–Civil War industrialization transformed the nature of women's work while altering women's daily lives and their relationships. She argues, from a feminist point of view, that the idea of "women's separate sphere," so emphasized by writers and reformers of the nineteenth century, was declining by the early twentieth century. Woman's place is continually stressed within the context of women's history

and the liberation movement. Strasser's subjectivity in this respect occasionally overshadows her excellent research. General subjects of housework are covered, as are more unusual subjects rarely discussed in other sources, such as boarding-house keeping, domestic service, consumerism, and the role of supermarkets and fast food in changing women's roles. This book is detailed and uses a wide variety of written and visual sources. *Never Done* is intended as a popular history, but it is also useful to scholars interested in labor, technology, social history, and women's studies.

Teleki, Gloria Roth. *The Baskets of Rural America.* New York: E. P. Dutton, 1975. xx+202 pp.; 20 illustrations, 74 illustrated entries, bibliography, index.

——. *Collecting Traditional American Basketry.* New York: E. P. Dutton, 1979. xxiii+131 pp.; 83 illustrations, 19 color plates, bibliography, index.

Teleki's two books provide a general survey of the types of American basket sought by today's collectors. The first provides information on construction techniques, including technical diagrams of weaving and stitching patterns, then moves on to examinations of baskets grouped by their ethnic or regional origins. The text attempts to place the baskets in their historical and functional context and is accompanied by a large section of photographic illustrations of various basket forms and types. The sequel fills in gaps in the first work and incorporates new research. Both books survey baskets of the nineteenth and twentieth centuries, many of recent manufacture. The text for both is largely derived from other published material and Teleki's own collecting experience.

Toulouse, Julian Harrison. *Fruit Jars: A Collectors' Manual.* Rev. ed. Nashville: Thomas Nelson; Hanover, Pa.: Everybodys Press, 1972. 542 pp.; 900 illustrations, glossary.

Toulouse outlines the technological and stylistic developments in the glass fruit-jar industry. The majority of the book is actually a chronology—in effect, a catalogue of different jar types organized according to their marks. Each catalogue entry contains a description of the marks, type of seal, approximate date, color, maker, and remarks. Additional chapters discuss famous innovators in fruit-jar history, changes in technology, methods of dating, patent chronology, and an explanation of glassmaking techniques in fruit jars. Toulouse includes a large section on seals (his major interest), an index of makers, and definitions and terms. This collector's guide covers one of the few classes of kitchen artifacts that are usually marked and can be documented.

Tyler, John D. "Eighteenth- and Nineteenth-Century Cast-Iron Cooking Utensils." *Early American Life* 9, no. 2 (April 1978): 29–31. 12 illustrations.

——. "Technological Development: Agent of Change in Style and Form of Domestic Iron Castings." In *Technological Innovation and the Decorative Arts*, edited by Ian M. G. Quimby and Polly Anne Earl, pp. 141–

65. Winterthur Conference Report 1973. Charlottesville: University Press of Virginia for the Henry Francis du Pont Winterthur Museum, 1974. 13 illustrations.

These two articles, one geared toward collectors and the other toward scholars, study the stylistic changes in cast-iron wares resulting from technological developments in the iron industry. The majority of each article is devoted to stylistic changes in pot and kettle legs, ears, general forms, and mold marks. Tyler also discusses the differences between fireplace and cookstove pots that result from the difference in cooking surfaces and the increasing mechanization in the iron production process. His 1978 article also contains advice on cleaning and caring for pots, while his earlier paper contains more information on the iron industry, European prototypes, and methods of documenting cast-iron pots, kettles, and early stoves and stove plates. Like Frank White's article on tin kitchens, Tyler provides a framework for a whole range of usually anonymous kitchen artifacts by documenting and analyzing a few specific examples.

White, Frank G. "Reflections on a Tin Kitchen." *Chronicle of the Early American Industries Association* 36, no. 3 (September 1983): 45–48, 61. 9 illustrations.

The tin reflector oven, or "tin kitchen," was one of the few specialized devices to be used for both stove and fireplace cooking. An important and innovative device for roasting, it almost completely replaced the open spit in America in the early and mid nineteenth century. White traces the history of the marked tin-reflector oven to gain a better understanding of its overall significance in the American kitchen. Through thorough and painstaking research with primary sources, he reveals rich documentation of tin reflector ovens and the closely related tin bakers. This article points out how, when properly researched, one or a few marked items can provide insight into an entire category of objects that had previously been mentioned only generally in collectors' books.

Plumbing, Heating, and Lighting

Ulysses Grant Dietz

This chapter covers what in today's architectural jargon is known as "systems." Modern architecture is essentially the skin that masks the innards of the electrical, climate-control, and plumbing systems of a building. In fact, modern building is far more akin to the human body than seventeenth- or eighteenth-century architecture, where systems were ancillary and usually not integrated into the body of the structure. Since the mid nineteenth century we have become so used to living with systems that comparatively little attention has been focused on how colonial, federal, and early Victorian America dealt with provisions for sanitation, heat, and light. Certain objects—andirons, mantels, chamber pots, and candlesticks—received attention after the rise of the colonial revival, but it was largely from a stylistic or an antiquarian point of view. Today the typical period room has an inordinate number of elegant candlesticks for even a wealthy family, and the mundane purpose of a rare Chinese export *bourdalou* or even rarer American pewter bedpan is often not made part of that object's interpretation. Charles F. Montgomery regaled his students with a story of selling a rare silver object to a collector, only to have her call him in a panic when she discovered that her flower-filled centerpiece was a bidet pan. Such is the seemingly willful ignorance that has veiled the artifacts of plumbing, heating, and lighting well into the twentieth century.

With the growing interdisciplinary focus of decorative arts studies, the social history of objects has become as vital as their aesthetic interest. This trend is reflected in the body of writings that have appeared in the last two decades. Lighting, because of the great number of surviving artifacts, has the largest body of work surrounding it and has the earliest scholarly origins; heating follows, and plumbing trails with a handful of publications covering its complex social and material history. It is not surprising that the scholarship on plumbing is of a more sophisticated overall quality, precisely because interest in the subject is more academic than aesthetic or antiquarian. Lighting has been more prone to amateur scholarship and popular writing. Heating falls between: studies of the objects are often far more superficial than are attempts to trace heating customs over time. The quality and content of the literature on heat and light varies enormously, and works of varying quality will be included here.

Ironically the most sophisticated discussion of plumbing is also the earliest: Siegfried Giedion's chapters on the bathroom in his 1948 *Mechanization Takes Command*. Giedion's complex philosophical approach to plumbing, part of his larger view of the mechanization of life, is also the least useful in many ways in understanding the development of indoor plumbing. Lawrence Wright's *Clean and*

Decent manages to be both scholarly and entertaining, covering toilet habits from Mesopotamia to modern times, as if it were tracing the adventures of some picaresque hero. Most of the plumbing scholars are, like Wright, British, probably because of England's importance in sanitation history. Roy Palmer's *Water Closet* is akin to Wright's, although less amusing, and Lucinda Lambton's *Temples of Convenience* is a slick, exhibition catalogue–like book that covers the same material in a condensed version. Wallace Reyburn's *Flushed with Pride* is more popular and suffers from being self-consciously cute, but is nonetheless a useful monograph on a famous British plumber. The brief article by R. Rhoades is included because it discusses an aspect of plumbing not dealt with elsewhere. Two American authors who have contributed to plumbing scholarship are May Stone, whose article in *Winterthur Portfolio* focuses on American plumbing history, and David Handlin, who includes a discussion of plumbing (and other household systems) in *American Home*. These last two are especially important because of the New World perspective they impart.

Heating scholarship dates as far back as 1914, with Henry Mercer's *Bible in Iron*. The revised and enlarged edition of 1961 remains a polished scholarly work, but it is of limited use due to its in-depth yet narrow focus on pre-1800 American cast-iron stove plates. The next efforts at tracing heating history date from the early 1950s. Charles Peterson's article on coal burning in fireplaces in colonial America is a valuable fragment, and Josephine Peirce's book on heating stoves remains the most scholarly and sweeping text on the history and design of stoves. Will and Jane Curtis's book is a good pictorial companion to Peirce's work, but it does not add much that is new from a scholar's viewpoint. Tammis Groft's excellent exhibition catalogue on Albany stove manufacturers is the most recent work done on stoves. It gives a geographically "local" viewpoint, which is nonetheless broadly applicable because of Albany's national importance as a stove center. Benjamin Walpert's and Eugene Ferguson's articles on central heating present important historical material but, in contrast with the less academic Peirce and Curtis books, are object poor.

This dichotomy in heating scholarship—theoretical and historical versus object-oriented stylistic analysis—is more apparent in the literature on fireplace equipment. Vrest Orton's strange homage to Count Rumford is a surprisingly complete technical manual on eighteenth-century fireplace building, while Henry Kauffman's books on fireplace equipment focus more on the design and fabrication of objects. In neither case is much attention given to the social history of fireplaces. Paul Revere Ladd's work, although an object book, does zero in on the social history of fireplace use, but its style is such that it seems antiquated and unacademic despite its correct premises. Bradford Rauschenberg's article on Charleston-made brass andirons is a classic example of careful, focused, in-depth object scholarship, but its usefulness is as limited as Mercer's equally lucid stove book.

Lighting is the most complex area of the three systems. Because its development occurred largely in the nineteenth century, when America moved from rushlights to light bulbs, careful analysis of lighting history is only fairly recent. Arthur Hayward's *Colonial Lighting*, a pioneering book in 1927, is now antiquated and is almost useless for a neophyte, but it demonstrates how much raw material was known even then. Although it is important as the first major work to deal with lighting, its flaws plagued all decorative arts scholarship at the time. Walter Hough's 1928 Smithsonian publication and Frederick Robins's 1939 book are similar to Hayward's effort (especially in the use of terrible photographs), but the latter is remarkably sophisticated, and Robins manages to cover his worldwide historical survey in a way that today's students would find helpful. These works all focus on technological history rather than stylistic change and yet do not give as much a sense of light-related social custom as Marshall Davidson's 1944 article for the *Metropolitan Museum of Art Bulletin*. By 1952 Bertram and Nina Little, as well as Malcolm Watkins, produced excellent articles giving solid sociohistorical background in lighting use through careful documentary research. Leroy Thwing's classic *Flickering Flames* (1958) and Larry Freeman's *Light on Old Lamps* (1955) are both too old-fashioned and amateurish for their dates and yet are considered standard American sources. William O'Dea's 1958 social history of lighting is, on the other hand, urbane, scholarly, and as fresh now as it was on publication. It provides the best overview of lighting's effect on human life. Lighting scholarship in America has had a hard time shaking off the antiquarian mantle of the 1920s. Not until Joseph Butler's 1965 chapter on lighting in his larger work on American antiques is there a lucid (although brief) attempt to combine correct technological history with stylistic analysis, and even this effort does not turn to social history. In his 1967 work on lighting, dealing with candlesticks, Butler does a fine job of combining the technological and stylistic, far better than the privately published book on candlesticks by John Grove, which is nonetheless useful because it shows numerous objects.

Loris Russell's *Heritage of Light* is probably the best overall book on lighting today. Russell coalesces technology, stylistic concern, and social history into one readable package. The wisdom of this book is condensed in his chapter in *Building Early America*. Catherine Thuro's recent books on kerosene lamps are more collector's handbooks than scholarly studies, but her work on glassmaking firms is important. Other seemingly narrow studies that have broader application are Denys Myers's top-notch work on gas-lighting and my own book on Dietz and Company of New York. Myers provides excellent technological, stylistic, and sociohistorical material. While less interested in technology, my study of the Dietz firm covers stylistic development and the social history of lighting in nineteenth-century America in depth, creating a cultural context in which to understand mid Victorian domestic lighting.

The most abstract writing on lighting and heating comes from Reyner Banham's *Architecture of the Well-Tempered Environment*. This academic and theoretical volume is useful largely as background, but it is important—like Giedion's writing—for its broader, non-object-bound perspective. Writers like Banham and Giedion are technological historians, not decorative arts writers. Their work represents the most highly intellectualized scholarship in the fields of plumbing, heating, and lighting, while the various recent books and articles focusing on night-lights, andirons, or specific manufacturing firms represent the more pragmatic side of decorative arts research—the identification, attribution, and understanding of objects and how they were used.

All the titles included in this chapter provide something useful for a researcher. Even outdated works have good information and are often documents of the history of scholarship itself. Whether they are theoretical, technical, or style oriented, a variety of works needs to be used to obtain a relatively complete overall view of the systems outlined here. More work needs to be done on the cultural and sociohistorical aspects of plumbing, heating, and lighting. Several important starts have been made, but there is much we have yet to understand about how and why the objects relating to household systems were used, and by whom.

PLUMBING

Giedion, Siegfried. "The Bath in the Nineteenth Century"; "The Bathroom Becomes Mechanized." In Siegfried Giedion, *Mechanization Takes Command: A Contribution to Anonymous History*, pp. 659–706. 1948. Reprint. New York: W. W. Norton, Norton Library, 1969. 39 illustrations.

Giedion's sociological analyses of bathroom evolution and bathing attitudes in the nineteenth and early twentieth centuries outline the influence of industry and mechanization as they hampered development of humanized equipment and related systems up to 1900 and as they ultimately promoted the invention of the "bath cell," or compact bathroom, by 1915 in America. He also discusses the use of the bath and shower as therapeutic and regenerative agents by the various hydropathic movements in the nineteenth century. Growing concern for public hygiene is considered the motivating force in the emergence of public and domestic bathing facilities. The effects of the bathroom on architectural plans are described, comparing especially the United States and England. *See also* "American Furniture, 1820–1920"; "Kitchen Artifacts and Housework."

Handlin, David P. "The Heart of the Home." In David P. Handlin, *The American Home: Architecture and Society, 1815–1915*, pp. 452–86. Boston: Little, Brown, 1979. Illustrations.

Handlin discusses the ambivalence of late nineteenth-century Americans toward the intrusion of modern systems into the sanctum of the home. The earth-closet campaign of George Waring's and J. P. Putnam's ventilating fireplace experiments are two examples that demonstrate the concern Americans felt about the possible ill side effects produced by plumbing and central-heating systems as they developed in the 1870s and 1880s. Handlin suggests how systems altered the way buildings were designed and the way people lived in them.

Lambton, Lucinda. *Temples of Convenience*. London: Gordon Fraser, 1978. 58 pp.; 112 color plates, bibliography.

The brief text covers the entire history of the toilet from ancient Rome, to Harington's first flush toilet of 1596, to Cummings's patent closet in 1775, when water-closet history commences. A historic survey of urban sanitary problems from the Middle Ages through the nineteenth century is documented with period citations. Bathtubs and washbasins are briefly noted, while the decorative aspects of plumbing fixtures are considered at some length. The bulk of the volume consists of color plates with detailed captions.

Palmer, Roy. *The Water Closet: A New History*. Newton Abbot: David and Charles, 1973. 141 pp.; 5 illustrations, 29 plates, bibliography, index.

Palmer begins with a brief but complete overview of sanitary facilities from ancient Egypt to the eighteenth century. His main thrust is on the development of the toilet and on the people who were instrumental in the process. A chronological approach is taken, starting with Harington's 1596 *Metamorphosis of Ajax*, which described the first flush toilet. Each technical version of the water closet is considered separately, and American usage is noted. Major manufacturers of sanitary wares (Twyfords, Doulton) and their history are covered, as are the founders of the American sanitary industry (such as the Maddockses in Trenton). The vagaries of the American toilet-bowl market, as well as the technical problems of toilet production, are outlined. Final chapters discuss the development of the tank or cistern and actual application of toilet facilities in public and private buildings, both in America and abroad.

Reyburn, Wallace. *Flushed with Pride: The Story of Thomas Crapper*. Englewood Cliffs, N.J.: Prentice-Hall, 1971. 95 pp.; illustrations.

Although general plumbing history is touched on, *Flushed with Pride* is essentially a monograph of a major English plumbing contractor and his work. Reyburn traces Crapper's life from his birth as a poor Yorkshire boy, through childhood plumbing apprenticeship, to ultimate success as the sanitary engineer to the Royal Family in London. The monograph focuses on his development of a water-waste-preventing cistern for the water closet, a quiet-flush mechanism, and other bathroom-related patents. His work for the Royal Family and his professional ties with the Twyfords sanitary-ware makers are explored. Ancillary chapters discuss the history of toilet paper and worldwide toilet-related euphemisms.

Rhoades, R. "Plumber's Tools for Lead Work." *Chronicle of the Early American Industries Association* 22, no. 3 (September 1969): 44–47. 16 illustrations.

Rhoades records the basic tools and operations involved in plumbing work done with lead pipes (soldering, joint wiping, bending, and beating). With the advent of copper, brass, and steel piping, the tools and techniques have become obsolete. This article preserves the information for posterity.

Stone, May N. "The Plumbing Paradox: American Attitudes toward Late Nineteenth-Century Domestic Sanitary Arrangements." *Winterthur Portfolio* 14, no. 3 (Autumn 1979): 283–309. 21 illustrations.

This work is important because of its focus on American usage and application of plumbing. Stone starts with a brief and lucid overview of plumbing history from ancient times to the nineteenth century. She discusses the development of waterworks in America and its direct influence on the creation of indoor plumbing. Sanitary manufacturing in all its phases is outlined, including pipes, sinks, hot-water heaters, and toilets. A strong emphasis is placed on the social history of plumbing; reformist movements and sanitary concerns in America and England are compared. The evolution of New York's water and sewerage systems is presented, with detailed discussion of the workings of effective domestic drainage systems as they appeared in England and America. Stone shows how the floor plans of New York row houses were adapted to the inroads of plumbing from 1830 to 1890. Kitchen-related plumbing is also covered.

Wright, Lawrence. *Clean and Decent: The Fascinating History of the Bathroom and the Water Closet and of Sundry Habits, Fashions, and Accessories of the Toilet, Principally in Great Britain, France, and America.* New York: Viking Press, 1960. xii+281 pp.; approximately 275 illustrations, bibliography, index.

Wright covers in great detail the entire history of the bathroom, from the palace of Knossos at Crete to the twentieth century. The first six chapters deal with ancient times through the Renaissance and provide historical background documenting sanitary arrangements throughout Europe. Chapters 7 through 18 are more relevant to American usage, beginning with a discussion of bathing in seventeenth- and eighteenth-century England and proceeding from the Cummings water-closet patent of 1775 to the rise of the modern bathroom. Such diverse topics as sanitary-related furniture (washstands, bidet cabinets), public-health movements, the development of the shower, and various flush mechanisms are considered individually. Although Wright focuses on England, American custom is noted, and application to this country is fairly straightforward. Final chapters include the history of soap, shaving equipment, toothbrushes, and towels.

HEATING

Cast with Style: Nineteenth-Century Cast-Iron Stoves from the Albany Area. Introduction and catalogue by Tammis Kane Groft; foreword by John J. Mesick. Exhibition catalogue. Albany: Albany Institute of History and Art, 1981. 101 pp.; 113 illustrations, appendix, bibliography.

Cast with Style is a regional exhibition catalogue with application for the entire United States. An essay, subdivided into long paragraphs by bold headings for quick reference, outlines the history of the stove and iron industry in the United States and the Albany and Troy region, beginning with jamb stoves in the 1720s and covering all facets through the late nineteenth century. Manufacturing methods, labor unions, fuels, and design are all touched on. The catalogue is divided into sections by type chronologically—for example, Franklin, box, parlor-column, and soapstone stoves. Sections on toy stoves, stove-related equipment, and cooking stoves are included. Appendixes list Albany and Troy stovemaking firms. Photographs are supplemented with reproductions of period advertising.

Curtis, Will, and Jane Curtis. *Antique Woodstoves: Artistry in Iron.* Ashville, Maine: Cobblesmith, 1974. 63 pp.; 202 illustrations.

This picture book begins with a brief historical sketch of stove use and production. Photographs are arranged in chapters chronologically by stove type (such as jamb, six-plate, ten-plate, Franklin, and column stoves) and again chronologically within each chapter. Historical background on each type is given, and captions provide pertinent data on every stove. Changing technology and manufacturing processes are noted. A chapter on cooking stoves is included.

Ferguson, Eugene S. "An Historical Sketch of Central Heating, 1800–1860." In *Building Early America*, edited by Charles E. Peterson, pp. 165–85. Radnor, Pa.: Chilton Book Co. for the Carpenters' Company of the City and County of Philadelphia, 1976. 19 illustrations.

Ferguson discusses the technological developments as well as the popular and scientific theories that played vital roles in the growth of "modern" heating. The development of hot-air, steam, and hot-water systems is traced from the late eighteenth century through key figures in the United States and England like Benjamin Franklin, Jacob and Angier Perkins, and Joseph Nason. Conflicting theories and philosophies of ventilation and fresh air in the nineteenth century are underscored. Included is a history of the ventilation and heating system installed at the United States Capitol (1855–61) under Montgomery Miegs, which demonstrates the conflict between the dogma of an engineer-inventor and more humane considerations for comfort and convenience. Excellent technical and popular illustrations from period sources are accompanied by detailed captions.

Gould, Mary Earle. "Foot Stoves and More Foot Stoves." *Spinning Wheel* 24, no. 11 (November 1968): 26–28, 40. 18 illustrations.

This brief article deals with a wide variety of personal heating devices not covered elsewhere. Gould sketches the use of foot stoves from the eighteenth through the nineteenth centuries, until central heating rendered them obsolete. Wood-, coal-, and oil-burning versions as well as hot-water-heated examples are included.

Kauffman, Henry, and Quentin Bowers. *Early American Andirons and Other Fireplace Accessories*. New York: Thomas Nelson, 1974. 192 pp.; 132 illustrations, bibliography, index.

This text opens with outlines of andiron usage in America and the stylistic development of andiron design. Three chapters document the design, materials, and manufacture of andirons in America from Jamestown, Virginia, to the mid nineteenth century, with an emphasis on the period between 1750 and 1800. Kauffman and Bowers discuss production processes (iron and brass founding) from the earliest-known American-used examples (1607) and include biographical sketches of major known makers, such as Henry Shrimpton of the seventeenth century, John Bailey of the 1770s, and the Whittinghams of the federal period. Fenders and grates are covered in separate chapters, with remaining fireplace equipment arranged alphabetically in the final chapter. Many pairs of andirons are illustrated for comparison.

Kauffman, Henry J. *The American Fireplace: Chimneys, Mantelpieces, Fireplaces, and Accessories*. Introduction by Joe Kindig III. Nashville and New York: Thomas Nelson, 1972. 352 pp.; approximately 200 black and white illustrations, color plates, bibliography, index.

Kauffman presents a history of the development of the fireplace, arranged in chronological chapters from the seventeenth through the twentieth centuries. Separate chapters deal with iron fireplaces (Franklin stoves), chimney improvements (the work of Benjamin Franklin and Benjamin Thompson [Count Rumford]), chimney sweeps, and fireplace equipment. Kauffman covers the changing form and architectural effect of chimneys and fireplaces from the primitive wood or wattle and daub of early settlements to the brick and stone chimneys of the eighteenth century. He includes regional variation as well as ethnic influences (Dutch, German, Swedish) in house plans and fireplace customs, and he traces the growth of ornament on the fireplace and outlines the life of Robert Wellford, a celebrated plaster-ornament producer of the federal period. The twentieth-century section deals largely with constructing efficient fireplaces in today's homes.

Ladd, Paul Revere. *Early American Fireplaces*. New York: Hastings House, 1977. 192 pp.; 202 illustrations, bibliography, index.

Early American Fireplaces is divided into three sections. The first covers the uses and development of the kitchen fireplace, enumerating varied household activities that occurred near or in it. Such diverse topics as brickmaking, lighting, and pewter casting are discussed. The second part is a gallery of pictures of extant kitchen fireplaces with commentary on objects and construction. The third section lists and defines tools used for fireplace maintenance (such as andirons and firebacks) and the utensils for fireplace-related activities (such as cooking, baking, and ironing). The book has a glossary-like but nonalphabetical format.

Mercer, Henry C. *The Bible in Iron: Pictured Stoves and Stoveplates of the Pennsylvania Germans*. 3d ed. Revised, corrected, and enlarged by Horace H. Mann; further amendments and additions by Joseph E. Sandford. Doylestown, Pa.: Bucks County Historical Society, 1961. xvi+256 pp.; 409 illustrations, bibliography, indexes.

The frequency with which biblical scenes and religious iconography were depicted on these stoves inspired the book's title. Mercer's landmark volume, published originally in 1914, is notable for its in-depth coverage and scientific approach in its focus entirely on box-form stoves of the five-plate (jamb) and six-plate (draft) types used before 1800. The first chapter outlines the origins and use of plate stoves in Europe and discusses their manufacture, construction, decoration, and transmission to America. Early scholars and collectors (pre 1914) are noted, and the various designs found are enumerated. The second chapter documents European stoves used in America before 1659 and records early iron production in Pennsylvania, New York, and New Jersey. Construction and casting differences between Europe and America are noted. Mercer discusses the plate designs and their German biblical sources, a topic that is augmented by a detailed analysis in a complete chapter by Sandford. Six-plate stoves and firebacks are considered more briefly but with the same format. Grouped awkwardly at the back of the book are 137 pages of annotations to the text and complex plate descriptions.

Orton, Vrest. *The Forgotten Art of Building a Good Fireplace*. Dublin, N.H.: Yankee [Magazine], 1969. 60 pp.; 8 illustrations.

A biographical sketch of Benjamin Thompson, American-born Count Rumford, is followed by a discussion of his and Benjamin Franklin's observations on fireplace construction. Using Rumford's principles, final chapters provide insight into building an efficient, smokeless fireplace in the eighteenth-century fashion.

Peirce, Josephine H. *Fire on the Hearth: The Evolution and Romance of the Heating-Stove*. Springfield, Mass.: Pond-Eckberg Co., 1951. xv+254 pp.; 145 illustrations, appendixes, bibliography, index.

Pierce presents the first broad survey of stove heating in the

United States. Five roughly chronological chapters start with a history of hearths and fireplaces from the Middle Ages to the nineteenth century. Stoves are considered by type and material (tile, soapstone, box, Franklin, airtight). Peirce presents extensive documentary citations of stove use and history. The ancient world and Europe are used as historical background, but the emphasis is on America, both for use and manufacture. Domestic stoves are considered separately from public stoves, and the various technological influences on production (iron production, ventilation controls) are discussed. Appendixes provide lists of American iron furnaces and patents for stoves, and some nineteenth-century advertisements are reproduced.

Peterson, Charles E. "American Notes: Early House-Warming by Coal-Fires." *Journal of the Society of Architectural Historians* 9, no. 4 (December 1950): 21–24. 1 illustration.

Peterson outlines the shift in America from wood burning to coal burning as early as 1750 in more urbanized areas such as Boston and New York. He documents the importation, shipping, and mining of coal in America from about 1769, as well as the use of coal in domestic heating in the eighteenth century.

Rauschenberg, Bradford L. "A School of Charleston, South Carolina, Brass Andirons." *Journal of Early Southern Decorative Arts* 5, no. 1 (May 1979): 26–75. 36 illustrations.

Rauschenberg proves the existence of a unique Charleston regional style of andiron by means of a detailed stylistic and structural analysis of fourteen pairs of surviving examples. Objects are grouped chronologically from circa 1780 to circa 1815, according to his theory of design drift and transition over time. Brass founders in Charleston from 1735 to 1820 are documented by means of newspaper advertisements.

Walbert, Benjamin L. "The Infancy of Central Heating in the United States: 1803–1845." Association for Preservation Technology, *Bulletin* 3, no. 4 (1971): 76–87. 3 illustrations, bibliography.

Walbert explores the early development of and experimentation with hot-air and hot-water heating systems in public buildings, institutions, and factories in the United States. He discusses the earliest recorded experiments by Benjamin Latrobe to heat the Capitol in Washington from 1803 to 1826, as well as other documented uses of central heating in almshouses, prisons, banks, and asylums. The first fully centrally heated building in America (Massachusetts Medical College, 1816) is described and illustrated. Appended is a list of pre-1845 manufacturers.

LIGHTING

Banham, Reyner. "A Dark Satanic Century"; "The Kit of Parts: Heat and Light." In Reyner Banham, *The Architecture of the Well-Tempered Environment*, pp. 29–44, 45–70. Chicago: University of Chicago Press, 1969. 4 illustrations, 11 illustrations.

Banham expresses concern with the changes in and effects of "environmental technology" (light, heat, and ventilation) from the mid nineteenth century to World War I. His works trace technical realities and theoretical perspectives from gas-lighting in the 1850s to the birth of electric light and its long infancy before 1900. There is a detailed discussion of electric light in the 1880–1910 years and its effect on architects and their buildings. Heating and ventilating are handled similarly, with technology and hygienic philosophy considered from early in the nineteenth century to the advent of embryonic air-conditioning after 1900. The background of lighting and heating history is briefly covered.

Butler, Joseph T. *Candleholders in America, 1650–1900: A Comprehensive Collection of American and European Candle Fixtures used in America.* New York: Crown Publishers, 1967. xiv+178 pp.; 136 illustrations, bibliography, index.

Candleholders in America is a chronological survey of objects documented as either made or used in America, with an emphasis on stylistic development. Each short chapter covers one basic style period (baroque, Queen Anne and Chippendale, neoclassicism, federal, historical revivalism, and art nouveau). The introductory chapter discusses the history of candles and candlemaking. Subsequent chapters cover a broad range of topics from the technological changes in manufacture, the various materials used (the stylistic importance of silver is stressed), the changing use of candles over time, and the diversity of candle-holding forms. High-quality photographs of objects are accompanied by reproductions of period illustrations. The Victorian period is less fully covered.

Butler, Joseph T. "Lighting Devices." In Joseph T. Butler, *American Antiques, 1800–1900: A Collector's History and Guide*, pp. 125–39. New York: Odyssey Press, 1965. 18 illustrations.

"Lighting Devices" covers candles, lamps, and gaslighted fixtures, with some emphasis on design and style. Technological development is traced briefly but thoroughly from Argand's tubular wick through the perfection of the flat-wick kerosene burner. Period illustrations accompany photographs of objects. Butler treats lighting from technological and stylistic viewpoints in this general antiques text.

Cooke, Lawrence S., ed. *Lighting in America: From Colonial Rushlights to Victorian Chandeliers.* Antiques Magazine Library, no. 4. New York: Main Street/Universe Books, 1975. 159 pp.; illustrations, index.

Lighting in America is a compilation of forty-one articles written between 1924 and 1972 on primitive lamps, oil lamps, candlesticks, and other devices. Earlier articles are strongly antiquarian and combine the use of period documents, the examination of surviving objects, and deductive guesswork. Terminology is considered at length in the chapter on primitive lamps. The chapter on oil lamps contains articles that discuss various types of fuels, burners, and materials (glass and metal) from the late eighteenth to the early nineteenth centuries. The chapter on candlesticks covers stylistic evolution and production techniques in various media. Old, blurred photographs mar the earliest articles, but numerous objects are illustrated and compared.

Cox, Henry Bartholomew. "Plain and Fancy: Incandescence Becomes a Household Word!" *Nineteenth Century* 6, no. 3 (Autumn 1980): 49–51. 9 illustrations.

Cox presents the designs of Bergmann and Company of New York, the largest early manufacturer of fixtures designed expressly for Thomas Edison's new electric lamp. The text is illustrated with reproductions from Bergmann's 1882 catalogue, from the plainest to the most ornate available fixtures, including on-off switches and bulb sockets. Cox includes rare documentation of pre-1900 electric-fixture design.

Darbee, Herbert C. *A Glossary of Old Lamps and Lighting Devices.* Technical Leaflet no. 30. Nashville: American Association for State and Local History, 1965. 16 pp.; 71 illustrations, bibliography.

Darbee's *Glossary* contains brief definitions of 179 lighting-related terms arranged alphabetically from *adamantine candle* to *worm candlestick.* Archaic terms and misnomers are noted. Inventors or patent holders are given within definitions. This work covers virtually every commonly used term.

Davidson, Marshall B. "Early American Lighting." *Metropolitan Museum of Art Bulletin,* n.s. 3 (Summer 1944): 30–40. 12 illustrations.

Davidson examines the customs and habits of American domestic lighting by means of eighteenth- and nineteenth-century documents. Historical rather than stylistic in approach, the text includes candles, primitive lamps, and various oil lamps from Argand onward. The relative cost of different fuels and the socioeconomic divisions in lighting usage are considered.

Dietz, Ulysses G. *Victorian Lighting: The Dietz Catalogue of 1860, with a New History of Dietz and Victorian Light-*

ing. Watkins Glen, N.Y.: American Life Foundation, 1982. 123 pp.; 37 black and white illustrations, 35 black and white and 6 color plates, bibliography.

This full-size facsimile of the 1860–65 catalogue of Dietz and Company of New York is accompanied by a three-part historical essay that focuses on the history of the firm and its founder, the development and sources of lighting design in the mid nineteenth century, and the sociohistorical context in which Victorian lighting and the Dietz firm were set. The essay is illustrated with period images and pictures of surviving objects produced by the firm. The catalogue facsimile shows large-format woodcuts of the firm's repertoire of lighting, from pieces designed in the 1840s to "new" objects of the 1860s. The emphasis is on the stylistic development and social history of lighting, with the technological aspects only touched on briefly as they affected the firm's output (such as its development of a successful kerosene burner in 1858). An annotated bibliography covers primary and secondary material.

Duncan, Alastair. *Art Nouveau and Art Déco Lighting.* London: Thames and Hudson, 1978. 208 pp.; 135 black and white illustrations, 36 color plates, glossary, bibliography, index.

Duncan's general handbook of the designers and their products is divided into two stylistic periods. The first section starts with a brief history of lighting as it affected lighting design, stressing the liberating impact of electricity on the lamp. The art nouveau style is analyzed, with discussion of motifs, materials, and artistic philosophies, as well as the changing role of the artist/artisan during the arts and crafts movement. The biographical chapter on art nouveau designers is subdivided by country, then alphabetically, covering major firms and individuals in the United States, Belgium, Great Britain, France, and northern Europe. A short biographical sketch of each designer is given with commentary on 1978 market prices of their work. Art deco receives similar treatment and is analyzed in contrast to its antithesis, art nouveau. The biographical chapter on art deco designers is not subdivided by country. Few of the color plates are of art deco work, but each maker is represented by black and white photographs.

Freeman, Larry. *New Light on Old Lamps.* 1968. Rev. ed. Watkins Glen, N.Y.: American Life Foundation, 1984. 224 pp.; 163 illustrations, 158 plates, bibliography, index.

In this expanded version of his 1968 *Light on Old Lamps,* with revisions and a new introduction by John Freeman, Larry Freeman focuses on later nineteenth-century lamps. This work is based on his collection, surviving period catalogues, and other documentation. A short sketch of primitive lighting to 1800 is followed by twenty chapters, roughly chronological, that cover lamp types by burner and material, including all varieties from early whale-oil burners to gaslights and early twentieth-century electric fixtures. Separate sections deal with the reassembly of old lamps, replacement parts, accessories, and specialty lamps (such as miniatures and art glass). Freeman provides a wealth of visual material found nowhere else, and his work is only slightly hampered by a quaintly archaic writing style and old photographs.

Grove, John Robert. *Antique Brass Candlesticks*. Queen Anne, Md.: By the author, 1967. 140 pp.; 169 illustrations.

Antique Brass Candlesticks is a picture book with brief paragraphs of descriptive commentary interspersed. The book is divided into five sections: two show a chronological series of candlesticks and tapersticks from the late Middle Ages to the late eighteenth century, a third illustrates other forms of brass candlesticks, a fourth offers silver candlesticks for comparison of design, and a fifth shows iron rushlights and candlesticks. Captions include notes on manufacture and approximate dating.

Hayward, Arthur H. *Colonial Lighting*. Introduction and supplement by James R. Marsh. 3d enl. ed. New York: Dover Publications, 1962. xxxi+198 pp.; 161 illustrations, line drawings, index.

Colonial Lighting is important as the first attempt to document lighting forms in America from the seventeenth to the early nineteenth centuries. After a brief background of ancient lighting usage, Hayward moves onto betty and other primitive lamps of early America. His wide-ranging discussion is subdivided loosely by fuel (candle, lard, whale oil, kerosene), material (pottery, glass, iron, tin, brass), and form (betty-type lamps, candlesticks, lanterns, tubular-wick lamps, rushlights). The text has a strong antiquarian emphasis, including numerous digressions that trace diverse topics such as the Bennington potteries, Sandwich Glass Company, Saugus Iron Works, the American whaling history, and Paul Revere's ride. Objects belonging to celebrated Americans are discussed individually. There is little discussion of chronology or style changes. Hundreds of objects are illustrated in old, cluttered photographs, and each is explained in the text. This work is a document in itself on early collecting attitudes.

Hebard, Helen B. *Early Lighting in New England, 1620–1861*. Rutland, Vt.: Charles E. Tuttle Co., 1964. 88 pp.; 11 illustrations, 35 plates, bibliography, index.

Early Lighting is a brief distillation by a collector for collectors. Focusing on New England usage, Hebard covers wood-burning lights (fireplaces, torches, cressets, rushlights), primitive grease lamps, candles and candlesticks, and various patent lamps, burners, and fuels up to the Civil War. Basic terminology is handled concisely and clearly. There is no emphasis on stylistic development, but social history is discussed briefly.

Hough, Walter. *Collection of Heating and Lighting Utensils in the United States National Museum*. Washington, D.C.: Government Printing Office, 1928. 113 pp.; 99 illustrations, index.

Collection is an early survey of broad scope that covers the worldwide chronological and technological development of lighting from prehistoric times to the late nineteenth century. The text is preceded by an illustration reference list that details each object. The author's emphasis is entirely technological, starting with torches and candles and drawing on various tribal, cultural, and regional materials, forms, and customs. Candlesticks are considered by form and material, and primitive lamps by region, material, and form. A study of wick-tube lamps is divided according to burner type and fuel from the late eighteenth to the late nineteenth centuries. Heating devices, including some American patent objects, are handled briefly. Hough largely focuses on food preparation and primitive heating devices. The illustrations are unaesthetic but clear; the text and illustrations are keyed to each other.

Little, Bertram K. "Street Lighting." *Chronicle of Early American Industries* 3, no. 17 (October 1948): 143–49.

Little briefly traces the history of documented outdoor lighting for public use in Europe and the United States in the eighteenth and nineteenth centuries. Efforts at street lighting in colonial Boston and Philadelphia are noted, as is the development of gas street lighting.

Little, Nina Fletcher. "Lighting in Colonial Records." *Old-Time New England* 42, no. 4 (April–June 1952): 96–101. 2 illustrations.

This article attempts to document lighting devices by means of advertisements and legal documents (wills and inventories). Little covers the seventeenth and eighteenth centuries, focusing on New England but including New York, Philadelphia, and some southern references. The paucity of lighting in pre-1700 America is compared with the relative opulence of candlelight after 1750 and the changeover to oil-lamp light from 1800. Period terminology is covered.

McDonald, Ann Gilbert. *Evolution of the Night Lamp*. Des Moines: Wallace-Homestead Book Co., 1979. 116 pp.; 136 black and white illustrations, 12 color plates, bibliography, index.

McDonald documents the use and popularity of small lamps, such as night-lights, throughout the nineteenth century. She focuses on the small, single-function lamp from colonial betty types to early twentieth-century versions, including whale-oil and kerosene lamps. Succeeding chapters deal with night-lights according to major manufacturers (both of glass and metal lamps), drawing on nineteenth-century commercial sources such as the *Crockery and Glass Journal*. There is a strong emphasis on the peak production period from 1880 to 1920, with chapters included on non-mass-produced forms (cameo glass, art glass) and on modern reproductions.

Myers, Denys Peter. *Gaslighting in America: A Guide for Historic Preservation*. Washington, D.C.: Department of the Interior, 1978. 279 pp.; 119 illustrations, appendix, bibliography, index.

Gaslighting in America is the only major work today that deals solely with gas fixtures. Although claiming to be a guide for preservationists, it is essentially a textbook on style and technology in gas-lighting devices. A brief introduction outlines the history of gas as a light source from the eighteenth century and offers suggestions on recreating gaslighted effects with modern installations. The main body of the text is chronological, and the pictures are either period illustrations or actual objects; the layout of the book is in two-page spreads with photographs facing commentaries. The chronology runs from English gas fixtures of 1815, to the earliest documented American usage (Boston, 1838), through the Welsbach gas mantle of 1890, to the waning of gaslight by 1910. Period terminology, major American manufacturers, and the function of gas fixtures and their placement in rooms are covered. An appendix lists the dates of local gas-company charters throughout the United States.

O'Dea, William T. *The Social History of Lighting*. London: Routledge and Paul, 1958. xiii+253 pp.; 59 illustrations, bibliography, indexes.

O'Dea's book is unique in its focus on the nature of varying sorts of light through the ages and on how light affected the lives of the people who used it. Beginning with a general overview of lighting history, from primitive lamps to fluorescent tubes, the rest of the text is divided into chapters by use: lighting in the home, in the workplace (including shops, mines, factories, hospitals), for travel and transportation, for worship and ritual, for entertainment, and for public events; and public lighting. A supplementary chapter deals with materials and methods for producing light. Each chapter begins with the most primitive form of light, such as shell lamps, and progresses chronologically to the most modern, with an emphasis on changing technology. This book is notable for its strong coverage of the early history of electric lighting before Thomas Edison. There are frequent literary and historical citations, along with illustrations gleaned from period sources. O'Dea's coverage is worldwide and cross-cultural, but America figures strongly.

Poese, William F. *Lighting through the Years: The Light in Darkness*. Des Moines: Wallace-Homestead Book Co., 1976. 99 pp.; 112 black and white illustrations, 9 color plates.

This work is a compendium of Poese's writings from various magazines, including *Antiques Journal*, *Relics*, and *Collector's World*. The seventeen chapters are loosely chronological, beginning with torches and candles, proceeding through primitive lamps and Argand types, to gaslighted and kerosene, patent, and electric lamps. The chapters are short and sparse, with cursory coverage of each topic. Chapters on such topics as fairy lamps, peg lamps, matches, and Royal Worcester porcelain snuffers cover material not found in other sources. Minimally captioned illustrations are not specifically referred to in the text.

Robins, Frederick W. *The Story of the Lamp (and the Candle)*. New York and London: Oxford University Press, 1939. xiv+155 pp.; 23 plates, bibliography, indexes.

Robins's work is the most sophisticated of the early lighting surveys. His focus is worldwide and outlines all lighting from the caveman to Thomas Edison, including the ancient world and the Orient. Three major sections, divided into twenty-nine short chapters, discuss torches, candles, primitive lamps, wick-type lamps, gaslights, and electric lights (the latter two are briefly but fully covered). A final section covers issues such as streetlights and lighthouses. Candlemaking is covered in special detail, and the evolution of the candlestick is fully traced. Post-Argand lamp development is more broadly handled, and not every burner variant is noted. Old-style, cluttered photographs are cross-referenced in the text but are still awkward to use.

Rushlight Club. *Early Lighting: A Pictorial Guide*. Boston: By the club, 1972. x+129 pp.; 463 illustrations, bibliography, index.

Early Lighting is a well-captioned photographic survey in thirteen chapters, each introduced by a concise historical paragraph. Subjects are divided by form and fuel (or burner), with supplementary sections on equipment and accessories. The text covers all aspects of lighting from ancient primitive lamps and rushlights to kerosene fixtures and includes nondomestic lighting (lanterns and ceremonial and work lighting). The focus is on technology, not style, but the roughly chronological layout provides a visual indication of the change over time. Materials of all sorts are considered (metal, glass, pottery), and some cross-cultural efforts are made for certain forms, including Near Eastern and Far Eastern examples, that relate to European and American variants. The terminology is accurate and current.

Rushlight Club. *Patented Lighting: A Special Issue in Honor of the United States Bicentennial*. Boston: By the club, 1976. 101 pp.; 81 illustrations.

Patented Lighting presents a selection of forty-one lighting patents, arranged by patent number, dating from 1812 to Thomas Edison's 1880 light-bulb patent. The selection is based on the importance of the invention, its ingenuity, and the survival of a production example of the device. The patent illustration and original text facsimiles are on facing pages. Each group of four patents is followed by photographs of actual examples.

Russell, Loris S. "Early Nineteenth-Century Lighting." In *Building Early America*, edited by Charles E. Peterson, pp. 186–201. Radnor, Pa.: Chilton Book Co., for the Carpenters' Company of the City and County of Philadelphia, 1976. 20 illustrations, bibliography.

Russell gives a chronological history of lighting devices from candles through fuel-burning lamps to gaslights. The text provides detailed discussions of varied sorts of candles, lamps, burners, and fuels, including descriptions of Argand, lard, burning fluid, whale oil, and kerosene burners. The emphasis is on technology, not style, and the illustrations underscore this focus. Gas-lighting is traced from its eighteenth-century beginnings through its phases to the Civil War, and technical information on early gas piping and meters is included.

Russell, Loris S. *A Heritage of Light: Lamps and Lighting in the Early Canadian Home*. Toronto: University of Toronto Press, 1968. 344 pp.; 190 illustrations, glossary, bibliography, index.

A Heritage of Light presents a detailed and scholarly survey of all lighting from rushlights to light bulbs. The chronological organization starts with splints and candles, moves to pan lamps (betty lamps and so forth), through the myriad wick-tube lamps of the 1800–1900 era, and finally to gas-lighting and electric lighting. The most extensive coverage is devoted to the wick-tube lamps; fuels, manufacturers, accessories, lamp forms, burners, and materials are all considered, as are candlemaking techniques. Diagrams illustrate major technological developments; some attention is given to stylistic changes. Major Canadian figures in lighting (like Abraham Gesner, who invented kerosene) are discussed. Terminology is handled carefully. A helpful glossary and a bibliography make this the first "modern" lighting textbook.

Smith, Frank R., and Ruth E. Smith. *Miniature Lamps*. New York and Toronto: Thomas Nelson and Sons, 1968. 285 pp.; 630 black and white illustrations, 13 color plates, appendix, bibliography.

This collector's handbook focuses on objects by size. A brief opening chapter, which outlines lighting history and the possible origins of miniature lamp forms, is followed by a catalogue of objects with brief descriptive captions. The appendix includes ten reproductions of United States miniature-lamp patents.

Thuro, Catherine M. V. *Oil Lamps: The Kerosene Era in North America*. Photographs by Ken Bell. Des Moines: Wallace-Homestead Book Co., 1976. 352 pp.; 990 black and white illustrations, 10 color plates, bibliography, index.

Oil Lamps is a collector's handbook that concentrates on glass lamps of the period from 1850 to 1900. The introductory material deals with lighting history of kerosene, outlines accessories, burner types, and glass manufacture, and provides research guidelines for collectors. The text is divided into chapters of photographs by form and material (glass lamps,

metal lamps), with a chronological order (pre 1880, 1880–1900, post 1900). There is a heavy emphasis on all- or partial-glass lamps and their makers and patterns, with chapters devoted to major glasshouses and their designs (Atterbury and Company, Hobbs, Brockunier, and Company). Thuro includes reproduced advertising material from the 1850s to the 1890s.

Thuro, Catherine M. V. *Oil Lamps II: Glass Kerosene Lamps*. Toronto: Thorncliffe House, 1983. 160 pp.; 213 black and white illustrations, 339 color plates, bibliography, index.

Thuro presents an extremely complex and sophisticated analysis of all- or partial-glass kerosene lamps marketed in America, with the goal of determining who was manufacturing and who was marketing. Using marked examples and advertisement documentation, various categories of lamps are compared and discussed regarding their possible attribution to various American and European firms. This is a unique and comprehensive effort with many clear photographs.

Thwing, Leroy. *Flickering Flames: A History of Domestic Lighting through the Ages*. Rutland, Vt.: Charles E. Tuttle Co. for the Rushlight Club, 1958. xvi+138 pp.; 10 illustrations, 93 plates, bibliography.

Flickering Flames is a historical and technical survey with no focus on style. The text covers lamps and candlesticks exclusively (no gas or electricity) in twenty-one short chapters, half of which focus on numerous variants of vertical wick-tube lamps and the remainder of which deal with ancient and primitive lamp types and candle-related materials. Thwing discusses evolving forms, fuels, and burner types. Terminology is considered extensively, but much is outdated. There is a strong antiquarian flavor to the text, which is reflected in cluttered and hard-to-use photographs. This is the first major survey to appear since those by Hayward (1927) and Hough (1928).

Watkins, C. Malcom. "Artificial Lighting in America, 1830–1860." In *Annual Report 1951*, Smithsonian Institution, pp. 385–407. Washington, D.C.: By the institution, 1952. 16 illustrations, bibliography.

Watkins discusses the boom in patent lighting between 1830 and 1860 against a background of urban growth and social change in the northeastern United States. He compares this with geographic, economic, and ethnic isolation at the same time in the South and the West and the archaic nature of lighting in rural regions. Although the focus is sociohistorical, technology and style are discussed. Public and domestic lighting are treated, including transportation and church usage. All major lighting substances from whale oil to kerosene and gas are outlined, with special mention of significant inventors (Miles, Jennings, Gesner).

Wills, Geoffrey. *Candlesticks*. New York: Clarkson N. Potter, 1974. 120 pp.; 117 black and white illustrations, 9 color plates, bibliography, index.

Candlesticks begins with a brief historical sketch covering decoration, manufacturing processes, and form changes over time. Wills deals with single candlesticks exclusively, focusing on English examples but drawing in American and Continental variants. The bulk of the book consists of large photographs, arranged chronologically from 1100 to 1890, each with a brief caption noting form, style, material, and date. The different materials used in making candlesticks are covered. The final chapter describes candles and candlemaking techniques into the nineteenth century.

Woodhead, E. I., C. Sullivan, and G. Gusset. *Lighting Devices in the National Reference Collection, Parks Canada*. Ottawa: Parks Canada, 1984. 86 pp.; 85 illustrations, bibliography.

Lighting Devices is an interesting and unusual study from an archaeological perspective. This chronological assemblage of lighting devices and related equipment retrieved from sites in Canada moves from primitive lamp forms and candles, to vertical wick-tube lamps (glass and metal), and finally to electric lights. Detailed diagrammatic drawings supplement fragmentary objects, and technical information accompanies each section. This is not an encyclopedic overview, but it is highly serviceable for specific usage of various forms.

Artisans and Culture

Craftsmen

The Arts and Crafts Movement in America

Craftsmen

Edward S. Cooke, Jr.

SCHOLARS FROM MANY DISCIPLINES have expressed great interest in American artisans or craftsmen, but few of these scholars have ever agreed on the proper way to analyze and interpret these historical figures. Instead, differences in training, source material, and definitions have balkanized the terrain. The effect of training is paramount. Art historians have been absorbed with the colonial craftsman, labor historians have focused only on factory workers, and intellectual historians have examined the artisan in the late nineteenth and early twentieth centuries. Each of these approaches possesses its own documents, analytic questions, and methodologies. Few scholars confidently or capably integrate all types of available materials to generate a full description of a craftsman and his product, process, and context. We are left with an unconnected view of American artisans rather than an understanding of the continuities and changes that affected them. For example, there is little consensus on what exactly a craftsman is and whether *artisan* and *craftsman* are interchangeable terms. Are master craftsmen worth studying? Is the working class ever the same as an artisanal class? Do craftsmen work only with certain materials?

A survey of the current literature on American artisans reveals three major coexisting thematic threads, each located in a specific temporal setting: preindustrial (1600–1800), industrial (1800–1880), and reform (1890–1920). Each of these possesses its own scholarly tradition. Understanding the strengths and weaknesses of these traditions is a critical prelude to mapping strategies for future research and writing.

Artisans comprised at least a fifth of America's preindustrial population. More individuals probably engaged in craft activity on a part-time basis. They also played an integral role in the exchange networks of the preindustrial economy and produced much of its built environment. Yet colonial historians have paid little attention to this segment of society. Two figures, Richard Morris and Carl Bridenbaugh, have dominated the field but have not yet probed deeply into the artisan's life. Morris's *Government and Labor in Early America* examines the legal position of free and unfree labor, points out regional differences of production and labor, and demonstrates how external and internal economic controls affected the producing part of the population. His study contains several perceptive observations about craftwork, but it is largely a descriptive sort of legal and economic history. Bridenbaugh's *Colonial Craftsman* also lacks any sort of analytic edge. Based almost entirely on newspaper advertisements, it is an impressionistic overview, the broad strokes of which camouflage the realities of an artisan's varied experiences and preclude any explanations for the patterns evident in a mechanic's career. Surprisingly, the shortcomings of *The Colonial Craftsman* have provoked only muted whispers from the new social and cultural historians, most of whom have focused on the agricultural production or commercial patterns of the colonial mixed economy and have been little interested in the service or production part of this economy.

Instead, the study of preindustrial craftsmen has been the domain of decorative arts scholars, most of whom have written object-oriented, descriptive biographies or compiled long lists of craftsmen with skeletal biographies. This approach, which had its origins in antiquarianism and is perpetuated by the predominant collector-dealer mentality of the field, results merely in the gathering of raw data to explain who the maker of a specific object was and when he produced it. Such information often increases an object's value in the marketplace. This genealogical approach has overemphasized master craftsmen who signed their work or advertised and those who produced the so-called decorative arts, especially furniture, clocks, silver, and pewter. Less attention has been focused on craftsmen who worked in brass or iron, and cordwainers, coopers, and other artisans responsible for more utilitarian products virtually have been ignored. Such biases inhibit possible conclusions about craft hierarchies, the role of bonded labor (journeymen, apprentices, or slaves), the context in which the craftsman worked and lived, and the artisan's values and aspirations. In short, the decorative arts studies lack provocative analysis or consideration of historical context.

Studies of early industrial artisans have been dominated by labor historians. Scholars writing earlier in the twentieth century followed a formal, institutional approach to the examination of nineteenth-century American artisans and workers that focused almost exclusively on the establishment of trade unions, the development of organized protest, and the strength of a labor political party. More recent studies have concentrated on the economic and cultural continuities and changes that accompanied industrialization. In charting the change from merchant capitalism to industrialism and the decline of the small-shop tradition, these new scholars have paid particular attention to technological continuity and invention, the importance of wages, the use of cheap labor, the growth of national markets, the importance of capital, the role of task specialization, the advent of mass production, social mobility, political behavior, changes in leisure and life-style, and family structure. These historians have used sophisticated record linkage and quantified analyses to explore the relationship between labor, which included many artisans, and the rest of society and to infer values and attitudes from observable patterns of behavior. The strength of these studies is the concern for contextual analysis within the workplace, the home, and the community.

While many labor history studies emphasize the perpetuation of certain preindustrial craft practices like outwork and small craft shops in certain industries and at certain times, they do not directly help our understanding of preindustrial craftsmen. A concern with large numbers of faceless workers or with an entire craft, a focus on journeymen or machine operatives, and an overemphasis on more utilitarian products make it difficult to compare the information from studies of industrial craftsmen with the data from decorative arts studies of preindustrial craftsmen. Furthermore, labor historians have seldom incorporated the actual products of their protagonists into their analysis. After all, tools and machines shaped products as well as lives. Any understanding of industrialization must incorporate material culture and consumerism.

Craftsmen

The late nineteenth century was a time in which the craftsman assumed major status within the nation's consciousness. Many Americans perceived problems with the nation's industrial economy but disagreed about the proper method to reform it. One group lamented the impersonal relationships, mechanical dependency, and poor design of the industrialized economy. Their romantic view of the preindustrial craftsman prompted their call for a return to the happier era of small-shop production in which craftsmen took time and care to make well-designed, honest things. A second group favored the precision and uniformity possible with new technology and held a less noble view of the craftsman. To these critics, craftsmen, who depended so heavily on inherited traditions and intuitive problem solving, were impediments to the perfection of America's industrial economy. Such reformers sought to continue task specialization and to base artisanal production more firmly on scientific principles by introducing a professional managerial class and a professional design class. Craftsmen were demoted to a menial status, while the new professional classes were elevated to a loftier level.

The romantic and scientific reformist views, which produced an abundance of writings, have greatly influenced the study of craftsmen from that period as well as studies of those active in other periods. By counterposing handworkmanship and mechanized industrialism and stressing the noble qualities of craftsmanship, the romantics denied the preindustrial craftsman economic identity. They emphasized the process and the final product, but rarely considered the viability of the producer. Many studies of this period have accepted romantic rhetoric at face value and have focused on the development of "traditional" practices and honestly constructed objects. Such writers celebrate the return to handcraftmanship and a democratization of craftwork. Actually there was great diversity in the production of household goods at the turn of the century: existing large-scale manufactories, small-scale shops, and operations in between simply altered their designs without changing their processes. Only a few well-to-do independent producers or avocational craftsmen could afford to concentrate solely on time-consuming individual production.

The scientific critics have also greatly influenced studies of the late nineteenth and early twentieth centuries. Scholars have relied on their writings to stress the exploitative power of the capitalists and professionals and the helplessness of the artisan to shape his own world. By emphasizing the rhetorical aspects of process propounded by the scientific critics, these scholars lament the degradation of work. They demonstrate little consideration of how the artisan's experience varied from industry to industry or from shop to shop, or how the artisan carved out his own niche. Like their colleagues who have relied on the writings of the romantic reformers, scholars also produce a skewed picture of artisanal life.

In the future we must move beyond simple genealogical information and object identification, mobility rates of faceless figures, or rhetorical postures. Instead we should combine the implicit strengths of the three different groups identified above: the detailed analysis of the artisans' products, a thorough exploration of their cultural and social context, and a balanced consideration of their techniques. We should construct solid theoretical frameworks that synthesize sophisticated historical analysis with sensitive treatment of craftsmen and craft processes and products. Essential to this task is the integration of information drawn from artifacts, account books, inventories and wills, tax lists, census records, town and church records, land deeds, genealogies, diaries, and any other pertinent material. The ultimate goal is an understanding of the fluid cultural networks in which craftsmen lived. In regard to production, we need to inquire about seasonal rhythms, the preferred time for certain tasks, the sources of tools and materials, the destinations of finished products, the initiation of transactions, the involvement of family members, the acceptable roles for women, children, and blacks, the strength of learned traditions, the varieties of productive units, the location of different productive tasks, and the hierarchy within the shop and within the craft. Less obvious and more sophisticated questions would focus on how the craftsman organized his production, how he altered his tasks in reaction to increased or decreased demand, how his production was determined by age or family development, how the work force was recruited or reproduced, and the source and rate of technical change. Pertinent questions regarding the craftsman within his community include his mobility, location, and kinship ties, the identity and relation of his customers, the common standards of artifactual language, the usual patterns of purchase, the relationship between shops within a town or region, and the extent of the market.

More sophisticated artifactual analysis combined with a deeper sense of historical processes will better enable us to understand the American artisan and artisanal culture. A certain synergism exists between craftsmen, their products, and the environments in which they lived and worked. The interpretation of each generates ideas, provides proof, and sheds light on the others. Case studies of American craftsmen should serve as building blocks for the analysis of the roots of the outwork system, the role of craftsmen in early industrialization, the strength of learned craft techniques, the extent of workers' control, the effect of architect-designed household furnishings, and the roots of financial difficulties faced by contemporary craftsmen. The following readings suggest the vast, untapped richness of a cultural and technical examination of the American craftsman in historical perspective.

Alexander, John D., Jr. *Make a Chair from a Tree: An Introduction to Working Green Wood*. Newtown, Conn.: Taunton Press, 1978. 125 pp.; illustrations, appendix, bibliography, index.

Alexander explores the intricacies of post-and-rung construction, the most economical type of chair produced in preindustrial America. Part learned treatise and part how-to manual, this book offers valuable information about wood properties, the use of tools, and the rationale behind construction.

Bishir, Catherine W. "Jacob W. Holt: An American Builder." *Winterthur Portfolio* 16, no. 1 (Spring 1981): 1–31. 44 illustrations.

Bishir reveals how a biographical study can provide deeper understanding of built products. Holt continued to use familiar organizational practices and construction techniques to build efficiently, but he used new pattern books and milled trim to incorporate current popular tastes in the mid nineteenth century.

Bivins, John, Jr. *The Moravian Potters in North Carolina*. Chapel Hill: University of North Carolina Press for Old Salem, 1972. xiii+300 pp.; 276 black and white illustrations, color plates, glossaries, bibliography, index.

Written records and archaeological evidence are used to recreate the original context in which the Moravian potters lived and worked. Bivins discusses the narrow type of technology and the broad understanding and practice of that technique. He points out the influence of learned tradition and the use of templates but cautions that an artisan's work "probably manifests some few attributes gleaned from apprenticeship, mixed with a large number of characteristics of design developed by the artisan himself" (pp. 115–16). *See also* "American Ceramics."

Boris, Eileen. *Art and Labor: Ruskin, Morris, and the Craftsman Ideal in America*. American Civilization series, edited by Allen F. Davis. Philadelphia: Temple University Press, 1986. xviii+261 pp.; 47 illustrations, index.

Boris describes the intellectual basis of the craftsman ideal—the reuniting of art and labor—then analyzes the social, cultural, and economic dimensions of this philosophical or romantic concept. In charting how these ideas were put into action, she includes chapters on the influences of arts and crafts societies on patrons and artisans, the desire to appropriate women's works for different ends, and the varied attempts to improve the environments and techniques of craftsmen. This is an insightful look at the ironies and hypocrisies of a period that continues to color our own views of craftsmanship. *See also* "The Arts and Crafts Movement in America."

Bridenbaugh, Carl. *The Colonial Craftsman*. 1950. Reprint. Chicago and London: University of Chicago Press, 1961. x+214 pp.; 17 illustrations, index.

Bridenbaugh relies on newspaper advertisements, diaries, and similar sources to emphasize the ideal craftsman, the few artisans who advertised during this period, or the atypical event. The sources result in the depiction of all village artisans as independent, self-sufficient, and respected townsmen and of all urban mechanics, who belonged to all levels of society, as ambitious entrepreneurs. Bridenbaugh neglects to consider the social diversity of the village craftsmen or the differing ideologies of the urban artisans. He uses craft processes and products only as illustrative ornament to an already developed argument rather than as integral source material. In spite of its shortcomings, this is an important book for its focus on the artisanal segment of society.

Burrison, John A. *Brothers in Clay: The Story of Georgia Folk Pottery*. Athens: University of Georgia Press, 1983. xviii+326 pp.; 154 illustrations, bibliography, checklist, index.

Brothers in Clay connects the actions of the shop floor to the activities of the community and to the larger external economy. The first two sections—one on the place of the potter in a preindustrial agrarian society and the other on the processes and techniques of potting—are especially helpful. Burrison sheds light on the workings of a domestic or family operation. *See also* "American Ceramics."

Campbell, R. *The London Tradesman. See* "Brass, Copper, Iron, and Tin."

Carpenter, Charles H., Jr. *Gorham Silver, 1831–1981*. New York: Dodd, Mead, 1982. xii+332 pp.; 295 black and white illustrations, 8 color plates, appendixes, bibliography, index.

This monograph helps to chart and explain changing silver shop practices and products in the nineteenth century.

Like Michael J. Ettema, in "Technological Innovation," Carpenter demonstrates that mechanization did not really overturn the economics of design. He points out the advantages of machinery: high consistent quality, sturdiness, more available time for elaboration than for mundane shaping, and more uniformity. The high cost of silver necessitated an increased reliance on volume sales. *See also* "American Silver and Gold."

Cooke, Edward S., Jr. *Fiddlebacks and Crooked-backs: Elijah Booth and Other Joiners in Newtown and Woodbury, 1750–1820*. Waterbury, Conn.: Mattatuck Historical Society, 1982. 120 pp.; 35 illustrations, appendixes.

Cooke's case study combines written records and artifactual evidence to explain the interrelationship between craftsmen's lives, their products, and their socioeconomic context. He discusses the need for additional microstudies before attempting a sophisticated general discussion of the craftsman in preindustrial New England. *See also* "American Furniture to 1820."

Dawley, Alan, and Paul Faler. "Working-Class Culture and Politics in the Industrial Revolution: Sources of Loyalism and Rebellion." *Journal of Social History* 9, no. 4 (June 1976): 466–80.

This study of shoemakers in Lynn, Massachusetts, in the second quarter of the nineteenth century discusses three broad responses to industrial capitalism. The traditionalists retained traditional values and behavior, the loyalists accepted the new moral order to improve themselves, and the rebels embraced the new morality in order to fight the system and to assert their traditional independence. This division of the artisanal classes has many broad implications for products, shop structure, and techniques.

Dibble, Ann W. "Major John Dunlap: The Craftsman and His Community." *Old-Time New England* 68, nos. 3–4 (Winter–Spring 1978): 50–58. 3 illustrations, 1 table.

Dibble uses Dunlap's account books to discuss the important features of preindustrial craftwork in a nonurban environment. She focuses on the use of familial labor, the seasonal rhythms of work, the broad spectrum of related craft activities, the purchasing patterns of neighbors and kin, and the circle of the local economy.

Douglas, Paul H. *American Apprenticeship and Industrial Education*. Studies in History, Economics, and Public Law, vol. 95, no. 2, whole no. 216. New York: Columbia University Press; London: P. S. King and Son, 1921. 348 pp.; bibliography, index.

This work is still the standard text that traces the vestigial forms of apprenticeship in the nineteenth century.

Dublin, Thomas. *Women at Work*. New York: Columbia University Press, 1979. 312 pp.; tables.

Dublin sheds light on the world of the farm daughters who worked in the early Lowell, Massachusetts, mills. He shows how the rural values of the girls, who had sought economic and social independence, were undermined first by technological reorganization and then by the cheap labor pool of immigrants.

Ettema, Michael J. "Technological Innovation and Design Economics in Furniture Manufacture." *See* "American Furniture, 1820–1920."

Fales, Martha Gandy. *Joseph Richardson and Family: Philadelphia Silversmiths. See* "American Silver and Gold."

Fix, Edward B. "A Long Island Carpenter at Work: A Quantitative Inquiry into the Account Book of Jedediah Williamson." *Chronicle of the Early American Industries Association* 32, no. 4 (December 1979): 61–63; and 33, no. 1 (March 1980): 4–8. 7 illustrations, 3 tables.

This study of a carpenter in the early national period demonstrates the correlation between family structure and craft activity. Fix explains the type and quantity of artisanal activities in light of the family needs or opportunities.

Forman, Benno M. "Delaware Valley 'Crookt Foot' and Slat-Back Chairs: The Fussell-Savery Connection." *Winterthur Portfolio* 15, no. 1 (Spring 1980): 41–64. 22 illustrations.

Forman combines thorough account book analysis and astute artifactual examination to study the business side of the eighteenth-century chairmaker: personnel organization in the shop, shop practices, and the wide range of products. He also documents the manner in which a craftsman thought about or approached a problem based on his training. *See also* "American Furniture to 1820."

Forman, Benno M. "German Influences in Pennsylvania Furniture." In Scott T. Swank et al., *Arts of the Pennsylvania Germans*, edited by Catherine E. Hutchins, pp. 102–70. New York: W. W. Norton for the Henry Francis du Pont Winterthur Museum, 1983. 61 black and white illustrations, color plates, 2 tables.

Artifactual analysis and written documents are used to explore the influence of Germanic traditions on the Anglo cabinetmakers and chairmakers. German immigrants applied traditional construction practices to English forms and details, incorporated new features into their traditional forms, and adapted techniques in response to American materials. In Philadelphia most Germans were confined to piecework or journeyman status, yet they had a great impact on constructional conventions. *See also* "American Furniture to 1820."

Forman, Benno M. "Urban Aspects of Massachusetts Furniture in the Late Seventeenth Century." In *Country Cabinetwork and Simple City Furniture*, edited by John D. Morse, pp. 1–33. Charlottesville: University Press of Virginia for the Henry Francis du Pont Winterthur Museum, 1970. 8 illustrations.

By following the shift from seventeenth-century joined oak furniture to dovetailed, veneered furniture and cane chairs, Forman attributes the technological and stylistic shifts to the influence of immigrant craftsmen and a changing socioeconomic climate.

Glassie, Henry. *Folk Housing in Middle Virginia: A Structural Analysis of Historic Artifacts*. Knoxville: University of Tennessee Press, 1975. xiv+231 pp.; 86 illustrations, bibliography, index.

Glassie explains that an artifact is the product of a complex transaction between competence, or the ability to compose, and performance, or the ability to relate composition to its context. He discusses the concept of transformational grammar. According to this structuralist model, the artisan analyzes new ideas or forms, breaks them down into comprehensible units, extracts what is permissible, and assimilates those features. Glassie's work is particularly important to the consideration of artifacts on their own terms, rather than from a presentist point of view, and to the understanding of each object as the product of specific people in specific contexts. *See also* "Domestic Architecture."

Gusler, Wallace B. *Furniture of Williamsburg and Eastern Virginia, 1710–1790*. Richmond: Virginia Museum, 1979. xxi+194 pp.; 126 black and white and color illustrations, appendix, bibliography, index.

Gusler's thesis is that the style and construction of a piece of furniture were affected by the prevailing economic and commercial conditions of that time and place and by the training and ethnic background of the maker. He musters documentary evidence to point out the great turnover of craftsmen in Williamsburg and the London training of many of them. Evidence from surviving furniture is used to show the various British urban cabinetmaking traditions transplanted to Williamsburg by immigrating craftsmen. *See also* "American Furniture to 1820."

Gutman, Herbert G. *Work, Culture, and Society in Industrializing America: Essays in American Working-Class and Social History*. New York: Vintage Books, 1976. xiv+343+xvi pp.; 3 tables, index.

The first essay, which shares the same title as the whole collection, stresses the necessity of understanding the background of a worker (the cultural system) and his or her environment (society). The resulting insights into behavior reveal the constant flux or tension between preindustrial cultures and an industrializing society. Gutman portrays the artisanal world of the nineteenth century as a very dynamic arena, one fed by a constant infusion of new craftsmen and new technologies.

Hazen, Edward. *The Panorama of Professions and Trades; or, Everyman's Book*. Philadelphia: Uriah Hunt, 1839. xii+320 pp.; illustrations.

Hazen's period book provides succinct descriptions of various trades during a period of economic change in which there was increased urban production, a rise in marketing, and a great dependence on rural outwork.

Hirsch, Susan E. *Roots of the American Working Class: The Industrialization of Crafts in Newark, 1800–1860*. Philadelphia: University of Pennsylvania Press, 1978. xx+170 pp.; 2 illustrations, 38 tables, appendixes, index.

Hirsch focuses on shoemaking, hatting, saddlemaking, jewelrymaking, trunkmaking, and leathermaking to demonstrate that industrialization was not a monolith. Rather, each trade or region had its own agents of change, pace and timing of change, and type of change. An important part of her argument is that artisans initiated much of the technological change.

Hobsbawm, E. J. *Labouring Men: Studies in the History of Labour*. New York: Basic Books, 1964. viii+401 pp.; tables, index.

Hobsbawm's study of labor deals with many varieties, including tramping, an informal custom to meet seasonal or irregular employment. Its role in preindustrial American trades, especially house joinery and pewter, remains to be explored. Chapters on the labor aristocracy and nineteenth-century customs, wages, and workloads focus on the British industrial experience, but their attention to the dynamics of change should be a model for American studies.

Hummel, Charles F. *With Hammer in Hand: The Dominy Craftsmen of East Hampton, New York*. See "American Furniture to 1820"; "Clocks and Watches."

Jobe, Brock, and Myrna Kaye, with the assistance of Philip Zea. *New England Furniture, the Colonial Era: Selections from the Society for the Preservation of New England Antiquities*. See "American Furniture to 1820."

Jones, Michael Owen. *The Hand Made Object and Its Maker*. Berkeley: University of California Press, 1975. xi+261 pp.; 102 illustrations.

Jones dismisses inferential studies of objects in isolation and proposes the need to examine production and consumption. In his discussion of a contemporary Kentucky chairmaker and his peers, he shows how many factors contributed to an ongoing, fluid style. These factors included the intended use of the object, the materials, tools, and techniques used in construction, the consumer's influence, and the needs and values of the craftsman.

Jones, Michael Owen. "The Study of Traditional Furniture: Review and Preview." *Keystone Folklore Quarterly* 12, no. 4 (Winter 1967): 233–45.

The questions that Jones asks of living craftsmen should guide the research agenda of those studying past craftsmen. His model encompasses function, technology, biography of the artisan, client taste, and craftsman-client interaction.

Kenney, John Tarrant. *The Hitchcock Chair: The Story of a Connecticut Yankee—L. Hitchcock of Hitchcocks-ville—and an Account of the Restoration of His Nineteenth-Century Manufactory*. See "American Furniture, 1820–1920."

Kranzberg, Melvin, and Joseph Gies. *By the Sweat of Thy Brow: Work in the Western World*. New York: G. P. Putnam's Sons, 1975. 248 pp.

This historical overview demonstrates the continuum of certain work organization forms from classical times to the present. In low-technology trades and where the commercial market was not fully developed, many crafts were organized in shops with less than twelve craftsmen and used outwork or cooperation among specialized shops to increase production.

Lasansky, Jeannette. *To Draw, Upset, and Weld: The Work of the Pennsylvania Rural Blacksmith, 1742–1935*. Lewisburg, Pa.: Oral Traditions Project of the Union County Historical Society, 1980. 80 pp.; illustrations, bibliography, index.

Lasansky is especially adept at depicting the world of the blacksmith. In spite of unchanged shop structures and tools, blacksmithing changed in the last half of the nineteenth century. Lasansky points out the overlapping of tasks, the two-edged effect of mass production (relief from monotony versus loss of steady small work), new uses for old tools, the effect of manuals and magazines, and the acceptance of new materials or fuels. This study emphasizes the flexibility and resilience of small-shop crafts. *See also* "Brass, Copper, Iron, and Tin."

Laurie, Bruce. *Working People of Philadelphia, 1800–1850*. Philadelphia: Temple University Press, 1980. xiii+273 pp.; 11 tables, bibliography, index.

Laurie distinguishes between five types of productive modes—factories, manufactures, sweatshops, outwork, and artisan shops—that were differentiated by scale, mechanization, and market orientation. The first chapter offers a good summary of the dynamic quality of the craft structure in the early national period. The depression of 1837 was the watershed whereby economic forces caused a change in the ethnic composition of the labor force and the size of productive units.

Light, John D., and Henry Unglik. *A Frontier Fur Trade Blacksmith Shop, 1796–1812*. Studies in Archaeology, Architecture, and History. Ottawa: Parks Canada, 1984. 130 pp.; 123 illustrations, 29 tables, bibliographies.

One of the few archaeological works that focus on a preindustrial craft shop, this work uses artifacts to determine the layout of the blacksmith's shop, identify the various work areas, describe daily activities, and document the range of work. The important role of archaeology in determining the shop-floor history of artisans is noted.

Montgomery, David. *Workers' Control in America: Studies in the History of Work, Technology, and Labor Struggles.* New York and London: Cambridge University Press, 1979. xi + 189 pp.

In this book, chapters 1 and 5 provide an understanding of the craftsman's role in the late nineteenth and early twentieth centuries. The first stresses that artisans could keep some control over production by retaining their traditional values. These were based on their functional autonomy (a result of their skill and discretion), their manly bearing toward their boss, and their brotherly bearing toward their fellow workers. Union work rules merely codified their informal ethical code. The fifth chapter identifies the first two decades of the twentieth century as the period in which artisanal control came under the heaviest attack.

Morris, Richard B. *Government and Labor in Early America.* 1946. Reprint. A Northeastern Classics Edition. Boston: Northeastern University Press, 1981. xxii + 557 pp.

Morris's overview of the fluid labor market in colonial America contrasts the use of free labor and indentured servitude in various regions. He also distinguishes between various craft activities and types of operations based on the number of necessary workers and the amount of required capital.

Moxon, Joseph. *Mechanick Exercises on the Whole Art of Printing (1683–4).* 1703. Reprint. New York: Praeger Publishers, 1970. 352 pp.; 26 plates.

The tools, techniques, and terminology of blacksmithing, joinery, carpentry, turning, brickmaking, and printing are discussed. Moxon provides an introduction but also reminds us, "Hand-Craft signifies Cunning, or sleight, or Craft of the Hands, which cannot be taught by Words, but only gained by Practice and Exercise."

Myers, Susan. "The Business of Potting, 1780–1840." In *The Craftsman in Early America*, edited by Ian M. G. Quimby, pp. 190–233. New York: W. W. Norton for the Henry Francis du Pont Winterthur Museum, 1984. 21 illustrations.

Myers examines the spectrum of the American ceramics industry in the early national period. Based on technology, raw materials, business organization, and the role of the craftsman, she identifies three different types of producers: the earthenware potter, who is proprietor/manufacturer/marketer; the stoneware potter, who allies his technical knowledge with the capital and sales connections of an en-

trepreneur; and the refined earthenware potter, who works in a large establishment.

Porter, Glenn. *The Workers' World at Hagley.* Wilmington, Del.: Eleutherian Mills–Hagley Foundation, 1981. 64 pp.; 65 illustrations.

In discussing the good and bad effects of industrialization at the end of the nineteenth century, Porter focuses on the relationship between owners, managers, and workers in industrial villages and company towns.

Pye, David. *The Nature and Art of Workmanship.* Cambridge and New York: At the University Press, 1968. 101 pp.; 31 plates, 9 line drawings, index.

Pye dismisses the arbitrary division between handwork and machine work; instead, he favors the term *workmanship*, of which there are two types: workmanship of risk, in which the result depends on judgment, dexterity, and care; and workmanship of certainty, in which the result depends on a jig or pattern. He makes the important point that skilled workmanship of risk could result in swift, efficient, and relatively uniform production. This concept of free work is essential to understanding large-scale production in preindustrial economies.

Quimby, Ian M. G. *Apprenticeship in Colonial Philadelphia.* Outstanding Dissertations in the Fine Arts, a Garland Series. New York: Garland Publishing, 1985. 10 + xiv + 215 pp.; illustrations, bibliography, appendixes.

This work focuses on the strength of the varieties of apprenticeship before the American Revolution. Quimby attributes this vitality to the success of the reciprocal relationships involved in apprenticeship. Youths were willing to commit themselves because they would be taught a skill for which there was sure demand. In the postrevolutionary period, social upheaval and the viability of larger productive units removed the master from daily contact, and commercial competition meant that skill did not guarantee a job, thus placing a greater emphasis on capital and organizational skills.

Reckman, Bob. "Carpentry: The Craft and Trade." In *Case Studies on the Labor Process*, edited by Andrew Zimbalist, pp. 73–102. New York: Monthly Review Press, 1979.

After refuting the degradation of skill theory by drawing a distinction between complementary and competitive technologies, Reckman shows that balloon framing and machine improvements in the first half of the nineteenth century were complementary technologies that increased the efficient use of labor and wood. In the last half of the nineteenth century, tools, techniques, and materials experienced little net change, but craftsmen lost control of design and construction of machines. Complementary trades (plumber, electrician), and competitive professions (architect, financier) and materials (iron, concrete) brought about the greatest changes.

Rink, Evald. *Technical Americana: A Checklist of Technical Publications Printed before 1831*. Foreword by Eugene S. Ferguson. Sponsored by the Eleutherian Mills Historical Library. Millwood, N.Y.: Kraus International Publications, 1981. xxviii+776 pp.; index.

This invaluable guide to period sources for overviews or manuals of many crafts also includes references to agriculture, milling, and commerce.

Rock, Howard B. *Artisans of the New Republic: The Tradesmen of New York City in the Age of Jefferson*. New York: New York University Press, 1979. xviii+340 pp.; illustrations, 13 tables, 1 map, bibliography, index.

Rock's study of urban artisans focuses on their political activities, entrepreneurial leanings, and labor conflicts. He proposes a difference between traditionally based crafts (goldsmith, baker, blacksmith, painter, sailmaker), licensed crafts (butcher, cartman), and conflict trades (shoemaker, cabinetmaker, clothier, house joiner, printer, shipbuilder, cooper).

Rorabaugh, W. J. *The Craft Apprentice: From Franklin to the Machine Age in America*. New York: Oxford University Press, 1986. xii+270 pp.; illustrations, appendix, index.

This descriptive work charts the decline of traditional apprenticeship between the Revolution and the Civil War. Rorabaugh attributes this transformation to economic and ideological forces: the concentration of capital, the development of technical and mechanical innovations, and the republican beliefs that stressed individualism and self-help. Documentation is drawn primarily from diaries and personal accounts but does not link craft structures to broader historical values.

St. George, Robert Blair. "Fathers, Sons, and Identity: Woodworking Artisans in Southeastern New England, 1620–1700." In *The Craftsman in Early America*, edited by Ian M. G. Quimby, pp. 89–125. New York: W. W. Norton for the Henry Francis du Pont Winterthur Museum, 1984. 4 illustrations, 12 tables.

St. George studies the English context of the first colonial craftsmen in order to understand their expectations and how these transformed in the New World. He then looks at generational, territorial, and vocational continuity of the first three generations of woodworkers. By 1700 fewer craftsmen found viable careers in the urban areas, where vocational values were high. More craftsmen lived outside these urban areas in towns where the emphasis was on familial values.

St. George, Robert Blair. "Style and Structure in the Joinery of Dedham and Medfield, Massachusetts, 1635–1685." In *American Furniture and Its Makers: Winterthur Portfolio 13*, edited by Ian M. G. Quimby, pp. 1–46. Chicago: University of Chicago Press for

the Henry Francis du Pont Winterthur Museum, 1979. 31 illustrations, appendixes.

The major theme of this article is cultural transfer—how an English regional artifactual style was preserved in a relatively homogeneous American settlement. Particularly valuable is the demonstration of drift between a master and his apprentice. *See also* "American Furniture to 1820."

Schwind, Arlene Palmer. "The Glassmakers of Early America." In *The Craftsman in Early America*, edited by Ian M. G. Quimby, pp. 158–89. New York: W. W. Norton for the Henry Francis du Pont Winterthur Museum, 1984. 12 illustrations.

Schwind focuses on the distinctive craft of glassmaking. The large physical plant, the expense of fuel and raw materials, and the number of craftsmen necessary to run the glasshouse made this craft different from most others. The small number of skilled craftsmen possessed simple tools but needed especially well developed skills and depended on others' capital and land. Schwind discusses the isolation of the glassworker: a physical location in a wooded rural area, workplace interaction with other foreign glassblowers, furnace-dictated work hours, and widespread drinking and disease. She also points out the early existence of such industrial practices as nonartisan supervision and the tramping craftsman who took along tools and techniques.

Scranton, Philip. *Proprietary Capitalism: The Textile Manufacture at Philadelphia, 1800–1885*. Cambridge and New York: At the University Press, 1983. xiii+431 pp.; illustrations, 3 maps, 47 tables, index.

While arguing against a depiction of industrialization as a linear progression from handwork to partial mechanization with outwork to integrated systems, Scranton laments the overemphasis on the corporations of nineteenth-century America. Instead, he concentrates on the small, separate, specialized firms in the Philadelphia area. These proprietary firms continued flexible, skill-intensive production by drawing on outwork, small shops, or specialized production. The shops and mills were built on past economic structures, but they smoothly incorporated new cultural and technological changes. Scranton introduces the notion of "the accumulation matrix." He reveals the full complexity of the manufacturing environment by demonstrating the interlocks between material, sociocultural, and external factors.

Smith, Merrit Roe. *Harpers Ferry Armory and the New Technology*. Ithaca: Cornell University Press, 1977. 363 pp.; 20 illustrations, bibliography, tables.

This extremely rich case study contrasts arms production at Harpers Ferry, West Virginia, and Springfield, Massachusetts, by examining the cultural traditions of the shop floor, economic changes, political intervention, market forces, and products. It is particularly strong in its examination of the traditional craft ethos, the new industrial perspective, and the relationship of artisanal culture to environment and change.

Sturt, George. *The Wheelwright's Shop.* 1923. Reprint. Cambridge: At the University Press, 1963. xii+200 pp.; 8 plates, 24 line drawings, glossary, index.

In spite of its romantic rhetoric, this book provides a great deal of insight into the craftsman's mind in a different economic environment, one based on social relations more than money. Particular subjects of interest are how work varied during the day, how craftsmen adjusted their tasks according to the time of day or the season, the importance of repairwork in making a living or learning new techniques, how small shops responded to increased demand, and the importance of social connections for raw materials, tools, labor, and patronage.

Upton, Dell. "Pattern Books and Professionalism: Aspects of the Transformation of Domestic Architecture in America, 1800–1860." *Winterthur Portfolio* 19, nos. 2/3 (Summer/Autumn 1984): 107–50. 38 illustrations.

Upton argues that an important change in the nineteenth century was the professionalization of architects (also implying the professionalization of designers in other trades). The need to differentiate designing as a market profession distinct from trades and to convince the public of the designer's value led to the development of architectural science (seen in builders' handbooks) and the concern with changing fashion (seen in stylebooks). *See also* "Domestic Architecture."

Victor, Stephen K. " 'From the Shop to the Manufactory': Silver and Industry, 1800–1970." In *Silver in American Life: Selections from the Mabel Brady Garvan and Other Collections at Yale University,* edited by Barbara McLean Ward and Gerald W. R. Ward, pp. 23–32. Boston: David R. Godine in association with the Yale University Art Gallery and the American Federation of Arts, 1979. 5 illustrations.

Victor describes the early use of mechanical processes in the making of silver and shows the cumulative effect of mechanization on style, consumption, and craftsmen's lives. He demonstrates how spinning, stamping, and other nineteenth-century techniques grew out of earlier practices and were beneficial in some ways to both artisan and consumer. *See also* "American Silver and Gold."

Vlach, John Michael. *Charleston Blacksmith: The Work of Philip Simmons.* Athens: University of Georgia Press, 1981. xvi+154 pp.; 82 illustrations, 2 maps, 30 line drawings, appendix, glossary.

Drawing on interviews, examination of surviving ironwork, studies of blacksmithing, and historical works on Charleston and black labor, Vlach composes a thorough biography of a contemporary South Carolina smith. The study sheds light on the mental and technical aspects of his work, explains his works, and shows his connections to the community. Vlach's methods, questions, and arguments have important implications for the human component of craft. *See also* "Brass, Copper, Iron, and Tin."

Wallace, Anthony F. C. *Rockdale: The Growth of an American Village in the Early Industrial Revolution.* Technical drawings by Robert Howard. New York and London: W. W. Norton, 1978. xx+553 pp.; approximately 45 illustrations, 3 tables, appendix, bibliography, index.

This study of the textile industry of southeastern Pennsylvania explores the fits and starts of early industrialization and deftly weaves together historical threads of family structure, social structure, technological change, economic beliefs, and political and religious ideology. It is a good model for the necessary level of sophistication and depth needed in the study of artisans.

Ward, Barbara McLean. "Boston Goldsmiths, 1690–1730." In *The Craftsman in Early America,* edited by Ian M. G. Quimby, pp. 126–57. New York: W. W. Norton, 1984. 9 illustrations, appendixes.

Ward's paper differs from all other studies of colonial goldsmiths in that the major focus is the mode of production. The objects are used as documents rather than as the purpose of the study. She is interested not so much in individual craftsmen, but in their interaction—craft hierarchy, wealth distribution, declining social mobility, working relationships among shop members, the range of work of each shop, and the difference between laboring artisan and merchant-producer. *See also* "American Silver and Gold."

Zea, Philip. "Clockmaking and Society at the River and the Bay: Jedidiah and Jabez Baldwin, 1790–1820." In *The Bay and the River, 1600–1900,* edited by Peter D. Benes, pp. 43–59. Boston: Boston University Scholarly Publications, 1982. 5 illustrations.

Zea's main thrust is the connection between the craftsman and his particular context. He follows the careers of two brothers who share the same training. Jedediah Baldwin settled in Hanover, where he ran a barter-based shop with regional clientele. He did not have to make occupation compromises, but balanced production and repairwork. His activity was connected to the annual rhythms of Dartmouth College. Jabez settled in Salem, where he used his training to maintain consistent production of specific silver items and entered into partnerships with craftsmen in Salem, Boston, and Providence. The greater density of population and the entrepreneurial economies of his hometowns allowed him to operate a specie-based retail shop.

Zimmerman, Philip D. "Workmanship as Evidence: A Model for Object Study." *See* "American Furniture to 1820."

The Arts and Crafts Movement in America

Cheryl A. Robertson

with contributions by Thomas Beckman and Robert L. Edwards

Unlike most other chapters in this volume, this one lists publications about a narrow period (1890–1920s) and about several media, notably furniture. The arts and crafts movement was a social phenomenon, an attitude toward work process, and an attempt to simplify and unify domestic architecture, interiors, and landscape. Hence, arts and crafts is not just a style, although some authors treat rectilinear, unornamented "mission oak" as the ineluctable physical manifestation of the ideas of English arts and crafts philosophers John Ruskin and William Morris and their American followers. It seems preferable to interpret the movement in America as a matrix of separate developments exhibiting a good deal of local color. The prevalent hierarchical approach of identifying "great men" (the current criteria are too often prolific writing and flamboyant personality) and tracing dissemination of their pronouncements and products distorts and over-simplifies a highly complex cultural phenomenon.

In the first issue of volume 2 of *Tiller*, four different concurrent cultural behaviors that fit under the rubric of arts and crafts are identified: craftsmen and communities that espoused "the simple life" and sought to create objects reflecting their ideals; individuals who valued handicraft and worked alone or in cooperative units to preserve and refine manual skills; designers who participated in avant-garde artistic activity but had only marginal ties to arts and crafts philosophy; and reformers and utopian experimenters whose chief concerns were thoughts and life-styles rather than chairs, pots, or hammered-silver tea sets.

Each category is represented in these entries. Two studies of communities—Byrdcliffe in Woodstock, New York, and Rose Valley in Moylan, Pennsylvania—draw on verbal documentation and extant objects to show how theory and practice were combined with limited success, at least in making and marketing furniture and ceramics. Andrea Callen and Harvey Jones give biographical facts and illustrate works by artist-craftsmen who valued handiwork either as a source of income or as a means to satisfy a personal creative impulse. Much of the painting, woodcarving, book illustration, and other decorative arts pictured in these texts is highly ornamental, in contrast to the output of certain contemporary designers headquartered in the Chicago area or California. H. Allen Brooks's *Prairie School* chronicles commissions by midwestern architects who sought to formulate not only a functionalist American architecture but also complementary, customized household furnishings. Randall Makinson expounds on the clean lines and elegant joinery characteristic of the constructional aesthetic of Pasadena architects Charles Sumner Greene and Henry Mather Greene. Charles Keeler's *Simple Home* is a period source demonstrative of the fourth classification—idealistic experimenters whose primary interest was how to live rather than what to make. Keeler's Berkeley utopia never came about, but he did found the Hillside Club to popularize his notions of harmony between natural and built environments.

Recently some historians have begun to scrutinize the ideological and sociological aspects of the arts and crafts movement. T. J. Jackson Lears and Robert Winter offer thoughtful insights on antimodernism and arts and crafts as secular religion and social salvation. Eileen Boris provides a comprehensive work that reports on reformist motivations and accomplishments not only in the aesthetic realm but also in manual training schools and settlement houses and among labor union activists and philanthropic capitalists.

Like Boris's book, Robert Clark's *Aspects of the Arts and Crafts Movement* is wide ranging, covering origins, design issues, and the social implications of style. Lionel Lambourne's *Utopian Craftsmen* is likewise notable for its attention to heterogeneous views and manifestations of the movement's intent. Coy Ludwig attempts a thematic organization by ideology, home life, communities and societies, craftsmen, and designers; he succeeds in showing diversity at the expense of commonality and mutuality.

Ludwig's work typifies the prevailing condition of much scholarship in the arts and crafts arena. Current emphasis is on cataloguing and surveying, a trend started by the ground-breaking Princeton University show and catalogue of 1972, *The Arts and Crafts Movement in America*, and continued twelve years later by Danforth Museum's *On the Threshold of Modern Design*. The cataloguing mentality is both a cause and an effect of antiquarianism. Collectors and dealers have been largely responsible for the spate of reprints that have fueled the adulation—and raised the retail value—of Roycroft, Craftsman, Stickley, Limbert, and other arts and crafts furniture. What gets reprinted appears to be determined by what is easily accessible and useful in the marketplace rather than by what is important to the development of typologies of versatile early twentieth-century tastemakers. Turn of the Century Editions' publications display sensitivity to the kinds of paper, ink, cover designs, and color schemes found in period trade booklets. Still, trade catalogue facsimiles, auction catalogues, collectors' volumes such as those by David Cathers and Charles Hamilton, and encyclopedias like those by James Mackay or Isabelle Anscombe and Charlotte Gere are alike in their presentation of partially digested, and sometimes misleading, data devoid of interpretive subtlety.

Perhaps macrocosmic analysis of arts and crafts must await additional microcosmic examinations of specific craftsmen, communities, guilds, and societies. What, for instance, do we really know about public and private philanthropic endeavors to preserve or reinvigorate traditional crafts in the Southwest or in Appalachia, or even in New England? Lonn Taylor and Dessa Bokides have devoted a chapter to the Spanish colonial revival in *New Mexican Furniture* (Santa Fe: Museum of New Mexico Press, 1987), but additional regional studies are needed to deepen understanding of the sources and transmutations of the important Hispanic and Indian strains in the American arts and crafts saga. New Hampshire Historical Society's 1986 exhibition, "They Put Their Trust in Their Hands," for which no catalogue was published, whets the appetite with references to five communities that initiated home industries producing Italian cutwork embroidery, raffia baskets, hooked or woven rugs, and other textiles and accessories in the 1898 to 1926 period. Although the midwestern cities of Chicago and Cincinnati have been studied for their respective contributions to "modern" architecture and fine ceramics, Kenneth Trapp points out in his introduction to Stephen Gray's *Arts and Crafts Furniture*, "Cincinnati has long been accorded preeminence for its art pottery, particularly for Rookwood. Although one of the nation's most prolific manufacturing centers in the nineteenth century, Cincinnati has not been much recognized for its Arts and Crafts furniture" (p. 3). Trapp goes on to identify a major flaw in current historical and art historical inquiries: the tendency to look to England for the standard by which arts and crafts in America should be measured. Continental innovators, particularly the secessionists in Germany and Austria, inspired progressive designs by the Shop of the Crafters, as well as by George Niedecken of Milwaukee and by Roycroft metalworker Karl Kipp. Sharon Darling, always worth reading because of her noteworthy blending of curatorial skills with the intellectual curiosity of the historian-detective, has unearthed little-known Chicago manual arts instructors, furniture makers, and decorative designers who set up cooperative ventures called the Crafters, Skokie Shop, Skylight Club, Windiknowe Shop, Craftsman's Guild, South Park Workshop Association, and so forth. *California Design 1910*, edited by Timothy Andersen, Eudorah Moore, and Robert Winter, plays a similar role for the West Coast in charting the territory with enticing but sketchy descriptions of complex personalities like Ernest Batchelder, who was a tilemaker, a teacher, an author, and a design theoretician.

Help in sorting out arts and crafts rhetoric, and the plethora of objects that reflected or, sometimes, contradicted it, is on the way. Museums deserve encouragement and praise for their efforts to collect, display, and bring scholarly scrutiny to bear on the artifactual and documentary legacies of the arts and crafts movement. Wendy Kaplan's 1987 catalogue of the traveling exhibition "The Art That Is Life" is encyclopedic in the lengthy entries and interpretive essays that bring together the combined wisdom of collectors, academics, and museum professionals. The thematic organization of the show and the catalogue does not always succeed, but it attempts to synthesize the varied manifestations of the movement in the intellectual, material, and social realms. The Boston-originated exhibition drew on, and sparked in turn, other museum exhibitions. For example, displays and catalogues about metalworker Samuel Yellin, art potter Frederick Hurten Rhead, and manual arts instructor Edward Worst, who was noted for his textile craftwork, preceded "The Art That Is Life." Appearing in 1987 were local studies of arts and crafts furniture at Grand Rapids Art Museum and of Addison B. Le Boutillier, best known as the chief designer for Grueby Pottery, at Andover Historical Society. *Arts and Crafts Quarterly*, launched in 1986, gives updates on museum projects, symposiums, and preservation and movement figures like furniture maker Charles Rohlfs (vol. 3, no. 1), who is the subject of a biography being prepared by Michael James.

Dissertations and books that are recently published or in progress bear witness to the dynamism of research into turn-of-the-century material life. Trapp is finishing a dissertation on Rookwood pottery (University of Illinois, Urbana-Champaign) and laying the groundwork for an exhibition in 1991 about the arts and crafts movement in California. Beverly Brandt has completed her dissertation,

"Mutually Helpful Relations: Architects, Craftsmen, and the Society of Arts and Crafts, Boston, 1897–1917" (Boston University, 1985) as well as two articles for *Tiller* (vol. 2, nos. 1, 5), the latter of which addresses the linkage between arts and crafts and colonial revival. Winterthur's *Colonial Revival in America*, edited by Alan Axelrod (New York: W. W. Norton, 1985), sheds additional light on the preindustrial mind set, handicraft emphasis, "simple life" reforms, and social agendas that the revivalists shared with numerous arts- and craftsmen. Another aspect of the colonial revival—the Hispanic past of the western United States—is the topic of Karen J. Weitze's *California Mission Revival* (Los Angeles: Hennessey and Ingalls, 1984). Weitze devotes a chapter to the historical intersection of mission symbols and arts and crafts icons. Bruce Kahler's dissertation explores the arts and crafts movement in Chicago from 1897 to 1910 (American Studies, Purdue University, 1986). Cleota Reed, author of *The Arts and Crafts Ideal: The Ward House, an Architect and His Craftsmen* (Syracuse, N.Y.: Institute for the Development of Evolutive Architecture, 1978), has published an important monograph, *Henry Chapman Mercer and the Moravian Pottery and Tile Works* (Philadelphia: University of Pennsylvania Press, 1987), the second chapter of which is devoted to the subject of Mercer and the arts and crafts movement. Jean France, who wrote a short catalogue on artist-architect Harvey Ellis for a 1973 exhibition jointly sponsored by the Strong Museum and the Memorial Art Gallery of the University of Rochester, has turned her attention to architect Claude Fayette Bragdon, a founder of Rochester Arts and Crafts Society in 1897. Mary Corbin Sies has gleaned excellent insights from period sources such as the shelter magazines *House Beautiful*, *American Homes and Gardens*, and *House and Garden*, to the end of producing a dissertation, "American Country House Architecture in Context: The Suburban Ideal of Living in the East and Midwest, 1877–1917" (University of Michigan, 1987).

Primary sources are what we urge not just scholars but also undergraduates, interior designers, and woodworkers to consult for a better comprehension of the movement and its legacy of craft studios, museum institutes, and industrial arts curricula in public schools. Even a small sample of *House Beautiful* issues that illustrate colonial revival and prairie-style rooms as equally fashionable alternatives, coupled with perusal of the *Craftsman* and the *Philistine*, wherein philosophy and advertising sometimes become philosophy of advertising, and a quick survey of professional journals like *Western Architect*, *Architectural Record*, and *Brickbuilder* will reveal how superficial and elementary many secondary sources are. We hope that teachers who incorporate the arts and crafts era into their courses will direct their students to the letters, drawings, business records, and other unpublished papers in archives throughout the country, a partial listing of which is contained in *Tiller* (vol. 1, no. 5). *The Art That Is Life*, *The Arts and Crafts Movement in New York State*, and *Chicago Furniture* have excellent footnotes and bibliographies that indicate additional manuscript and printed works of the late nineteenth and early twentieth centuries. Research libraries, sometimes in concert with museums, are becoming increasingly active in procuring special collections of verbal and artifactual documents relating to artist-craftsmen. A stellar example is the announcement in mid 1987 by Huntington Library, in conjunction with Gamble House, of the creation of a center devoted to Greene and Greene's works.

The following entries are by no means an exhaustive compilation of all the published material pertaining to aspects of the arts and crafts movement. Since our focus is the United States, we have excluded writings about British protagonists, except Gillian Naylor's "classic," which is quoted by almost everyone who has penned thoughts about the movement in the United States. Individuals closely identified with specific media, be it Adelaide Alsop Robineau in ceramics or Bernard Maybeck in architecture, are not treated for two reasons: first, their histories are the purview of other sections of this bibliography; second, their significant contributions lie outside the realm of the decorative arts per se. Entries on the art of the book and on prairie school material are included as reminders that fine printing and innovative architecture attracted the creative energy of the most vocal and talented arts and crafts proponents. Furniture is well represented, in part because many analyses of the movement focus on furniture and because a furniture emphasis is to be expected in a movement in which architects played a central role. Whether one looks at Greene and Greene, Ellis, William Price, or Frank Lloyd Wright, one finds a preoccupation with furniture as a key aspect of furnishing schemes that complete the harmonious, unified domestic environment. Date of publication was an important criterion for our selections since original works or reprints that have appeared in the last few years are more readily available in bookstores and libraries than are earlier editions. However, a sizable percentage of these books is either museum catalogues or products of small presses. In some cases, they may be more difficult to locate than periodicals from the turn of the century.

I want to express my thanks to the two colleagues who assisted me in preparing the annotations. Robert L. Edwards has curated and lent to arts and crafts shows and has authored or published new research on known and unknown artist-craftsmen; he brought verbal and visual knowledge to this project. To my strengths in the prairie school and arts and crafts home life, Thomas Beckman added a generalist's perspective derived from a long-standing interest in book arts and in nineteenth- and early twentieth-century architectural pattern books, from many years as a museum registrar and from personal experience as an arts and crafts house dweller.

Andersen, Timothy J., Eudorah M. Moore, and Robert W. Winter, eds. *California Design 1910*. Rev. ed. Santa Barbara and Salt Lake City: Peregrine Smith, 1980. 144 pp.; 320 illustrations, index.

California Design is an enthusiastic survey of California domestic architecture, landscape painting, and decorative arts from the 1890s to the 1920s. The essays and catalogue entries on media and individual practitioners are of varying length and quality. The authors attempt to illustrate "how the forms and values of the [arts and crafts] movement were influenced and changed by the nature and surroundings of the Californians" (p. 4). The introductory essay is devoted exclusively to Pasadena and should be balanced by a reading of Leslie M. Freudenheim and Elizabeth S. Sussman, *Building with Nature: Roots of the San Francisco Bay Tradition* (Santa Barbara: Peregrine Smith, 1974). One tantalizingly brief essay focuses on education in arts and crafts design. There is little exploration of Hispanic or native American influences, and there is almost no mention of arts and crafts communities, societies, or guilds.

Anscombe, Isabelle, and Charlotte Gere. *Arts and Crafts in Britain and America*. New York: Rizzoli International Publications, 1978. 232 pp.; 334 black and white and color illustrations, bibliography, index.

Although arranged in encyclopedia format with thumbnail sketches of artists, organizations, and companies, the lack of a systematic organization (entries are not even alphabetical) assumes that readers already have more knowledge of the arts and crafts movement than the basic information provided in the book. The index must be used to discover all the references to one artist, which may be scattered through seven chapters with vague titles such as "Towards a Free Style" and "The Emergence of a 'Polychromatic' Idiom." The introduction features a long discussion of the American arts and crafts movement that is rife with misinformation and therefore mistaken interpretation. A caption identifies an L. and J. G. Stickley bookcase and a table as being Gustave Stickley's Craftsman furniture. The early work of Charles Sumner Greene and Henry Mather Greene is characterized as Craftsman, a term specific to Gustave Stickley that should not be used either in a generic sense or in relation to elaborate Greene and Greene furniture. The "original aspirations of Shaker furniture" (p. 19) as an influence on William Price's Gothic-style Rose Valley furniture is, without a footnote, news from nowhere. One cannot determine why some objects or makers were included and others were not. Why was Grueby Faience Company included but not Teco? Why was a company as peripheral to the movement as Herter Brothers accorded an illustration as well as a "biography," while E. W. Godwin, a designer of major status, was allowed neither? The book is without original research and draws on previously published illustration materials. Conclusions are sometimes opinions inadequately supported by facts.

Arts and Crafts Quarterly. Edited by David Rago. Trenton, N.J., 1986–.

Issued in an 8-by-11-inch newsletter format, this journal increased from eight to twenty-two pages per issue during its first year. Most valuable for its "Current and Coming" column and exhibition previews, it also publishes brief articles on contemporary craftsmen as well as turn-of-the-century masters. Articles on Europeans are to be included in future issues. Contributors are usually enthusiasts and collectors rather than scholars. The high point of the journal thus far is the previously unknown sources cited in an essay on the philosophy of Charles Rohlfs (vol. 1, no. 3). The "Good/Better/Best" section borrows its format from Albert Sack's *Fine Points of Furniture* and is equally subjective.

Ayres, William, ed. *A Poor Sort of Heaven, a Good Sort of Earth: The Rose Valley Arts and Crafts Experiment.* Exhibition catalogue. Chadds Ford, Pa.: Brandywine River Museum, 1983. 134 pp.; illustrations, illustrated catalogue, bibliography.

This exhibition catalogue includes brief essays of varying quality by seven authors on aspects of a Philadelphia-area utopian crafts fellowship that was active from 1901 to 1907. Founded by architect William Price (1861–1916), Rose Valley comprised about fifty people, chiefly Price's friends and relatives. Its activities and philosophy are documented in surviving minute books and its journal, the *Artsman.* The most significant product of the Rose Valley shops is Price's expensive, carved, neo-Gothic furniture that was produced by immigrant artisans who were never fully integrated into the community. Also important are the dwellings that Price designed for the area; ranging from cottages to mansions, many exhibit contemporary British influences in both massing and details. Most of the authors make no attempt to place the Rose Valley experiment within the broader context of the American arts and crafts movement.

Bavaro, Joseph J., and Thomas L. Mossman. *The Furniture of Gustav Stickley: History, Techniques, and Projects.* New York: Van Nostrand Reinhold Co., 1982. 175 pp.; illustrations, bibliography, index.

In this work, divided into five sections, the intent of Bavaro and Mossman is to give Stickley's biography, set forth his philosophy, chronicle his achievements as part of fin de siècle American and European art developments, and explicate Craftsman materials and methods, as well as provide step-by-step procedures, working drawings, and exploded views for nine examples of furniture: mirror, screen, combination bookcase-table, rocker, recliner, settle, dining table, bookcase, and clock case. Five of these projects were culled from the Home Training in Cabinet-Work series published in the *Craftsman.* Both Bavaro and Mossman are design professors at Los Angeles Valley College; their sketches and comments on the fabrication of Stickley furniture carry more weight than their forays into historical analysis. Used in conjunction with H. H. Windsor's *Mission Furniture*, this work is a valuable tool for students seeking do-it-yourself experience with what Stickley termed "the structural style in cabinetmaking."

Boris, Eileen. *Art and Labor: Ruskin, Morris, and the Craftsman Ideal in America.* American Civilization Series, edited by Allen F. Davis. Philadelphia: Temple University Press, 1986. xviii+261 pp.; 47 illustrations, index.

The enormous amount of material compiled in this volume begins to fill the need for substantial, high-quality scholarship missing in most of the literature about the arts and crafts movement in America. Boris's text is so packed with researched information that there is little room for narrative or interpretation. Labor—including the social and economic forces associated with industrialization, as well as "progressive" antimodern concerns—is emphasized, along with aesthetics, as a moral imperative and a powerful agent for cultural assimilation and redemption. American women's role in the movement is highlighted, reflecting the currently popular concept that the arts and crafts movement provided an opportunity for women to free themselves from the constricting male domination suffered by their Victorian predecessors. Boris describes arts and crafts societies and communities, philanthropic endeavors, manual training, museum-sponsored education schemes, and societal and industrial reforms. She elaborates on the tenet that through beauty, growing out of and integral to the work process, everyone could achieve a high quality of living. Unfortunately, the resulting arts and crafts objects expressive of, and often at odds with, the ideals of the movement are discussed neither sufficiently nor from firsthand experience. Such contradictions as hammer marks on copper goods, where handiwork amounted to little more than assembling machine-produced parts, deserve more scholarly scrutiny. This study would have been twice as long if it had treated objects as thoroughly as ideals. *See also* "Craftsmen."

Brooks, H. Allen. *The Prairie School: Frank Lloyd Wright and His Midwest Contemporaries.* 1972. Reprint. New York: W. W. Norton, 1976. xxiii + 373 pp.; 247 illustrations, index.

Brooks's treatise places the work of mentor Louis Sullivan and chief protagonist Frank Lloyd Wright in the cultural framework of architectural reform emanating from Chicago between 1900 and World War I. Some twenty architects are studied in relation to their indebtedness not only to the masters of the prairie style but also to transatlantic compatriots such as Charles Ashbee and Baillie Scott and continental modernists publicized through international periodicals and expositions. In several instances (George W. Maher and Robert Spencer, for example), personal preference results in a less than thorough account of an architect's contributions. Since prairie school practitioners believed movable furnishings should be custom designed to fit the needs of the client and to harmonize with the form and ornament of the house shell, many interior photographs appear alongside plans and elevations. The text derives from careful research in unpublished materials, from interviews, and from period journals such as *Western Architect* (1902–31), the only architectural publication to record prairie school commissions consistently and extensively. *The Prairie School* should be supplemented by Brooks's *Prairie School Architecture: Studies from "the Western Architect"* (Toronto: University of Toronto Press, 1975).

The Byrdcliffe Arts and Crafts Colony: Life by Design. Exhibition catalogue. Wilmington: Delaware Art Museum, 1984. 31 pp.; 30 illustrations.

Written as an adjunct to an exhibition originated by Delaware Art Museum, this catalogue concentrates on human relationships and motivations rather than connoisseurship. Two essays—"Byrdcliffe: Life by Design" by Robert L. Edwards and "White Pines Pottery: The Continuing Arts and Crafts Experiment" by Jane Perkins Claney—report on and draw conclusions from a trove of scrap and record books, glaze samples, drawings for textiles and painted-wood decoration, and correspondence to describe the work process and intent in a utopian colony where living the simple life was more important than commercial or artistic success.

Callen, Anthea. *Angel in the Studio: Women Artists of the Arts and Crafts Movement, 1870–1914.* London: Astragal Books, 1979. viii + 232 pp.; illustrations, appendixes, bibliography, index.

Thought-provoking comments about class structure, feminism, and political conflict are presented in the introductory and concluding chapters. Intervening chapters are organized by media—ceramics, needlework, lacemaking, metalworking, woodcarving and furniture making, and printing and bookbinding. Four groups of women active in the movement are identified: working-class or peasant women employed in the revival of traditional-rural cottage industries; aristocrats and middle-class women who were philanthropically inclined to support household endeavors in the countryside but design schools in the cities; destitute gentlewomen, both free-lancers at home and wage earners in commercial workshops; and the inner circle of daughters, wives, and friends allied to male leaders in the arts and crafts movement. Callen is stronger in English rather than American source material, but her partisan view that women were and are outsiders in a patriarchal culture colors her discussions of both countries.

Cathers, David M. *Furniture of the American Arts and Crafts Movement: Stickley and Roycroft Mission Oak.* Photography by Peter Curran. New York: New American Library, 1981. 275 pp.; approximately 145 illustrations, appendixes, bibliography, index.

Cathers's title suggests a far more comprehensive work than the contents provide. The Roycrofters are given fleeting treatment with only a few of the many photographs devoted to their furniture. L. and J. G. Stickley and Stickley Brothers Company are mentioned perfunctorily. The book is primarily a survey of recently marketed Gustave Stickley furniture. A system of dating based on types of Stickley labels is offered, yet several well-known types are omitted. The standard for rarity seems to have been determined by the inventory of a single retail outlet. Some of the photographs depict pieces so altered by restoration as to be misrepresentative. One appendix is an interview with ninety-three-year-old Barbara Wiles, Stickley's daughter. Her family stories are touching and humorous, but her memory is not accurate enough to provide reliable information about furniture production and sales.

Champney, Freeman. *Art and Glory: The Story of Elbert Hubbard.* New York: Crown Publishers, 1968. 248 pp.; illustrations, bibliography, index.

Art and Glory is the best of several memoirs and biographies of Hubbard (1856–1915), a flamboyant entrepreneur of the American arts and crafts movement. A successful businessman who retired in his thirties to devote himself to writing, Hubbard established Roycroft Press in East Aurora, New York, in 1895. Hundreds of laborers found employment with the expanding Roycroft Shops, which produced furniture, copperwork, and leather goods in addition to books and periodicals. Not quite the bohemian he was often thought to be, Hubbard was a strong believer in the work ethic and spent much of his later career writing and lecturing on employee initiative and the values of big business. Champney puts Hubbard's "brilliance, bombast, sentimentality, calculated sincerity, pretense, and self-revelation" into context (p. 2), but in so doing neglects the products of his shops and their makers.

Clark, Robert Judson, ed. *The Arts and Crafts Movement in America, 1876–1916.* Exhibition catalogue. Princeton: Princeton University Press, 1972. 190 pp.; 295 illustrations, bibliography.

Published as a catalogue for the 1972 show of the same name, this work has been the standard overall survey of both the movement's ideas—in essays by Clark, Martin Eidelberg, David Hanks, and Susan Otis Thompson—and its objects. The catalogue is divided into five sections: the eastern seaboard, the Midwest, the Pacific coast, book arts, and art pottery. The last is the least successful section because the art pottery movement, while sometimes falling into the realm of arts and crafts, has a longer and different history. Much has been learned since the catalogue was published, particularly about furniture. For example, entries for L. and J. G. Stickley Company and Stickley Brothers Company state that their products were inferior to Craftsman furniture made by Gustave Stickley. All these factories used veneers and laminations, and each had some fine original designs. In spite of mistakes in details that have become obvious with time, a surprising proportion of the objects illustrated have remained classic examples of the movement's production. *See also* "Surveys."

Clark, Robert Judson, ed. *Aspects of the Arts and Crafts Movement in America. Record of the Art Museum*, Princeton University, 34, no. 2 (1975). 44 pp.; 33 illustrations.

This work contains six of the eight symposium papers delivered in conjunction with the 1972 exhibition, "The Arts and Crafts Movement in America, 1876–1916." Edgar Kaufmann, Jr., points out progressive and reactionary tendencies in the international arts and crafts arena, postulating that the movement derived as much from the Enlightenment as from the industrial revolution. Martin Eidelberg and Marilyn Johnson Bordes trace stylistic aspects of pottery and furniture and demonstrate Americans' indebtedness to European ceramics developments and Anglo-Japanese aestheticism. Robert Koch focuses on Louis Tiffany's painterly approach to ornamental glass, while Robert Winter comments on the redemptive, progressivist traits of the Anglo-American arts and crafts movement as revealed in the writings of Arthur Mackmurdo, Charles Ashbee, Gustave Stickley, and Mary Ware Dennett of Boston Arts and Crafts Society. Carl Schorske's observations stress the polarity between the genteel, urban(e) arts and crafts movement and the sturdy, petit bourgeois movement.

Conforti, Michael P. "Orientalism on the Upper Mississippi: The Work of John S. Bradstreet." *Minneapolis Institute of Art Bulletin* 65 (1981–82): 2–35. 30 illustrations.

In the "frontier" cities of Minneapolis and St. Paul, Bradstreet created commercial and domestic interiors that mirrored changing trends in American high-style design of the late nineteenth and early twentieth centuries. He worked in Gothic, Moorish, art nouveau, Japanese, and arts and crafts styles, but adapted each to reflect his personal taste and that of his local clients. Bradstreet was both an imitator and an innovator. His Crafthouse was derivative of William Morris's Kelmscott Manor, yet his *jin-di-sugi* paneling and furniture represented a novel American translation of traditional Japanese woodworking techniques. Conforti's methodological blend of historical and art historical analysis results in a well-rounded picture of the artist, his times, and his regional culture. See also Ronald L. M. Ramsay, "John Scott Bradstreet and the Minneapolis Crafthouse," *Tiller* 1, no. 4 (March–April 1983): 37–48.

Crichton, Laurie W. *Book Decoration in America, 1890–1910*. Revised by Wayne G. Hammond and Robert L. Volz. Exhibition catalogue. Williamstown, Mass.: Chapin Library, Williams College, 1979. 87 pp.; illustrations, index.

This attractive catalogue, which accompanied an exhibition of seventy books assembled from diverse collections in the Williams College library, deals with typography and ornamentation, not descriptive illustrations, and includes information on binding design (for more on this subject, see Charles Gullans and John Espey, "American Trade Bindings and Their Designers, 1880–1915," in *Collectible Books: Some New Paths*, ed. Jean Peters [New York: R. R. Bowker Co., 1979], pp. 32–67). Crichton builds on Susan Otis Thompson's *American Book Design* in examining a variety of stylistic influences in addition to that of William Morris. Crichton emphasizes designers rather than publishers and treats important practitioners neglected by Thompson. Although the works of each graphic artist are usually grouped together, the groups appear to be randomly organized, and the use of the index is mandatory.

Darling, Sharon. *Chicago Furniture: Art, Craft, and Industry, 1833–1983. See* "American Furniture, 1820–1920."

The Domestic Scene (1897–1927): George M. Niedecken, Interior Architect. Exhibition catalogue. Milwaukee: Milwaukee Art Museum, 1981. 108 pp.; black and white and color illustrations, checklist, bibliography, index.

This catalogue accompanied an exhibition based on materials owned by or lent to Milwaukee Art Museum's Prairie Archives. Interior designer Niedecken (1878–1945), a Milwaukee native, is best remembered for his intermittent collaboration as muralist and furniture manufacturer with Frank Lloyd Wright. The catalogue reveals that Niedecken was the designer of some furniture heretofore attributed to Wright and that he occasionally modified other Wright furnishings produced in his workshops. Niedecken's training and practice as a professional interior designer is described, and his 1913 "Relationship of Decorator, Architect, and Client" is reprinted. The text also explains how Niedecken was able to synthesize the academic-revivalist mentality and arts and crafts secessionist theory by designing simultaneously in several styles. Client profiles and information on furniture construction techniques are included.

Farnam, Anne. "The Arts and Crafts Tradition in Essex County." *Essex Institute Historical Collections* 113, no. 1 (January 1977): 1–15. 12 illustrations.

This article was written in conjunction with a loan exhibition at the Essex Institute in 1977. Farnam sheds light on macrocosmic aspects of the arts and crafts movement—the establishment of village industries and cooperative societies of craftsworkers, perseverance of individualistic designer-craftsmen, and development of progressive curricula in museum institutes, fine arts colleges, or summer classes in rural resorts—through microcosmic studies of Arthur E. Baggs and Marblehead Pottery, silversmith Franklin Porter, and art composition instructor Arthur Wesley Dow. In each instance, Farnam indicates how the picturesque landscape and colonial artifacts of New England affected both the content and the method of these twentieth-century artist-preservationists.

Finlay, Nancy. *Artists of the Book in Boston, 1890–1910.* Exhibition catalogue. Cambridge, Mass.: Department of Printing and Graphic Arts, Houghton Library, Harvard College Library, 1985. xiv+114 pp.; 56 illustrations, bibliography, indexes.

Boston was important in the book arts at the turn of the century due to the discriminating taste of its publishers and the technical abilities of its many printers. This attractive catalogue documents publications produced in Boston (although not necessarily designed there) through a brief introductory essay, 100 entries, and thirty-eight artists' biographies that offer much information not available elsewhere. Finlay's emphasis is on illustrators rather than typographers. Several of the designers were architects or painters, and posters as well as books are included. Except in the work of Bertram Grosvenor Goodhue, the influence of William Morris was minimal, although conventionalized decoration in line, mass, and pattern prevailed. Design sources from England, France, and Japan are discussed, as is art nouveau. Two-thirds of the entries are devoted to trade books of the 1890s; only after 1900 was there a significant number of private press editions created for bibliophiles.

Freeman, John Crosby. *The Forgotten Rebel: Gustav Stickley and His Craftsman Mission Furniture.* Watkins Glen, N.Y.: Century House, 1966. 112 pp.; illustrations, bibliography, index.

Out of print and obsolete, Freeman's augmented University of Delaware thesis must be credited for its early recognition of Stickley as a major force in the American arts and crafts movement. The book includes part of a 1909 Stickley catalogue, two overlapping bibliographies, and an unreliable but nonetheless useful index of authors found in the *Craftsman.* Some family and business history included here is not published elsewhere.

Freeman, John Crosby, ed. *Mission and Art Nouveau.* Antique Furniture Handbooks, no. 5. Watkins Glen, N.Y.: Century House, 1966. [102] pp.; illustrations.

In the tradition of Freeman's eccentric productions, this paperback (which is no longer in print) has an impressive table of contents covering a wide range of subjects. This is a reprint of the Popular Mechanics Company handbook *Mission Furniture* by H. H. Windsor, now available in several other reprints, and, more important, of a catalogue from Joseph P. McHugh Company. Aside from his claims to be the first producer of mission furniture, McHugh offered inventive designs that were mass produced at the time (the catalogue is undated, but 1902 appears on some illustrations).

Gilbert, James B. "Reviving the Work Ethic: The Arts and Crafts Movement." In James B. Gilbert, *Work without Salvation: America's Intellectuals and Industrial Alienation, 1880–1910,* pp. 83–96. Baltimore: Johns Hopkins University Press, 1977.

Gilbert provides concise coverage of philosophical aspects of the arts and crafts movement and emphasizes the discontinuity between prevailing and ideal relationships of the individual to the factory system in particular and to urban society in general. The movement's romanticized view of both medieval guilds and America's preindustrial past produced a conservative ideology which "proposed to put the old order back together again and sought to reestablish the hegemony of the work ethic," but overlooked "movements in psychology and philosophy that attempted to restate the relationship of mankind to work in a new, behaviorist form." Ambiguities and contradictions within the movement are noted but are not rigorously analyzed. Gilbert's conclusions are based on a limited reading of primary sources and reveal a lack of familiarity with arts and crafts designers and their works.

Grand Rapids Bookcase and Chair Company. *Life-Time Furniture: The Cloister Styles.* Ca. 1910. Reprint. New York: Turn of the Century Editions, 1981. iii+109 pp.; illustrations.

Unlike Charles P. Limbert Company, Grand Rapids Bookcase and Chair Company touted its efficient production, which was made possible by state-of-the-art machines and systematic division of labor. *Cloister Styles* was one of two catalogues issued yearly by this Michigan furniture manufacturer; the other featured "Mahogany and Oak Dining Room Furniture in Period and Modern Styles." Chairs and library furniture, whether bookcases, desks, or desk-tables, are the common offerings. Also prominent are settees and buffets that are constructed in the same manner as rockers and armchairs, with pinned mortise-and-tenon joints and panel or slat sides and backs. Captions for the different forms are limited to measurements, with the exception of drop-leaf, gateleg, and turn-top tables, which are afforded several descriptive sentences.

Gray, Stephen, ed. *Arts and Crafts Furniture: Shop of the Crafters at Cincinnati.* Introduction by Kenneth R. Trapp. 1906. Reprint. New York: Turn of the Century Editions, 1983. 71 pp.; 185 illustrations.

The contents of this book differ from other reprinted trade literature in three ways: Germanic references outweigh English ones in the mission designs illustrated; the preponderance of hall clocks, smokers' cabinets, cellarettes, shaving stands, tables, and other forms for the library indicates a calculated bid for male clients; and handcraftmanship is not linked with any particular style. For instance, quality construction characterizes superficially different tall-case clocks labeled "Colonial," "Empire," "Van Dyke," and "Viennese." Austro-Hungarian sources were preeminent for the German workers at the Shop of the Crafters. Paul Horti, who participated in the Hungarian exhibit at the St. Louis Fair of 1904, originated some Crafter designs. Captions for many of the more expensive Cincinnati pieces specify inlaid colored woods imported from Austria. Sixteen plates of contemporary secession interiors are provided as home decoration suggestions. See also Kenneth R. Trapp, "The Shop of the Crafters at Cincinnati, 1904–20," *Tiller* 2, no. 5 (February 1986): 8–25.

Gray, Stephen, ed. *The Mission Furniture of L. and J. G. Stickley.* New York: Turn of the Century Editions, 1983. 189 pp.; illustrations.

Mission Furniture is divided into five sections: a brief history of the Fayetteville, New York, company by Mary Ann Clegg Smith; a discussion by Robert L. Edwards of the ideas and construction techniques behind the mission furniture of Gustave Stickley's younger brothers, Leopold and John George; the sketches from the Onondaga Shops, including the first label used by the L. and J. G. partnership; a compilation of the pages and crayon drawings from the 1910 *Handcraft Furniture* catalogue; and the advertising plates and unpublished designs (ca. 1910–16) assembled from original illustrations lent by Alfred Audi, current owner of L. and J. G. Stickley Company. This anthology should be compared with Stickley Brothers Company's *Quaint Furniture in Arts and Crafts* since John George had been associated with the Grand Rapids enterprise and Leopold with the Eastwood factory before they joined forces in Fayetteville.

Gray, Stephen, and Robert Edwards, eds. *Collected Works of Gustav Stickley.* New York: Turn of the Century Editions, 1981. 165 pp.; illustrations.

Gray presents a sampling of line drawings, renderings, and photographs excerpted from the *Craftsman*, promotional materials distributed to Stickley retailers, and trade literature such as *Things Wrought* by United Crafts (1902), and *Hand-Wrought Metal Work from the Craftsman Workshops* (1905). Pages 57 to 116 are devoted to Catalogue D, *Cabinet Work from the Craftsman Workshops* (ca. 1904), which was notable for its decorative vignettes of accessories tastefully arranged atop tables and case furniture that was advertised in mahogany, fumed oak, or silver-gray maple. Explanations of coloring and finishes for wood, as well as comments on the evolution and social implications of Craftsman furniture, are extracted from other Stickley publications ranging from 1901

to 1914. Much of the visual data included here is not reproduced elsewhere, but the lack of text elucidating Stickley's philosophy about democratic art and domestic harmony undermines Gray's stated intent to produce a reference book useful to a heterogeneous audience of collectors, aestheticians, and cultural historians.

Hamilton, Charles F. *Roycroft Collectibles.* New York: A. S. Barnes, 1980. 128 pp.; 107 black and white illustrations, 10 color plates, index.

Elbert Hubbard's Roycroft Shops, in business from 1895 to 1938, produced books and periodicals, furniture, leather goods, and copperwork. The dust-jacket copy for *Roycroft Collectibles* claims that the brief text covers "the full range of items related to Elbert Hubbard," but this is mere hyperbole. Furniture, for example, is alloted just half a page. Sprinkled with errors and contradictions, and illustrated exclusively with items from the author's collection, this book is useful chiefly to the souvenir hunter. Hamilton has also written *Little Journeys to the Homes of the Roycrofters* (East Aurora, N.Y.: S-G Press, 1963), which includes interviews with eight former Roycrofters, and has edited *As Bees in Honey Drown* (New York: A. S. Barnes, 1973), a sequence of maudlin love letters between Hubbard and his longtime mistress.

Hanks, David A. *The Decorative Designs of Frank Lloyd Wright.* New York: E. P. Dutton, 1979. xx+232 pp.; 219 black and white illustrations, 24 color plates, index.

Hanks documents the unity between Wright's buildings and furnishings in both commercial and domestic settings from the 1890s to the 1950s. Chapters treat the decorative arts in three distinct but interrelated ways: chronologically, by commission; generically, by media; and technically, by method of production. Furniture receives the most attention, followed by art glass and graphic designs. Metals and textiles receive minimal attention, and murals are noted only in passing. Hanks's strength lies in critical assessment of visual relationships rather than in interpretation of historical context. The chapter on Wright's connection to the arts and crafts movement is superficial, but the biographical list of craftsmen and manufacturers who executed decorative arts for Wright is an important data source for cultural historians.

[Hubbard, Elbert]. *The Book of the Roycrofters.* Reprint of two catalogues, 1919 and 1926. East Aurora, N.Y.: House of Hubbard, 1977. 82 pp.; illustrations.

[———]. *Catalog of Roycroft Furniture and Other Things.* 1906. Reprint. New York: Turn of the Century Editions, 1981. 47 pp.; illustrations.

[———]. *Roycroft Hand Made Furniture.* 1912. Reprint. East Aurora, N.Y.: House of Hubbard, 1973. 61 pp.; 134 illustrations.

Hubbard's 1906 Roycroft furniture catalogue instructed customers "not to class [their] products as . . . so-called 'Mission Furniture'" (p. 3) (the preceding year's catalogue characterized their furniture as "Aurora Colonial"). But Hubbard was a pragmatic businessman alert to marketing trends, and his 1912 catalogue declared that the furniture's "simplicity of design and intent are strictly Mission" (p. 1). Not all this furniture was in the arts and crafts mode. Dining room tables, for example, were modified pedestal types of the 1890s. Hubbard owned logging camps and a sawmill, but only a portion of his lumber was obtained locally. Almost everything in the 1906 and 1912 catalogues could be had in African or Santo Domingan mahogany as well as in mission oak. Furniture production ceased about 1920, but smaller gift items (books, leather goods, copperwork) continued to be made in great numbers, especially after 1915, when retail store franchises were introduced to supplement mail-order sales. The 1919 and 1926 catalogues, intended for retailers, illustrate objects that were produced by the Roycroft Shops until their demise during the 1930s. All four catalogues include price lists.

Jones, Harvey L. *Mathews: Masterpieces of the California Decorative Style*. Exhibition catalogue. 1972. Rev. ed. Santa Barbara and Salt Lake City: Peregrine Smith, 1980. 127 pp.; 72 black and white illustrations, color plates, bibliography, index.

This catalogue was prepared for a 1972 exhibition based on Oakland Museum's archive of more than 1,000 items by San Francisco artist-designer Arthur F. Mathews (1860–1945) and his pupil-wife, Lucia (1870–1955). The work of Arthur Mathews—director of California School of Design for sixteen years, mural and easel painter, furniture and graphic designer, decorator, writer, and publisher—somewhat resembles William Morris's. Unlike Morris, however, whose inspiration was medieval and whose influence was international, Mathews was affected by the classical world and had, partially by choice, only a local reputation. An anemic catalogue essay emphasizes the couple's paintings and pays less attention to their furniture shop, where as many as fifty craftsmen produced both domestic and commercial custom-designed, carved, and polychromed furniture and accessories. There is little mention of the Mathewses' city planning magazine, *Philopolis*, or the limited editions published by their Philopolis Press.

Kaplan, Wendy. *"The Art That Is Life": The Arts and Crafts Movement in America, 1875–1920*. Exhibition catalogue. Boston: Little, Brown for the Museum of Fine Arts, a New York Graphic Society Book, 1987. xiv+410 pp.; 7 black and white illustrations, color plates, illustrated catalogue, index.

Architect William Price termed *work* "the art that is life." This handsome catalogue, with contributions by eighteen authors, deals with not only the aesthetics of objects but also the nature of work, production, and consumption and the conduct of life. It expands themes introduced in the groundbreaking 1972 Princeton exhibition "The Arts and Crafts Movement in America" and consolidates recent scholarship. While the Museum of Fine Arts exhibition included 20 percent fewer objects than the Princeton show, most are examined in context and in much greater depth. The overall premise is the concept of reform. The essays and catalogue entries discuss the changing attitudes toward the design, fabrication, and use of objects in all media, integrated domestic environments, and the dissemination of reform ideals. Objects are related to their makers' intentions, with a conservative to progressive range of stylistic influences explored. The essay on style betrays an architectural bias, but entries on architecture lack imagination. The essay on dress reform seems out of place, since this topic antedates the arts and crafts era, and only four costumes are included. Entries on ceramics and metals are particularly informative. Furniture, ceramics, metals, and architecture comprise 75 percent of the catalogue entries, which are confusingly grouped and integrated in a somewhat strained thematic framework. More than 80 percent of the entries are from the latter half of the exhibition's date range. An important contribution to the literature of American design, this catalogue should remain the standard reference on the American arts and crafts movement into the next century. *See also* "Surveys."

Keeler, Charles. *The Simple Home*. New introduction by Dimitri Shipounoff. 1904. Reprint. Santa Barbara and Salt Lake City: Peregrine Smith, 1979. xliv+55 pp.; illustrations.

In consort with visual art reformers, California poet and ornithologist Keeler (1871–1937) believed that dwellings reflected the nature of their occupants and should be suited to their individual needs. His guide to planning, furnishing, and landscaping a San Francisco Bay–area house is significant as much for its principle of restraint as for its specific recommendations (veneered furniture and mechanically printed wallpaper are eschewed in favor of mission oak and Japanese prints). Like William Morris, Keeler regarded architecture as the sovereign of the arts; unlike Morris, he accepted society as it was, regarding the home as a "shelter from the world." His own house was the first independent commission of arts and crafts/beaux arts architect Bernard Maybeck, and *The Simple Home* is dedicated to him. The new introduction by Shipounoff places Keeler in the context of his time.

Lambourne, Lionel. *Utopian Craftsmen: The Arts and Crafts Movement from the Cotswolds to Chicago*. Salt Lake City: Peregrine Smith, 1980. vii+218 pp.; 255 black and white illustrations, color plates, bibliography, index.

An overview of British and American arts and crafts designers, *Utopian Craftsmen* is unusual in its attempts to illustrate the movement's influence up to the present. A section on American achievements cites Walt Whitman's effect on British craftsmen and the Shakers' devotion to a utopian simple life. The volume overemphasizes contributions of Gustave Stickley and Frank Lloyd Wright and does not even mention designers like William Price or Ralph Whitehead, who actually attempted utopian schemes. Lambourne recognizes parallel developments (the influence of the church, design reform, and social reform) within the movement, thereby counteracting the distortions that result from discussions of the movement as a homogeneous entity.

Lears, T. J. Jackson. "The Figure of the Artisan: Arts and Crafts Ideology." In T. J. Jackson Lears, *No Place of Grace: Antimodernism and the Transformation of American Culture, 1880–1920*, pp. 60–96. New York: Pantheon Books, 1981.

No Place of Grace is a Marxist/psychoanalytic approach to selected arts and crafts tenets, based chiefly on articles in Gustave Stickley's *Craftsman*, New Clairvaux colony's *Country Time and Tide*, Rose Valley's *Artsman*, and Boston Society of Arts and Crafts' *Handicraft*. Dealing with social salvation ideology rather than design reform, Lears comes to the conclusion, "despite its origins as a reaction against modern overcivilization, the craft revival served to intensify the modern preoccupation with individual fulfillment" (p. 83), and "American craft leaders transformed what might have been an alternative to alienated labor into a revivifying hobby for the affluent" (p. 93). Lears overstates the case, taking no notice of the art pottery movement, for example, which began with hobbyists and was later modified. Here the intellectual historian neglects evidence from material culture studies. Several factual errors are corrected in a 1983 paperback edition. This work is a provocative interpretation that is not to be missed.

[Limbert, Charles P.] *The Arts and Crafts Furniture of Charles P. Limbert*. Two catalogues with an introduction by Robert L. Edwards. Facsimile. Watkins Glen, N.Y.: American Life Foundation, 1982. [20]+52+56 pp.; illustrations.

[———]. *Limberts Holland Dutch Arts and Crafts Furniture*. Reprints of Charles P. Limbert Company Cabinetmakers, Grand Rapids and Holland, Michigan, books 112 and 119. New York: Turn of the Century Editions, 1981. 128 pp.; approximately 86 catalogue plates.

While Turn of the Century Editions produces a higher-quality reprint than American Life Foundation, the latter makes the better selection in content. Its Limbert reprint includes the autumn 1905 catalogue featuring bookcases with floral-pattern leaded-glass doors and chairs inlaid with metal. These options, as well as alternatives in type of wood and upholstery, are reduced or curtailed in Booklet 100, published after Limbert moved his offices from Grand Rapids to Holland, Michigan, but are included in the American Life Foundation volume. In all the catalogues, the influences of Scotsman Charles Rennie Mackintosh and American competitor Gustave Stickley are apparent. Ironically, Dutch influence is not obvious in the illustrations, despite efforts made by Limbert in the texts of Booklets 100, 112, and 119 to link his furniture to Netherlandish prototypes of the fifteenth to seventeenth centuries. Booklet 119 has the great-

est range of forms, but the pieces are less subtle and varied in design than earlier Limbert offerings.

Ludwig, Coy L. *The Arts and Crafts Movement in New York State, 1890–1920s*. Exhibition catalogue. Hamilton: Gallery Association of New York State, 1983. ix+118 pp.; approximately 100 black and white and color illustrated entries, bibliography, index.

This catalogue accompanied a survey exhibition summarizing responses to queries made to more than seventy historical agencies about arts and crafts activities in every region of New York. The purpose of the show and catalogue was "to provide an introduction to the quality and to the extraordinary array of the work its practitioners created, and to convey the flavor of those ingredients—publications, communities, studios, shops—which made arts and crafts more than simply a style" (p. 10). While the definition of arts and crafts set forth in the opening paragraph stresses humanistic attitudes and social concerns, most of the text is a descriptive account of significant dates and commissions in the careers of movement leaders. Of special note are two lists that record personnel, addresses, products, and primary references for arts and crafts shops and handicraft schools.

Mackay, James. *Turn-of-the-Century Antiques: An Encyclopedia*. New York: E. P. Dutton, a Dutton Visual Book, 1974. 320 pp.; black and white illustrations, color plates, bibliography.

Although this work is not specifically about the arts and crafts movement, the majority of the entries are relevant if only by contrast. The organization is clear, and the photographs show seldom-published objects. The credibility of the text is compromised by a full-page color illustration of "Americana" in which appears fake scrimshaw, brass buckles, and firemarks, the kind of slight all too common in British books about American decorative arts. As a basic background source for collectors, this work is more than adequate. The illustrations are the most valuable part of the book; however, Mackay makes no attempt to interpret the objects.

Makinson, Randell L. *Greene and Greene: Furniture and Related Designs*. Santa Barbara and Salt Lake City: Peregrine Smith, 1979. 161 pp.; approximately 225 black and white illustrations and 14 color plates, bibliography, index.

Pasadena architects Charles Sumner Greene (1868–1957) and Henry Mather Greene (1870–1954) are remembered chiefly for their "ultimate bungalows," meticulously constructed timber and shingle homes exhibiting both arts and crafts and oriental influences in their design. This volume is a companion to Makinson's *Greene and Greene: Architecture as a Fine Art* (Layton, Utah: Peregrine Smith, 1977) and presupposes a fairly thorough knowledge of the Greene brothers and their careers. Furniture, which (with few exceptions) was the work of Charles, is almost Makinson's sole subject. The "related designs," from textiles to stained glass to fireplace tools, get short shrift. The text is principally descriptive, providing little analysis. Neither meaningful comparisons with the work of other designers nor sources for the oriental influences on the brothers' forms are offered. Furniture construction techniques are better understood by reading Alan Marks, "Greene and Greene: A Study in Functional Design," *Fine Woodworking* (September 1978): 40–45. *See also* "American Furniture, 1820–1920."

Marek, Don. *Arts and Crafts Furniture Design: The Grand Rapids Contribution, 1895–1915*. Exhibition catalogue. Grand Rapids, Mich.: Grand Rapids Art Museum, 1987. 77 pp.; 72 black and white and duotone illustrations.

Grand Rapids was the capital of American furniture design, fabrication, and marketing at the turn of the century. This fascinating catalogue documents arts and crafts production within the city's forty furniture factories, where 10,000 skilled workmen employed a combination of hand and machine techniques to produce an immense variety of forms. In a biannual Grand Rapids Furniture Market, one local firm exhibited 3,000 different designs. While Grand Rapids furniture is sometimes denigrated today, Marek demonstrates that local firms produced avant-garde forms in advance of Gustave Stickley and other well-known arts and craftsmen. As early as 1900 *Grand Rapids Furniture Record* was publishing work by Charles Ashbee, Henry Van de Velde, and various Frenchmen. Both an arts and crafts society and Grand Rapids School of Furniture Design were founded in 1902, and within two years several local firms were applying the descriptor "modern English" to furniture influenced not only by Scotsman Charles Rennie Mackintosh but also by Viennese designers. Glasgow school and Austrian influences were especially evident in the work of Charles P. Limbert Company. Half of this catalogue's entries are devoted to Limbert, but brief biographies of nine additional companies and eleven designers and craftsmen are also provided. Thirty-five other individuals and firms are noted, but too little use has been made of local trade journals.

Naylor, Gillian. *The Arts and Crafts Movement: A Study of Its Sources, Ideals, and Influence on Design Theory*. 1971. Reprint. Cambridge, Mass.: MIT Press, 1980. 208 pp.; 101 black and white and color plates, bibliography, index.

Naylor provides an overview of personalities and societies that they founded to foster the handicraft aesthetic in England, from Augustus-Charles Pugin in the 1830s through the Design and Industries Association started in 1915. His hypothesis is that twentieth-century modernism is complementary, not antithetical, to the efforts of John Ruskin, William Morris, Arthur Mackmurdo, Walter Crane, Charles Ashbee, and their reformer colleagues who championed the human spirit and manual labor over industrial efficiency and machine precision. Naylor's commentary relies on books and essays of the 1835 to 1935 era rather than analysis of the

"state" or "cottage" artifacts produced by design schools and craft guilds; thus, illustrations are rarely discussed in the text. Writers on American arts and crafts often cite this work for background on the English movement because the biographies and institutional histories are concise and quotations from primary sources abound.

On the Threshold of Modern Design: The Arts and Crafts Movement in America. Exhibition catalogue. Framingham, Mass.: Danforth Museum of Art, 1984. 55 pp.; approximately 90 illustrations, checklist.

This catalogue was prepared for an exhibition of 275 objects in all media lent from Boston-area collections. Two-thirds of the items were produced by Massachusetts or New York makers; 40 percent are ceramic objects. Roger T. Dunn's brief introductory essay accepts Nicholas Pevsner's 1936 thesis that the philosophy of the arts and crafts movement led directly to the international style and, disregarding more recent developments such as postmodernism, asserts that arts and crafts principles are now "more operative than ever in determining the look of our environments and their furnishings" (p. 10). The exhibition contains no objects that would defend this viewpoint, but does include works by significant makers (such as the Shop of the Crafters) that were ignored in the 1972 Princeton show, "The Arts and Crafts Movement in America," as well as less common objects by more familiar names (for example, Gustave Stickley's 1901 pansy-form tea table). Unfortunately, most of the illustrations are small and rather muddy.

Sanders, Barry, ed. *The Craftsman: An Anthology*. Designed by Richard Firmage. Santa Barbara and Salt Lake City: Peregrine Smith, 1978. xvi+328 pp.; illustrations.

Sanders presents "a sample of the most well written, interesting and informative pieces" (p. ix) from Gustave Stickley's magazine, which ran for some 190 issues. Almost every subject relative to the arts and crafts movement was treated at one time or another, from architecture to music and from education to agriculture. This book is an enjoyable taste of the kind of material Stickley published, but one must go back to the originals to appreciate fully the editorial perspective of the *Craftsman*.

Smith, Mary Ann. *Gustav Stickley: The Craftsman*. Syracuse, N.Y.: Syracuse University Press, 1983. xiv+186 pp.; 116 illustrations, index.

Smith intends to place Stickley in the design context of his time by exploring the role of his complementary interests in furniture design, publishing, and architecture in the formulation of a utopian philosophy of life. Smith emphasizes house plans from the *Craftsman*, for she considers Stickley's architectural prescriptions to be the summation of his arts and crafts ideals. The chapter "Influences from Europe" is especially disappointing because it offers speculation but no convincing scholarship on Stickley's personal experience with international reform of the home and work processes. Readers should be wary of Smith's interpretations because she fails to recognize that Stickley's advertising ploys and propagandist impulses may be couched in moral language.

Stickley, Gustav. *The Best of Craftsman Homes*. Santa Barbara and Salt Lake City: Peregrine Smith, 1979. ix+245 pp.; illustrations.
——. *Craftsman Homes: Architecture and Furnishings of the American Arts and Crafts Movement*. 1909. 2d ed. Reprint. New York: Dover Publications, 1979. 205 pp.; 292 illustrations.

These two works by Stickley are more useful than catalogue reprints because the many illustrations of interiors show how Stickley and his designers intended Craftsman furnishings to be used. The works include every type of arts and crafts house, from an elaborate bungalow designed by Greene and Greene to a modest cottage for a single woman. *The Best of Craftsman Homes* includes excerpts from *Craftsman Homes* (1909) and *More Craftsman Homes* (1912). Many of Stickley's published designs were actually built from specifications that included stain colors for woodwork and type of hardware. The books suggest color schemes, floor treatments, and curtains to accompany Craftsman furniture. The house plans that Stickley published were neither innovative nor particularly original. Their prosaic quality exemplified the "democratic" Craftsman ideal.

Stickley, Gustav. *What Is Wrought in the Craftsman Workshops: A Brochure Published in the Interests of the Homebuilders Club*. 1904. Reprint. Watkins Glen, N.Y.: American Life Foundation, 1982. 92 pp.; approximately 65 illustrations.

The upsurge in popularity of mission furniture in the late 1970s spawned a rash of catalogue reprints. Those who have examined the *Craftsman* and other catalogue reprints will not need to ferret out this difficult-to-find facsimile because most of the information is available in Stickley's other publications. However, the information, condensed as it is here, highlights Stickley's zeal for the fumed-oak finish, which is discussed in poetic detail. His artisanal pretensions are exposed in the form of a photograph showing him posed in a blacksmith's leather apron. No evidence exists to indicate that he had any metalworking skills, and the apron covers a white shirt, vest, and bow tie.

Stickley, Gustav. *Catalogue of Craftsman Furniture Made by Gustav Stickley at the Craftsman Workshops*. 1909. Reprint. Watkins Glen, N.Y.: American Life Foundation, 1978. 127 pp.; illustrations.
[Stickley, L. and J. G.]. *The Arts and Crafts Furniture Work of L. and J. Stickley*. [1909]. Facsimile catalogue. Watkins Glen, N.Y.: American Life Foundation, 1978. 55 pp.; illustrations.
Stickley Craftsman Furniture Catalogs . . . : "Craftsman Fur-

niture Made by Gustav Stickley" and *"The Work of L. and J. G. Stickley."* New introduction by David M. Cathers. N.d. Reprint. New York: Dover Publications, 1979. viii+182 pp.; illustrations.

The Dover and American Life Foundation reprints cover some of the same material, although the difference of one year in the original Craftsman catalogues gives the American Life Foundation edition the advantage. It includes designs not found in the Dover version, like the so-called Spindle line. Dover, on the other hand, shows pages of willow furniture. The two L. and J. G. catalogues are identical. If the publishers had selected catalogues covering more years than these reprints do, one could determine when specific "lines" or designs were introduced and look for the first appearance and subsequent transformations of certain forms (plate racks, library tables, or reclining chairs) that are unique aspects of arts and crafts interiors. Catalogues should not be used as a substitute for studying real objects, even by those primarily interested in the ideas of the movement. Dealers and collectors will have the most use for the three reprints because they describe and identify specific objects.

[Stickley Brothers Company]. *Quaint Furniture in Arts and Crafts*. Ca. 1908. Reprint. New York: Turn of the Century Editions, 1981. 80 pp.; illustrations.

Quaint Furniture shows fumed-oak slat-back chairs and settees, Spanish Moroccan leather upholstery, and hand-beaten copper accessories by the Grand Rapids manufactory of John George and Albert Stickley, younger brothers of Gustave Stickley. The brothers assert that quaint furniture is suitable for every room in the home as well as for clubs, cafés, and hotels because each rocker, table, or ensemble exhibits the fundamental principles of modern decoration: simplicity, harmony, durability, comfort, and inexpensiveness. The furniture is of tongue-and-groove construction, with drawer fronts of solid walnut and no veneers. Copperware, which includes brass or wrought-iron accents, is described as strictly handmade by the sons and grandsons of metalsmiths. The measurements and price for each item are given. Despite the catalogue's title, the advertising format is straightforward, and the illustrations are neither unusual nor oldfashioned. They bear comparison with machine-made merchandise sold by other Grand Rapids firms aiming at the same bungalow-dwelling audience.

Thompson, Susan Otis. *American Book Design and William Morris*. New York and London: R. R. Bowker Co., 1977. xvii+258 pp.; 111 illustrations, appendix, bibliography, index.

Morris established his Kelmscott Press in 1891, printing limited-edition, handcrafted books, the designs of which were inspired by medieval illuminated manuscripts, fifteenth-century typefaces, and early woodcuts. Thompson explores the Kelmscott influence in the United States, dealing with periodicals as well as books and with trade publishers as well as private presses. Typography and, to a lesser extent, illustrations are emphasized at the expense of bindings, in which Morris showed little interest. Morris's ornate decorative schemes and densely spaced lettering were but one source of inspiration for Americans. Will Bradley's graphic designs, for example, show the influence of Kelmscott and Renaissance ornament (antithetical to Morris), art nouveau, and such disparate artists as Aubrey Beardsley and William Nicholson. Thompson's illustrations are large and clear but are too few to represent adequately the scope of her text.

Tiller: A Bimonthly Devoted to the Arts and Crafts Movement. Edited by Robert L. Edwards. Vol. 1–, no. 1–. Bryn Mawr, Pa.: Artsman, September–October 1982–.

Two or three articles, plus an editor's foreword, appear in each issue of *Tiller*. The editorial policy of the periodical fosters exploration of all aspects of the arts and crafts movement not yet investigated. This fine-quality publication maintains the arts and crafts ideals of combining beauty and utility and the movement's philosophy and practice. Hand-colored, tipped-in illustrations or reproductions of period photographs documenting little-known or destroyed examples of architecture, interior decoration, and individual objects accompany essays ranging from customized prairie school residences to forward-looking chair designs by David Kendall for mass production in Grand Rapids. From time to time, *Tiller* includes book reviews, notes on institutional holdings of primary materials, reprints from turn-of-the-century periodicals, and letters to the editor.

Traubel, Horace, Hawley McLanahan, and Will Price, eds. *The Artsman.* Vol. 1, no. 1–vol. 4, no. 3 (1903–7). Reprint. Introduction by Gertrude Traubel and Joseph Niver, Sr. Millwood, N.Y.: Kraus Reprint Co., 1979. 1,192 pp.; illustrations, index.

The reprinting of the entire run of the *Artsman* is a boon to researchers. The *Artsman* presents arts and crafts movement rhetoric with a sincerity apparently unadulterated by the merchandising interests that afflicted some of the periodicals offered by other communities and cooperatives. Line drawings, although taken from photographs in many instances, provide better representations of the intended effect of the furniture, interiors, and buildings of the Rose Valley community than a camera could. "The House of the Democrat," Price's ideal arts and crafts shelter which was actually built at Rose Valley, is depicted (vol. 3, no. 132). Articles such as "Do We Attack the Machine" and "Ugly Homes and Bad Morals," together with the regular reviews presented in "Artsmanship in Recent Literature," elucidate the important issues of the time and serve an audience larger than Rose Valley residents.

Triggs, Oscar Lovell. *Chapters in the History of the Arts and Crafts Movement.* 1902. Reprint. New York: Benjamin Blom, 1971. 198 pp.; illustrations, plates.

Chicago-based Triggs translated the arts and crafts gospel according to Thomas Carlyle, John Ruskin, and William Morris into American terms. He diluted Carlyle's and Ruskin's strong statements to make them more palatable to Americans: "Another fundamental proposition in Ruskin's theory of industry is that all good work must be free handwork. Probably Ruskin would admit to himself that his antagonism to the machine was too extreme" (p. 42). Morris, however, is extensively quoted verbatim. Triggs's description of the Rookwood pottery as an ideal workshop is interesting because it provides a contemporary interpretation of the proper application of arts and crafts principles.

Ulehla, Karen Evans, ed. and comp. *The Society of Arts and Crafts, Boston: Exhibition Record, 1897–1927.* Boston: Boston Public Library, 1981. 289 pp.; chronology, bibliography.

The national significance of Boston's Society of Arts and Crafts for the movement makes this listing of the members of the society, the years during which they were members, and the particular crafts they practiced essential to anyone studying specific people in the movement. Craftsmen from across the country joined the society because it gave their work considerable publicity and provided contact with other craftsmen.

Windsor, H. H. *Mission Furniture: How to Make It.* Abbreviated ed. of 3 vols. published 1909, 1910, and 1912. Santa Barbara and Salt Lake City: Peregrine Smith, 1976. 120 pp.; approximately 80 illustrations.

Forty objects are pictured in finished form and in detailed line drawings. Tables, chairs, chests, desks, lamps, a hall clock, and a combination billiard table–davenport are among the selections. Windsor's illustrations document the popular rather than the avant-garde aspect of the arts and crafts. The audience for this publication was the handyman or manual-training student. Descriptions that accompany each project encapsulate a central contradiction of the arts and crafts movement: employment of industrial technology to create domestic furnishings evocative of the preindustrial agrarian world. The final chapter on techniques and tools gives recipes for mission stains and finishes, directions for bending wood and for making screws hold in the end grain, and advice on fuming oak and cutting tenons. In 1980 Dover Publications produced an unabridged one-volume replication of the three-part *Mission Furniture*, which features ninety-eight projects and 213 illustrations; the author cited is Popular Mechanics Company.

Notes on Contributors

KENNETH L. AMES is professor, Winterthur Program in Early American Culture, Winterthur Museum, Winterthur, Delaware.

GERALD W. R. WARD is curator, Strawbery Banke Museum, Portsmouth, New Hampshire.

DONNA R. BRADEN is associate curator of domestic arts, Edison Institute, Henry Ford Museum and Greenfield Village, Dearborn, Michigan.

BARBARA G. CARSON is lecturer, George Washington University, Washington, D.C., and College of William and Mary, Williamsburg, Virginia.

EDWARD S. COOKE, JR., is assistant curator, American Decorative Arts and Sculpture, Museum of Fine Arts, Boston, Massachusetts.

ELLEN PAUL DENKER is a museum consultant, writer, and lecturer specializing in American ceramics history, Wilmington, Delaware.

ULYSSES GRANT DIETZ is curator of decorative arts, Newark Museum, Newark, New Jersey.

DEBORAH A. FEDERHEN is an independent scholar, Chadds Ford, Pennsylvania.

ADRIENNE D. HOOD is curatorial fellow, Textile Department, Royal Ontario Museum, Toronto.

ANN SMART MARTIN is research fellow, Department of Archaeological Research, Colonial Williamsburg Foundation, Williamsburg, Virginia.

THOMAS S. MICHIE is assistant curator of decorative arts, Museum of Art, Rhode Island School of Design, Providence.

GEORGE L. MILLER is collections research specialist, Department of Archaeological Research, Colonial Williamsburg Foundation, Williamsburg, Virginia.

KIRK NELSON is curator of glass, Sandwich Glass Museum, Sandwich, Massachusetts.

SUSAN ROACH-LANKFORD is an independent scholar, Ruston, Louisiana.

CHERYL A. ROBERTSON is assistant professor, Winterthur Program in Early American Culture, Winterthur Museum, Winterthur, Delaware.

RODRIS ROTH is curator, Division of Domestic Life, Smithsonian Institution, Washington, D.C.

DAVID SCHUYLER is professor, American Studies Program, Franklin and Marshall College, Lancaster, Pennsylvania.

SUSAN BURROWS SWAN is curator and in charge of textiles, Winterthur Museum, Winterthur, Delaware.

NEVILLE THOMPSON is librarian in charge, Printed Book and Periodical Collection, Winterthur Museum.

BARBARA MCLEAN WARD is director of interpretation and publications, Essex Institute, Salem, Massachusetts.

THOMAS BECKMAN is registrar, Delaware Historical Society, Wilmington.

ROBERT L. EDWARDS is an artist, Swarthmore, Pennsylvania.

Index

"A. H. Davenport and Company," Anne Farnam, 122

Aaron Dodd Crane, Frederick Shelley, 298

Abbott, Henry G., *Watch Factories*, 303

Abel Buell, Lawrence C. Wroth, 157

"Abraham Kimball," Kathleen M. Catalano, 119

"Account Book of John Gould," Benno M. Forman, 275

Accounts of . . . Furniture Makers, trans. and ed. Alan G. Keyser et al., 96

Adams, William Howard, ed., *Eye of Thomas Jefferson*, 43

Adamson, Jack E., *Illustrated Handbook of Ohio Sewer Pipe Folk Art*, 188

Adelaide Alsop Robineau, ed. Peg Weiss, 194

Adirondack Furniture, Craig Gilborn, 124

Adrosko, Rita J.: "Anatomy of a Quilted Counterpane," 271; *Natural Dyes*, 271

"Aesthetic Forms in Ceramics," Alice Cooney Frelinghuysen, 185

"Aesthetic Principles in Afro-American Quilts," Maude Southwell Wahlman and John Scully, 263

Afro-American Folk Art, ed. William Ferris, 47

Afro-American Tradition, John Michael Vlach, 56

Agius, Pauline, *British Furniture*, 115

Ahlborn, Richard, "Peter Glass," 115

Albany Silver, Norman S. Rice, 155

Albright, Frank P., *Johann Ludwig Eberhardt*, 292

Alexander, John D., Jr., *Make a Chair*, 336

Alexander, Robert L., "Neoclassical Wrought Iron," 170

"Alexander Parris, B. Henry Latrobe, and the John Wickham House,"

Edward F. Zimmer and Pamela J. Scott, 75

"Alexander Roux," Dianne D. Hauserman, 125

All Sorts of . . . Cloth, Martha Coons and Katherine Koob, 273

All That Glisters, Marc Simpson, 176

Allentown Art Museum, *Early American Pewter*, 162

Allgemeines Lexikon, Ulrich Thieme and Felix Becker, 35

Allix, Charles, *Carriage Clocks*, 288

America in the Kitchen, Linda Campbell Franklin, 312

America Underfoot, Anthony N. Landreau, 244

American Antique Furniture, Edgar G. Miller, Jr., 98

American Antiques from the Israel Sack Collection, 87

American Apprenticeship, Paul H. Douglas, 337

American Architectural Books, Henry-Russell Hitchcock, 30

American Art, ed. Charles F. Montgomery and Patricia E. Kane, 52, 99

"American Art," Rodris Roth, 130

American Art Auction Catalogues, comp. Harold Lancour, 30

American Art Journal, 35

American Art Nouveau, Diane Chalmers Johnson, 50

American Art Nouveau Glass, Albert Christian Revi, 233

American Basketry, William C. Ketchum, Jr., 314

American Belleek, Mary Frank Gaston, 185

American Book Design, Susan Otis Thompson, 356

American Bottles, Helen McKearin and Kenneth M. Wilson, 230

American Bungalow, Clay Lancaster, 71

American Carpet Manufacture, Arthur H. Cole and Harold F. Williamson, 242

American Case Furniture, Gerald W. R. Ward, 105

American Ceramics, comp. Ruth Irwin Weidner, 187

American Chairs, John T. Kirk, 96

American Clock, Edwin A. Battison and Patricia E. Kane, 288

American Clock, William H. Distin and Robert Bishop, 289

American Clock Making, Henry Terry, 299

American Clocks, Carl W. Dreppard, 289

American Collector, 35

American Copper and Brass, Henry J. Kauffman, 174

American Decorative Arts, David M. Sokol, 32

American Decorative Arts, Robert Bishop and Patricia Coblentz, 44

American Decorative Tiles, Thomas P. Bruhn, 184

American Eagle, ed. Clarence P. Hornung, 49

American Family Home, Clifford Edward Clark, Jr., 67

American Fireplace, Henry J. Kauffman, 324

American Folk Art, Milwaukee Art Museum, 52

American Folk Art, Simon J. Bronner, 29

American Furniture, Charles F. Montgomery, 98

American Furniture, Elizabeth Bidwell Bates and Jonathan L. Fairbanks, 87, 118

American Furniture, Helen Comstock, 88

American Furniture, Joseph Downs, 90

American Furniture and the British Tradition, John T. Kirk, 96

American Furniture at Chipstone, Oswaldo Rodriquez Roque, 102

American Furniture Craftsmen, comp. Charles J. Semowich, 103

American Furniture in the Metropolitan Museum, Morrison H. Heckscher, 94

American Furniture in the Museum of Fine Arts, Richard H. Randall, Jr., 102

American Furniture of the Nineteenth Century, Celia Jackson Otto, 129

American Glass, George S. McKearin and Helen McKearin, 230

American Glass Cup Plates, Ruth Webb Lee and James H. Rose, 229

American Gold, Peter J. Bohan, 148

American Hand-Woven Coverlets, comp. Margaret E. White, 280

American Hearth, 310

American Heritage, Edmund P. Hogan, 152

American Heritage History of Antiques, ed. Marshall B. Davidson, 46

American Historical Views on Staffordshire China, Ellouise Baker Larsen, 211

American Home, David P. Handlin, 70

American Horological Journal. See Jewelers' Circular, 290

American House, Mary Mix Foley, 68

"American Houses," Vincent Scully, 73

American Ice Boxes, Joseph C. Jones, Jr., 314

American Interiors, Harold L. Peterson, 53

American Majolica, M. Charles Rebert, 186

American Needlework, Georgiana Brown Harbeson, 251

American Needlework Treasures, Betty Ring, 253

"American Neoclassical Furniture," Donald L. Fennimore, 123

"American Notes," Charles E. Peterson, 325

American Painted Furniture, Dean A. Fales, Jr., 91, 122

American Patriotic and Political China, Marian Klamkin, 210

"American Pewter," Elizabeth M. Ely, 164

American Pewter, J. B. Kerfoot, 165

American Pewter, John Meredith Graham II, 164

American Pewter (Flint Institute), 162

American Pewter (Museum of Fine Arts), 162

American Pewter (Virginia Museum), 162

American Pewter (Yale), 162

American Pewterer, Henry J. Kauffman, 165

American Porcelain, Alice C. Frelinghuysen, 185

American Presidential China, Susan G. Detweiler, 206

American Pressed Glass, Albert Christian Revi, 233

American Quilts, ed. L. Thomas Frye, 260

"American Quilts," Phillip H. Curtis, 260

American Reed Organ, Robert F. Gellerman, 123

American Renaissance, Brooklyn Museum, 45

American Rugs, Helene Von Rosenstiel, 246

American . . . Rugs, Joel Kopp and Kate Kopp, 244

American Sampler, National Gallery of Art, 53

"American Samplers," Elisabeth Donaghy Garrett, 249

American Samplers, Ethel Stanwood Bolton and Eva Johnston Coe, 248

American Seating Furniture, Benno M. Forman, 92

American Silver Flatware, Noel D. Turner, 155

American Silver, C. Louise Avery, 147

American Silver, Graham Hood, 153

American Silver, John Marshall Phillips, 154

American Silver, Kathryn C. Buhler, 148

American Silver, Kathryn C. Buhler and Graham Hood, 148

American Silver, Martha Gandy Fales, 150

American Silverplate, Dorothy T. Rainwater and H. Ivan Rainwater, 155

American Silversmiths, Stephen G. C. Ensko, 150

American Stonewares, Georgeanna H. Greer, 185

American Watch Papers, Dorothea E. Spear, 305

American and British Pewter, ed. John Carl Thomas, 167

American and English Pewter, David L. Barquist, 162

American and European Jewelry, Charlotte Gere, 151

American and European Pressed Glass, Jane Shadel Spillman, 234

America's . . . Fabrics, Florence H. Pettit, 277

Ames, Kenneth: "Battle of the Sideboards," 116; "George Henkels," 116

Ames, Kenneth L.: *Beyond Necessity*, 43; "Designed in France," 116; "Material Culture as . . . Communication," 116; "Meaning in Artifacts," 116; "Sitting in (Néo-Grec) Style," 116; "What Is the Néo-Grec," 117

Ames, Kenneth L., ed., *Victorian Furniture*, 117

"Analysis . . . of Coverlets," Connie Ulasewicz et al., 280

Analysis of . . . Ceramics, Teresa Majewski and Michael J. O'Brien, 211

"Analysis of . . . Pewter," Janice H. Carlson, 163

"Ananias Hensel," Warren E. Roberts, 130

Anatomy of English Wrought Iron, John Seymour Lindsay, 175

"Anatomy of a Quilted Counterpane," Rita J. Adrosko, 271

Andersen, Timothy J., et al., eds., *California Design*, 347

Anderson, Clarita, "Coverlet Bibliography," 271

Anderson, Clarita, et al., "Analysis . . . of Coverlets," 280

Anderson, Susan H., *Most Splendid Carpet*, 242

Andrews, Carol Damon, "John Ritto Penniman," 303

Andrews, Deborah C., and William D. Andrews, "Technology and the Housewife," 310

Andrews, Edward Deming, and Faith Andrews: *Religion in Wood*, 117; *Shaker Furniture*, 117

Andrews, Faith, and Edward Deming Andrews: *Religion in Wood*, 117; *Shaker Furniture*, 117

Andrews, John, *Price Guide to . . . Furniture*, 117

Andrews, William D., and Deborah C. Andrews, "Technology and the Housewife," 310

Angel in the Studio, Anthea Callen, 349

Anscombe, Isabelle, and Charlotte

Gere, *Arts and Crafts in Britain and America,* 347

Ansonia Clock Company, *Illustrated Catalogue,* 292

Antiquarian, 35

Antique Brass Candlesticks, John Robert Grove, 327

Antique Fakes and Reproductions, Ruth Webb Lee, 229

Antique Metalware, ed. James R. Mitchell, 176

Antique or Fake, Charles H. Hayward, 86

Antique Pewter, Ronald F. Michaelis, 166

Antique Woodstoves, Will Curtis and Jane Curtis, 323

Antiques (magazine), 35

Antiques and Collectibles, Linda Campbell Franklin, 30

Antiques Book of Victorian Interiors, comp. Elisabeth Donaghy Garrett, 68

Antiques of American Childhood, Katharine Morrison McClinton, 51

Antonelli, Marylu, and Jack Forbes, *Pottery in Alberta,* 188

"Appreciating American Samplers," Susan Burrows Swan, 255

Apprenticeship, Ian M.G. Quimby, 340

"Archaeological Investigation of Blacksmith Shops," John D. Light, 175

Archer, Michael, and Brian Morgan, *Fair as China Dishes,* 203

Archer, Michael, and F. H. Garner, *English Delftware,* 207

Architectural Treatises, Janice G. Schimmelman, 31

Architecture, Men, Women, and Money, Roger G. Kennedy, 70

"Architecture of Urban Housing," Richard Pommer, 72

Archives of American Art: *Arts in America,* 29; *Collection of Exhibition Catalogs,* 29

Arman, David, and Linda Arman, *Historical Staffordshire,* 203

Arman, Linda, and David Arman, *Historical Staffordshire,* 203

Arntzen, Etta, and Robert Rainwater, *Guide to . . . Art History,* 29

Art and Antiques, ed., *Nineteenth Century Furniture,* 118

Art and Glory, Freeman Champney, 349

Art and History of the Potting Business, William Evans, 207

Art and Labor, Eileen Boris, 337, 348

Art Books, E. Louise Lucas, 30

Art Books, Wolfgang M. Freitag, 30

"Art Furniture," Marilynn Johnson, 126

Art Index, 29

Art Nouveau . . . Lighting, Alastair Duncan, 326

Art . . . of Creating Medallion Quilts, Jinny Beyer, 259

"Art of Indiana Coverlets," Peggy S. Gilfoy, 275

Art of the European Silversmith, Carl Hernmarck, 146

Art of the Potter, ed. Diana Stradling and G. Garrison Stradling, 187

Art of the Weaver, ed. Anita Schorsch, 279

Art Pottery, Paul Evans, 184

"Art That Is Life," Wendy Kaplan, 50, 353

"Artifact and Culture, Architecture and Society," Henry Glassie, 69

"Artifacts and Status Differences," John Solomon Otto, 215

Artifacts of the Spanish Colonies, Kathleen Deagan, 197

"Artificial Lighting," C. Malcom Watkins, 329

Artisans, Howard B. Rock, 341

Artistic Houses, 118

Artists of the Book, Nancy Finlay, 351

Arts and Architecture of German Settlements, Charles van Ravenswaay, 56

Arts and Crafts Furniture, [Charles P. Limbert], 354

Arts and Crafts Furniture, Don Marek, 355

Arts and Crafts Furniture, ed. Stephen Gray, 351

Arts and Crafts Furniture Work, [L. and J. G. Stickley], 356

Arts and Crafts in Britain and America, Isabelle Anscombe and Charlotte Gere, 347

Arts and Crafts in New England, comp. George Francis Dow, 33

Arts and Crafts in New York, Rita Susswein Gottesman, 33

Arts and Crafts in North Carolina, James H. Craig, 32

Arts and Crafts in Philadelphia, Maryland, and South Carolina, comp. Alfred Coxe Prime, 34

Arts and Crafts Movement, Gillian Naylor, 355

Arts and Crafts Movement in America, ed. Robert Judson Clark, 45, 349

Arts and Crafts Movement in New York, Coy L. Ludwig, 354

Arts and Crafts Quarterly, 348

"Arts and Crafts Tradition," Anne Farnam, 351

Arts in America, Archives of American Art, 29

Arts in America, Louis B. Wright et al., 57

Arts in America, Wendell D. Garrett et al., 48

Arts in Early American History, 29

Arts of Independence, Elisabeth Donaghy Garrett, 250

Arts of the Anglo-American Community, ed. Ian M. G. Quimby, 54, 102

Arts of the Pennsylvania Germans, Scott T. Swank, 56

Arts of the United States, ed. William H. Pierson, Jr., and Martha Davidson, 54

Artsman, ed. Horace Traubel et al., 357

Ashton, Thomas Southcliffe, *Eighteenth Century Industrialist,* 303

Aspects of the Arts and Crafts Movement, ed. Robert Judson Clark, 349

At Home, George Talbot, 73

At Home in Upper Canada, Jeanne Minhinnick, 72

Atterbury, Paul, ed., *English Pottery and Porcelain,* 203

Austin, John C., *Chelsea Porcelain at Williamsburg,* 204

Authentic Decor, Peter Thornton, 85

Authority, Liberty, and Automatic Machinery, Otto Mayr, 302

Autobiography, [Levi Hutchins], 297

"Availability and Selection of Ceramics to Silcott," Lina P. Gaw, 207

Avery, Amos, *New England Clocks,* 288

Avery, C. Louise: *American Silver,* 147; *Early American Silver,* 147

Axminster Carpets, Bertram Jacobs, 244

Ayensu, Edward S., and Philip Whitfield, eds., *Rhythms of Life,* 300

Ayres, Edward, et al., *"Poor Potter,"* 188

Ayres, William, ed., *Poor Sort of Heaven,* 348

Bailey, Beth, "Learning to Accept the Sewing Machine," 311

Bailey, Chris H.: *From Rags to Riches,* 292; "One Hundred Sixty Years of Seth Thomas Clocks," 293; *Two*

Hundred Years of American Clocks and Watches, 288

Bailey, Chris H., and Dana J. Blackwell, *Heman Clark and . . . Shelf Clocks*, 293

Baillie, G. H., et al., *Britten's Old Clocks and Watches*, 288

Baillie, Granville H.: *Clocks and Watches*, 288; *Watchmakers and Clockmakers*, 288

Baker, Vernon G., *Historical Archaeology at Black Lucy's Garden*, 204

Baltimore Album Quilts, Dena S. Katzenberg, 262

Baltimore Furniture, 87

"Baltimore Glass Trade," Dwight P. Lanmon, 229

Baltimore Painted Furniture, 118

Banham, Reyner: "Dark Satanic Century," 325; "Kit of Parts," 325

Banjo Timepiece, Chipman P. Ela, 290

Barber, Edwin AtLee: *Marks of American Potters*, 184; *Pottery and Porcelain*, 184; *Tulip Ware*, 188

Barber, Kate, and Andrew L. Winton, *Norwalk Potteries*, 194

Barber, Laurence Luther, "Clockmakers of Ashby," 293

Barclay, Miriam A., *Daniel Pratt, Jr.*, 293

Barka, Norman F., et al.: "Impermanent Architecture," 67; "*Poor Potter*," 188

Barlow, Raymond E., and Joan F. Kaiser, *Glass Industry*, 226

Baroque and Rococo Silks, Peter Thornton, 280

Barquist, David L., *American and English Pewter*, 162

Barr, Elaine, *George Wickes*, 144

Barr, Lockwood Anderson, *Eli Terry . . . Clocks*, 293

Barrett, Richard Carter, *Bennington Pottery*, 188

Bartlett, J. Neville, *Carpeting the Millions*, 242

Bartlett, Lu, and William Voss Elder III, *John Shaw*, 90

Basketry, Sue H. Stephenson, 317

Baskets of Rural America, Gloria Roth Teleki, 317

Bates, Elizabeth Bidwell, and Jonathan L. Fairbanks, *American Furniture*, 87, 118

Bath, Virginia Churchill, *Lace*, 248

"Bath in the Nineteenth Century," Siegfried Giedion, 322

"Bathroom Becomes Mechanized," Siegfried Giedion, 322

Battison, Edwin A., and Patricia E. Kane, *American Clock*, 288

"Battle of the Sideboards," Kenneth Ames, 116

Baumgarten, Linda R., "Textile Trade," 271

Bavaro, Joseph J., and Thomas L. Mossman, *Furniture of Gustav Stickley*, 348

Baylor, H. W., and William Ewers, *Sincere's History of the Sewing Machine*, 312

Bayou Bend, David B. Warren, 57, 106

Beaudry, Mary C., "Ceramics in York County," 204

Beaudry, Mary C., et al., "Vessel Typology for Early Chesapeake Ceramics," 204

Becker, Felix, and Ulrich Thieme, *Allgemeines Lexikon*, 35

Beckman, Elizabeth D., *In-Depth Study of . . . Watch and Clockmakers*, 293

Bed Hangings, comp. Abbott Lowell Cummings, 273

Bed Ruggs, Wadsworth Atheneum, 255

Beer, Alice Baldwin, *Trade Goods*, 271

Belden, Louise Conway: *Festive Tradition*, 44; *Marks of American Silversmiths*, 147

Bemiss, Elijah, *Dyer's Companion*, 271

Benes, Peter, *Two Towns*, 44

Bennington Pottery, Richard Carter Barrett, 188

Bensch, Christopher, *Blue and the Gray*, 188

Bent Wood and Metal Furniture, ed. Derek E. Ostergard, 129

Berney, Esther S., *Collector's Guide to Pressing Irons*, 311

Best of Craftsman Homes, Gustav Stickley, 356

Betts, Richard J., "Woodlands," 66

Beyer, Jinny, *Art . . . of Creating Medallion Quilts*, 259

Beyond Necessity, Kenneth L. Ames, 43

"Beyond . . . Women's Traditional Arts," Joyce Ice and Judith Shulimson, 261

Bible in Iron, Henry C. Mercer, 324

Bibliographic Guide to Books on Ceramics, Peter H. Weinrich, 218

Bibliography of . . . Architecture, Frank J. Roos, Jr., 31

Bigelow, Francis Hill, *Historic Silver*, 148

Bird, Michael, and Terry Kobayashi, *Splendid Harvest*, 271

Birmingham Brass Candlesticks, Jean M. Burks, 171

Bishir, Catherine W., "Jacob W. Holt," 336

Bishop, Barbara, and Martha Hassell, eds., *Your Obdt. Servt., Deming Jarves*, 226

Bishop, Robert, *Centuries and Styles of the American Chair*, 118

Bishop, Robert, and Carleton L. Safford: "Candlewick Spread," 279; "Double Weave Coverlet," 279; "Jacquard Coverlet," 279; "Overshot Coverlet," 279; "Summer and Winter Coverlet," 279

Bishop, Robert, and Elizabeth Safanda, *Gallery of Amish Quilts*, 259

Bishop, Robert, and Patricia Coblentz: *American Decorative Arts*, 44; *World of Antiques, Art, and Architecture*, 44

Bishop, Robert, and William H. Distin, *American Clock*, 289

Bishop, Robert, et al., *Quilts, Coverlets, Rugs, and Samplers*, 259

Bivins, John, Jr.: *Furniture of Coastal North Carolina*, 87; *Moravian Potters*, 189, 336

Bivins, John, Jr., and Paula Welshimer, *Moravian Decorative Arts*, 44

Bjerkoe, Ethel Hall, *Cabinetmakers of America*, 87

Blackburn, Roderick H., *Cherry Hill*, 66

Blacksmith, ed. Vernon S. Gunnion and Carroll J. Hopf, 173

Blackwell, Dana J., and Chris H. Bailey, *Heman Clark and . . . Shelf Clocks*, 293

Blair, Claude, ed., *History of Silver*, 144

Blaszczyk, Regina Lee, "Ceramics and the Sot-Weed Factor," 204

Block, Jean F., *Hyde Park Houses*, 66

Bloomfield, Anne, "Real Estate Associates," 66

Blue and the Gray, Christopher Bensch, 188

Blue Book, Philadelphia Furniture, William Macpherson Hornor, Jr., 94

Bogdonoff, Nancy Dick, *Handwoven Textiles*, 272

Bohan, Peter, and Philip Hammerslough, *Early Connecticut Silver*, 148

Bohan, Peter J., *American Gold*, 148

Bokides, Dessa, and Lonn Taylor, *New Mexican Furniture*, 104, 133

Bolingbroke, Judith M., *William and Mary Fabrics*, 272

Bolton, Charles Knowles, *Bolton's American Armory*, 148

Bolton, Ethel Stanwood, and Eva Johnston Coe, *American Samplers*, 248

Bolton's American Armory, Charles Knowles Bolton, 148

Bonnin, Alfred, *Tutenag and Paktong*, 171

Bonnin and Morris, Graham Hood, 191

Book Decoration, Laurie W. Crichton, 349

Book of American Clocks, Brooks Palmer, 291

Book of Glass, Gustav Weiss, 234

Book of Rookwood Pottery, Herbert Peck, 192

Book of Shaker Furniture, John Kassay, 126

Book of Silver, Eva Link, 146

Book of Sun-Dials, Mrs. Alfred Gatty, 304

Book of the Roycrofters, [Elbert Hubbard], 352

Book of Time, ed. John Grant and Colin Wilson, 301

Bordes, Marilynn Johnson, "Christian Herter," 118

Boris, Eileen, *Art and Labor*, 337, 348

"Boston Empire Furniture," Page Talbott, 133

"Boston Furniture Industry," Edward S. Cooke, Jr., 120

Boston Furniture of the Eighteenth Century, 87

"Boston Goldsmiths," Barbara McLean Ward, 156, 342

Bottle Makers, Julian Harrison Toulouse, 234

Bottles, Flasks, and Dr. Dyott, Helen McKearin, 230

Boultinghouse, Marquis, *Silversmiths, Jewelers, Clock and Watch Makers*, 293

Bowers, Quentin, and Henry Kauffman, *Early American Andirons*, 324

Bracket Clock, Deryck Roberts, 291

Bradbury, Frederick, *History of Old Sheffield Plate*, 144

Bradley, H. G., ed., *Ceramics of Derbyshire*, 204

Bradshaw, James Stanford, "Grand Rapids," 119

Branin, M. Lelyn: *Early Makers of . . . Earthenware*, 189; *Early Potters and Potteries*, 189

Branyan, Lawrence, et al., *Worcester Blue and White Porcelain*, 204

Brass Book, Peter Schiffer et al., 176

Brass Candlesticks, Rupert Gentle, 172

Bray, Hazel V., *Potter's Art*, 189

Brears, Peter C. D., *English Country Pottery*, 204

Brett, Katharine B., and John Irwin, *Origins of Chintz*, 276

Brett, Vanessa: *Phaidon Guide to Pewter*, 162; *Sotheby's Directory of Silver*, 144

Bridenbaugh, Carl, *Colonial Craftsman*, 337

Brill, Robert H., et al., "Some Blown 'Three-Mold' Suspicions," 229

"Britannia in America," Nancy A. Goyne, 164

British Furniture, Pauline Agius, 115

British Pewter (Currier Gallery), 162

Britten, Frederick James, *Britten's Watch and Clock Maker's Handbook*, 288

Britten's Old Clocks and Watches, G. H. Baillie et al., 288

Britten's Watch and Clock Maker's Handbook, Frederick James Britten, 288

Broadlooms and Businessmen, John S. Ewing and Nancy P. Norton, 242

Bromley, John, ed., *Clockmaker's Library*, 289

Bronner, Simon J., *American Folk Art*, 29

Bronson, J. and R., *Early American Weaving*, 272

Brooklyn Museum, *American Renaissance*, 45

Brooks, H. Allen, *Prairie School*, 349

Brothers in Clay, John A. Burrison, 189, 337

Brown, Marley R., III, "Ceramics from Plymouth," 205

Brown, Michael K., et al., *Marks of Achievement*, 157

Bruhn, Thomas P., *American Decorative Tiles*, 184

Bruton, Eric: *Clocks and Watches*, 289; *Clocks and Watches, 1400–1900*, 289; *Dictionary of Clocks and Watches*, 289; *Longcase Clock*, 289

Buckeye Horology, James W. Gibbs, 296

Buckley, Jerome Hamilton, *Triumph of Time*, 300

Buferd, Norma Bradley, and Patricia Cooper, *Quilters*, 260

Buhler, Kathryn C.: *American Silver*, 148; *Colonial Silversmiths*, 148

Buhler, Kathryn C., and Graham Hood, *American Silver*, 148

Building Early America, ed. Charles E. Peterson, 72

Building the Dream, Gwendolyn Wright, 75

Bulkeley, Houghton, *Contributions to Connecticut Cabinet Making*, 88

Bulletin of the National Association of Watch and Clock Collectors, 289

Bulletin of the Pewter Collectors' Club of America, 163

Bunting, Bainbridge, *Houses of Boston's Back Bay*, 66

Burchill, Frank, and Richard Ross, *History of the Potters' Union*, 205

"Bureau Table in America," Nancy A. Goyne, 93

Burke, Doreen Bolger, et al., *In Pursuit of Beauty*, 45

Burks, Jean M., *Birmingham Brass Candlesticks*, 171

Burnham, Dorothy K.: "Constructions Used by . . . Weavers," 272; *Comfortable Arts*, 272; *Unlike the Lilies*, 272; *Warp and Weft*, 272

Burnham, Dorothy K., and Harold B. Burnham, *"Keep Me Warm One Night,"* 273

Burnham, Harold B., and Dorothy K. Burnham, *"Keep Me Warm One Night,"* 273

Burrison, John A., *Brothers in Clay*, 189, 337

Burrows, G. Edmond, *Canadian Clocks*, 293

Burt, Edwin B., Sr., and Fraser R. Forgie, *Clockmakers*, 293

Burt, Jo, and Owen Burt, "Walter H. Durfee," 293

Burt, Jo, and Owen H. Burt, *Welch, Spring*, 294

Burt, Owen, and Jo Burt, "Walter H. Durfee," 293

Burt, Owen H., and Jo Burt, *Welch, Spring*, 294

Burton, E. Milby: *Charleston Furniture*, 88; *South Carolina Silversmiths*, 149

Burton, Stanley H., *Watch Collection*, 303

"Business of Potting," Susan Myers, 340

Butler, Joseph T.: *Candleholders*, 325; "Lighting Devices," 325; *Sleepy Hollow Restorations*, 88

Butler, Joseph T., et al., *Arts in America*, 48

By the Sweat of Thy Brow, Melvin Kranzberg and Joseph Gies, 339

Byrdcliffe . . . Colony, 349

Byron, Joseph, *New York Interiors*, 67

Cabinet Makers' Assistant, John Hall, 124

Cabinetmakers of America, Ethel Hall Bjerkoe, 87

"Cabinetmaking in Philadelphia," Kathleen M. Catalano, 119

Calder, Charles A., *Rhode Island Pewterers*, 163

California Design, ed., Timothy J. Andersen et al., 347

Callen, Anthea, *Angel in the Studio*, 349

Calvert, Karin, "Cradle to Crib," 119

Calvert, Karin, et al., *Century of Childhood*, 49

Cambridge Glass, Lura Woodside Watkins, 234

Cameron, Elisabeth, *Encyclopedia of Pottery and Porcelain*, 197

Camp, Hiram, *Sketch of the Clock Making Business*, 294

Campbell, R., *London Tradesman*, 171

Canadian Clocks, G. Edmond Burrows, 293

Canadian Silversmiths, John E. Langdon, 146

Candleholders, Joseph T. Butler, 325

Candlesticks, Geoffrey Wills, 329

Candlesticks, Rupert Gentle, 172

"Candlewick Spread," Carleton L. Safford and Robert Bishop, 279

Canedy, Ruth Mary, and Barrows Mussey, *Terry Clock Chronology*, 298

"Canton *famille-rose* Porcelain . . . Mandarin," John Quentin Feller, 198

"Canton *famille rose* Porcelain . . . Rose Medallion," John Quentin Feller, 198

Cantor, Jay E., *Winterthur*, 45

Carlisle, Lilian Baker, "New . . . Findings on Curtis and Dunning," 294; *Vermont Clock and Watchmakers*, 294

Carlson, Janice H., "Analysis of . . . Pewter," 163

Carpenter, Charles H., Jr.: *Gorham Silver*, 149, 337; *Tiffany Silver*, 149

Carpenter, Charles H., Jr., and Mary Grace Carpenter, "Shaker Furniture," 119

Carpenter, Mary Grace, and Charles H. Carpenter, Jr., "Shaker Furniture," 119

"Carpentry," Bob Reckman, 340

Carpeting the Millions, J. Neville Bartlett, 242

"Carpets," W. G. Thompson, 246

Carriage Clocks, Charles Allix, 288

Carson, Cary, et al., "Impermanent Architecture," 67

Carson, Jane, *Colonial Virginia Cookery*, 311

Cast with Style, 323

Castleford Pottery, Diana Edwards Roussel, 215

Catalano, Kathleen M.: "Abraham Kimball," 119; "Cabinetmaking in Philadelphia," 119

Catalog of Roycroft Furniture, [Elbert Hubbard], 352

Catalogue of Craftsman Furniture, Gustav Stickley, 356

Catalogue of the Henry P. Strause Collection of Clocks, Virginia Museum of Fine Arts, 292

Catalogue of Tools for Watch and Clock Makers, 304

Cathers, David M., *Furniture of the American Arts and Crafts Movement*, 349

Caughley and Worcester Porcelains, Geoffrey A. Godden, 208

Cavallo, Adolph S., *Needlework*, 248

Celoria, F., and D. G. Vaisey, "Inventory of George Ecton," 217

Celoria, Francis, "Reports . . . on the Staffordshire Potteries," 205

Central Pennsylvania Redware Pottery, Jeannette Lasansky, 191

Centuries and Styles of the American Chair, Robert Bishop, 118

Century of Ceramics, Garth Clark, 184

Century of Childhood, Mary Lynn Stevens Heininger et al., 49

"Century of Revivals," Ulysses G. Dietz, 121

Ceramic Art, Jennie J. Young, 187

Ceramic Art of Great Britain, Llewellynn Jewitt, 210

"Ceramic Imports of Frederick Rhinelander," Arlene Palmer Schwind, 200, 215

Ceramic Marks from Old Sacramento, Mary Praetzellis et al., 214

"Ceramic Supply in an Economically Isolated Frontier Community," George L. Miller and Silas D. Hurry, 212

"Ceramics and the Sot-Weed Factor," Regina Lee Blaszczyk, 204

"Ceramics at the Crossroads," Ellen Paul Denker, 190

"Ceramics from Plymouth," James J. F.

Deetz, 206

"Ceramics from Plymouth," Marley R. Brown III, 205

"Ceramics from Suffolk County," Garry Wheeler Stone, 216

"Ceramics from the John Hicks Site," Garry Wheeler Stone, 216

Ceramics in America, ed. Ian M. G. Quimby, 199

"Ceramics in Providence," Barbara Gorely Teller, 216

"Ceramics in St. Mary's County," Lynne L. Herman et al., 209

"Ceramics in York County," Mary C. Beaudry, 204

Ceramics of Derbyshire, ed. H. G. Bradley, 204

Cescinsky, Herbert, *Gentle Art of Faking Furniture*, 85

"Chairs for the Masses," Mary Ellen Yehia, 135

Champlin, Richard L.: "James Wady," 294; "Quaker Clockmakers," 294; "Thomas Claggett," 294; *William Claggett*, 294

Champney, Freeman, *Art and Glory*, 349

Chandlee, Edward E., *Six Quaker Clockmakers*, 294

"Changing Iconography of Father Time," Samuel L. Macey, 302

Chapters in . . . the Arts and Crafts Movement, Oscar Lovell Triggs, 357

Chapuis, Alfred, *De horologiis in arte*, 300

Charleston, R. J., ed.: *English Porcelain*, 205; *World Ceramics*, 197

Charleston, R. J., and Donald Towner, *English Ceramics*, 205

Charleston, Robert J., *Masterpieces of Glass*, 226

Charleston Blacksmith, John Michael Vlach, 177, 342

Charleston Furniture, E. Milby Burton, 88

Chase, Ada R., "Two Eighteenth-Century Craftsmen," 295; "Two Eighteenth-Century Clockmakers," 295

"Checklist of American Pewter," Elizabeth M. Ely, 164

Checklist of European Treatises on Art, Janice G. Schimmelman, 31

Checklist of . . . Weavers, comp. John W. Heisey, 276

Chelsea Porcelain at Williamsburg, John C. Austin, 204

Cherry Hill, Roderick H. Blackburn, 66

"Chest of Drawers in America,"
  Benno M. Forman, 92

Chester County Clocks, Arthur E. James,
  297

Chicago Ceramics and Glass, Sharon S.
  Darling, 190

Chicago Furniture, Sharon Darling, 120

Chicago Metalsmiths, Sharon S. Darling,
  150, 171

Child's Comfort, Bruce Johnson, 261

China Collecting, Alice Morse Earle, 207

China Hunter's Club, [Annie Slossen],
  215

China Trade, Carl L. Crossman, 46

Chinese Export Porcelain, Herbert
  Schiffer et al., 200

Chinese Export Porcelain, Jean McClure
  Mudge, 199

Chinese Export Silver, H. A. Crosby
  Forbes et al., 145

Chinnery, Victor, *Oak Furniture*, 83

Chinoiserie, Hugh Honour, 49

Choice of Sundials, Winthrop W. Dolan,
  304

"Christian Herter," Marilynn Johnson
  Bordes, 118

"Christopher Townsend, Jr.'s, Watch
  Paper," Robert P. Emlen, 304

Churchill, Edwin A., *Simple Forms and
  Vivid Colors*, 120

Cipolla, Carl M., *Clocks and Culture*, 300

City of Hills and Kilns, William C. Gates,
  Jr., 190

Clabburn, Pamela, *Needleworker's Dictionary*, 249

Clark, Clifford E., Jr., "Domestic Architecture," 67

Clark, Clifford Edward, Jr., *American
  Family Home*, 67

Clark, Garth, *Century of Ceramics*, 184

Clark, Hyla M., *Tin Can*, 311

Clark, Ricky, ed., *Quilts and Carousels*,
  259

Clark, Robert Judson, ed.: *Arts and
  Crafts Movement in America*, 45, 349;
  *Aspects of the Arts and Crafts Move-
  ment*, 349

Clarke, Hermann Frederick: *John
  Coney*, 149; *John Hull*, 149

Clarke, Hermann Frederick, and Henry
  Wilder Foote, *Jeremiah Dummer*,
  150

Clarke, Mary Washington, *Kentucky
  Quilts*, 259

Classical America, 45, 88

Classical Language of Architecture, John
  Summerson, 34

Classical Presence in American Art, Milo
  M. Naeve, 99

"Classification and Economic Scaling
  of . . . Ceramics," George L. Miller,
  212

Clay in the Hands of the Potter, 189

Clayton, Michael, *Collector's Dictionary
  of the Silver and Gold*, 144

Clean and Decent, Lawrence Wright,
  323

"Cleanliness," Harvey Green, 313

Cloak, Evelyn Campbell, *Glass Paperweights*, 226

Clock and Watch Designs, John Ittman,
  290

Clock and Watchmakers, John E.
  Langdon, 290

Clock Book, Wallace Nutting, 291

Clock Collection, William H. Distin, 289

Clockmaker, Thomas Chandler
  Haliburton, 301

Clockmaker's Library, ed. John Bromley,
  289

"Clockmakers of Ashby," Laurence
  Luther Barber, 293

Clockmakers of Concord, Edwin B. Burt,
  Sr., and Fraser R. Forgie, 293

Clockmakers of Concord (Concord Antiquarian Society), 295

Clockmakers of Lancaster, Stacy B. C.
  Wood, Jr., et al., 299

*Clockmakers Outcry against . . . Tristram
  Shandy*, 300

"Clockmaking and Society," Philip Zea,
  342

Clocks, Douglas H. Shaffer, 292

"Clocks and Chronology," Samuel L.
  Macey, 302

Clocks and Culture, Carl M. Cipolla, 300

Clocks and the Cosmos, Samuel L. Macey,
  302

Clocks and Watches, Eric Bruton, 289

Clocks and Watches, Granville H. Baillie,
  288

Clocks and Watches, William E. Drost,
  295

Clocks and Watches, 1400–1900, Eric
  Bruton, 289

Clocks in Home Decoration, 300

Clocks of Shenandoah, Philip Whitney,
  299

Clocks That Time Us, Martin C. Moore-
  Ede et al., 302

Clockwork Man, Lawrence Wright, 303

Clockwork Universe, ed. Klaus Maurice
  and Otto Mayr, 302

Clunie, Margaret Burke, et al., *Furniture at the Essex Institute*, 88

Clutton, C., et al., *Britten's Old Clocks
  and Watches*, 288

Clutton, Cecil, and George Daniels,
  Watches, 304

Coblentz, Patricia, and Robert Bishop,
  American Decorative Arts, 44; *World of
  Antiques, Art, and Architecture*, 44

Cocks, Dorothy, *Pewter Collection of the
  New Canaan Historical Society*, 163

Coe, Eva Johnston, and Ethel Stanwood
  Bolton, *American Samplers*, 248

Coffin, Margaret, *History and Folklore of
  . . . Tinware*, 171

Cogswell, Elizabeth Agee, "Henry Lippitt House," 120

Cohen, Lizabeth A., "Embellishing a
  Life of Labor," 67

Cohn, Jan, *Palace or the Poorhouse*, 68

Colby, Averil, *Quilting*, 260

Cole, Arthur H., "Tempo of Mercantile
  Life," 300

Cole, Arthur H., and Harold F.
  Williamson, *American Carpet Manufacture*, 242

Collard, Elizabeth, *Nineteenth-Century
  Pottery and Porcelain in Canada*, 205

Collard, Frances, *Regency Furniture*, 83

Collected Works of Gustav Stickley, ed.
  Stephen Gray and Robert Edwards,
  352

*Collecting American Nineteenth Century
  Silver*, Katharine Morrison
  McClinton, 153

Collecting American Pewter, Katherine
  Ebert, 164

*Collecting and Restoring Wicker Furni-
  ture*, Richard Saunders, 131

Collecting Traditional American Basketry,
  Gloria Roth Teleki, 317

Collecting Watch Fobs, John M. Kaduck,
  305

Collection of Exhibition Catalogs, Archives
  of American Art, 29

*Collection of Heating and Lighting Uten-
  sils*, Walter Hough, 327

Collector's Dictionary of Quilt Names,
  Yvonne M. Khin, 262

*Collector's Dictionary of the Silver and
  Gold*, Michael Clayton, 144

*Collector's Guide to American Wicker Fur-
  niture*, Richard Saunders, 131

Collectors' Guide to . . . Ceramics, Marvin
  D. Schwartz, 187

Collector's Guide to Pressing Irons, Esther
  S. Berney, 311

Colonial Craftsman, Carl Bridenbaugh, 337

Colonial Furniture, Luke Vincent Lockwood, 97

Colonial Furniture of New England, Irving Whitall Lyon, 97

Colonial Grandeur, Nicholas B. Wainwright, 56

Colonial Ironwork, Philip B. Wallace, 177

Colonial Kitchens, Frances Phipps, 316

Colonial Lighting, Arthur H. Hayward, 327

"Colonial Revival and American Nationalism," William B. Rhoads, 73

Colonial Silversmiths, Kathryn C. Buhler, 148

Colonial Virginia Cookery, Jane Carson, 311

"Colorful Ceramics," Lura Woodside Watkins, 218

Comfortable Arts, Dorothy K. Burnham, 272

Comfortable House, Alan Gowans, 70

Commemorative Pottery, John May and Jennifer May, 212

"Common Houses, Cultural Spoor," Peirce F. Lewis, 71

Common Places, ed. Dell Upton and John Michael Vlach, 74

Complete Book of American Kitchen and Dinner Wares, Lois Lehner, 186

Complete . . . Glass, Estelle Sinclaire Farrar and Jane Shadel Spillman, 227

Complete Guide to . . . Watches, Cooksey Shugart, 305

Comstock, Helen: "Eighteenth-Century Floorcloths," 242; *American Furniture*, 88; *Looking Glass in America*, 88

Comstock, Helen, ed., *Concise Encyclopedia of American Antiques*, 32

"Concepts of Shelter," John F. Moe, 72

"Concerning the Simon Willard Legend," George H. Kernodle, 298

Concise Encyclopedia of American Antiques, ed. Helen Comstock, 32

Conforti, Michael P., "Orientalism," 349

Congram, Marjorie, "Haircloth Upholstery," 273

Connecticut Clockmakers, Penrose R. Hoopes, 297

Connecticut Furniture, 89

Connecticut Pewter, John Carl Thomas, 167

Conrad, Henry Clay, *Old Delaware Clockmakers*, 295

"Constructions Used by . . . Weavers," Dorothy K. Burnham, 272

Contribution of Joseph Ives, Kenneth D. Roberts, 298

Contributions to Connecticut Cabinet Making, Houghton Bulkeley, 88

Cook, Clarence, *House Beautiful*, 120

Cooke, Edward S., Jr.: "Boston Furniture Industry," 120; *Fiddlebacks*, 337; *Fiddlebacks and Crooked-backs*, 89; *Upholstery*, 89

Cooke, Lawrence S., ed., *Lighting*, 326

"Cooking and Heating," Jeanne Minhinnick, 315

Coons, Martha, and Katherine Koob, *All Sorts of . . . Cloth*, 273

Cooper, Grace Rogers: *Copp Family Textiles*, 249; *Sewing Machine*, 311

Cooper, Patricia, and Norma Bradley Buferd, *Quilters*, 260

Cooper, Ronald G., *English Slipware Dishes*, 205

Cooper, Wendy, A., *In Praise of America*, 45, 89

Copeland, Robert, *Spode's Willow Pattern*, 205

Copp Family Textiles, Grace Rogers Cooper, 249

Copper for America, Maxwell Whiteman, 177

Corbett, Cynthia Arps, *Useful Art*, 189

Cornelius, Charles Over, *Furniture Masterpieces of Duncan Phyfe*, 89

Cosentino, Geraldine, and Regina Stewart, *Kitchenware*, 312

Cotterell, Howard Herschel, *Old Pewter*, 163

Cotterell, Howard Herschel, et al., *National Types of Old Pewter*, 163

Country Arts, Nina Fletcher Little, 51

Country Cabinetwork, ed. John D. Morse, 99

Country Clocks, Brian Loomes, 290

Country Cloth, Sandra Rambo Walker, 280

Country House Floors, Christopher Gilbert et al., 243

Country Life International Dictionary of Clocks, ed. Alan Smith, 292

Cousins, Frank W., *Sundials*, 304

"Coverlet Bibliography," Clarita Anderson, 271

Coverlets, Mildred Davison and Christa C. Mayer-Thurman, 274

Covill, William E., Jr., *Ink Bottles and Inkwells*, 226

Cowan, Ruth Schwartz, *More Work for Mother*, 312

Cox, Alwyn, and Angela Cox, *Rockingham Pottery and Porcelain*, 206

Cox, Angela, and Alwyn Cox, *Rockingham Pottery and Porcelain*, 206

Cox, Henry Bartholomew, "Plain and Fancy," 326

Coysh, A. W., and R. K. Henrywood, *Dictionary of Blue and White Printed Pottery*, 206

"Cradle to Crib," Karin Calvert, 119

Craft Apprentice, W. J. Rorabaugh, 341

Craft of the Clockmaker, Eric John Tyler, 292

Craftsman, ed. Barry Sanders, 355

Craftsman Homes, Gustav Stickley, 356

Craftsman in Early America, ed. Ian M. G. Quimby, 54

Craftsman's Handbook, Henry Lapp, 127

"Craftsmen and Machines," Polly Anne Earl, 122

Craig, James H., *Arts and Crafts in North Carolina*, 32

Crawley, W., *Is It Genuine*, 86

Crazy Quilts, Penny McMorris, 262

Creamware, Donald Towner, 217

Creamware and Other English Pottery at Temple Newsam, Peter Walton, 217

Creamware and Pearlware, Terence A. Lockett and Pat A. Halfpenny, 211

"Creamware to Pearlware," Ivor Noël Hume, 213

Creation of the Rococo Decorative Style, Fiske Kimball, 50

Crescent City Silver, 150

"Crewel Embroidered Bed Hangings," Ann Pollard Rowe, 254

Crichton, Laurie W., *Book Decoration*, 349

Crom, Theodore R.: *Horological Shop Tools*, 304; *Horological Wheel Cutting Engines*, 304

Crossman, Carl L., *China Trade*, 46

Crosson, Janet Gray, *Let's Get Technical*, 273

Crystal Palace Exhibition, 120

Culme, John, *Nineteenth-Century Silver*, 145

"Cultural Pluralism and Pots," Meta F. Janowitz et al., 198

Culture and Comfort, Katherine C. Grier, 48

Cummings, Abbott Lowell, *Framed Houses*, 68

Cummings, Abbott Lowell, comp., *Bed Hangings*, 273

Cummings, Abbott Lowell, ed., *Rural Household Inventories*, 32

Cummins, J. M., "Small . . . Clocks," 304

Cunningham, Patricia A., "Ohio's Woven Covelets," 274

Curtis, Jane, and Will Curtis, *Antique Woodstoves*, 323

Curtis, Phillip H.: "American Quilts," 260; "Production of Tucker Porcelain," 190

Curtis, Will, and Jane Curtis, *Antique Woodstoves*, 323

Cushion, J. P., comp., *Handbook of Pottery and Porcelain Marks* 197

Cutten, George Barton: *Silversmiths, Watchmakers, and Jewelers of . . . New York*, 295; *Silversmiths of Georgia*, 295; *Silversmiths of Virginia*, 295

Dalia, Maria M., and Andrew Hayes Miller, *Survey of American Clocks*, 291

"Daniel Pabst," David A. Hanks and Page Talbott, 125

Daniel Pratt, Jr., Miriam A. Barclay, 293

Daniels, George, *English and American Watches*, 304

Daniels, George, and Cecil Clutton, *Watches*, 304

Darbee, Herbert C., *Glossary of Old Lamps*, 326

"Dark Satanic Century," Reyner Banham, 325

Darley, Gillian, and Philippa Lewis, *Dictionary of Ornament*, 34

Darling, Sharon, *Chicago Furniture*, 120

Darling, Sharon S.: *Chicago Metalsmiths*, 150, 171; *Chicago Ceramics and Glass*, 190

Dated English Delftware, Louis L. Lipski, 211

Davenport Pottery and Porcelain, Terence A. Lockett, 211

David Rittenhouse, Brooke Hindle, 296

Davidson, Caroline, *Woman's Work*, 312

Davidson, Marshall B., "Early American Lighting," 326

Davidson, Marshall B., ed., *American Heritage History of Antiques*, 46

Davidson, Martha, and William H. Pierson, Jr., eds., *Arts of the United States*, 54

Davies, Jane B., "Gothic Revival Furniture Designs," 121

Davis, John D., *English Silver at Williamsburg*, 145

Davis, Myra Tolmach, *Sketches in Iron*, 171

Davis, Pearce, *Development of the American Glass Industry*, 226

Davison, Mildred, and Christa C. Mayer-Thurman, *Coverlets*, 274

Dawley, Alan, and Paul Faler, "Working-Class Culture," 337

De horologiis in arte, Alfred Chapuis, 300

Deagan, Kathleen, *Artifacts of the Spanish Colonies*, 197

Deas, Alston, *Early Ironwork of Charleston*, 172

Decorated Furniture, Henry M. Reed, 130

Decorated Stoneware Pottery, Donald Blake Webster, 187

"Decorative Arts," Berry B. Tracy, 134

Decorative Arts Newsletter, 35

Decorative Arts of New Hampshire, 295

Decorative Designs of Frank Lloyd Wright, David A. Hanks, 352

Deerfield Embroidery, Margery Burnham Howe, 251

Deetz, James, *In Small Things Forgotten*, 46

Deetz, James J. F., "Ceramics from Plymouth," 206

de Jonge, C. H., *Delft Ceramics*, 197

de Jonge, Eric, "Johann Christoph Heyne," 163

Delaware Cabinetmakers, Charles G. Dorman, 90

"Delaware Valley . . . Chairs," Benno M. Forman, 92, 338

Delft Ceramics, C. H. de Jonge, 197

Denker, Bert, and Ellen Denker: *Main Street Pocket Guide to . . . Pottery*, 184; *Rocking Chair Book*, 121

Denker, Ellen, and Bert Denker: *Main Street Pocket Guide to . . . Pottery*, 184; *Rocking Chair Book*, 121

Denker, Ellen Paul: "Ceramics at the Crossroads," 190; *Kirkpatricks' Pottery*, 190

Department of American Decorative Arts and Sculpture and Museum of Fine Arts, Boston, *Frontier America*, 52

DePasquale, Dan, et al., *Red Wing Stoneware*, 190

DePasquale, Gail, et al., *Red Wing Stoneware*, 190

Derwich, Jenny B., and Mary Latos, *Dictionary Guide to . . . Pottery and Porcelain*, 184

"Designed in France," Kenneth L. Ames, 116

de Solla Price, Derek J., *On the Origin of Clockwork*, 301

Detroit Institute of Arts, *Quest for Unity*, 46

Detweiler, Susan G., *American Presidential China*, 206

Detweiler, Susan Gray, *George Washington's Chinaware*, 197, 206

Deutsch, Davida Tenenbaum, "Samuel Folwell," 249

Deutsch, Davida Tenenbaum, and Betty Ring, "Homage to Washington," 249

Development of the American Glass Industry, Pearce Davis, 226

DeVoe, Shirley S., "Hopkins and Alfred," 295

DeVoe, Shirley Spaulding: "Painted Floor-Cloths," 242; *Tinsmiths of Connecticut*, 172

Diaz Collection, David L. Felton and Peter D. Schulz, 207

Dibble, Ann W., "Major John Dunlap," 337

Dickstein, Robert, and Lester Dworetsky, *Horology Americana*, 289

Dictionary Guide to . . . Pottery and Porcelain, Jenny B. Derwich and Mary Latos, 184

Dictionary of American Clock and Watch Makers, Kenneth A. Sposato, 292

Dictionary of Architecture, Nikolaus Pevsner et al., 34

Dictionary of Blue and White Printed Pottery, A. W. Coysh and R. K. Henrywood, 206

Dictionary of Clocks and Watches, Eric Bruton, 289

Dictionary of Dyes, K. G. Ponting, 277

Dictionary of English Furniture, Percy Macquoid and Ralph Edwards, 84

Dictionary of Ornament, Philippa Lewis and Gillian Darley, 34

Dietz, Ulysses G.: "Century of Revivals," 121; *Victorian Lighting*, 326

Dining in America, ed. Kathryn Grover, 49

Directly from China, Christina H. Nelson, 199

Directory: Historical Agencies in North America, 32

Directory of Boston . . . Watch and Clock Makers, Paul J. Fredyma and Marie-Louise Fredyma, 296

Directory of Connecticut . . . Watch and Clock Makers, John J. Fredyma, 296

Directory of Maine . . . Watch and Clock Makers, James P. Fredyma, 296

Directory of Vermont . . . Watch and Clock Makers, Paul J. Fredyma, 296

Distin, William H., *Clock Collection*, 289

Distin, William H., and Robert Bishop, *American Clock*, 289

Dixie Clockmakers, James W. Gibbs, 296

Documentary History of American Interiors, Edgar de N. Mayhew and Minor Myers, Jr., 51, 71

Documentation of Collections, comp. Rosemary Reese, 31

"Documented Use of Cup Plates," Jane S. Shadel, 234

"Documents Relating to English Ceramics," Arnold R. Mountford, 213

Dolan, Winthrop W., *Choice of Sundials*, 304

Domestic American Textiles, Beverly Gordon, 250

"Domestic Architecture," Clifford E. Clark, Jr., 67

Domestic Pottery, ed. Sarah Peabody Turnbaugh, 193

Domestic Scene, 349

"Domestic Textile Industry," David-Thiery Ruddel, 279

Dorman, Charles G., *Delaware Cabinet-makers*, 90

Doros, Paul E., *Tiffany Collection of the Chrysler Museum*, 227

"Double Weave Coverlet," Carleton L. Safford and Robert Bishop, 279

Douglas, Diane M., "Machine in the Parlor," 312

Douglas, Paul H., *American Apprenticeship*, 337

"Dover Manufacturing Company," Caroline Sloat, 279

Dow, George Francis, comp., *Arts and Crafts in New England*, 33

Downing, A. J., "Furniture," 121

Downs, Joseph, *American Furniture*, 90

Drakard, David, and Paul Holdway, *Spode Printed Ware*, 206

Dreppard, Carl W., *American Clocks*, 289

Drost, William E., *Clocks and Watches*, 295

Dublin, Thomas, *Women at Work*, 337

Dubrow, Eileen, and Richard Dubrow,

Furniture Made in America, 121

Dubrow, Richard, and Eileen Dubrow, *Furniture Made in America*, 121

Duncan, Alastair, *Art Nouveau . . . Lighting*, 326

Duncan Phyfe and the English Regency, Nancy McClelland, 98

Dunlaps and Their Furniture, 90

Dutch Trade and Ceramics, Charlotte Wilcoxen, 200

Dworetsky, Lester, and Robert Dickstein, *Horology Americana*, 289

Dyer's Companion, Elijah Bemiss, 271

Earl, Polly Anne, "Craftsmen and Machines," 122

Earl, Polly Anne, and Ian M. G. Quimby, eds. *Technological Innovation and the Decorative Arts*, 54

Earle, Alice Morse: *China Collecting*, 207; "Flax Culture and Spinning," 274; "Handweaving," 274; "Wool Culture and Spinning," 274; *Sun Dials and Roses*, 304

Early American Andirons, Henry Kauffman and Quentin Bowers, 324

Early American Clocks, ed. Don Maust, 291

Early American Fireplaces, Paul Revere Ladd, 324

Early American Folk Pottery, Harold F. Guilland, 185

Early American Furniture, John T. Kirk, 96

Early American House, Mary Earle Gould, 313

Early American Ironware, Henry J. Kauffman, 174

"Early American Lighting," Marshall B. Davidson, 326

"Early American Look," Jane Nylander, 245

Early American Pewter, Allentown Art Museum, 162

Early American Silver, C. Louise Avery, 147

Early American Silver, ed. Jane Bentley Kolter, 153

Early American Silver, Martha Gandy Fales, 150

Early American Taverns, Kym S. Rice, 55

Early American Textiles, Frances Little, 277

Early American Weaving, J. and R. Bronson, 272

Early American Wooden Ware, Mary Earle Gould, 313

Early American Wrought Iron, Alfred H. Sonn, 177

Early Canadian Pottery, Donald Webster, 194

"Early Colonial Clockmakers," Carolyn Wood Stretch, 299

Early Connecticut Silver, Peter Bohan and Philip Hammerslough, 148

"Early Delaware Clockmakers," James W. Gibbs, 296

Early English Delftware, Ivor Noël Hume, 213

Early Furniture Made in New Jersey, 90

Early Furniture of Louisiana, Jessie J. Poesch, 101

Early Ironwork of Charleston, Alston Deas, 172

Early Lighting, Helen B. Hebard, 327

"Early . . . Lighting," Loris S. Russell, 328

Early Lighting, Rushlight Club, 328

Early Makers of . . . Earthenware, M. Lelyn Branin, 189

Early New England Potters, Lura Woodside Watkins, 194

Early Ontario Potters, David L. Newlands, 192

Early Potters and Potteries, M. Lelyn Branin, 189

Early Potters and Potteries of New York, William C. Ketchum, Jr., 191

"Early Work of Charles F. McKim," Richard Guy Wilson, 75

"East Liverpool Pottery," William C. Gates, Jr., and Dana E. Ormerod, 191

Eastern Shore . . . Raised-Panel Furniture, James R. Melchor et al., 98

Eastlake, Charles L., *Hints on Household Taste*, 122

Eastlake-Influenced American Furniture, Mary Jean Madigan, 127

Ebert, Katherine, *Collecting American Pewter*, 164

Eckhardt, George, *United States Clock and Watch Patents*, 289

Eckhardt, George H., *Pennsylvania Clocks*, 295

"Editor's Attic," [Homer Eaton Keyes], 305

"Edmund Currier," David R. Proper, 298

"Edward Winslow's Sugar Boxes," Edward J. Nygren, 154

Edwardes, Ernest L., *Grandfather Clock*, 290

Edwards, Ralph, *Shorter Dictionary of English Furniture*, 83

Edwards, Ralph, and Percy Macquoid, *Dictionary of English Furniture*, 84

Edwards, Robert, and Stephen Gray, eds., *Collected Works of Gustav Stickley*, 352

"Eighteenth- and Nineteenth-Century Cast-Iron Cooking Utensils," John D. Tyler, 317

Eighteenth and Nineteenth Century Maryland Silver, Jennifer Faulds Goldsborough, 152

Eighteenth-Century American Arts, Edwin J. Hipkiss, 94

Eighteenth-Century Ceramics from Fort Michilimackinac, J. Jefferson Miller II and Lyle M. Stone, 199, 213

"Eighteenth-Century Cultural Process in Delaware Valley Folk Building," Henry Glassie, 69

"Eighteenth-Century Floorcloths," Helen Comstock, 242

Eighteenth-Century Houses of Williamsburg, Marcus Whiffen, 74

Eighteenth Century Industrialist, Thomas Southcliffe Ashton, 303

Ela, Chipman P., *Banjo Timepiece*, 290

Elder, William Voss, III, and Lu Bartlett, *John Shaw*, 90

Elgin Reminiscences, 304

Eli Terry, Edward Ingraham et al., 297

Eli Terry, Kenneth D. Roberts, 298

Eli Terry . . . Clocks, Lockwood Anderson Barr, 293

Ely, Elizabeth M.: "American Pewter," 164; "Checklist of American Pewter," 164

"Embellishing a Life of Labor," Lizabeth A. Cohen, 67

"Emery Attributions," Robert F. Trent, 105

Emery, Irene, *Primary Structures of Fabrics*, 274

Emlen, Robert P.: "Christopher Townsend, Jr.'s, Watch Paper," 304; "Masterful William Claggett Clock," 295

Encyclopaedia of British Pottery and Porcelain Marks, Geoffrey A. Godden, 208

Encyclopedia of American Cut and Engraved Glass, J. Michael Pearson, 232

Encyclopedia of American Silver Manufacturers, Dorothy T. Rainwater, 154

Encyclopedia of Glass Paperweights, Paul Hollister, Jr., 227

Encyclopedia of Pottery and Porcelain, Elisabeth Cameron, 197

English and American Watches, George Daniels, 304

English and Oriental Carpets, Mildred B. Lanier, 244

English and Scottish Earthenware, G. Bernard Hughes, 210

English Art Pottery, Malcolm Haslam, 209

English Blue and White Porcelain, Bernard Watney, 218

English Brass and Copper, Henry Hamilton, 173

English Brown Stoneware, Adrian Oswald, 214

English-Canadian Furniture, Donald Blake Webster, 85

"English Carpets," Ruth Page, 245

English Ceramics, R. J. Charleston and Donald Towner, 205

English China, Geoffrey A. Godden, 208

English Church Plate, Charles Oman, 147

English Country Pottery, Peter C. D. Brears, 204

English Decorative Ironwork, John Harris, 174

English Delftware, F. H. Garner and Michael Archer, 207

English Domestic Brass, Rupert Gentle and Rachael Feild, 172

English Domestic Needlework, Therle Hughes, 252

English Furniture, Edward T. Joy, 126

English Furniture, Maurice Tomlin, 85

English Furniture Designs, Peter Ward-Jackson, 85

English Furniture Styles, Ralph Fastnedge, 83

English Goldsmiths, Charles Jackson, 146

English Needlework Carpets, M. J. Mayorcas, 244

English Porcelain, ed. R. J. Charleston, 205

English Pottery and Porcelain, ed. Paul Atterbury, 203

English Printed Textiles, 274

English Silver at Williamsburg, John D. Davis, 145

English Slipware Dishes, Ronald G. Cooper, 205

"English Tools," Charles F. Hummel, 305

English Transfer-Printed Pottery and Porcelain, Cyril Williams-Wood, 219

English Yellow-Glazed Earthenware, J. Jefferson Miller II, 213

Enigma of Time, ed. Peter T. Landesberg, 301

Ensko, Stephen G. C., *American Silversmiths*, 150

"Entrepreneurship in . . . the American Clock Industry," John Joseph Murphy, 291

Essex County Furniture, Dean A. Fales, Jr., 91

Ettema, Michael J.: "Forum: History, Nostalgia, and American Furniture," 122; "Technological Innovation and Design Economics," 122

European Porcelain, Peter Wilhelm Meister and Horst Reber, 199

Evans, Joan, *Pattern*, 46

Evans, Paul, *Art Pottery*, 184

Evans, William, *Art and History of the Potting Business*, 207

"Evolution and Horizon," Stanley South, 216

Evolution of the Night Lamp, Ann Gilbert McDonald, 327

Evolution of the Sad-Iron, A. H. Glissman, 313

Ewers, William, and H. W. Baylor, *Sincere's History of the Sewing Machine*, 312

Ewing, John S., and Nancy P. Norton, *Broadlooms and Businessmen*, 242

Examples of Early English Pottery, John Eliot Hodgkin and Edith Hodgkin, 210

Exhibition of Connecticut Pewter, New Haven Colony Historical Society, 166

Eye of the Beholder, 83

Eye of Thomas Jefferson, ed. William Howard Adams, 43

Fabian, Monroe H., *Pennsylvania-German Decorated Chest*, 90

Fabrics for Historic Buildings, Jane C. Nylander, 277

Failey, Dean F., *Long Island Is My Nation*, 47, 91

Fair as China Dishes, Michael Archer and Brian Morgan, 203

Fairbanks, Jonathan L., and Elizabeth Bidwell Bates, *American Furniture*, 87, 118

Fairbanks, Jonathan L., and Robert F. Trent, *New England Begins*, 47, 91

Faler, Paul, and Alan Dawley, "Working-Class Culture," 337

Fales, Dean A., Jr.: *American Painted Furniture*, 91, 122; *Essex County Furniture*, 91; *Furniture of Historic Deerfield*, 91

Fales, Martha Gandy: *American Silver*, 150; *Early American Silver*, 150; *Joseph Richardson*, 150

Fales, Martha Gandy, and Henry N. Flynt, *Heritage Foundation Collection of Silver*, 151

Falkner, Frank, *Wood Family of Burslem*, 207

Farm and Cottage Inventories, ed. Francis W. Steer, 34

Farnam, Anne: "A. H. Davenport and Company," 122; "Arts and Crafts Tradition," 351

Farnam, Anne, et al., *Furniture at the Essex Institute*, 88

Farrar, Estelle Sinclaire, and Jane Shadel Spillman, *Complete . . . Glass*, 227

"Fashion for Carpets," Audrey Michie, 245

Fastnedge, Ralph, *English Furniture Styles*, 83

"Father Time," Erwin Panofsky, 303

"Fathers, Sons, and Identity," Robert Blair St. George, 341

Faÿ-Hallé, Antoinette, and Barbara Mundt, *Porcelain of the Nineteenth Century*, 198

Feeny, Bill, and Dorothy Robinson, *Official Price Guide to American Pottery*, 186

Feild, Rachael, and Rupert Gentle, *English Domestic Brass*, 172

Feller, John Quentin: "Canton *famille rose* Porcelain . . . Mandarin," 198; "Canton *famille-rose* Porcelain . . . Rose Medallion," 198

Felton, David L., and Peter D. Schulz, *Diaz Collection*, 207

Fendelman, Helaine W., *Tramp Art*, 123

Fennimore, Donald, "Religion in America," 151

Fennimore, Donald L.: "American Neoclassical Furniture," 123; "Thomas Fletcher and Sidney Gardiner," 151; *Silver and Pewter*, 164

Ferguson, Eugene S., "Historical Sketch of Central Heating," 323

Ferris, William, "Pecolia Warner," 260

Ferris, William, ed., *Afro-American Folk Art*, 47

Festive Tradition, Louise Conway

Belden, 44

Fiddlebacks, Edward S. Cooke, Jr., 337

Fiddlebacks and Crooked-backs, Edward S. Cooke, Jr., 89

"Figure of the Artisan," T. J. Jackson Lears, 354

Fikioris, Margaret A., "Neoclassicism in Textile Designs," 274

Findley, Ruth E., *Old Patchwork Quilts*, 260

Fine Points of Furniture, Albert Sack, 102

Finer, Ann, and George Savage, eds., *Selected Letters of Josiah Wedgwood*, 207

Finkelstein, Barbara, et al., *Century of Childhood*, 49

Finlay, Nancy, *Artists of the Book*, 351

Finley, John, and Jonathan Holstein, *Kentucky Quilts*, 261

Fire on the Hearth, Josephine H. Peirce, 324

"First Orreries," Harrold E. Gillingham, 305

Fiske, Patricia L., ed., *Imported and Domestic Textiles*, 274

Fitzgerald, Oscar P.: *Green Family of Cabinetmakers*, 123; *Three Centuries of American Furniture*, 92, 123

Fix, Edward B., "Long Island Carpenter," 338

"Flax Culture and Spinning," Alice Morse Earle, 274

Fleming, E. McClung, "Symbols of the United States," 47

Fleming, J. Arnold, *Scottish Pottery*, 207

Fleming, John, and Hugh Honour, *Penguin Dictionary of Decorative Arts*, 33

Fleming, John, et al., *Dictionary of Architecture*, 34

Flickering Flames, Leroy Thwing, 329

"Floor Coverings," Charles F. Hummel, 244

Floor Coverings, Nina Fletcher Little, 244

Floor Coverings, Rodris Roth, 245

"Flow-Blue," Susan R. Williams, 219

Flowering of American Folk Art, Alice Winchester and Jean Lipman, 51

Flushed with Pride, Wallace Reyburn, 322

Flynt, Henry N., and Martha Gandy Fales, *Heritage Foundation Collection of Silver*, 151

Foley, Mary Mix, *American House*, 68

Folk Housing in Middle Virginia, Henry Glassie, 69, 338

Food, Audrey Noël Hume, 316

Food on the Frontier, Marjorie Kreidberg, 314

"Foot Stoves," Mary Earle Gould, 324

Foote, Henry Wilder, and Hermann Frederick Clarke, *Jeremiah Dummer*, 150

For Generations to Come, Forrest M. Holly, 297

Forbes, H. A. Crosby, et al., *Chinese Export Silver*, 145

Forbes, Jack, and Marylu Antonelli, *Pottery in Alberta*, 188

Forgie, Fraser R., and Edwin B. Burt, Sr., *Clockmakers*, 293

Forgie, Fraser R., et al., *Eli Terry*, 297

Forgotten Art of Building a Good Fireplace, Vrest Orton, 324

Forgotten Rebel, John Crosby Freeman, 351

"Form, Function, and Meaning in . . . Fabric Furnishings," Susan Prendergast Schoelwer, 279

Forman, Benno M.: "Account Book of John Gould," 275; *American Seating Furniture*, 92; "Chest of Drawers in America," 92; "Delaware Valley . . . Chairs," 92, 338; "German Influences in . . . Furniture," 92, 338; "Urban Aspects of . . . Furniture," 338

"Forum: History, Nostalgia, and American Furniture," Michael J. Ettema, 122

Four Hundred Trademarks on Glass, Arthur G. Peterson, 232

Framed Houses, Abbott Lowell Cummings, 68

Franklin, Benjamin, "How to Make a Striking Sundial," 301

Franklin, Linda Campbell: *America in the Kitchen*, 312; *Antiques and Collectibles*, 30

Franklin Institute, *Horological Books*, 290

Fraser, Esther Stevens, "Some Colonial . . . Decorative Floors," 243

Fraser, J. T., *Of Time, Passion, and Knowledge*, 301

Fraser, J. T., ed., *Voices of Time*, 301

Fredyma, James P., *Directory of Maine . . . Watch and Clock Makers*, 296

Fredyma, John J., *Directory of Connecticut . . . Watch and Clock Makers*, 296

Fredyma, Marie-Louise, and Paul J. Fredyma, *Directory of Boston . . . Watch and Clock Makers*, 296

Fredyma, Paul J., *Directory of*

Vermont . . . Watch and Clock Makers, 296

Fredyma, Paul J., and Marie-Louise Fredyma, *Directory of Boston . . . Watch and Clock Makers,* 296

Freedman, Jonathan, et al., *In Pursuit of Beauty,* 45

Freeman, John Crosby, *Forgotten Rebel,* 351

Freeman, John Crosby, ed., *Mission and Art Nouveau,* 351

Freeman, Larry, *New Light,* 326

Freeman, Roland, ed., *Something to Keep You Warm,* 260

Freitag, Wolfgang M., *Art Books,* 30

Frelinghuysen, Alice C., *American Porcelain,* 185

Frelinghuysen, Alice Cooney, "Aesthetic Forms in Ceramics," 185

Frelinghuysen, Alice Cooney, et al., *In Pursuit of Beauty,* 45

French, Hollis, *Jacob Hurd,* 151

French, Neal, et al., *Worcester Blue and White Porcelain,* 204

Friends of the Cabildo, *New Orleans Architecture,* 68

"From Pure Coin," Deborah Dependahl Waters, 157

From Rags to Riches, Chris H. Bailey, 292

"From the Shop," Stephen K. Victor, 342

Frontier America, Museum of Fine Arts, Boston, and the Department of American Decorative Arts and Sculpture, 52

Frontier Fur Trade, John D. Light and Henry Unglik, 339

Fruit Jars, Julian Harrison Toulouse, 317

Frye, L. Thomas, ed., *American Quilts,* 260

Fuller, Charles A., et al., *Clocks That Time Us,* 302

"Furniture," A. J. Downing, 121

Furniture, Eric Mercer, 84

Furniture and Its Makers of Chester County, Margaret Berwind Schiffer, 103

Furniture at Temple Newsam House and Lotherton Hall, Christopher Gilbert, 83

Furniture at the Essex Institute, Margaret Burke Clunie et al., 88

Furniture by New York Cabinetmakers, V. Isabelle Miller, 98

"Furniture by the Lejambre Family,"

Peter L. L. Strickland, 132

"Furniture Designs of Henry W. Jenkins," John H. Hill, 125

Furniture in Maryland, Gregory R. Weidman, 106, 134

"Furniture in Philadelphia," Cathryn J. McElroy, 98

Furniture Made in America, Richard Dubrow and Eileen Dubrow, 121

Furniture Making, R. W. Symonds, 86

Furniture Masterpieces of Duncan Phyfe, Charles Over Cornelius, 89

Furniture of Coastal North Carolina, John Bivins, Jr., 87

Furniture of Gustav Stickley, Joseph J. Bavaro and Thomas L. Mossman, 348

Furniture of Historic Deerfield, Dean A. Fales, Jr., 91

Furniture of John Henry Belter, Marvin D. Schwartz et al., 131

Furniture of Our Forefathers, Esther Singleton, 103

Furniture of the American Arts and Crafts Movement, David M. Cathers, 349

Furniture of the Georgia Piedmont, Henry D. Green, 93

"Furniture of the Lower Connecticut River Valley," Nancy E. Richards, 102

Furniture of the New Haven Colony, Patricia E. Kane, 95

Furniture of the Pilgrim Century, Wallace Nutting, 100

Furniture of Williamsburg, Wallace B. Gusler, 93, 338

Furniture Treasury, Wallace Nutting, 101

G. Washington, Margaret Brown Klapthor and Howard Alexander Morrison, 50

Gallagher, Constance Dann, *Linen Heirlooms,* 275

Gallery of American Samplers, Glee F. Krueger, 252

Gallery of Amish Quilts, Robert Bishop and Elizabeth Safanda, 259

Garner, F. H., and Michael Archer, *English Delftware,* 207

Garoutte, Sally, "Marseilles Quilts," 249

Garrett, Elisabeth Donaghy: "American Samplers," 249; *Arts of Independence,* 250; "Theodore H. Kapnek Collection," 250

Garrett, Elisabeth Donaghy, comp., *Antiques Book of Victorian Interiors,* 68

Garrett, Wendell D., et al., *Arts in America,* 48

Garvan, Anthony N. B., "New England Porringer," 151

Garvan, Beatrice B., *Pennsylvania German Collection,* 93

Garvan, Beatrice B., and Charles F. Hummel, *Pennsylvania Germans,* 48

Garvin, James L., "Mail-Order House Plans," 69

Gaslighting, Denys Peter Myers, 328

Gaston, Mary Frank, *American Belleek,* 185

Gates, William C., Jr., *City of Hills and Kilns,* 190

Gates, William C., Jr., and Dana E. Ormerod, "East Liverpool Pottery," 191

Gatty, Mrs. Alfred, *Book of Sun-Dials,* 304

Gaudy Welsh China, Howard Y. Williams, 218

Gaw, Lina P., "Availability and Selection of Ceramics to Silcott," 207

Gehret, Ellen J.: *Rural Pennsylvania Clothing,* 250; *This Is the Way I Pass My Time,* 250

Geijer, Agnes, *History of Textile Art,* 275

Gellerman, Robert F., *American Reed Organ,* 123

Gentle, Rupert: *Brass Candlesticks,* 172; *Candlesticks,* 172

Gentle, Rupert, and Rachael Feild, *English Domestic Brass,* 172

Gentle Art of Faking Furniture, Herbert Cescinsky, 85

"George Henkels," Kenneth Ames, 116

"George M. Coates," George L. Miller, 212

George Washington's Chinaware, Susan Gray Detweiler, 197, 206

George Wickes, Elaine Barr, 144

Georgian Furniture, Victoria and Albert Museum, 85

Gerdts, William H., and James L. Yarnall, comps., *National Museum of American Art's Index to American Art Exhibition Catalogues,* 32

Gere, Charlotte, *American and European Jewelry,* 151

Gere, Charlotte, and Isabelle Anscombe, *Arts and Crafts in Britain and America,* 347

"German Influences in . . . Furniture," Benno M. Forman, 92, 338

Gerstell, Vivian S., *Silversmiths of Lancaster*, 152

Gibb, George Sweet, *Whitesmiths of Taunton*, 152

Gibbs, James W.: *Buckeye Horology*, 296; *Dixie Clockmakers*, 296; "Early Delaware Clockmakers," 296; "Horologic Rhode Island," 296; "Horology in Vermont," 296

Gibbs, James W., and Robert W. Meader, "Shaker Clockmakers," 296

Giedion, Siegfried: "Bath in the Nineteenth Century," 322; "Bathroom Becomes Mechanized," 322; "Mechanization Encounters the Household," 313; *Mechanization Takes Command*, 123

Gies, Joseph, and Melvin Kranzberg, *By the Sweat of Thy Brow*, 339

Giffen, Jane C., "Susanna Rowson," 250

Gilbert, Christopher: *Furniture at Temple Newsam House and Lotherton Hall*, 83; *Life and Work of Thomas Chippendale*, 84

Gilbert, Christopher, et al., *Country House Floors*, 243

Gilbert, James B., "Reviving the Work Ethic," 351

Gilborn, Craig, *Adirondack Furniture*, 124

Gilfoy, Peggy S., "Art of Indiana Coverlets," 275

Gillingham, Harrold E., "First Orreries," 305

Gillon, Edmund V., Jr., and Clay Lancaster, *Victorian Houses*, 69

Gilman, Carolyn, *Where Two Worlds Meet*, 48

Gingerbread Age, John Maass, 71

Ginsburg, Cora, "Textiles," 250

Glanville, Philippa, *Silver in England*, 145

Glasgow, Vaughn L., "Textiles of the Louisiana Acadians," 275

Glass, Ada Polak, 232

Glass, Ivor Noël Hume, 231

Glass Industry in Sandwich, Raymond E. Barlow and Joan F. Kaiser, 226

Glass of the British Military, Olive R. Jones and E. Ann Smith, 228

Glass Paperweights, Evelyn Campbell Cloak, 226

"Glass Production," Arlene Palmer, 232

Glass Salt Shakers, Arthur G. Peterson, 232

Glasser, Richard, *Time in French Life*, 301

Glassie, Henry: "Artifact and Culture," 69; "Eighteenth-Century Cultural Process in Delaware Valley Folk Building," 69; *Folk Housing in Middle Virginia*, 69, 338

"Glassmakers of Early America," Arlene Palmer Schwind, 341

"Glastenbury Glass Factory," Kenneth M. Wilson, 235

Glissman, A. H., *Evolution of the Sad-Iron*, 313

Gloag, John, *Short Dictionary of Furniture*, 84

Glossary of Old Lamps, Herbert C. Darbee, 326

Godden, Geoffrey, *Staffordshire Porcelain*, 208

Godden, Geoffrey A.: *Caughley and Worcester Porcelains*, 208; *Encyclopaedia of British Pottery and Porcelain Marks*, 208; *English China*, 208; *Godden's Guide to Mason's China*, 208; *Jewitt's Ceramic Art of Great Britain*, 208; *Minton Pottery and Porcelain*, 208; *Porcelains*, 209

Godden's Guide to Mason's China, Geoffrey A. Godden, 208

Goldsborough, Jennifer Faulds: *Eighteenth and Nineteenth Century Maryland Silver*, 152; *Silver in Maryland*, 152

Gombrich, E. H., *Sense of Order*, 48

Goodison, Nicholas: *Ormolu*, 172; "Victoria and Albert Museum's . . . Metal-Work Pattern Books," 173, 305

Gordon, Beverly: *Domestic American Textiles*, 250; "Rugs and Floor Coverings," 243; *Shaker Textile Arts*, 276

"Gorgas Family," Elizabeth W. Shaub, 298

Gorham Silver, Charles H. Carpenter, Jr., 149, 337

"Gothic Revival Furniture Designs," Jane B. Davies, 121

Gothic Revival Style, Katherine S. Howe and David B. Warren, 49, 125

Gottesman, Rita Susswein, *Arts and Crafts in New York*, 33

Gould, Mary Earle: *Early American House*, 313; *Early American Wooden Ware*, 313; "Foot Stoves," 324

Government and Labor, Richard B. Morris, 340

Gowans, Alan: *Comfortable House*, 70; *Images of American Living*, 69

Gowans, Alan, et al., *Arts in America*, 48

Goyne, Nancy A.: "Britannia in America," 164; "Bureau Table in America," 93

Graham, John Meredith, II, *American Pewter*, 164

Grand Domestic Revolution, Dolores Hayden, 70

"Grand Rapids," James Stanford Bradshaw, 119

Grand Rapids Bookcase and Chair Company, *Life-Time Furniture*, 351

Grandfather Clock, Ernest L. Edwardes, 290

Grandma's Tea Leaf Ironstone, Annise Doring Heaivilin, 209

Grant, Alison, *North Devon Pottery*, 209

Grant, John, and Colin Wilson, eds., *Book of Time*, 301

Gray, Stephen, ed.: *Arts and Crafts Furniture*, 351; *Mission Furniture of L. and J. G. Stickley*, 352

Gray, Stephen, and Robert Edwards, eds., *Collected Works of Gustav Stickley*, 352

Great River, 93

Green, Harvey: "Cleanliness," 313; *Light of the Home*, 48

Green, Harvey, et al., *Century of Childhood*, 49

Green, Henry D., *Furniture of the Georgia Piedmont*, 93

Green Family of Cabinetmakers, Oscar P. Fitzgerald, 123

Greene, Leslie A., "Late Victorian Hallstand," 124

Greene and Greene, Randell L. Makinson, 128, 354

Greenlaw, Barry A., *New England Furniture at Williamsburg*, 93

Greentown Glass, James Measell, 231

Greenwich Time, Derek Howse, 301

Greer, Georgeanna H., *American Stonewares*, 185

Grier, Katherine C., *Culture and Comfort*, 48

Griffith, Lee Ellen, *Pennsylvania Spice Box*, 93

Grimwade, Arthur G., *London Goldsmiths*, 145

Groce, George C., and David H. Wallace, *New-York Historical Society's Dictionary of Artists*, 33

Grove, John Robert, *Antique Brass Candlesticks*, 327

Grover, Kathryn, ed., *Dining in America*, 49

Groves, Sylvia, *History of Needlework Tools*, 251

Gruber, Alain, *Silverware*, 145

Guide to American Pewter, Carl Jacobs, 165

Guide to American Trade Catalogs, Lawrence B. Romaine, 31

Guide to . . . Art History, Etta Arntzen and Robert Rainwater, 29

Guide to Artifacts, Ivor Noël Hume, 53, 199

Guide to Watch Holders, James J. Niehaus, 305

Guilland, Harold F., *Early American Folk Pottery*, 185

Gunnion, Vernon S., and Carroll J. Hopf, eds., *Blacksmith*, 173

Gusler, Wallace B., *Furniture of Williamsburg*, 93, 338

Gusset, G., et al., *Lighting Devices*, 329

Gustav Stickley, Mary Ann Smith, 355

Gutcheon, Beth, *Perfect Patchwork Primer*, 261

Gutman, Herbert G., *Work, Culture, and Society*, 338

Haders, Phyllis, *Sunshine and Shadow*, 261

Hadley Chest, Clair Franklin Luther, 97

Haedeke, Hanns-Ulrich, *Metalwork*, 173

"Haircloth Upholstery," Marjorie Congram, 273

Halfpenny, Pat A., and Terence A. Lockett, *Creamware and Pearlware*, 211

Haliburton, Thomas Chandler: *Clockmaker*, 301; *Sam Slick*, 301

Hall, Carrie A., and Rose G. Kretsinger, *Romance of the Patchwork Quilt*, 261

Hall, John, *Cabinet Makers' Assistant*, 124

Hamilton, Charles F., *Roycroft Collectibles*, 352

Hamilton, Henry, *English Brass and Copper*, 173

Hamilton, Suzanne, "Pewter of William Will," 164

Hammerslough, Philip, and Peter Bohan, *Early Connecticut Silver*, 148

Hand Made Object, Michael Owen Jones, 339

Handbook of Pottery and Porcelain Marks, comp. J. P. Cushion, 197

Handcraft to Industry, Susan H. Myers, 192

Handlin, David P.: *American Home*, 70; "Heart of the Home," 322

"Handweaving," Alice Morse Earle, 274

Handwoven Textiles, Nancy Dick Bogdonoff, 272

Handy Things, Loris S. Russell, 317

Hanks, David A.: *Decorative Designs of Frank Lloyd Wright*, 352; *Innovative Furniture in America*, 124; *Isaac E. Scott Reform Furniture*, 124

Hanks, David A., and Donald C. Peirce, *Virginia Carroll Crawford Collection*, 124

Hanks, David A., and Page Talbott, "Daniel Pabst," 125

Hanks, David A., et al., *In Pursuit of Beauty*, 45

Hanley, Hope, *Needlepoint in America*, 251

Harbeson, Georgiana Brown, *American Needlework*, 251

Hargrove, John, comp., *Weavers Draft Book*, 276

Harpers Ferry Armory, Merrit Roe Smith, 341

Harris, H. G., *Nineteenth Century American Clocks*, 290

Harris, John, *English Decorative Ironwork*, 174

Harris, John, and Jill Lever, *Illustrated Glossary of Architecture*, 33

Harrison, Molly, *Kitchen in History*, 314

Haslam, Malcolm, *English Art Pottery*, 209

Hassell, Martha, and Barbara Bishop, eds., *Your Obdt. Servt., Deming Jarves*, 226

Hatcher, John, and T. C. Barker, *History of British Pewter*, 164

Hauserman, Dianne D., "Alexander Roux," 125

Hawaiian Furniture, Irving Jenkins, 126

Hawaiian Quilts, Stella M. Jones, 261

Hayden, Dolores, *Grand Domestic Revolution*, 70

Hayward, Arthur H., *Colonial Lighting*, 327

Hayward, Charles H., *Antique or Fake*, 86

Hayward, Helena, ed., *World Furniture*, 84

Hayward, Helena, and Pat Kirkham, *William and John Linnell*, 84

Hayward, Mary Ellen, "Urban Vernacular Architecture," 70

Hazen, Edward, *Panorama of Professions*, 339

Heaivilin, Annise Doring, *Grandma's Tea Leaf Ironstone*, 209

"Heart of the Home," David P. Handlin, 322

Hearth and Home, George W. McDaniel, 51

"Hearth Rug," Jane C. Nylander, 245

Hearts and Crowns, Robert F. Trent, 105

Hebard, Helen B., *Early Lighting*, 327

Heckscher, Morrison H., *American Furniture in the Metropolitan Museum*, 94

Hedges, Ernest S., *Tin*, 165

Heffner, Syvilla L., ed., *Ohio Clock Exhibit*, 296

Hefford, Wendy: "Patents for Strip-Carpeting," 243; "Thomas Moore," 243

Heilpern, Gisela, comp., *Josiah Wedgwood . . . Bibliography*, 209

Heininger, Mary Lynn Stevens, et al., *Century of Childhood*, 49

Heisey, John W., comp., *Checklist of . . . Weavers*, 276

Heman Clark and . . . Shelf Clocks, Chris H. Bailey and Dana J. Blackwell, 293

"Henry Lippitt House," Elizabeth Agee Cogswell, 120

Henrywood, R. K., and A. W. Coysh, *Dictionary of Blue and White Printed Pottery*, 206

Here Lies Virginia, Ivor Noël Hume, 53

Hering, Daniel Webster: *Key to the Watches in the James Arthur Collection*, 290; *Lure of the Clock*, 290

Heritage Foundation Collection of Silver, Henry N. Flynt and Martha Gandy Fales, 151

Heritage of Country Furniture, Howard Pain, 84

Heritage of Light, Loris S. Russell, 329

Herman, Bernard L.: "Multiple Materials, Multiple Meanings," 209; "Time and Performance," 70

Herman, Lynne L., et al., "Ceramics in St. Mary's County," 209

Hernmarck, Carl, *Art of the European Silversmith*, 146

Hewitt, Benjamin A., et al., *Work of Many Hands*, 94

Hill, John H., "Furniture Designs of Henry W. Jenkins," 125

Hillier, Bevis: *Master Potters*, 209; *Pottery and Porcelain*, 198, 210

Hindle, Brooke, *David Rittenhouse*, 296

Hints on Household Taste, Charles L. Eastlake, 122

Hipkiss, Edwin J., *Eighteenth-Century American Arts*, 94

Hirsch, Susan E., *Roots of the . . . Working Class*, 339

"Historic Clay Tobacco Pipemakers," Byron Sudbury, 187

Historic Silver, Francis Hill Bigelow, 148

Historical Archaeology at Black Lucy's Garden, Vernon G. Baker, 204

Historical Needlework, Margaret B. Schiffer, 254

"Historical Sketch of Central Heating," Eugene S. Ferguson, 323

Historical Staffordshire, David Arman and Linda Arman, 203

History and Folklore of . . . Tinware, Margaret Coffin, 171

History of American Art, Daniel M. Mendelowitz, 52

History of American Ceramics, Susan R. Strong, 187

History of American Pewter, Charles F. Montgomery, 166

History of British Carpets, Creassey Edward Cecil Tattersall, 245

History of British Pewter, John Hatcher and T. C. Barker, 164

History of Metals, James A. Mulholland, 176

History of Needlework Tools, Sylvia Groves, 251

History of Old Sheffield Plate, Frederick Bradbury, 144

History of Silver, Claude Blair, ed., 144

History of Textile Art, Agnes Geijer, 275

History of the American Clock Business, Chauncey Jerome, 297

History of the Gear-Cutting Machine, Robert S. Woodbury, 305

History of the Potters' Union, Frank Burchill and Richard Ross, 205

History of the Staffordshire Potteries, Simeon Shaw, 215

History of the . . . Watch Case, Warren H. Niebling, 305

History of Thimbles, Edwin F. Holmes, 251

Hitchcock, Henry-Russell, *American Architectural Books*, 30

Hitchcock Chair, John Tarrant Kenney, 126

Hitchings, Sinclair, "Thomas Johnston," 305

Hoadley, R. Bruce, *Understanding Wood*, 86

Hobsbawm, E. J., *Labouring Men*, 339

Hodgkin, Edith, and John Eliot Hodgkin, *Examples of Early English Pottery*, 210

Hodgkin, John Eliot, and Edith Hodgkin, *Examples of Early English Pottery*, 210

"Hoff Family," Stacy B. C. Wood, Jr., 299

Hogan, Edmund P., *American Heritage*, 152

"Hogarth and . . . Time," Samuel L. Macey, 302

Holdway, Paul, and David Drakard, *Spode Printed Ware*, 206

Holgate, David, *New Hall and Its Imitators*, 210

Holland, Margaret, *Old Country Silver*, 146

Hollister, Paul, and Dwight P. Lanmon, *Paperweights*, 227

Hollister, Paul, Jr., *Encyclopedia of Glass Paperweights*, 227

Holly, Forrest M., *For Generations to Come*, 297

Holmes, Edwin F.: *History of Thimbles*, 251; *Thimbles*, 251

Holstein, Jonathan, *Pieced Quilt*, 261

Holstein, Jonathan, and John Finley, *Kentucky Quilts*, 261

"Homage to Washington," Davida Tenenbaum Deutsch and Betty Ring, 249

Homespun Textile Tradition, Pennsylvania Farm Museum, 277

Homespun to Factory Made, 276

Honour, Hugh: *Chinoiserie*, 49; *Neo-Classicism*, 49

Honour, Hugh, and John Fleming, *Penguin Dictionary of Decorative Arts*, 33

Honour, Hugh, et al., *Dictionary of Architecture*, 34

Hood, Graham: *American Silver*, 153; *Bonnin and Morris*, 191

Hood, Graham, and Kathryn C. Buhler, *American Silver*, 148

Hoopes, Penrose R.: *Connecticut Clockmakers*, 297; *Shop Records of Daniel Burnap*, 297

Hopf, Carroll J., and Vernon S. Gunnion, eds., *Blacksmith*, 173

"Hopkins and Alfred," Shirley S. DeVoe, 295

Hornor, William Macpherson, Jr., *Blue Book, Philadelphia Furniture*, 94

Hornsby, Peter R. G., *Pewter of the Western World*, 165

Hornung, Clarence P., ed., *American Eagle*, 49

"Horologic Rhode Island," James W. Gibbs, 296

Horological Books, Franklin Institute, 290

Horological Shop Tools, Theodore R. Crom, 304

Horological Wheel Cutting Engines, Theodore R. Crom, 304

Horology Americana, Lester Dworetsky and Robert Dickstein, 289

"Horology in Vermont," James W. Gibbs, 296

Hough, Walter, *Collection of Heating and Lighting Utensils*, 327

Hounshell, David A., "Sewing Machine," 314

Hour Glasses, Joseph Sternfield, 305

House Beautiful, Clarence Cook, 120

"Household Art," Martha Crabill McClaugherty, 127

Houses of Boston's Back Bay, Bainbridge Bunting, 66

Housewares Story, Earl Lifshey, 315

"How to Make a Striking Sundial," Benjamin Franklin, 301

Howard, David Sanctuary, *New York and the China Trade*, 198

Howe, Katherine S., and David B. Warren, *Gothic Revival Style*, 49, 125

Howe, Katherine S., et al., *Marks of Achievement*, 157

Howe, Margery Burnham, *Deerfield Embroidery*, 251

Howse, Derek, *Greenwich Time*, 301

[Hubbard, Elbert]: *Book of the Roycrofters*, 352; *Catalog of Roycroft Furniture*, 352; *Roycroft Hand Made Furniture*, 352

Hughes, G. Bernard: *English and Scottish Earthenware*, 210; *Victorian Pottery and Porcelain*, 210

Hughes, Graham, *Modern Silver*, 146

Hughes, Therle, *English Domestic Needlework*, 252

Hummel, Charles F.: "English Tools," 305; "Floor Coverings," 244; "Samuel Rowland Fisher's Catalogue," 305; *With Hammer in Hand*, 86, 297; *Winterthur Guide to American Chippendale Furniture*, 95

Hummel, Charles F., and Beatrice B. Garvan, *Pennsylvania Germans*, 48

Humphreys, Sherry B., and Johnell L. Schmidt, *Texas Pottery*, 191

Hunter, Frederick William, *Stiegel Glass*, 227

Hurry, Silas D., and George L. Miller, "Ceramic Supply in an Economically Isolated Frontier Community," 212

Husher, Richard W., and Walter W. Welch, *Study of Simon Willard's Clocks*, 297

[Hutchins, Levi], *Autobiography*, 297

Hyde Park Houses, Jean F. Block, 66

Ice, Joyce, and Judith Shulimson, "Beyond . . . Women's Traditional Arts," 261

Ilbert, C. A., et al., *Britten's Old Clocks and Watches*, 288

Illinois Horology, Andrew Hayes Miller and Dalia M. Miller, 298

Illustrated Catalogue, Ansonia Clock Company, 292

Illustrated Dictionary of Glass, Harold Newman, 231

Illustrated Glossary of Architecture, John Harris and Jill Lever, 33

Illustrated Guide to Liverpool Herculaneum Pottery, Alan Smith, 216

Illustrated Guide to Staffordshire Salt-Glazed Stoneware, Arnold R. Mountford, 213

Illustrated Guide to Worcester Porcelain, Henry Sandon, 215

Illustrated Handbook of Ohio Sewer Pipe Folk Art, Jack E. Adamson, 188

Illustrated History of Needlework Tools, Gay Ann Rogers, 254

Illustrated History of Silver Plate, Charles Jackson, 146

Images of American Living, Alan Gowans, 69

"Impermanent Architecture," Cary Carson et al., 67

Imported and Domestic Textiles, ed. Patricia L. Fiske, 274

"In a Feasting Posture," Barbara McLean Ward, 156

In Praise of America, Wendy A. Cooper, 45, 89

In Pursuit of Beauty, Doreen Bolger Burke et al., 45

In Small Things Forgotten, James Deetz, 46

In-Depth Study of . . . Watch and Clockmakers, Elizabeth D. Beckman, 293

Indiana Stoneware, 191

"Infancy of Central Heating," Benjamin

L. Walbert, 325

"Influence of . . . Eastlake," Mary Jean Smith Madigan, 127

Ingerman, Elizabeth A., "Personal Experiences of an Old New York Cabinetmaker," 125

Ingraham, Edward, et al., *Eli Terry*, 297

Ink Bottles and Inkwells, William E. Covill, Jr., 226

Innes, Lowell, *Pittsburgh Glass*, 228

Innovative Furniture in America, David A. Hanks, 124

"Introduction of the Jacquard Loom," Natalie Rothstein, 277

"Inventory of George Ecton," D. G. Vaisey and F. Celoria, 217

Iron and Brass Implements, J. Seymour Lindsay, 175

Irwin, John, and Katharine B. Brett, *Origins of Chintz*, 276

Irwin, John Price, *People and Their Quilts*, 261

Is It Genuine, W. Crawley, 86

Isaac E. Scott Reform Furniture, David A. Hanks, 124

Ittman, John, *Clock and Watch Designs*, 290

Jackson, Charles: *English Goldsmiths*, 146; *Illustrated History of Silver Plate*, 146

Jacob Hurd, Hollis French, 151

"Jacob W. Holt," Catherine W. Bishir, 336

Jacobs, Bertram, *Axminster Carpets*, 244

Jacobs, Carl, *Guide to American Pewter*, 165

"Jacquard Coverlet," Carleton L. Safford and Robert Bishop, 279

James, Arthur E.: *Chester County Clocks*, 297; *Potters and Potteries of Chester County*, 191

James, Michael, *Quiltmaker's Handbook*, 261

James and Charles Whitehead . . . Designs, James Whitehead and Charles Whitehead, 218

"James and Ralph Clews," Frank Stefano, Jr., 216

"James Clews," Frank Stefano, Jr., 216

"James Wady," Richard L. Champlin, 294

Janowitz, Meta F., et al., "Cultural Pluralism and Pots," 198

Jenkins, Irving, *Hawaiian Furniture*, 126

Jeremiah Dummer, Hermann Frederick

Clarke and Henry Wilder Foote, 150

Jerome, Chauncey, *History of the American Clock Business*, 297

Jewelers' Circular and Horological Review, 290

Jewelers' Review. See Jewelers' Circular, 290

Jewelers' Weekly. See Jewelers' Circular, 290

Jewitt, Llewellynn, *Ceramic Art of Great Britain*, 210

Jewitt's Ceramic Art of Great Britain, Geoffrey A. Godden, 208

Jobe, Brock, and Myrna Kaye, *New England Furniture*, 95

"Johann Christoph Heyne," Eric de Jonge, 163

Johann Ludwig Eberhardt, Frank P. Albright, 292

John, Hatcher, and T. C. Barker, *History of British Pewter*, 164

John, W. D., and Katherine Coombes, *Paktong*, 174

John and Thomas Seymour, Vernon C. Stoneman, 104

John Brown House Loan Exhibition of Rhode Island Furniture, 95

John Coney, Hermann Frederick Clarke, 149

"John Holker's . . . *Livre d'Enchantillons*," Florence M. Montgomery, 277

John Hull, Hermann Frederick Clarke, 149

"John Ritto Penniman," Carol Damon Andrews, 303

John Shaw, William Voss Elder III and Lu Bartlett, 90

Johnson, Bruce, *Child's Comfort*, 261

Johnson, Diane Chalmers, *American Art Nouveau*, 50

Johnson, Marilynn, "Art Furniture," 126

Johnson, Marilynn, et al., *In Pursuit of Beauty*, 45

"Joiners of Seventeenth Century Hartford County," Patricia E. Kane, 95

Jones, E. Alfred, *Old Silver of American Churches*, 153

Jones, Harvey L., *Mathews*, 353

Jones, Joseph C., Jr., *American Ice Boxes*, 314

Jones, Michael Owen: *Hand Made Object*, 339; "Study of . . . Furniture," 339

Jones, Olive R., and E. Ann Smith, *Glass of the British Military*, 228

Jones, Stella M., *Hawaiian Quilts*, 261

Joseph Richardson, Martha Gandy Fales, 150

"Josiah Wedgwood and . . . Commercialization," Neil McKendrick, 211

Josiah Wedgwood . . . Bibliography, comp. Gisela Heilpern, 209

Journal of Early Southern Decorative Arts, 35

Journal of Glass Studies, 228

Joy, Edward T., *English Furniture*, 126

Jug and Related Stoneware, Cornelius Osgood, 192

Kaduck, John M., *Collecting Watch Fobs*, 305

Kaiser, Joan F., and Raymond E. Barlow, *Glass Industry*, 226

Kane, Patricia E.: *Furniture of the New Haven Colony*, 95; "Joiners of Seventeenth Century Hartford County," 95; *Three Hundred Years of American Seating Furniture*, 95

Kane, Patricia E., and Charles F. Montgomery, eds., *American Art*, 52, 99

Kane, Patricia E., and Edwin A. Battison, *American Clock*, 288

Kane, Patricia E., et al., *Work of Many Hands*, 94

Kaplan, Wendy, "*Art That Is Life*," 50, 353

Kassay, John, *Book of Shaker Furniture*, 126

Katzenberg, Dena S., *Baltimore Album Quilts*, 262

Kauffman, Henry, and Quentin Bowers, *Early American Andirons*, 324

Kauffman, Henry J.: *American Pewterer*, 165; *American Copper and Brass*, 174; *American Fireplace*, 324; *Early American Ironware*, 174

Kaye, Myrna, and Brock Jobe, *New England Furniture*, 95

Keeler, Charles, *Simple Home*, 353

"*Keep Me Warm One Night*," Harold B. Burnham and Dorothy K. Burnham, 273

"Keeping Clean," Jeanne Minhinnick, 315

Kelso, William M., et al., "Impermanent Architecture," 67

Kennedy, Doris Finch, and Sadye Tune Wilson, *Of Coverlets*, 280

Kennedy, Roger G., *Architecture, Men, Women, and Money*, 70

Kenney, John Tarrant, *Hitchcock Chair*, 126

Kentucky Furniture, 95

Kentucky Quilts, Jonathan Holstein and John Finley, 261

Kentucky Quilts, Mary Washington Clarke, 259

Keown, J. R., "Willard and Nolen," 305

Kepes, Gyorgy, ed., *Man-Made Object*, 50

Kerfoot, J. B., *American Pewter*, 165

Kernan, John Devereux, et al., *Chinese Export Silver*, 145

Kernodle, George H., "Concerning the Simon Willard Legend," 298

Ketchum, William C., Jr.: *American Basketry*, 314; *Early Potters and Potteries of New York*, 191; *Pottery and Porcelain Collector's Handbook*, 185

Kettell, Russell Hawkes, *Pine Furniture*, 96

Key to the Watches in the James Arthur Collection, Daniel Webster Hering, 290

[Keyes, Homer Eaton], "Editor's Attic," 305

Keyser, Alan G., et al., trans. and eds., *Accounts of . . . Furniture Makers*, 96

Khin, Yvonne M., *Collector's Dictionary of Quilt Names*, 262

Kimball, Fiske, *Creation of the Rococo Decorative Style*, 50

Kindig, Joseph K., III, *Philadelphia Chair*, 96

King of Desks, Betty Lawson Walters, 134

"Kinship Quilt," Susan Roach, 263

Kirk, John T.: *American Chairs*, 96; *American Furniture and the British Tradition*, 96; *Early American Furniture*, 96

Kirkham, Pat, and Helena Hayward, *William and John Linnell*, 84

Kirkpatricks' Pottery, Ellen Paul Denker, 190

"Kit of Parts," Reyner Banham, 325

"Kitchen," Russell Lynes, 315

Kitchen Antiques, Mary Norwak, 316

Kitchen in History, Molly Harrison, 314

"Kitchens," Jeanne Minhinnick, 315

Kitchenware, Geraldine Cosentino and Regina Stewart, 312

Klamkin, Marian, *American Patriotic and Political China*, 210

Klapthor, Margaret Brown, *Official White House China*, 198, 210

Klapthor, Margaret Brown, and Howard Alexander Morrison, *G. Washington*, 50

"Knapp Dovetailing Machine," Patricia M. Tice, 133

Kobayashi, Terry, and Michael Bird, *Splendid Harvest*, 271

Koch, Robert, *Louis C. Tiffany*, 228

Kolter, Jane Bentley, ed., *Early American Silver*, 153

Koob, Katherine, and Martha Coons, *All Sorts of . . . Cloth*, 273

Kopp, Joel, and Kate Kopp, *American . . . Rugs*, 244

Kopp, Kate, and Joel Kopp, *American . . . Rugs*, 244

Kornwolf, James D., et al., *In Pursuit of Beauty*, 45

Kovel, Ralph, and Terry Kovel, *Kovels' Collector's Guide to . . . Pottery*, 186

Kovel, Terry, and Ralph Kovel, *Kovels' Collector's Guide to . . . Pottery*, 186

Kovels' Collector's Guide to . . . Pottery, Ralph Kovel and Terry Kovel, 186

Kramer, Stephen E., III, et al., *Clockmakers of Lancaster*, 299

Kranzberg, Melvin, and Joseph Gies, *By the Sweat of Thy Brow*, 339

Kreidberg, Marjorie, *Food on the Frontier*, 314

Kretsinger, Rose G., and Carrie A. Hall, *Romance of the Patchwork Quilt*, 261

Krueger, Glee, *New England Samplers*, 252

Krueger, Glee F., *Gallery of American Samplers*, 252

Kubler, George, *Shape of Time*, 50

La fabrication artisanale des tissus, 277

"L'aménagement intérieur," Robert-Lionel Séguin, 279

L'amour de maman, 276

"L'equipement technique," Robert-Lionel Séguin, 279

Labouring Men, E. J. Hobsbawm, 339

Lace, Virginia Churchill Bath, 248

Ladd, Paul Revere, *Early American Fireplaces*, 324

Lambourne, Lionel, *Utopian Craftsmen*, 353

Lambton, Lucinda, *Temples of Convenience*, 322

Lancaster, Clay, *American Bungalow*, 71

Lancaster, Clay, and Edmund V. Gillon, Jr., *Victorian Houses*, 69

Lancour, Harold, comp., *American Art Auction Catalogues*, 30

Landes, David S., *Revolution in Time*, 301

Landesberg, Peter T., ed., *Enigma of Time*, 301

Landreau, Anthony N., *America Underfoot*, 244

Lane, Rose Wilder, *Woman's Day Book of American Needlework*, 252

Langdon, John E.: *Canadian Silversmiths*, 146; *Clock and Watchmakers*, 290

Lanier, Mildred B., *English and Oriental Carpets*, 244

Lanmon, Dwight P., "Baltimore Glass Trade," 229

Lanmon, Dwight P., and Paul Hollister, *Paperweights*, 227

Lanmon, Dwight P., et al., "Some Blown 'Three-Mold' Suspicions," 229

Lantz, Louise K., *Old American Kitchenware*, 315

Lapp, Henry, *Craftsman's Handbook*, 127

Larsen, Ellouise Baker, *American Historical Views on Staffordshire China*, 211

Lasansky, Jeannette: *Central Pennsylvania Redware Pottery*, 191; *Made of Mud*, 191; *To Cut, Piece, and Solder*, 174; *To Draw, Upset, and Weld*, 175, 339; *Willow, Oak, and Rye*, 315

"Late Victorian Hallstand," Leslie A. Greene, 124

Latos, Mary, and Jenny B. Derwich, *Dictionary Guide to . . . Pottery and Porcelain*, 184

Laughlin, Ledlie Irwin, *Pewter in America*, 165

Laurie, Bruce, *Working People*, 339

Laury, Jean Ray, *Quilted Clothing*, 262

"Le costume," Robert-Lionel Séguin, 279

Lea, Zilla Rider, ed., *Ornamented Tray*, 175

"Learning to Accept the Sewing Machine," Beth Bailey, 311

Lears, T. J. Jackson, "Figure of the Artisan," 354

Lee, Jean Gordon, *Philadelphians and the China Trade*, 199

Lee, Ruth Webb: *Antique Fakes and Reproductions*, 229; *Sandwich Glass*, 229

Lee, Ruth Webb, and James H. Rose, *American Glass Cup Plates*, 229

Leeds Pottery, Donald Towner, 217

"Legend of Eli Whitney," Robert S. Woodbury, 300

Lehner, Lois: *Complete Book of American Kitchen and Dinner Wares*, 186; *Ohio Pottery and Glass Marks*, 192

Leibowitz, Joan, *Yellow Ware*, 186

Leone, Diana, *Sampler Quilt*, 262

Let Virtue Be a Guide to Thee, Betty Ring, 253

Let's Get Technical, Janet Gray Crosson, 273

Lever, Jill, and John Harris, *Illustrated Glossary of Architecture*, 33

Lewis, Alfred Allan, *Mountain Artisans Quilting*, 262

Lewis, Griselda, and John Lewis, *Pratt Ware*, 211

Lewis, John, and Griselda Lewis, *Pratt Ware*, 211

Lewis, Peirce F., "Common Houses, Cultural Spoor," 71

Lewis, Philippa, and Gillian Darley, *Dictionary of Ornament*, 34

Life and Work of Thomas Chippendale, Christopher Gilbert, 84

Life of Josiah Wedgwood, Eliza Meteyard, 212

Life-Time Furniture, Grand Rapids Bookcase and Chair Company, 351

Lifshey, Earl, *Housewares Story*, 315

Light of the Home, Harvey Green, 48

Light, John D., "Archaeological Investigation of Blacksmith Shops," 175

Light, John D., and Henry Unglik, *Frontier Fur Trade*, 339

Lighting, ed. Lawrence S. Cooke, 326

Lighting, William F. Poese, 328

Lighting Devices, E. I. Woodhead et al., 329

"Lighting Devices," Joseph T. Butler, 325

"Lighting in Colonial Records," Nina Fletcher Little, 327

[Limbert, Charles P.]: *Arts and Crafts Furniture*, 354; *Limberts Holland . . . Furniture*, 354

Limberts Holland . . . Furniture, [Charles P. Limbert], 354

Lindsay, J. Seymour, *Iron and Brass Implements*, 175

Lindsay, John Seymour, *Anatomy of English Wrought Iron*, 175

Linen Heirlooms, Constance Dann Gallagher, 275

Link, Eva, *Book of Silver*, 146

Lipman, Jean, and Alice Winchester, *Flowering of American Folk Art*, 51

Lipski, Louis L., *Dated English Delftware*, 211

List of Architectural Books, Helen Park, 31

Litchfield County Furniture, 97

Little, Bertram K., "Street Lighting," 327

Little, Frances, *Early American Textiles*, 277

Little, Nina Fletcher: *Country Arts*, 51; *Floor Coverings*, 244; "Lighting in Colonial Records," 327

Lockett, Terence A., *Davenport Pottery and Porcelain*, 211

Lockett, Terence A., and Pat A. Halfpenny, *Creamware and Pearlware*, 211

Lockwood, Luke Vincent, *Colonial Furniture*, 97

Lohr, N. Gordon, et al., *Eastern Shore . . . Raised-Panel Furniture*, 98

Lomax, James, et al., *Country House Floors*, 243

London Goldsmiths, Arthur G. Grimwade, 145

London Tradesman, R. Campbell, 171

Long, Janet, et al., "Vessel Typology for Early Chesapeake Ceramics," 204

"Long Island Carpenter," Edward B. Fix, 338

Long Island Is My Nation, Dean F. Failey, 47, 91

Longcase Clock, Eric Bruton, 289

Longcase Clock, Tom Robinson, 291

Look at White Ironstone, Jean Wetherbee, 187, 218

Looking Glass in America, Helen Comstock, 88

Loomes, Brian: *Country Clocks*, 290; *White Dial Clock*, 291

Losch, John C., et al., *Eli Terry*, 297

Louis C. Tiffany, Robert Koch, 228

Lubell, Cecil, ed., *Textile Collections*, 277

Lucas, E. Louise, *Art Books*, 30

Ludwig, Coy L., *Arts and Crafts Movement in New York*, 354

Lure of the Clock, Daniel Webster Hering, 290

Luther, Clair Franklin: *Hadley Chest*, 97; *Supplemental List of Hadley Chests*, 97

Lynes, Russell: "Kitchen," 315; *Tastemakers*, 71

Lynn, Catherine, et al., *In Pursuit of Beauty*, 45

Lyon, Irving Whitall, *Colonial Furniture of New England*, 97

Maass, John: *Gingerbread Age*, 71; *Victorian Home in America*, 71
McClaugherty, Martha Crabill, "Household Art," 127
McClelland, Nancy, *Duncan Phyfe and the English Regency*, 98
McClinton, Katharine Morrison: *Antiques of American Childhood*, 51; *Collecting American Nineteenth Century Silver*, 153
McCoubrey, John W., et al., *Arts in America*, 57
McDaniel, George W., *Hearth and Home*, 51
McDonald, Ann Gilbert, *Evolution of the Night Lamp*, 327
McElroy, Cathryn J., "Furniture in Philadelphia," 98
Macey, Samuel L.: "Changing Iconography of Father Time," 302; "Clocks and Chronology," 302; *Clocks and the Cosmos*, 302; "Hogarth and . . . Time," 302
"Machine in the Parlor," Diane M. Douglas, 312
Mackay, James, *Turn-of-the-Century Antiques*, 354
McKearin, George S., and Helen McKearin: *American Glass*, 230; *Two Hundred Years of American Blown Glass*, 230
McKearin, Helen, *Bottles, Flasks, and Dr. Dyott*, 230
McKearin, Helen, and George S. McKearin: *American Glass*, 230; *Two Hundred Years of American Blown Glass*, 230
McKearin, Helen, and Kenneth M. Wilson, *American Bottles*, 230
M'Kee and Brothers, *M'Kee Victorian Glass*, 231
M'Kee Victorian Glass, M'Kee and Brothers, 231
McKendrick, Neil, "Josiah Wedgwood and . . . Commercialization," 211
McKinstry, E. Richard, *Trade Catalogues at Winterthur*, 30
McLanahan, Hawley, et al., eds., *Artsman*, 357
MacLeod, Anne Scott, et al., *Century of Childhood*, 49
McMorris, Penny, *Crazy Quilts*, 262
Macquoid, Percy, and Ralph Edwards,

Dictionary of English Furniture, 84
Maddock, Archibald M., II, *Polished Earth*, 186
Made in Ohio, 127
Made of Mud, Jeannette Lasansky, 191
Madigan, Mary Jean, *Eastlake-Influenced American Furniture*, 127
Madigan, Mary Jean Smith, "Influence of . . . Eastlake," 127
"Mail-Order House Plans," James L. Garvin, 69
Main Street Pocket Guide to . . . Pottery, Ellen Denker and Bert Denker, 184
Mainardi, Patricia, "Quilts," 262
Majewski, Teresa, and Michael J. O'Brien, *Analysis of . . . Ceramics*, 211
"Major John Dunlap," Ann W. Dibble, 337
Make a Chair, John D. Alexander, Jr., 336
Makers of Surveying Instruments, Charles E. Smart, 176
Makinson, Randell L., *Greene and Greene*, 128, 354
Man and Time, J. B. Priestly, 303
Mankowitz, Wolf, *Wedgwood*, 212
Man-Made Object, ed. Gyorgy Kepes, 50
"Man Who Made Brass Works," Mabel M. Swan, 305
"Man Who Made . . . Clock Cases," Mabel M. Swan, 305
Mannerism, John Shearman, 55
"Mansion People," Kevin M. Sweeney, 73
Marek, Don, *Arts and Crafts Furniture*, 355
"Marketing American Pottery," Susan H. Myers, 192
"Marketing Ceramics," George L. Miller, 212
Marks of Achievement, David B. Warren et al., 157
Marks of American Potters, Edwin AtLee Barber, 184
Marks of American Silversmiths, Louise Conway Belden, 147
"Marseilles Quilts," Sally Garoutte, 249
"Mary Balch's Newport Sampler," Betty Ring, 253
Maryland Queen Anne and Chippendale Furniture, 98
Maryland Silversmiths, J. Hall Pleasants and Howard Sill, 154
Masonic Symbols in American Decorative Arts, 51

Master Craftsmen of Newport, Michael Moses, 99
Master Potters, Bevis Hillier, 209
"Masterful William Claggett Clock," Robert P. Emlen, 295
Masterpieces of American Silver, Virginia Museum of Fine Arts, 156
Masterpieces of Glass, Robert J. Charleston, 226
"Material Culture and Folk Arts of the Norwegians," Marion J. Nelson, 128
"Material Culture as . . . Communication," Kenneth L. Ames, 116
Material History Bulletin, 36
Mathews, Harvey L. Jones, 353
Mattera, Joanne, ed., *Quiltmaker's Art*, 262
Maurice, Klaus, and Otto Mayr, eds., *Clockwork Universe*, 302
Maust, Don, ed., *Early American Clocks*, 291
May, Jennifer, and John May, *Commemorative Pottery*, 212
May, John, and Jennifer May, *Commemorative Pottery*, 212
Mayer-Thurman, Christa C., and Mildred Davison, *Coverlets*, 274
Mayhew, Edgar de N., and Minor Myers, Jr., *Documentary History of American Interiors*, 51, 71
Mayorcas, M. J., *English Needlework Carpets*, 244
Mayr, Otto, *Authority, Liberty, and Automatic Machinery*, 302
Mayr, Otto, and Klaus Maurice, eds., *Clockwork Universe*, 302
Meader, Robert W., and James W. Gibbs, "Shaker Clockmakers," 296
"Meaning in Artifacts," Kenneth L. Ames, 116
Measell, James, *Greentown Glass*, 231
Mechanick Exercises, Joseph Moxon, 340
"Mechanization Encounters the Household," Siegfried Giedion, 313
Mechanization Takes Command, Siegfried Giedion, 123
Meister, Peter Wilhelm, and Horst Reber, *European Porcelain*, 199
Melchor, James R., et al., *Eastern Shore . . . Raised-Panel Furniture*, 98
Melchor, Marilyn S., et al., *Eastern Shore . . . Raised-Panel Furniture*, 98
"Memorial Embroideries," Betty Ring, 253
Mendelowitz, Daniel M., *History of American Art*, 52
Mercer, Eric, *Furniture*, 84

Mercer, Henry C., *Bible in Iron*, 324

"Metalwares," Barbara McLean Ward, 157, 168

Metalwork, Hanns-Ulrich Haedeke, 173

Meteyard, Eliza, *Life of Josiah Wedgwood*, 212

"Methodological Study in . . . Chippendale Furniture," Philip D. Zimmerman, 106

Michaelis, Ronald F.: *Antique Pewter*, 166; *Old Domestic Base-Metal Candlesticks*, 175

Michie, Audrey, "Fashion for Carpets," 245

Miller, Andrew Hayes, and Dalia M. Miller, *Illinois Horology*, 298

Miller, Andrew Hayes, and Maria M. Dalia, *Survey of American Clocks*, 291

Miller, Dalia M., and Andrew Hayes Miller, *Illinois Horology*, 298

Miller, Edgar G., Jr., *American Antique Furniture*, 98

Miller, George L.: "Classification and Economic Scaling of . . . Ceramics," 212; "George M. Coates," 212; "Marketing Ceramics," 212; "Tenant Farmer's Tableware," 212

Miller, George L., and Silas D. Hurry, "Ceramic Supply in an Economically Isolated Frontier Community," 212

Miller, Henry M., et al., "Vessel Typology for Early Chesapeake Ceramics," 204

Miller, J. Jefferson, II, *English Yellow-Glazed Earthenware*, 213

Miller, J. Jefferson, II, and Lyle M. Stone, *Eighteenth-Century Ceramics from Fort Michilimackinac*, 199, 213

Miller, V. Isabelle: *Furniture by New York Cabinetmakers*, 98; *Silver by New York Makers*, 153

Milwaukee Art Museum, *American Folk Art*, 52

Minhinnick, Jeanne: *At Home in Upper Canada*, 72; "Cooking and Heating," 315; "Keeping Clean," 315; "Kitchens," 315

Miniature Lamps, Frank R. Smith and Ruth E. Smith, 329

Minton Pottery and Porcelain, Geoffrey A. Godden, 208

Mission and Art Nouveau, ed. John Crosby Freeman, 351

Mission Furniture, H. H. Windsor, 357

Mission Furniture of L. and J. G. Stickley, ed. Stephen Gray, 352

Mitchell, James R., ed., *Antique Metalware*, 176

"Mitchell and Rammelsberg," Donald C. Peirce, 129

Modern Silver, Graham Hughes, 146

Moe, John F., "Concepts of Shelter," 72

Montgomery, Charles F.: *American Furniture*, 98; *History of American Pewter*, 166

Montgomery, Charles F., and Patricia E. Kane, eds., *American Art*, 52, 99

Montgomery, David, *Workers' Control*, 340

Montgomery, Florence M.: "John Holker's . . . *Livre d'Enchantillons*," 277; *Printed Textiles*, 277; *Textiles in America*, 277

Moore, Charles W., *Timing a Century*, 305

Moore, Eudorah M., et al., eds., *California Design*, 347

Moore, J. Roderick, "Wythe County . . . Punched Tin," 128

Moore, N. Hudson, *Old Clock Book*, 291

Moore-Ede, Martin C., et al., *Clocks That Time Us*, 302

Moralism and the Model Home, Gwendolyn Wright, 75

Moravian Decorative Arts, John Bivins, Jr., and Paula Welshimer, 44

Moravian Potters, John Bivins, Jr., 189, 336

More Work for Mother, Ruth Schwartz Cowan, 312

Morgan, Brian, and Michael Archer, *Fair as China Dishes*, 203

Morgan, Kate T., et al., "Cultural Pluralism and Pots," 198

Morris, Richard B., *Government and Labor*, 340

Morrison, Howard Alexander, and Margaret Brown Klapthor, *G. Washington*, 50

Morse, Edward W., ed., *Silver in the Golden State*, 153

Morse, John D., ed., *Country Cabinetwork*, 99

Moses, Michael, *Master Craftsmen of Newport*, 99

Mossman, Thomas L., and Joseph J. Bavaro, *Furniture of Gustav Stickley*, 348

Most Splendid Carpet, Susan H. Anderson, 242

Mountain Artisans Quilting, Alfred Allan Lewis, 262

Mountford, Arnold R.: "Documents Relating to English Ceramics," 213; *Illustrated Guide to Staffordshire Salt-Glazed Stoneware*, 213

Mourning Becomes America, Anita Schorsch, 254

Moxon, Joseph, *Mechanick Exercises*, 340

"Mrs. Saunders' and Miss Beach's Academy," Betty Ring, 253

Mudge, Jean McClure, *Chinese Export Porcelain*, 199

Mulholland, James A., *History of Metals*, 176

Muller, Charles R., and Timothy D. Rieman, *Shaker Chair*, 128

"Multiple Materials, Multiple Meanings," Bernard L. Herman, 209

Murphy, John Joseph, "Entrepreneurship in . . . the American Clock Industry," 291

Museum of Fine Arts, Boston, *Paul Revere's Boston*, 52, 99

Museum of Fine Arts, Boston, and the Department of American Decorative Arts and Sculpture, *Frontier America*, 52

Mussey, Barrows, *Young Father Time*, 298

Mussey, Barrows, and Ruth Mary Canedy, *Terry Clock Chronology*, 298

Myer Myers, Jeanette Rosenbaum, 155

Myers, Denys Peter, *Gaslighting*, 328

Myers, Louis Guerineau, *Some Notes on American Pewterers*, 166

Myers, Minor, Jr., and Edgar de N. Mayhew, *Documentary History of American Interiors*, 51, 71

Myers, Susan, "Business of Potting," 340

Myers, Susan H.: *Handcraft to Industry*, 192; "Marketing American Pottery," 192

Naeve, Milo M., *Classical Presence in American Art*, 99

National Gallery of Art, *American Sampler*, 53

National Museum of American Art's Index to American Art Exhibition Catalogues, comp. James L. Yarnall and William H. Gerdts, 32

National Types of Old Pewter, Howard Herschel Cotterell et al., 163

Natural Dyes, Rita J. Adrosko, 271

Nature . . . of Workmanship, David Pye, 340

Naylor, Gillian, *Arts and Crafts Movement*, 355

Neal, D. B., and L. W. Neal, *Pressed Glass Salt Dishes*, 231

Neal, L. W., and D. B. Neal, *Pressed Glass Salt Dishes*, 231

Neat Pieces, 128

Needlepoint in America, Hope Hanley, 251

Needlework, Adolph S. Cavallo, 248

Needlework, ed. Betty Ring, 254

Needleworker's Dictionary, Pamela Clabburn, 249

Neff, Larry M., et al., trans. and eds., *Accounts of . . . Furniture Makers*, 96

Neiman, Fraser D., et al., "Vessel Typology for Early Chesapeake Ceramics," 204

Nelson, Christina H.: *Directly from China*, 199; "Transfer-Printed Creamware and Pearlware," 213

Nelson, Marion J., "Material Culture and Folk Arts of the Norwegians in America," 128

"Neoclassical Wrought Iron," Robert L. Alexander, 170

Neo-Classicism, Hugh Honour, 49

"Neoclassicism in Textile Designs," Margaret A. Fikioris, 274

Never Done, Susan Strasser, 317

New England Begins, Jonathan L. Fairbanks and Robert F. Trent, 47, 91

New England Clocks, Amos Avery, 288

New England Furniture, 99

New England Furniture, Brock Jobe and Myrna Kaye, 95

New England Furniture at Williamsburg, Barry A. Greenlaw, 93

New England Glass, Kenneth M. Wilson, 235

"New England Porringer," Anthony N. B. Garvan, 151

New England Samplers, Glee Krueger, 252

New England Silversmith, 154

"New . . . Findings on Curtis and Dunning," Lilian Baker Carlisle, 294

New Hall and Its Imitators, David Holgate, 210

New Hampshire Clocks, Charles S. Parsons, 298

New Haven Colony Historical Society, *Exhibition of Connecticut Pewter*, 166

New Jersey Pottery, 192

New Light, Larry Freeman, 326

New London County Furniture, 100

"New London County Joined Chairs," Robert F. Trent, 105

New Mexican Furniture, Lonn Taylor and Dessa Bokides, 104, 133

New Orleans Architecture, Friends of the Cabildo, 68

New York and the China Trade, David Sanctuary Howard, 198

New York Furniture, John L. Scherer, 103

New York Furniture before 1840, 100

New-York Historical Society's Dictionary of Artists, George C. Groce and David H. Wallace, 33

New York Interiors, Joseph Byron, 67

Newcomb Pottery, Jessie Poesch, 193

Newlands, David L., *Early Ontario Potters*, 192

Newman, Harold, *Illustrated Dictionary of Glass*, 231

Newport Mansions, Preservation Society of Newport County, 72

Nicholson, Alice, and Don Nicholson, *Novelty and Animated . . . Clocks*, 291

Nicholson, Don, and Alice Nicholson, *Novelty and Animated . . . Clocks*, 291

Niebling, Warren H., *History of the . . . Watch Case*, 305

Niehaus, James J., *Guide to Watch Holders*, 305

Nineteenth Century, 36

Nineteenth-Century America, 53, 100, 129

Nineteenth Century American Clocks, H. G. Harris, 290

Nineteenth Century Ceramics . . . in the Eastern Ozark Border Region, Cynthia R. Price, 214

Nineteenth Century Furniture, ed. Art and Antiques, 118

Nineteenth-Century Glass, Albert Christian Revi, 233

Nineteenth-Century Pottery and Porcelain in Canada, Elizabeth Collard, 205

Nineteenth-Century Silver, John Culme, 145

Noël Hume, Audrey, *Food*, 316

Noël Hume, Ivor: "Creamware to Pearlware," 213; *Early English Delftware*, 213; *Glass*, 231; *Guide to Artifacts*, 53, 199; *Here Lies Virginia*, 53; "Pearlware," 213; *Pottery and Porcelain in Colonial Williamsburg's . . . Collections*, 214; "Rise and Fall of English White Salt-Glazed Stone-

ware," 214; "What, Who, and When of English Creamware Plate Design," 214

North Devon Pottery, Alison Grant, 209

Norton, Nancy P., and John S. Ewing, *Broadlooms and Businessmen*, 242

Norton, Paul F., et al., *Arts in America*, 48

Norwak, Mary, *Kitchen Antiques*, 316

Norwalk Potteries, Andrew L. Winton and Kate Barber, 194

Novelty and Animated . . . Clocks, Don Nicholson and Alice Nicholson, 291

Nowotny, H., "Time Structuring," 303

Numismatic Art, Cornelius Vermeule, 156

Nutting, Wallace: *Clock Book*, 291; *Furniture of the Pilgrim Century*, 100; *Furniture Treasury*, 101

Nygren, Edward J., "Edward Winslow's Sugar Boxes," 154

Nylander, Jane, "Early American Look," 245

Nylander, Jane C.: "Hearth Rug," 245; *Fabrics for Historic Buildings*, 277; "Some Print Sources of . . . Schoolgirl Art," 253

Oak Furniture, Victor Chinnery, 83

Objects for Preparing Food, 316

O'Brien, Michael J., and Teresa Majewski, *Analysis of . . . Ceramics*, 211

O'Dea, William T., *Social History of Lighting*, 328

Of Coverlets, Sadye Tune Wilson and Doris Finch Kennedy, 280

Of Time, Passion, and Knowledge, J. T. Fraser, 301

Official Museum Directory, 34

Official Price Guide to American Pottery, Dorothy Robinson and Bill Feeny, 186

Official White House China, Margaret Brown Klapthor, 198, 210

Ohio Clock Exhibit, ed. Syvilla L. Heffner, 296

Ohio Pottery and Glass Marks, Lois Lehner, 192

"Ohio's Woven Covelets," Patricia A. Cunningham, 274

Oil Lamps, Catherine M. V. Thuro, 329

Oil Lamps II, Catherine M. V. Thuro, 329

Old American Kitchenware, Louise K. Lantz, 315

Old Clock Book, N. Hudson Moore, 291

Old Country Silver, Margaret Holland, 146

Old Delaware Clockmakers, Henry Clay Conrad, 295

Old Domestic Base-Metal Candlesticks, Ronald F. Michaelis, 175

Old European Pewter, A. J. G. Verster, 168

Old Furniture, Nancy A. Smith, 86

Old Patchwork Quilts, Ruth E. Findley, 260

Old Pewter, Howard Herschel Cotterell, 163

Old Pots, Phil Schaltenbrand, 193

Old Silver of American Churches, E. Alfred Jones, 153

Oman, Charles, *English Church Plate*, 147

On the Origin of Clockwork, Derek J. de Solla Price, 301

On the Threshold of Modern Design, 355

"One Hundred Sixty Years of Seth Thomas Clocks," Chris H. Bailey, 293

"Oriental Carpets," Sarah B. Sherrill, 245

"Orientalism," Michael P. Conforti, 349

Origins of Chintz, John Irwin and Katharine B. Brett, 276

Orlofsky, Myron, and Patsy Orlofsky, *Quilts in America*, 253, 262

Orlofsky, Patsy, and Myron Orlofsky, *Quilts in America*, 253, 262

Ormerod, Dana E., and William C. Gates, Jr., "East Liverpool Pottery," 191

Ormolu, Nicholas Goodison, 172

Ornamented Tray, ed. Zilla Rider Lea, 175

Orton, Vrest, *Forgotten Art of Building a Good Fireplace*, 324

Osborne, Harold, ed., *Oxford Companion to the Decorative Arts*, 34

Osgood, Cornelius, *Jug and Related Stoneware*, 192

Ostergard, Derek E., ed., *Bent Wood and Metal Furniture*, 129

Oswald, Adrian, *English Brown Stoneware*, 214

Otto, Celia Jackson, *American Furniture of the Nineteenth Century*, 129

Otto, John Solomon, "Artifacts and Status Differences," 215

"Overshot Coverlet," Carleton L. Safford and Robert Bishop, 279

Oxford Companion to the Decorative Arts, ed. Harold Osborne, 34

Page, Ruth, "English Carpets," 245

Pain, Howard, *Heritage of Country Furniture*, 84

"Painted Floor-Cloths," Shirley Spaulding DeVoe, 242

Paktong, W. D. John and Katherine Coombes, 174

Palace or the Poorhouse, Jan Cohn, 68

Palmer, Arlene, "Glass Production," 232

Palmer, Brooks: *Book of American Clocks*, 291; *Treasury of American Clocks*, 291

Palmer, Roy, *Water Closet*, 322

Panofsky, Erwin, "Father Time," 303

Panorama of Professions, Edward Hazen, 339

Paperweights, Paul Hollister and Dwight P. Lanmon, 227

Park, Helen, *List of Architectural Books*, 31

Parsons, Charles S., *New Hampshire Clocks*, 298

"Part One: Furniture of Early Texas," Donald Lewis Stover, 132

Patchwork Quilts, Susan Roach-Lankford, 263

Patented Lighting, Rushlight Club, 328

"Patents for Strip-Carpeting," Wendy Hefford, 243

Pattern, Joan Evans, 46

"Pattern Books and Professionalism," Dell Upton, 74, 342

Paul Revere—Artisan, Businessman, and Patriot, 154

Paul Revere's Boston, Museum of Fine Arts, Boston, 52, 99

Payne, Christopher, *Price Guide to . . . Furniture*, 129

Peal, Christopher A., *Pewter of Great Britain*, 166

"Pearlware," Ivor Noël Hume, 213

Pearson, J. Michael, *Encyclopedia of American Cut and Engraved Glass*, 232

Peck, Herbert, *Book of Rookwood Pottery*, 192

"Pecolia Warner," William Ferris, 260

Peirce, Donald C., "Mitchell and Rammelsberg," 129

Peirce, Donald C., and David A. Hanks, *Virginia Carroll Crawford Collection*, 124

Peirce, Josephine H., *Fire on the Hearth*, 324

Péladeau, Marius B., "Silas Hoadley," 298

Penguin Dictionary of Decorative Arts, John Fleming and Hugh Honour, 33

Pennsylvania Clocks, George H. Eckhardt, 295

Pennsylvania Farm Museum, *Homespun Textile Tradition*, 277

Pennsylvania German Collection, Beatrice B. Garvan, 93

Pennsylvania-German Decorated Chest, Monroe H. Fabian, 90

Pennsylvania Germans, Beatrice B. Garvan and Charles F. Hummel, 48

Pennsylvania Spice Box, Lee Ellen Griffith, 93

People and Their Quilts, John Price Irwin, 261

Perfect Patchwork Primer, Beth Gutcheon, 261

"Personal Experiences of an Old New York Cabinetmaker," Elizabeth A. Ingerman, 125

Perspectives on American Folk Art, ed. Ian M. G. Quimby and Scott T. Swank, 54

Perspectives on American Furniture, ed. Gerald W. R. Ward, 105

"Peter Glass," Richard Ahlborn, 115

Peterson, Arthur G.: *Four Hundred Trademarks on Glass*, 232; *Glass Salt Shakers*, 232

Peterson, Charles E., "American Notes," 325

Peterson, Charles E., ed., *Building Early America*, 72

Peterson, Harold L., *American Interiors*, 53

Peterson, Larry, et al., *Red Wing Stoneware*, 190

Pettit, Florence H., *America's . . . Fabrics*, 277

Pevsner, Nikolaus, et al., *Dictionary of Architecture*, 34

Pewter Collection of the New Canaan Historical Society, Dorothy Cocks, 163

Pewter Collectors' Club, *Pewter in American Life*, 167

Pewter in America, Ledlie Irwin Laughlin, 165

Pewter in America (Currier Gallery), 167

Pewter in American Life, Pewter Collectors' Club, 167

Pewter Marks, D. Stara, 167

Pewter of Great Britain, Christopher A. Peal, 166

Pewter of the Western World, Peter R. G. Hornsby, 165

"Pewter of William Will," Suzanne Hamilton, 164

Pewter Wares from Sheffield, Jack Scott, 167

Phaidon Guide to Pewter, Vanessa Brett, 162

Philadelphia, Philadelphia Museum of Art, 54

Philadelphia: Three Centuries of American Art, 101

Philadelphia Chair, Joseph K. Kindig III, 96

Philadelphia Furniture, ed. John J. Snyder, Jr., 103

Philadelphia Georgian, George B. Tatum, 74

Philadelphia Museum of Art, *Philadelphia*, 54

Philadelphians and the China Trade, Jean Gordon Lee,199

Phillips, John Marshall, *American Silver*, 154

Phipps, Frances, *Colonial Kitchens*, 316

Pictorial Dictionary of British Nineteenth Century Furniture, 130

Pieced Quilt, Jonathan Holstein, 261

"Pieces of History," Rodris Roth, 131

Pierson, William H., Jr., and Martha Davidson, eds., *Arts of the United States*, 54

Pilgrim Century Furniture, ed. Robert F. Trent, 105

Pine Furniture, Russell Hawkes Kettell, 96

Pittsburgh Glass, Lowell Innes, 228

Plain and Elegant, Rich and Common, 101, 130

"Plain and Fancy," Henry Bartholomew Cox, 326

Plain and Fancy, Susan Burrows Swan, 255

Plain and Ornamental, 101

Pleasants, J. Hall, and Howard Sill, *Maryland Silversmiths*, 154

"Plumber's Tools," R. Rhoades, 322

"Plumbing Paradox," May N. Stone, 323

Poesch, Jessie, *Newcomb Pottery*, 193

Poesch, Jessie J., *Early Furniture of Louisiana*, 101

Poese, William F., *Lighting*, 328

Polak, Ada, *Glass*, 232

Polished Earth, Archibald M. Maddock II, 186

Pommer, Richard, "Architecture of Urban Housing," 72

Ponting, K. G., *Dictionary of Dyes*, 277

"Poor Potter," Norman F. Barka et al., 188

Poor Sort of Heaven, ed. William Ayres, 348

Porcelain of the Nineteenth Century, Antoinette Faÿ-Hallé and Barbara Mundt, 198

Porter, Glenn, *Workers' World*, 340

Potter's Art, Hazel V. Bray, 189

Potters and Potteries of Chester County, Arthur E. James, 191

Pottery and Porcelain, Bevis Hillier, 198, 210

Pottery and Porcelain, Edwin AtLee Barber, 184

Pottery and Porcelain Collector's Handbook, William C. Ketchum, Jr., 185

Pottery and Porcelain in Colonial Williamsburg's . . . Collections, Ivor Noël Hume, 214

Pottery in Alberta, Marylu Antonelli and Jack Forbes, 188

Pottery Industry, U.S. Department of Commerce, 217

Pottery Trade and North Staffordshire, Lorna Weatherill, 218

Pottinger, David, *Quilts from the Indiana Amish*, 262

Praetzellis, Mary, et al., *Ceramic Marks from Old Sacramento*, 214

Prairie School, H. Allen Brooks, 349

Pratt Ware, John Lewis and Griselda Lewis, 211

Preservation Society of Newport County, *Newport Mansions*, 72

Pressed Glass Salt Dishes, L. W. Neal and D. B. Neal, 231

Price, Cynthia R., *Nineteenth Century Ceramics . . . in the Eastern Ozark Border Region*, 214

Price, Will, et al., eds., *Artsman*, 357

Price Guide to . . . Furniture, Christopher Payne, 129

Price Guide to . . . Furniture, John Andrews, 117

Priestly, J. B., *Man and Time*, 303

Primary Structures of Fabrics, Irene Emery, 274

Prime, Alfred Coxe, comp., *Arts and Crafts in Philadelphia, Maryland, and South Carolina*, 34

Printed Textiles, Florence M. Montgomery, 277

Pritchett, William F., et al., *Eli Terry*, 297

"Production of Tucker Porcelain," Phillip H. Curtis, 190

Proper, David R., "Edmund Currier," 298

Proprietary Capitalism, Philip Scranton, 341

Pye, David, *Nature . . . of Workmanship*, 340

Quaint Furniture, [Stickley Brothers Company], 356

"Quaker Clockmakers," Richard L. Champlin, 294

Quest for Unity, Detroit Institute of Arts, 46

"Quilt Making," Susan Roach and Lorre Weidlich, 263

"Quilt Traditions," Earl F. Robacker and Ada F. Robacker, 263

Quilted Clothing, Jean Ray Laury, 262

Quilters, Patricia Cooper and Norma Bradley Buferd, 260

Quilting, Averil Colby, 260

"Quilting," John Michael Vlach, 263

Quiltmaker's Art, ed. Joanne Mattera, 262

Quiltmaker's Handbook, Michael James, 261

Quilts, Marie Daugherty Webster, 263

"Quilts," Patricia Mainardi, 262

Quilts, Coverlets, Rugs, and Samplers, Robert Bishop et al., 259

Quilts and Carousels, ed. Ricky Clark, 259

Quilts from the Indiana Amish, David Pottinger, 262

Quilts in America, Patsy Orlofsky and Myron Orlofsky, 253, 262

Quimby, Ian M. G., *Apprenticeship*, 340

Quimby, Ian M. G., ed.: *Arts of the Anglo-American Community*, 54, 102; *Ceramics in America*, 199; *Craftsman in Early America*, 54

Quimby, Ian M. G., and Polly Anne Earl, eds., *Technological Innovation and the Decorative Arts*, 54

Quimby, Ian M. G., and Scott T. Swank, eds., *Perspectives on American Folk Art*, 54

Rainwater, Dorothy T., *Encyclopedia of American Silver Manufacturers*, 154

Rainwater, Dorothy T., ed., *Sterling Silver Holloware*, 154

Rainwater, Dorothy T., and H. Ivan

Rainwater, *American Silverplate*, 155

Rainwater, H. Ivan, and Dorothy T. Rainwater, *American Silverplate*, 155

Rainwater, Robert, and Etta Arntzen, *Guide to . . . Art History*, 29

Raised in Clay, Nancy Sweezy, 193

Randall, Richard H., Jr., *American Furniture in the Museum of Fine Arts*, 102

Rasmussen, William M. S., "Sabine Hall," 72

Rauschenberg, Bradford L., "School of Charleston . . . Andirons," 325

"Real Estate Associates," Anne Bloomfield, 66

Reber, Horst, and Peter Wilhelm Meister, *European Porcelain*, 199

Rebert, M. Charles, *American Majolica*, 186

Reckman, Bob, "Carpentry," 340

Recreating the Historic House Interior, William Seale, 73

Red Wing Stoneware, Dan DePasquale et al., 190

Reed, Henry M., *Decorated Furniture*, 130

Rees, Abraham, *Rees's Clocks*, 305

Rees's Clocks, Abraham Rees, 305

Reese, Rosemary, comp., *Documentation of Collections*, 31

"Reflections on a Tin Kitchen," Frank G. White, 318

Regency Furniture, Frances Collard, 83

Regional Aspects of American Folk Pottery, 193

Reilly, George, et al., "Some Blown 'Three-Mold' Suspicions," 229

"Religion in America," Donald Fennimore, 151

Religion in Wood, Edward Deming Andrews and Faith Andrews, 117

"Reports . . . on the Staffordshire Potteries," Francis Celoria, 205

Revi, Albert Christian: *American Art Nouveau Glass*, 233; *American Pressed Glass*, 233; *Nineteenth-Century Glass*, 233

"Reviving the Work Ethic," James B. Gilbert, 351

Revolution in Glassmaking, Warren C. Scoville, 233

Revolution in Time, David S. Landes, 301

Reyburn, Wallace, *Flushed with Pride*, 322

Rhoades, R., "Plumber's Tools," 322

Rhoads, William B., "Colonial Revival and American Nationalism," 73

Rhode Island Pewterers, Charles A. Calder, 163

Rhythms of Life, ed. Edward S. Ayensu and Philip Whitfield, 300

Rice, Kym S., *Early American Taverns*, 55

Rice, Norman S., *Albany Silver*, 155

Richards, Nancy E., "Furniture of the Lower Connecticut River Valley," 102

Ridgway Porcelains, Geoffrey A. Godden, 209

Rieman, Timothy D., and Charles R. Muller, *Shaker Chair*, 128

Riff, Adolphe, et al., *National Types of Old Pewter*, 163

Ring, Betty: *American Needlework Treasures*, 253; *Let Virtue Be a Guide to Thee*, 253; "Mary Balch's Newport Sampler," 253; "Memorial Embroideries," 253; "Mrs. Saunders' and Miss Beach's Academy," 253; "Saint Joseph's Academy," 254; "Samplers and Pictorial Needlework," 254

Ring, Betty, ed., *Needlework*, 254

Ring, Betty, and Davida Tenenbaum Deutsch, "Homage to Washington," 249

Rink, Evald, *Technical Americana*, 341

"Rise and Fall of English White Salt-Glazed Stoneware," Ivor Noël Hume, 214

Rise of the Staffordshire Potteries, John Thomas, 217

Rivers, Betty, et al., *Ceramic Marks from Old Sacramento*, 214

Roach, Susan, "Kinship Quilt," 263

Roach, Susan, and Lorre Weidlich, "Quilt Making," 263

Roach-Lankford, Susan, *Patchwork Quilts*, 263

Robacker, Ada F., and Earl F. Robacker: "Quilt Traditions," 263; *Spatterware and Sponge*, 214

Robacker, Earl F., and Ada F. Robacker: "Quilt Traditions," 263; *Spatterware and Sponge*, 214

"Robert Sanderson," Albert S. Roe and Robert F. Trent, 155

Roberts, Deryck, *Bracket Clock*, 291

Roberts, Kenneth D.: *Contribution of Joseph Ives*, 298; *Eli Terry*, 298; *Some Observations concerning Connecticut Clockmaking*, 298

Roberts, Warren E.: "Ananias Hensel," 130; "Turpin Chairs," 130

Robins, Frederick W., *Story of the Lamp*, 328

Robinson, Dorothy, and Bill Feeny, *Official Price Guide to American Pottery*, 186

Robinson, Tom, *Longcase Clock*, 291

Rock, Howard B., *Artisans*, 341

Rockdale, Anthony F. C. Wallace, 342

Rocking Chair Book, Ellen Denker and Bert Denker, 121

Rockingham Pottery and Porcelain, Alwyn Cox and Angela Cox, 206

Rodriquez Roque, Oswaldo, *American Furniture at Chipstone*, 102

Roe, Albert S., and Robert F. Trent, "Robert Sanderson," 155

Rogers, Gay Ann, *Illustrated History of Needlework Tools*, 254

Rogers, Stephen T., and Samuel D. Smith, *Survey of Historic Pottery Making*, 193

Rohr, René R. J., *Sundials*, 305

Romaine, Lawrence B., *Guide to American Trade Catalogs*, 31

Romance of the Patchwork Quilt, Carrie A. Hall and Rose G. Kretsinger, 261

Roos, Frank J., Jr., *Bibliography of . . . Architecture*, 31

Roots of the . . . Working Class, Susan E. Hirsch, 339

Rorabaugh, W. J., *Craft Apprentice*, 341

Rose, James H., and Ruth Webb Lee, *American Glass Cup Plates*, 229

Rosenbaum, Jeanette, *Myer Myers*, 155

Ross, Lester A., "Transfer Printed Spodeware," 215

Ross, Richard, and Frank Burchill, *History of the Potters' Union*, 205

Roth, Rodris: "American Art," 130; *Floor Coverings*, 245; "Pieces of History," 131; *Tea Drinking*, 55

Rothschild, Nan A., et al. "Cultural Pluralism and Pots," 198

Rothstein, Natalie, "Introduction of the Jacquard Loom," 277

Roussel, Diana Edwards, *Castleford Pottery*, 215

Rowe, Ann Pollard, "Crewel Embroidered Bed Hangings," 254

Roycroft Collectibles, Charles F. Hamilton, 352

Roycroft Hand Made Furniture, [Elbert Hubbard], 352

Ruddel, David-Thiery, "Domestic Textile Industry," 279

"Rudy Stoner," Stacy B. C. Wood, Jr., 299

"Rugs and Floor Coverings," Beverly Gordon, 243

Rural Household Inventories, ed. Abbott Lowell Cummings, 32

Rural Pennsylvania Clothing, Ellen J. Gehret, 250

Rushlight Club: *Early Lighting*, 328; *Patented Lighting*, 328

Russell, Loris S.: "Early . . . Lighting," 328; *Handy Things*, 317; *Heritage of Light*, 329

"Sabine Hall," William M. S. Rasmussen, 72

Sack, Albert, *Fine Points of Furniture*, 102

Safanda, Elizabeth, and Robert Bishop, *Gallery of Amish Quilts*, 259

Safford, Carleton L., and Robert Bishop: "Candlewick Spread," 279; "Double Weave Coverlet," 279; "Jacquard Coverlet," 279; "Overshot Coverlet," 279; "Summer and Winter Coverlet," 279

St. George, Robert Blair: "Fathers, Sons, and Identity," 341; "Set Thine House in Order," 73; "Style and Structure," 102, 341; *Wrought Covenant*, 102

"Saint Joseph's Academy," Betty Ring, 254

Sam Slick, Thomas Chandler Haliburton, 301

Sampler Quilt, Diana Leone, 262

"Samplers and Pictorial Needlework," Betty Ring, 254

"Samuel Folwell," Davida Tenenbaum Deutsch, 249

Samuel McIntire . . . and the Sandersons, Mabel M. Swan, 104

"Samuel Rowland Fisher's Catalogue," Charles F. Hummel, 305

Sanders, Barry, ed., *Craftsman*, 355

Sandon, Henry, *Illustrated Guide to Worcester Porcelain*, 215

Sandon, John, et al., *Worcester Blue and White Porcelain*, 204

Sands, John O., et al., "Ceramics in St. Mary's County," 209

Sandwich Glass, Ruth Webb Lee, 229

Saunders, Richard: *Collecting and Restoring Wicker Furniture*, 131; *Collector's Guide to American Wicker Furniture*, 131

Savage, George, and Ann Finer, eds.,

Selected Letters of Josiah Wedgwood, 207

Savannah Furniture, Mrs. Charlton M. Theus, 105

Savory Suppers, Susan Williams, 57

Schaeffer, Herwin, "Tiffany's Fame," 233

Schaltenbrand, Phil, *Old Pots*, 193

Schecter, Daniel, et al., "Ceramics in St. Mary's County," 209

Scherer, John L., *New York Furniture*, 103

Schiffer, Herbert, et al.: *Brass Book*, 176; *Chinese Export Porcelain*, 200

Schiffer, Margaret B., *Historical Needlework*, 254

Schiffer, Margaret Berwind, *Furniture and Its Makers of Chester County*, 103

Schiffer, Nancy, et al.: *Brass Book*, 176; *Chinese Export Porcelain*, 200

Schiffer, Peter, et al.: *Brass Book*, 176; *Chinese Export Porcelain*, 200

Schimmelman, Janice G.: *Architectural Treatises*, 31; *Checklist of European Treatises on Art*, 31

"Schindler, Roller," Peter L. L. Strickland, 132

Schmidt, Johnell L., and Sherry B. Humphreys, *Texas Pottery*, 191

Schoelwer, Susan Prendergast, "Form, Function, and Meaning in . . . Fabric Furnishings," 279

"School of Charleston . . . Andirons," Bradford L. Rauschenberg, 325

Schorsch, Anita, *Mourning Becomes America*, 254

Schorsch, Anita, ed., *Art of the Weaver*, 279

Schulz, Jeanette K., et al., *Ceramic Marks from Old Sacramento*, 214

Schulz, Peter D., and David L. Felton, *Diaz Collection*, 207

Schwartz, Marvin D., *Collectors' Guide to . . . Ceramics*, 187

Schwartz, Marvin D., et al., *Furniture of John Henry Belter*, 131

Schwind, Arlene Palmer: "Ceramic Imports of Frederick Rhinelander," 200, 215; "Glassmakers of Early America," 341

Scott, Jack, *Pewter Wares from Sheffield*, 167

Scott, Pamela J., and Edward F. Zimmer, "Alexander Parris, B. Henry Latrobe, and the John Wickham House," 75

Scottish Pottery, J. Arnold Fleming, 207

Scoville, Warren C., *Revolution in Glassmaking*, 233

Scranton, Philip, *Proprietary Capitalism*, 341

Scully, John, and Maude Southwell Wahlman, "Aesthetic Principles in Afro-American Quilts," 263

Scully, Vincent, "American Houses," 73

Seale, William: *Recreating the Historic House Interior*, 73; *Tasteful Interlude*, 55

Secord, William, et al., *Quilts, Coverlets, Rugs, and Samplers*, 259

Séguin, Robert-Lionel: "L'aménagement intérieur," 279; "Le costume," 279; "L'equipement technique," 279

Selected Letters of Josiah Wedgwood, ed. Ann Finer and George Savage, 207

Semowich, Charles J., comp., *American Furniture Craftsmen*, 103

Sense of Order, E. H. Gombrich, 48

"Set Thine House in Order," Robert Blair St. George, 73

1776, 55

Seventeenth-Century Interior Decoration, Peter Thornton, 85

Sewing Machine, Grace Rogers Cooper, 311

"Sewing Machine," David A. Hounshell, 314

Shadel, Jane S., "Documented Use of Cup Plates," 234

Shaffer, D. H., *Survey History of the American Spring Driven Clock*, 292

Shaffer, Douglas H., *Clocks*, 292

Shaker, 131

Shaker Chair, Charles R. Muller and Timothy D. Rieman, 128

"Shaker Clockmakers," James W. Gibbs and Robert W. Meader, 296

Shaker Furniture, Edward Deming Andrews and Faith Andrews, 117

"Shaker Furniture," Mary Grace Carpenter and Charles H. Carpenter, Jr., 119

Shaker Textile Arts, Beverly Gordon, 276

Shape of Time, George Kubler, 50

"Share of Honour," 55

Shaub, Elizabeth W., "Gorgas Family," 298

Shaw, Simeon, *History of the Staffordshire Potteries*, 215

Shearman, John, *Mannerism*, 55

Shelley, Frederick, *Aaron Dodd Crane*, 298

Sheriden, Christine, et al., "Poor Potter," 188

Sherrill, Sarah B., "Oriental Carpets," 245

Shop Records of Daniel Burnap, Penrose R. Hoopes, 297

Short Dictionary of Furniture, John Gloag, 84

Short History . . . and a Catalogue of Pewterware, Worshipful Company of Pewterers, 168

Shorter Dictionary of English Furniture, Ralph Edwards, 83

Shugart, Cooksey, *Complete Guide to . . . Watches*, 305

Shulimson, Judith, and Joyce Ice, "Beyond . . . Women's Traditional Arts," 261

"Silas Hoadley," Marius B. Péladeau, 298

Sill, Howard, and J. Hall Pleasants, *Maryland Silversmiths*, 154

Silver and Pewter, Donald L. Fennimore, 164

Silver by New York Makers, V. Isabelle Miller, 153

Silver in American Life, ed. Barbara McLean Ward and Gerald W. R. Ward, 157

Silver in England, Philippa Glanville, 145

Silver in Maryland, Jennifer Faulds Goldsborough, 152

Silver in the Golden State, ed. Edward W. Morse, 153

Silversmiths, Jewelers, Clock and Watch Makers, Marquis Boultinghouse, 293

Silversmiths, Watchmakers, and Jewelers of . . . New York, George Barton Cutten, 295

Silversmiths of Georgia, George Barton Cutten, 295

Silversmiths of Lancaster, Vivian S. Gerstell, 152

Silversmiths of New Jersey, Carl M. Williams, 299

Silversmiths of New York City, Paul von Khrum, 156

Silversmiths of Virginia, George Barton Cutten, 295

Silverware, Alain Gruber, 145

Simon Willard, John Ware Willard, 299

Simple Forms and Vivid Colors, Edwin A. Churchill, 120

Simple Home, Charles Keeler, 353

Simpson, Marc, *All That Glisters*, 176

Sincere's History of the Sewing Machine, William Ewers and H. W. Baylor, 312

Singleton, Esther, *Furniture of Our Forefathers*, 103

"Sitting in (Néo-Grec) Style," Kenneth L. Ames, 116

Six Quaker Clockmakers, Edward E. Chandlee, 294

Sketch of the Clock Making Business, Hiram Camp, 294

Sketches in Iron, Myra Tolmach Davis, 171

Sleepy Hollow Restorations, Joseph T. Butler, 88

Sloat, Caroline, "Dover Manufacturing Company," 279

[Slossen, Annie], *China Hunter's Club*, 215

"Small . . . Clocks," J. M. Cummins, 304

Smart, Charles E., *Makers of Surveying Instruments*, 176

Smith, Alan, *Illustrated Guide to Liverpool Herculaneum Pottery*, 216

Smith, Alan, ed., *Country Life International Dictionary of Clocks*, 292

Smith, E. Ann, and Olive R. Jones, *Glass of the British Military*, 228

Smith, Eugene Randolph, and Grace Howard Smith, *Watch Keys*, 305

Smith, Frank R., and Ruth E. Smith, *Miniature Lamps*, 329

Smith, Grace Howard, and Eugene Randolph Smith, *Watch Keys*, 305

Smith, Mary Ann, *Gustav Stickley*, 355

Smith, Merrit Roe, *Harpers Ferry Armory*, 341

Smith, Nancy A., *Old Furniture*, 86

Smith, Robert C., et al., *Arts in America*, 57

Smith, Ruth E., and Frank R. Smith, *Miniature Lamps*, 329

Smith, Samuel D., and Stephen T. Rogers, *Survey of Historic Pottery Making*, 193

Snyder, Ellen Marie, "Victory over Nature," 132

Snyder, John J., Jr., ed., *Philadelphia Furniture*, 103

Snyder, John J., Jr., et al., *Clockmakers of Lancaster*, 299

Social History of Lighting, William T. O'Dea, 328

Society of Arts and Crafts, ed. and comp. Karen Evans Ulehla, 357

"Sociological Aspects of Quilting," Susan Stewart, 263

Sokol, David M., *American Decorative Arts*, 32

Soltow, Lee, "Watches and Clocks," 303

"Some Blown 'Three-Mold' Suspicions," Dwight P. Lanmon et al., 229

"Some Colonial . . . Decorative Floors," Esther Stevens Fraser, 243

Some Notes on American Pewterers, Louis Guerineau Myers, 166

Some Observations concerning Connecticut Clockmaking, Kenneth D. Roberts, 298

"Some Print Sources of . . . Schoolgirl Art," Jane C. Nylander, 253

Something to Keep You Warm, ed. Roland Freeman, 260

Sonn, Alfred H., *Early American Wrought Iron*, 177

Sotheby's Directory of Silver, Vanessa Brett, 144

South, Stanley, "Evolution and Horizon," 216

South Carolina Silversmiths, E. Milby Burton, 149

Southern Furniture, 103

Southern Silver, 155

Spanish, French, and English Traditions in the Colonial Silver of North America, 155

Spatterware and Sponge, Earl F. Robacker and Ada F. Robacker, 214

Spear, Dorothea E., *American Watch Papers*, 305

Spillman, Jane Shadel, *American and European Pressed Glass*, 234

Spillman, Jane Shadel, and Estelle Sinclaire Farrar, *Complete . . . Glass*, 227

Spivack, Steven M., et al., "Analysis . . . of Coverlets," 280

Splendid Harvest, Michael Bird and Terry Kobayashi, 271

Spode, Leonard Whiter, 218

Spode Printed Ware, David Drakard and Paul Holdway, 206

Spode's Willow Pattern, Robert Copeland, 205

Sposato, Kenneth A., *Dictionary of American Clock and Watch Makers*, 292

Staffordshire Porcelain, Geoffrey Godden, 208

Staffordshire Romantic Transfer Patterns, Petra Williams, 219

Stanek, Edward J., et al., *Furniture of John Henry Belter*, 131

Stara, D., *Pewter Marks*, 167

Steer, Francis W., ed., *Farm and Cottage Inventories*, 34

Stefano, Frank, Jr.: "James and Ralph Clews," 216; "James Clews," 216

Stein, Roger B., et al., *In Pursuit of Beauty*, 45

Stephenson, Sue H., *Basketry*, 317

Sterling Silver Holloware, ed. Dorothy T. Rainwater, 154

Sternfield, Joseph, *Hour Glasses*, 305

Stewart, Regina, and Geraldine Cosentino, *Kitchenware*, 312

Stewart, Susan, "Sociological Aspects of Quilting," 263

Stickley, Gustav: *Best of Craftsman Homes*, 356; *Catalogue of Craftsman Furniture*, 356; *Craftsman Homes*, 356; *What Is Wrought*, 356

[Stickley, L. and J. G.], *Arts and Crafts Furniture Work*, 356

[Stickley Brothers Company], *Quaint Furniture*, 356

Stickley Craftsman Furniture Catalogs, 356

Stiegel Glass, Frederick William Hunter, 227

Stone, Garry Wheeler: "Ceramics from the John Hicks Site," 216; "Ceramics from Suffolk County," 216

Stone, Garry Wheeler, et al.: "Impermanent Architecture," 67; "Vessel Typology for Early Chesapeake Ceramics," 204

Stone, Lyle M., and J. Jefferson Miller II, *Eighteenth-Century Ceramics from Fort Michilimackinac*, 199, 213

Stone, May N., "Plumbing Paradox," 323

Stoneman, Vernon C.: *John and Thomas Seymour*, 104; *Supplement to John and Thomas Seymour*, 104

Stonewares and Stone Chinas of Northern England, 216

Story of the Lamp, Frederick W. Robins, 328

Stoudt, John Joseph, *Sunbonnets and Shoofly Pies*, 56

Stover, Donald L., *Tischlermeister Jahn*, 132

Stover, Donald Lewis, "Part One: Furniture of Early Texas," 132

Stradling, Diana, and G. Garrison Stradling, eds., *Art of the Potter*, 187

Stradling, G. Garrison, and Diana Stradling, eds., *Art of the Potter*, 187

Strasser, Susan, *Never Done*, 317

"Street Lighting," Bertram K. Little, 327

Stretch, Carolyn Wood, "Early Colonial Clockmakers," 299

Strickland, Peter L. L.: "Furniture by the Lejambre Family," 132; "Schindler, Roller," 132

Strong, Susan R., *History of American Ceramics*, 187

"Study of . . . Furniture," Michael Owen Jones, 339

Study of Simon Willard's Clocks, Richard W. Husher and Walter W. Welch, 297

Sturt, George, *Wheelwright's Shop*, 342

"Style and Structure," Robert Blair St. George, 102, 341

Sudbury, Byron, "Historic Clay Tobacco Pipemakers," 187

Sullivan, C., et al., *Lighting Devices*, 329

Sulzman, Frank M., et al., *Clocks That Time Us*, 302

"Summer and Winter Coverlet," Carleton L. Safford and Robert Bishop, 279

Summerson, John, *Classical Language of Architecture*, 34

Sun Dials and Roses, Alice Morse Earle, 304

Sunbonnets and Shoofly Pies, John Joseph Stoudt, 56

Sundials, Frank W. Cousins, 304

Sundials, René R. J. Rohr, 305

Sunshine and Shadow, Phyllis Haders, 261

Supplement to John and Thomas Seymour, Vernon C. Stoneman, 104

Supplemental List of Hadley Chests, Clair Franklin Luther, 97

Supplementary Catalogue of Pewterware, Worshipful Company of Pewterers, 168

Survey History of the American Spring Driven Clock, D. H. Shaffer, 292

Survey of American Clocks, Andrew Hayes Miller and Maria M. Dalia, 291

Survey of Historic Pottery Making, Samuel D. Smith and Stephen T. Rogers, 193

"Susanna Rowson," Jane C. Giffen, 250

Swan, Mabel M.: "Man Who Made Brass Works," 305; "Man Who Made . . . Clock Cases," 305; *Samuel McIntire . . . and the Sandersons*, 104

Swan, Susan B., "Worked Pocketbooks," 255

Swan, Susan Burrows: "Appreciating American Samplers," 255; *Plain and Fancy*, 255; *Winterthur Guide to American Needlework*, 255

Swank, Scott T., *Arts of the Pennsylvania Germans*, 56

Swank, Scott T., and Ian M. G. Quimby, eds., *Perspectives on American Folk Art*, 54

Sweeney, Kevin M., "Mansion People," 73

Sweezy, Nancy, *Raised in Clay*, 193

Swisegood School of Cabinetmaking, 104, 133

"Symbols of the United States," E. McClung Fleming, 47

Symonds, R. W., *Furniture Making*, 86

Talbot, George, *At Home*, 73

Talbott, Page, "Boston Empire Furniture," 133

Talbott, Page, and David A. Hanks, "Daniel Pabst," 125

Tasteful Interlude, William Seale, 55

Tastemakers, Russell Lynes, 71

Tattersall, Creassey Edward Cecil, *History of British Carpets*, 245

Tatum, George B., *Philadelphia Georgian*, 74

Tatum, George B., et al., *Arts in America*, 57

Taylor, Lonn, and David B. Warren, *Texas Furniture*, 133

Taylor, Lonn, and Dessa Bokides, *New Mexican Furniture*, 104, 133

Tea Drinking, Rodris Roth, 55

Technical Americana, Evald Rink, 341

"Technological Development," John D. Tyler, 317

"Technological Innovation and Design Economics," Michael J. Ettema, 122

Technological Innovation and the Decorative Arts, ed. Ian M. G. Quimby and Polly Anne Earl, 54

"Technology and the Housewife," William D. Andrews and Deborah C. Andrews, 310

Teleki, Gloria Roth: *Baskets of Rural America*, 317; *Collecting Traditional American Basketry*, 317

Teller, Barbara Gorely, "Ceramics in Providence," 216

Temples of Convenience, Lucinda Lambton, 322

"Tempo of Mercantile Life," Arthur H. Cole, 300

"Tenant Farmer's Tableware," George L. Miller, 212

Terry, Henry, *American Clock Making*, 299

Terry Clock Chronology, Barrows Mussey and Ruth Mary Canedy, 298

Texas Furniture, Lonn Taylor and David B. Warren, 133

Texas Pottery, Sherry B. Humphreys and Johnell L. Schmidt, 191

Texas Quilts, Suzanne Yabsley, 263

Textile Collections, ed. Cecil Lubell, 277

Textile History, 280

"Textile Trade," Linda R. Baumgarten, 271

"Textiles," Cora Ginsburg, 250

Textiles in America, Florence M. Montgomery, 277

"Textiles of the Louisiana Acadians," Vaughn L. Glasgow, 275

"Theodore H. Kapnek Collection," Elisabeth Donaghy Garrett, 250

Theus, Mrs. Charlton M., *Savannah Furniture*, 105

Thieme, Ulrich, and Felix Becker, *Allgemeines Lexikon*, 35

Thimbles, Edwin F. Holmes, 251

This Is the Way I Pass My Time, Ellen J. Gehret, 250

Thomas, John, *Rise of the Staffordshire Potteries*, 217

Thomas, John Carl, *Connecticut Pewter*, 167

Thomas, John Carl, ed., *American and British Pewter*, 167

"Thomas Claggett," Richard L. Champlin, 294

Thomas Day, Cabinetmaker, 133

"Thomas Fletcher and Sidney Gardiner," Donald L. Fennimore, 151

"Thomas Johnston," Sinclair Hitchings, 305

"Thomas Moore," Wendy Hefford, 243

Thompson, E. P., "Time, Work-Discipline," 303

Thompson, Susan Otis, *American Book Design*, 356

Thompson, W. G., "Carpets," 246

Thonet, Christopher Wilk, 134

Thornton, Peter: *Authentic Decor*, 85; *Baroque and Rococo Silks*, 280; *Seventeenth-Century Interior Decoration*, 85

Three Centuries of American Furniture, Oscar P. Fitzgerald, 92, 123

Three Hundred Years of American Seating Furniture, Patricia E. Kane, 95

Thuro, Catherine M. V.: *Oil Lamps*, 329; *Oil Lamps II*, 329

Thwing, Leroy, *Flickering Flames*, 329

Tice, Patricia M., "Knapp Dovetailing Machine," 133

Tiffany Collection of the Chrysler Museum, Paul E. Doros, 227

Tiffany Silver, Charles H. Carpenter, Jr., 149

"Tiffany's Fame," Herwin Schaeffer, 233

Tiller, 357

"Time, Work-Discipline," E. P. Thompson, 303

"Time and Performance," Bernard L. Herman, 70

Time in French Life, Richard Glasser, 301

"Time Structuring," H. Nowotny, 303

Timepieces Quarterly, 292

Timing a Century, Charles W. Moore, 305

Tin, Ernest S. Hedges, 165

Tin Can, Hyla M. Clark, 311

Tinsmiths of Connecticut, Shirley Spaulding DeVoe, 172

Tischlermeister Jahn, Donald L. Stover, 132

To Cut, Piece, and Solder, Jeannette Lasansky, 174

To Draw, Upset, and Weld, Jeannette Lasansky, 175, 339

Toher, Jennifer, et al., *In Pursuit of Beauty*, 45

Tomlin, Maurice, *English Furniture*, 85

Touching Gold and Silver, 147

Toulouse, Julian Harrison: *Bottle Makers*, 234; *Fruit Jars*, 317

Towner, Donald: *Creamware*, 217; *Leeds Pottery*, 217

Towner, Donald, and R. J. Charleston, *English Ceramics*, 205

Tracy, Berry B., "Decorative Arts," 134

Trade Catalogues at Winterthur, E. Richard McKinstry, 30

Trade Goods, Alice Baldwin Beer, 271

Traditional Pottery of Alabama, 193

Tramp Art, Helaine W. Fendelman, 123

"Transfer-Printed Creamware and Pearlware," Christina H. Nelson, 213

"Transfer Printed Spodeware," Lester A. Ross, 215

Traubel, Horace, et al., eds., *Artsman*, 357

Treasury of American Clocks, Brooks Palmer, 291

Trent, Robert F.: "Emery Attributions," 105; *Hearts and Crowns*, 105; "New London County Joined Chairs," 105

Trent, Robert F., ed., *Pilgrim Century Furniture*, 105

Trent, Robert F., and Albert S. Roe, "Robert Sanderson," 155

Trent, Robert F., and Jonathan L. Fairbanks, *New England Begins*, 47, 91

Trent, Robert F., et al., *Furniture at the Essex Institute*, 88

Triggs, Oscar Lovell, *Chapters in . . . the Arts and Crafts Movement*, 357

Triumph of Time, Jerome Hamilton Buckley, 300

True, Douglas K., et al., *Furniture of John Henry Belter*, 131

Tulip Ware, Edwin AtLee Barber, 188

Turn-of-the-Century Antiques, James Mackay, 354

Turnbaugh, Sarah Peabody, ed., *Domestic Pottery*, 193

Turner, Noel D., *American Silver Flatware*, 155

Turner, William, ed., *William Adams*, 217

Turners and Burners, Charles G. Zug III, 194

"Turpin Chairs," Warren E. Roberts, 130

Tutenag and Paktong, Alfred Bonnin, 171

"Two Eighteenth-Century Clockmakers," Ada R. Chase, 295

"Two Eighteenth-Century Craftsmen," Ada R. Chase, 295

Two Hundred Twenty-Five Years of Timepieces, Stacy B. C. Wood, Jr., 299

Two Hundred Years of American Blown Glass, George S. McKearin and Helen McKearin, 230

Two Hundred Years of American Clocks and Watches, Chris H. Bailey, 288

Two Towns, Peter Benes, 44

Tyler, Eric John, *Craft of the Clockmaker*, 292

Tyler, John D.: "Eighteenth- and Nineteenth-Century Cast-Iron Cooking Utensils," 317; "Technological Development," 317

U.S. Department of Commerce, *Pottery Industry*, 217

Ulasewicz, Connie, et al., "Analysis . . . of Coverlets," 280

Ulehla, Karen Evans, ed. and comp., *Society of Arts and Crafts*, 357

Uncoverings, 263

Understanding Wood, R. Bruce Hoadley, 86

Unearthing New England's Past, 200, 217

Unglik, Henry, and John D. Light, *Frontier Fur Trade*, 339

United States Clock and Watch Patents, George Eckhardt, 289

Unlike the Lilies, Dorothy K. Burnham, 272

Upholstery, Edward S. Cooke, Jr., 89

Upton, Dell: "Pattern Books and Professionalism," 74, 342; "Vernacular Domestic Architecture," 74

Upton, Dell, and John Michael Vlach, eds., *Common Places*, 74

Upton, Dell, et al., "Impermanent Architecture," 67

"Urban Aspects of . . . Furniture," Benno M. Forman, 338

"Urban Vernacular Architecture," Mary Ellen Hayward, 70

Useful Art, Cynthia Arps Corbett, 189

Utopian Craftsmen, Lionel Lambourne, 353

Vaisey, D. G., and F. Celoria, "Inventory of George Ecton," 217

Vandell, Kathy, et al., *Century of Childhood*, 49

van Ravenswaay, Charles, *Arts and Architecture of German Settlements*, 56

Vermeule, Cornelius, *Numismatic Art*, 156

Vermont Clock and Watchmakers, Lilian Baker Carlisle, 294

"Vernacular Domestic Architecture," Dell Upton, 74

Verster, A. J. G., *Old European Pewter*, 168

"Vessel Typology for Early Chesapeake Ceramics," Mary C. Beaudry et al., 204

Vetter, Robert M., et al., *National Types of Old Pewter*, 163

Victor, Stephen K., "From the Shop," 342

Victoria and Albert Museum, *Georgian Furniture*, 85

"Victoria and Albert Museum's . . . Metal-Work Pattern Books," Nicholas Goodison, 173, 305

Victorian Chair for All Seasons, 134

Victorian Furniture, ed. Kenneth L. Ames, 117

Victorian Home in America, John Maass, 71

Victorian Houses, Edmund V. Gillon, Jr., and Clay Lancaster, 69

Victorian Lighting, Ulysses G. Dietz, 326

Victorian Pottery and Porcelain, G. Bernard Hughes, 210

"Victory over Nature," Ellen Marie Snyder, 132

Virginia Carroll Crawford Collection, David A. Hanks and Donald C. Peirce, 124

Virginia Museum of Fine Arts: *Catalogue of the Henry P. Strause Collection of Clocks*, 292; *Masterpieces of American Silver*, 156

Vlach, John Michael: *Afro-American Tradition*, 56; *Charleston Blacksmith*, 177, 342; "Quilting," 263

Vlach, John Michael, and Dell Upton, eds., *Common Places*, 74

Voices of Time, ed. J. T. Fraser, 301

von Khrum, Paul, *Silversmiths of New York City*, 156

Von Rosenstiel, Helene, *American Rugs*, 246

Voorsanger, Catherine Hoover, et al., *In Pursuit of Beauty*, 45

Wadleigh, William L., Jr., et al., *Eli Terry*, 297

Wadsworth Atheneum, *Bed Ruggs*, 255

Wahlman, Maude Southwell, and John Scully, "Aesthetic Principles in Afro-American Quilts," 263

Wainwright, Nicholas B., *Colonial Grandeur*, 56

Walbert, Benjamin L., "Infancy of Central Heating," 325

Walker, Sandra Rambo, *Country Cloth*, 280

Wallace, Anthony F. C., *Rockdale*, 342

Wallace, David H., and George C. Groce, *New-York Historical Society's Dictionary of Artists*, 33

Wallace, Philip B., *Colonial Ironwork*, 177

"Walter H. Durfee," Owen Burt and Jo Burt, 293

Walters, Betty Lawson, *King of Desks*, 134

Walton, Peter, *Creamware and Other*

English Pottery at Temple Newsam, 217

Ward, Barbara McLean: "Boston Goldsmiths," 156, 342; "In a Feasting Posture," 156; "Metalwares," 157, 168

Ward, Barbara McLean, and Gerald W. R. Ward, eds., *Silver in American Life*, 157

Ward, Gerald W. R., *American Case Furniture*, 105

Ward, Gerald W. R., ed., *Perspectives on American Furniture*, 105

Ward, Gerald W. R., and Barbara McLean Ward, eds., *Silver in American Life*, 157

Ward, Gerald W. R., et al., *Work of Many Hands*, 94

Ward-Jackson, Peter, *English Furniture Designs*, 85

"Wares and Chairs," Deborah Dependahl Waters, 134

Warp and Weft, Dorothy K. Burnham, 272

Warren, David B., *Bayou Bend*, 57, 106

Warren, David B., and Katherine S. Howe, *Gothic Revival Style*, 49, 125

Warren, David B., and Lonn Taylor, *Texas Furniture*, 133

Warren, David B., et al., *Marks of Achievement*, 157

Watch Collection, Stanley H. Burton, 303

Watch Factories, Henry G. Abbott, 303

Watch Keys, Grace Howard Smith and Eugene Randolph Smith, 305

Watches, Cecil Clutton and George Daniels, 304

"Watches and Clocks," Lee Soltow, 303

Watchmakers and Clockmakers, Granville H. Baillie, 288

Watchmaking in England, Leonard Weiss, 305

Water Closet, Roy Palmer, 322

Waters, Deborah Dependahl, "From Pure Coin," 157; "Wares and Chairs," 134

Watkins, C. Malcom, "Artificial Lighting," 329

Watkins, Lura Woodside: *Cambridge Glass*, 234; "Colorful Ceramics," 218; *Early New England Potters*, 194

Watney, Bernard, *English Blue and White Porcelain*, 218

Weatherill, Lorna, *Pottery Trade and North Staffordshire*, 218

Weavers Draft Book, comp. John Hargrove, 276

Webster, Donald, *Early Canadian Pottery*, 194

Webster, Donald Blake: *Decorated Stoneware Pottery*, 187; *English-Canadian Furniture*, 85

Webster, Marie Daugherty, *Quilts*, 263

Wedgwood, Wolf Mankowitz, 212

Weidlich, Lorre, and Susan Roach, "Quilt Making," 263

Weidman, Gregory R., *Furniture in Maryland*, 106, 134

Weidner, Ruth Irwin, comp., *American Ceramics*, 187

Weinrich, Peter H., *Bibliographic Guide to Books on Ceramics*, 218

Weiser, Frederick S., et al., trans. and eds., *Accounts of . . . Furniture Makers*, 96

Weiss, Gustav, *Book of Glass*, 234

Weiss, Leonard, *Watchmaking in England*, 305

Weiss, Peg, ed., *Adelaide Alsop Robineau*, 194

Weissman, Judith Reiter, et al., *Quilts, Coverlets, Rugs, and Samplers*, 259

Welch, Spring, Owen H. Burt and Jo Burt, 294

Welch, Walter W., and Richard W. Husher, *Study of Simon Willard's Clocks*, 297

Wells-Cole, Anthony, et al., *Country House Floors*, 243

Welsh, Peter C., *Woodworking Tools*, 86

Welshimer, Paula, and John Bivins, Jr., *Moravian Decorative Arts*, 44

Wetherbee, Jean, *Look at White Ironstone*, 187, 218

"What, Who, and When of English Creamware Plate Design," Ivor Noël Hume, 214

"What Is the Néo-Grec," Kenneth L. Ames, 117

What Is Wrought, Gustav Stickley, 356

Wheelwright's Shop, George Sturt, 342

Where Two Worlds Meet, Carolyn Gilman, 48

Whiffen, Marcus, *Eighteenth-Century Houses of Williamsburg*, 74

White, Frank G., "Reflections on a Tin Kitchen," 318

White, Margaret E., comp., *American Hand-Woven Coverlets*, 280

White Dial Clocks, Brian Loomes, 291

Whitehead, Charles, and James Whitehead, *James and Charles*

Whitehead . . . Designs, 218

Whitehead, James, and Charles Whitehead, *James and Charles Whitehead . . . Designs*, 218

Whiteman, Maxwell, *Copper for America*, 177

Whiter, Leonard, *Spode*, 218

Whitesmiths of Taunton, George Sweet Gibb, 152

Whitfield, Philip, and Edward S. Ayensu, eds., *Rhythms of Life*, 300

Whitney, Philip, *Clocks of Shenandoah*, 299

Wilcoxen, Charlotte, *Dutch Trade and Ceramics*, 200

Wilk, Christopher, *Thonet*, 134

Wilkins, Ruth S., et al., *Chinese Export Silver*, 145

Willard, John Ware, *Simon Willard*, 299

"Willard and Nolen," J. R. Keown, 305

William Adams, ed. William Turner, 217

William and John Linnell, Helena Hayward and Pat Kirkham, 84

William and Mary Fabrics, Judith M. Bolingbroke, 272

William Claggett, Richard L. Champlin, 294

Williams, Carl M., *Silversmiths of New Jersey*, 299

Williams, Howard Y., *Gaudy Welsh China*, 218

Williams, Petra, *Staffordshire Romantic Transfer Patterns*, 219

Williams, Susan, *Savory Suppers*, 57

Williams, Susan R., "Flow-Blue," 219

Williamson, Harold F., and Arthur H. Cole, *American Carpet Manufacture*, 242

Williams-Wood, Cyril, *English Transfer-Printed Pottery and Porcelain*, 219

Willow, Oak, and Rye, Jeannette Lasansky, 315

Wills, Geoffrey, *Candlesticks*, 329

Wilson, Colin, and John Grant, eds., *Book of Time*, 301

Wilson, Kenneth M.: "Glastenbury Glass Factory," 235; *New England Glass*, 235

Wilson, Kenneth M., and Helen McKearin, *American Bottles*, 230

Wilson, Richard Guy, "Early Work of Charles F. McKim," 75

Wilson, Sadye Tune, and Doris Finch Kennedy, *Of Coverlets*, 280

Winchester, Alice, and Jean Lipman,

Flowering of American Folk Art, 51

Windsor, H. H., *Mission Furniture*, 357

Winter, Robert W., et al., eds., *California Design*, 347

Winterthur, Jay E. Cantor, 45

Winterthur Guide to American Chippendale Furniture, Charles F. Hummel, 95

Winterthur Guide to American Needlework, Susan Burrows Swan, 255

Winterthur Portfolio, 36

Winton, Andrew L., and Kate Barber, *Norwalk Potteries*, 194

With Hammer in Hand, Charles F. Hummel, 86, 297

Woman's Day Book of American Needlework, Rose Wilder Lane, 252

Woman's Work, Caroline Davidson, 312

Women at Work, Thomas Dublin, 337

Wood, Stacy B. C., Jr.: "Hoff Family," 299; "Rudy Stoner," 299; *Two Hundred Twenty-Five Years of Timepieces*, 299

Wood, Stacy B. C., Jr., et al., *Clockmakers of Lancaster*, 299

Wood Family of Burslem, Frank Falkner, 207

Woodbury, Robert S.: *History of the Gear-Cutting Machine*, 305; "Legend of Eli Whitney," 300

Woodhead, E. I., et al., *Lighting Devices*, 329

"Woodlands," Richard J. Betts, 66

Woodworking Tools, Peter C. Welsh, 86

"Wool Culture and Spinning," Alice Morse Earle, 274

Wooton Patent Desks, 135

Worcester Blue and White Porcelain, Lawrence Branyan et al., 204

Work, Culture, and Society, Herbert G. Gutman, 338

Work of Many Hands, Benjamin A. Hewitt et al., 94

"Worked Pocketbooks," Susan B. Swan, 255

Workers' Control, David Montgomery, 340

Workers' World, Glenn Porter, 340

"Working-Class Culture," Alan Dawley and Paul Faler, 337

Working People, Bruce Laurie, 339

"Workmanship as Evidence," Philip D. Zimmerman, 106

World Ceramics, ed. Robert J. Charleston, 197

World Furniture, ed. Helena Hayward, 84

World of Antiques, Art, and Architecture,
Robert Bishop and Patricia Coblentz,
44

Worshipful Company of Pewterers of
London: *Short History . . . and a Catalogue of Pewterware,* 168; *Supplementary Catalogue of Pewterware,* 168

Wright, Gwendolyn: *Building the
Dream,* 75; *Moralism and the Model
Home,* 75

Wright, Lawrence: *Clean and Decent,*
323; *Clockwork Man,* 303

Wright, Louis B., et al., *Arts in America,*
57

Wroth, Lawrence C., *Abel Buell,* 157

Wrought Covenant, Robert Blair St.
George, 102

"Wythe County . . . Punched Tin,"
J. Roderick Moore, 128

Yabsley, Suzanne, *Texas Quilts,* 263

Yarnall, James L., and William H.
Gerdts, comps., *National Museum of
American Art's Index to American Art
Exhibition Catalogues,* 32

Yehia, Mary Ellen, "Chairs for the Masses," 135

Yellow Ware, Joan Leibowitz, 186

Young, Jennie J., *Ceramic Art,* 187

Young Father Time, Barrows Mussey,
298

Your Obdt. Servt., Deming Jarves, ed.

Barbara Bishop and Martha Hassell,
226

Zea, Philip, "Clockmaking and Society," 342

Zimmer, Edward F., and Pamela J.
Scott, "Alexander Parris, B. Henry
Latrobe, and the John Wickham
House," 75

Zimmerman, Philip D.: "Methodological Study in . . . Chippendale Furniture," 106; "Workmanship as Evidence," 106

Zug, Charles G., III, *Turners and
Burners,* 194

LIBRARY OF CONGRESS CATALOGUING-IN-PUBLICATION DATA

Decorative arts and household furnishings in America, 1650–1920 : an annotated
bibliography / edited by Kenneth L. Ames & Gerald W. R. Ward.
     p.   cm.
   ISBN 0–912724–19–6
     1. Decorative arts—United States—Bibliography.   2. House
furnishings—United States—Bibliography.   I. Ames, Kenneth L.
II. Ward, Gerald W. R.
Z5956.D3D43   1989
[NK805]   89–20010
016.745′0973—dc20   CIP

Decorative Arts and
Household Furnishings in America
1650 – 1920
An Annotated Bibliography

was composed and printed by Meriden-Stinehour Press. The text type is Janson Text with Snell Roundhand for display, all set on a Linotronic-300. The text paper is Mohawk Superfine, Eggshell Finish; the endleaves are Rainbow Felt; the book is bound in Tex-Linen by Acme Bookbindery.

Design and oversight of production by Christopher Kuntze.
Production editing and indexing by Patricia R. Lisk.
Copy editing by Deborah G. Huey.